The Reform of UK Personal Property Security Law

There has been much discussion in the last ten years about the need to reform the law governing company charge registration, with many bodies including the Department of Trade and Industry (now re-named the Department for Business, Innovation and Skills) and Law Commissions considering the case for reform of this area in the context of a wider scheme of personal property security reform. This has culminated in the coming into force of Part 25 of the Companies Act 2006, which is concerned with company charge registration.

This major new book features the work of international experts on personal property security law. It focuses on the reform of UK company charge law and argues that the Companies Act 2006 did not go far enough in reforming the law. It addresses the question as to whether the UK should follow the lead of other jurisdictions that have adopted US Article 9-type personal property security schemes. As well as considering current UK law, the book also addresses the changes proposed by the Law Commissions and, despite current government inaction, considers whether these reform proposals should be adopted.

The book contains major international comparisons and, in particular, looks at law reform in the USA, Canada, Australia, New Zealand, Singapore and Europe. This comparative treatment gives the reader a full perspective on this difficult and constantly developing area of law.

John de Lacy is a Senior Lecturer in Law at the University of Sheffield.

The Reform of UK Personal Property Security Law

Comparative Perspectives

Edited by
John de Lacy

Routledge-Cavendish
Taylor & Francis Group
LONDON AND NEW YORK

First published 2010
by Routledge-Cavendish
2 Park Square, Milton Park, Abingdon, Oxon OX14 4RN

Simultaneously published in the USA and Canada
by Routledge-Cavendish
711 Third Ave, New York, NY 10017

Routledge-Cavendish is an imprint of the Taylor & Francis Group, an informa business

Typeset in Baskerville by Keyword Group Ltd.

British Library Cataloguing in Publication Data
A catalogue record for this book is available from the British Library.

Library of Congress Cataloging in Publication Data
The reform of personal property security law in the UK: comparative perspectives / Edited by John de Lacy.
p. cm.
Includes bibliographical references and index.
ISBN 978-1-85941-891-8 (alk. paper)
1. Security (Law)–Great Britain. 2. Personal property–Great Britain.
3. Security (Law) 4. Personal property. I. De Lacy, John.
KD1755.R45 2009
346.4104'7–dc22
2009023245

ISBN10: 1–85941–891–0 (hbk)
ISBN10: 0–20386–512–X (ebk)

ISBN13: 978–1–85941–891–8 (hbk)
ISBN13: 978–0–20386–512–5 (ebk)
ISBN13: 978–0–41563–154–9 (pbk)

This book is dedicated to my mother, Alice and late father, Eddie, to whom I owe so much.

Contents

Table of Statutes

For statutes from non-UK jurisdictions the name of the statute has been qualified by placing the name of the jurisdiction after it, e.g. 'Air Navigation Act 1920 (Australia)'. UK statutes are not qualified.

Table of Cases

Notes on contributors

Spiros Bazinas is Senior Legal Officer Trade Law Division of the United Nations Office of Legal Affairs, UNCITRAL. He is currently the Secretary of Working Group VI, preparing an Annex to the UNCITRAL Guide on Secured Transactions.
Joanna Benjamin is a reader in law at the London School of Economics and a Member of the Bank of England's Financial Markets Law Committee.
David Brown is Associate Professor of law at the University of Adelaide, Australia.
Richard Calnan is a Partner at Norton Rose LLP, Solicitors, London.
Iwan Davies holds the Sir Julian Hodge Chair in Asset Finance Law at Swansea University.
Ulrich Drobnig is Professor and Emeritus Director and Scientific Member of the Max Planck Institute for Comparative and International Private Law, Hamburg, Germany.
Simon Fisher is a barrister in Brisbane, Queensland, Australia.
Roy Goode is Emeritus Professor of law and Fellow of St John's College, Oxford University.
George Gretton is Lord President Reid Professor of law at Edinburgh University and currently serves as a Law Commissioner at the Scottish Law Commission, since his appointment in May 2006.
Louise Gullifer is a reader in commercial law and tutor in law at Harris Manchester College, Oxford University.
John de Lacy is a senior lecturer in law at Sheffield University.
Jacqueline Lipton is a Professor of law at Case Western Reserve University, School of Law, Cleveland, Ohio, USA.
Gerard McCormack is Professor of International Business Law at Leeds University.
Yock Lin Tan is Professor of Law at the National University of Singapore.
Jacob Ziegel is Professor of Law Emeritus University of Toronto, Canada.

Foreword

This collection of essays by scholars and practitioners from this country and overseas makes an important contribution to an ongoing debate on the role and content of a modern law of security in personal property. A focal point of the papers assembled in *The Reform of UK Personal Property Security Law* is the (English) Law Commission's report *Company Security Interests*, published in 2005 with the expectation that what was then the Companies Bill would include power to make regulations along the lines of those drafted by the Law Commission as an Appendix to its report. That this did not happen is no fault of the Law Commission, which was throughout working under the extreme time constraints imposed by the need to meet the legislative timetable.

These constraints resulted in a considerable watering down on what had been proposed in the Law Commission's consultative report published the previous year. This was a fine, bold piece of work embodying a thorough and carefully worked-out set of recommendations which drew on tried-and-tested legislation of long-standing in the United States, Canada and, more recently, New Zealand, and adapted it to the particular needs and practices of English business enterprises and financiers. If implemented, the report would have given England its very first clear and comprehensive legislation on security interests in personal property.

Unhappily it did not come to pass. Although much of what was proposed received support, there was opposition from some sectors of the practising profession, stemming partly from conservatism – most of us tend to be resistant to change – but perhaps more importantly from the lack of adequate time for consultation and for involvement of consultees in the process. In consequence, in its final report the Law Commission retreated from several of its earlier proposals, abandoning the central idea of a unified security interest and undermining the conceptual clarity of its earlier consultative report. Even this reduced set of proposals would have been worth saving, but in the end the Companies Act, already by far the largest on the statute book, failed to include the necessary regulation-making power.

This is not the end of the road. An initiative is already on foot to revive the proposals in the consultative report and engage with industry, commerce and the professions to iron out any remaining problems, taking whatever time is needed to ensure that all interest sectors have a proper opportunity to contribute to the outcome. So the appearance of this volume comes at a particularly opportune time. An extensive first chapter by the editor, Dr John de Lacy, traces the history of English personal property security law and the various attempts to persuade legislators to provide a modern statutory regime: the Crowther Report in 1971, the Cork Report in 1982, the Diamond Report in 1989 and now the Law Commission report, all urging a new legislative framework governing security interests in personal property.

Dr de Lacy's introduction provides an excellent springboard for the subsequent contributions by leading academics and practitioners from the UK and overseas which examine the Law Commission's proposals from the perspective of existing or impending legislation in their own countries, as well as in the context of developments in Europe and of specialist areas, such as intellectual property. The volume concludes with an overview of the UNCITRAL legislative guide to secured transactions.

This is a rich feast which will provide invaluable material for those working in the field. Not all the contributions are supportive of the Law Commission's proposals. There are some which, while acknowledging the quality of what has been done, consider that existing English law, though not without its faults, is broadly satisfactory. It is important that these critical voices should be heard and their arguments addressed, because, as Megarry J put it in *Cordell* v. *Second Clanfield Properties Ltd* [1969] 2 Ch. 9, when taking a view diametrically opposed to what he himself had said in his own co-authored textbook on real property, an author

> has to form his views without the aid of the purifying ordeal of skilled argument on the specific facts of a contested case. Argued law is tough law. This is as true today as it was in 1409 when Hankford J. said: 'Home ne scaveroit de quel metal un campane fuit, si ceo ne fuit bien battu, quasi diceret, le ley per bon disputacion serra bien conus'.

This excellent volume should be read by everyone having an interest in the reform of the law governing secured transactions in personal property, for it combines history with rigorous analysis, an awareness of commercial needs and practices and a keen understanding of the philosophy and concepts of the legislation described in it.

Roy Goode
Oxford, 4 June 2009

Introduction

John de Lacy

The idea for this book came following the publication of the Law Commission's Consultation Paper *Registration of Security Interests: Company Charges and Property other than Land* in 2002.[1] This document seemed to herald the beginning of a new era for personal property security interest law in the UK.[2] The Law Commission acknowledged that the time was now right for fundamental reforms to be brought in modelled on Article 9 of the US Uniform Commercial Code. The Law Commission's Consultation Paper set out proposals that, at that time, seemed likely to become law when the government finally got around to introducing reforming company law legislation following the earlier Company Law Reform Project.[3] Although the Commission's proposed scheme to implement law reform was not ideal, based on a dual strategy of implementing reform first for companies via a new Companies Act to be followed, at a later date, by reform for other categories of debtor, it did at least seem to offer the real prospect of fundamental reform to this area, which had been crying out for reform since the publication of the Crowther Report in 1971.[4] It was on this basis that the authors of the chapters in this collection undertook their commissions. However, the reform project was beset by delays and problems and, rather than publishing a final report, the Commission was forced to publish a second consultation paper in 2004[5] before its *Final Report* eventually appeared in 2005.[6]

Unfortunately, by the time the Law Commission published its *Final Report* in 2005, the promising ideals of reforming this area, that were manifested in their 2002 Paper, had gone and a more limited scheme based on the pragmatic reality of getting City practitioners to agree to reform was produced. Sadly, even the more limited reform scheme of 2005 was ultimately rejected by the government when the

1 See Law Commission Consultation Paper No. 164 (London, TSO, 2002).
2 The Scottish Law Commission was also working on a similar project at this time; see Scottish Law Commission Discussion Paper 121 *Registration of Rights in Security by Companies* (Edinburgh, TSO, 2002).
3 On which see John de Lacy (ed.) *The Reform of UK Company Law* (London, Cavendish Publishing, 2002).
4 (1971) Cmnd 4596.
5 See Consultation Paper No. 176 *Company Security Interests: A Consultative Report* (London, TSO, 2004).
6 See Law Commission Report No. 296 *Company Security Interests* (2005) Cm 6654.

Companies Act 2006, Part 25 (covering company charge registration) was eventually passed. These vacillations caused many problems for commentators attempting to guess the future course of law reform. Many academics had hoped to see a new modern personal property security law enacted in the UK based on North American precedent. However, that was not to be and we are now left, following the most extensive law reform review ever undertaken, with essentially the same law on company charges as we had before. This is a major source of disappointment. Nevertheless, the current law is so outmoded that fundamental reform is still needed. Although successive governments have continued to balk at implementing fundamental reforms and rejected all the major reform initiatives that have been made since 1971, the case for reform is still strong and, it is submitted, will ultimately have to be met. This volume contains the work of leading international authorities and examines the case for law reform, offering suggestions on what future shape the law might take.

I am most grateful to all the contributors in this volume who have shown great patience with the project as it has progressed. However, the book is now able to tell the complete story of the reform of PPS law in the UK up and until 2009, the year in which the belated company charge registration provisions of the Companies Act 2006 came into force.[7] The latter can, at best, be regarded as a stopgap pending more fundamental reforms. With reform in mind, the collection includes full comparative treatment and readers can see the developments in other jurisdictions which have taken a lead that the UK has, so far, declined to follow.

7 The provisions came into force on 1 October 2009; see SI 2008/2860.

1 The evolution and regulation of security interests over personal property in English law

John de Lacy

Introduction

The passage and coming into force of the company charge provisions of the Companies Act 2006,[1] has, for the time being at any rate, signalled the end of serious debate about the reform of English personal property security (PPS) law.[2] Given the amount of work that has gone into reforming this area, it is a modest statement to say that the 'new' company charge provisions are a disappointment. The topic of reform has been on the agenda since 1998 when the Company Law Review project started, but the reform issue has a much longer pedigree stretching back to the early 1970s.[3] This chapter will charter the evolution of security interests under English law and the regulatory response to the growth and take-up of security which has fuelled the economy since the earliest days of the Industrial Revolution. Given the current economic crisis that started with excessive risk taking in the financial sector,[4] which quickly spread to the general economy, it is opportune to consider the fundamentals of security and the risk management process that the taking of security implies.

The concept and meaning of 'security interest'

Fundamental to the basis of this chapter is the notion of security and it is, therefore, appropriate at this stage to consider the basic concept of a security interest. The question of classifying the nature of a security interest has prompted much conflicting academic debate[5] and it is safe to say that the security concept, in a definitional sense,

1 See generally Companies Act 2006, Part 25, ss. 860–877.
2 That is to say at governmental levels, at any rate.
3 See the Crowther Report (1971) Cmnd 4596, which is discussed in this volume, pp. 43–47.
4 The so-called 'credit crisis' which began in the USA in mid-2007 and quickly spread to the UK in September 2007 with the collapse of the Northern Rock Bank plc, which had to be nationalised by the UK government. By October 2008 the crisis had intensified in the UK and a wholesale 'bail-out' of the UK's banking system was under way. In February 2009 the UK government admitted that the economy had entered into the worst recession since the 1930s.
5 The most notable examples of this debate are the articles by Allan and Goode entitled: 'Security: some mysteries, myths and monstrosities' (Allan) and 'Security: a pragmatic conceptualist's response' (Goode), (1989) 15 *Monash Law Review* 337 and 361 respectively; see also: Goode *Legal Problems of Credit and Security* (3rd edn, 2003), pp. 1–38; Oditah *Legal Aspects of Receivables Financing* (1991), pp. 4–14; Gretton 'The concept of security', in Cusine (ed.), *A Scots Conveyancing Miscellany* (1987), pp. 126–51; Sykes *The Law of Securities* (5th edn, 1993), pp. 3–27.

remains one of the more elusive notions in legal science. On a general level there is no statutory concept[6] of a security interest and one is forced to look to the common law to furnish an answer.

Under the broad rubric of security it is possible to find two main types of situation in which the term is used:

(a) **consensual security** which arises by way of contractual agreement; and[7]
(b) **legal security** which arises by operation of law.[8]

A further sub-division, applicable to both types of security, is also warranted in that both can be sub-divided into:

(a) real security; and
(b) quasi security.

The difference between these sub-classes is that in the case of real security we are concerned with the grant of an interest by way of security, whereas in the case of quasi security recourse is gained against some form of proprietary interest otherwise than by way of grant. This essay is primarily concerned with the regulation of consensual security interests and it is to them that we must now turn.

The consensual security interest

We must, therefore, now address our attention to consensual security interests. This heading has been subdivided into real security and quasi security to encompass two main threads of reasoning behind the main heading, although some commentators

6 A notable exception is provided by the Insolvency Act 1986, ss. 248(b)(i) and 425(4) which state that 'security' means 'any mortgage, charge, lien or other security'. Section 93 of the Companies Act 1989 would have introduced a new s. 395(2) providing that a 'charge' means 'any form of *security interest* (fixed or floating) over property, other than an interest arising by operation of law' (author's emphasis); this provision is discussed in this chapter, p. 29.

7 It should be noted that the concept of personal security also falls under this heading. This arises where a third party undertakes to the creditor that he will assume some form of responsibility should the debtor default in the performance of his obligation. This type of security interest does not involve any form of proprietary rights and it will not be dealt with in this chapter. As this type of security is personal in nature its efficiency is dependent on the continued solvency of the third-party guarantor, which makes proprietary security so much more valuable in practice. However, there is no reason why a creditor cannot make use of both personal and proprietary security; see *China & South Sea Bank Ltd* v. *Tan* [1990] 1 AC 536. Sykes has doubted the legitimacy of the label personal security because it does not involve the exercise of any proprietary rights: 'The transaction [i.e. personal security] merely super-adds one personal obligation to another and the personal obligation of the guarantor in itself is merely enforceable by action of debt in the same manner as the obligation of the original debtor himself ... It is thought, therefore, that the so-called personal security is not security at all, that is to say, all securities are "real"' (op. cit., Sykes, fn 5, p. 11).

8 There are numerous specified situations where both statute and common law recognise security in favour of a debtor generally by imposition of a lien over property until a debt is paid. The policy behind such security is to protect a potentially vulnerable creditor who might not be in a position to contract for such protection. It is for this reason that most registration systems contain an express exemption from the registration requirement in favour of security rights arising by operation of law.

would deny that there is any division at all.[9] To a layperson the concept of possessing a right of security might be described (if one will forgive the tautology) 'as the condition of being secure'.[10] Given such a definition, one would simply look at a commercial transaction and see if the lender was 'secure' in the event of the debtor's failure to repay a debt or perform some other type of obligation, in order to determine whether a security interest could be said to exist. The condition of being 'secure' under such a test would probably remain a subjective assessment, although in practice it would mean no more than that the debtor had some additional means of recovering the debtor's deficiency, from whatever source.

From a legalistic approach, the question of defining a consensual security interest is more problematic. Although the lay definition given above is general enough to cover a real security interest, the legal definition is far more circumspect. It may be described as follows: a real security interest arises by agreement of the contracting parties and involves the grant of an interest over the property of the debtor (i.e. the person who owes the obligation) in order to secure the performance of the primary duty or obligation the debtor is under.[11] For these purposes a declaration of trust by a debtor that he holds property as a trustee in order to secure his performance of a duty or obligation towards the creditor/beneficiary also creates a security interest. The existence of a real security postulates at least a two-party consensual agreement to such effect, since a person cannot have a charge over his own property because

9 See: Allan, op. cit., fn 5; Oditah, op. cit., fn 5. Although Oditah (p. 11) does use the term quasi-security, he uses it as a residual class covering types of arrangements outside his own definition (p. 8) and not to cover arrangements such as retention of title, which, it will be argued, are not forms of real security interest known to law. See generally pp. 28–37.

10 See OED (2nd edn, 1989), vol. 14, p. 853, point 1. However, 'security' is also defined in more legalistic terms as: 'Property deposited or made over, or bonds, recognizances, or the like entered into, by or on behalf of a person in order to secure his fulfilment of an obligation, and forfeitable in the event of non-fulfilment' (Ibid., p. 854, point 8). See also *Re Marwalt plc* [1992] BCC 32,42H–43A, *per* Judge Paul Baker, QC (use of the word 'security' is a 'wide expression' which did not, on the facts of the case, cover a registrable charge interest).

11 In many cases this will simply involve the repayment of money, but security can be taken to ensure the performance of any obligation, e.g. the building of a house; see also *Santley* v. *Wilde* [1899] 2 Ch. 474 (security given, *inter alia*, to secure payment of business profits). Most of today's secured loan transactions will in addition to securing the duty to repay the sum advanced also place the debtor under secondary duties, such as the upkeep of the security interest, insurance thereof, etc. These secondary duties will independently of the repayment obligation also give rise to enforcement against the property subject to the security if they are not performed by the debtor by accelerated repayment of the outstanding debt. Nevertheless, where security is taken to secure the performance of a non-monetary obligation, the enforcement of such security must, ultimately, be quantified in monetary damages resulting from the debtor's non-performance of that obligation. Note that the security interest can also be created by a third party over his property in favour of the creditor, despite the fact that the third party is under no liability for the performance of the original duty or obligation the debtor undertakes to perform: see *Barclays Bank plc* v. *O'Brien* [1993] QB 109; such a position is expressly recognised by Arts 9–105 (d) of the UCC which define the scope of the term 'debtor' to include such a third party who undertakes this type of liability. See, for example: *Re Reliable Manufacturing Corp.* 703 F.2d 996 (7th Cir., 1983); Arts 9–112 (third-party debtor's rights against secured party). However, third-party debtor situations might well be open to scrutiny under the various avoidance mechanisms contained in the Insolvency Act 1986; see *Re Answerfone Inc.* 48 *Bankr.* 24 (Bankr. E. D. Ark., 1985) (such a security caught as a fraudulent conveyance under the Bankruptcy Code 1978, s. 548).

there is nothing to secure in one's own favour.[12] A real security is always an ancillary or secondary right that only becomes enforceable upon the debtor's default in performing the primary duty or obligation.[13] However, it appears that the holder of a security interest may, by virtue of that interest, be also entitled 'in appropriate, and no doubt rare, circumstances' to restrain the conduct of a third party whose conduct in relation to his own property may in some way indirectly imperil the value of that security interest.[14] Although the security interest is, in theory, designed to ensure that

12 *Re Charge Card Services Ltd* [1987] Ch. 150, p. 175C, *per* Millet J. (conceptually impossible to have a charge over one's own debt); see also (1991) 107 LQR 679, p. 680; *National Westminster Bank Ltd* v. *Halesowen Presswork & Assemblies Ltd* [1972] AC 758, pp. 802C–E, *per* Viscount Dilhorne, 810F–G, *per* Lord Cross (impossible for a bank to have a lien over a customer's account since the property represented by the account belongs to the bank); *Rye* v. *Rye* [1962] AC 496 (owner of land cannot grant himself a lease over that land). The proposition in the main text is undoubtedly correct, if only as a matter of basic contract theory, however, the wider authority of *Re Charge Card* denying the validity of a charge-back transaction (i.e. the ability of a creditor to grant security over a debt owed by the debtor back to the debtor) is not free from difficulty such that the case was doubted in *Welsh Development Agency* v. *Export Finance Ltd* [1990] BCC 393, p. 408F, *per* Browne-Wilkinson VC, but followed 'in the interests of preserving consistency in matters which have an important general commercial impact'. The doubts of Browne-Wilkinson VC on this point were indorsed, *obiter*, in the Court of Appeal on appeal (overruling *Welsh Development Agency* v. *Export Finance Ltd* [1990] BCC 393) by Dillon LJ who stated: 'I have very considerable difficulty with the view expressed by Millett J' [1992] BCC 270, p. 284F; the other members of the Court of Appeal preferred not to express an opinion on the matter. Indeed, the *Final Report of the Legal Risk Review Committee* (October 1992), Appendix 2, recommended the statutory reversal of the *Re Charge Card*. Charge-backs caused many problems, but the registrar of companies did accept for registration an attempt by a bank to take a charge over its indebtedness (although such practice in no way affects the legal validity of the 'charge'). But the point was finally resolved by the House of Lords in *Re BCCI (No. 8)* [1998] AC 214 where it was found that charge-backs were perfectly valid, overturning *Re Charge Card*; see further McCormack *Secured Credit under English and American Law* (Cambridge: Cambridge University Press, 2004), pp. 249–62.

13 'The promise to pay the debt, which is the subject of the personal covenant of the debtor, and the security for that obligation are distinct': *Equiticorp Finance Group Ltd* v. *Cheah* [1991] 1 NZLR 299, p. 301, *per* Richardson J. A notable exception to this rule concerns a legal mortgage of realty. Since the mortgage gives the mortgagee a legal title upon the execution of the conveyance, he has an immediate right to enter into possession of the property 'before the ink is dry on the mortgage', *per* Harman J, *Four-Maids Ltd* v. *Dudley Marshall (Properties) Ltd* [1957] Ch. 317, p. 320, even if the mortgagor is not in default, and thus has a primary right by virtue of his security; see *Birch* v. *Wright* (1786) 1 TR 378, p. 383, *per* Buller J; *Four-Maids Ltd*; this right is maintained by the Law of Property Act 1925, s. 87(1). However, the parties can contract out of this right and in practice unless the debtor is in default or the property is in some way threatened, it is unlikely that a mortgagee would want to be troubled with the burdens associated with going into possession; indeed in *Four-Maids Ltd* case, p. 321, Harman J referred to the mortgage allowing the mortgagee immediate possession as 'an old-fashioned type of mortgage'. Such a rule, by necessary implication, would also apply to the mortgage of personalty, but it is thought, as a matter of practical convenience, that the parties would expressly negate the mortgagee's automatic right to possession. In the case of a mortgage of personalty by an individual, the Bills of Sale Act (1878) Amendment Act 1882, s. 7 would also effectively negate the mortgagee's common law right to possession.

14 See *Standard Chartered Bank* v. *Walker* [1992] 1 WLR 561, p. 567C, *per* Vinelott J (shareholder prevented from exercising his vote at an extraordinary general meeting against a reconstruction proposal supported by the company's major creditors and security holders; cf. *Pender* v. *Lushington* (1877) 6 Ch. D 70).

the debtor performs the primary duty or obligation,[15] in practice it merely provides the holder with a right of recourse against some specified form of property and arises independently of the primary agreement.[16] A real security interest is designed to protect the interests of its holder by giving him a real right in addition to any personal liability his debtor may be under to him. At the present time the common law only recognises four types of transaction as conferring a security interest: (i) the mortgage; (ii) the charge; (iii) the pledge; and (iv) the consensual lien.[17] It can be seen that these security transactions are either possessory[18] or non-possessory in character.[19]

A quasi-security interest can be defined as any form of arrangement that secures the debtor's performance of the duty or obligation he is under. Essentially, this involves looking at each transaction in order to determine whether its function is to provide the creditor with security. It will be noted that this test is basically the same as that given above under the layperson's concept. The main distinguishing feature between the real security interest and the quasi-security interest is that the former concept only involves rights over the property of the debtor, whereas under the latter concept the location of strict proprietary interests is irrelevant.

A good example of this distinction is provided by the leading case of *Armour* v. *Thyssen Edelstahlwerke AG*.[20] The case concerned a dispute between the appellants, a West German manufacturer and supplier of steel, and the respondent, the receiver of a Scottish manufacturing and engineering company, as to the ownership of a quantity of steel in the receiver's possession which had not been paid for. This steel had been supplied by the appellants subject to a retention-of-title clause which provided that title to the steel would not pass until the purchaser had paid 'all debts' owing to the supplier. It was argued on the behalf of the receiver that the clause was void, as a security interest which was only valid under Scots law if accompanied by a transfer of possession to the security holder (which had not taken place).[21] However, the House of Lords was unanimous in rejecting this argument, that such a retention-of-title clause could be regarded as a security interest in law, since there was no element of creation in the transaction whereby security rights were transferred to the supplier. The leading speech was given by Lord Keith who explained the position as follows:

> I am, however, unable to regard a provision reserving title to the seller until payment of all debts due to him by the buyer as amounting to the creation by the buyer of a right of security in favour of the seller. Such a provision does in

15 The ability of a debtor to give security undoubtedly makes it easier to raise finance and will also affect the rate of interest charged for a loan – the better the security, the lower the rate of interest.

16 In the sense that the security right is only triggered upon failure of the primary agreement.

17 See *Re Cosslett (Contractors) Ltd* [1998] Ch. 495, p. 508, *per* Millett LJ. The proposition that there are but limited categories of transaction recognised by the common law as security interests (a numerus clausus) has been rejected by some commentators, see: op. cit., Allen, fn 5; op. cit., Oditah, fn 5. However, it is submitted in this chapter (pp. 28–37) that their claims are misguided (i.e. that there need not be an element of creation in order to constitute a security interest), since the four transactions (i)–(iv) are the only ones that at present exist whereby a debtor can confer an interest over his own property. But see p. 37 *et seq.* in this chapter for the Insolvency Act approach to security interests.

18 I.e. types (iii) and (iv).

19 I.e. types (i) (ii).

20 [1991] 2 AC 339; see de Lacy 'All-sums retention of title: a failure of consideration?' (1991) 5 JIBL 201.

21 I.e. the 'traditio' rule, a long-established principle of Scottish property law; see fn 51.

a sense give the seller security for the unpaid debts of the buyer. But it does so by way of a legitimate retention of title, not by virtue of any right over his own property conferred to the buyer.

In all cases where a right of security is conferred, the debtor retains an ultimate right[22] over the subject matter in question. The creditor, having realised out of that subject matter a sufficient sum to meet the debt, is obliged to account to the debtor for any surplus. Where, however, the seller of goods retains title until some condition has been satisfied, and on failure of such satisfaction repossesses them, then he is not obliged to account to the buyer for any part of the value of the goods. Where the condition is to the effect that the price of the goods shall have been paid and it has not been paid, then in the situation where the market price of the goods has risen, so that they are worth more than the contract price, the extra value belongs to the unpaid seller. That is clearly the position where the condition relates to payment of the price of the actual goods, and goes to show that the retention of title provision is not one creating a right of security, forming an exception to the general rule requiring possession by the creditor. The same is true, in my opinion, where the provision covers not only the price of the very goods which are the subject of the particular contract of sale, but also all debts due to the seller under other contracts.[23]

The evolution and early regulation of security interests under English law

In the early days, before the Industrial Revolution took off, the English economy was predominantly rural/agricultural in nature. From a security interest point of view, possession was all and the devices of the pledge and the lien were the only forms of security interest that were recognised. Indeed the main mechanism for signalling the conveyance of property was a transfer of possession. Such a society was reliant on the barter as the main method of exchange before coinage became established[24] via the recognition of currency. The old expression 'possession is nine-tenths of the law' stems from this rather (from today's perspective) primitive maxim. However, in a technologically challenged medieval (and pre-medieval) society, physical dominance of property via possession was the only real method of demonstrating control and therefore implicit ownership of property. In such a simple (and perhaps hypothetical) economy possession is power. That is to say, all property claims and titles are manifested in the person with actual possession of the same. Conveyance by contract is unknown and property transfers are manifested by physical delivery or assumption of possession. Perhaps the oldest forms of property transfer, namely transactions by way of barter and pledge, are the best examples of commercial exchange in such an economy. In a non-literate and isolated society one might expect to find these types of transaction as the basic and exclusive method of exchange. This description has a feudal air and, from a modern perspective, would be rejected out of hand as

22 I.e. the equity of redemption. See also: *Re Bond Worth Ltd* [1980] Ch 228, p. 248 E–F, *per* Slade J; *Re George Inglefield Ltd* [1933] 1 Ch1, p. 27, *per* Romer LJ.

23 [1991] 2 AC 339, p. 353A–E and note: *Bristol Airport plc.* v. *Powdrill* [1990] Ch. 744, p. 760C–D, *per* Browne-Wilkinson VC; *The Manchester, Sheffield & Lincolnshire Railway Co.* v. *The North Central Wagon Co.* (1888) 13 App. Cas. 554, p. 567, *per* Lord Macnaghten.

24 Particularly coinage of precious metal, such as gold or silver.

an economic, or even legal, model on which to base a society.[25] Commercial activity based upon a freely available exchange of goods and services would be largely frustrated if the legal regime were to be exclusively based upon possessory concepts. Nevertheless, historically, English law has shown a reverence for possessory concepts which, until the mid-nineteenth century, were to dominate the regulation of proprietary assignments. Despite this, the modern industrialised economy fuelled by a free supply of credit could not have evolved into its present state if possessory rules had remained unchecked. Thus, contract developed as the main method of conveyance, aided by an increasingly literate society with a less isolationist and more international outlook. Economic growth could only be sustained by increasing markets and production which could not be achieved if productive assets were only susceptible to possessory security interests. Nevertheless, the moment contractual conveyance mechanisms began to take off, the certainty of proprietary rights was lost for ever. The separation of title and possession to property meant that no longer could an assignee assume without more that the potential assignor in possession had an indefeasible title to convey. Even today English law is still struggling to accommodate this separation, which in the domain of security interests began to manifest itself when the mortgage and charge replaced the pledge and lien as the main methods of security assignment. Registration systems developed to meet the challenge posed by these developments although, as we shall see, they have met with conflicting degrees of success.

Curiously, English law has never articulated any consistent objectives that form the basis of any of the myriad of registration schemes[26] that currently exist. Instead, security registers have developed piecemeal in response to the simple pragmatic concerns that befell each passing generation. For example, historically, the preoccupation of the law (in terms of its attempts to regulate security transactions) has been with preventing fraud. Although such concerns can be traced at least as far back as 1376,[27] the generally accepted starting point is 1571 and the Statute of Fraudulent Conveyances. This statute[28] provided that all transfers of property made with the 'intent to delay, hinder, or defraud creditors and others' were void and that the value of such a transfer could be recovered. However, the importance of the statute lies, not so much in its wording, but upon the interpretation given to it by the court of the Star Chamber in the celebrated *Twyne's Case*.[29] Here, Twyne was indebted to two parties A and B. After being sued by B to recover his debt, Twyne secretly assigned all his property to A, in satisfaction of his debt, prior to B's writ being heard.

25 Such a society existed in England until the fifteenth century when the common law began to recognise contractual-based conveyance mechanisms in personal property, although it was not until the eighteenth century that this trend became firmly established in both the domain of sales and security transactions. See: Holdsworth *A History of English Law* (5th edn, 1942), vol. 3, pp. 354–5; *Cochrane* v. *Moore* (1890) 25 QBD 57, pp. 70–1, *per* Fry LJ.

26 For a list of the main security registers, see the Diamond Report *A Review of Security Interests in Personal Property* (London: DTI, 1989), p. 67, para. 12.1.2; Goode *Commercial Law* (3rd edn, 2004), pp. 650–1.

27 50 Edw. 3, c. 6, An Act to avoid collusive gifts in favour of execution creditors.

28 13 Eliz.1, c. 5; see ss. 1 and 2; see now the Insolvency Act 1986, s. 423. Reference should also be made to the statute of 27 Eliz. c. 4, 1585: 'An Act Against Covinous And Fraudulent Conveyances' which provided similar protection to purchasers of land; see now the Law of Property Act 1925, s. 173.

29 (1601) 3 Coke 80b. It has been remarked that *Twyne's Case* 'inextricably mixed though it may be with Lord Coke's gloss has become part of the statute itself'; Elkus and Glenn *A Treatise on Secret Liens and Reputed Ownership* (1910), p. 3.

Twyne was allowed to remain in possession of the property after the alleged transfer with full powers of disposition and to deal with it as his own, despite the transfer to A. The court struck down the transaction as a fraud within the Statute because of Twyne's continued possession of the property after the alleged transfer with full powers of disposition and was not satisfied as to its bona fides.[30] As is stated in the report of the case: 'because fraud and deceit abound in these days more than in former times ... all statutes made against fraud should be liberally and beneficially expounded to suppress fraud'.[31] The case was to have wide ramifications for commercial practice over the following centuries because, in certain quarters, the judgment was distilled down to the principle that the continued possession of property by an assignor was taken as being proof that the transaction as a whole was fraudulent and to be avoided. Thus, in *Edwards* v. *Harben*[32] the rule was proclaimed that any absolute assignment of property in goods which was not accompanied by the delivery of possession to the assignee was at law fraudulent against creditors.[33] Again in *Wordall* v. *Smith*[34] Lord Ellenborough is reported as stating: 'There must be an exclusive possession [in the assignee] under the assignment, or it is fraudulent and void as against creditors'.[35] Professor Goode has commented that '[u]ntil 1854 the non-possessory chattel mortgage was almost invariably doomed to failure, for the debtor's continuance in possession after granting a security bill of sale was regarded as nearly conclusive evidence

30 The court found six badges of fraud in the transaction: (a) the assignment covered all the debtor's property; (b) the debtor continued in possession of the property with full powers of disposition; (c) the assignment was made in secret; (d) the assignment was made pending a writ; (e) the assignment was to operate as a trust 'and fraud is always apparelled and clad with a trust, and a trust is the cover of fraud' (1601) 3 Coke 80b, p. 81a; and (f) the assignment stated that it was made bona fide, which was suspicious as to the true intent of the parties.

31 (1601) 3 Coke 80b, p. 82a. It transpires that apart from being an early form of creditor protection statute the Statute of Fraudulent Conveyances was also intended as a revenue measure for the benefit of the Crown, since by virtue of s. 3 of the Act, one-half the value of the property transferred by the offending conveyance went to the Crown, with the other half to the persons aggrieved, which may, in part, explain the court's eagerness to 'liberally and beneficially' expand its ambit; see Glenn *Fraudulent Conveyances and Preferences* (rev. edn, 1940), pp. 87–94.

It should be noted that the avoidance power could only be exercised in favour of a judgment creditor, or creditor having some other process which authorised seizure, since prior to attaining that status, the creditor would have no interest over the debtor's estate (i.e. the right to interfere in the fraudulent disposition); 'When a conveyance is said to be void against creditors, the reference is to such parties when clothed with their legal judgments and executions, or such other titles as the law has provided for the collection of debts', *Van Heusen* v. *Radcliff* (1858) 17 NY 580; and see *Noble* v. *Holmes* (1843) 5 Hill 194 to like effect. Likewise the assignor/debtor had no *standi* to invoke the Statute; *Robinson* v. *M'Donnell* (1818) 2 B & Ald 134.

32 (1788) 2 TR 587.

33 Although the assignment was expressed to be absolute, it was in fact by way of security with the assignor being given 14 days in which to repay the debt, or possession would be taken. Ironically the court was to acknowledge that not all assignments without a transfer of possession were fraudulent 'if the want of immediate possession be consistent with the deed' (1788) 2 TR 587, p. 597, *per* Buller J. However, the fact that the assignment was expressed to be by way of bill of sale seems to have been taken as requiring an immediate delivery of the goods in order to be consistent with the expressed transaction.

34 (1808) 1 Camp 332.

35 (1808) 1 Camp, p. 334.

of an intent to defraud creditors within the Fraudulent Conveyances Act 1571'.[36] Similar sentiments are also to be found elsewhere.[37] Nevertheless, these views amount to a gross simplification and distort the true picture at that time.[38] For example, the rule enunciated in *Edwards* v. *Harben* was contrary to that already established at the time of the decision in *Ryall* v. *Rolle*[39] where Burnet J, after reviewing the cases, was to explain:

> From all these cases it appears, that upon the construction of the statute of the 13th of Eliz. [i.e. Fraudulent Conveyances Act 1571] there is no room to make a distinction betwixt conditional and absolute sales of goods, if made to defraud creditors, but a court or jury are left to consider of this from the circumstances of the case.[40]

In a case prior to *Wordall* v. *Smith* Lord Ellenborough had not been prepared to state so bold a rule such that an assignor's continued possession 'was, in some measure, indicative of fraud; but was not conclusive'.[41]

It is strange how the retention of possession by the assignor equalled fraud notion ever gained credence. Certainly *Twyne's Case* did not support so simple a proposition, more that retention of possession by an assignor was an ingredient to look for in ascertaining a fraudulent motive.[42] More important, the Statute of Fraudulent Conveyances said nothing about possession as an element in the fraud equation and even emphasised that transactions made in good faith and upon good consideration were unaffected.[43] It is, perhaps, more accurate to state the law at the time of the decisions in *Edwards* and *Wordall* as being that if an assignor remained in possession of property, it would raise a rebuttable presumption of fraud until the assignee could demonstrate to the court his good title and the reason why he allowed the assignor to remain in possession.[44] Post *Edwards* and *Wordall* there is no evidence to support any fraud in possession rule.

36 *Commercial Law* (3rd edn, London: Penguin, 2004), p. 586. The proposition is qualified by Goode (fn 57), such that in case of an absolute transfer, failure to take possession was 'conclusive evidence of fraud', citing *Edwards* v. *Harben* (1788) 2 TR 587. However, in the case of a security transfer the failure to take possession 'was very strong evidence of fraud' but not conclusive in point of law.

37 Davies (1988) 37 ICLQ 465: '[*Twyne's Case*] demonstrated a simple rule which was that in order to obtain priority in an asset over third parties, it was not only necessary to receive consent of the prior owner but also possession of the chattel'; Diamond (1960) 23 MLR 399: 'Originally, the courts were prepared to presume fraud in any transfer of property where the grantor remained in possession...' (p. 400, citing *Twyne's Case*).

38 I.e. pre-1854.

39 (1749) 1 Atk 165.

40 (1749) 1 Atk, p. 169.

41 *Hoffman* v. *Pitt* (1803) 5 Esp. pp. 22, p. 25.

42 See fn 30.

43 See s. 5.

44 See: *Bucknal* v. *Roiston* (1709) Prec. Ch 285; *Ryall* v. *Rolle*, fn 40 and the main text thereat, *per* Burnet J; *Cadogan* v. *Kennett* (1776) 2 Cowp 432; *Holbird* v. *Anderson* (1793) 5 TR 235; *Arundell* v. *Phipps* and see fn 45, *per* Lord Eldon LC.

Indeed, these cases were to be readily distinguished,[45] although sidestepped might be a more accurate description.[46] By 1820 the cases were openly criticised,[47] such that from that point onwards the 'rule', if it ever existed, was rejected as a matter of routine.[48] To return to Professor Goode's observation,[49] it can now, perhaps, be rephrased so that prior to 1854 an assignor's continued possession of personal property would almost inevitably be subject to legal challenge upon the ground that it was a fraudulent transfer.[50] However, the success of any such challenge would be dependent on factors other than merely establishing the retention of possession by the assignor.[51]

Although the development of non-possessory security assignments, sanctioned by the rejection of the fraud in possession rule, is to be welcomed, it did produce a significant injustice to other creditors of the debtor/assignor who might seek to levy execution or, likewise, take an absolute or security assignment over the encumbered property. This injustice was caused by the fact that creditors, or indeed potential creditors, had no means of ascertaining the true state of affairs other than via the goodwill of the debtor. Thus, creditors were faced with the prospect of prior undisclosed interests materialising when they sought to levy execution or enforce their own proprietary assignment against the debtor. It would be wrong to apportion any blame upon assignees for this state of affairs, since they could not be expected to remedy this information problem. How could an assignee be expected to disclose his non-possessory interest to the world? What emerged was a classic lesser of two evils problem. Economic growth depended upon the availability of non-possessory secured credit. However, the availability of this type of credit, although serving to stimulate the economy, created a problem of ostensible ownership, since third parties dealing with a debtor would have no independent method of discovering the existence of prior interests. The growth of the industrialised economy ensured that the interests of non-possessory secured finance prevailed in this conflict. Since fraud has

45 Given the nature of the cases prior to *Edwards* and *Wordall*, it is submitted that there was in fact no precedent in their favour; see *Arundell* v. *Phipps* (1804) 10 Ves Jun 139, p. 145, *per* Lord Eldon LC: 'The mere circumstance of possession of chattels, however familiar it may be to say, that it proves fraud, amounts to no more than, that it is prima facie evidence of property in the man possessing, until a title, not fraudulent, is shewn, under which that possession has followed'.

46 See: *Kidd* v. *Rawlinson* (1800) 2 Bos & Pul 59; *Meux* v. *Howell* (1803) 4 East 1; *Benton* v. *Thornhill* (1816) 7 Taunt 150; *Jozeph* v. *Ingram* (1817) 8 Taunt 837.

47 See: *Steward* v. *Lombe* (1820) 1 Brod & B 506, p. 511, *per* Dallas CJ '*Edwards* v. *Harben* has been dissented from often'; *Eastwood* v. *Brown* (1825) R & M 312, 313, *per* Abbott LCJ: 'I cannot agree to the doctrine laid down in [*Wordall* v. *Smith*]'.

48 See: *Benton* v. *Brown* (1825) R & M 312; *Latimer* v. *Batson* (1825) 4 B & C 652; *Eastwood* v. *Brown* (1825) R & M 312; *Martindale* v. *Booth* (1832) 3 B & A 495; *Reeves* v. *Capper* (1838) 5 Bing NC 136.

49 See fn 36.

50 See *Cookson* v. *Swire* (1884) 9 App. Cas. 653, p. 665, *per* Lord Blackburn.

51 Cf. the 'traditio' rule of Scottish common law which states that there cannot be an effective security unless there is a transfer of possession. This rule has caused considerable problems with the extended retention-of-title clause; see generally: de Lacy [1989] Conv. 364; *Armour* v. *Thyssen Edelstahlwerke AG* [1991] 2 AC 339. The rule was also criticised by the Diamond Report (see fn 26), as being 'no longer compatible with modern business needs' (para. 8.2.3). Prior to the introduction of the Sale of Goods Act 1893, ss. 17(1), 18r.1 in Scotland, property in goods would generally not pass unless the buyer took delivery; see Brown, *The Sale of Goods* (1895), p. 80 – the position was different in England (see fn 76).

always tended to be a minority occupation, the interests of the majority were always bound to triumph.

The Statute of Fraudulent Conveyances suffered from three main defects: first, it was difficult to prove a fraudulent intent behind property assignments; second, it only covered dispositions of the debtor's property; and, third, it did nothing to cure the ostensible ownership problem caused by the recognition of a separation between title and possession to property. In an attempt to meet these problems the Bankruptcy Act 1623 introduced the concept of reputed ownership into English law.[52] This Act provided that upon a bankruptcy any goods or chattels in the possession of the bankrupt, with the consent of the true owner such that the bankrupt appeared to be the reputed owner of the same were available to the bankruptcy commissioners in order to realise them for the benefit of general creditors. In short any assignee who failed to take possession[53] or, demand possession (so as to deny consensual possession remaining with the bankrupt)[54] prior to the bankruptcy of a debtor would lose the benefit of his assignment. The Act was strictly construed and in all cases where the debtor was in consensual possession title would be lost upon bankruptcy, despite the fact that this would render the value of much non-possessory security illusory.[55] This statutory provision is the classic example of ostensible ownership regulation and was introduced as a direct result of contractual conveyance mechanisms beginning to replace the traditional possession based forms of conveyance. As Lee LCJ was to explain:

> [T]he Act of 21 Jac. 1 [i.e. Bankruptcy Act 1623] supposes a fair conveyance, but deprives the party of any preference, because he does not give proper notice of his conveyance, and it seems to me that the cases upon this statute are more like the cases that may happen upon the registering acts, where a person does not register, and so loses the priority of the security: so here the donee is not to suffer the donor to continue in such possession, as is prescribed against by the Act.[56]

It was earlier remarked[57] how strange it was that the fraud in possession rule came to be associated with the Statute of Fraudulent Conveyances. Certainly that Statute, nor the majority of cases decided directly under it, supported such a rule. Nevertheless, the reputed ownership provision was often invoked as an alternative mechanism to avoid assignments upon bankruptcy and it is probable that the two notions became, in some minds, intertwined. A leading US case graphically illustrates this process where it was stated:

> But I take it, where the motive of the sale is merely security to the vendee, and the owner is permitted to retain all the visible marks of ownership, for no other reason than the convenience of the parties, the contract will be void, although the reasons for the arrangement be inserted, and the provision be consistent with the deed. *The law will not and ought not to permit the owner of personal property*

52 See s. 11.

53 See: *Robinson* v. *M'Donnell* (1818) 2 B & Ald 134, p. 136, *per* Abbott CJ; *Storer* v. *Hunter* (1824) 3 B & C 368.

54 See: *Carruthers* v. *Payne* (1828) 5 Bing 270; *Smith* v. *Topping* (1833) 5 B & Ald 674.

55 See *Ryall* v. *Rolle* (1749) 1 Atk 165, p. 173 *per* Burnet J. Note also: *Shuttleworth* v. *Hernaman* (1857) 1 DeG & J 322; *Re Ginger* [1897] 2 QB 461.

56 *Ryall* v. *Rolle*, p. 180.

57 See p. 11.

> *to create an interest in another, either by mortgage or absolute sale, and still continue to be the ostensible owner; and where the creating of such an interest is the sole object, the conveyance will be fraudulent,* whether it contain a stipulation for retention of possession or not; for to indulge the motive that led to the arrangement, would be against true policy.[58]

Despite the apparent simplicity of the reputed ownership rule, by the nineteenth century it was beginning to be construed increasingly restrictively by the courts.[59] Exceptions to the rule, based on trade customs, emerged which slowly began to erode at the efficacy of the doctrine.[60] Consensual possession per se in a bankrupt was not enough to attract the doctrine; rather, reputed ownership had to be proved in fact.[61] Clearly, the forces that had destroyed the establishment of a fraud in possession rule under the 1571 Act were at work again. As Parke B. was to explain:

> Whatever may have been the state of commerce in the time of James 1, it is evident that, at the present day, a trader does not obtain credit by the possession and apparent ownership of other persons' goods, but in consequence of his general estimation as a merchant.[62]

Indeed, later versions of the Bankruptcy Act were to restrict the ambit of the reputed ownership doctrine, so that it only applied where the bankrupt was a trader and did not cover any goods held on trust or, significantly, to things in action other than debts due in the course of the bankrupt's business.[63] More importantly, the notion of 'reputed ownership' became discredited and the exception rather than the rule in bankruptcy. Such became the numbers of exceptions that it became 'virtually impossible'[64] to apply the reputed ownership doctrine which, by the twentieth century, was an 'irrelevance'.[65] However, it was not until the passage of the Insolvency Act 1985[66] that the doctrine was finally repealed. Significantly, the rule never applied to companies.[67]

Both the Statute of Fraudulent Conveyances and the reputed ownership doctrine only applied indirectly to assignments by way of security. The first legislation to target directly a transaction operating by way of security was the 1604 Act Against Brokers.[68]

58 *Clow* v. *Woods* (1819) 5 Serg & Rawle 275, *per* Gibson J (author's emphasis); see also Davies, fn 37.

59 See: *Ex parte Watkins* (1873) LR 8 Ch. App. 520, p. 532, *per* Lord Selborne LC; *Ex parte Kemp* (1874) LR 9 Ch. App. 383, p. 389, *per* Mellish LJ.

60 See, for example: *Watson* v. *Peache* (1834) 1 Bing (NC) 327; *Mullett* v. *Green* (1838) 8 C & P 382; *Ex parte Watkins* (1873) LR 8 Ch.

61 See *Ex parte Watkins* (1873) LR 8 Ch, p. 528, *per* Lord Selborne LC.

62 *Belcher* v. *Bellamy* (1848) 2 Ex 303, p. 309.

63 See: the Bankruptcy Act 1869, s. 15; later replaced by Bankruptcy Acts 1883, s. 44; 1914, s. 38(c).

64 See: Cork Report (1982) Cmnd 8558, para. 1088; Blagden Report (1957) Cmnd 222, para.110 to like effect. Note also *Salford Van Hire Ltd* v. *Bocholt Developments Ltd* [1995] CLC 611.

65 See: Cork Report, para. 1092; *Stoneleigh Finance Ltd* v. *Phillips* [1965] 2 QB 537, p. 566C, *per* Sellers LJ (goods subject to hire-purchase terms do not convey the impression of ownership so as to induce unjustified credit); *Salford Van Hire.*

66 See s. 235(3) and Schedule 10 Part 3, repealing s. 38(c) of the Bankruptcy Act 1914.

67 See: Re Crumlin Viaduct Works Company (1879) 11 Ch. D. 755; *Gorringe* v. *Irwell India Rubber & Gutta Percha Works* (1886) 34 Ch. D. 128.

68 1 Jac.1 c.21 (1604).

This Act targeted the pledge/pawn of goods and was designed to target the fencing of stolen property which was becoming a problem in London at that time. The Act, and its successors,[69] attempted to regulate the trade of pawnbroking by, for example, establishing a system of licensed pawnbrokers and other forms of regulation of the trade. It also abolished the market overt rule in respect of pawns of stolen goods and imposed basic forms of accountability where it was suspected that property had been stolen and pawned on. In many ways this pawnbroking legislation was an early form of consumer protection law and it is not surprising to learn that the legislation was later to be subsumed/repealed by the Consumer Credit Act 1974 (as amended). However, in respect of security interests, the Act is of only passing significance, since it only affected the pledge of goods to a pawnbroker. More significant developments were to occur with the passage of the first Bills of Sale Act in 1854.

To return to our earlier theme. The main problem with the reputed ownership doctrine had always been that it was limited to bankruptcy situations and could not be invoked merely because a secondary assignee had been misled. Despite this, the legislature was not adverse to the plight in the minority situation where a debtor would fraudulently conceal information about his prior assignments. Thus, in 1854 the first Bills of Sale Act was passed with the express intention of preventing debtors keeping up the appearance of being in good circumstances and possessed of property when in reality their assets were encumbered.[70] Under this Act, any documentary assignment (whether absolute or conditional) which allowed the assignor to remain in possession of personal chattels[71] while granting the assignee the right to seize or take possession was rendered 'null and void' in the event of the assignor's bankruptcy or against execution creditors, unless the document was registered within 21 days of its creation.[72] The Act established the first universal register of personal property assignments and enabled, in theory, any person dealing with a debtor the ability to ascertain the true state of encumbrances against the debtor's estate.[73] From this point onwards the argument that a debtor's continued possession of property after an assignment was fraudulent in law effectively died.[74] The Bills of Sale Act was clearly passed to deal with an established phenomenon, non-possessory assignment, and its provisions were a reaction to the lack of information sanctioned by such assignment. Those that have championed the myth of the fraud in possession rule overlook the fact that this legislation contained no repeal of the common law, nor any enabling

69 See generally various Pawnbrokers Acts: 30 Geo.2 c.24 (1757); 24 Geo.3 c.42 (1784); 25 Geo.3 c.48 (1785); 27 Geo.3 c.37 (1787); 28 Geo.3 c.50 (1788); 29 Geo.3 c.57 (1789); 31 Geo.3 c.52 (1791); 36 Geo.3 c.87 (1796); 39 & 40 Geo.3 c.99 (1800); 19 & 20 Vict. c.27 (1856); 22 & 23 Vict. c.14 (1859); 20 & 21 Vict. c. 21 (1860); 35 & 36 Vict. c.93 (1872); Pawnbrokers Act 1960.

70 See the preamble to the Bills of Sale Act 1854.

71 Although the Bills of Sale Acts were originally confined to assignments of chattels certain assignments of book debts were required to be registered under the Bills of Sale Act 1878 by virtue of the Bankruptcy Act 1914, s. 43; see now the Insolvency Act 1986, s. 344.

72 s. 1. The registration period was later reduced to seven days; see the Bills of Sale Act 1878, s. 8.

73 See ss. 3 and 4. In order to protect the free flow of commerce not all bills of sale required registration and transfers of goods made in the ordinary course of business; bills of lading; other documents of title/control of goods and choses in action, among other things were excluded from the Act; see s. 7.

74 A few (unsuccessful) cases are still to be found in the law reports after this time, but they are very much in a minority when compared with the reported cases pre-1854; see: *Alton* v. *Harrison* (1869) LR 4 Ch. 622; *Ex parte Games* (1879) 40 LT 789.

provisions to sanction non-possessory assignment, a fact that conclusively destroys any arguments to the contrary.[75]

In the sale of goods arena it was also established law that, unless a contrary intention appeared, property in specific goods was transferred at the date of the contract despite the fact that the buyer might not have taken possession.[76]

One final development occurred in this period, namely the emergence of the rule in *Dearle* v. *Hall*.[77] This case concerned a simple priority dispute between two rival assignees of the benefit of a trust fund. The issue to be determined was which assignee should take priority: the first assignee in time or, the first assignee to give notice of his assignment to the trust fund holder? The court held that the first assignee to give notice to the fund holder would take priority. Although this case concerned the question of priority relating to successive assignments of a trust fund, the case has since had wide ramifications for assignments of choses in action in general and become the main rule of priority in this type of situation. Originally the court in *Dearle* v. *Hall* based its decision, in part,[78] on the erroneous belief that by requiring an assignee to give notice to the fund holder that this was the equivalent of taking possession of goods which was required to pass title.[79] However, the case is now regarded as an example of the common law imposing a perfection requirement on the assignee if he is to be able to assert title legally to a chose in action, following the assignment, in priority to any third-party rival assignee. The case of *Dearle* v. *Hall* is important because it provides a rare example of the common law adapting to the needs of commercial exchange and providing us with a simple rule of priority.

The needs of commerce ensured that, by the turn of the nineteenth century, English law had long since cast off the shackles imposed by an exclusive possession-based conveyance mechanism of title to goods/choses in action.[80] This was the very conundrum facing the court in *Dearle* v. *Hall*.[81] Even today English law is still struggling to

75 See *Ex parte Allen* (1870) LR 11 Eq 209, p. 211, *per* Bacon CJ. Note also the Statute of Frauds 1677, s. 17, which provided that any contract for the sale of goods for a price of more than £10 'shall not be allowed to be good' unless: the buyer actually received part of the good; paid part of the price or gave something in earnest to bind the bargain; or a memorandum in writing evidenced the contract signed by the parties. This statute was yet another expressed to suppress the 'many fraudulent practices of the time'; see preamble. Nevertheless, the Act did expressly acknowledge both contract-based and possession-based conveyance mechanisms in the sale-of-goods arena. The Act was, however, a conspicuous failure in terms of preventing fraud and although the provision was later replaced by s. 4 of the Sale of Goods Act 1893, which, in turn, was repealed in 1954.

76 See: *Blackstone's Commentaries* (1766) vol. 2, pp. 448–9; *Blackburn on Sale* (1st edn, 1845), p. 147; *Ryall* v. *Rowles* (1749) 1 Ves 348, p. 361, *per* Burnet J; *Phillimore* v. *Barry* (1808) 1 Camp 513, p. 515, *per* Lord Ellenborough; *Rugg* v. *Minelt* (1809) 11 East 210, p. 219, *per* Bayley J; *Simmons* v. *Swift* (1826) 5 B & C 857, p. 862, *per* Bayley J; *Tarling* v. *Baxter* (1827) 6 B&C 360, p. 364, *per* Bayley J; *Dixon* v. *Yates* (1833) 5 B & Ad 313, p. 340, *per* Parke J.

77 (1823) 3 Russ 1.

78 There were two other grounds for the judgment: (a) notice to the fund holder was necessary to convert the fund holder into a trustee for the assignee; (b) notice to the fund holder was necessary to prevent the assignor from making any further fraudulent assignments and thereby misleading third-party assignees who would be unable to verify the title of the assignor in the absence of the fund holder having notice of prior assignments; see *Dearle* v. *Hall* (1823) 3 Russ 1, pp. 12–13, 22–3, *per* Sir Thomas Plummer MR.

79 This belief was ultimately founded on a simple interpretation of *Twyne's Case* and serves as yet another example of the confusion in the law at the time.

80 See fn 25.

81 (1828) 3 Russ 1.

accommodate this separation, which in the domain of security interests began to manifest itself when the mortgage and charge replaced the pledge and lien as the main methods of security assignment.[82] Outside the context of bankruptcy, registration systems developed (the first being the Bills of Sale Act 1854) to meet the information challenge posed by these developments, although they were largely confined to the domain of security assignments.[83] No general system existed to record the non-security assignments.[84] Instead, protection was afforded in limited circumstances by virtue of successive Factors Acts based on the principle of ostensible ownership/authority.[85] These developments were entirely statutory. The moment English common law recognised contract as a method of assignment in its own right no longer could a party in physical possession be regarded as possessing the exclusive proprietary interest. Henceforth, some active representation was required to destroy the title of a party not in possession and the *nemo dat* rule and its equitable counterpart were the main regulating principles in the event of any title conflict.[86] *Dearle* v. *Hall* emerged as an exception to this trend and was a judge-made attempt to regulate what, in other areas, was to become the prerogative of Parliament.

The Bills of Sale Act 1854 was far from perfect and contained a number of inherent limitations. It assumed that proprietary assignments would inevitably be contained in written documents – hence the Act's title – and therefore oral assignments were unaffected, remaining secret within the vice that the Act was intended to cure. Second, the Act contained no priority rule for competing assignments, so that the common law would continue to regulate priority disputes. Perhaps, more alarming was the fact that an unregistered bill of sale was not avoided against a later registered interest, so that absent formal bankruptcy proceedings, according to the common law priority rules, the prior unregistered and undisclosed interest would generally prevail. Finally, and this is a feature which has served to undermine all English personal property security registers to this day, the scheme only covered dispositions by the debtor and, therefore, quasi-security interests were excluded. Some of these deficiencies were plugged by the successor Act of 1878 which introduced a new statutory priority rule according to the date a bill of sale was registered,[87] thus ensuring the greater reliability of the register for secured creditors.

The Act of 1878 was supplemented by an Act of 1882 which, henceforth, governed all security transfers by way of bill of sale.[88] The latter Act returned to the theme of fraud and can best be described as an early form of consumer protection measure since it was intended to protect the public from the usurer who would 'extract extortionate

82 It is ironic that in a possession-oriented environment such devices as the pledge and lien were countenanced, since they sanctioned a separation of title and possession to goods. That is to say a genuine possession-based conveyance rule can only be based on the principle that possession = ownership. Quaere the status of theft in the latter system: can a thief pass good title to a bona fide purchaser? See further Ames (1889–90) 3 Harv LR 23.

83 See: Companies (Clauses) Act 1845, s. 45 (statutory companies); Companies Act 1862, s. 43 (companies incorporated by registration) – see now Part 25 of the Companies Act 2006; Bills of Sale Act 1854 (individuals) – see now Bills of Sale Acts 1878–91.

84 However, the Bills of Sale Acts of 1854 and 1878 did apply to certain absolute assignments of chattels, but such assignments were, by their nature, in the minority when compared to security assignments.

85 See Factors Acts 1823–77, later replaced by Factors Act 1889.

86 See *Johnson* v. *Crédit Lyonnais Co.* (1877) 3 CPD 32.

87 Bills of Sale Act 1878, s. 10.

88 The Act of 1878 still governs non-security assignments, although these are now very much minority transactions.

bargains from needy persons in comparative safety behind security bills of sale'.[89] Protection was offered by specifying a minutiae of details that had to be complied with otherwise the bill would be void.[90] Interestingly, if such a bill was not registered within seven days of execution, it was rendered completely void, even against the grantor.[91] Although the measure prescribed great formalities for the execution of security bills of sale, it did not provide that all security assignments be in documentary form and thus oral security remained excluded from the regime. The 1882 Act is really the first example of a registration regime seeking to go beyond publication of information and priority service and actually regulate an internal contractual relationship.[92]

Both the Acts of 1878 and 1882 are still in force governing assignments by individuals.[93] However, they both suffer from the fundamental defect that they only deal with one type of information problem, that is, assignments by a debtor of an interest in his property. Therefore, transactions by way of conditional sale, hire purchase, lease, to name but a few, have always remained immune from the registration machinery.[94] This is despite the fact that these types of transactions ostensibly perform the same function as the bill of sale and cause the same information and priority problems that led to the introduction of public registration in 1854. The problem has long been appreciated, but we are still awaiting a solution. As Lord Herschell LC was to state in the leading case of the time:

> If a transaction of that description [i.e. a conditional sale] is within the mischief of the Bills of Sale Act, then the Bills of Sale Act needs amendment. I do not say whether it is so or is not; but it seems to me impossible to bring this case within the Bills of Sale Act because the transaction may bear a resemblance to a transaction which would be within it on the ground that it is within the mischief, when the initial step of bringing the Bills of Sale Act into operation at all fails, namely, that there should have been an assurance, or an assignment, or a licence to seize, or any of the other matters referred to in the Bills of Sale Act given by the bankrupt to some other person.[95]

Whatever limitations accompanied the Bills of Sale legislation, at least they appeared to recognise the basic information problem caused by an assignment of personal property without the simultaneous transfer of possession. Nevertheless, it remains a mystery why intangible property assignments, and in particular assignments of debts, remained excluded from this registration machinery. Possession of intangible property is generally a physical impossibility unless it is susceptible to reduction into documentary form.[96] The most common example of this would be

89 Waldock *The Law of Mortgages* (2nd edn, 1950), p. 79.

90 See generally the Bills of Sale Act (1878) Amendment Act 1882, ss. 4, 5, 9 and Schedule.

91 Ibid., s. 8.

92 It is generally agreed that this Act failed in all its goals and the prescribed level of formality was so great that it had the effect of 'removing the mortgage on goods out of the realm of responsible, respectable financial business'; see Diamond in Sauvelplanne (ed.), *Security over Corporeal Moveables* (1974), p. 34.

93 The position in respect of company assignments is discussed below, p. 20 *et seq.*

94 I.e. quasi-security interests.

95 *McEntire* v. *Crossley* [1895] AC 457, p. 466. See also *Helby* v. *Matthews* [1895] AC 471, p. 482, *per* Lord Macnaghten, to like effect in the context of a hire-purchase transaction.

96 E.g. a negotiable instrument. The common law was to recognise the bill of lading as a document of title to goods at an early stage; see *Lickbarrow* v. *Mason* (1787) 2 TR 64.

an assignment of a debt. Since a debt has no physical existence other than as an acknowledgement by a person of an existing monetary obligation in favour of another, it is clearly impossible to take possession of this abstract right. Therefore, the notion of possessory security could never exist to regulate this type of disposition. It might be thought that a registration scheme would provide a unique vehicle to regulate such transactions. This thought did not occur to the nineteenth-century legislature and these transactions remained immune from registration. The reason for this omission is probably because no substantial problems had materialised at that time with regard to this type of proprietary assignment. The type of ostensible ownership situation that had caused problems in the field of personal property assignments (i.e. chattels) was rejected when applied to debt assignments for, as Pollock CB was to explain: 'in reality no man has an apparent ownership of debts, or obtains credit by means of them, since debts are generally unknown'.[97] Such sentiments undoubtedly ensured that this type of assignment was excluded from the Bills of Sale Act 1854.[98] Viewed from the perspective of the modern receivables financing industry, the statement of Pollock CB demonstrates the utmost naivety. However, at that time, such financial techniques were at best in their infancy, but later to develop at a pace.[99] Nevertheless, the earlier case of *Dearle* v. *Hall*[100] appeared to have already settled the problem by providing a quasi-possessory rule that the assignee should give notice to the fund holder in order to perfect his assignment against the world. The problem was later solved in so far as it related to a general assignment of existing or future book debts by a business person which was required to be registered under the Bills of Sale Act 1878 if it were to be effective against a trustee in bankruptcy.[101]

The passage of the Bills of Sale Acts marked the high-water point in terms of the regulation of security interests in relation to individual debtors. The Acts were important from a conceptual point of view because they demonstrated that the 'solution' (at least temporarily) to the problem of a separation of ownership (or other qualified form of proprietary interest) and possession was to introduce a public register disclosing incumbrances against a debtor's estate coupled with a simple priority rule of first in time.[102] Although this legislation had grasped the basic principles of any efficient registration system, namely notice and priority, in practice the Bills of Sale Acts, at least going into the twentieth century, were a conspicuous failure, virtually destroying the ability of debtors to give, or lenders to receive, security interests over personal property.[103] Despite an almost universal acceptance of the failure of the Bills of Sale Acts, they still remain the main source of regulation in this area, but are rarely used in practice.

Instead, the twentieth century saw the development of new forms of debt financing in the individual debtor market. Transactions such as hire-purchase and conditional sale became the norm, later replaced by credit card finance and unsecured loans based on the debtor's perceived credit worthiness. Larger-scale finance for business would invariably be secured by guarantees and/or security over real property

97 See *Belcher* v. *Bellamy* (1848) 2 Ex 303, p. 308.
98 S. 7; see now the Bills of Sale Act 1878, s. 4; but see fn 101 below for a limited exception to this.
99 See *Tailby* v. *Official Receiver* (1888) 13 App Cas 523.
100 (1828) 3 Russ 1.
101 See Bankruptcy Act 1914, s. 43; see now Insolvency Act 1986, s. 344.
102 There was no intrusion of construction notice in this scheme.
103 See the comments of Professor Diamond, fn 92.

(invariably the family home).[104] The regulatory response to these developments was the formal development of modern consumer credit legislation which was to emerge in 1974 to repeal and replace the earlier attempts to regulate these new consumer transactions via the Hire Purchase Acts and Moneylenders legislation. The Consumer Credit Act 1974 (as amended)[105] does not regulate security interests per se but, instead, regulates the provision of credit and those authorised to give credit to the public. Under English law the giving of real security over personal property is now almost exclusively the prerogative of companies. It is to the emergence of corporate security that we must now turn.

The evolution of corporate security interest regulation

The regulation of company charges has a relatively long history and can be traced back to the Companies (Clauses) Act 1845.[106] This required all companies[107] incorporated by Special Act of Parliament (incorporating the standard clauses the Act of 1845 laid down) to keep a register of mortgages and bonds, which were to be entered on the register within fourteen days of creation. The only information required on this register were the names of the parties involved in the security and the amount thereby secured. A right of inspection[108] was provided for the shareholders of the chargor company, the chargee, and 'any person interested'[109] in the security could also inspect the register at 'all reasonable times'. Nevertheless, the section was largely permissive in effect since there was no penalty for failure to comply and it did not govern priorities, rendering it extremely limited as a matter of practice.

With the passage of the Companies Act 1862 – the 'Magna Carta'[110] of modern company law – the importance of the 1845 Act was greatly diminished. The consolidation of the diffuse statutes regulating the corporate form that the 1862 Act brought about was to mark the beginning of a period of rationalisation and growth. No longer was the aspiring company required to go through the cumbersome process of obtaining incorporation by Special Act of Parliament or via the limited provisions of the Joint Stock Companies Act 1844,[111] for the means of obtaining incorporation were now readily provided for under the new Act. As a result the 1845 Act can for most purposes be forgotten.[112]

104 See *Barclays Bank plc* v. *O'Brien* [1996] 1 AC 180.
105 See also Consumer Credit Act 2006.
106 See s. 45 and Schedules C and D for the forms of mortgage and bond.
107 As a matter of fact the duty was placed on the company secretary; cf. the Companies Act 1862 discussed below, pp. 21–26.
108 Such inspection was to be 'without fee or reward'.
109 This category was not defined by the Act, although subsequent developments have left this Statute largely redundant, so perhaps the question never needed to be canvassed.
110 See *Palmer's Company Law* (1st edn, 1898) p. 1, now (25th edn, 1992) vol. 1, para. 1.110.
111 For a fuller discussion of the history of incorporation, see: *Palmer's Company Law* (1992), paras. 1.106–1.108; Gower's *Principles of Modern Company Law* (London: Sweet & Maxwell, 5th edn, 1992), chs 2–3.
112 Indeed by 2006 there were only 50 companies registered by Special Act of Parliament, compared with the 2.1m that were on the register for the whole of Great Britain during the period 2005 to 2006; see the report *Companies in 2005–2006* (London, TSO, 2006) HC 1534, Tables E3 and A1.

Section 43 of the 1862 Act required companies to keep a register of 'all mortgages and charges[113] specifically affecting property of the company', the register to contain a short description of the property mortgaged or charged; the amount secured thereby and the names of parties entitled to the security. However, in contrast with the 1845 Act, no time period was specified for registration. Nevertheless, the new provision went one stage further than the 1845 Act and actually imposed a criminal penalty[114] for default. This penalty applied to every director, manager or officer of the company who 'knowingly and wilfully' authorised, or permitted non-registration of such securities. Although this development was obviously introduced to ensure compliance, the sanction appears to have made little or no impact on the practice of registration. As the Loreburn Report was to comment on this section 'the penalty for non-compliance with this section was rarely exacted, and practically, therefore, little reliance could be placed on the register thus provided for'.[115] Despite the dubious link between criminal penalties and compliance with the registration requirement, another significant drawback with these registration provisions concerned the ability to inspect the register. The only categories of person allowed access were the members and creditors of the chargor company. Thus, a potential creditor had no means of ascertaining the state of encumbrances on a company's property without the company's prior agreement. This approach can be contrasted with the 1845 Act which allowed any person interested in the registered securities a right of inspection which, presumably, would have covered potential secured creditors?[116] It is a strange irony that the legislature appears to have striven for compliance with the registration requirement, while at the same time restricting the utility of the register due to the limited categories of person entitled to inspect it. The change was probably designed to ensure that corporate information remained private and reflected the perception that the persons most likely to derive any benefit from the provision was the company membership in that the majority of company finance at this time came from internal sources.[117]

Despite the Act's express stipulation that the failure to register a prescribed charge would render the executives of the company in default liable to a financial penalty, for a time the courts also developed their own more potent sanction, that of invalidation. In what was to become known as the equitable rule against directors, the courts, in a series of cases,[118] refused to allow an unregistered security to be enforced against creditors held by a director or other officer of the company in default. As James LJ was to explain:

113 Note the change from the 1845 Act which required bonds to be registered. This change is accounted for on the basis that the bond created a purely personal obligation to repay the loan, which lenders were increasingly reluctant to accept wanting more specific forms of security giving them a proprietary interest.

114 The penalty was a fine not exceeding £50.

115 (1906) Cd. 3052, para. 35. It appears that matters have not changed in this respect. see the Diamond Report, fn 26, para. 24.1.1.

116 But see fn 109.

117 This register can be readily contrasted with that established under the Bills of Sale Act 1854 which was a public register open to inspection 'by all persons at all reasonable times'; s. 3. See now Bills of Sale Act (1878) Amendment Act 1882, s. 16.

118 See: *Re Wynn Hall Coal Co.* (1870) 10 LR Eq. 515; *Re Patent Bread Machinery Co.* (1872) 7 Ch. App. 289; *Re Native Iron Ore Co.* (1876) 2 Ch. D. 345; *Re Dublin Drapery Co.* (1884) 13 LR Ir. 174.

> it is the duty of the officers of the company to see that every charge specifically affecting property of the company is registered, I am of the opinion that no director, manager, or other officer of the company, can avail himself of a charge which is not registered. Everyone standing in a fiduciary position towards the company is bound to see that the company obeys the directions of the legislature; and I am of the opinion that the failure of the Appellant to do so is fatal to his case.[119]

It is interesting to note that even at this early stage the courts appreciated that the most effective penalty for failing to register a security was invalidation against other creditors and that the financial penalty by itself was not enough. In more modern terms the courts were, in effect, imposing a perfection requirement,[120] although the requirement was of a limited ambit. Therefore, an unregistered security in the hands of a creditor who did not stand in a fiduciary position towards the company was unaffected by the rule.[121] The rule also did not cover the shareholders of the company,[122] the company's bankers[123] or a third party taking a sub-mortgage from a director who would have been affected.[124]

Despite these limitations on the ambit of the equitable rule, it was not without critics.[125] Indeed this criticism was supported by the House of Lords in overruling the equitable rule in the case of *Wright* v. *Horton.*[126] Here, the House refused to invalidate an unregistered charge held by a company director on the basis that s. 43 could not be imputed with such a sanction. As Lord Watson was to explain:

> I have come to the conclusion that the effect of the rule is to inflict upon persons who may fail to perform the duty imposed upon them by s. 43, severe penal consequences which the legislature has not enacted and cannot be held to have contemplated. The creation of such penalties, in addition to the pecuniary mulct which the legislature has thought fit to attach to the wilful neglect of the statutory duty of registration, is, in my opinion, altogether beyond the functions of a Court of Equity.[127]

The importance of *Wright* v. *Horton* was that it established that, save for the financial penalty for non-compliance with s. 43, all unregistered securities (in the absence of fraud) remained fully enforceable. The case also demonstrated that the practice of evasion of s. 43 was widespread, although such events were often due to inadvertence rather than design. Nevertheless, it was clear that the purpose of s. 43 in attempting

119 *Re Patent Bread* (1872) 7 Ch. App. 289, p. 291.
120 I.e. an additional step imposed after the security interest has been created in order that it be enforceable against third parties.
121 See *Re General South American Co.* (1876) 12 Ch. App. 337.
122 See Re General Provident Assurance Co. (1872) 14 Eq. 507.
123 Re General Provident Assurance Co. (1872) 14 Eq. 507.
124 See *Re International Pulp Paper Co.* (1877) 6 Ch. D. 556. The rule also did not affect a partnership, one of whom happened to be a director of the chargor company in default; *Re Underbank Mills Manufacturing Co.* (1885) 31 Ch. D. 226.
125 Note in particular the judgments of Jessel MR in: *Re Borough of Hackney Newspaper Co.* (1876) 3 Ch. D. 669; *Re International Pulp and Paper Co.*; *Re The Globe & New Patent Iron & Steel Co.* (1878) 48 LJ Ch. 295. It is interesting to note that the cases establishing the equitable rule appeared to overlook the mental element of 'knowingly and wilfully' required by s. 43.
126 (1887) 12 App. Cas. 371.
127 (1887) 12 App Cas 371, pp. 380–1. However, the House expressed no opinion on the question of active concealment of a charge in order to induce creditors to provide finance.

to publicise mortgages and charges, albeit to a limited category of person, was being frustrated. The cases establishing the equitable rule had demonstrated that it was only the sanction of invalidation that was likely to prove of any effect, since such a penalty would deprive the charge holder of their security, thereby adding a perfection requirement via registration.

Nevertheless, despite the fact that the decision in *Wright* v. *Horton* ended the challenge to unregistered securities held by directors and officers of a company, there still remained another method of invalidation under the Bills of Sale Acts. Until 1890 it appears to have been accepted that the Bills of Sale Acts applied to companies as well as individuals.[128] However, in that year it was held that the Bills of Sale Acts 1878 and 1882 did not affect the debentures of a company and, by implication, any charge or mortgage by way of security.[129] Despite the wide ambit of this judgment, doubt persisted whether companies were exempted and it was to take the decision of the Court of Appeal in *Re Standard Manufacturing Co.*[130] to settle the matter.[131]

It is obvious that the machinery afforded for the registration of mortgages and charges under the Companies Act 1862 was inadequate and failed in its objective to provide a source for the disclosure of encumbrances on the specific property of a company. The limited treatment of company securities at this time can be readily contrasted with the provisions applicable to individual persons under the Bills of Sale Acts, and the fact that these Acts had been invoked in the case of companies demonstrated the dissatisfaction with the existing company provisions.[132] However, it is important to stress that the Bills of Sale Acts were passed with one aim in mind: that of regulating personal securities when given by way of bill of sale. The Companies Acts, already mentioned, were passed with a different purpose in that they were intended to regulate the corporate form, with the limited provisions relating to the registration of security an incidental feature. Registration was seen as an internal management issue for the benefit of the company membership alone. The security interest register was but one form of register companies were required to maintain, others existed covering the company membership and directors.[133] Indeed, as it is recognised that since the modern company was effectively only created as a result of the Companies Act 1862 it is hardly surprising that scant regard was paid towards the regulation of securities. The Bills of Sale Acts were based on centuries of experience in attempting to counter the various frauds relating to personal, and indeed real, property by individuals. The legislators of the company form had no such experience on which they could draw, for

128 See: *Shears* v. *Jacob* (1866) LR 1 CP 513; *Deffel* v. *White* (1866) LR 2 CP 144; *Re Cunningham & Co. Ltd* (1885) 28 Ch D 682; *Edmonds* v. *Blaina Furnaces Co.* (1887) 36 Ch. D. 215; *Levy* v. *Abercorris Slate & Slab Co.* (1887) 37 Ch. D. 260; *Jenkinson* v. *Brandley Mining Co.* (1887) 19 QBD 568; *Brocklehurst* v. *Railway Printing & Publishing Co.* [1884] WN 70. However, there were cases to the contrary see: *Re Asphaltic Wood Pavement Co. Ltd* (1883) 49 LT 159; *John Welsted & Co. Ltd* v. *Swansea Bank Ltd* (1889) 5 TLR 332; *Re Marine Mansions* (1867) LR 4 Eq. 601.

129 See *Read* v. *Joannon* (1890) 25 QBD 300, p. 303.

130 [1891] 1 Ch. 627.

131 The history of this issue is reviewed in *Slavenburg's Bank* v. *Intercontinental Ltd* [1980] 1 WLR 1076, pp. 1094A–1098H.

132 Although some of this dissatisfaction can be attributed to the imprudent creditor (see p. 25, fn 148 below and the main text thereat) anxious to utilise any means for improving his position, it is a reasonable deduction that genuine misfortune was caused by the company provisions which were clearly defective in their operation.

133 See: Companies Act 1862, ss. 25 and 45; Companies (Clauses) Act 1845, ss. 9 and 63.

even the limited types of corporation that existed pre-1862 'were not bodies in the habit of committing frauds of this sort'.[134] A further demonstration of the point is that the Companies Act 1862 only required the registration of charges affecting the specific property of the company, which was later to prove inadequate in dealing with the floating security that was to become fashionable during the 1870s and onwards, as investors searched for increasingly novel methods of security.[135] The 1862 Act also said nothing in relation to the priority of registered security interests.

Although the incidence of company trade was relatively low pre-1862, such that the availability of security interests does not appear to have caused major problems, post-1862 it was appreciated that the availability of security interests in the corporate sector caused an identical problem of ostensible ownership as had occurred with individual debtors pre-1854. It is not surprising that calls for reform soon began to be made. The first such call was made by the Registrar of Joint Stock Companies to the Parliamentary Committee on the Companies Acts 1862 and 1867 that reported in 1877.[136] Although the registrar was under no obligation at this time to keep a register of mortgages and charges, it appears that he was in the habit of filing such information when provided to him and that such information was regularly requested by third parties from the registrar,[137] for even the persons entitled to inspect companies' own registers often met with 'impediments'.[138] In the opinion of the registrar, there was a stigma attached to requesting an inspection of an individual company's register which made creditors reluctant to inquire. The only solution was to give the registrar the power to maintain a similar register to that imposed upon companies, with every company being obliged to file prescribed information upon penalty.

However, it was only as a result of the Companies Amendment Bill 1884[139] that any attempt was made to alter the existing provisions contained in the Companies Act 1862. This Bill recognised the force of the recommendations made earlier by the Registrar of Companies and sought to impose a duty on every company to provide a copy of their register of mortgages and charges at least once a year for filing by him.[140] As with the existing s. 43, neglect of this duty would have rendered the company liable to a financial penalty. Nevertheless, it was also proposed that companies' own registers would be open to public inspection.[141] Similar bills were also

134 See *Re Standard Manufacturing Co.* [1891] 1 Ch 627, p. 645, *per* Bowen LJ.

135 However, the problem was later appreciated see: Companies Bill 1895 (HC No. 91) clause 3 provided for the amending of s. 43 so that all property, whether specific or general, required registration. For a more detailed account on the growth of floating security see: Pennington (1960) 23 MLR 630; Manson (1897) 13 LQR 418.

136 (1877) *Reports Committees*, VIII, p. 438 *et seq.*

137 Indeed, the House of Lords Select committee on the Companies Bill 1896 discovered that about 100 people a day examined the companies annual summary filed with the registrar; see (1896) *Reports Committees* IX, p. 1407.

138 See *Reports Committees*, VIII, p. 400. Note also: *Re Credit Co.* (1879) 11 Ch. D. 256; *Nelson* v. *Anglo-American Land Mortgage Agency Co.* [1897] 1 Ch. 130.

139 HC No. 38, 6 February 1884.

140 Cl. 89. Nevertheless, as the case of *Wright* v. *Horton* (1887) 12 App. Cas. 371 was to demonstrate many companies were not even in the habit of maintaining their own register, let alone supplying a copy to the registrar.

141 Cl. 88.

introduced in 1887,[142] 1888,[143] 1890,[144] 1894[145] and 1895,[146] although none made any headway, but at least the principle of effective disclosure was by now becoming universally appreciated.[147]

Despite the increasing calls that were being made at this time for the wider disclosure of, and rights to inspect, company securities, it appears that as a matter of practice creditors were not in the habit of utilising such information even when it was freely available. As Lindley LJ was to remark in a leading case of the time:

> It is idle to say that persons dealing with companies are protected by s. 43 of the Companies Act 1862, which requires mortgages of limited companies to be registered, and entitles creditors to inspect the register. It is only when a creditor begins to fear he might not be paid that he thinks of looking at the register; and until a person is a creditor he has no right of inspection. *As a matter of fact, persons do not ask to see the mortgage registers before they deal with limited companies; and this is perfectly well known to everyone acquainted with the actual working of the Companies Acts and the habits of business men.*[148]

Nevertheless, whatever the practical realities appeared to be, general opinion favoured reform and as the Davey Report on company law reform was to state: 'a more efficient system of registration of mortgages and in particular floating charges is demanded in the interests of creditors'.[149] The basis of the findings of the Davey Report was that important information relating to matters such as the solvency and credit worthiness of a company should be freely available for all to see. This type of information might not in practice be used by individual parties, but at least the opportunity was there for such persons to avail themselves of it: 'It is a trite observation that legislation cannot protect people from the consequences of their own imprudence, recklessness, or want of experience'.[150] However, there was not unanimity of opinion in the evidence presented before the Davey Commission supporting this finding. A leading solicitor of the time remarked:

> The reason that these inquiries [i.e. relating to a company's mortgages and charges] are not made at the present time is fear of competition by others who

142 HC No. 218, 5 April 1887.
143 HC No. 144, 27 February 1888.
144 HC No. 146, 4 December 1890.
145 HC No. 278, 11 June 1894.
146 HC No. 91, 11 February 1895.
147 Indeed, the latter half of the nineteenth century marked the foundation of the various systems relating to the registration of security interests as we now know them; see also: (a) Merchant Shipping Act 1854, s. 66 (see now Merchant Shipping Act 1993, s. 6 and Schedule 1); (b) Mortgage Debenture Acts 1865 and 1870, ss. 7 and 32 (repealed by the Statute Law Revision Act 1958); (c) Land Transfer Act 1875, s. 22 (see now Land Registration Act 1925, s. 26 (as amended); (d) Yorkshire Registries Act 1884 (as amended), ss. 4 and 7 (this register was closed by the Law of Property Act 1969, see 37 *Halsbury's Statutes* (4th edn, 1982, p. 514); (e) Stannaries Act 1887, s. 19; (f) Land Charge Registration and Searches Act 1888, s. 5(1) (see now Land Charges Act 1972, s. 3).
148 *Broderip* v. *Salomon* [1895] 2 Ch 323, p. 339, approved at [1897] AC 22, p. 40, *per* Lord Watson; see also *Re The Dublin Drapery Co. Ltd* (1884) 13 LR Ir. 174, p. 184, *per* Porter MR – contrast with the evidence of the registrar at fn 137 above and the main text thereat.
149 See (1895) c.7779, para. 7.
150 Ibid., para. 4.

will dispense with inquiry, or the fact that the average trader relies upon his general knowledge of the nature and extent of business done by the company and its general standing, in the same way as he knows similar particulars with reference to a private individual ...

The outcry for publicity of every kind in connection with joint stock companies is to a great extent *ad captandum*, and proceeds not from the thinking person of the community, but from those who have invested blindfold, and now have a wild sort of idea that the criticism of the press on published details will protect them in future, and enable them to invest in safety without prudent consideration of the risks[151] incident to such matters.[152]

These views express no more than the general spirit of laissez-faire that had been the main force behind the Victorian trade explosion at this time. However, such sentiments were beginning to give way to the desire for more effective regulation and the Davey Report was to reject the relevance of the maxim caveat emptor continuing in this area without adequate safeguards.[153] In what was to be the precursor of the Companies Act 1900, the Davey Report set out a draft bill for the reform of the existing law. The importance of the bill was that the principle of invalidity against prescribed parties was adopted as the main sanction for unregistered securities and for the first time it was proposed to establish a public register of such securities with open inspection to all.[154]

It was not until the passage of the Companies Act 1900, s. 14 that the main proposals of the Davey Report were finally implemented. The reason for this five-year delay was the 'prolonged investigation'[155] carried out by the House of Lords into the various bills introduced to effect such reform.[156] The President of the Board of Trade was to describe the broad principle behind the new Act as being 'to ensure the fullest information being available to all those who desire to take part in companies or invest their capital'.[157] This was particularly appropriate with regard to what he termed the 'evil'[158] of unregistered securities although, as we shall see, the provisions were, and still are, deficient in providing a comprehensive information service in this regard.

It is a remarkable indictment that until the passage of the 1900 Act, a security granted by an individual trader with unlimited liability to his creditors would invariably

151 Perhaps the classic example of the risk attendant with dealing with the limited liability company is *Salomon* v. *Salomon & Co.* [1897] AC 22; see also *Re London Pressed Hinge Co. Ltd* [1905] 1 Ch 576, p. 581, *per* Buckley J.

152 See the *Davey Report* (1895) c.7779, Appendix, pp. 76–7.

153 Ibid., para. 5.

154 Ibid., App., Pt 2, cl. 20.

155 *Hansard* 4th Series (1900), vol. 84. p. 1141.

156 See the reports of the House of Lords' Select Committees on the Companies Bills, 1896, 1897 and1898.

157 *Hansard* 4th Series (1900), vol. 84, p. 1141; see also vol. 87, p. 395, *per* Lord Davey. The courts have also interpreted the purpose of charge registration under the Companies Act in this way: *Re Jackson & Bassford Ltd* [1906] 2 Ch 467, p. 476; *Re Cardiff Workmen's Cottage Co. Ltd* [1906] 2 Ch. 627, p. 629; *Esberger & Sons Ltd* v. *Capital & Counties Bank* [1913] 2 Ch. 366, p. 374; *Dublin City Distillery Ltd* v. *Doherty* [1914] AC 823, p. 854; *Re Wallis & Simmons Ltd* [1974] 1 WLR 391, p. 404H; *Re Bond Worth Ltd* [1980] Ch 228, p. 274C; *Re Brightlife Ltd* [1987] Ch 200, pp. 215A–D; *Smith* v. *Bridgend County BC* [2001] 3 WLR 1347, p. 134D, *per* Lord Hoffmann.

158 See *Hansard* 4th. Series (1900), vol. 84, p. 1143.

have required registration under the Bills of Sale Acts, whereas such a security when granted by a company with limited liability, was for all practical purposes exempt from a similar duty, save for the remote possibility of a financial penalty.[159] The sheer proliferation in the number of companies being registered[160] meant that whatever the effects on accepted commercial practice, reform along the lines of the provisions applicable to individuals had to be introduced.[161] Another factor was the shift in the main sources of company finance.[162] Whereas it had been common for companies to be financed from their internal membership, by the end of the nineteenth century external institutions such as the banks were increasingly taking over as the dominant providers of finance. These bodies naturally wanted their interests adequately protected by security and so the rise in the numbers of security interests being taken must, by necessary implication, have been commensurate with the growth in the numbers of companies as a whole. Obviously, it was undesirable that the company debtor remained the exclusive source of information and the ostensible ownership problem needed to be checked.

Despite later consolidations, the purpose of charge registration under the Companies Act 2006 remains the same – that of providing for the adequate disclosure of encumbrances[163] over the property of a company. The 'potent' sanction of invalidation was also retained as the main method of ensuring compliance with the registration requirement.[164] Nevertheless, the Companies Act has largely failed in its attempts to provide a reliable source of information via the establishment of a public registration system.

Registrable company charge security interests 1900–1985

The Companies Act 1900 is notable in that it introduced the first public system of charge registration for companies.[165] However, this new system was far from comprehensive and only the following categories of charge required registration:

(a) a mortgage or charge for the purpose of securing any issue of debentures;
(b) a mortgage or charge on uncalled capital of the company;
(c) a mortgage or charge created or evidenced by an instrument, which, if created by an individual would require registration as a bill of sale; and
(d) a floating charge on the undertaking or property of the company.

159 It appears that by 1897 no company had been fined for breach of s. 43 despite the apparent wholesale evasion; see (1897) *Reports Committees* vol. X, paras 1196–7.

160 See *Companies In 2005–2006*, fn 112, p. 15 Table A4 where it is stated that during the period 1862–9, 5,000 companies were incorporated, however by the period 1890–9 the figure had risen to 36,600; from 1862 to 1890 there were 32,900 incorporations.

161 'The provisions in the Act of 1862 for registration had become a dead letter, and that dead letter had carried more misfortune to shareholders and creditors than probably any other portion of the company law' *per* Sir Albert Rollit, *Hansard* (1900) 4th series, vol. 87, p. 111.

162 See the Cork Report (1982) Cmnd 8558, para. 1474.

163 Although the scheme is severely limited due to the fact that it is only specified categories of charge that must be registered, see p. 27–8 below.

164 Diamond Report, fn 26, para. 24.1.2.

165 See generally Companies Act 1900, s. 14.

Charges had to be registered within 21 days of creation, otherwise they would be void against the liquidator or any creditor of the company.[166] The list of registrable charges was not intended to be fixed and the Companies Act 1907 added to the list of registrable charges:

(e) a mortgage or charge on any land, wherever situate, or any interest therein; and
(f) a mortgage or charge on any book debts of the company.

The Companies Act 1928 then added further categories of registrable charge:

(g) a mortgage or charge on calls made but not paid;
(h) a mortgage or charge on a ship or any share in a ship; and
(i) a mortgage or charge on goodwill, on any patent or licence under a patent, on any trademark or on any copyright or licence under a copyright.

These provisions were eventually consolidated[167] in the Companies Act 1985 with very minor modifications.[168] It is clear then that the categories of registrable security charge/mortgage in relation to corporate assignments closed in 1928.[169] As will be seen later this closed list has caused many problems in the intervening years, as challenges both successful and unsuccessful have been continually made as to whether a particular transaction amounted to a registrable charge security interest or not. The confusion thereby engendered has remained a formidable obstacle to accepting the Companies Act registration scheme as a legitimate and workable scheme serving the interests of its users. Despite numerous attempts to change and reform the system even today it remains essentially the same creature as that which emerged in 1928 based on the model introduced in 1900. Significantly, despite the company charge provisions being introduced in 1900 (after the Bills of Sale legislation) no priority rule has ever featured in any of the Companies Acts legislation to date.

Consensual security interests and the effects of the Companies Act 1989

For the purposes of the former Companies Act 1985 (unamended), the notion of a company possessing a security interest had been of little practical relevance to the academic commentator. Rather, the question had always been, was there a registrable

166 Unregistered charges were also made void against administrators following the introduction of the administration order procedure under the Insolvency Act 1986.
167 Via consolidations in the Companies Acts 1929 and 1948.
168 Category (i) was later abbreviated in an amendment to the 1985 Act s. 396(1)(j) so that only charges over 'goodwill' and 'intellectual property' became registrable. However, for these purposes 'intellectual property' was defined to cover the elements previously in category (i) listed in the main text above; see s. 396[3A], as amended by the Copyright, Designs and Patents Act 1988, s. 303(1).
169 A notable amendment came via the Financial Collateral Arrangements (No. 2) Regulations 2003, S. I. 2003/3226, Regulation 4 of which disapplied the Companies Act 1985, s. 395 so that charges over a financial collateral arrangement (i.e. over cash, financial instruments, company shares, bonds) would be exempt from the registration requirement. This reform was brought in to implement the European Parliament Council Directive 2002/47/EC on financial collateral arrangements. The Banking Act 2009, s. 252 also exempts certain specified banks, such as the Bank of England, from the new company charge registration scheme under the Companies Act 2006, Part 25.

security charge for the purposes of the Act?[170] Since if there was, and it had not been registered, it would be void against certain specified categories of person. This was made clear by s. 395(1):

> a charge created by a company ... and being a charge to which this section applies is, so far as any security on the company's property or undertaking is conferred by the charge, void against the liquidator or administrator and any creditor of the company, unless the prescribed particulars of the charge ... are delivered to or received by the registrar of companies for registration ...

Nevertheless, the ill-fated Companies Act 1989 was intended to repeal this section and replace it by substituted provisions.[171] This led to it being argued that should the substituted provisions become law, it would be no longer necessary to create a security interest, but that, for example, a security interest could be retained, so that a retention-of-title clause would become a registrable charge security for the purposes of the Companies Act 1985 (as amended).[172] This argument was based on the fact that a 'charge' was to be expressly defined under the 1989 amendments as 'any form of security interest (fixed or floating) over property, other than an interest arising by operation of law'.[173] The argument goes[174] that because a retention-of-title clause is a security interest, now that the element of creation is omitted from the definition of a charge, it must be regarded as a registrable interest for the purpose of the Companies Act.[175]

The argument that the Companies Act 1989 had changed matters was, remarkably, advanced by academics, despite the House of Lords' decision in *Armour* v. *Thyssen*[176] being reported in 1990. The first such argument was made by Oditah who argued against the grant theory as being solely responsible for the creation of security.[177] As he explains:

> The test of a security interest is whether the debtor has an equity of redemption in the property, the subject-matter of the alleged security. If this be so, the question

170 This, perhaps, explains the description of a retention of title clause as a 'security' interest by some courts, which must now be read as references to quasi-security interests *post Armour*, see for example: *Borden Ltd* v. *Scottish Timber Products Ltd* [1981] Ch. 25, p. 44C *per* Templeman LJ; *Clough Mill Ltd* v. *Martin* [1985] 1 WLR 111, pp. 115G, 119D, 121A *per* Robert Goff LJ; 122 E–F *per* Oliver LJ; 125 C–D *per* Donaldson MR; *E. Pfeiffer Weinkellerei-Weineinkauf GmbH & Co.* v. *Arbuthnot Factors Ltd* [1988] 1 WLR 150, p. 159C *per* Phillips J; *Tatung (UK) Ltd* v. *Galex Telesure Ltd* (1989) 5 BCC 325, p. 332B *per* Phillips J; cf. *Aluminium Industrie Vaasen B.V.* v. *Romalpa Aluminium Ltd* [1976] 1 WLR 676, pp. 688C, 690A where Roskill LJ uses the words 'secure' and 'protect' to describe the effect of a title retention clause. Indeed, the courts now appear to have grasped the point, see *Compaq Computer Ltd* v. *Abercorn Group Ltd* [1991] BCC 484, p. 493C, *per* Mummery J. who uses the word 'protect' to describe the sellers purpose in retaining title to goods. In the case of an individual, likewise, the question has been whether there was a registrable bill of sale for the purpose of the Bills of Sale Acts 1878–1891.

171 Sections 95, 93 introducing new sections 398(1) and 395(2) respectively.

172 Op. cit., Oditah, fn 5, pp. 6, 92–93.

173 See Companies Act 1985 (as amended), s. 395(2).

174 See fn 172.

175 Cf. *Clough Mill* v. *Martin* [1985] 1 WLR 111.

176 [1991] 2 AC 339.

177 See fn 5.

> is really whether in a transaction under which an owner of property reserves title until he is paid, the buyer has an equity of redemption. It is submitted that the buyer does indeed have an equity of redemption. Where he has paid part of the purchase price before the goods are repossessed, there are in reality two proprietary interests: the seller's interest and the buyer's. If the seller resells, he must account to the buyer for this interest. It follows that whatever the seller is liable to account to the buyer under the contract, constitutes the buyer's equity of redemption. It matters little whether, as a matter of legal analysis, the seller's liability is described as arising from a contractual obligation to account in cases where the contract is still afoot, or from the buyer's restitutionary right to recover as on a failure of consideration, in those cases where the sale contract has already determined.[178]

Although it cannot be disputed that any real security interest will leave the debtor with an equity of redemption,[179] such that there is nothing exceptional in the definition quoted, its use to widen the concept of security outside the confines of the grant theory is disputed.

Contrary to Oditah's argument (that where there has been part payment of the purchase price there are in reality two proprietary interests) there is only one proprietary interest over goods in the retention-of-title situation: that belonging to the seller who has reserved title to himself alone. The interest of the buyer is merely possessory in nature subject to whatever rights are given to him by the seller in the contract of supply/purchase. Therefore, it is difficult to see how it is possible to classify the buyer as having any form of proprietary right.[180] The observation of Lord Denning MR: '[i]n a hire-purchase transaction there are two proprietary interests: the finance company's interest and the hirer's interest'[181] relied upon to support this argument is to be disregarded and, indeed, represents no more than infelicitous language in a difficult case.[182] Indeed, when sitting in the House of Lords, Lord Denning had earlier acknowledged that the hire-purchase transaction was not a form of real security.[183] Another case that has been relied upon to support the hirer's proprietary interest, *Whiteley Ltd.* v. *Hilt*[184] is similarly to no avail.[185] In that case Swinfen Eady MR stated:

> The whole terms of the [hire-purchase] agreement show that the contract was not merely a bailment for reward, *but that it conferred on the bailee an interest in the chattel.*[186]

178 See op. cit., Oditah, fn. 5, p. 6 (footnotes omitted).
179 See *Armour* v. *Thyssen*, quoted at fn 22 above and the main text thereat and the authorities there cited.
180 See: *Hendy Lennox Ltd* v. *Graham Puttick Ltd* [1984] 1 WLR 485, pp. 492C–E, *per* Staughton J; *Clough Mill Ltd* v. *Martin* [1985] 1 WLR 111, pp. 116B–C *per* Robert Goff LJ, 122B–C, *per* Oliver LJ, 125C *per* Donaldson MR; *McEntire* v. *Crossley* [1895] AC 457.
181 See *Wickham Holdings Ltd* v. *Brooke House Motors Ltd* [1967] 1 WLR 295, p. 300H.
182 See Goode *Hire Purchase Law & Practice* (2nd edn, 1970), pp. 36, 584–6. Cf. the Insolvency Act 1986 approach to the hire-purchase transaction which equates it with the security form for certain purposes; discussed, p. 37 below.
183 See *Bridge* v. *Campbell Discount Co. Ltd* [1962] AC 600, p. 626 'it is as well to remember what is the nature of a hire-purchase transaction ... It is, in effect, though not law, a mortgage of goods'.
184 [1918] 2 KB 808.
185 See Oditah (1992) 108 LQR 459, p. 485.
186 [1918] 2 KB 808, pp. 817–18.

This quotation is used to support the contention that the hirer has a proprietary interest in the subject matter of the transaction. However, it ignores the question as to the nature of the hirer's interest in the chattel, for as Swinfen Eady MR went on to explain:

> It did not amount to a contract of sale, as the hirer was not bound to purchase on complying with the provisions of the agreement. *But it did confer on the hirer an absolute right to purchase on complying with the provisions of the agreement.*[187]

Thus, far from having a proprietary interest in the chattel, it is clear that the interest of the hirer is the contractual right to purchase, and thereby acquire property in the chattel.[188] It cannot be denied that the hire-purchase transaction causes many conceptual problems of functional classification and that it has been described as a 'monstrosity' of confused concepts.[189] Nevertheless, it can be said that the device is not a form of real security, whatever problems remain with its operation in other spheres.

It is also submitted, that the basis of Oditah's argument, that the buyer acquires an equity of redemption in 'whatever the seller is liable to account to the buyer under the contract', is misplaced. It may well be that should a buyer, under a conditional sale contract, default in his payment obligation so that the seller accepts the breach, terminates the contract, repossessing the goods and reselling them, thereby becomes liable to the buyer for any payments made prior to the breach on the basis of a failure of consideration.[190] However, the liability of a seller in this situation is purely personal in nature. The courts by imposing a liability to refund part payments are merely striving to prevent unjust enrichment, thereby ensuring that the seller does not profit from the buyer's misfortune.[191] Indeed, any liability the seller may be under would, in many cases, be extinguished by set-off damages in respect of the buyer's initial breach of contract by failing to pay the price. Should the contract contain a forfeiture clause, then, prima facie, the seller will be under no liability for part payments.[192] Part payments by way of deposit will be irrecoverable.[193] Thus, in the latter two situations there will be no liability and therefore no scope for any 'equity of redemption' in the first place.

Although a liability to refund part payments may bear a superficial resemblance to an equity of redemption, its nature is fundamentally different. As has already been explained, all real security arises by way of grant. The debtor creates an interest over his property in favour of the creditor to secure his performance of the underlying

187 [1918] 2 KB 808, pp. 817–18. Although Warrington LJ spoke of the contract conferring a proprietary interest (p. 822) his judgment agreed with that of Swinfen Eady MR and must be taken in the same context as explained in the main text. Indeed, it is clear from earlier remarks of Warrington LJ (p. 820) that he viewed the hirer's interest as purely contractual.

188 A point made clear in *Helby* v. *Matthews* [1895] AC 471, p. 481 *per* Lord Macnaghten. Cf. *Transag Haulage Ltd* v. *Leyland Daf Finance plc* [1994] BCC 356, p. 365E *per* Knox J where the interest of a defaulting hirer is classified as proprietary.

189 See Sykes, op. cit., fn 5, p. 6.

190 See *Clough Mill Ltd* v. *Martin* [1985] 1 WLR 111, at 117H–118A *per* Robert Goff LJ. A similar position exists where goods have not been delivered to the buyer; *Dies* v. *British & International Mining* [1939] 1 KB 724, pp. 744–5 *per* Stable J. For a persuasive argument against there being a failure of consideration under a conditional sale contract, see Mance [1992] LMCLQ 35.

191 I.e. that the seller get to keep both the goods and part payments; see *Dies* v. *British & International Mining* [1939] 1 KB 724.

192 *Stockloser* v. *Johnson* [1954] 1 QB 476; *Else (1982) Ltd* v. *Parkland Holdings Ltd* [1994] 1 BCLC 130.

193 See *Howe* v. *Smith* (1884) 27 Ch. D. 89.

obligation. Should the creditor be called upon to enforce his security, he is exerting rights against property which have been granted to him for the purpose of discharging the obligation alone. It follows that should the realisation produce a surplus this will be held on trust by the creditor on behalf of the debtor to whom it must be re-vested. No such obligation exists in the case of a creditor repossessing goods supplied subject to retention-of-title terms. The seller is under no obligation to account to the debtor for any surplus remaining after the goods have been realised.[194] This follows from the simple fact that the buyer (i.e. debtor) has no interest in the goods in the first place.

If Oditah's arguments were accepted it would render the determination of the existence of security arbitrary and capricious.[195] The following examples, applying Oditah's concept of security, serve to illustrate the point:

(a) Goods are supplied subject to retention-of-title terms. The buyer defaults prior to making any payments. No security interest exists because the seller has no proceeds to refund.
(b) As in (a) but the buyer makes part payment prior to defaulting. However, the part payment is by way of deposit, or the contract contains a forfeiture clause. No security exists because the seller is under no obligation to make a refund of the payments.[196]
(c) As in (a) but the buyer makes part payment prior to default. Prima facie the seller comes under a duty to refund any payments, but his damages claim against the buyer for his breach of contract is equal to, or greater than, this sum. The liability is extinguished via set off along with the 'equity of redemption' and it follows that there is no security.
(d) As in (c) but the claim in damages is below the sum represented by the part payment. A security interest will exist because the seller is under a liability to refund the excess.

These examples serve to demonstrate that the application of Oditah's theory would make it virtually impossible to tell in advance whether any particular transaction operated by way of security.[197] It must be remembered that the date of creation of the 'security' in these cases would be the date the contract was entered into.[198] However, no party could ever be sure whether at some point later in time 'real security' would materialise.[199] In short the provenance of security would become a lottery.

194 See *Armour* v. *Thyssen*, above fn 23 and the main text thereat *per* Lord Keith. Indeed, the seller will be under no general obligation to realise the goods in the first place.
195 *A priori* this comment would apply to the operation of the Companies Act registration provisions; cf. *Esberger & Son Ltd* v. *Capital & Counties Bank* [1913] 2 Ch. 366, p. 374, *per* Sargant J.
196 In the case of a forfeiture clause it is debatable whether an equitable jurisdiction exists in which the courts can grant the debtor relief; see *Stockloser* v. *Johnson* [1954] 1 QB 476; cf. *Transag Haulage Ltd* v. *Leyland Finance plc* [1994] BCC 356, pp. 367B–C, *per* Knox J (jurisdiction exists to grant relief against forfeiture under a hire purchase contract).
197 Excluding transactions by way of mortgage, charge, pledge or lien.
198 It should be noted that provided the debtor has purported to create a security interest that interest will be deemed to have been created at that time, despite the fact that the debtor may have had no interest in the relevant property, or there being no underlying debt in existence at such time, so long as the missing element is later satisfied; see *Independent Automatice Sales Ltd* v. *Knowles & Foster* [1962] 1 WLR 974, p. 985 *per* Buckley J.
199 I.e. attachment occurs.

A similar argument was made in 1995 by a group of academics who sought to argue that under the amended definition of a registrable charge interest under the Companies Act 1985 (as amended by the 1989 Act), because the new definition had been expanded to include expressly the words 'any form of security interest ... over property', retention-of-title clauses which had hitherto remained outside the registration provisions would become registrable devices if, and when, the Act ever came into force.[200] Their argument was because 'any form of security interest over property' is now registrable under the Act the concept of 'security interest' is no longer limited under the Act to security interests arising by way of mortgage or charge. Both the latter types of security interest involved the grant of a proprietary interest by way of security by the debtor to secure his performance of the relevant obligation that was the subject of the security grant. However, because under the 1989 reforms the term 'security interest' was not restricted to mortgage or charge-type interests, any form of transaction that operated by way of security interest would now be registrable. In their opinion this would mean that retention-of-title clauses would now be caught by the registration requirement because (in their view) the retention-of-title clause was a security interest arising by way of reservation by a seller of goods. In short, their argument is that security interests can arise by way of grant or reservation. In effect this argument amounted to the proposition that English common law adopts a functional approach to security interests looking at the purpose of the arrangement in order to determine whether or not a transaction amounts to a security interest. In support of their argument they cite the speech of Viscount Cave in the tax case of *Singer* v. *Williams*[201] where the word 'securities' was defined as:

> the normal meaning of the word 'securities' is not open to doubt. The word denotes a debt or claim the payment of which is in some way secured. The security would generally consist of a right to resort to some fund or property for payment; but I am not prepared to say that other forms of security (such as personal guarantee) are excluded. In each case, however, where the word is used in its normal sense, some form of secured liability is postulated.

It is clear that the above definition is a casual, almost shorthand, off-the-cuff definition given for ease of use, rather than precise definition intended for binding effect. Indeed, if we were to take the source offered as the definition for registrable security interests under the 1989 Act, then presumably personal guarantees when given by companies would have become registrable company charges? The fact that Viscount Cave is apparently describing the word 'securities' rather than then more precise 'security interest' is also significant since, at least from today's perspective, the word 'securities' seems more apt to describe an interest in company shares.[202] A close inspection of the definitional text above reveals that it more begs the question rather than answering the question of

200 See Cowan, Clark and Goldberg 'Will English *Romalpa* clauses become registrable securities?' [1995] CLJ 43.

201 [1921] 1 AC 41, p. 49.

202 See also the essay by Benjamin below, p. 223 fn. 1 for an example of this usage. Indeed *Singer* v. *Williams* concerned a dispute over tax liability for dividend payments on shares held by a UK citizen in the US company Singer Manufacturing of New Jersey and whether these shares were either 'foreign securities' or 'foreign possessions' for the purposes of tax legislation each phrase attracting a different tax treatment, the House of Lords holding that

what is a 'security interest'? The definition states (after ironically stating the definition of 'securities 'is not open to doubt'!) that: 'The word [securities] denotes a debt or claim the payment of which is in some way secured'. But this definition merely begs the question as to how is a party 'secured' and what does 'secured' mean in this context? The only answer we are given to these questions is, to take up the definition again: 'The security would generally consist of a right to resort to some fund or property for payment'. But again this is not a definition per se of the word 'security', for the sentence says 'The security', presupposing that the word 'security' is here being used as an umbrella term, a generic description of charge, mortgage, pledge or lien – the only type of security that English law recognises and all arising by way of grant. It is stretching credibility to use this brief description, in a tax case unconnected with the rigours that our analysis demands, as a source from which all transactions would be measured in order to determine if a registrable company 'security interest' existed in a given case. One only has to project through some of the implications of this reclassification of 'security interest' to realise the folly. All security interests give the 'debtor' an equity of redemption, since the purpose of a security interest is merely the performance of the duty (usually the repayment of debt) once the duty is performed in full the security comes to an end and the creditor must account for any surplus. It would come as a shock to sellers of goods, those involved in hire-purchase transactions, or chattel leases, to know that their arrangement had become registrable and an equity of redemption existed in the corporate domain. Indeed, in the article advancing this argument it is acknowledged that at least one government minister at the time feared that the use of the word 'security interest' might cause confusion.[203] The words 'security interest' used in the Companies Act 1989 were used in a strict legal sense as has just been explained.[204] This point is reinforced by the fact that The Insolvency Act 1986 had already introduced the administration order procedure,[205] which included a moratorium on the enforcement of security rights. Although the Insolvency Act defined 'security' as including 'or other security'[206] the Act (unamended)[207] also went on to state:

> s. 10(1)(b).
>
> no steps may be taken [following the presentation of an administration order petition] to enforce any security over the company's property, or to repossess goods in the company's possession under any hire purchase agreement,[208] except with leave of the court ...

the shares came under 'foreign possessions' since shares could not be classed as securities under the relevant tax legislation.

203 See [1995] CLJ 43, p. 50, n. 42 quoting Lord Strathclyde 'To define charge [in the Companies Act 1989] as including any security in relation to England and Wales might therefore give rise to ambiguity as to whether certain contractual provisions which are not at present registrable because they do not constitute a mortgage, lien, pledge or (in the strict sense) charge, have thereby been made registrable'.

204 See the main text above.

205 See generally Insolvency Act 1986 (unamended), ss. 8–27.

206 See Insolvency Act 1986, s. 248(b)(i) 'security' means: 'any mortgage, charge, lien or other security'.

207 I.e. the 1986 version, pre-Enterprise Act 2002 amendments.

208 For these purposes 'hire-purchase agreement' includes 'conditional sale agreements, chattel leasing agreements and retention of title agreements'; see Insolvency Act 1986 (unamended) s. 10(4).

If English common law had already recognised retention-of-title clauses as security interests, then this drafting would not have been necessary. Nor would the amendments made to the Insolvency Act 1986, by virtue of the Enterprise Act 2002, have replicated these provisions. It is submitted that this fact, coupled with the decision of the House of Lords in *Armour* v. *Thyssen* destroys any arguments to the contrary. Indeed, in *Singer* v. *Williams* itself Lord Shaw was to caution:

> The word 'securities' has no legal significance which necessarily attaches to it on all occasions of the use of the term. It is an ordinary English word used in a variety of collocations; and it is to be interpreted without the embarrassment of a legal definition and simply according to the best conclusion one can make as to the real meanings of the term as it is employed in, say, a testament, an agreement, or a taxing or other statute as the case may be. The attempt to transfer legal definitions derived from one collocation to another leads to confusion and sometimes to a defeat of true intention ...[209]

Further, the amended s. 398(1) of the Companies Act 1985 stated '[i]t is the duty of a company which *creates* a charge' (author's emphasis) to deliver the prescribed particulars to the registrar for registration. The definition of a charge is contained in an ancillary section purely as a matter of convenience and was certainly not intended to override the primary section placing the company under a duty to deliver the prescribed particulars of a charge it has created to the registrar. Therefore, even indulging those who have argued that English common law adopts a wide construction to 'security interest', the point should never have arisen in the first place.

For the sake of finality, one further argument which pre-dates the 1989 Companies Act should be briefly considered. The late Professor Allan, for example, had argued[210] that real security does not depend on the theory that a debtor grants an interest over property in order to secure the debt such that the common law recognises only a numerus clausus of types of security interest.[211] Instead Allan argues that '[a]nything that performs the function of security must be security'.[212] The function of security in this context is to give the creditor rights of preference and pursuit. From this, security is defined as:

> If one is trying to create or establish a security, or if one is trying to characterise a transaction as a security, these are the rights one seeks [i.e. rights of preference and pursuit]. It should follow that a form of transaction which confers these rights on the creditor is a security, and a transaction which does not ... is not a security.[213]

For the purpose of this inquiry one is only concerned with the external effects of the transaction, that is, the ability of the creditor to assert rights of preference and pursuit against third parties.[214] The internal effects of the transaction, namely debtor and

209 See [1921] 1 AC 41, p. 57.
210 See fn 5 above. Reference should also be made to the response to this argument by op. cit., Goode, fn 5, whose arguments are adopted here.
211 I.e. security by way of mortgage, charge, pledge or lien.
212 Op. cit., Allan, fn 5, p. 345.
213 Op. cit., Allan, fn 5, p. 346.
214 Op. cit., Allan, fn 5, p. 350.

creditor, otherwise known as attachment is 'meaningless and misleading'[215] in attempting to identify whether a security interest exists. It follows in Allan's view that one needs to ask the question if the transaction confers rights of pursuit and preference in order to determine whether it is a security interest rather than merely asking whether the transaction meets 'a ready-made concept of security with pre-determined incidents'.[216] Allan's classification of security is more expansive than that argued for here, since it would embrace retention-of-title transactions because such a transaction produces the key external validity characteristics of preference and pursuit.[217]

It is submitted that Allan's arguments in relation to the establishment of security are misguided. For example, it is now established beyond any doubt[218] that the conditional sale transaction, in which title is retained by the seller pending the buyer's payment of the price or other stipulations,[219] does not operate by way of security interest.[220] This confirmation came from the House of Lords where it was stated that security arises by way of grant and not by reservation or any other method.[221] It is a fundamental rule that the debtor must have a proprietary interest which he is capable of conveying by way of security. This is why one must look at the internal effects of a transaction (i.e. attachment) before the external effects can be adequately gauged.[222]

Despite these criticisms of the arguments advanced by those that doubt the grant theory of security interest creation, it cannot be denied that their desire to see transactions such as title-retention contracts recognised as real security interests are not without merit. What is objected to, however, are the tenuous arguments that have been used in order to bring about such a result under existing common law. English common law on security interests is now effectively crystallised in terms of the formal requisites to establish this status. If a wider functional criterion is required, embracing transactions as conditional sale or hire purchase, then statutory intervention is a prerequisite. Indeed, absent a statutory definition of security, there is no substantive case law that supports anything other than the grant theory of security interest creation.[223]

It is now possible to summarise the present criteria for ascertaining whether a charge security interest is registrable under the current Companies Act 2006, thereby becoming perfected[224] against certain categories of third party. In order that a charge

215 Op. cit., Allan, fn 5, p. 352 point (iii).

216 Op. cit., Allan, fn 5, p. 352 point (i). The 'ready-made concept' in this context is the concept of attachment in the framework of a transaction expressed to be by way of mortgage, charge, pledge, or lien; transactions which, of course, produce the result that the creditor will have the rights of pursuit and preference.

217 Op. cit., Allan, fn 5, p. 350.

218 Cf. the arguments of Oditah and others discussed, p. 29 *et seq.*

219 See Sale of Goods Act 1979, ss. 17, 19(1).

220 See *Armour* v. *Thyssen* [1991] 2 AC 339.

221 See *Armour v. Thyssen* [1991] 2 AC 339.

222 As Goode has aptly remarked: 'The creation of real rights as between creditor and debtor is a necessary springboard for the assertion of real rights against third parties, which certainly cannot derive from purely personal contractual rights against the debtor'; op. cit., Goode, fn 5, p. 363, see also p. 365.

223 See also the Australian case *General Motors Acceptance Corp.* v. *Southbank Traders* [2007] HCA 19.

224 Perfection refers to the need to perform some additional act (such as registration) after the creation of the security interest in order that the interest is validated, or 'perfected', against the claims of third parties unconnected with the initial grant of the security interest.

becomes registrable under the Act, and also becomes liable to avoidance if registration is not effected, it must meet the following criteria:

(i) The charge must cover the property[225] of the company.
(ii) The charge must fall within one of the listed categories specified by the Act.[226]
(iii) The charge must be created by the company.[227]

If any of the above elements is absent from a particular transaction, then, whatever its real nature, it cannot be a registrable charge for the purposes of the Act.[228] Although these criteria might appear simple and predictable, their practical application has proved far from being so, and the identification of registrable charge security interests remains, as will be seen, as problematic as ever. This is a leading reason why the present company charge registration provisions cry out for reform and envious eyes remain focused on our fellow common law neighbours who have moved on to adopt modern personal property security regimes based on Article 9 of the US Uniform Commercial Code (UCC).[229]

Insolvency act implications

The restrictive and limited concept of 'security interest' that we have seen operating under the Companies Act can be usefully contrasted with developments that were brought in under the Insolvency Act 1986. Under the latter Act, for the first time, attempts were made to broaden the ambit traditionally seen when regulating 'security interests' so that what had been termed quasi-security interests were caught.[230] This new approach to regulating security interests was particularly noticeable in respect of the new administration order procedure that the Act introduced in an attempt to remove the shortcomings of the prior legislation in respect of companies experiencing financial difficulty by placing constraints upon the exercise of certain security rights against property held by the company.[231] In the original (unamended) version of the Insolvency

225 This includes future property; see *Independent Sales Ltd* v. *Knowles & Foster* [1962] 1 WLR 974, p. 985, *per* Buckley J (future book debts registrable); see also: *Tailby* v. *The Official Receiver* (1888) 13 App. Cas. 523; *Re Bush Aggregates Ltd.* [1983] BCLC 320; *Elders Pastoral Ltd.* v. *Bank of New Zealand (No. 2)* [1990] 1 WLR 1478.

226 See s. 860(7).

227 See s. 860(1). However, if a company acquires property subject to an existing charge it will still be registrable under s. 862(1) despite the absence of the element of creation on the part of the acquirer. For present purposes we are only concerned with those charges that meet all three elements of the criteria outlined above, the key element of which is creation, for it is only where this element is present that the charge can be avoided for want of registration; see s. 874(1), i.e. we are dealing with a perfection requirement. Where the company acquires property subject to an existing charge and fails to register under s. 862(1) then the only penalty, by virtue of s. 862(4), is a fine against the company and every officer of it who is responsible for ensuring registration is effected, i.e. the charge is not required to be perfected.

228 But see fn 227 above.

229 Note also the chapters by Brown and Fisher (pp. 328 and 366) in this volume on the positions of New Zealand and Australia respectively.

230 See generally above, p. 3 *et seq.*

231 See Insolvency Act 1986, s. 8. The new procedure was described by Nicholls LJ as representing 'a major reform in the law relating to companies which are insolvent or likely to become so'; *Re Atlantic Computer Systems plc* [1992] Ch. 505, p. 525C.

Act 1986,[232] s. 11(3)(c) provided that during the period an administration order was in force 'no other steps may be taken to enforce any security over the company's property ... except with the consent of the administrator or the leave of the court'.[233] 'Security' was defined under this Act as 'any mortgage, charge, lien or other security'.[234] This definition of security was more expansive than that used under the Companies Act, since security interests arising by operation of law were not expressly excluded. Thus, the statutory right[235] of an airport authority to detain an aircraft in respect of unpaid airport charges has been held to amount to a 'lien or other security' for the purposes of the Insolvency Act.[236] This approach can be readily contrasted with the security interest concept used under the Companies Act which is only directed at consensual interests and does not apply to interests conferred by statute. As Browne-Wilkinson VC has stated, 'it would not be right to give the general words "other security" a narrower meaning than they would normally bear since that would tend to frustrate the purposes of ... the [Insolvency] Act of 1986'.[237] Further, the Act also extended its coverage beyond strict security rights and s. 11(3)(c) also prevented the repossession of any goods in the company's possession subject to a hire-purchase agreement. The term 'hire-purchase agreement' was widely construed[238] and included conditional sale agreements, chattel-leasing agreements and retention-of-title agreements.[239] This expansion was the first example of the legislature taking on board the limitations of the strict security interest concept when applied to company transactions at common law. Thus, the moratorium procedure also covered many arrangements which would be described as quasi-security interests.

232 The Act was later to be amended by the Enterprise Act 2002.

233 For the position of the court in granting leave see: *Royal Trust Bank* v. *Buchler* [1989] BCLC 130; *Re Atlantic Computer Systems plc* [1992] Ch. 505; *Re David Meek Access Ltd* [1993] BCC 175. Reference should also be made to the former s. 11(3)(d) which provided that during the continuation of an administration order: 'no other proceedings and no execution or other legal process may be commenced or continued, and no distress may be levied against the company or its property except with the consent of the court'.

234 s. 248(b)(i) although it might be remarked that the latter part of the definition of 'security' as including 'or other security' is not particularly helpful in promoting understanding exactly what security is and effectively throws one back upon the common law definition. It is thought that the only other type of 'other security' would be the pledge, see p. 7 above. Cf. Sale of Goods Act 1979, s. 62(4) which provides that the Act does not apply to 'any transaction in the form of a contract of sale which is intended to operate by way of mortgage, pledge, charge or other security'.

235 See Civil Aviation Act 1982, s. 88(1).

236 See *Bristol Airport plc* v. *Powdrill* [1990] Ch. 744. It is submitted that this type of statutory right should be classified as a lien, since there is no other type of 'other security' it could possibly be. If this is not achieved the expression 'other security' threatens to undermine the accepted legal basis of the security interest; see *Exchange Travel Agency Ltd* v. *Triton Property Trust plc.* [1991] BCC 341, discussed, p. 39 *et seq.*

In *Re Sabre International Products Ltd* [1991] BCLC 470 it was held that a transport company's refusal to deliver goods (belonging to a company in administration) to the administrator on the basis of prior outstanding indebtedness entitling them to a lien over the goods was caught by s. 11(3)(c) and the refusal to hand over the goods amounted to the enforcement of security.

237 See *Bristol Airport plc* v. *Powdrill* [1990] Ch. 744, pp. 761A–B.

238 See s. 10(4).

239 See s. 251 for a definition of this term.

However, the history of these new provisions is important because at first the courts were prepared to give a wide and overly generous interpretation of the reach of these provisions. For example, Harman J in *Exchange Travel Agency Ltd* v. *Triton Property Trust plc*[240] ignored the first principles of security law and held that a leasehold provision allowing a landlord the right of re-entry upon the tenant's non-payment of rent amounted to the enforcement of a security interest and was caught under s. 11(3)(c) of the Act.

This conclusion was reached because the proviso for re-entry upon non-payment of rent was generally regarded in equity as security for the unpaid rent.[241] The proposition was supported by ample authority.[242] However, before it could be concluded that because the right of re-entry has been described as a 'security' it automatically fell within the ambit of the then s. 11(3)(c), it was necessary to examine the context in which the description was applied. This is something that Harman J failed to do. An examination of the authorities[243] where the word 'security' had been used revealed that it had been used merely as a label of convenience to describe the function and purpose of the proviso for re-entry. In no respects could the use of the word in this context be used to support it as coming under the accepted legal definition. The use of the label 'security' in this sphere amounted to no more than a description, rather than a term of legal art and provides yet another example of the state of general misuse in which the term is used.[244] It is clear that if one examines the key elements of real security,[245] the following points may be made:

(a) security must cover the property of the grantor;[246]
(b) security leaves the debtor with an equity of redemption;
(c) security arises by way of grant or operation of law; and
(d) there are only four recognised types of security interest.

240 [1991] BCC 341; endorsed in *Re Olympia & York Canary Wharf Ltd* [1993] BCC 154.
241 See *Halsbury's Laws of England* (4th edn, 1981) vol. 27, p. 346, para. 442.
242 See: *Wadman* v. *Calcraft* (1804) 10 Ves Jun 67, p. 69, *per* Sir William Grant MR 'there is no doubt equity will relieve against the forfeiture; considering the purpose of the clause of re-entry to be only to secure the payment of rent; and that, when the rent is paid, the end is obtained'; *Howard* v. *Fanshawe* [1895] 2 Ch. 581, p. 588, *per* Stirling J 'The object of the proviso [i.e. the right of re-entry] ... is to secure the landlord the payment of his rent'; see also *Belgravia Insurance Co. Ltd* v. *Meah* [1964] 1 QB 436, p. 443 *et seq. per* Lord Denning MR; *Shiloh Spinners Ltd* v. *Harding* [1973] AC 691 for the scope of equity in this area.
243 See fn 242.
244 See also, p. 35, fn 209 and the main text thereat above. The problem is not new and the term 'charge' has also been abused in a similar way, see: *Ashby, Warner & Co Ltd* v. *Simmons* [1936] 2 A11 ER 697, p. 708 *per* Greene LJ; *Borden (UK) Ltd* v. *Scottish Timber Products Ltd* [1979] 2 Lloyd's Rep. 168, 172 *per* Judge Rubin (overturned, on a different point, on appeal at [1981] Ch. 25); *Re BCCI (No. 8)* [1998] AC 214 and note also *London County & Westminster Bank Ltd* v. *Tompkins* [1918] 1 KB 515 (distinction between mortgage and equitable charge).
245 See also, p. 3 *et seq.* for a discussion of the basics of security under English law.
246 By virtue of s. 248(a) 'secured creditor' means: 'in relation to a company, means a creditor of the company who holds in respect of his debt a security over *property of the company* ...' (author's emphasis). It should be noted that the grantor of the security will not necessarily be the party under the duty to perform the obligation to the debtor of which the grant of the security was intended to secure.

If these points are applied to the landlord's right of re-entry, then it should have become clear that such a right could not possibly be classified as a real security:

(a) The lessee has no property which is covered by security interest. Although the lessee undoubtedly has a proprietary interest in the subject matter of the demise, such an interest is at all times subject to the superior title of the lessor who is merely creating a subsidiary interest over his estate. Thus, upon the lessee's failure to pay rent, his interest in the demise automatically comes to an end (subject to the court's discretionary power of relief against forfeiture) and the lessor is merely recovering possession of his own property. As Shaw LJ has explained:

> The nature of the action [i.e. for re-entry] is the same in every case, namely, that the right and interest of the lessee to possession has been terminated before its natural expiry in pursuance of a contractual provision in his lease so that he becomes a trespasser if he continues in occupation of the premises. The obverse of this situation is that the lessor becomes entitled to possession on forfeiture of the lessee's interest. The action for re-entry is in the nature of an action for trespass. It is not a remedy against the property of the debtor in respect of a debt, notwithstanding that the occasion of the forfeiture is default in payment of the rent reserved by the lease. The consequence of forfeiture (subject to the power of the court to grant relief) is to determine the lessee's interest.[247]

(b) There is no equity of redemption present under a lease transaction. Upon the lessee's default in paying the rent and the landlord's re-entry, the lessee's interest in the property is terminated (subject to intervention by the court) and any dealings with the property by the landlord are free from any interest of the former lessee.

(c) It is clear that under a lease transaction the lessee is not granting any interest by way of security to his landlord. On the contrary the contractual agreement is merely to the effect that the lease will be 'terminated before its natural expiry'.[248] Although the courts may be prepared to exercise an equitable jurisdiction to relieve the lessee against forfeiture, in no way can this be said to amount to the existence of security by operation of law. The use of the term 'security' in this context is merely a functional label to justify the possible intervention of the courts. As Shaw LJ has explained:

> [T]he phrase 'security for rent' is not to be understood in the strict legal sense as something equivalent to a mortgage as security for a debt. It is rather a means of putting the lessee in the position that if he does not pay the rent he will risk losing his lease.[249]

(d) The landlord's right of re-entry cannot be classified as a: (i) mortgage; (ii) charge; (iii) pledge; or (iv) lien.

From this analysis it becomes obvious that the only possible 'security' classification that can be applied to the right of re-entry is that it is a quasi-security interest.[250]

247 See *Ezekiel* v. *Orakpo* [1977] QB 260, pp. 267H–268A.
248 See fn 247 above and the main text thereat, *per* Shaw LJ.
249 See *Ezekiel* v. *Orakpo* [1977] QB 260, p. 269B; see also, by way of analogy, *Royscot Trust Ltd* v. *Rogerson* [1992] 2 QB 297, p. 309C where Ralph Gibson LJ refers to a hire-purchase agreement as giving the hirer 'security' by virtue of his ownership of the goods subject to the contract of hire.
250 See generally above, p. 7 *et seq.*

Nevertheless, English law does not recognise this type of security interest and it can only be regarded as a mere label of convenience (albeit a source of confusion). Therefore, it can be concluded that the judgment of Harman J in the *Exchange Travel Agency* case amounted to an illegitimate extension of the security interest concept. Although his decision was clearly based on the spirit of the decision of the Court of Appeal in the *Bristol Airport* case,[251] that the word 'security' should not be given a narrower meaning than it normally bears in order to prevent the purpose of the administration procedure being frustrated,[252] neither should the word 'security' be given an extended meaning in order to cover supposed defects in the operation of the procedure if that were not done.[253]

Unfortunately, for a time the decision of Harman J was followed by the courts despite its fundamental failings in respect of the application of 'security interest'.[254] When the point was fully taken and, in particular, the case of *Ezekiel* v. *Orakpo*[255] cited in respect of the true meaning and scope of 'security interest' the courts realised their error and declined to follow the *Exchange Travel Agency* case.[256] Although this change of direction was clearly correct and necessary, Lord Neuberger has since expressed his 'regret'[257] in having to take this approach in rejecting the *Exchange Travel Agency* case.[258] The policy of the Insolvency Act in seeking to prevent the enforcement of security interests in administration order cases was clearly equally desirable in both real and quasi-security interest situations. But, as Lord Neuberger acknowledged '[t] he courts cannot correct defective draughtsmanship if it would amount to a subversion

251 [1990] Ch. 744.

252 See Insolvency Act 1986 (unamended), s. 8(3) for the purposes of granting an administration order. See now Insolvency Act 1986 (as amended), s. 8 and Schedule B1, para. 3(1)(a)–(c).

253 However, there was a second ground to the judgment of Harman J in that the landlord's peaceable re-entry to the premises was caught by s. 11(3)(d), quoted at fn 233. As he explained the position: 'It seems to me that "legal process" [as used in s. 11(3)(d)] is exactly how one would describe the exercise of a right by a person not in a contractual relationship with his tenant but holding a relationship by privity of estate between them. In my judgment it is a correct use of words to describe a landlord who has legal rights, arising out of the privity of estate, which he exercises by the process of peaceable re-entry as exercising "legal process". It seems to me, therefore, that if this exercise of the right of re-entry be not a security, it is quite certainly the commencement of another legal process, and, as I see it, that must have been one of the purposes for which Parliament plainly intended the Act to operate'; see [1991] BCC 341, p. 345G–H.

In *Re Olympia & York Canary Wharf Ltd* [1993] BCC 154, p. 158C Millett J rejected this construction of s. 11(3)(d) in holding that the words 'legal process' meant a process which required the assistance of the court so that the service of a contractual notice purporting to make time of the essence or to terminate a contract by reason of the company's repudiatory breach did not require the consent of the administrator or the leave of the court, and see also: *McMullen & Sons Ltd* v. *Cerrone* [1994] BCC 25; *Scottish Exhibition Centre Ltd* v. *Mirestop Ltd* [1994] BCC 845; *Re a Debtor 13A10 of 1994* [1996] BCC 57, to like effect; however Millett J endorsed the main ground of Harman J's judgment in the *Exchange Travel Agency* case.

254 See: *Re Olympia & York Canary Wharf Ltd* [1993] BCC 154, p. 158C, *per* Millett J; *Doorbar* v. *Alltime Securities Ltd (No. 2)* [1995] BCC 728, p. 734E, *per* Knox J; *March Estates plc* v. *Gunmark plc* [1996] 2 BCLC 1, pp. 7C–8A, *per* Lightman J.

255 [1977] QB 260.

256 [1991] BCC 341.

257 See Neuberger 'Company law reform: the role of the courts' in de Lacy (ed.), *The Reform of UK Company Law* (London, Cavendish Publishing, 2002) 59, p. 64.

258 The cases rejecting *Exchange Travel Agency* were: *Razzaq* v. *Pala* [1998] BCC 66 and *Re Lomax Leisure Ltd* [2000] BCC 352.

of legal principle'.[259] Parliament was aware of this limitation and moved quickly to plug this gap following the courts' reversal, and the administration order procedure now bites equally in this situation, so that the landlord's right of re-entry is now classified by the Insolvency Act as a security interest.[260] Despite the fact that the law is now clear in this area, for a period of seven years there was confusion and a fundamental misapplication of the law of security interests.

A further interesting feature of the Insolvency Act concept of security is that the term 'property' was defined so as to depart from the normal association of the term[261] with 'the full rigour of a technical work of art'.[262] By virtue of s. 436 of the Act: 'property includes money, goods, things in action, land and every description of property, wherever situated, and also obligations and every description of interest, whether present or future or vested or contingent, arising out of, or incidental to, property'.[263] Therefore, it has been held that the interest of a lessee under a contract for the lease of an aircraft is proprietary in nature for the purposes of this definition.[264]

259 Op. cit., Neuberger, fn 257.

260 See Insolvency Act 2000, s. 9. The law is now found in Insolvency Act 1986 (as amended) s. 8 and Schedule B1 at para. 43(4).

261 I.e. title/property is an absolute concept and lies where the parties intend it to be so that, for example, a reservation of title clause under the Sale of Goods Act 1979, ss. 17 and19 conveys no proprietary interest to the buyer in possession prior to his performance of the stipulated conditions.

262 See *Re Paramount Airways Ltd* [1990] BCC 130, p. 136B, *per* Harman J, affirmed, *sub. nom. Bristol Airport* v. *Powdrill* [1990] Ch. 744.

263 'It is hard to think of a wider definition of property' *Bristol Airport* v. *Powdrill* [1990] Ch. 744, p. 759D, *per* Browne-Wilkinson VC. Cf. *Welsh Development Agency* v. *Export Finance Co. Ltd* [1992] BCC 270 where it was found that the term 'property' as used in s. 234(3) (relating to, *inter alia*, administrative receivers immunity for seizing property that does not belong to the company) did not cover choses in action and the term was, in its natural sense, only applicable to tangible property therefore, the proviso in s. 436 'except in so far as the context otherwise requires' applied. The courts have also been keen to expand the ambit of 'property' in other contexts, see, for example, *Fairfold Properties Ltd* v. *Exmouth Docks Co. Ltd* (*No. 2*) [1993] Ch. 196, p. 204B (charges under Solicitors Act 1974, s. 73 can cover untaxed costs).

264 See *Bristol Airport* v. *Powdrill* [1990] Ch. 744, p. 759D–G, *per* Browne-Wilkinson VC; *Re Paramount Airways Ltd* [1990] BCC 130, p. 136D–F, *per* Harman J. There appear to have been two grounds for finding the interest of a lessee to be proprietary in nature. The first is based on the valuable possessory interest held by the lessee which can be realised by assignment 'for in many cases substantial capital sums' *per* Harman J, above. This approach would certainly appear to accord with the wider definition of 'property' used by the Act which includes 'every description of interest'; see *Re Rae* [1995] BCC 102, p. 113D–G, *per* Warner J. Although the Court of Appeal upheld the decision of Harman J on this point, Browne-Wilkinson VC, above, also based his decision on the fact that the lessee held an 'equitable right of some kind' on the basis that a court would have ordered specific performance of the leasing contract. This approach was necessary because, although s. 11(3)(c) provided that goods subject to a hire purchase contract (defined in s. 10(4) to include conditional sale agreements, chattel leasing agreements and retention of title agreements) could not be repossessed during the period of the administration order (this covers goods in the company's possession despite the fact that the contract originally granting the right of possession may have been terminated prior to the administration; *Re David Meek Access Ltd* [1993] BCC 175), in this case the security right of detention was exercised by a third party creditor and would, thus, have exposed a lacuna in the provisions. Nevertheless, outside the confines of the Insolvency Act the interests of a buyer

Nevertheless, as the *Exchange Travel Agency*[265] case demonstrated, the more relaxed attitude towards the constitution of proprietary interests, needs to be limited to a construction of that Act alone and should not be widened without parliamentary intervention. If this is not done, then the whole fabric of English personal property law, as we now know it, could be threatened and potential chaos arise out of the multiplicity of proprietary interests thereby sanctioned, contrary to existing public policy. Having said this, the experience of the Insolvency Act illustrates a major shift from conventional wisdom with its rigid adherence to the location of title. It can reasonably be speculated that the subtle influence of Article 9 of the UCC and the movement for the reform of English law on personal property security is behind this policy shift.[266] Whatever its antecedents, it certainly marks a new chapter in the field of English company security law and acknowledges the willingness of the legislature to respond to the ever-changing commercial environment.[267] Nevertheless, and so far at any rate, beyond the confines of insolvency law, the legislature has shown a marked reluctance to implement law reform, as opposed to discussing and commissioning reform projects in the field of personal property security law.

The reform of English personal property security interest law 1971–2005

The reform of personal property security law has a long and distinguished history stretching back nearly forty years. Our period of inquiry covers the years 1971 to 2005, the latter date being the completion of the work of the English Law Commission. For the sake of convenience, this discussion will be considered under the following sub-headings.

The Crowther Report *1971*

The publication of the Crowther *Report*[268] in 1971 was a momentous occasion for UK lawyers involved in PPS issues. For the first time Article 9 of the US Uniform Commercial Code (UCC) was introduced to a mainstream UK audience. The Americans had long grappled with similar problems faced by the UK in terms of regulating assignments of personal property, whether absolute or by way of security. By the 1950s the 'solution' to the various problems was found to be the enactment of the new comprehensive Uniform Commercial Code regulating most of the types of commercial transaction that were then found. In the context of PPS law Article 9 of the UCC became, in the US, the exclusive source of regulation in all US states. Although Article 9 emerged in the 1950s, and has since been revised and updated

under a retention of title clause has been denied proprietary status; *Armour* v. *Thyssen* [1991] 2 AC 339. Note also Swadling 'The proprietary effect of a hire of goods' in Palmer and McEndrick (eds), *Interests in Goods* (1993), pp. 17–22 (a general essay refuting arguments that a hirer's interest in goods is proprietary in nature).

265 [1991] BCC 341.

266 The reform movement is discussed below (pp. 43–76).

267 See the general observations of Harman J in *Re Paramount Airways Ltd* [1990] BCC 130, pp. 139G–140D.

268 See *Consumer Credit*, Report of the Committee on Consumer Credit Chaired by Lord Crowther (1971) Cmnd 4596 (London: HMSO, 1971).

several times, it still remains along with the entire UCC the main source of regulation for commercial transactions in the US. By 1971 the influence of Article 9 began to permeate the UK's shores. The Crowther *Report* described Article 9 as having 'outstanding merits'[269] such that 'It forms the basis of much of the thinking underlying this part of our Report'.[270] Apart from borrowing concepts and ideas from Article 9, the major new development for the UK came from the Crowther *Report*'s new approach to addressing the concepts behind many of the then (and still current) forms of commercial transactions. This new approach came in the form of adopting a functionalist approach to classifying the nature and hence legal treatment of commercial transactions. Up until Crowther we had seen a formalistic approach to commercial transaction construction based upon the language and forms of transactions that commercial parties undertook. The latter approach had developed over the past hundred or so years in direct response to both common law and statutory developments aimed at particular types of commercial transaction, such as the conditional sale or hire-purchase transaction. Whereas under the new scheme proposed by Crowther, a new functionalist approach[271] would be used to classify the nature of a transaction and the law's treatment of it as a consequence. This new approach rested upon two fundamental points:

i. Recognition that the extension of credit in a sale or hire-purchase transaction is in reality a purchase-money loan and that the reservation of title under a hire-purchase or conditional sale agreement or finance lease is in reality a chattel mortgage securing a loan.
ii. Replacement of what are at present distinct sets of rules for different security devices by a legal structure applicable uniformly to all forms of security interest.[272]

Under the new proposals there would be a new generic statutory definition of 'security interest' designed to ensure that any type of transaction that involved the use of personalty in order to secure the performance of an obligation would be caught by the new scheme, irrespective of the law at the time the Report was published or, the type of transaction used, be it by way of recognised security interest or absolute proprietary assignment, such as a conditional sale of goods or finance lease.[273]

The Crowther *Report* (unlike some of its successor reports on PPS law reform)[274] did not go into minutiae in detailing the reformed law it proposed. Instead it adopted a broad-brush approach to setting out the principles and policies that should underpin

269 Crowther *Report*, fn 268, p. 183, para. 5.15.
270 Ibid., para. 5.2.9.
271 'The fundamental concept is that transactions should be regulated according to their function, not according to their form, and that an agreement which, though purporting to reserve the full title, is intended as a security agreement should be treated as such by the legislation'; ibid., p. 196, para. 5.5.1.
272 Crowther *Report*, fn 268, p. 186, para. 5.2.8.
273 'Though in general restricted to security interests, the [new PPS (based on our recommendations)] Act would also regulate outright sales of accounts receivable, since in the commercial world such sales are recognised as in reality financing transactions and in practice it is often extremely difficult to know whether the transaction is a sale or a loan'; ibid., p. 196, para. 5.5.2.
274 These reports are discussed below.

the new PPS law for the UK. Fundamental to this new law was Article 9, which was 'in concept and structure an admirable prototype for a modern law of personal property security'.[275] The new scheme would comprehensively regulate all security interests from the moment of creation to enforcement and provide for a uniform set of rules to promote a simple and efficient system of law. Therefore, in order to be enforceable, a security interest would have to be in writing and signed by the debtor, or the secured party would have to take possession of the security, or documents representing it.[276] Linked to this, the concept of 'attachment' would have to be fulfilled, namely a valid security interest be in existence whereby the secured party had given value and also the debtor had proprietary rights in the subject matter of the security.[277] Security interests could also extend to cover after-acquired property by the debtor.[278] Given that the nature of the scheme was to regulate security interests, it followed that the rights of the debtor would have to be clearly spelled out in order to reflect the fact that the debtor had, at all times, an equity of redemption which must be respected by the secured party even after default such that any realisation of the security interest would be solely for the purposes of covering the debt plus interest and that alone.[279] Likewise, it was proposed that the new scheme would also provide a comprehensive scheme of remedies for the secured party upon the debtor's default.[280]

Perhaps the most fundamental part of the new scheme concerned the scheme of priorities. The *Report* noted that current UK law on priority conflicts was in a 'chaotic state', producing much 'injustice'.[281] Crowther proposed a new scheme of priority rules which were based upon the new functionalist approach to regulating what appeared to be a myriad of distinct transactions but were, in reality, unified under a common purpose, namely providing for security for debt/obligation.[282] The new priority rules like much of the *Report* were 'much influenced by Article 9'.[283] Underlying the system of priorities was the concept of 'perfection'[284] whereby a secured party is placed under an obligation, in addition to attachment, in order that its interest is enforceable (i.e. it is perfected) against third parties. Under the new scheme there would be two basic methods of perfection and priority, namely via possession of the security (particularly where it involved documents of title/negotiable instruments), or registration/notice filing of the security interest. Under the new scheme a secured party would be required to register its security interest if they wanted to gain priority over the claims of third parties. The act of registration would also give notice to other creditors, particularly putative secured parties that particular items of property of the debtor might be encumbered. The new computerised registration system would be based on the notice file principle, whereby a secured party files a financing statement with the public registrar indicating that the secured party has, or intended to take, a security interest over defined items of the debtor's personal property.[285] Once filed, a financing statement would remain on the register for a

275 Crowther *Report*, fn 268, p. 197, para. 5.5.6.
276 Ibid., p. 200.
277 Ibid., p. 578, para. 11 (IV Attachment).
278 Ibid., pp. 200–1.
279 Ibid., pp. 201–2.
280 Ibid., pp. 202 5.
281 Ibid., p. 206, para. 5.7.1.
282 Crowther *Report*, fn 268, p. 206, para. 5.7.2.
283 Ibid., para. 5.7.3.
284 Ibid., pp. 222–3.
285 Ibid., pp. 218–22 for a general description on how the registry would operate.

period of five years before it became necessary to renew it – each act of filing being valid for a continuous five-year period.[286] The system would only apply in respect of security interests securing a sum in excess of £300.[287] Regarding the priority of interests under the new scheme, the basic rule of priority would be that perfected interests took priority over unperfected interests. Within this broad rule, priority would generally be afforded on the first-to-file principle, even if the first to file had notice of a prior unperfected interest.[288] There would be special priority rules, in addition to the basic scheme, such as a buyer in the ordinary course of business would defeat the claims of a perfected security interest holder and, also, the claims of purchase-money security interest holders would be recognised.[289]

The new Crowther scheme would apply to all categories of debtor be they corporation, partnership or individual. However, security interests in 'consumer goods' would not require filing.[290] Of note, with regard to corporate security interests, was Crowther's proposal that the Companies Act registration provisions would continue to operate alongside the new regime. However, the penalty of avoidance for non-registration under the Companies Act would be removed such that the new scheme would be the exclusive arbitrator of priority. As the new scheme only applied to PPS interests, the Companies Act scheme would remain wider in terms of coverage in some respects, since it covered charges over land and required possessory security to be registered in some cases. Crowther recognised that the Companies Act scheme had been intended purely as an information-based register of interests for the benefit of corporate investors, as well as potential secured creditors.[291] Linked to this was the proposal that the floating charge would continue under the new scheme, despite the fact that a fixed security over shifting assets would now be possible under the new scheme. As Crowther explained: 'this form [i.e. the floating charge] of security agreement is so widely used that it would in our view be wrong to deprive the financial world of the ability to continue to use it'.[292]

Despite stating that reform of UK PPS law was 'vitally needed'[293] and gaining 'broad agreement'[294] and 'strong support'[295] from the Law Commission, the Law Society, the Law Society of Scotland and Professor Aubrey Diamond the recommendations of the Crowther *Report* in respect of PPS reform came to nothing. The more wide-ranging aspects of the *Report* concerning consumer credit were later adopted by the government in the Consumer Credit Act 1974 later amended in 2005.[296] However, no reforms were forthcoming in respect of the radical reform of PPS law. In rejecting the Crowther *Report*'s recommendations for reforming PPS law in the

286 Ibid., p. 221, para. 5.7.56. There would be exceptions in the case of the five-year validity period for corporate debentures and debenture stock which would remain valid for an indefinite period following initial filing.
287 Ibid., p. 218, para. 5.7.47.
288 Crowther *Report*, fn 268, pp. 224–5, para. 5.7.68.
289 Ibid., pp. 225–7 for the general scheme with respect to special priority situations.
290 'Consumer goods' were defined as 'goods used or acquired for use primarily for personal, family or household purposes'; ibid., p. 574, para. 3.
291 Ibid., pp. 217–18.
292 Ibid., p. 227, para. 5.7.77.
293 Crowther *Report*, fn 268, p. 196, para. 5.5.1.
294 Ibid., p. 196, para.5.5.3.
295 Ibid.
296 See Consumer Credit Act 2005 and note White Paper *Fair, Clear Competitive: the Consumer Credit Market in the 21st Century* (2003) Cmnd 6040.

UK, the government stated that it did not have 'sufficient evidence either of a need for such a major recasting of the law on new principles or of general support for the particular solution proposed by the Committee'.[297]

Given the nature of the Crowther *Report* and the extensive preparatory work that went into producing it, this viewpoint appears incredulous, although, as we shall see, it was to reappear with regularity over the coming decades.

The Diamond Report 1989

Despite the almost summary rejection of the case for reform by the government in the early 1970s, by the mid-1980s the question of reforming PPS law was back on the agenda. Many problems emerged highlighting the sheer unpredictability and uncertainty of application of the company charge registration provisions and the basic nature of security interests. Perhaps the most important development post-Crowther was the emergence of retention-of-title clauses as a mainstream credit finance tool. Although such devices had a long pedigree and, as long ago as 1895, the House of Lords had held that no registrable security interest was created[298] in 1976 the Court of Appeal extended their utility by holding that a seller could recover not only the original goods supplied but also any proceeds received by the seller via authorised depositions of the goods.[299] This finding was to revolutionise commercial practice and such devices became commonplace. A protracted legal battle then also began to rage, as the contours of the enforceability of such clauses began to be chartered by the courts in a long series of cases where such clauses were challenged as being unenforceable as amounting to unregistered charges.[300] Much uncertainty was thereby created and, although from today's perspective this debate has died down, the underlying principles are still far from settled.[301] Although the re-emergence of retention-of-title clauses was the most notable development post-Crowther, there were also other areas that underlined the inadequacies of the law relating to company charges/security interests issues – such as the ability to differentiate between a fixed and floating charge,[302] the use of a trust rather than a charge[303] and the sheer unpredictable application of the registration of charge provisions[304] – were common features of the case law landscape.

297 See White Paper *Reform of the Law on Consumer Credit* (1973) Cmnd 5427, para. 14.

298 See *McEntire* v. *Crossley Bros. Ltd* [1895] AC 457.

299 See *Aluminium Industrie Vaassen BV* v. *Romalpa Aluminium Ltd* [1976] 1 WLR 676.

300 See generally de Lacy '*Romalpa* theory and practice under retention of title in the sale of goods' (1995) 24 Anglo-Am L Rev 327.

301 For example, how can the case of *Tatung Ltd* v. *Galex Telesure Ltd* (1989) 5 BCC 325 (High Court holding that any attempt by a seller of goods to claim the proceeds of sub-sale amounts to a registrable company charge) be reconciled with the Court of Appeal decision in the *Romalpa* case [1976] 1 WLR 676?

302 See *Siebe Gorman & Co. Ltd* v. *Barclays Bank Ltd* [1979] 2 Lloyd's Rep 142.

303 See *Carreras Rothmans Ltd* v. *Freeman Mathews Treasure Ltd* [1985] Ch. 207.

304 See *Re Welsh Irish Ferries Ltd* [1986] Ch. 471, p. 480C, *per* Nourse J '[the question of registrability] has caused me considerable concern because if the lien falls within [the registration requirement] it is clear that it will come as something of a shock to those who deal with matters of this kind'. Note also *Slavenburg's Bank* v. *Intercontinental Natural Resources Ltd* [1980] 1 WLR 1076 (a charge created by an overseas company with a place of business in England is void for non-registration under the Companies Act even though the then practice of the registrar of companies was to refuse to register such charges when presented

In December 1985 the government appointed Professor Aubrey Diamond (a consultee to the Crowther *Report* Committee) to examine the need to reform the law relating to PPS. In particular Diamond was asked to reconsider whether the time might now be right to take forward the original Crowther *Report* which had been in abeyance since 1971. The result of Diamond's work was the publication of the Diamond Report in 1989.[305] The Report noted that there were 'major problems in the present law' and that there was 'weighty support for reform'.[306] The main conclusion of the Report being:

> I have come to the clear conclusion that radical changes should be made and that something on the lines of the Crowther recommendations is necessary.[307]

The Diamond Report proposed that a new PPS scheme should be introduced based on the 'well-tried model in Canada and the United States'.[308] Although there had been some minor problems with Article 9 in the US, on the whole the Article 9 regime had 'worked well' and been a 'vast improvement' on the previous law such that few Americans would wish to return to the position prior to its introduction.[309] This being the case, it followed that any new legislation in the UK 'should be based closely on Article 9 of the American Uniform Commercial Code and the Personal Property Security Acts introduced into several Canadian provinces, though it need not slavishly follow any of the precedents ...'.[310] The new scheme would establish a computerised register based on notice filing which would be applicable to all types of debtor engaged in business be they companies, partnerships or individuals.[311] It was envisaged that the new registration scheme would be self-financing from fee income raised from users of the system.[312] The register could be operated by a government agency or private corporation but there would be 'great advantages' in having the new system run by Companies House, the current managers of the Companies Act registration provisions.[313] The new system would be the virtual preserve of commercial parties, particularly companies, and it followed that by having Companies House operate the scheme it would be more efficient, since it would be easy to check the status of corporate actors whether they be debtors or secured creditors. This would be particularly important since companies have a unique identification number on their

unless the company first registered/applied to be registered under the Companies Act); *Grove* v. *Advantage Healthcare (T10) Ltd* [2000] 1 BCLC 661 (wrong company number put on the prescribed particulars form and sent to registrar for registration held to comply with the Companies Act 1985, s. 395(1) despite the fact that a search of the charges register under the correct name of the chargor company would not reveal the charge).

305 Diamond Report, fn 26.

306 Ibid., p. 196, para. 5.5.3, p. 1, para. 1.7 and p. 31 para. 8.2.3; the report stated that 'English law is in urgent need of reform'.

307 Diamond Report, fn 26, pp. 1–2, para. 1.7. The report also referred to the findings of the *Cork Report* of 1982, Cmnd 8558, p. 366 para. 1623, that 'there is a considerable body of informed opinion which supports the recommendations of the Crowther Committee'; p. 6, para. 2.11.

308 Ibid., p. 2. para. 1.9.

309 Ibid., p. 15 paras 4.13 and 4.17.

310 Ibid., p. 35, para. 9.2.2.

311 Ibid., p. 2, paras 1.11–1.12.

312 Ibid., p. 63, para. 11.6.2.

313 Ibid.

incorporation[314] which would remove a common source of error in some North American schemes particularly in relation to consumer debtors. The fact that the Diamond Report recommended that consumer goods be exempt from the need for filing would be significant in this respect.[315] With regard to non-corporate business debtors identification would be via VAT registration number or, where that did not exist, a social security number or date of birth or, possibly, some combination of numbers in case of doubt such that debtor identification mistakes should not be a problem.[316]

There would be no obligation to file security interests nor any time period within which filing/registration would have to be made.[317] However, if a security interest was not filed with the registrar within 21 days of its creation and the debtor became insolvent within one year of the security interest being filed, then the security interest would not be protected by the act of 'late' filing.[318] The parties would have a choice as to the length of time a registration would last. Based on the Saskatchewan scheme in Canada, the parties would pay a fee based on the number of years the entry was to remain on the register which might range from one year to an indefinite period of time.[319] An exception to the need to file security interests in order to perfect them against third-party claims would operate in favour of the holders of possessory security interests, such as under a pledge.[320] But this exception would only operate in cases where the secured party retained possession of the goods. Should possession be given up, even if for a temporary purpose, then the secured party would be required to file his claim in order to maintain perfected status.[321] Following the Crowther *Report*,[322] the Diamond *Report* also recommended an exception from filing in the case of consumer goods which would have the effect of giving a purchaser a good title where a security interest existed over such goods but the security interest would remain effective against other third-party claims, such as an insolvency official or other creditors of the debtor.[323] Unlike Crowther, Diamond did not favour having any exception from the filing requirement in order to perfect a security interest in respect of small-cost transactions, such as Crowther's proposed £300 minimum value of the secured transaction.[324]

The basic priority rule under the new system would be that the first to file wins.[325] The scheme would also adopt a functionalist approach to categorising security interests such that it was the function of the transaction, rather than its form, which was

314 See Companies Act 2006, s. 1066. Cf. *Grove* v. *Advantage Healthcare (T10) Ltd* [2000] 1 BCLC 661.

315 'Since the registration of security interests in consumer goods would be excluded, virtually all registrations would be related to business activities'; Diamond Report, fn 26, p. 63, para. 11.6.3.

316 Ibid., p. 63, para. 11.6.4.

317 Cf. this with the current obligation to register company charges within 21 days of their creation; see Companies Act 2006, s. 870.

318 Diamond Report, fn 26, p. 58, para. 11.3.9.

319 Ibid., p. 65, para. 11.8.6.

320 Diamond Report, fn 26, p. 60, para.11.5.7.

321 Ibid., p. 60, para. 11.5.7; cf. the current position at common law where this is not the case and a pledge remains effective if possession is only given up on a temporary basis for a specific purpose, see *Reeves* v. *Capper* (1838) 5 Bing NC 136.

322 See fn 290.

323 Diamond Report, fn 26, p. 61, para. 11.5.12.

324 Ibid., p. 62, para. 11.5.17. Compare this with the Crowther Report, above fn 287.

325 Ibid., p. 64 para. 11.7.4.

the determinative factor in indicating whether parties were dealing with a security interest:[326]

> The definition of security interest should be such that it would include not only mortgages, charges and security in the strict sense but also any other transfer or retention of any interest in or rights over property other than land which secures the payment of money or the performance of any other obligation.[327]

Diamond also stressed the need for new legislation to make clear that the doctrine of constructive notice did not apply to the register of finance statements which would be established under the new system. As the Report explained:

> The [new] system works because priorities are determined by reference to the date of filing, and there is no assumption or presumption that anyone has looked at the register. It is there to be looked at – or rather searched – if people wish to do so, but they are not taken to have done so if they have not.[328]

Like Crowther before, Diamond also recommended that the new scheme should be extended to cover any lease of goods for a period of not less than three years, even if it could be said that the transaction was not intended to perform a security function, since, if it were otherwise, there would be difficult border-line cases where it might be difficult to come to an answer as to the 'real' function of the lease in question, such a debate being unproductive.[329] There would be exceptions to the basic first-to-file priority rule. For example, the claims of purchase-money secured financiers would prevail over prior perfected security interests.[330] Likewise, the claims of a buyer in the ordinary course of business would defeat the claim of a prior perfected security interest. As the Report explained:

> There should be a ... principle ... that a debtor in possession of goods subject to a security interest who sells the goods in the ordinary course of business (or who appears to a reasonable person to do so) can pass a good title free of the security interest to an innocent purchaser ...
>
> In these proposals it is recognised that in most cases the filing of a financing statement is irrelevant. One would not expect a purchaser who buys goods from a person who appears to be selling in the ordinary course of business to search in a register of security interests. Moreover, even if the purchaser knows of the existence of a security interest, that should not hinder his acquisition of a good title. As we know from the use of the floating charge and of retention of title clauses, the retention of a security interest is not incompatible with a power of sale in the ordinary course of business. Only if the purchaser actually knows that the sale to him is in breach of a term in the security agreement should he be prevented from obtaining a good title.[331]

326 Ibid., pp. 11–12, para. 3.10.
327 Diamond Report, fn 26, p. 35, para. 9.3.2.
328 Ibid., p. 66, para. 11.9.5.
329 Ibid., fn 26, p. 42, para. 9.7.16 for the recommendation; pp. 38–42 generally for a discussion of the role of leasing.
330 Diamond Report, fn 26, pp. 64–5, paras 11.7.6–11.7.8.
331 Ibid., p. 77, paras 13.6.5 and 13.6.8. On the general issues relating to *nemo dat*, see the chapter by Gullifer in this volume (pp. 188–222).

The security agreement between the parties would also be regulated under the Diamond proposals. There would be a requirement that the security agreement was in writing and signed by the debtor clearly identifying the subject matter of the security interest. Failure to establish a written security agreement would render any alleged security interest unenforceable even between the parties (i.e. debtor/creditor) but the creditor could still prove for any debt underlying the alleged agreement (i.e. on a non-secured basis).[332] The requirement for writing would not, however, apply in respect of possessory security interests (except in consumer cases regulated by the Consumer Credit Act 1974).[333] In respect of non-possessory security interests the act of registration would be effected by filing a prescribed financing statement with the relevant registrar responsible for maintaining the new register.[334] Likewise, the new scheme would contain a comprehensive codification of the remedies available to the parties subject to the security interest. These remedies would be the same as explained in the Crowther *Report*[335] and could not 'be regarded as controversial' being based on the principle that the relationship between both parties to any security interest is 'essentially that of mortgagor and mortgagee'.[336]

Although the new scheme would become the main source of regulation for PPS assignments, Diamond recognised that several existing specialised registers would continue to operate alongside the new register. Unlike the Crowther *Report*,[337] in respect of company charges Diamond proposed that the new scheme would replace the Companies Act scheme at least in respect of all charges/security interests created after the new scheme came into operation (the old scheme remaining to govern existing charges until they expired).[338] Regarding other specialist registers covering interests over ships, aircraft, etc., dual registration would follow under both the new scheme and the existing registers with the latter governing priority disputes between conflicting security interests and avoidance in insolvency situations under the later scheme if a party did not perfect under the new scheme.[339] In respect of non-corporate debtors, however, the Bills of Sale Acts would be repealed and the registers closed after the new scheme came into force.[340] However, the repeal of the Bills of Sale Acts would bring with it the need to protect consumer debtors from their own potential follies. This would entail the need 'to prohibit the grant of a security interest on after-acquired goods' by consumers.[341] A minor exception to this would cover a purchase-money security interest created by consumers whereby goods were acquired after the security interest was created but within a specified period of time.[342]

332 Diamond Report, fn 26, p. 46, paras 10.3.16–10.3.18.
333 Ibid., p. 47, para. 10.4.5.
334 Ibid., p. 51, para. 10.5.5.
335 See p. 45 fn 280.
336 Diamond Report, fn 26, p. 79, paras 14.2 and 14.3.
337 See generally p. 46.
338 Diamond Report, fn 26, p. 68 paras 12.2.2, 12.2.5.
339 Diamond Report, fn 26, p. 69, para. 12.3.5. The Diamond Report did not consider the possibility that this might lead to circular priority problems where an interest was registered under the specialist register but not under the new scheme thereby giving the secured party priority against competing security interests under the specialist register but that interest being avoided against creditors in insolvency under the new scheme post Diamond.
340 Ibid., p. 69, para. 12.4.2.
341 Ibid., p. 92, para. 18.1.9.
342 Ibid., p. 92, para. 18.1.9.

Like Crowther before, the Diamond Report also acknowledged that the floating charge 'is here to stay'.[343] Parties would be free to use floating charges under the new system, subject to filing a financing statement which would perfect the security interest and fix the priority point. The debtor would be free to dispose of encumbered property in the ordinary course of business and the security interest would continue in any proceeds thereby received.[344] The common negative-pledge clause found in most floating charges would be added to the list of particulars to be filed on the financing statement thereby warning third parties of the true ambit of the security interest and, from a conceptual viewpoint, the floating charge concept of 'crystallisation would lose all or most of its importance'.[345] The accommodation of the floating charge under the new regime would also pose questions as to its role and compatibility with measures aimed specifically at it under the Insolvency Act 1986.[346] However, Diamond did not think that there would be any problems in this respect and explained:

> I am now satisfied that the courts would have no difficulty in identifying a security interest [i.e. a floating charge] which applied to after-acquired property and permitted the debtor to dispose of property to which the security interest had attached as being similar to a floating charge within section 175 [of the Insolvency Act 1986], and I do not think the introduction of the new scheme should bring about any change in the position of preferred creditors. Again the legislation should spell this out.[347]

The foregoing measures were the main part of the Diamond Report's recommendations. However, as an interim measure and 'in no way a substitute for or alternative'[348] to them *Diamond* also recommended 'as interim measures',[349] even if only on a 'short-term'[350] basis, that it was possible to 'make big improvements in the register of company charges'.[351] Therefore, Part 3 of the Report made specific recommendations for the reform of Part 12 of the, then current, charge registration measures under the Companies Act 1985. Diamond noted that there were 'serious

343 Ibid., p. 84, para. 16.7.

344 See generally ibid., pp. 80–1. Regarding unauthorised dispositions of secured property and the ability of the secured party to trace *Diamond* recommended that 'it would be desirable for the new legislation to spell out the details with some precision, and in my view it should be made clear that ... the right to trace does not depend on the presence of a fiduciary relationship'; p. 82, para. 15.2.3.

345 Diamond Report, fn 26, p. 85, para. 16.11.

346 See in particular, Insolvency Act 1986, s. 175 which gives priority to the holders of preferential debts over the claims of a floating charge holder. The Enterprise Act 2002, s. 252 also added a new s. 176A to the Insolvency Act which, in certain circumstances, requires an insolvency official to 'make a prescribed part of the company's net property available for the satisfaction of unsecured debts' in priority to the claims of any floating charges. The rules regarding 'prescribed part' are set out in the Insolvency (Prescribed Part) Order 2003, SI 2003/2097. Note also *Re International Sections Ltd* [2009] EWHC 137 (Ch.).

347 Diamond Report, fn 26, p. 85, para. 16.14.

348 Ibid., p. 97, para. 20.4.

349 Ibid., p. 87, para. 20.4.

350 Diamond Report, fn 26, p. 97, para. 20.3.

351 Ibid., p. 97, para. 20.3.

problems'[352] with the company charges registration scheme under the Companies Act 1985. To solve these problems a number of recommendations were made with the aim of creating 'an efficient and up-to-date register of charges that fulfils its purposes without unnecessarily hindering legitimate business activities'.[353]

These recommendations were that:[354]

(a) There should no longer be a duty to submit the original (or copy) instrument creating the registrable charge. Instead all that should be required is the submission, to the registrar of companies, of a prescribed form containing the relevant information in relation to the registrable charge.[355]
(b) The new register of charges would be the register containing the prescribed forms submitted to the registrar. The registrar would not review the form and reject registrations on the basis that he considered it did not contain a charge that required registration under the Act.[356]
(c) In order to ensure that the register of charges was accurate the chargee would only be able to rely on the information in relation to his charge as disclosed on the registered form submitted to the registrar. The conclusive certificate of registration issued by the registrar would also be amended to reflect this.[357]
(d) Negative-pledge clauses contained in floating charges would become registrable particulars of the charge and would be entered on the register of charges.[358]
(e) The decision of the High Court in *Re Welsh Irish Ferries Ltd*[359] be reversed by the statute and a shipowner's charge/lien over sub-freights under a charter party be expressly exempted from the registration requirement.[360]
(f) The list of registrable charges be extended to include: charges over insurance policies;[361] extended retention-of-title clauses;[362] hire-purchase and conditional sale contracts;[363]charges over shares.[364]
(g) The present registrable charge found under Companies Act 2006, section 860(7)(b)[365] (i.e. if executed by an individual would require registration as a bill of sale) be replaced by a new simpler version removing reference to the bills of sale legislation which was 'verbose and unclear'.[366] The new charge to cover a security interest over goods.[367]

352 Ibid., p. 97, para. 20.1.
353 Ibid., p. 98, para. 21.4.
354 See generally ibid., Part III, p. 97 *et seq.* Note also pp. 138–9 of the report for more minor technical recommendations that are not dealt with here.
355 Ibid., pp. 99–101.
356 Ibid., pp. 101–2.
357 Diamond Report, fn 26, pp. 102–3.
358 Ibid., p. 104.
359 [1986] Ch. 471.
360 Diamond Report, fn 26, pp. 111–12.
361 Ibid., p. 112.
362 Ibid., p. 114, para. 23.6.9.
363 Ibid., pp. 114–15, para. 23.7.4.
364 Ibid., p. 117, para. 23.8.13.
365 Formerly Companies Act 1985, s. 396(1)(c).
366 Diamond Report, fn 26, p. 119, para. 23.9.14.
367 Ibid., p. 120 para. 23.9.18 for details.

(h) The present registrable charge found under Companies Act 2006, section 860(7)(f)[368] (i.e. over book debts) be amended so as to provide a definition of book debts.[369]

(i) The Companies Act should spell out the priority rules for competing charges and be based on the principle that the first charge registered wins subject to stated exceptions. The doctrine of constructive notice would have no role in the new rules of priority. Protection would also be afforded to innocent purchasers of goods without knowledge of prior charges on them.[370]

(j) It would no longer be necessary to apply to the court[371] to register a charge which was not registered within the prescribed time period, provided the omission was accidental or due to inadvertence. Instead a direct application for late registration could be made to the registrar of companies.[372]

(k) In order to ensure that potential chargees could rely on the accuracy of the register for priority purposes Diamond recommended that a system of provisional registration should be introduced. This would allow a chargee to register a prescribed form detailing his charge but omitting the date of creation. This form would be registered and confer a provisional priority for a period of 21 days. If the chargee then registered a newly created charge within the 21-day period, the date of the first 'provisional' registration would then be the priority date. This new procedure would ensure that a chargee who searched the register could be sure of his priority without a secret charge being registered in between the search of the register and the subsequent creation and registration of the charge.[373]

(l) Reform of the *Slavenburg*[374] decision was needed.[375] It should be made clear that the registration requirement should only apply to overseas companies registered under the Companies Act.[376] An overseas company registering under the Companies Act should also be placed under a duty to deliver to the registrar of companies a list of charges already covering its property located in England at the time the company registered under the Companies Act.[377] However, although failure to register a charge created after the company had registered under the Act would invalidate it, failure to register charges in existence at the time the company registered under the Act would not and the only penalty would be a fine against the company.[378] This would leave the situation where an overseas-registered company created a charge over property which was subsequently brought into England. In order to prevent unfairness and an unreasonable registration duty on the company[379] Diamond recommended a system of purely voluntary registration in this situation with no penalty where registration

368 Formerly Companies Act 1985, s. 396(1)(e).
369 Diamond Report, fn 26, p. 121, para. 23.9.22 for details.
370 Ibid., at pp. 125–6.
371 See generally Companies Act 2006, s. 873.
372 Diamond Report, fn 26, p. 128 para. 25.3.3.
373 Diamond Report, fn 26, pp. 129–130, paras 26.6–26.7.
374 [1980] 1 WLR 1076. See p. 47 fn 304.
375 Diamond Report, fn 26, p. 133, para.27.10.
376 Ibid., p. 133 para. 27.11.
377 Ibid., p. 133 para. 27.12.
378 Ibid., p. 133 para. 27.13.
379 Ibid., p. 134 para. 27.15.

was not effected.[380] All other charges created by an overseas company would be governed by the normal *lex situs* rule.[381]

(m) Should alterations occur to the charge after it has been created and registered, then these changes should be made registrable upon sanction that the changes would become unenforceable against the prescribed parties.[382]

(n) It should be obligatory to submit to the registrar information that the registered charge had been discharged and the assets charged released in whole or in part from the charge.[383]

In April 1991 the government gave its considered opinion on the main proposals of the Diamond Report for fundamental reform of the law. The (then) Secretary of State for Trade and Industry (Peter Lilley MP) explained:

> A clear majority of those representing interests governed by English law argued against major reform. Reform would be complex and, in view of the proposed registration arrangements, potentially costly to the Government and business. It could be contemplated only if there was a strong commercial justification. That did not emerge from the consultation and I have therefore decided not to accept the recommendations in Part II of the report for England and Wales. However, the report served a useful purpose in airing these important issues.[384]

The Companies Act 1989

Despite the fact that the Diamond Report was rejected by the government, its publication in 1989 also coincided with the passage of the Companies Act 1989, which was intended to amend the 1985 Act.[385] The 1989 Act was intended to repeal the existing Part 12 of the Companies Act 1985 and replace it with substitute provisions. The basic scheme and principles behind the original 1985 version of company charge registration were to remain intact under the changes but several important modifications would have been brought about had the 1989 Act ever become law.

380 Ibid., p. 134 para. 27.16.

381 Ibid., p. 134 para. 27.14.

382 Diamond Report, fn 26, p. 136 paras 28.1.3 and 28.1.6.

383 Ibid., 6, p. 137 para. 28.2.1.

384 See (1991) *Hansard* HC vol.189 col. 482, 24 April 1991. The Law Society of England and Wales was also opposed to any major reform of the law and had the following comments to make on the Diamond Report: 'whilst the Committee accepts that the current law is open to the criticisms made by Professor Diamond, it is believed that in practice few real problems arise. Accordingly on balance the Committee are of the view that the given costs to government and industry in implementing any change as against the relatively few areas where the existing law creates a real difficulty in practice, a major change in the law of the nature suggested is probably not warranted.'; see 'Comments on "a review of security interests in property" by Professor A. L. Diamond', by the Law Society Company Law Committee (London, Law Society, November 1989), p. 4.

385 Interestingly, the 1989 Act was intended to fuse the law of company charge registration under the one regime for both England and Wales and Scotland (subject to minor qualifications) in Part 12 of the Companies Act 1985 which had previously been divided into two parts Chapters 1 (England and Wales, ss. 395–409) and 2 (Scotland, ss. 410–424), on which see Appendix 3 of this volume.

The reforms were intended to tidy up the existing law and make the register of charges more reliable to users and more efficient to operate by the registrar of companies. Of particular note were the following reforms:

(a) A new statutory definition of 'charge' was added to the Act.[386]
(b) Changes were made to the list of registrable charges to improve the system,[387] including a new power to the Secretary of State to make regulations in respect of adding or removing categories of registrable charge.[388] Provision was also made for the possibility of automatic crystallisation clauses in floating charges being made registrable.[389]
(c) The doctrine of constructive notice was put on a statutory footing in respect of registered charges insofar as it related to subsequent chargees alone.[390]
(d) The certificate of conclusivity in respect of registered charges was limited to the date of registration alone.[391]
(e) It was now possible to register changes to the registered charge to correct the registered details so as not to mislead searchers of the register.[392] Failure to register such changes would render them void insofar as the details registered would mislead searchers of the register as to the correct position.[393]
(f) A duty was placed on the chargor company to deliver the prescribed particulars of the charge to the registrar for registration. However, the chargor no longer had to supply a copy of the original charge (if it existed) nor did the registrar have to check the details of the charge but was placed under an obligation to file the prescribed particulars supplied on the company charges register. This was intended to simplify and speed up the registration process.[394]
(g) In respect of non-registered charges these were now also avoided against 'any person who for value acquires an interest on or right over property subject to the charge'.[395] But unregistered charges were not avoided against a party expressly acquiring an interest in the property subject to the avoided charge.[396]
(h) A chargee holding an avoided charge was given power to pass good title to property subject to the avoided charge in favour of a good faith purchaser for valuable consideration.[397] However, any proceeds thereby received were held on trust by the chargee for the benefit of specified parties under the Act.[398]

386 See Companies Act 1989, s. 93 introducing a new s. 395(2). This measure is discussed in detail, p. 28 *et seq* above.
387 See Companies Act 1989, s. 93 introducing: a new s. 396(1)(b) requiring a charge over goods to be registrable replacing the old bills of sale charge under s. 396(1)(c); a new s. 396(2)(g) stating that a shipowner's lien on sub-freights was not a registrable charge (repealing *Re Welsh Irish Ferries Ltd* [1986] Ch. 471).
388 Ibid., s. 93, introducing a new s. 396(4).
389 Ibid., s. 100, introducing a new s. 410.
390 Ibid., s. 103, introducing s. 415.
391 Ibid., s. 94 introducing s. 397(5).
392 Ibid., s. 96 introducing s. 401.
393 Ibid., s. 96 introducing s. 402.
394 Ibid., s. 95 introducing s. 398.
395 See Companies Act 1989, s. 95 introducing s. 399(1)(b).
396 Ibid., s. 99 introducing s. 405(1).
397 Ibid., s. 99 introducing s. 406(1) and (4)(c).
398 Ibid., s. 99 introducing s. 406(2).

(i) The Secretary of State was given a general power to amend the company charge provisions of the amended Companies Act Part 12.[399]
(j) It was now possible to register a charge outside the 21-day registration period without the need to make an application to court.[400]
(k) The *Slavenburg*[401] decision was reversed and the law changed such that only overseas companies actually registered under the Companies Act were under a duty to register charges and a new registration regime was brought in specifically for such companies.[402]

The above measures would certainly have brought about a modest improvement in the company charge scheme. However, they were never brought into force and the relevant provisions of the Companies Act 1989 were repealed by the 2006 Act.[403] The reasons why the 1989 Act measures were not brought into force was explained by the government as being:

> These provisions [i.e. the 1989 company charge reforms] have not been brought into force, partly because the loss of the conclusive certificate proved unwelcome to presenters and users of the register and partly because of problems of interaction between Part IV and the land registration system.[404]

Despite the rejection of both the Diamond Report and the failure to implement the 1989 reforms in 1994 the government published new proposals on how company charge law might be reformed.

DTI 1994 Consultative Reform Document

In 1992 the government (as part of a wider review of company law being undertaken at that time) set up a working party of interested parties to examine both systems of company charge regulation under the 1985 and 1989 Companies Acts. The fruits of this work were published in November 1994 in a new Consultative Document[405] which canvassed possible ways forward in which the law light be reformed. This Document explained that the DTI saw 'the main objective of the register as being to provide information on the indebtedness of companies. It has also been seen as a way of regulating the order of priority of charges'.[406] The Consultative Document noted that the current law under the 1985 Act needed reforming and that law had been criticised as 'causing inconvenience and, in some cases, loss to lenders and delays to business'.[407]

399 Ibid., s. 102 introducing s. 413.
400 Ibid., s. 95 introducing s. 400 (there were qualifications as to the enforceability of late registered charges).
401 [1980] 1 WLR 1076.
402 See Companies Act 1989, s. 105 and Schedule 15 introducing new ss. 703A–N.
403 See Companies Act 2006, s. 1180.
404 See DTI Consultative Document *Company Law Review: Proposals for Reform of Part XII of the Companies Act 1985* (London, DTI, November 1994), p. 4 para. 2; and note also at pp. 8–9, para. 8 for further elaboration of these points.
405 See *Company Law Review: Proposals for Reform of Part XII of the Companies Act 1985*, above n. 404.
406 See Consultative Document, above fn 404, p. 4 para. 1.
407 Ibid.

In order to remedy these problems the Document put forward three possible options for reform, upon which it invited comment. The three options were:

i) Retain the present system under Part 12 of the Companies Act 1985 unamended.[408]
ii) Retain the 'core'[409] elements of Part 12 of the 1985 Act but incorporate into the Act certain provisions of the 1989 Act reforms together with a system of provisional registration for charges.[410]
iii) Introduce a new notice file system – the 'more radical option'.[411]

Perhaps, unsurprisingly, given the history of reform it can come as no surprise to learn that the first option was to prevail in this consultation exercise. As the English Law Society's Company Law Committee was to state in its submission to the DTI in response to the Consultative Document:

> We have no reason to believe that the retention of the present law would give rise to any unacceptable risks. The present system of registration had worked tolerably well in the past[412] and it is not in urgent need of reform.

Therefore, in the space of little more than five years the government had commissioned or proposed three separate reform measures all of which were to be rejected or dropped.[413] Nor, were matters to rest here, for in 1998 the reform question was to be resurrected once again as part of the Company Law Review.

The Company Law Review 1998–2001

In March 1998 the government launched the Company Law Review,[414] the most comprehensive review of UK company law ever undertaken, a process which was to

408 See generally ibid., p. 10. The main reason for continuing with the current system despite its acknowledged flaws was the familiarity with which users had with it and the costs and uncertainty that might result from introducing changes/reforms to it.
409 These being the retention of the conclusive certificate of registration and the registrar of companies current role and functions operating the register of charges; see generally the Consultative Document, above fn 404, at p. 11 paras 16–17.
410 See generally the Consultative Document, above fn 404, at p. 11–24.
411 Ibid., pp. 5 point C and 24–28.
412 See Company Law Committee Memorandum No. 311 *Proposals for Reform of Part XII of The Companies Act 1985* (London, Law Society, February 1995), p. 1 para. 1.1.
413 The government's response to the 1994 consultation came in the form of a letter dated November 1995 from the DTI. The letter revealed that there were 60 responses to the 1994 consultation the 'large majority' of which favoured the second option. Support for option three based on notice filing was 'very low' and a 'minority' of respondents favoured the first option and maintaining the status quo. On this basis the government proposed to follow the second option and undertake further work on developing reform measures. However, the letter acknowledged 'It is not yet possible to give a precise indication of when we shall be able to present Parliament legislation to give effect to our proposals for the reform of the law on the registration of company charges'. No further public measures were taken before the Company Law Review was started in 1998.
414 See consultation document *Modern Company Law for a Competitive Economy* (London: DTI, 1998). For a full treatment of the company law review see the essays in op. cit., de Lacy,

last three years, and a further five years to follow, before a new reformed Companies Act was passed. As part of this review the topic of company charges was addressed in October 2000 with the publication of the consultation document *Registration of Company Charges*.[415] The document noted that the respondents to the 1994 consultation had been 'strongly in favour'[416] of the second option and the notice file option had been rejected at that time because 'the costs would have been heavy and the benefits a little speculative'.[417]

Nevertheless, although the notice file option had been 'strongly rejected' in 1994, the Company Law Review Steering Group noted that it might be prepared to consider such a scheme if the Steering Group's consultation led 'to a strong call for it'.[418] Previous reform initiatives led the Steering Group to believe that 'the best approach'[419] would be to continue the work of the 1994 consultation based on developing the second option. This would entail reforming the existing system and incorporating parts of the 1989 reforms along with any other reforms that the current consultation exercise revealed. In short, its proposals would be 'aimed at improving the present system by providing more information, simplifying procedures and, where possible, reducing costs both in the business and professional communities and at Companies House'.[420] Before reaching any firm conclusions on reform, the consultation document posed forty-three questions[421] relating to basic issues concerning the system of company charge registration to which respondents were invited to make submissions before the closing date of 5 January 2001.

Given the previous hostility to notice filing proposals following consultation exercises and the rather pessimistic tone of the 2000 consultation, we could be forgiven for thinking that the results of the consultation would merely have endorsed the provisional views of the Steering Group based on the second option from 1994. However, when the Final Report of the Company Law Review Steering Group was published in June 2001,[422] it came as something of a surprise to learn that the notice file system was firmly back on the agenda as the basis for reforming the system of company charge registration. The respondents to the 2000 consultation were 'almost unanimous' that some form of system was required for the registration of company charges.[423] Although it was noted that:

> But, while there was little consensus on any of the main issues, convincing arguments in favour of radical change were advanced in some responses.[424]

fn 257. For a general history of the review, see the chapter by Jonathan Rickford, pp. 3–42.

415 See *Modern Company Law: Registration of Company Charges* (London, DTI, 2000) by the Company Law Review Steering Group Document No.7, URN 00/1213.

416 Ibid., p. 8, para. 1.14.

417 Ibid., p. 9, para. 2.4.

418 Ibid., p. 12, para. 2.12.

419 Ibid., p. 13, para. 3.1.

420 Ibid., p. 13, para. 3.1.

421 Ibid., pp. 41–5.

422 See Company Law Review Steering Group *The Final Report* (London, DTI, 2001) in two volumes.

423 *The Final Report*, fn. 422, p. 245, para. 12.7.

424 *The Final Report*, fn. 422, p. 247, para. 12.7.

Of the respondents to the 2000 consultation about half of them favoured a new notice file system 'and opposition to it was much weaker than in previous consultations'.[425]

Given the new found support for (or rather lack of opposition to) notice filing the Steering Group provisionally recommended that a new notice file system should be introduced for company charges based upon the following basic principles:[426]

> The registration system would be based on the notice file principle whereby registration is made by filing a financing statement giving notice that a charge has been taken or is proposed to be taken over a designated asset of the debtor company.[427]
>
> Registered charges would be prioritised according to the date of registration (or filing). Unregistered/filed charges would lose priority to later created and registered/filed charges.
>
> Unregistered/filed charges would be void against a liquidator, administrator.
>
> There would be a right to apply to the court for relief from the sanction of invalidity.
>
> If the court granted relief against invalidity following an application, it would not be able to change the relative priority of registered charges.

The new notice file system would remain entirely optional but the chargee would run the risk of losing priority were charges to remain unregistered under the new system.[428] The prescribed particulars to be supplied to the registrar would be:

(a) the chargor's name and registration number;
(b) whether the chargor was acting as trustee of the property;
(c) the chargee's name and, if a company, its registration number;
(d) the property charged;
(e) the nature of the charge, i.e. fixed or floating;
(f) the nature of the obligation secured and, if a monetary debt, the sum secured which might be 'all monies';
(g) whether there was an automatic crystallisation clause;
(h) in Scotland only, whether the charge included a negative-pledge clause;

425 See *The Final Report*, fn. 422, p. 249, para.12.15. In early 2001 a seminar was held in Oxford to discuss the review at the invitation of Professor Sir Roy Goode, QC and this seminar 'contributed to a more radical view being adopted on company charges'; see op. cit, Rickford, fn 414 p. 41.

426 See generally *The Final Report*, fn. 422, p. 251, para. 12.19.

427 The Steering Group also recommended that the practice of keeping two registers in respect of companies, one for the prescribed particulars (on which see Companies Act 2006, s. 860(1)) and a second made by the registrar containing short particulars of the charge and other listed information (see Companies Act 2006, s. 869), be amended so that the latter register was abolished saving time and costs to the registry such that the amended register would be made up solely of filed forms containing prescribed information in relation to the registered charges (on which see paras (a)–(i) in the main text below); see *The Final Report*, fn. 422, p. 270, para. 12.69.

428 See *The Final Report*, fn. 422, para. 12.48: 'The combination of the sanction of invalidity together with the establishment of priority should be sufficient to ensure that registrable charges are registered under a system of notice filing'. The report noted that in situation where the chargor was not responsible for filing and the charge had yet to be created at the time of filing then the party filing should be required to verify that the chargor had consented to the filing. It would be an offence to knowingly file inaccurate particulars under the new scheme.

(i) whether the charge has already been created; and
(j) the name of the party registering the charge and, if not the chargor and the charge has yet to be created, confirmation that the chargor had given its written consent.

In addition to the above particulars the following two points would be optional:

(k) In England and Wales only, whether the charge included a negative-pledge clause; and
(l) whether the charge was a market charge under the Companies Act 1989, s. 73.

Regarding the categories of registrable charge a dual approach was recommended in that the new scheme should specify what was and what was not registrable. Under this approach, floating charges, charges over goods (except where the chargee obtained possession of the goods) and charges covered by a specialist registry would be registrable.[429] With regard to other types of charge it was recommended that they be registered unless covered by a specified exemption.[430] Although priority would be generally governed by the date of registration, the doctrine of constructive notice would also apply[431] in respect of subsequent chargees who would be deemed to have notice of all entries on the register.[432] The certificate of conclusivity issued by the registrar of companies would remain for registered charges but would only be conclusive as to the date a charge was registered.[433] In respect of defective particulars on the register a charge would only be valid in respect of property covered by the registered particulars and the original security/charge agreement.[434] In respect of any potential civil liability for inaccurate particulars the Steering Group recommended that the registrar should not be liable for any errors but, instead, the chargee should

429 A 'clear majority of consultees' to the 2000 consultation favoured keeping the dual registration requirement for ease of use whereby credit reference agencies could make one search at Companies House to learn about the state of encumbrances on the company's property. However, the Steering Group hoped that technological advances would lessen the burden of registration in the future via cooperation between registries and transfers of information; see *The Final Report*, fn. 422, p. 264, para.12.56.

430 The exemptions listed being: (a) simple retention of title clauses; (b) a charge, as such, for the purpose of securing any issue of debentures; (c) the deposit by way of security of a negotiable instrument given to secure the payment of a debt; (d) charges over shares; (e) charges over marine insurance policies which insure goods which are exported, and insurance policies in respect of goods over which charges are not registrable; (f) contractual liens over sub-freights; (g) charges over cash or securities, including shares, bonds, money market instruments and units in collective investment schemes in such securities; see *The Final Report*, fn. 422, p. 266, para. 12.61. It had been argued that Lloyds underwriters suffered from the current system and should also be given an exception from registration but the Steering Group believed that their new scheme based on notice filing with no time limit within which registration had to be effected would benefit them with no need for any exception but they were unable to consult on this; see *The Final Report*, fn. 422, pp. 268–9.

431 See *The Final Report*, fn. 422, p. 262.

432 This would only be of practical significance in respect of registered floating charges with an optional registered negative pledge clause forbidding the chargor from granting later charges in priority over the encumbered property.

433 *The Final Report*, fn. 422, p. 251, para. 12.20.

434 Ibid., p. 255, para. 12.29.

be liable for all errors irrespective of the party responsible for supplying the (inaccurate) prescribed particulars to the registrar.[435]

Although the new scheme would be based on voluntary registration with no time period within which registration had to be made, the Steering Group recommended that a charge filed after it had been created and also after insolvency proceedings had begun would be avoided. The onset of insolvency proceedings would be the cut-off point by which time registration/filing would have to be made if the charge was not to be subject to the avoidance sanction. In reaching this conclusion the Steering Group expressly rejected any arguments that a special time-cut-off point[436] might be needed to protect unsecured creditors from collusion by the company to conceal its correct credit position via a heavily encumbered property estate which was not disclosed on the register but would be quietly registered on the eve of insolvency.[437] The Steering Group succinctly noted that all unsecured creditors run the risk of secured creditors intervening at some point whether they register or not; it is inherent to their status that they have decided to run the risk.[438]

Finally, the Steering Group recommended that companies should no longer be required to maintain their own internal register of charges. Although in theory this register is much wider than the public register of charges at Companies House because it applies to 'all'[439] charges covering any property of the company rather than a numerus clausus, in practice the register is rarely kept and compliance was stated to be 'poor'. Nevertheless, it was recommended that a company's members and creditors should continue to have the right to inspect copies of instruments creating charges.[440]

The Steering Group was mindful that its proposals were confined in application to companies and the reform of the Companies Act 1985. However, the topic of company charges was intricately linked to the concept of security interests in general and reforming this topic could not sensibly be considered without its application to non-corporate debtors. Therefore, the proposals made in the *Final Report* were stated to be only 'provisional'[441] and needed to be tested via wider consultation. It was recommended, therefore, that the DTI refer the topic, via the Lord Chancellor's Department, to the Law Commissions for further work.[442]

Given the history of company charge reform and governments, to this date, rejection of reform schemes based on notice filing, it is not surprising that the Steering Group also made more limited recommendations for reforming the present system in case its main proposals were rejected. The Steering Group recommended that the current system of registration should be made optional and that the criminal penalty

435 *The Final Report*, fn. 422, p. 256, para. 12.32.

436 It was also suggested that a criminal penalty or invoking the Company Director Disqualification Act 1986 might also be used here; see *The Final Report*, fn. 422, p. 261, para. 12.49.

437 Cf. Insolvency Act 1986, s. 245 (avoidance of certain floating charges created without the provision of new value within a relevant time).

438 *The Final Report*, fn. 422, p. 261, para. 12.49.

439 See now Companies Act 2006, s. 876.

440 See *The Final Report*, fn. 422, p. 2710, para. 12.69. The right to inspect copies of instruments is now found in Companies Act 2006, s. 877(4) which also allows inspection by 'any other person upon payment of such fee as may be prescribed' (a new right which was not available under the old Companies Act 1985, s. 408).

441 *The Final Report*, fn. 422, p. 247, para. 12.8.

442 Ibid.

for non-registration within 21 days of the charge's creation be abolished.[443] Instead, unregistered charges would simply be avoided, as at present, if not registered within that time. However, as with the notice file proposals, the Steering Group thought that the avoidance power might breach the European Convention on Human Rights and, in order to make it Convention compliant, a new power for a chargee to apply to the court for relief from avoidance should be added to the Act.[444] The current provision making the debt secured by the avoided charge becoming repayable immediately would also be repealed.[445]

In order to improve the efficiency of the present system the Steering Group recommended that chargees only be required to supply the prescribed information to the registrar and not that relating to the instrument of charge as well.[446] In respect of the prescribed particulars to be supplied these would be similar to those in respect of the notice file scheme but with the additional factor that the date of the charge's creation would be added.[447] Once registered, a certificate of registration would be issued which would only be conclusive as to the date of registration. A chargee would only be able to rely on his charge security interest to the extent that it was accurately revealed in the prescribed particulars supplied to the registrar and shown on the register of charges which would be made up of that prescribed form alone. Should there be any errors on the form, then the charge would not be avoided due to the error but, as has just been stated, the chargee could only rely on the public record of his charge to the extent that that entry reflected the true nature of the charge as in the original charge security itself.[448] Although the 21-day registration period would remain, it would be possible to register a charge outside this time without the need to apply to court (as is presently required) so long as winding-up procedures had not commenced and any charge registered later would rank behind any charges already registered at that time (even if the later registered charge was created before them).[449] In all other respects the Steering Group recommended that its proposals for notice filing should also be adopted in respect of the more modest reforms to be made if notice filing was rejected including the categories of charge to be registrable[450] under the Companies Act.[451]

The Law Commission Proposals 2002–2005

Following the recommendation of the Company Law Review Steering Group in its *Final Report*,[452] a ministerial reference from the DTI was made to the Law Commission to review the law on company security interests. This was to lead to a three-year period of review and consultation starting with the publication, in June 2002, of the

443 See *The Final Report*, fn. 422, p. 271, para. 12.73; as to the current criminal penalty see Companies Act 2006, s. 860.
444 See *The Final Report*, fn. 422, p. 271, para. 12.71. It is submitted that the avoidance power is Convention compliant and no such measure is necessary; see further de Lacy 'Company charge avoidance and human rights' [2004] JBL 448.
445 See Companies Act 2006, s. 874(3).
446 See generally *The Final Report*, fn. 422, pp. 273–4, para. 12.82.
447 See generally, pp. 60–1 for these particulars.
448 See *The Final Report*, fn. 422, p. 274, para. 12.80.
449 Ibid., p. 272, para. 12.76.
450 See p. 61 above for the categories of registrable charge.
451 See *The Final Report*, fn. 422, p. 274 para. 12.83.
452 See fn 442.

consultation paper *Registration of Company Security Interests: Company Charges Other than Land*.[453] The terms of the Law Commission's reference were to:

1. examine the law on the registration, perfection and priority of company charges;
2. consider the case for a new scheme of registration and priority of company charges, including charges created by
   a) companies having their registered office in England or Wales, wherever the assets charged are located; and
   b) overseas companies and companies having their registered office in Scotland, where the charge is subject to English law;
3. consider whether such a scheme should apply both to security in the strict sense and to 'quasi-security' interests such as conditional sales, retention of title clauses, hire-purchase agreements and finance leases, including the extent to and means by which such interests should be made subject to the law governing securities;
4. examine the law relating to the granting of security and 'quasi-security' interests by unincorporated businesses and individuals over property other than land, including the feasibility of extending any new scheme for company charges to such interests, and the extent to and means by which such 'quasi-security' interests should be made subject to the law governing securities; and
5. make recommendations for reform.[454]

Although the Law Commission intended to make recommendations affecting the reform of the law on security interests irrespective of the nature of the entity creating the security, be it corporate or non-corporate debtor, the fact that the DTI was at this time actively reviewing company law in general with a view to introducing a new Companies Act meant that the Commission was forced to adopt a 'split treatment'[455] in its review of this area. This approach meant formulating proposals that would initially only apply to companies and would be brought into force under a new Companies Act via secondary legislation. This would then be followed by a second phase under which the law applicable to non-companies would be reformed via primary legislation at which time the law would be consolidated and the provisions formally only applicable to companies be repealed and replaced by the new statute.[456] The Law Commission did not favour this dual approach,[457] but it was the only way

453 Law Commission Consultation Paper No. 164; available at www.lawcom.gov.uk.

454 See Law Commission Consultation Paper No. 164, above fn 453, p. 5 para. 1.16.

455 Ibid., p. 5, para. 1.18.

456 The Law Commission did consider the need to reform non-corporate security interests in the Consultation Paper and came firmly to the conclusion that the law needed fundamental reforms similar to those it recommended for companies. The Commission found five main reasons why the law needed reforming: (a) it was too complex particularly the Bills of Sale legislation; (b) the avoidance power for unregistered bills of sale was potentially incompatible with the ECHR; (c) the law made it difficult for businesses and individuals to create fixed charges; (d) the law made it impossible for non-companies to create floating charges; (e) the law failed to give adequate public notice of security and quasi-security interests. See generally Law Commission Consultation Paper No. 164, above fn 453, pp. 221–6.

457 As the Law Commission noted: 'It is this reasoning that compels the divided structure of this Consultation Paper, rather than it being our preferred approach'; see ibid., p. 6, para. 1.18.

in which law reform could be quickly implemented given the fact that any reforms would demand much parliamentary time. This then offered the current company law reform project what was thought an opportune moment to effect law reform. This pragmatic approach was unfortunate and was to dog the entire reform project perhaps even being, in part, responsible for the government's decision not to implement the findings in the Companies Act 2006. As the Law Commission was to explain:

> In order to meet the legislative time-scale imposed on the project by the DTI's reference, we have had to prepare this Consultation Paper in much shorter time than would be normal. Consequently we have not been able to do as much research into some issues, particularly the operation of other notice-filing systems, as we would have wished.[458]

The starting point for the Law Commission was that some form of registration system for company charges was essential and the basic question was not should we have a system to regulate security interests, but, rather, what form of system should we have?[459] Whatever system might be used it would/should perform two basic functions,[460] namely:

(a) provide a source of information 'about the extent to which assets that may appear to be owned by the company are in fact subject to securities in favour of other parties'; and
(b) regulate the priorities of security interests.

The Law Commission was of the view that the system of company charge registration under the then Companies Act 1985 Part 12 failed to perform any of these functions in a satisfactory manner.[461] Therefore, following in the wake of the predecessor Crowther and Diamond Reports, the Law Commission proposed that a new notice file scheme should be introduced to replace the current scheme under Part 12 of the Act. The new notice file scheme would rest on three principles:[462]

> filing is not necessarily about specific transactions, but is about giving public notice that a person has taken or intends to take a non-possessory security interest over a designated asset or class of assets of the debtor;
> the secured party can file a notice to protect the security interest either before or after the security interest is actually created, and priority will be determined by the date of filing in either case;
> the notice filed as a public document contains specified information in relation to the security interest and is not the actual document of charge/security or a copy of it thereby allowing a purely automated system to operate it, with the

458 See Consultation Paper No. 164, fn 453, p. 17, para. 1.58.
459 Consultation Paper No. 164, fn 453, p. 46.
460 Ibid., pp. 46–7, para. 3.4. The Law Commission also noted that the system 'should also provide clear rules of purchasers who buy assets that are subject to security interests'; p. 47, para. 3.6.; see generally the chapter by Gullifer in this volume (pp. 188–222) for a treatment of this issue.
461 Ibid., p. 48, para. 3.9.
462 Ibid., pp. 61–2, para. 4.9.

searcher then making secondary inquiries of the debtor/chargor company or the secured party if further information is desired/required.

The introduction of this new system would bring about four principal changes to the existing system of company charge registration.[463] First, the amount of detailed information in relation to the relevant security interest or charge would be greatly reduced. The new system would be based on the filing of a notice in relation to a security interest or proposed security interest as opposed to the registration of an actual charge transaction as exists at present. Registration or filing would be effected by supplying the registrar with a standard form financing statement containing prescribed information[464] in relation to the security interest. This new process would allow a quicker and more efficient system to operate, since the public officials responsible for maintaining the public register would no longer have to check, or attempt to summarise, the nature of the security. This would also be important since the system would be computerised and fully automated. Indeed, there would be no need for any human input via Companies House meaning that 'the party filing would take responsibility for the accuracy of the particulars in the financing statement and would bear the risk of any mistakes'.[465]

The second important change is that the system would allow prospective filing of security interests. That is to say an 'interest' could be filed before any actual security interest materialised. This would remove the current problem of invisibility in that a charge has only to be registered within 21 days of its creation[466] in order to be perfected but priority is accorded to the date the security charge is actually created. This means that any chargee cannot be sure that prior interests are not in existence at the date such chargee's security charge is taken at which point in time the public register might be free of registered charges but, a prior chargee exists and is making the most of the 21-day period of grace before effecting registration. Notice filing allows the prospective secured creditor to file his interest in the confidence that if the register is clear at the date of filing he will be assured of priority if, and when, the actual security interest is created subsequently. Additional benefits are that convenience is afforded due to the fact that notice filing is not dependent on actual security transactions, therefore a prospective secured assignee of a company's debts can file a single interest which will then cover all future dealings/assignments made to him by way of security.

The third important change would be that the new notice file system would regulate priorities which the current scheme does not do.[467] The basic rule of priority, underpinning the new system, would be that security interests are prioritised according to the date upon which they are filed at the public registry. The first to file a security interest would generally prevail in any conflict of priorities and this would have the significant

463 See generally Consultation Paper No. 164, fn 453, pp. 62–3.

464 Ibid., p. 66, para. 4.21 and pp. 68–9, para. 4.29 for their recommendations in respect of this prescribed information. The prescribed information is almost identical to that proposed by the Company Law Review Steering Group in their 2001 *Final Report*, on which see pp. 60–1.

465 See Consultation Paper No. 164, above fn 453, p. 62, para. 4.11. Note also at pp. 122–4 for other liability issues discussed by the Law Commission.

466 See generally Companies Act 2006, s. 870(1)(a).

467 The fact that the Companies Act does not contain any priority rules for charges other than the fact that unregistered charges are liable to be avoided has caused much confusion over the years and some have suggested that the doctrine of constructive notice applies in respect of registered charges, but this can be doubted; see further de Lacy 'Constructive notice and company charge registration' [2001] Conv. 122.

effect of removing the artificial distinction that currently exists between legal and equitable interests over property.[468] However, an exception to perfection via notice filing would be in respect of possessory security interests, particularly the pledge and where a security interest was taken via a pledge prior to any later interest being perfected by filing, in which case the pledge interest would prevail in the event of any conflict.[469] Not all security interests would require filing[470] under the Law Commission's proposals and in a situation where there was a conflict between a filed security interest and an unfiled interest covered by an exception, then the general rule would be that priority would be determined by the date upon which the interests had been perfected.[471]

Linked to the priority question is the issue of the ambit upon which the security interest is recognised, particularly where the debtor deals in some way with encumberd assets. The Law Commission favoured that a security interest should automatically extend to proceeds and the interest be continuously perfected where the proceeds (of the debtor's dealing) were money, or similar property or the proceeds came within the description of the property originally covered by the financing statement, or that statement stated that it also covered proceeds of the original property. In other cases it was proposed that where the proceeds were not continuously perfected, then they should be perfected for a short period of time allowing the secured party time to file a new financing statement in respect of the proceeds and they would then gain priority over those proceeds according to the priority enjoyed by the first filing.[472] A secured party would also be able to tack advances onto the original debt such that the secured party would also enjoy priority for any future advances, provided that the financing statement (and the security agreement) made reference to this.[473]

A notable exception to the rule that priorities are generally determined according to the date of filing would be in respect of the purchase-money security interest. Even in a case where there existed a prior filing covering relevant property of the debtor in a situation where that debtor acquired more of such property financed by a purchase-money security interest by way of such a transaction as a conditional sale or hire-purchase, then the latter interest would prevail. Even under current law[474] this interest is expressly recognised by the law as a special situation meriting protection, since it enables a debtor to secure fresh funding over unique property, so long as it can be demonstrated that the secured party's funding led, and was intended to lead, directly to the acquisition of particular property.[475]

A new development concerned the Law Commission's proposals in respect of purchasers of goods subject to security interests.[476] At present there is no specific legislation on this topic which is governed by a host of specialist statutes and common

468 For these purposes notice would also be irrelevant and a second security interest holder would prevail over the claims of a prior security interest holder if the second were the first to file despite having notice of the prior interest; see Consultation Paper No. 164, fn 453, p. 97, para. 4.123.

469 Ibid., p. 103, para. 4.145.

470 See the main text below for these exceptions.

471 See Consultation Paper No. 164, fn 453, p. 104, para. 4.148.

472 See generally Consultation Paper No. 164, fn 453, p. 112, para. 4.172.

473 Ibid., pp. 106–7.

474 See further de Lacy 'The purchase money security interest: a company charge conundrum?' [1991] LMCLQ 531.

475 See further Consultation Paper No. 164, fn 453, pp. 107–9.

476 For a specific discussion of this area in relation to the Law Commission's work, see the chapter by Gullifer in this volume (pp. 188–222).

law principles.[477] However, the Law Commission made a number of proposals that would, in general, have served to protect purchasers in this situation and generally give them good title to encumbered goods, provided that they were sold in the ordinary course of business.[478]

A final point on the priority of security interests under the new scheme concerned the role of the floating charge.[479] The Law Commission noted that 'we would expect companies to continue to use the floating charge' even if their notice file proposals were adopted.[480] Any security interest that allowed the debtor to utilise the encumbered property in the ordinary course of business (particularly via sale and use of the proceeds) could accurately be classified as a floating charge whatever the parties chose to call their arrangement.[481] This would mean that any such security would continue to be caught by the measures contained in the Insolvency Act 1986 (as amended) that are specifically aimed at floating charges.[482] However, a potential problem is that, at common law, it has been found that the ability of a debtor to continue to deal with an encumbered property also covers the ability to create subsequent security charges in priority over a floating charge (as long as the second chargee was without notice of any particular restriction in the first charge).[483] This would mean that under the new regime a filed 'floating charge' might be said to lose out to a later filed 'fixed' charge over the same assets. In order to remove this possibility the Law Commission recommended that the new scheme should make it clear that a floating charge would no longer give the debtor the power/authority to create subsequent charges in priority to the earlier floating charge.[484] Another area of concern for the Law Commission concerned crystallisation clauses and their effects on potential purchasers of goods who might not be aware that the debtor's authority to deal had been withdrawn. In order to prevent arguments as to the debtor's authority to pass good title in this type of situation it was recommended that it would be a requirement to register the fact that a floating charge had crystallised pursuant to an automatic crystallisation clause.[485]

The fourth main change brought about by the proposals would concern the interrelationship between the company charge register, maintained by the registrar of companies at Companies House, and the more specialised title-based registers that currently exist, such as those covering land, ships and aircraft. Under current law priority conflicts can occur, since both systems exist on a mutually exclusive basis. In order to remove any conflicts the Law Commission proposed that in future the specialist registers would prevail and govern all priority matters. Although the Law Commission expressed no firm views on the matter of whether certain interests might be required to be filed on an information-only basis under the reformed company only scheme.[486]

477 For a general treatment of this area, see Beale, Bridge, Gullifer and Lomnika *The Law of Personal Property Security* (Oxford: Oxford University Press, 2007), ch.13.
478 See generally Consultation Paper No. 164, fn 453, pp. 112–19.
479 Note also the work of Crowther on this, fn 268, p. 70, n. 292.
480 See Consultation Paper No. 164, fn 453, p. 100, para. 4.130.
481 See *Agnew* v. *Commissioner of Inland Revenue* [2001] 2 AC 710.
482 Note in particular Insolvency Act 1986, ss. 175, 175A, 245.
483 See generally: *English & Scottish Mercantile Investment Co. Ltd* v. *Brunton* [1892] 2 QB 700; *Re Benjamin Cope & Sons Ltd* [1914] 1 Ch. 800; *Re Automatic Bottle Makers Ltd* [1926] Ch. 412.
484 See Consultation Paper No. 164, fn 453, p. 102, para. 4.142.
485 See Consultation Paper No. 164, fn 453, p. 103, para. 4.144.
486 Ibid., p. 63, para. 4.14, p. 121, para. 4.211.

With regard to the coverage and application of the proposed notice file scheme the Law Commission was of the view that it should apply to all charges subject to specified exceptions.[487] They justified this new approach on the basis that:

> a system working on the basis that the parties to a transaction would expect most charges to be registrable unless on a finite list would perhaps be easier to operate and would reflect the commercial reality that in practice most companies or creditors seek to register all charges 'just in case'. In addition, such an approach would go towards making the section 'future-proof' in respect of security over new types of assets. This would avoid repetition of the difficulty now felt over whether charges over [certain types of asset] are registrable.[488]

The exceptions to the new notice file regime would include: security arising by operation of law (the system being confined to consensual interests alone);[489] possessory security,[490] set-off,[491] special purpose trusts;[492] charges over property already covered by an existing specialist register; charges over bank accounts under the control of the chargee; charges on goods and on insurance policies on goods where the goods are abroad at sea, or are imported goods before they are delivered to a buyer, or deposited in a warehouse or store.[493] However, the Law Commission rejected the idea that small-cost transactions should be excluded from the scheme.[494]

Linked to the categories of interest covered by the proposed notice file scheme was its application to quasi-security interests. The Law Commission was well aware of the prior work of both Crowther and Diamond and the fundamental principle that came out of each of their reports was that a reformed law of security needed to be based on the function, rather than the form, of a transaction. Linked to this functional approach and of growing importance in the modern world was the 'international dimension', as the Law Commission described it,[495] which has been more aptly described as the global dimension.[496] The Commission noted:

> We wonder whether there might be a risk that in time overseas investors may be hesitant before investing in United Kingdom companies if we persist in having a system that does not take a functional approach, instead retaining the

487 Ibid., p. 130, para. 5.6.
488 See Consultation Paper No. 164, fn 453, p. 129, para. 5.5.
489 Ibid., p. 65, para. 4.18.
490 See Consultation Paper No. 164, above fn 453, at p. 64 para. 4.17. The exception would also include charges over shares and investment securities where the secured party has possession of the certificate, or has control by being registered as owner; see Consultation Paper No. 164, at p. 162 para. 5.123 Point (2). But the transfer of shares and investment securities under a 'repo' would not be subject to filing; see Consultation Paper No. 164, at p. 196, para. 7.50.
491 Ibid., p. 196 para. 7.52.
492 Ibid., pp. 196–7.
493 See generally ibid., p. 162, para. 5.123.
494 Ibid., pp. 204–5.
495 See Consultation Paper No. 164, fn 453, p. 184, para. 7.10.
496 The drive for the reform of the law on security interests is internationally driven and has been led by the USA with Article 9 of the UCC followed by Canada, New Zealand and Australia. Note also the chapters by Zeigel, Brown and Fisher in this volume (pp. 117, 328 and 366 respectively) for an international approach to the reform of this area.

application of any system only to charges. We do not know how great such a risk might be, but we certainly think it is a factor that should be considered.[497]

With this in mind the Commission recommended that the new scheme should adopt the functional approach to security interests shown by other international systems,[498] and introduce a new statutory concept of 'security interest' which would extend the present concept beyond the narrow concepts of proprietary assignments by way of security to any transaction which was intended to operate by way of security, irrespective of the location of property under the relevant transaction, thereby bringing the quasi-security interest within the new scheme.[499] This extension of the traditional ambit of the 'security interest' would mean that the new scheme would extend, according to the Law Commission recommendations, to hire-purchase and conditional sales contracts (including retention of title),[500] sales of receivables,[501] and possibly, depending on the response to consultations, to consignments of goods[502] and finance leases.[503]

So far the provisional findings of the Law Commission were essentially in respect of introducing a new notice file scheme governing the priorities of security interests. However, the Law Commission was aware that fundamental reforms of this area in other countries had gone much wider than this to encompass an entire restatement of the law on security interests. Given that the Law Commission had proposed that the law of security interests under a notice file scheme should see the unification of real and quasi-security interests under the same notice file scheme, the Commission thought it only logical that other areas of the law in relation to the creation and enforcement of security should receive the same treatment. Therefore, the Law Commission proposed that the scheme should extend to regulate such security interests from the moment and method of their creation, to their priority of enforcement and, finally, to their extinguishment via enforcement and payment of the secured debt to the rules of distribution of any surplus.[504] However, given the time demands placed on the reform project and the fact that a dual stage of reform was envisaged, starting with a companies-only scheme under a reformed Companies Act, the Commission recommended that the implementation of any restatement of the law should be postponed until the full reform package was introduced, so that a unified system of law reform would be in place affecting all categories of debtor be they companies or other form of trader/individual.[505]

Although the Law Commission was firmly of the view that the way forward was by comprehensive reform, entailing a new notice file-based system coupled with a restatement of the law on security interests, it also submitted proposals for amending the current system as an alternative, in the event that its main proposals were rejected. Such a path had been followed by the Company Law Review Steering Group[506] and

497 See Consultation Paper, No. 164, fn 453, p. 185, para. 7.10.
498 On which, see fn 496 above.
499 See Consultation Paper No. 164, fn 453, p. 187, para. 7.20. See also p. 3 *et seq.* in this volume for a general discussion of the concept of security.
500 See Consultation Paper No. 164, fn 453, pp. 188–9.
501 See Consultation Paper No. 164, fn 453, pp. 194–5, para. 7.45.
502 Ibid., pp. 189–90.
503 See generally ibid., pp. 190–1.
504 See generally ibid., pp. 243–55 and pp. 289–308.
505 Ibid., p. 254, para. 11.46.
506 See pp. 62–3.

the Diamond Report[507] but the Law Commission was keen to stress that to adopt an amendment to the current system 'would be a less satisfactory approach' to following its main recommendations for fundamental reform.[508] These amendment proposals[509] were essentially similar to the proposals made by both the Steering Group and *Diamond Report*[510] but stressed that a new priority rule should be introduced to the company charge registration system based upon the date of registration and that even this reformed 'old' system should be based upon notice filing such that potential chargees could register/file their prospective interests in advance of their actual creation.[511]

In August 2004 the Law Commission published the follow up to its consultation paper of 2002 in the shape of *Company Security Interests: a Consultative Report.*[512] The Law Commission received a total of sixty-eight responses to its earlier paper, and the Commission noted that its proposals for a new notice file scheme to replace Part 12 of the Companies Act 1985 had 'received broad support of all but a handful of consultees'.[513] The only concern revealed by the consultation was that the proposal to extend the coverage of the scheme to catch quasi-security interests 'proved to be more controversial'.[514] However, although the reform proposals had generated support, most of the consultees had expressed concern that in order to give the new scheme full support and be able to express full and detailed comments on the proposals, they would need to see what any legislation that might result from the proposals would look like. In order to meet their concerns the Law Commission took the step of producing a second consultation document, pending its final report, so that it could receive a more considered response which would ensure that any resulting recommendations had been given full and frank scrutiny by interested groups.[515] The *Consultative Report* of 2004 was limited to companies and limited liability partnerships, due to time constraints imposed by the DTI and the fact that its implementation would have to be under secondary legislation derived from the anticipated new Companies Act.[516] However, the Commission wanted the scheme to apply to all categories of business debtor, but in order to get its proposals implemented, a more pragmatic initial approach was warranted, and wider reform could follow at a later date. The Commission noted that:

> We are in any event of the view that the introduction of a scheme just for companies would have sufficient benefits to warrant adopting such a course, rather than insisting on an 'all or nothing' approach.[517]

507 See pp. 52–5.
508 See Consultation Paper No. 164, fn 453, p. 273, para. A.3.
509 On which see generally ibid., pp. 273–88.
510 On which see pp. 62–3 and pp. 52–5.
511 See Consultation Paper No. 164, fn 453, p. 286, para. A.45.
512 See Law Commission Consultation Paper No. 176 (London: The Stationery Office, 2004), hereafter the *Consultative Report.* The closing date for comments on this paper was 23 November 2004.
513 *Consultative Report*, fn. 512, p. 4, para. 1.12.
514 Ibid.
515 See generally *Consultative Report*, fn. 512, p. 5, paras 1.14, 1.17; the Law Commission intended to publish its final report by the summer of 2005.
516 *Consultative Report*, fn. 512, pp. 5–6, paras 1.16, 1.19.
517 *Consultative Report*, fn. 512, p. 5, para. 1.16; with regard to consumer debtors the Commission noted that 'we have not at this stage reached any conclusions as to security interests created by consumer debtors'.

In effect the *Consultative Report* of 2004 was a fleshed-out version of the earlier Consultation Paper of 2002, the Law Commission stating that its new proposed scheme 'is in its essentials the same as that proposed in the Consultation Paper' of 2004.[518] However, the 2002 Consultation Paper had had the benefit of revealing that the Commission's secondary proposals[519] for a more limited approach of amending Part 12 of the Companies Act had produced 'very little support', with only four consultees bothering to comment on their worth.[520]

Responses to the *Consultation Paper* had confirmed the Law Commission's view that the current system had failed to meet the two basic functions of a registration system, namely that of providing an effective system of information/notice and also priority in relation to security interests.[521] Therefore the Commission was now confident that notice filing was the only sensible way forward. The Commission identified seven main benefits of introducing a new notice file system:[522]

Electronic, online filing would be simple, fast and (in the long term) cheap. The same would be true of searching.

The risk of errors would be very small particularly in a companies-only scheme, since debtors' names can be cross-checked against registration number upon incorporation.[523]

The risk of inaccuracies in the description of the collateral would be reduced, because a simple description would suffice, and the danger to third parties greatly reduced, as a security interest would not be effective as regards collateral that is not within the description in the financing statement.

It would be possible to file while a security agreement is being negotiated to protect the lender's priority position.

Dual registration of security interests over land, many registered ships, registered aircraft, patents, trade marks and registered designs would no longer be necessary.

There would be a clear statement of priority rules affecting security interests better suited to modern conditions.

The distinction between the fixed and floating charge would all but disappear under the new system. It would be possible to create a security interest with priority according to the date of filing but which would still give the debtor the power to deal in the ordinary course of business.[524]

518 *Consultative Report*, fn. 512, p. 7, para. 1.23.
519 On which see generally pp. 70–1.
520 *Consultative Report*, fn. 512, p. 14, para. 2.7.
521 *Consultative Report*, fn. 512, pp. 12–13.
522 See *Consultative Report*, fn. 512, pp. 22–3.
523 See Companies Act 2006, s. 1066. Cf. *Grove* v. *Healthcare (T10) Ltd* [2000] 1 BCLC 661.
524 See generally the *Consultative Report*, fn. 512, pp. 27–9. Note also at p. 68 for the former views of the Commission in *Consultation Paper No. 164*. One possible problem of the new scheme would concern the applicability of the Insolvency Act 1986 measures aimed specifically at the floating charge. The Commission stated that its recommendations were intended to be 'insolvency neutral'. In order to accommodate the Act the Commission recommended that the new scheme should identify the specific types of collateral that would be covered by a floating charge and expressly give priority to the claims of preferential creditors over these assets; see the *Consultative Report*, p. 29, para. 2.60.

Although the Commission was keen to promote the benefits of the new scheme, it was also made aware of possible limitations and some of the responses to its earlier Consultation Paper had expressed reservations about the reform proposals.[525] However, the Commission was of the opinion that these possible limitations were of no great significance and the benefits of moving over to a new electronic notice file scheme would outweigh any disadvantages particularly in the long term once the changeover was complete. The Law Commission concluded:

> Thus, while we are not in a position to make an accurate assessment of the costs and benefits of the scheme, our provisional view is that the costs of changing from the current scheme of registration and priority of company charges to the notice-filing scheme outlined earlier would not be great and would be relatively slight compared to the benefits to be obtained. This conclusion and the nearly unanimous support for this change from those who responded to our Consultation Paper lead us to recommend that, unless the response to this consultative report reveals convincing reasons to the contrary, a notice-filing scheme for company charges should be adopted.[526]

The rest of the *Consultative Report* was concerned with explaining how the new scheme would operate in practice. A most notable feature of the document was that the Law Commission included a draft statement of the new scheme to be implemented by secondary legislation. These draft regulations were heavily influenced by Article 9 of the UCC and the Saskatchewan Personal Property Security Act 1993 (with appropriate modifications) and listed 74 draft clauses providing a detailed exposition of exactly what form and shape the new law would look like if ever implemented. The regulations were very comprehensive and covered:[527] Part 1 Introduction (meaning of terms and scope of new law); Part 2 Effectiveness of Security Agreements (requirements for attachment, requests for information from secured party); Part 3 Perfection and Priorities (methods of perfection and statement of priority rules); Part 4 Filing (general rules in relation to the operation of the register of security interests); Part 5 Rights and Remedies on Default (general rules governing the enforcement of security interests and the distribution upon realisation); Part 6 Supplementary Provisions (general provisions in relation to the scheme and its interrelationship with other areas of law). In short the reader was given a comprehensive treatment of exactly what the reform process would entail in terms of a new legislative regime. The basic principles remained the same as had already been set out in *Consultation Paper No.164* but their practical implementation could now be fully assessed.

In August 2005 the Law Commission published its *Final Report* on reforming this area.[528] It had received 70 responses to the 2004 *Consultative Report*, but 'it was not easy to analyse the responses'.[529] Although there was universal agreement that the current system had 'significant weaknesses' there was no consensus on agreeing on a new reformed law to replace the current system.[530] Despite this apparent cooling

525 *Consultative Report*, fn. 512, pp. 23–9 for these reservations.
526 *Consultative Report*, fn. 512, p. 31, para. 2.67.
527 *Consultative Report*, fn. 512, pp. 289–345.
528 See Law Commission Report No. 296 *Company Security Interests* (2005) Cmnd 6654; hereafter the *Final Report*.
529 *Final Report*, fn. 528, p. 7, para. 1.20.
530 Ibid.

from consultees to introducing a new system of company charge registration, the Law Commission remained convinced that there was a 'business case' for it.[531] Having analysed its own proposals, the Commission was firmly of the view that its proposed new scheme would bring major benefits for users of the system and its implementation would render the law more effective and efficient than the current system.[532]

The final scheme proposed by the Law Commission contained significant changes from that proposed in its *Consultative Report* of 2004. Opposition, particularly from the legal community (largely led by City solicitors) meant that the Commission dropped its proposals to extend the scheme to cover quasi-security interests (including retention-of-title transactions) and also that the scheme include a statement of the rights and remedies of the parties to security interest transactions. Instead, the Commission decided to keep the scheme focused on its traditional ambit, namely company charges/mortgages.[533] Thus, the 'new' scheme would be limited to 'any charge or pledge created by a company registered in England and Wales over any of its property (wherever situated)'.[534] However, in a major new shift, the scheme did extend to cover sales of receivables,[535] despite opposition from lawyers.[536] Therefore under these proposals the law would change from the current numerus clausus approach to registrable charges[537] to a simple rule that all charges are registrable unless covered by an exemption.[538] If a charge was not registered, then the penalty would be avoidance in insolvency against prescribed parties[539] and also against execution creditors, but the process of registration would be entirely optional and there would be no duty on any party to register, nor any criminal penalties for not so doing.[540] Nor would companies be required to keep their own register of charges.[541] The new scheme would be entirely electronic with online filing and searching based upon measures that had already been proposed.[542]

The new scheme also included comprehensive priority rules to regulate any conflicts between charges. Fundamental to the priority rules was the basic principle that all registered charges rank according to the date of registration,[543] rather than creation as at present. However, in keeping with its previous recommendations, the Commission

531 *Final Report*, fn. 528, p. 23, para. 2.2.
532 *Final Report*, fn. 528, pp. 23–32 for the reasons for this view.
533 See generally the *Final Report*, fn. 528, p. 9, paras 1.29–1.30.
534 *Final Report*, fn. 528, p. 162 Draft Regulation 2(1)(a).
535 *Final Report*, fn. 528, p. 162 Draft Regulation 2(1)(b); the term 'receivables' was defined in Regulation 3.
536 The Law Commission was particularly influenced in pressing this change due to the fact that the trade body for the factoring and discounting industry, the Factors and Discounters Association were strongly in favour of a new filing scheme for receivables that regulated priority issues. The City of London Law Society, Financial Law Committee was against such a move and favoured keeping the law as it stood. See generally the *Final Report*, fn. 528, pp. 107–8.
537 On which, see pp. 27–8.
538 The proposed exemptions are set out in the *Final Report*, fn. 528, p. 164, Regulation 4; notable listed exemptions are a lien or charge arising by operation of law, a fixed charge over registered land and registered under the Land Registration Act 2002, certain Lloyd's trust fund/deposit charges.
539 *Final Report*, fn. 528, p. 180 Regulation 20; the prescribed parties being an administrator or liquidator.
540 See generally, the *Final Report*, fn. 528, p. 49, paras 3.72–3.73.
541 See the *Final Report*, fn. 528, p. 101, para. 3.300.
542 See generally the *Final Report*, fn. 528, pp. 147–50.
543 See generally the *Final Report*, fn. 528, p. 68, para. 3.155(2), 184 Regulation 24(3).

kept the principle that advance registration or filing of a charge interest would be possible even before the charge was actually created,[544] with priority being afforded at that date should an actual charge later materialise. The scheme also extended to cover the majority of other situations in which priority disputes might arise,[545] but the Commission declined to give purchase-money security charges any special priority under the new scheme.[546] A further change came in relation to the floating charge which the Commission had proposed to scrap, in effect, under its *Consultative Report*.[547] However, following comments from consultees,[548] the Commission decided to retain the floating charge as a distinct form of charge security interest.[549] Although the Commission believed that there was a 'good case'[550] for removing the present distinction between fixed and floating charges and that the Insolvency Act could be suitably amended to accommodate this change[551] 'we recognise that insolvency law has undergone significant changes in recent years, and there is great unwillingness to see further changes in the immediate future'.[552] Therefore the current position was maintained, but the Commission recommended that the issue be revisited when insolvency law was reviewed in the future.[553] Nevertheless, from a priority point of view, the position of the retained floating charge was enhanced under the Law Commission's *Final Report* because all priority issues were determined according to the date of registration/filing and therefore devices such as the negative pledge or automatic crystallisation clause were greatly diminished in importance.[554]

As with the *Consultative Report* the end of the *Final Report* contained a draft set of regulations to be implemented by a future Companies Act. These draft regulations were divided into six parts and contained 43 draft regulations covering: Part 1 (Introduction); Part 2 (Registration of Charges and Sales of Receivables); Part 3 (Effectiveness of Charges); Part 4 (Priority); Part 5 (Financial Collateral);[555] Part 6 (Miscellaneous and Supplementary). Although the scheme was limited to companies, the Commission was firmly of the view that the new scheme should be extended to all businesses in the future and that further work would be undertaken with that in

544 See generally the *Final Report*, fn. 528, p. 54 para. 3.91, 166 Regulation 6(1)(a).

545 See generally the *Final Report*, fn. 528, p. 184 Regulation 24 (residual priority rules) and Regulation 25 (conflicts with specialist registers).

546 *Final Report*, fn. 528, p. 67, para. 3.146.

547 See fn 524 and the main text thereat.

548 The Commission did note, however, that the responses were 'particularly difficult to analyse' and 'it has been hard to gauge whether there is real opposition to our proposals when correctly understood' such that: 'The scheme proposed [in the *Consultative Report*] was designed to enable fixed and floating charges as they currently exist to be superseded by a new single form of charge that would be more flexible and give the lender better protection. We believe that in terms of the law of security there is a good case for this change'; see the *Final Report*, fn. 528, pp. 70–1, para. 3.164.

549 *Final Report*, fn. 528, p. 69, para. 3.158.

550 *Final Report*, fn. 528, p. 73, para. 3.171.

551 On which see the *Final Report*, fn. 528, p. 72.

552 *Final Report*, fn. 528, p. 73, para. 3.172.

553 *Final Report*, fn. 528, p. 73, para. 3.175.

554 *Final Report*, fn. 528, p. 74, para. 3.180. This recommendation would have led to possible circular priority conflicts in insolvency situations where there were preferential creditors and the Commission also made recommendations to prevent this; see ibid., fn. 528, p. 76, para. 3.187.

555 See generally the *Final Report*, fn. 528, Part 5, for the Law Commission's recommendations in respect of this topic. Note also the essay by Benjamin in this volume at pp. 260–4.

mind once the new companies-only scheme had been implemented.[556] Likewise, with regards to having a statement of rights and remedies in the new scheme, the Commission proposed to review this area again to see if support could be gained for having such a statement implemented in the future.[557]

DTI Economic Impact Consultation 2005

Prior to the publication of the Law Commission's *Final Report* in July 2005, the DTI published a consultation document *The Economic Impact of the Law Commissions' Proposals*.[558] The purpose of this document was to enable the government to make a Regulatory Impact Assessment on the possible options for reforming the law on security interests prior to any Companies Bill being introduced in Parliament. In order to facilitate this task the Law Commission supplied an advance copy of its Draft Regulations on company charge registration (which were printed in an Annex to the consultation document), so that consultees could comment on them[559] in advance of the publication of its *Final Report* which was to follow in August 2005. The document also included reference to the work of the Scottish Law Commission which had produced a separate report recommending changes to the law in Scotland but rejecting the case for fundamental reform and the introduction of a new notice-file-type scheme.[560] The government was particularly interested in finding which of the following three options consultees favoured:

(a) do nothing;[561]
(b) implement either or both of the Law Commissions' recommendations; or[562]
(c) improve the current scheme for England and Wales.[563]

Depending on which particular option consultees favoured, the government also sought views and information on the costs and benefits to consultees of implementing any of these options.[564]

So the Law Commission's review of this area took three years, entailing three major consultation documents, coupled with a government-produced impact assessment. Those interested in the reform of company charges and personal property security interests were kept very busy in what was to be one of the most comprehensive reform projects ever undertaken by either the government or the Law Commission of England and Wales.

556 *Final Report*, fn. 528, p. xiv, fn. 528, paras 23–4.
557 *Final Report*, fn. 528, para. 22. Likewise the Commission also proposed to review the area of retention of title clauses again; see *Final Report*, fn. 528, p. xiv, para. 21.
558 Document URN 05/1366 (London, DTI, 2005); hereafter *Economic Impact*.
559 The closing date for submissions was 7 October 2005.
560 As to the position in Scotland, see the chapter by Gretton in this volume (pp. 270–84).
561 *Economic Impact*, fn. 558, pp. 25–6; the main benefit of adopting this approach was stated to be 'continuity'.
562 *Economic Impact*, fn. 558, pp. 26–9; numerous advantages were listed as flowing from the adoption of this option for both countries.
563 *Economic Impact*, fn. 558, pp. 29–30; this option would bring the benefits of 'continuity' and more modest benefits than option (b) above.
564 *Economic Impact*, fn. 558, pp. 3–4.

The Companies Act 2006

On 8 November 2006 the new Companies Act 2006 received Royal Assent, although Part 25 of the Act which introduced the 'new' company charge registration scheme was not to be brought into force until 1 October 2009.[565] Remarkably, given the amount of work that had preceded the Act, no substantive reforms to company charge law were brought about when the Act came into force. Instead the company charge provisions were an almost carbon copy of their predecessor sections from Part 12 of the Companies Act 1985, subject to minor cosmetic rearrangements of wording and order of presentation.[566] Therefore the duty[567] remains upon a company creating a specified charge[568] to deliver the prescribed particulars[569] of that charge to the registrar of companies for registration[570] within the prescribed time limit,[571] otherwise the charge will be liable to be avoided against prescribed parties.[572] The company is also still required to maintain its own register of charges,[573] and both that register and the register kept by the registrar of companies are open to public inspection.[574]

Despite the fact that the new provisions are a virtual re-enactment of their predecessor provisions from the 1985 Act, there are three areas where significant change has been brought about. First, the new provisions do not expressly apply to charges created by overseas companies.[575] Second, there are new provisions allowing for 'information sharing arrangements',[576] which will give the Secretary of State power to make orders to allow for the sharing of information between the register of company charges and special registers[577] such that duplicate registration is not necessary in appropriate cases[578] and, for example, the details of a charge registered on a

565 See the Companies Act 2006 (Commencement No. 8 Transitional Provisions and Savings) Order 2008 SI 2008/2860 Regulation 3(h).

566 For a comprehensive review of the new law on company charge under the Companies Act 2006, see *Annotated Companies Acts* (Oxford: Oxford University Press), John Birds (ed.), vol. 2, part 25.

567 Companies Act 2006, s. 860(1).

568 Ibid., s. 860(7).

569 Ibid., s. 869(4) and The Companies (Particulars of Company Charges) Regulations 2008, SI 2008/2996 (the prescribed particulars are identical to those under the former Act).

570 Ibid., s. 869. Once registered, the registrar will issue the company with a certificate of registration and that certificate is 'conclusive evidence' that the registration requirement has been complied with; see s. 869(6).

571 Ibid., s. 870.

572 Ibid., s. 874(1).

573 Ibid., s. 876.

574 Ibid., s. 869(7) (public register of charges), s. 877(4)(companies internal register).

575 I.e. there is no counterpart to the former Companies Act 1985, s. 409 which extended the registration scheme to all overseas companies who created charges on property located in England and Wales or acquired property subject to an existing charge over property in England and Wales. However, this is now subject to The Overseas Companies (Execution of Documents and Registration of Charges) Regulations 2009, S.I. 2009/1917 which applies a new charge registration scheme similar to that found in Part 25 of the Act to overseas companies that have opened a branch/establishment in the UK and registered with the registrar of companies under The Overseas Companies Regulations 2009, S.I. 2009/1801.

576 Companies Act 2006, s. 893.

577 These are likely to include the registers in relation to registered land under the Land Registration Act or Merchant Shipping Act and see footnote below.

578 The government has stated that 'there are no immediate plans to use these powers other than so that floating charges registered in the Scottish register of floating charges do not have to be

special register can then be provided automatically to the registrar of companies for entry on the register of company charges. Given that the dual registration of company charges covering interests over land, ships and aircraft are still necessary, this may be a useful provision in the future when appropriate measures are in place to allow for information sharing. Third, and finally, section 894 of the Act provides:

> (1) The Secretary of State may by regulations under this section–
>
> amend this Part by altering, adding or repealing provisions,
> make consequential amendments or repeals in this Act or any other enactment (whether passed or made before this Act).

This new provision is a rare example of the Act adopting an express recommendation of the Law Commission and it will allow the registration scheme to be amended in the future by means of secondary legislation without the need for a new Act of Parliament. The government has stated in relation to this new power that:

> The purpose of the power is to make changes within the confines of the existing system ... We intend to use that power to address the many imperfections of the present system, particularly those noted by the Company Law Review in its final report.
>
> In particular, we intend to use it to update the list of charges to which the provisions apply, to provide that a copy of the instrument, rather than the instrument itself, be delivered to the Registrar of Companies, and for other measures to improve the existing system to reduce the burdens on companies and on the Registrar of Companies. But we do not expect to use the power immediately. Rather, we intend to consult fully, building on the discussions that have been continuing for some time, and to take account of changes in the pipeline to enable electronic conveyancing in England and Wales and automated land transfer in Scotland.[579]

So it is clear that the government already envisages that reforms will be necessary to the company charge scheme but, unlike the full Law Commission recommendation which envisaged a power to bring in a new scheme, only minor reforms will be available in the future.

The question remains as to why the government virtually ignored the work of the Law Commission when enacting the Companies Act 2006? The short answer to this question is that major reforms were not brought in because:

> It was clear from the consultation [i.e. the Economic Impact consultation of 2005] that there is not a consensus of support for the proposals.[580]

The main opposition to reform came from the legal profession, and centred on objections made by City of London solicitors. Typical of this was the response of the City

registered with the Registrar of Companies'; see www.berr.gov.uk section 'Charges/Security interests'.

579 *Hansard* (HL) (2006) 2 November, at col. 480, *per* Lord Sainsbury.

580 See (2005) *Hansard* (HC) written ministerial statements, 3 November, *per* Alun Michael (Minister for Industry), at col. 57WS.

of London Law Society's Financial Law Committee who, in responding to the DTI 2005 Impact Assessment consultation, stated:

> There is no demand amongst those who use the system for major change. The costs of doing so would far outweigh any marginal benefits which it would produce. In practice, the current system works well, and achieves the objective of providing those dealing with companies with the information which they need about security created by companies.[581]

Coming in the wake of the House of Lords' decision in the case of *Re Spectrum Plus Ltd*,[582] a decision which overturned 25 years' established banking practice in what were believed to be fixed charges over book debts, but which the House of Lords found to be floating charges,[583] this is quite a remarkable statement. The fact that the government took notice of this is even more remarkable, given the trend of reform and modernisation in company law. We need only consider the law on directors' duties, particularly in relation to the duty of care when taking company decisions, to see how out of touch this approach was.

The Companies Act 2006, s. 174 introduced a new statutory restatement of the level of a director's duty of skill and care to his company. However, historically, the traditional approach to this under English common law had been relatively low and undemanding. Thus, we had cases where a 6-month-old baby (the Marquis of Bute) was appointed to a directorship of a bank on which board he served for many years until the bank's failure due to a fraud. An attempt to render the Marquis liable for the affairs of the bank failed due to his virtually complete lack of involvement in the management or directorship of the bank. The defence of 'I did nothing and knew nothing' was held good at law and it seemed that only active participation in, or wilful ignorance of the fraud, would found liability. In another leading case it was proclaimed that a director need not exhibit any experience or knowledge in the field of which the company he serves operates.[584] The standard of skill and care was established as a subjective standard and 'a director need not exhibit in the performance of his duties a greater degree of skill than may reasonably be expected from a person of his knowledge and experience'.[585] This standard had its plaudits and served to encourage persons to act as directors and display entrepreneurial spirit or risk taking. Nevertheless, the economic recession of the 1970s, coupled with corporate scandals

581 See document 'The Registration of Companies' Security Interests (Company Charges)' comments in response to the DTI's Consultation Document of July 2005, p. 5, para. 5. Cf. Calnan 'Taking security in English law', in Bridge and Stevens (eds), *Cross-Border Security and Insolvency* (2001), p. 33 who states in relation to English laws priority rules for security interests: 'The priority rules are a potential minefield for secured creditors'; 'it is very difficult to be confident of the outcome of any dispute'.

582 [2005] UKHL 41. For further treatment of this area, see Getzler and Payne (eds) *Company Charges: Spectrum and Beyond* (Oxford. Oxford University Press, 2006).

583 Overruling the case of *Siebe Gorman & Co. Ltd* v. *Barclays Bank Ltd* [1979] 2 Lloyd's Rep 142. Problems with floating charges have been a regular feature before our High Court and above with Goode noting that there had been 48 judgments in a five-year period up to 2006; see Goode 'The case for the abolition of the floating charge', in Getzler and Payne (eds), above fn 582, p. 21.

584 See *Re Brazilian Rubber Plantation* [1911] 1 Ch. 425, p. 436, *per* Neville J.

585 See *Re City and Equitable Fire Insurance Co. Ltd* [1925] 1 Ch. 407, pp. 428–9, *per* Romer J.

in the late 1980s and early 1990s led to a reassessment of this standard. By 1993 the test had been superseded by a new joint subjective–objective test based upon s. 214 of the Insolvency Act 1986.[586] From that point on company directors could not rely upon lack of involvement in the affairs of their company as a defence to an action for breach of duty.[587]

To return to our theme and continuing the analogy, if, during the passage of what was to become the Companies Act 2006, anybody (City solicitor or layperson) had sought to argue that since the decision in *Salomon*'s case[588] that caveat emptor remains the philosophy of those dealing with companies and everybody knows that there is a risk in such dealing and can, therefore, contract around that risk (by taking security or personal guarantees from the company or its directors) such that there was no need for s. 174 or a change in the common laws approach,[589] they would have been laughed out of town. The argument might have continued that a subjective standard of the duty of care had served UK companies well since Victorian times and numbers had steadily risen to over two million,[590] the standard served to encourage risk taking and a successful economy. Since the Maxwell scandal,[591] and the emergence of corporate governance as a mainstream subject binding on all listed companies,[592] no such arguments were advanced in the mainstream. At the time of writing, the current 'credit crunch' and financial scandals affecting the banking sector[593] continue to make any such argument unlikely.

Therefore, it is strange that in relation to company charges a similar backward argument was advanced and went unchallenged in government circles despite a near 40-year movement for reform, starting with the publication of the Crowther *Report* in 1971 and concluding with major new recommendations from the government-sponsored Law Commission. The law on company charges is truly out of step with mainstream company law reform policies of modernisation and efficient updating to reflect modern conditions. Remarkably, law reform was denied on the basis of 21 responses from practitioners to the Law Commission's *Final Report* of 2005,[594] despite the fact that there are currently over two million registered companies to which the registration system applies. Few, if any, companies responded to the various law reform consultations which may reflect the fact that this topic is 'lawyer's law' but, given the fact that simplification and accessibility were aims of the law reform project, this fact still remains disappointing and means the end result might well be unrepresentative of the views of the majority of the system's users.[595]

586 See *Re D'Jan* [1993] BCC 646.
587 See, for example: *Bishopsgate Investment Management* v. *Maxwell* [1993] BCC 130; *Re Simmon Box (Diamonds) Ltd* [2001] 1 BCLC 776.
588 [1897] AC 22.
589 See *Re D'Jan* [1993] BCC 646.
590 See *Companies in 2005–2006* (London: TSO, 2006) HC 1534, p. 13 Table A1 where it is stated that there were 2.1m companies on the register during this period; whereas in the period 1890–9 there were 36,000 companies registered; see p. 15 Table A4.
591 On which see DTI Report *Mirror Group Newspapers plc* (London, TSO, 2001).
592 See generally the Combined Code on Corporate Governance (June 2008), available at www.frc.org.uk, which is rendered mandatory for listed companies by virtue of Rule 12.43A of the London Stock Exchange Listing Rules.
593 See generally the *Turner Review Report* (March 2009) available at www.fsa.gov.uk.
594 See the *Final Report*, fn. 528, p. 7, para. 1.19.
595 Cf. the expectation of the then President of the Board of Trade, Margaret Beckett MP, who, on launching the Company Law Review in 1998, stated 'It will be an open review,

Conclusions

This introduction has shown that problems emerged under English law the moment the law recognised contract as a legitimate method of transferring property/title to personal property rather by means of possession alone. This natural development enabled trade and the economy to flourish but at the expense of certainty in relation to property interests. The common law attempted to meet some of these concerns based on the rule in *Dearle* v. *Hall*[596] and estoppel principles and there were also more limited statutory measures under bankruptcy law but none were effective. It was only by virtue of the introduction of registration systems under the Bills of Sale Acts (in relation to individuals) and Companies Acts that this problem began to be managed. However, these registers never really developed to meet the changing commercial environment. Essentially, English law in relation to personal property security interests has remained regulated by eighteenth- and nineteenth-century common law principles with Victorian legislation superimposing a registration system. Given the tremendous developments in relation to security interests, particularly quasi-security, in the twentieth and now twenty-first centuries, it is hardly surprising that major problems remain and continue to emerge with this system. It is true that the recognition of the consumer debtor is one area that has not caused many problems in recent years and various consumer credit legislation has successfully regulated this particular category of debtor. However, in the business sector major problems remain and the Companies Act 2006 has done little, if anything, to deal with them.

Given the emergence of the American Uniform Commercial Code in the 1950s and the recognition of its benefits in regulating secured transactions under Article 9 by the Crowther *Report* in 1971, there is no excuse based on ignorance for the way forward.[597] Developments in the Commonwealth since then, particularly in Canada, have served to educate on the potential 'solutions' to regulating company charges and the wider question of security interests in the business sector. In short, English law is currently stuck in a time warp from which it shows no sign of being keen to emerge. Given the rejection of the Law Commission's recommendations and the passage of the Companies Act 2006, Part 25, it appears that fundamental law reform is some way off.[598] However, we can be certain that it will not be too long before we see yet more High Court decisions which serve only to demonstrate the weaknesses of the current system. It is remarkable that this area of law has generated such a mass of reform proposals and so little action. Although we are currently

with wide consultation. I want to hear from all parts of business, both large and small, what changes they believe would enhance their competitiveness or, better still, give them a competitive advantage'; see *Modern Company Law for a Competitive Economy* (DTI, March 1998) at p. i.

596 (1828) 3 Russ 1.

597 Indeed, even the senior members of the English judiciary have now recognised that personal property security law reform may be the way forward; see *National Westminster Bank plc* v. *Spectrum Plus Ltd* [2004] EWCA (Civ) 670, para. 99, *per* Lord Phillips MR.

598 Indeed, the former Law Commissioner responsible for the company charges reform project, Professor Hugh Beale, has since stated that 'there is very little immediate prospect of radical reform'; see op. cit., Beale et al., fn 477, p. vi. The Law Commission have stated that they were 'disappointed' that the government did not include their recommendations in The Companies Act 2006. However, the commission still 'await a formal decision on whether the Government accepts our recommendations and, if so, how it intends to implement them.' See Law Commission, *Annual Report 2008–09* (2009) HC 811 at p. 64.

witnessing a period of 'reform fatigue',[599] we can be certain that it will not be too long in the future before the reform agenda is raised yet again, we can only hope that, when it is, the outcome will result in some form of modern personal property security registration system.[600] Until that time we can but look to our Commonwealth neighbours[601] who are leading the way and to whom we must surely eventually join in enacting modern personal property security legislation.

599 See the chapter by Fisher in this volume (p. 385).

600 An interesting parallel can be seen in the recent economic woes to affect our financial sector where it has been recognised that failure to modernise the regulatory structure to reflect the substance rather than form of transactions was a major contributory factor in the problems; see the speech by Lord Adair Turner (Chairman FSA) 'The financial crisis and the future of financial regulation'; speech to the *Economist*'s Inaugural City Lecture, 21 January 2009: 'The third key priority is to ensure that in future financial activities are always regulated according to their economic substance not their legal form. One of the striking features of the years running up to the crisis ... was that a core banking function – maturity transformation – was increasingly being performed by institutions which were not legally banks, but the off balance sheet vehicles of banks, investment banks and mutual funds. To different degrees in different countries these "near banks" or shadow banks escaped the capital, leverage and liquidity regulation which would apply to banks ... In future it is essential that if an economic activity is bank-like and poses a significant risk to consumer or financial stability, regulators can extend banking-style regulation. And essential that accounting treatment reflects the economic reality of risks being taken'; available at www.fsa.gov.

601 Particularly Canada, New Zealand and, it appears, Australia. Note also the chapters by Ziegel, Brown and Fisher respectively, in this volume (pp. 117–61, pp. 328–65 and pp. 366–86).

2 Pressured by the paradigm

The Law Commission and company security interests

Gerard McCormack

Introduction

In the Ireland of yesteryear there was a song much in vogue about being on the one road – the road to God knows where. The same might or might not be said about the European Union after the failure of the Constitution project. Part of the reason for the failure may be continental concerns about the intentions of the Anglo-Saxons. In the Anglo-Saxon lands they do things differently. They speak a different language and with a different accent. But it would be unwise to assume too much. The Anglo-Saxon lands are not all alike. There are superficial similarities but, as regards each other, there is a wealth of differences. Personal property security law is a case in point. For over 30 years successive official bodies and government reports have endorsed the idea of reforming the English law of personal property security along the lines of Article 9 of the United States Uniform Commercial Code (UCC) which was first adopted in the 1950s and whose influence has since spread to the common law provinces of Canada, New Zealand and it appears to Australia.[1] Practitioners have generally been at best, indifferent, and at worst, outrightly hostile to the idea. Their general stance is best encapsulated in the maxim that the present law, while it may do with the occasional incremental adjustment, works well and if it is not broke, there is no need to fix it. The Law Commission started on the project of comprehensive personal property security law reform in 2001 following a reference from the Company Law Review Steering Group.[2] The way forward then seemed clear. There was a strong steer from the Company Law Review suggesting that legislation based on Article 9 of the UCC was the appropriate path to follow. The Law Commission endorsed this approach in the Consultation Paper *Registration of Security Interests* (July 2002)[3] and the basic approach was confirmed and extended in the Consultative

1 See generally the chapters by Brown and Fisher in this volume, pp. 328–65 and pp. 366–86. Note also: P. Ali *The Law of Secured Finance* (Oxford: Oxford University Press, OUP, 2002); G. McCormack *Secured Credit under English and American Law* (Cambridge: Cambridge University Press, 2004). It should be noted that Australia is also actively considering similar reforms. For up-to-date information on the reform process in Australia. see www.ag.gov.au/pps.

2 See *Modern Company Law for a Competitive Economy* (London: The Stationery Office, 2001).

3 See Law Commission Consultation Paper No. 164 *Registration of Security Interests: Company Charges and Property other than Land* (London: The Stationery Office, 2002); hereafter Consultation Paper. See generally on the consultation paper, Gullifer 'Will the Law Commission sink the floating charge?' [2003] LMCLQ 125; McCormack 'Quasi-securities and the Law Commission Consultation Paper on security interests – a brave new world' [2003] LMCLQ

Report *Company Security Interests* (September 2004).[4] However, in its *Final Report*, the Law Commission had a major change of heart.[5] In crude terms, one might say that the Law Commission 'bottled it'. Elements of the United States analysis would have remained under the proposals but substantially watered down.[6] In particular, the comprehensive cutting edge of Article 9 has been blunted in a big way. The Law Commission also shied away from amendments to insolvency legislation.[7] The appetites of users of the system were not sufficiently robust to stomach such changes. More generally, the change of heart by the Law Commission demonstrates the persuasive power of professional lobby groups. In this chapter I shall single out the pressure applied by two such groups – the City of London Law Society[8] – and the Financial Markets Law Committee.[9] The Financial Law Committee of the City of London Law Society proved particularly influential. As the Law Commission noted,

80; note also Davies 'The reform of English personal property security law: functionalism and Article 9 of the Uniform Commercial Code' (2004) 24 LS 295.

4 See Law Commission Consultation Paper No. 176 *Company Security Interests: a Consultative Report* (London: The Stationery Office, 2004); hereafter, Consultative Report and on which see McCormack 'The Law Commission Consultative Report on Company Security Interests: an irreverent riposte' (2005) 68 MLR 286.

5 See Law Commission Report No. 296 *Company Security Interests* (London: The Stationery Office, 2005), (2005) CM 6654, hereafter *The Final Report*; all the Law Commission papers are available at www.lawcom.gov.uk/.

6 See Ziegel 'The travails of English chattel security law reform – a transatlantic view' [2006] LMCLQ 110, p. 119: 'In my view ... the Law Commission's revised proposals, as reflected in the draft Regulations, do not by any reasonable yardstick amount to a mini-Art 9 style Code and, it is safe to assume, were not meant to do so. They contain important building blocks in the realization of such a goal but in their present form too many critical blocks are missing to justify such an ambitious claim.' For a different perspective, see the paper by Law Commissioner Hugh Beale 'The exportability of North American chattel security regimes: the fate of the English Law Commission's proposals' [2006] *Canadian Business Law Journal*.

7 See generally M. Bridge 'The Law Commission's proposals for the reform of corporate security interests', in (eds) J. Getzler and J. Payne, *Company Charges: Spectrum and Beyond* (Oxford: Oxford University Press, 2006), p. 267 and who concludes at p. 289: 'Those who have participated in international gatherings will be acutely aware that the absence of a presentable package of English commercial law is a major hindrance to its international influence.'

8 I will look primarily at the response of the Financial Law Committee of the City of London Law Society and for the sake of brevity I will refer to it generally as the City of London Solicitors' Group. Its comments on the Law Commission proposals can be found on the website (www.citysolicitors.org/). The chair of the working group which produced this response was Richard Calnan of Norton Rose and he has synopsised the report in an article 'The reform of company security interests' in [2005] *Butterworths Journal of International Banking and Financial Law* 28. This article will be referred to as Calnan [2005] BJIBFL 28. The Insolvency Law Committee of the City of London Law Society has also commented on, and been critical of, the Law Commission proposals, stating, para. 1.5, of its response: 'There is no doubt that the current filing system contained ... is inefficient, costly, cumbersome and burdensome, and in principle we support its replacement with a more efficient system. As to the substantive law, we readily acknowledge that the current state of the law on the characterisation of charges is unsatisfactory. However, we do not consider that the deficiencies of small parts of the current regime justify the wholesale replacement of that regime. To do so is unnecessary, will lead to confusion and uncertainty and will necessitate an ongoing revision and amendment of the laws relating to insolvency.' This response can also be found on the website: www.citysolicitors.org/.

9 See www.fmlc.org.

this committee 'examined our proposals in particular depth, and their response was adopted by a further 11 respondents, some of whom added comments and clarifications of their own'.[10]

The government's response to the work of the Law Commission was the introduction of Part 25 Companies Act 2006 in October 2009 which simply re-enacts the existing law on registration of company charges contained in Part 12 Companies Act 1985 with some rearrangement in the sequencing of sections but without changes of substance. This legislative re-enactment does not preclude the possibility of further legislative provisions implementing the Law Commission recommendations in the medium term. The very act of legislative re-enactment renders such change more unlikely however.

This chapter will set out the fundamentals of the current law; then at the scheme originally advocated by the Law Commission followed by an examination of the scheme it produced in its *Final Report*. The chapter will then dissect the change of heart by the Law Commission and finally canvass the prospects for the revised scheme receiving legislative approval in the medium term.

The current English law on security interests

The present law on security interests in England is contained in a multitude of sources. A security right or interest is basically a right over property to ensure the payment of money, or the performance of some other obligation.[11] The security giver may itself have secured the obligation, or it may be that it is the interest of some third party which is secured. Property law determines the kinds of security right that may be created and there are four types of security right known to English law: mortgages, charges (fixed and floating), pledges and liens. Mortgages and charges are both non-possessory consensual rights. They are created by agreement between security giver and security taker. Moreover, the security giver retains possession of the property that serves as security. In *NatWest Bank plc* v. *Spectrum Plus Ltd*[12] Lord Scott ventured the view that the essential characteristic of a floating charge, the characteristic that distinguishes it from a fixed charge, is that the 'asset subject to the charge is not finally appropriated as a security for the payment of the debt until the occurrence of some future event. In the meantime, the charge giver was left free to use the charged asset and to remove it from the security.'

10 See *The Final Report*, fn 5, at para. 1.19. There was a total of 70 responses to the Consultative Report, including 21 from practitioners and practitioner organisations, 10 from banks and banking organisations and 12 from academics – 'Inevitably, we received more responses from lawyers and lenders than from companies … '. The City Solicitors' Group also produced a follow-up document 'The registration of companies' security interests' whose appearance more or less coincided with the appearance of the Law Commission *Final Report*. This document will be referred to in this essay and appears on the City of London Law Society website: www.citysolicitors.org/. The group continues to be critical of the Law Commission proposals.

11 *Re Paramount Airways Ltd* [1990] BCC 130, p. 149, *per* Browne-Wilkinson VC; see also the statement of Lord Scott in *Smith* v. *Bridgend County Borough Council* [2002] 1 AC 336, p. 355 that a 'contractual right enabling a creditor to sell his debtor's goods and apply the proceeds in or towards satisfaction of the debt is a right of a security character'.

12 [2005] 2 AC 680, para. 111.

Sometimes, the expression 'mortgage' and 'charge' (meaning a fixed charge) are used interchangeably.[13] On other occasions, however, the expression 'charge' may be used as a general umbrella concept that also embraces mortgages; [14] but it has been suggested that there is a narrow technical difference between a mortgage and a charge. A mortgage involves the transfer of ownership to the security taker, with a retransfer once the obligation secured has been discharged, whereas the charge involves no transfer of ownership but merely a right of recourse against the property to ensure the discharge of the relevant obligation.[15] The decision of the House of Lords in *Re Leyland Daf Ltd: Buchler* v. *Talbot*[16] serves to blur the distinction however. *Leyland Daf* also calls into question the analysis, increasingly gaining currency, which suggests the floating charge is a charge over a fund of assets and likens the floating charge to a trust fund.[17] In both cases, powers of management belong to a 'legal' owner but another party enjoys beneficial rights.

The pledge is also created by agreement between security giver and security taker but it differs from the mortgage or charge in that actual or constructive possession of the property serving as security, or documents representing the same,[18] is handed over to

13 The Law of Property Act 1925, s. 205(1)(xvi) states that 'mortgage' includes any charge or lien on any property for securing money or money's worth and see also Insolvency Act 1986, s. 248.

14 The Companies Act 2006, s. 861(5) provides that 'charge' includes 'mortgage'.

15 See the comments of Slade J in *Re Bond Worth Ltd* [1980] Ch. 228, p. 250 but compare however Lord Hoffmann in *Re BCCI (No. 8)* [1998] AC 214, p. 226E–F where he described an equitable charge as 'a species of charge, which is a proprietary interest granted by way of security. Proprietary interests confer rights in rem which, subject to questions of registration and the equitable doctrine of purchaser for value without notice, will be binding upon third parties and unaffected by the insolvency of the owner of the property charged. A proprietary interest provided by way of security entitles the holder to resort to the property only for the purpose of satisfying some liability due to him (whether from the person providing the security or a third party) and, whatever the form of the transaction, the owner of the property retains an equity of redemption to have the property restored to him when the liability has been discharged.'

16 See *Re Leyland Daf Ltd: Buchler* v. *Talbot* [2004] 2 AC 298, para. 51 where Lord Millett suggested that where property is charged, irrespective of whether the charge is a fixed or floating charge, it belongs to the charge holder to the extent of the amount secured. Only the equity of redemption remains the property of the chargor and falls within the scope of the chargor's liquidation. Lord Hoffmann, para. 30, also suggested that assets subject to a floating charge belong beneficially to the debenture holder. In *Buchler* v. *Talbot* it was decided that general liquidation expenses could not be paid out of floating charge assets but the decision has been reversed on this point by the Companies Act 2006, s. 1282.

17 See generally Nolan 'Property in a fund' (2004) 120 LQR 108. For accounts of the juridical nature of the floating charge, see Ferran 'Floating charges – the nature of the security' [1988] CLJ 213; Worthington 'Floating charges – an alternative theory' [1994] CLJ 81; Naser 'The juridical basis of the floating charge' (1994) 15 *Company Lawyer*; Gregory and Walton 'Fixed charges over changing assets – the possession and control heresy' [1998] CFILR 68. See also Getzler 'The role of security over future and circulating capital: evidence from the British economy circa 1850–1920', in (eds) J. Getzler and J. Payne, *Company Charges: Spectrum and Beyond* (Oxford: Oxford University Press, 2006), p. 227.

18 See *Harrold* v. *Plenty* [1901] 2 Ch. 314.

the security taker.[19] A lien can take at least two forms.[20] The common law lien is perhaps the most straightforward and gives the lien holder the right to retain possession of items originally delivered for some other purpose until some outstanding indebtedness is discharged.[21] The lien holder has a passive power to retain possession, and no power of sale over the assets, though statute sometimes brings into existence such a power of sale.[22] The equitable lien, on the other hand, is essentially an equitable charge over property, arising by operation of law, rather than by agreement between the parties.[23]

Whereas property law serves to determine what security rights may be created, contract law sets out the formalities for the creation of consensual security rights. These requirements are not onerous. In the generality of cases, a simple oral contract is all that is required although, in practice, there will be writing in considerable and expensive detail. For security interests relating to land the writing requirement is mandatory under the Law of Property (Miscellaneous Provisions) Act 1989 and, before that, the Statute of Frauds.

Registration and priorities

Once a security right has been created, then it is good, not only as between the security giver and the security taker, but also with respect to third parties. Chapter 25 of the Companies Act 2006 lays down however, that particulars of certain types of charge created by a company, along with the original instrument of charge, must be delivered to Companies House within 21 days of the date of creation of the charge. If this is not done, then the charge is invalid in the event of the corporate charge giver going into liquidation or administration. Registration requirements apply to the most common types of charge, including floating charges and fixed charges over land, goods, debts, ships, aircraft and intellectual property rights. The list of registrable charges is set out in the Companies Act 2006, s. 860(7) and only if a charge is on the list is it registrable. To use American Article 9 legal jargon, the requirement of registration is a 'perfection'

19 The Privy Council explained the nature of a pledge in *Official Assignee of Madras* v. *Mercantile Bank of India Ltd* [1935] AC 53, pp. 58–9: 'At common law a pledge could not be created except by a delivery of possession of the thing pledged, actual or constructive. It involved a bailment. If the pledgor had the actual goods in his physical possession, he could effect the pledge by physical delivery; in other cases he could give possession by some symbolic act, such as handing over the key of the store in which they were held. If, however, the goods were in the custody of a third person, who held for the bailor so that in law his possession was that of the bailor, the pledge could be effected by a change of the possession of the third party, that is by an order to him from the pledgor to hold for the pledgee, the change being perfected by the third party attorning to the pledgee, that is acknowledging that he thereupon held for him; there was thus a change of possession and a constructive delivery and the goods in the hands of the third party became by this process in the possession constructively of the pledgee.'

20 In *Re Cosslett (Contractors) Ltd* [1998] Ch. 495, p. 508G Millett LJ referred to a contractual lien and distinguished it from a pledge stating that, in the case of pledge the owner delivers possession to the creditor as security, whereas, in the case of a lien, the creditor retains possession of goods previously delivered to him for some other purpose. It should be noted that under the draft Company Security Regulations 2006 published as an appendix to the Law Commission *Final Report*, fn 5, a contractual lien is considered to be a pledge.

21 See *Tappenden* v. *Artus* [1964] 2 QB 185.

22 See *Bristol Airport plc* v. *Powdrill* [1990] Ch. 744.

23 For descriptions of equitable liens, see *Re Bond Worth Ltd* [1980] Ch. 228, p. 251; *Re Bernstein* [1925] Ch. 12, pp. 17–18.

requirement. Another way of putting it is to say that Part 25 Companies Act 2006 must be complied with before the enumerated categories of charge become effective against certain parties, i.e. companies in administration or liquidation.[24]

The purpose behind Part 25 appears to be principally the provision of information.[25] The existence of registration requirements results in the disclosure of information as to a company's secured lending practices. This information may be of use to such persons as later lenders, rating or credit reference agencies, potential investors or financial analysts. Essentially Part 25 prevents the implication of false wealth. Turning to users of the system, the City of London Law Society's Financial Law Committee has said:[26]

> In our experience, the information provided by Companies House about charges created by companies is very useful to those dealing with companies – not just secured creditors, but also unsecured creditors and others considered dealing with the company concerned. In this respect, the Charges Register provides a useful public service …

It also has an incidental effect in determining priorities in that an unregistered but registrable charge is void in a company's liquidation or administration. According to Lord Hoffmann in *Smith* v. *Bridgend County Borough Council*: 'The plain intention of the legislature was that property subject to a registrable but unregistered charge should be available to the general body of creditors (or a secured creditor ranking after the unregistered charge) as if no such charge existed.'[27] Part 25, however, plays no comprehensive role in determining priorities. Priority between competing security interests in the same property turns on a number of factors as well as the fact of registration, such as the order of creation of the respective security interests; whether the security interest in question is a fixed or floating charge, and whether one security interest holder had notice of another earlier security interest before taking its later security interest. Where the security interests are charges, the order of priority is roughly as follows: assuming that all the charges have been duly registered, fixed

24 Lord Hoffmann remarked in *Smith* v. *Bridgend County Borough Council* [2002] 1 AC 336 at pp. 347–348: 'Section 395 [of the Companies Act 1985] … was intended for the protection of the creditors of an insolvent company. It was intended to give persons dealing with a company the opportunity to discover, by consulting the register, whether its assets were burdened by floating and certain fixed charges which would reduce the amount available for unsecured creditors in a liquidation. Whether this was a realistic form of protection and whether the choice of registrable charges was entirely logical is not presently relevant.'

25 According to the DTI in 'Regulatory impact assessment on proposals for the registration of companies' security interests' (London: DTI, July 2005), para. 2.7, the system for registration of company charges is needed to address the following risks:

- the concealment of secured credit with markets being misled by the apparent unencumbered ownership by companies of assets which in fact are encumbered in favour of prior creditors,
- uncertainty over the rights of secured parties in the event of the borrower's insolvency,
- uncertainty over the rights of those who buy assets that are subject to security interests.

26 For judicial doubts as to how the system works in practice, see *Smith* v. *Bridgend County Borough Council* [2002] 1 AC 336, para. 19, *per* Lord Hoffmann: *NatWest Bank plc* v. *Spectrum Plus Ltd* [2005] 2 AC 680, para. 156, *per* Lord Walker.

27 [2002] 1 AC 336, para. 68.

charges rank ahead of floating charges irrespective of the order of creation unless the floating charge contains a restrictive or negative pledge that forbids the creation of subsequent fixed charges having priority and the fixed charge has actual notice, not just constructive notice, of the restrictive clause.[28]

The basic priority position is complicated further by the freedom-of-contract principles that underlie English law. Security interest holders are free to alter the order of priority among each other by contractual provision.[29] Moreover, while there is a finite list of security interests, parties can often achieve the functional equivalent of security through other legal strategies. The retention of title by the seller of goods pending payment of the purchase price serves the same legal effect as a loan of money on the security of goods. In the same way, the assignment of debts owing to a company to a finance house, will provide the company with immediate funds to the same extent as a loan of money on the security of the debts. Both these kinds of transaction are referred to as 'quasi-security', i.e. functionally equivalent legal devices to security rights strictly so-called. Moreover, quasi-security rights are generally stronger than security rights since the holder of the quasi-security right has ownership of the asset in question.

The earlier Law Commission proposals in the consultation papers

The Law Commission consideration of the law relating to security interests arose from a reference by the Company Law Review Steering Group and must be understood against that backdrop. As part of a thorough review of Company Law the Steering Group was considering the registration of company charge provisions. In a 2000 consultation paper *Registration of Company Charges*[30] the Steering Group suggested that a modest tinkering with what is now Part 25 was all that was required. The *Final Report* of the Steering Group in July 2001 *Modern Company Law for a Competitive Economy* manifested a radical change of approach however. It seems that there was some determined and sustained arm-twisting behind the scenes by convinced and highly placed advocates of the UCC Article 9 philosophy. Professor Sir Roy Goode is one advocate and did not mince his words when criticising the present English position in strident terms.[31] He has added that:[32]

> this state of affairs continues to be tolerated in the 21st century, when the United States and Canada have for many years had highly developed, market-responsive

28 See generally: *G & T Earle Ltd* v. *Hemsworth Rural District Council* (1928) 44 TLR 605; *Re Standard Machine Co Ltd* (1906) 95 LT 829: *Wilson* v. *Kelland* [1910] 2 Ch. 306. For possible circularity problems, see *Re Portbase Clothing Ltd* [1993] Ch. 388 and *Re Woodroffes (Musical Instruments) Ltd* [1986] Ch. 366.

29 See: *Cheah* v. *Equiticorp Finance Group Ltd* [1992] BCC 98, *Re SSSL Realisations Ltd* [2004] EWHC 1760; *Re Maxwell Communications Corp (No 2)* [1993] 1 WLR 1402; *Re British & Commonwealth Holdings plc (No. 3)* [1992] 1 AC 472. Note also: Ferran 'Subordination of secured and unsecured debt', in *Company Law and Corporate Finance* (Oxford: Oxford University Press, 1999), ch. 16; Nolan 'Less equal than others' [1995] JBL 485.

30 Company Law Review Steering Group (London: DTI, October 2000).

31 See generally Goode 'Insularity or leadership? The role of the United Kingdom in the harmonisation of commercial law' (2001) 50 ICLQ 751, pp. 759–60. Professor Goode acted as a consultant to the Law Commission during the Company Security Interests project.

32 See *Legal Problems of Credit and Security* (London: Sweet & Maxwell, 3rd edn, 2003), p. 156.

legislation which has worked and when successive government reports have recommended the adoption of similar legislation in this country, is a shocking indictment of the indifference of successive governments to the modernisation of our commercial law.

Goode also endorsed the Law Commission's subsequent 'excellent' Consultation Paper stating that in it 'the groundwork is being laid for a modern personal property security law which responds to the needs of the market rather than being rooted in outdated concepts and doctrine'.[33]

In the Consultation Paper, and the subsequent consultative report, the Law Commission voiced certain criticisms of the registration of charge provisions in particular, and the English law of personal property security in general. The registration-of-charge provisions were criticised as far from being comprehensive. They apply to an important but, comparatively, limited range of security interests and registration does not serve as the overriding reference point for determining priorities between competing security interests. Quasi-security interests are also outwith the registration system. Moreover, the system it embodies is one of transaction filing, rather than notice filing. The original instrument of charge has to be submitted, along with the requisite particulars, to Companies House. The latter compares the two and, if satisfied that the filed particulars are accurate, issues a certificate of due registration which is stated to be conclusive evidence that all the requirements of the legislation as to registration have been observed.[34] There is a considerable administrative burden imposed on staff at Companies House against a backdrop of potential liability to prejudicially affected parties if it transpires that the certificate of due registration was issued in error. Transaction filing relates necessarily to a single transaction, rather than to a chain of potential transactions. Additionally, filing is, by definition, *ex post facto*. It is not possible to file in advance of the conclusion of a security agreement.

Article 9 is based on notice filing.[35]A secured party may file a notice which simply states that the creditor may have a security interest in a person's property. Filing is the generally accepted method of perfecting a security interest or making it effective against third parties although, in certain circumstances, handing possession over to the secured party may serve as an alternative to filing. Moreover, certain security interests are automatically perfected, i.e. no filing is necessary and, for certain types of intangible property investing the secured party with control over the property, is a superior method of perfection. The notice may be filed before any security interest

33 Op. cit., Goode, fn 32.

34 Companies Act 2006, s. 869(6)(b). For cases on the conclusiveness of the registrar's certificate, see *Re CL Nye Ltd* [1971] 1 Ch. 442; *Re Central Bank of India Ltd* [1986] QB 1114.

35 For an explanation of the distinction between notice filing and transaction filing, see the Scottish Law Commission discussion paper *Registration of Rights in Security by Companies* (Edinburgh: The Stationery Office, October 2002), p. 8: 'The most characteristic difference between notice filing and traditional systems of registration is that notice filing is parties-specific rather than transaction-specific. What is filed are not the details of a particular security but notice that certain parties have entered into, or may in future enter into, a secured transaction in relation to specified property. This approach has certain implications. A notice may be filed in advance of the transaction and the proposed transaction may never take place. The same notice may serve a series of connected transactions. And the information given on the register is necessarily rather general in character, being an invitation to further inquiry rather than a full account of the right in security.'

is concluded and a single filing may relate to a series of security interests between the parties. If there is more than one security interest over the same item of property, then priority is normally determined by the application of a first to file has priority principle although there are exceptions to this principle for purchase-money security interests (PMSIs). A PMSI is a loan of money, or more generally the extension of credit, that is conditioned on the acquisition of particular property and where the credit provider takes a security interest in the property that is thereby acquired. The PMSI will outrank an earlier general creditor whose security interest extends to the later property by virtue of an after-acquired property clause in the security agreement.[36] The Article 9 filing and priority rules also extend, in the main, to the assignment of receivables and to title-retention devices, although finance leases have posed particular problems for the conceptual and practical design of an Article 9 scheme. Article 9 therefore has some of the comprehensiveness that the English company charge registration system lacks.

The Law Commission was convinced of the merits of Article 9 as a suitable guide for English law to follow. It suggested that a new English system would be modelled along the lines of Article 9 and the Personal Property Security Acts in the common law provinces of Canada and in New Zealand. Overseas legislation was used as a guide, the Law Commission explained, partly because of the constraints of time but also because the Law Commission saw 'no need to re-invent the wheel'.[37] It was said that there was not necessarily an assumption that what has worked well in North America will work well in England but 'the fact that Article 9 and the PPSAs [Personal Property Security Acts] have been so successful means that they deserve very careful consideration'.[38] The Law Commission thought that notice filing could be applied to a broader range of transactions, and not just the current list of registrable charges set out in what is now Companies Act 2006, s. 860(7). In particular, it singled out factoring, i.e. the assignment of receivables, and retention-of-title clauses in sale of goods transactions. The first tranche of reform would involve the introduction of notice filing for an amended list of company charges and, in its view, preferably also for 'quasi-security' interests with the vehicle of reform being regulations made under a new Companies Act. Later on, the reform might be extended to non-corporate legal actors and a further stage of reform would entail a comprehensive restatement of the law of security interests.

A major selling point used by the Law Commission to advance the cause of reform was that of registration of security interests over the Internet. Registration could be effected online, without the active intervention of Companies House, other than the provision of the necessary facilities. This would produce a saving of staff time for the latter and cut down generally on administrative inconvenience. The Law Commission

36 For a theoretical justification of PMSI super priority, see the discussion in the Diamond Report *A Review of Security Interests in Property* (London: HMSO, 1989), para.17.7, (Chairman Professor A. L. Diamond); and for a law and economics perspective, see Kanda and Levmore 'Explaining creditor priorities' (1994) 80 *Virginia Law Review* 2103, pp. 2138–41. Note also Schwartz 'The continuing puzzle of secured debt' (1984) 37 *Vanderbilt Law Review* 1051 who argues that whereas a general financier takes account of average risk, the PMSI lender may have particular skills and is able to lend on particularly advantageous terms because of its special knowledge of the collateral.

37 See Consultative Report, fn 4, para. 1.20.

38 Ibid., para. 1.5.

stated that notice filing would be advantageous primarily for the following reasons:[39]

(a) Electronic filing would be fast, simple and cheap in the long run.
(b) In a companies-only scheme, the risk of an error that might invalidate a filing would be very small since companies have a unique registration number.
(c) A simple description of the secured property – the 'collateral' would suffice. This would reduce the risk of inaccurate descriptions and also protect third parties because a security interest would not be effective as regards property that fell outside the description in the financing statement.
(d) Filing would become permissible in advance of a security agreement being concluded and this would enable a lender to protect its priority position while negotiations over security were continuing.
(e) Dual registration would become generally a thing of the past. Security interests over land, ships, aircraft and intellectual property rights would remain registrable in the specialist asset registers but would no longer be registrable at Companies House though, to ensure that there was no loss of valuable information, there would be an automatic forwarding of information from the Land Register to Companies House.
(f) The time of filing would become the crucial reference point for determining priorities where there was more than one security interest over the same property, subject to the recognised Article 9 exception for PMSIs. In the Law Commission's view the rules 'of priority will be more rational and better suited to modern conditions, for example in relation to assignments of receivables. They will still be complicated but they will be significantly clearer than under current law.'[40]
(g) The Law Commission suggested that the fixed/floating charge distinction could disappear under the new system. No longer would complicated boundary demarcation exercises of the kind necessarily engaged in by the Privy Council in *Re Brumark Ltd*[41] and the House of Lords in *Re Spectrum Plus Ltd*[42] be the order of the day. The floating charge would be superseded by a single type of security interest that would have all the advantages of the floating charge but fewer disadvantages to the lender.

The list of supposed advantages articulated by the Law Commission in respect of notice filing did not go without challenge. In particular, some of the points mentioned by the Law Commission bore no connection with the introduction of a notice-filing system. Indeed a Companies House strategy document canvassed the possibility of developing an online service for the registration of mortgages and charges.[43]

39 Ibid., para. 2.43.
40 See Consultative Report, fn 4, para. 2.43.
41 *Re Brumark Ltd*: *Agnew* v. *CIR* [2001] 2 AC 710.
42 [2005] 2 AC 680.
43 See the Companies House Strategy document (April 2003) *Strategic Direction 2003/2006*: *the Future for Companies House*, pp. 6–7: '[W]e will investigate the potential to develop an on-line service for the registration of mortgages and charges. However, as both company and land registration law is changing over the life of this plan we need to make a careful assessment of when it would be appropriate to invest in the delivery of this new service.' According to the DTI in 'Regulatory impact assessment on proposals for the registration of companies' security

This would be done in conjunction with the existing company charge registration framework. Moreover, in practice under the existing system, given the fact that companies have a unique registration number and given the certificate of due registration issued by Companies House, there is not an appreciable risk of an error in the registration process that would invalidate a complete filing. Simple descriptions of the secured property, while making it easy to file for a secured party, also provide less information to a potential searcher of the register. Divorcing registration from the actual conclusion of a security agreement also opens up the possibility that the state of the register may become remote from the factual realities concerning the state of a debtor's secured borrowings. A notice on the register may relate not to an actual transaction but to one of a multitude of possible transactions that never in the event materialised.

The presence or absence of dual registration has nothing to do with notice filing. One could have a transaction-filing system with registration not being required in respect of security interests that are the subject of separate registration in an asset-based register. Equally one could introduce a notice filing system that also includes security interests that are the subject of separate registration in an asset-based register. Dual registration, or the absence thereof, and notice filing are logically separate and distinct concepts. There is no necessary connection between the two.

Moreover, notice filing, and the first to file has priority principle, are logically separate and distinct concepts. One could devise a system which makes notice filing, whether before or after the formalisation of a security agreement, a condition of the validity of certain security interests in certain circumstances, but which leaves priority between two or more security interests in respect of the same property turn on factors other than filing. Equally, one could have a transaction-filing system where the time of registration determines priority questions. Indeed, the current asset-based registers for ships, aircraft, and so on, involve a variant of this approach. Notice filing, and the statutory or judicial recognition of PMSIs are also independent from one another. The purchase-money security interest is not inherently a part and parcel of a notice-filing system. Alternatively, one could have special priority status for the PMSI even under a transaction filing system and, arguably, this is the case at the moment. In *United Malayan Banking Corp* v. *Aluminex*[44] courts in Malaysia recognised the PMSI on the basis of old English authorities like *Re Connolly Bros Ltd* (*No. 2*)[45] and *Wilson* v. *Kelland*.[46] In England, more recently the Court of Appeal in *Whale* v. *Viasystems Ltd*[47] gave further judicial blessing to the PMSI and reinforced the comments of Professor Sir Roy Goode about 'the inequity that would result in allowing the prior

interests' (London: DTI, July 2005) the idea of computerised registration of company security interests had almost universal support.

44 (1993) 3 MLJ 587. For discussion of the case, see Tjio 'Personal property security interests in Singapore and Malaysia' (1995) 16 *Company Lawyer* 28.

45 [1912] 2 Ch. 25.

46 [1910] 2 Ch. 306.

47 [2002] EWCA Civ. 480. See the comments of Jonathan Parker LJ, para. 72: 'It must now be taken as settled law that, in the context of an issue as to priorities between equitable interests, the court will have regard to the substance, rather than the form of the transaction or transactions which give rise to the competing interests; and in particular that conveyancing technicalities must give way to considerations of commercial and practical reality ... [T]his approach is not limited to cases involving the purchase of a property coupled with the grant of a mortgage or charge to secure repayment of the funds which were required to enable completion of the purchase to take place ... [I]t falls to be adopted generally, in every case where an issue arises as to priority as between equitable interests.'

chargee a windfall increase in his security brought about not with the debtor's money or new funds injected by the prior chargee but with financing provided by a later incumbrancer'.[48] Finally, while the floating charge is a time-honoured feature of English law, fixed and floating charges could be assimilated without doing undue violence to the current transaction filing system. Indeed, a noted critic of the Law Commission consultation documents, Richard Calnan of the law firm Norton Rose, while being sharply critical of notice filing, has also endorsed assimilation of fixed and floating charges or at least similar treatment of the two for most salient purposes.[49]

Practitioner objections to the original Law Commission proposals

There were some practitioner objections to the proposals contained in the Law Commission consultation paper entitled 'Registration of Security Interests' of 2002 but these were muted, in the main. As time went on, the objections began to harden.[50] The Law Commission noted in its Consultative Report of 2004 *Company Security Interests* that 'at least one respondent representing legal practitioners may now have moved to a position where it considers only minor reform of the law relating to registration of company charges is desirable'.[51] It is believed that this was a reference to the Financial Law Committee of the City of London Law Society[52] and one of the leading lights in this group, Richard Calnan, had warned graphically about the dangers of throwing out the baby with the bathwater. He suggested that there was nothing

48 *Legal Problems of Credit and Security* (London: Sweet & Maxwell, 2nd edn, 1988), pp. 99–100 and see now the third edition, fn 32, pp. 192–3.

49 See Calnan 'Floating charges: a proposal for reform' [2005] *Butterworths Journal of International Banking and Financial Law* 341. Note also Calnan's chapter in the present volume, pp. 162–87.

50 It should be noted that the Scottish Law Commission refused to recommend a notice-filing system for Scotland; see *Report on Registration of Rights in Security by Companies* Scottish Law Commission Report No. 197 (Edinburgh: The Stationery Office, September 2004), para. 1.5. In its view, a notice-filing system could not readily be modified to accommodate the very different structures and concepts of Scots property law. See generally D. Cabrelli 'Joined up thinking? An analysis of the Scottish and English Law Commissions' proposals for the reform of rights in security and charges granted by companies' [2004] *Journal of Corporate Law Studies* 385. The provisions of the Bankruptcy and Diligence etc. (Scotland) Act 2007 should be noted. These implement generally the recommendations of the Scottish Law Commission.

51 See Consultative Report, para 2.7, n. 21.

52 The City Solicitors' Group may not agree with this assessment of its position by the Law Commission. Its commentary on the Law Commission's Consultation Paper No. 164 in 2002 (available at www.citysolicitors.org) is generally critical of the Law Commission proposals and concludes, para. 115, by saying 'Although we understand why a functional registration scheme is being proposed, we believe that it cannot be considered in relation to "quasi-security" generally, but only in relation to individual financing arrangements. Registration of a particular type of arrangement should only be required if:

(a) it is, in substance, a financing arrangement;
(b) there would be certainty as to the types of transaction which are included;
(c) registration would serve a useful purpose in terms of the provision of information or the regulation of priorities: and
(d) the practical problems of implementation would not outweigh the advantages of registration.'

fundamentally wrong with the present system that a bit of incremental amendment could not mend,[53] whereas the Law Commission's[54] 'imperative seemed to be to introduce a US-style functional system as a wholesale replacement for our current system. On a cost–benefit analysis, this seems difficult to justify. The implementation costs will be very large, and it is difficult to see what material benefits will result from it.'

He added that one of the advantages of English law for domestic and international investors was the ease of creation of security and quasi-security and it would be most unfortunate if the effect of the Law Commission proposals were to make it more complicated and expensive to do so.

In a sense, resistance from practitioners to the Law Commission proposals should hardly occasion surprise in that earlier proposals for the introduction of an Article 9-type system by the Crowther Committee Report on consumer credit in 1971[55] and in the Diamond Report in 1989[56] met with stubborn practitioner resistance, and ultimately floundered. In 1991 it was announced that the government would not be proceeding with the Diamond recommendations. It was suggested that Article 9-style reforms would be costly and, in view of proposed registration requirements, difficult to implement, as well as cutting across potential EC initiatives.[57] Moreover, there was no major demand for such reforms.

The City of London solicitors group has made the same point in relation to the Law Commission recommendations while, at the same time, emphasising its own objectivity:

> [W]e believe that there is no desire amongst those who use the English law of security for a wholesale change, and we have a real concern that the proposed changes will reduce the efficiency, effectiveness and competitiveness of London as an international financial centre. We are concerned that the only beneficiaries of the changed law will be lawyers, whose services will be in demand to advise clients on the implications of the proposals and to litigate areas of uncertainty. We believe it right to make this observation: looking to the long-term health of the UK economy and against our firms' immediate financial interest.

There are some, perhaps cynical, observers who might take these professions of impartiality and disinterestedness at less than face value. It is worth noting however that the introduction of PPSA reforms in New Zealand did not meet with similar levels of opposition from the practising legal profession and there are some suggestions that the legal profession in New Zealand saw reform in the personal property

53 Calnan 'The reform of the law of security' [2004] BJIBFL 88.

54 Op. cit., Calnan, fn 53, p. 92. For a response by the then Law Commissioner responsible for the Commercial and Common Law team, Professor Hugh Beale, 'Reform of the law of security – another view' [2004] BJIBFL 117.

55 See *Report of the Committee on Consumer Credit* (London: HMSO, 1971) Chairman Lord Crowther Cmnd 4596, Parts IV and V.

56 See *A Review of Security Interests in Property* (London: DTI, 1989); on which see generally Prentice 'The registration of company charges: ripe for reform' (1985) 101 LQR 330; Davies 'The reform of English personal property security law' (1990) 30 *Malaya Law Review* 88; Lawson 'The reform of the law relating to security interests in property' [1989] JBL 287; Diamond 'The reform of the law of security interests' (1989) 42 CLP 231.

57 See (1991) HC debates vol. 189, col. 482, 24 April 1991, *per* Peter Lilley MP, the then Secretary of State for Trade and Industry.

security sphere as potentially a valuable source of new business, with a similar view being taken in Australia.[58]

The City of London solicitors voiced some general criticism of the reform proposals in terms of fragmentation of the law, lack of flexibility, additional complication, constraints on contractual freedom and the introduction of increased uncertainty. Land was excluded from the scheme, so that one was left with one set of rules applicable on default in the case of land, and a different set for personal property. Also major capital assets, such as ships and aircraft, were excluded. The overall effect would be a fragmented enforcement system, whereas much security consisted of fixed and floating charge debentures over all corporate assets. Also, they believed that the imposition of mandatory duties, and the requirement to treat transactions which did not create security as if they did, resulted in artificial distinctions, making it more difficult for the parties to be able to document the transaction which they actually wanted to enter into. It was also felt that the introduction by the Law Commission of American concepts produced complexity. Many of the Law Commission proposals, it was suggested, would make the law less flexible and more uncertain than was currently the case, would provide less information to those dealing with companies, as well as placing unnecessary restraints on freedom of contract in business transactions.[59] The City of London Solicitors explained:

> We do not believe that there is any desire for a wholesale change of the law of security by those who use it in practice, whether they are lenders, borrowers, lawyers or other professionals. They recognise the great benefits of the way in which the English law of security works at the moment, and do not wish to jeopardise it. It was suggested that change should only be implemented by primary legislation; after there has been a proper analysis of the economic effect of the proposals; once its inter-relationship with insolvency law has been established clearly; and in the context of an overall reform of the priority rules relating to property law generally, and following on from a detailed consultation on all the issues involved.

The new revised Law Commission proposals

Following practitioner resistance, the Law Commission changed its proposals and the original reform agenda was watered down considerably.[60] A new system of electronic notice filing for companies was proposed that would apply to traditional security interests (essentially mortgages and charges) and also to sales of receivables.

58 See the chapters in this volume by Brown and Fisher, pp. 328–65 and pp. 366–86. More generally on the New Zealand system see the official website www.ppsr.govt.nz; note also M. Gedye, R. Cuming and R. Wood *New Zealand Personal Property Securities Act* (Wellington: Thomson, 2002); L. Widdup and L. Mayne *Personal Property Securities Act: a conceptual approach* (Wellington: Butterworths, 2002); B. Allan *Guidebook to New Zealand Personal Property Securities Law* (Auckland: CCH, 2002).

59 See the City Solicitors' Group 2004 submission, fn 8, p. 3.

60 For a synopsis of the revised proposals, see 'Company security interests: developing a final scheme' (May 2005) available on the Law Commission website (www.lawcom.gov.uk/). The *Final Report* was published after this document at the end of August 2005; see Law Commission Report No. 296, fn 5.

However, the new scheme would not extend to title-retention techniques, such as finance leases and simple reservation of title under sale of goods contracts.

The new scheme included specific proposals on financial collateral[61] and, while priority would be linked to the date of registration, the scheme would also preserve the fixed–floating charge distinction, particularly in the context of insolvency. These proposals were said to 'make the floating charge simpler and more effective as a security' with the opportunity being taken to deal with various problems under current law and 'generally to clarify and simplify it'.[62] While the Law Commission envisaged specific rules to deal with financial collateral, it now ruled out particular legislative rules giving super priority to purchase-money security interests. Also excluded from the legislative agenda is a statutory statement of the rights and remedies of the parties to a security agreement and the imposition of obligations on secured parties to disclose information about the charge.

In *The Final Report* the general thrust of the notice-filing proposals were preserved from the original consultation documents but there were very considerable variations in detail. For example, in the revised proposals, the Law Commission suggest that ships, aircraft and intellectual property rights should still be registrable for validity purposes at Companies House and, for priority purposes, under the specialist asset registers. In the original scheme, registration at the specialist asset registers was all that would have been required. Consultees were of the view that double registration in both the specialist register and at Companies House was worthwhile because of the advantages in finding information at one source. As far as land was concerned, Companies House would simply serve as a reception point for information transmitted from the Land Registry with the validity and priority of charges over land being dependent solely on rules of land law.[63]

The change of heart dissected: floating charges

The Law Commission's *Final Report* of 2005 advocated a 'first to file has priority' principle but its preservation of the fixed–floating charge distinction renders this less

61 See Regulations 36–41 of the draft Company Security Regulations 2006 which are found as an appendix to the Law Commission *Final Report*, fn 60. This essay will not discuss financial collateral in detail but basically as an alternative to registration the regulations allow a charge holder to take 'control' of financial collateral. Taking 'control' renders the charge effective in the debtor company's liquidation and also confers priority advantages over a charge rendered effective through registration.

62 See 'Company security interests: developing a final scheme', fn 60, para. 1.3. See also 'Regulatory impact assessment on proposals for the registration of companies' security interests' (London: DTI, July 2005), p. 66: 'The effectiveness of floating charges will be enhanced … [I]t will no longer be necessary to employ negative pledge clauses to preserve the priority of a floating charge against subsequent charges. Nor will it be necessary to use automatic crystallisation clauses to prevent seizure of the property by other [execution] creditors. Both types of clause are unreliable in their operation and add significantly to the complexity of the current law.' On the latter points, see Regulations 24 and 45 of the draft Company Security Regulations contained in *The Final Report*, fn 5.

63 But see 'Regulatory impact assessment on proposals for the registration of companies' security interests', fn 25, p. 12 'This may depend on the introduction of e-conveyancing in England and Wales. The target date for starting this process is 2007. It is unlikely that the new scheme for company charges would be brought into effect before that date in any event.'

important in practice. To use an inexact metaphor, the Law Commission deliberations on the fixed–floating charge issue may remind one of the old dance – 'she steps out, she steps in and she steps out again'. In the original Consultation Paper, the Law Commission proposed the retention of the floating charge. It suggested that 'a charge that permits the debtor to dispose of the assets in the ordinary course of business free of the charge may still be described accurately as a floating charge'.[64] Therefore, it was still subject to the provisions of the Insolvency Act 1986 giving priority to preferential creditors and to s. 245 which invalidates floating charges granted to secure past indebtedness in the immediate run-up to liquidation or administration. There was criticism of this approach, for practitioners would not only have to get used to a new notice-filing system they would also have to bear in mind the fixed–floating charge distinction and its continued importance.[65] Moreover, while pre-Article 9 United States law did not have any functional equivalent of the floating charge[66] as such, floating charges were an important part of the commercial landscape in Canada and New Zealand before the reforms of personal property security legislation.[67] The original Personal Property Security Act in Ontario in 1967 tried to retain the floating charge but this approach was widely considered to be unsatisfactory and later PPSAs went for the approach of assimilating the fixed and floating charges. In *Royal Bank of Canada* v. *Sparrow Electric Corp*[68] the Supreme Court of Canada declared that the legislative effect was to abolish the old fixed and floating charge distinction together with that between legal and equitable security interests. As one commentator remarks: 'In a PPSA statutory regime, all security interest attach on the debtor's acquisition of rights in the collateral, regardless of whether the collateral is specific or circulating, and regardless of the scope of the debtor's licence to deal. In thus establishing a unitary attachment regime independent of the concept of crystallisation, the PPSA legislators had effectively signalled to the courts that all security interests were henceforth to be characterised as fixed and legal in their proprietary effect.'[69]

64 See Consultation Paper No. 164, fn 3, para. 4.133.

65 See, for example, Gullifer 'Will the Law Commission sink the floating charge?' [2003] LMCLQ 125, p. 144.

66 See *Zartman* v. *First National Bank of Waterloo* (1907) 189 NY 267; *Benedict* v. *Ratner* (1925) 268 US 353; note also J. O. Honnold, S. L. Harris and C. W. Mooney *Security Interests in Personal Property* (New York: Foundation Press, 3rd edn, 2001), pp. 452–6. The progenitor of Article 9, Professor Grant Gilmore, has argued that if floating charges had been accepted in the US, then some of the pressure for change which brought about Article 9 would have been absent; see *Security Interests in Personal Property* (Boston: Little Brown, 1965), pp. 359–61. Note also the comments of Lord Walker in *NatWest Bank Plc* v. *Spectrum Plus Ltd* [2005] 2 AC 680, para. 133.

67 See generally G. McCormack 'The floating charge in England and Canada', in (ed.) J. de Lacy, *The Reform of United Kingdom Company Law* (London: Cavendish, 2002), p. 389.

68 (1997) 143 DLR (4th) 385; on which see generally Davis 'Priority of Crown claims in insolvency' (1997) 29 CBLJ 145.

69 See Catherine Walsh 'The floating charge is dead: long live the floating charge', in (ed.) Agasha Mugasha, *Perspectives on Commercial Law* (St Leonards NSW: Prospect, 1999), p. 146: 'Although the court ultimately divided, the majority and minority opinions were ad idem on the proprietary character of the bank's PPSA security interest in the debtor's inventory: it was fixed and legal in nature ... In a PPSA statutory regime, all security interests attach on the debtor's acquisition of rights in the collateral, regardless of whether the collateral is specific or circulating, and regardless of the scope of the debtor's licence to deal. In thus establishing a unitary attachment regime independent of the concept of crystallisation, the PPSA legislators had effectively signalled to the courts that all security interests were henceforth to be characterised as fixed and legal in their proprietary effect.'

As far as New Zealand is concerned, Lord Millett remarked in *Re Brumark Ltd: Agnew* v. *Commissioner of Inland Revenue*:[70]

> A curiosity of the case is that the distinction between fixed and floating charges, which is of great commercial importance in the United Kingdom, seems likely to disappear from the law of New Zealand when the Personal Property Security Act 1999 comes into force.

In the Consultative Report of 2004 *Company Security Interests* the Law Commission changed tack from the earlier 2002 Consultation Paper and seemed to accept that its proposals would see the disappearance of the floating charge, as we traditionally know it. What instead would appear on the horizon would be this super security interest that would have all the advantages of the floating charge in terms of ease of creation and management autonomy over the charged assets as far as the debtor is concerned yet, at the same time, none of the disadvantages, such as inferior priority status to the fixed charge.[71] Legal commentators have written elegies to the floating charge[72] and that is perhaps one of the reasons why the Law Commission was so coy about its disappearance in the Consultative Report. In *Re Brumark Ltd: Agnew* v. *Commissioner of Inland Revenue*[73] Lord Millett remarked:

> The floating charge is capable of affording the creditor, by a single instrument, an effective and comprehensive security upon the entire undertaking of the debtor company and its assets from time to time, while at the same time leaving the company free to deal with its assets and pay its trade creditors in the ordinary course of business without reference to the holder. Such a form of security is particularly attractive to banks, and it rapidly acquired an importance in English commercial life which … should not be underestimated.

70 [2001] 2 AC 710, p. 716.

71 Professor Sir Roy Goode has long propounded this view arguing that 'a unified concept of security interests in which rules of attachment, perfection and priority are clearly laid out and are designed to produce results that are fair in the typical case is greatly preferable to the uncodified and unsystematised collocation of rules we have painfully developed in this country over the past century'; see 'The exodus of the floating charge', in (eds) D. Feldman and F. Meisel, *Corporate and Commercial Law: Modern Developments* (London: Lloyds of London Press, 1996), ch. 10, pp. 202–3.

72 See R. Mokal 'An elegy to the floating charge', in (ed.) S Worthington, *Commercial Law and Commercial Practice* (Oxford: Hart Publishing, 2003), p. 479.

73 [2001] 2 AC 710. In *NatWest Bank plc* v. *Spectrum Ltd* [2005] 2 AC 680 Lord Scott, paras 95–7, explained the history and development of the floating charge. He said 'By the middle of the 19th century industrial and commercial expansion in this country had led to an increasing need by companies for more capital. Subscription of share capital could not meed this need and loan capital had to be raised. But the lenders required security for the loans. Traditional security, in the form of legal or equitable charges on the borrowers' fixed assets, whether land or goods, could not meet the need. The greater part of most entrepreneurial companies' assets would consist of raw materials, work in progress, stock-in-trade and trade debts. These were circulating assets, replaced in the normal course of business and constantly changing. Assets of this character were not amenable to being the subject of traditional forms of security. Equity, however, intervened.'

Lord Scott pointed out that by the last decade of the 19th century the 'floating security' had become firmly established and in regurlar use. This new form of security was not the creature of statute but had been bred by equity lawyers and judges out of the needs of the commercial and industrial entrepreneurs of the time.

The Crowther Committee on consumer credit back in 1971 went so far to observe that the floating charge was so fundamentally a part of commercial lending practice that its abolition could not seriously be contemplated.[74]

In its *Final Report*, the Law Commission did a turnaround and reverted to the thinking in its original Consultation Paper – so that the distinction would remain between fixed and floating charges though priority between competing charges, whether fixed or floating, would be by date of filing, unless otherwise agreed between the parties involved.[75] As the Law Commission explained:

> Under current law, chargees use negative pledge clauses to attempt to alter the 'default' priority position for a floating charge that enables a charger to grant subsequent fixed charges that will rank ahead of the floating charge. However, such clauses are not always effective against subsequent chargees. Dating priority from time of registration will make it unnecessary for a chargee to rely on a negative pledge clause in order to prevent subsequent charges gaining priority.[76]

But why the volte-face? This was explained on the basis that the complete assimilation of fixed and floating charges would mean major implications for insolvency law and matters such as the unsecured creditors' lifeboat.[77] Under the Insolvency Act 1986, s. 176A (introduced by virtue of the Enterprise Act 2002) a proportion of floating charge recoveries, calculated on a sliding scale, but not fixed charge recoveries, are required to be set aside for the benefit of unsecured creditors. Also under the Insolvency Act 1986, ss. 40 and 175 if unsecured assets are insufficient to discharge preferential debts, the latter can be recouped out of floating charge assets but not fixed charge assets.[78] The Law Commission suggested that for these provisions there was an appropriate replacement – preferential creditors and the unsecured creditors' fund should have first claim on:

(a) any inventory or receivables belonging to the company; and
(b) any other assets of the company that, under the charge agreement, the company had the right to dispose of free from the charge.

In its view, the effects of adopting this test would be broadly 'insolvency neutral' and furthermore, the test would be easier to apply than the current one.[79]

74 See Crowther Report, fn 55, para. 5.7.77.

75 See *The Final Report*, fn 5, para. 3.158: '[I]n the light of responses to the CR we have decided that, for the time being at least, the distinction between fixed and floating charges should be retained.'

76 'Company security interests: developing a final scheme', fn 60, para. 1.16, n. 5. See also Regulation 24 of the draft Company Security Regulations 2006, fn 61.

77 See *The Final Report*, fn 5, para. 3.166 'It is true that, were the scheme set out in the CR to be implemented, significant numbers of consequential amendments would be needed in particular to the Insolvency Act 1986.'

78 Moreover, and very importantly, under the Insolvency Act 1986 (as amended), Schedule B1 para. 99, costs and expenses incurred by an administrator can be paid out of floating charge assets but not fixed charge assets. The Enterprise Act 2002 continues to enshrine the fixed–floating charge distinction in various respects, including giving the holder of a qualifying floating charge the power to appoint an administrator out of court.

79 See: 'Company security interests: developing a final scheme', fn 60, para. 1.31; *The Final Report*, fn 5, para. 3.170.

There are other possible solutions. One could, for instance, earmark a proportion of all charge recoveries, irrespective of how the charge is categorised, for preferential creditors and for unsecured creditors thereby building upon the Insolvency Act 1986, s. 176A and the Enterprise Act reforms. The 'solution' envisaged by the Law Commission is not free from difficulty.[80] What about 'receivables' factored by the company? Would they be caught by the provision? A similar provision in New Zealand has generated substantial difficulties not least in terms of drafting and has had to be amended twice.

The Law Commission however stepped back from the brink recognising 'that insolvency law has undergone significant change in recent years, and that there is great unwillingness to see further changes in the immediate future'. As a result, the Law Commission was not minded to recommend the steps that would result in the distinction between fixed and floating charges being rendered obsolete. Pusillanimity to the nth degree or a sensible bow to the prevailing political winds?[81] The reader is left to make up his or her own mind.

It is submitted that the end result of the Law Commission proposals is a somewhat messy and anomalous priority picture. A floating charge may have priority over the fixed charge under the first-to-file principle yet, in a receivership, administration or liquidation, a fixed charge outranks all other creditors, whereas a floating charge is subject to the claims of preferential creditors[82] and to the unsecured creditors' lifeboat etc. Regulation 45 of the draft Company Security Regulations 2006 attempted to square this particular circle by adopting what might be referred to as the 'statutory subrogation' solution. In other words, the floating charge would step into the shoes of the fixed charge so that, as against the preferential creditors and the unsecured creditors' fund, the floating charge should have priority to the extent of any fixed charges over which it had priority.[83]

The change of heart dissected: title retention and purchase-money security interests

In its earlier consultative exercises, the Law Commission was pretty adamant that title-retention devices should be included in the new legislative scheme, even at the

80 See the response of the Insolvency law Committee of the City of London Law Society to the Law Commission at pp. 6–7; available on www.citysolicitors.org/.

81 In the Consultative Report, fn 4, the Law Commission recognised that insolvency matters were a political hot potato stating, para. 2.60, that: 'Policy issues relating to insolvency are issues for the Government rather than the Law Commission: our brief does not include insolvency. However, it is clear that if the scheme we provisionally propose were to be implemented, a good deal of consequential amendment would be needed to the current insolvency legislation. We have discussed our scheme with the Insolvency Service, and although we have identified some areas that will need amendment, we are continuing to work on this area.'

82 Insolvency Act 1986, ss. 40 and 175. The general costs and expenses of liquidation, however, cannot be met out of floating charge realisations; see *Re Leyland Daf Ltd*: *Buchler* v. *Talbot* [2004] 2 AC 298.

83 See 'Regulatory impact assessment', fn 62, p. 84 and for analogous examples under current law, see *Re Portbase Clothing Ltd* [1993] Ch. 388; *Re Woodroffes (Musical Instruments) Ltd* [1986] Ch. 366.

'companies-only' stage.[84] The Law Commission recognised that its proposals meant a major expansion of the filing system in that the penalty for failure to register a deemed security interest would be loss of the security interest in the debtor's insolvency.[85]

Take two implications of this proposal.[86] The first concerns finance leases which were deemed by legislative fiat to constitute a security interest. If the lessor fails to file notice against the lessee then, effectively, the lessor will lose its ownership of the property if the lessee declines into insolvency. Likewise with the supplier of raw materials who relies upon a simple retention-of-title clause in a sale of goods contract. If the buyer becomes insolvent the seller will not be able to reclaim the goods even in their original, unprocessed state because the seller is deemed to have a security interest and this interest will be invalid for want of registration in the buyer's insolvency.[87]

In effect, two types of contractor, the finance lessor and the simple retention of title supplier, who never considered that they were bringing into existence a security interest at all, are magically transformed by legislation into doing what they never wanted to do.[88] Article 9 legislation deems the parties to have done something that

84 Consultative Report, fn 4, para. 2.87.

85 The New Zealand Personal Property Securities Act provides protection in this situation by allowing an unregistered security interest to remain valid in liquidation. Failure to file means loss of priority to competing parties claiming an 'ownership' or security interest in the goods; see, e.g., New Zealand Personal Property Securities Act 1999, s. 52. Note also the New Zealand Law Commission Report No. 8 *A Personal Property Securities Act for New Zealand* (Wellington, 1989), p. 115: 'In practice, only two parties are possibly misled by the absence of a registration statement. The first is the prospective creditor who would normally advance credit only against a first ranking security in a debtor's goods. Under the proposed statute, if such a creditor files a registration statement, it is protected against any unperfected security interests ... Creditors, who supply goods or funds on an unsecured basis are generally either not concerned about the presence of outstanding interests or assume that such interests exist. Prospective buyers and lessees, like prospective secured creditors, also rely heavily on the ostensible ownership of their transferor. Accordingly, they are protected from unperfected security interests ... unless they have knowledge of the security interest.'

86 See generally McCormack 'Quasi-securities and the Law Commission Consultation Paper on security interests – a brave new world' [2003] LMCLQ 80.

87 Current law suggests, however, that a retention-of-title clause is only likely to be valid insofar as it applies to goods in their original unprocessed state and, to the extent that it secures the unpaid purchase price of those goods, and, perhaps, other obligations owing by the buyer to the seller; see: *Clough Mill Ltd* v. *Martin* [1985] 1 WLR 111; *Armour* v. *Thyssen Edelstahlwerke AG* [1991] 2 AC 339. A claim by a seller to resale proceeds and to products manufactured out of the goods supplied is likely to be held to constitute a registrable security interest; see *Compaq Computer* v. *Abercorn Group Ltd* [1991] BCC 484; *Borden* v. *Scottish Timber Products Ltd* [1981] Ch. 25; *Modelboard* v. *Outer Box Ltd* [1992] BCC 945; *Ian Chisholm Textiles Ltd* v. *Griffiths* [1994] BCC 96. For a different view, see the decision of the High Court of Australia in *Associated Alloys Pty Ltd* v. *CAN* (2002) 202 CLR 588.

88 See the comment by I. Davies 'The reform of English personal property security law' [2004] LS 295, p. 321: 'The difficulty with the functionalism as applied in Article 9-type regimes is that it can be both over-inclusive and also under-inclusive at the same time. A more appropriate approach in any reform of English personal property security law is to operate within the existing legal landscape rather than to seek to transform it.'

they expressly did not want to do and this 'recharacterisation', if you can call it that, has troubled even arch exponents of an Article 9-type regime:[89]

> There are two features of the UCC, Article 9 approach that appear to be troublesome even to those who are attracted to it. The first is the total reconceptualisation that it requires in the context of types of transactions that traditionally are not viewed as secured financing devices ... The second feature ... is the extent to which it requires a bifurcated approach to the characterisation of certain types of transactions. Since a title retention sales contract or a lease falls within a secured financing regime because it functions as a security device, it follows that the seller or lessor is not the owner of the goods sold or leased ... What is troublesome is that outside this regime, the recharacterisation might not be acceptable with the result that same transaction is viewed differently depending on the legal issues being addressed.

The Law Commission was appreciative of the point that the questions of whether or not the new framework should include title-retention devices, and whether this inclusion was warranted at the companies-only stage, were 'difficult and controversial'.[90] Nevertheless, the Law Commission favoured inclusion even though it admitted that there was no obvious advantage for a retention-of-title supplier. It did point out, however, that filing online would be cheap and easy. Moreover, for high volume users, such as suppliers who normally used retention-of-title clauses in their conditions of sale, special arrangements were envisaged under which information entered into a secured party's own system could be forwarded to the registry without further data input.[91]

The Law Commission was even dismissive of the view that it would be inappropriate to include title-retention devices in a companies-only scheme because the law would become unnecessarily complicated if different rules applied that depended on whether the lessee/hirer/buyer as the case may be, was either a corporate or an unincorporated entity. The opportunity, afforded by the slot given to the Companies Bill in the government and legislative timetable, was an opportunity that, in its view, should not be missed:[92]

> The anticipated Companies Bill gives us an opportunity to establish the notice-filing scheme for companies. If we do not seize that opportunity, we reduce the chance that any of the scheme will ever reach the statute book. A Bill introducing this scheme from scratch would require much more Parliamentary time and Departmental effort than to take powers, and have regulations made, under a Companies Bill. It is true that primary legislation would then be needed in order to extend the scheme to unincorporated debtors; but it would in substance be merely a re-enactment of the companies scheme with a wider scope of application. That should require much less Parliamentary time and Departmental effort. It would be ideal to insist on enactment of the entire scheme all at one but those

89 Professor Ronald Cuming 'The internationalisation of secured financing law', in (ed.) Ross Cranston, *Making Commercial Law: Essays in Honour of Roy Goode* (Oxford: Oxford University Press, 1997), pp. 522–3.

90 See Consultative Report, fn 4, para. 2.132.

91 Ibid., para. 2.103.

92 Ibid., para. 2.122.

> with close knowledge of the legislative process have advised us not to recommend an all-or-nothing approach.

Certain critics of the inclusion of title-retention devices, apart from the illegitimacy of deeming parties to have done what they had no intention of doing, focused on the complexity of the resultant legislative scheme. Statutory recognition of the purchase-money security interest is meant to accommodate title-retention devices and to preserve, roughly speaking, the present priority position. Under current law if a creditor can claim ownership of property in a debtor's insolvency, the creditor's ownership interest will prevail against charge holders who are also laying claim to the property; but, in their case, through the debtor. With a new scheme there are difficult questions about how the super priority of the purchase-money security interest holder should extend into proceeds, and products, of the original goods supplied. Another issue is the conditions that must be satisfied before PMSI status can be obtained and whether a distinction should be drawn, as in some schemes, between inventory and capital equipment, with PMSI status in the latter being more difficult to establish. The present position is basically that a retention-of-title claim is valid with respect to goods in their original condition but claims by the supplier to proceeds or products of the goods are likely to fall by the wayside. It would seem extraordinary if all any future legislation was doing was reproducing this general pattern, but doing so in a very complicated way, by introducing a new registration apparatus and complicating this with a new conceptual structure.

The City of London Solicitors' group argued strongly that there was no material benefit to be obtained from requiring quasi-security to be registered, 'both because of the very material uncertainty which will result and because the requirement to recharacterise quasi-security will unnecessarily interfere with the ability of the parties to structure their business transactions as they wish'. It was suggested out that parties in international financial transactions, including sale and repurchase agreements (repos), choose English law precisely because of their confidence that the English courts will not generally engage in a recharacterisation exercise:[93]

> The effect of the proposed regulations would be, in the case of the lease, to treat the lessee as if it owned the asset which it had never intended to own and, in the case of the stock loan, to treat the lender as if it had retained an interest in the asset which it never intended to retain. It is hard to see why this should be required. This is not a case of looking to the substance rather than the form of the transaction it is a matter of overriding both the form and the substance of a transaction because it could have been effected in a different way.

The committee was concerned that the recharacterisation of quasi-security would create unforeseen, and unintended, consequences and this would, in turn, lead parties to seeking legal advice more frequently than they did at the moment. The maxim 'when in doubt, file' was not necessarily of assistance in this context since the definition of 'quasi-security' covered transactions that parties would not regard as financing transactions. In the committee's view, there was a fundamental distinction between a company granting an interest over its own asset and a company obtaining limited rights in someone else's assets. This was not an arcane legal concept which

93 See Calnan [2005] BJIBFL 25, p. 28.

served to obscure the reality of the transaction but, instead, was the reality of the transaction. In the second scenario, the company never owned the asset and so could not grant security over it. The inclusion of quasi-security in the legislative scheme would alter these fundamental legal conceptions.[94]

The distinguished legal commentator, Philip Wood, of Allen & Overy, has also been vehement against the inclusion of title finance devices.[95] In his view, it would be a seriously retrograde step for England to make title finance subject to filing and to the surplus, and other rules, of security interests. His language is strong but basically the objections boil down to the following: notice filing can be punitive in its effects, providing a windfall benefit for third-party creditors of the debtor if there has been a failure to file. The principle against false wealth is weak, and is not honoured for major items of property. Filing would be required in respect of many trivial transactions – small ticket retention of title cases and small leases. The inclusion of sales and leases would interfere with predictability and also breed litigation and uncertainty. It was putting the cart before the horse to have a blanket inclusion of all transactions like security and then carve out those transactions considered to be acceptable without registration. This was the wrong way around. The inclusion would mean more form filling and bureaucracy in the legal system.

The function of the Financial Markets Law Committee (FMLC) is to identify issues of legal uncertainty or misunderstanding, insofar as they might affect the financial markets, and generate material risks.[96] Therefore, the committee confined its consideration of the Law Commission proposals to these issues. It did add however, that 'many practising lawyers have great reservations about various proposals contained in the Consultation Paper (which introduces many radical changes in the law)…'.[97]

The FMLC noted that many security instruments, including long-term debenture stock and secured bond issues, had negative-pledge clauses against the creation of any other security interest. These clauses might permit companies to carry out transactions that were not presently recognised by the law as constituting security interests. A change in the law, however, could cause existing quasi-security arrangements to fall within the negative-pledge clauses and cause the borrower to be in default. This might bring existing funding arrangements to an end, or lead to an increase in funding costs. This might trigger cross-default provisions and the worst-case scenario would be a domino effect, leading to financial collapse. On title retention, it was suggested that the Law Commission give further consideration 'to whether, having regard to the legal uncertainty created, it is right to recharacterise title retention on sale of goods as a quasi-security, or whether the present situation is preferable'.[98]

94 Op. cit., Calnan, fn 93, p. 29. For a different perspective, see Ziegel 'The travails of English chattel security law reform – a transatlantic view' [2006] LMCLQ 110, p. 116 'a conditional sale agreement is only a short form of chattel mortgage and that in each case the seller or mortgagee merely retains or obtains title as security for performance of the buyer's obligation'.

95 See Phillip R. Wood 'Comment on Law Commission's Proposals to adopt Article 9 regime for company security interests' (23 November 2004), pp. 21–2, on file with the author.

96 For more details of the committee, see its website www.fmlc.org. The committee is presently chaired by Lord Woolf and its membership included the former Law Commission President, Sir Roger Toulson (who left the Law Commission in August 2006).

97 See FMLC response to the Law Commission, p. 1, which is available on the website (www.fmlc.org).

98 See FMLC response, fn 97, p. 3.

The final proposals signalled a major climbdown by the Law Commission:[99]

> Commissioners have decided not to recommend including title-retention devices as part of the companies-only scheme. They have provisionally decided that such devices should be further considered in the light of the proposed study of transfer of title by non-owners that has been included in the Law Commission's Ninth programme of Law Reform. This will allow examination of title-transfer issues in a wider context than just company security interests.

The Law Commission also noted simply that the priority rules on PMSIs were included in the Consultative Report on the assumption that title-retention devices were to be covered and, given the fact that the initial stages of reform would not include such devices, PMSI rules would also be excluded.[100]

There had been a lot of opposition to inclusion of purchase-money super priority in the scheme from legal professionals. One commentator remarked:[101]

> The underlying policies supporting this super-priority are questionable. There have to be strong reasons in favour of a super-priority preference. Bank finance is itself mainly purchase money in the broadest sense – bank finance buys the debtor's assets and funds the employees and the purchases which build the assets. More importantly these PMSIs result in the splitting of the assets between creditors which complicates work-outs if the debtor is in trouble and makes the management of a rescue much more difficult.

The City of London Solicitors' group observed:[102]

> It is by no means self-evident that a creditor which can identify funds lent by it to acquire a particular asset should be in a better position than a creditor which has taken general security over all the company's assets and which has provided it with the benefit of working capital. Who is to say that one is more valuable than the other? The effect of these arrangements will be to prefer vendor credit to lender credit. The implications of such a change in a market which has traditionally relied on lender credit are difficult to establish. We do not believe that such a major change should be contemplated without proper economic investigation of its effects.

Assignment of receivables

The Law Commission was still of the view that absolute assignments of receivables should be subject to notice-filing requirements and to the 'first to file has priority'

99 'Company security interests: developing a final scheme', fn 60, para. 1.26; and see *The Final Report*, fn 5, para. 1.66. However, it should be noted that the Law Commission has yet to get around to looking at transfer of title by non-owners; see further the chapter by Gullifer in the present volume, pp. 188–222.

100 See *The Final Report*, fn 5, para. 3.146.

101 Op. cit., Wood, fn 95, p. 24.

102 See Calnan [2005] BJIBFL 25, p. 30.

principle. There are essentially two reasons for this. The first is the very narrow defining line between absolute assignments of receivables and security assignments.[103] The latter, where executed by a company, are registrable under present law as charges over book debts but, on the other hand, absolute assignments are outwith the company charge registration system. Second, the present rules for determining priorities between competing assignments of the same debt are widely considered to be unsatisfactory. Under the rule in *Dearle* v. *Hall*[104] priority goes to the first assignee to give notice to the debtor, unless that assignee has actual or constructive notice of an earlier assignment at the time that the later assignment was taken. The Law Commission pointed out that it was not practicable to check 'with each account debtor to find out whether a notice of assignment of the debt has been given, nor will the assignee always wish to give notice simply in order to preserve its priority as against a competing assignment'.[105] The Commission was also against trying to draw a distinction between sales of receivable, with recourse against the assignor, from those without recourse. In its view, it was so hard to distinguish between assignments that resemble a secured transaction and those that do not. Nevertheless, in any reforming legislation some fine distinctions would have to be drawn to avoid undue disturbance in the financial markets. In the United States, financial intangibles i.e. where the account debtor's principal obligation is a monetary one, are excluded from filing requirements. This was done to safeguard the loan participation market where parts of loans may be in sold in an intense, fast-moving market.[106] Market participants felt that filing obligations would be inapposite in this context and it is difficult to see financial professionals in England coming to a different conclusion.

The City of London Solicitors' group has also expressed opposition to the inclusion of outright sales of receivables in the legislative scheme. As it understood, the reason for including factoring transactions was to avoid some of the uncertainties that might otherwise arise in defining quasi-security:

> This is doubtless a laudable intention, but it completely turns the problem on its head. The difficulty of defining quasi-security should not result in extending the

103 See generally *Re George Inglefield Ltd* [1933] Ch. 1; *Lloyds & Scottish Finance* v. *Cyril Lord (Carpet Sales) Ltd* [1992] BCLC 609; *Crown Finance Ltd* v. *Orion* [1996] BCC 621.

104 (1828) 3 Russ 1 and for criticism of the rule see Oditah 'Priorities: equitable versus legal assignments of book debts' (1989) 9 OJLS 521. Note also de Lacy 'Reflections on the ambit of the rule in *Dearle* v. *Hall* and the priority of personal property assignments – II' (1999) 28 *Anglo-American Law Review* 197, p. 214 who comments: 'the rule in *Dearle* v. *Hall* is no longer suitable to meet the requirements of information and priority in an efficient or satisfactory manner. The only effective solution to this problem is to replace the fund-holder with a centralised public register onto which information regarding assignments could be stored. This would solve the problem relating to the quality and objectivity of the fund holder that, at present, besets the operation of the rule. The establishment of a centralised register should also be coupled with a priority rule according to the date that assignments are registered. This would produce a simple and readily ascertainable priority point free of any issue relating to the doctrine of notice.'

105 See Consultative Report, fn 4, para. 2.87.

106 For an explanation see generally Bjerre 'Secured transactions inside out: negative pledge covenants, property and perfection' (1999) 84 *Cornell Law Review* 305, p. 392; Harris and Mooney 'How successful was the revision of UCC Article 9?: Reflections of the reporters' (1999) 74 *Chicago-Kent Law Review* 1357, pp. 1369–73.

concept of security beyond quasi-security to outright transfer. It rather suggests that the attempt to include quasi-security should be abandoned.

The FMLC was also critical, noting that extending filing requirements to outright assignments of receivables was 'completely new law and it may take some time for businessmen to become accustomed to the new requirements'.[107] The Law Commission canvassed the possibility of exempting 'isolated' assignments – an assignment which did not by itself or in conjunction with other assignments to the same assignee transfer a significant part of the assignor's outstanding accounts. The FMLC, while not doubting the praiseworthy nature of these sentiments, said that concerns were likely to arise as to what might be meant by 'a significant part' and how the line should be drawn. 'Again a series of definitional cases are likely to be needed and this is the type of issue which may be subject to differences of judicial view.'

The Law Commission tried to meet some of the concerns of practitioners by adopting a deliberately narrow definition of receivables in the draft Company Security Regulations:[108] 'The requirement to register sales of receivables applies only to the kinds of monetary obligation that are commonly sold by companies to factors or discounters. It does not apply, for example, to rent or payments under mortgages or credit card loans.' According to Regulation 20, however, there is no obligation to register a sale of receivables if it 'is of such a small proportion of the assignor's receivables that it would not influence a reasonable person deciding whether to make an advance to the company'.[109] Moreover, and by a process of statutory magic, such a sale of receivables is regarded as having been automatically registered at the date of sale. Critics might say that this provision is likely to be a hostage to fortune and to give rise to considerable interpretative difficulties.[110] Regulation 35 also provides that a term in the contract giving rise to the receivable that purports to prohibit or restrict assignment of the receivable (other than an assignment in part) will not be effective against the assignee. The Law Commission suggested that this provision 'removes a serious but often unintended obstacle to many small companies obtaining receivables financing'.[111] On the other hand, anti-assignment clauses are often used in

107 See fn 97, p. 4; available on the website www.fmlc.org.

108 See Regulation 2, fn 61.

109 See 'Regulatory impact assessment on the proposal for the registration of companies' security interests' (July 2005), fn 62, p. 67.

110 In 'The registration of companies' security interests' (31August 2005), fn 52, p. 18, the City of London Solicitors' Group commented caustically 'What price certainty if that were the law? We understand that the Law Commission only intend to cover cases of "receivables financing" but their inability to produce a clear definition of what that means shows how dangerous the approach is. This kind of uncertainty can only adversely affect the desirability of doing factoring business in relation to English debtors.' More generally the group remarked 'We do not believe that there is any material advantage to be gained by requiring that the priority of assignments over receivables is to be determined by the date of registration … There is much to be said for the concept that the priority of assignments or charges over receivables should, as a general rule, depend on the date notice is given to the person who owes the receivable. Not least, this is because the person who owes the receivable will get a good discharge by paying the creditor unless he has been notified of the assignment or charge.'

111 See 'Regulatory impact assessment on the proposal for the registration of companies' security interests' (July 2005), fn 62, p. 66 and see also *The Final Report*, fn 5, paras 4.35–4.40. According to the Law Commission, para. 4.38: 'Much of the opposition … was based on a

contracts and serve the legitimate objective of preventing the contract debtor from being brought into direct relations with someone he would not choose to contract with directly.[112] They are particularly used in the construction industry where personal relationships between the parties tend to be crucial in the completion of a project.[113] The draft regulation, however, would not have precluded their continued use in this context since 'receivables' was defined narrowly to mean monetary obligations, whether or not earned by performance, arising principally from the supply of goods or services.[114]

The bare bones of the new Law Commission scheme: notice filing as opposed to transaction filing

Stripped down to its bare bones, the essence of the revised and final Law Commission scheme was for the application of notice filing to security interests (narrowly so-called). However, the current list of charges that must be registered, now listed in the Companies Act 2006, s. 860(7) would be replaced by a provision that any charge was registrable unless specifically exempted.[115] The Law Commission considered that this was more in line with practitioner thinking about going about registration where there was the slightest doubt that the transaction constituted a registrable security – when in doubt, register. In this sense, it was accepted that the Law Commission proposals did not change anything much in practice but they might, however, have the affect of altering the language in which the debate was framed. At the moment, one can focus on the wording of what is now Companies Act 2006, s. 860(7) and ask whether a particular transaction is a registrable charge within that list.[116] Under the Law Commission's proposed new regime, the debate will focus not on any list but whether the transaction amounts to a 'charge' in the first place and that question might not be susceptible of easy answer, given the long-standing debate about debt subordination trusts, and so on.[117]

misplaced concern that it would apply to loan agreements, or that there is no demand for the change. The latter is simply incorrect: the industry concerned supports the change strongly.'

112 See generally Allcock 'Restrictions on the assignment of contractual rights' [1983] CLJ 328; Goode 'Inalienable rights' (1979) 42 MLR 553; McCormack 'Debts and non-assignment clauses' [2000] JBL 422.

113 See the comments of Lord Browne-Wilkinson in *Linden Gardens* v. *Lenesta Sludge* [1994] 1 AC 385, p. 429: 'The reason for including the contractual prohibition viewed from the contractor's point of view must be that the contractor wishes to ensure that the deals, and deals only, with the particular employer with whom he has chosen to deal. Building contracts are pregnant with disputes: some employers are more reasonable than others in dealing with such disputes.'

114 See generally *The Final Report*, fn 5, at paras 4.19–4.25.

115 'Company security interests: developing a final scheme', fn 62, at para. 1.13; *The Final Report*, fn 5, at paras 3.14–3.16

116 To be registrable a security interest must constitute a 'charge'; be created by a company and also come within the list set out in the section; see generally H. Bennett 'Registration of company charges', in (eds) J. Armour and H. Bennett, *Vulnerable Transactions in Corporate Insolvency* (Oxford: Hart Publishing, 2003), p. 243.

117 'Charge' is defined by the Companies Act 2006, s. 861(5) but there is no other amplification of the term in the statute.

What is the magic about notice filing that so attracted the Law Commission even though civil law jurisdictions have remained largely immune to its charms? [118] The Law Commission said that[119] 'it will be necessary only to provide brief particulars of the charge in a simple, electronic format. It will no longer be necessary to send the original charge document. Charges will appear on the register and be searchable on-line as soon as the registration procedure has been complied with: thus there will be no period of "invisibility" between submission of the particulars and their appearance on the register.'

Responsibility for filing would be transferred from the corporate charge giver to the secured party. In practice, it is the latter that attends to registration at the moment, although the charge giver is subject to the theoretical possibility of a criminal penalty if there is no registration. Currently, failure to file renders the charge invalid in an administration or liquidation. This would continue under the proposals, though the 21-day time limit from the date of creation for registering a charge would disappear. So too would the checking function performed by Companies House. The instrument of charge would not have to be delivered to Companies House and, consequently, no longer would there be any scope for Companies House to compare the submitted particulars against the instrument of charge. As a result, Companies House would no longer issue a conclusive certificate of registration although registration could be proved by the electronic record, a copy of which would be sent to the secured party. It is part of the proposed scheme that a secured party may not rely on rights that are in excess of those referred to in the particulars delivered for registration.[120]

Some of these proposals are very worthwhile. Removing the invisibility gap and cutting down on staff time at Companies House are worthwhile endeavours. On the other hand, the invisibility gap may not be very significant in practice.[121] Borrowers do not normally create two or more near contemporaneous charges without one

118 According to the Scottish Law Commission, the only civil law jurisdictions to have introduced notice filing are Quebec and Louisiana; see Discussion Paper *Registration of Rights in Security by Companies* (Edinburgh, October 2002), para. 1.28. See further, Harrell 'A guide to the provisions of Article 9 of Louisiana's Commercial Code' (1990) *Loyola Law Review* 711; Bridge, Macdonald, Simmonds and Walsh 'Formalism, functionalism and understanding the law of secured transactions' (1999) 44 *McGill Law Journal* 567. Indeed, the Scottish Law Commission in a Discussion Paper state: 'Existing models of notice filing presuppose Anglo-American property law and turn on distinctions between creation, attachment and perfection which are unknown in Scots law or in other systems drawn from the Germanic stream of the civil law tradition. A system of notice filing suited to English property law could not readily be modified or adapted to accommodate the very different structures and concepts of Scots property law'; see Scottish Law Commission Discussion Paper No. 121 *Registration of Rights in Security by Companies* (Edinburgh, October 2002), para. 1.28. Note also the Final Report by the Scottish Law Commission entitled *Registration of Rights in Security by Companies* (Edinburgh, September 2004), para. 1.5. See further the essay by Gretton in this volume at pp. 270–284.

119 See 'Company security interests: developing a final scheme', fn 62, at para. 1.8; and see also *The Final Report*, fn 5, paras 3.107–3.109.

120 See *The Final Report*, fn 5, paras 3.74–3.76 and 3.124–3.131. Note also 'Regulatory impact assessment', fn 62, p. 71 'the charge will not be effectively registered in respect of collateral that was omitted from the description of the collateral'.

121 See the comment by the City Solicitors' Group, p. 9 of 'The registration of companies' security interests' (31August 2005), fn 8, 'We do not believe that this is a material issue in practice. It is not something which, in our experience concerns lenders.' To deal with the issue the group suggests a priority notice system of the kind used by the Land Registry in relation to registered land for many years.

credit provider knowing about the other. Moreover, a credit provider can always insist on an interval of at least 21 days between the execution of a charge and the release of funds.

What is more problematic is that removing the time limit for registration opens up the possibility that the register might become seriously out of date and not provide a complete picture as to a company's secured borrowings. It also creates the risk of last minute filings by connected parties.[122] Indeed, the Law Commission was very concerned about this prospect in its earlier consultation exercises.

The Law Commission stressed that, with notice filing, it would be possible to file in advance of the transaction and that a single filing may cover a series of similar transactions between the same parties.[123] With the assignment of receivables, the Law Commission pointed out that if filing had to be made separately for each sale, there would be difficulties.[124] 'Receivables financing is often done on a "facilitative" basis: that is, the agreement is that the company may be entitled to decide which receivables to offer to a factor, and the factor may be entitled to decide which to accept. There is no sale or agreement to sell until a particular batch has been offered and accepted. It would be inconvenient were it not possible to register in advance of the sale and to cover all the sales that might be made under the agreement.'

But with security interests in the strict sense, rather than quasi-securities, such as retention-of-title clauses, these supposed advantages are very small beer. First of all, how likely is it that a prospective borrower would be in contact with a number of potential lenders and that each of the latter would wish to file to protect its position lest some other secured party sneak into the breach in the meantime? A lender can always make it a condition of the loan that there are no other charges on the property with breach of the condition rendering the loan immediately repayable.[125] Moreover, a single charge can cover an ongoing credit facility with the borrower having general or limited drawdown facilities.

The question arises whether all the supposed advantages of notice filing could equally be achieved in a reformed transaction filing system such as currently exists under the Companies Act 2006, Part 25 and the answer to that question seems to be in the affirmative. Some jurisdictions require the filing of transactions but there is no checking of documents performed by the equivalent of Companies House. The applicant simply gets a statement – perhaps computer generated – that the particulars of the transaction have been filed on such and such a date.[126] Doing away with the

122 To reduce this risk, the Law Commission recommended the amendment of the Insolvency Act 1986, s. 245 which invalidates floating charges that have been granted to secure past indebtedness within a certain period prior to liquidation or administration. The amendment would cover floating charges that were filed within the relevant period even though they may have been created earlier. On this see *The Final Report*, fn 5, para. 3.85.

123 See *The Final Report*, fn 5, para. 1.32: 'This will be particularly important for sales of receivables ...'.

124 Ibid., para. 3.88.

125 Another approach would be for the lender to wait 21 days from the grant of the charge before extending credit facilities.

126 For details of the Irish position, see Irish Companies Act 1963, s. 99 and, for reforms envisaged by the Irish Company Law Review Group, see the website (www.clrg.org/). The Singapore system under its Companies Act, s. 131 involves the electronic submission of particulars without the instrument of charge being produced as a matter of course. The registrar of companies is still required to issue a notice or certificate of due registration. The position of Singapore in relation to PPSA reform is discussed in the chapter by Tan in the present volume, pp. 387–443.

conclusive evidence of due registration certificate issued by Companies House[127] may cause anxiety to some. A similar provision in the Companies Act 1989, Part IV which made various changes to the company charge registration procedure and which was heavily criticised may have scuppered implementation of Part IV. The Land Registry required evidence in the form of the certificate of due registration that a company charge over land had been duly registered at Companies House before allowing registration at the Land Registry. A way around the problem was not found at that time but the problem disappears if the formal requirement of dual registration in the case of charges over land was abolished. The charge would be registered at the Land Registry which would, in turn, forward the information to Companies House for information-purposes only.[128]

Also the criminal sanction for failure to register is not a necessary part of a transaction-filing system. Indeed, as the Law Commission noted, the sanction is rarely applied at the moment and could usefully be scrapped.[129] Likewise, the time limit for failure to register under a transaction-based registration system could be removed with registration being permissible at any stage up until the commencement of liquidation or administration coupled with, presumably, some sanction to prevent last minute filing by corporate insiders or other connected persons. Whether or not this would be a wise step to take is another question entirely. If disclosure of charges were to become in this sense 'voluntary', then the register would lose some of its utility in providing information about the state of a company's secured borrowings to potential lenders and investors, and other secured parties.

With regard to the Law Commission notice-filing proposals, the City of London Solicitors' Group pointed out that the 'voluntary' nature of the registration, and the fact that it could be made at any time before the company underwent insolvency proceedings, made it much easier for security to be given to connected parties without this information becoming publicly available.[130] In its view, if the security was not registered within a comparatively short period, the security, but not the secured indebtedness, should become void. The group's strong preference was for a registration system for all charges with appropriate penalties for failure to comply.

In this respect, it is questionable whether the Law Commission proposals would comply with the guiding principles drawn up by the European Bank for Reconstruction and Development (EBRD) for the development of a charges registry in the transitional economies of Central and Eastern Europe. The EBRD pointed out:[131]

> In some legal systems publicity is a condition for the creation of a charge, or is even the act which creates the charge. In others it is merely the means by which the chargeholder acquires prior ranking against other persons with a claim in the

127 What is now the Companies Act 2006, s. 869(6)(b) (formerly Companies Act 1985, s. 401(2)(b) and for cases on the provision see: *Re CL Nye Ltd* [1971] 1 Ch. 442; *Re Central Bank of India* [1986] QB 1114).

128 As is pointed out in 'Regulatory impact assessment', fn 62, p. 14. much depends on whether the Land Registry's proposals for electronic conveyancing go ahead as anticipated.

129 See 'Company security interests: developing a final scheme', fn 60, para. 1.9; *The Final Report*, fn 5, at paras 1.32(4) and 3.77.

130 See Calnan [2005] BJIBFL 25 at p. 30.

131 See *EBRD Guiding Principles for the Development of a Charges Registry* available on the EBRD website (www.ebrd.com/st guiding principle no. 4). Note also Dahan and Simpson 'Publicity of security rights: setting standards for charges registries' [2005] Law in Transition 16.

> charged asset. Whatever the approach adopted, the effect in practice of a failure to publicise should be the same: no charge in the register means no security right that can be effective against third parties. This is essential for ensuring a sufficient level of certainty for assets to be freely bought and sold, or offered as collateral.

The earlier Model Law on Secured Transactions drawn up by EBRD was based firmly on transaction filing and required the submission of a registration statement to the relevant registry within 30 days of the execution of an instrument of charge. There is no provision for advance registration.[132] Accordingly, registration must relate to a specific transaction although the Model Law provides for an 'enterprise charge' – roughly the equivalent of an English-style floating charge. The most recent material from EBRD avoids a preference for notice filing over transaction filing or vice versa. It is simply noted that the 'concept of a registration system (whether called notice filing, public recording or whatever) dedicated to publicising security rights created by debtors over their movable assets has certainly gained prominence in the last 15 years or so'. The EBRD emphasises strongly however the principle of electronic filing suggesting that the 'case for an electronic system of registration is too compelling to give serious consideration to the option of a paper-based registry'. In its view, a computer-based system will greatly increase the simplicity, speed and efficiency of recording and retrieving information as compared to a paper-based system.

There is no reason why the current paper-based English company charge registration regime could not be switched to online. Indeed, Companies House is currently exploring the possibility[133]and, now that the Law Commission proposals appear to have fallen by the wayside, the changeover should be carried through as a matter of urgency. Indeed, one of the unintended effects of the Law Commission reform project may be a degree of 'planning blight'. That is to say much needed, and important, incremental reforms are not carried because of the possibility of medium to longer-term major reforms.

It can be seen that most of the advantages of notice filing can be achieved through a revamped transaction-filing system. All that appears to be left is the 'small beer' of advance filing and a single filing to cover a multiplicity of transactions between the parties. Moreover, the latter is not much of an issue where the system does not cover quasi-securities. On 'advance filing', one critic has suggested that the notice-filing system may lead to the underproduction of valuable information in that a searcher of the register does not know whether a particular registration relates to an actual transaction or to an intended transaction that never in fact materialised. Furthermore, fewer details of the transaction are available than under transaction filing,[134] although the Law Commission has now addressed the latter concern by allowing a full description of the property subject to the charge.[135]

132 See Articles 8 and 33 of the Model Law. See generally on the Model Law, Mistelis (1998) 5 *Parker School Journal of East European Law* 455; McCormack and Dahan [1999] CfiLR 65.

133 See the Companies House Strategy document (April 2003) *Strategic Direction 2003/2006: the Future for Companies House*, pp. 6–7: '[W]e will investigate the potential to develop an on-line service for the registration of mortgages and charges. However, as both company and land registration law is changing over the life of this plan we need to make a careful assessment of when it would be appropriate to invest in the delivery of this new service.'

134 Calnan 'The reform of the law of security' [2004] BJIBFL 88, pp. 89–90 'the effect of the proposals would be to make the system less informative and reliable'.

135 See 'Regulatory impact assessment', fn 62, at para. 3.2. 'A brief general description will suffice, but there will be a facility to enable the party filing to copy a full description from

More generally, the Law Commission responded by saying that the risk of clutter was small for two reasons:[136]

> First, filing will only be effective if done with the debtor's consent and it can be expected that debtors will be circumspect in giving their consent to a filing. Secondly, if further finance is sought from another secured party, it will insist before anything else that any filings that are not concerned with existing security agreements are removed.

In response, one might say the expense in getting unnecessary registrations removed may cause delay in financing transactions and also add to transaction costs. The EBRD, for one, have been sceptical about the merits of allowing advance registration, or pre-registration, stating that 'the advantages of allowing a potential creditor to take priority during the negotiations are debatable'.[137] There is a practitioner perspective that advance filing is a 'useful add-on but is largely tidying up'.[138]

Even across the Atlantic in the US, not all commentators are necessarily convinced about the importance of the notice-filing system as a key ingredient of a successful mercantile economy and the following, perhaps slightly tongue-in-cheek, comments have been added:[139]

> The filing system is an integral part of the most sophisticated secured lending system known to mankind. Only by an effective filing system can a secured lender know of other lenders and only by it can later secured lenders and unsecured lenders be encouraged to lend. Without such a system, lenders would grow wary, commerce would be hobbled, and the manifold commercial ends that are met by commercial lenders would be stunted, rendered more costly, or stymied altogether ... I can see generations of law students writing this down and repeating this incantation in negotiations, in court, and elsewhere. This view even extends to Americans abroad who approach the English, Dutch and Germans with an air of superiority, asserting the superiority of our filing system and belittling the European efforts to put together a filing system worthy of the name.

Conclusions

The Law Commission started out with a big plan to make the English law of security interests very much like the American – notice filing, extension of the scheme to cover quasi-securities, new rules on priorities and a comprehensive restatement of the law of security interests. The Law Commission stuck to its guns for a couple of

the charge document into the financing statement'. See also *The Final Report*, fn 5, paras, 1.32(7) and 3.107–3.109.

136 See Consultative Report, fn 4, para. 2.54.

137 See *Publicity of Security Rights: EBRD Guiding Principles for the Development of a Charges Registry* (December 2004), p. 14; available on the EBRD website (www.ebrd.com/st).

138 See *Comment on Law Commission's Proposals to Adopt Article 9 Regime for Company Security Interests*, by Phillip R. Wood (23 November 2004), fn 95, p. 4.

139 White 'Reforming Article 9 priorities in light of old ignorance and new filing rules' (1995) 79 *Minnesota Law Review* 529, p. 530.

years but all the huffing and puffing failed to convince influential practitioner groups whose basic message was: stick to the basics of what we have got at the moment and do not go down the American path.[140]

The Law Commission message to the practitioner and to business lobby groups was that notice filing, and so on, would provide all the advantages in terms of flexibility, comprehensive coverage, and so on, that the present system offers, but also it would add something much more. The additional benefits would include ease of registration, greater simplicity and convenience in structuring transactions plus simpler and more coherent priority principles. But it is a bit difficult to persuade financial lawyers that somebody else knows best for them and it is not surprising that, ultimately, the Law Commission failed in its task.[141] The whole saga may remind one of the story about 'charge-backs'.[142] Basically, banks wanted to take charges in situations of reciprocal indebtedness, e.g. charges over credit balances. The courts said this was not possible legally.[143] The banker–customer relationship was a debtor–creditor one and a charge equalled a property or ownership right and how could a bank have a charge – an ownership right – in a credit balance – a debt that it owed? In any event, charges were not necessary because banks could achieve the same objectives through other means.[144] The banks, and their legal advisers, were not appeased, however, and after lobbying for legislative change,[145] got their way through judicial decision.[146] It is very difficult to persuade banks, and their legal advisers, that they are not the best judges of their own best interests.[147]

After being repulsed with its 'big plan', the Law Commission then came back with little plan – notice filing and a few add-ons. The American antecedents of the little plan are still fairly obvious. Nevertheless, the scheme has been very much watered down. So much so, that any advantages it yields could substantially be

140 See Calnan 'The reform of the law of security' [2004] BJIBFL 88, p. 92: 'The Law Commission's imperative seems to be to introduce a US-style functional system as a wholesale replacement for our current system. On a cost–benefit analysis, this seems difficult to justify. The implementation costs will be very large, and it is difficult to see what material benefits will result from it.' Note also the chapter by Calnan in the present volume, pp. 162–87.

141 That is not to say of course that the Law Commission was necessarily wrong!

142 See *Re BCCI (No. 8)* [1998] AC 214.

143 See: *Re Charge Card Services Ltd* [1987] Ch. 150; *Re BCCI (No. 8)* [1996] 2 All ER 121 (CA).

144 See the comments of Millett J in *Re Charge Card Services Ltd* [1987] Ch. 150, p. 177: 'It does not, of course, follow that an attempt to create an express mortgage or charge of a debt in favour of the debtor would be ineffective to create a security. Equity looks to the substance not the form, and while, in my judgment, this would not create a mortgage or charge, it would no doubt give a right of set off which would be effective against the creditor's liquidator or trustee in bankruptcy.'

145 See the Final Report of the Legal Risk Committee (1992), p. 42. The Legal Risk Committee is one of the predecessors of FMLC.

146 [1998] AC 214. According to Lord Hoffmann in the case the law should be slow to declare a practice of the commercial community to be conceptually impossible, given the fact that the law was fashioned to suit the practicalities of life.

147 It is interesting to note that Regulation 44 of the draft Company Security Regulations 2006 confirms the results in *Re BCCI (No. 8)* [1998] AC 214 by expressly validating charge-backs.

achieved by technological adjustments to the present system.[148] In other words, Internet registration to go hand in hand with the current transaction-based, company charge registration regime. As noted at the outset, the Companies Act 2006, Part 25 simply re-enacts the former registration of charge provisions contained in the Companies Act 1985, Part 12. It does not contain any specific measures to implement the Law Commission recommendations and, one feels that, the fact of re-enactment may exhaust what is already a poor appetite for reform. Nevertheless, the Law Commission, perhaps somewhat optimistically, observes on its website:[149]

> The DTI has not yet reached a final decision on whether to accept our recommendations. We have been told that discussions will continue with interested parties about the merits of the proposals.

148 The City of London Solicitors' Group has suggested in 'The registration of companies security interests' (31 August 2005), fn 6, p. 1, that a few, fairly small changes would make the present system work better, these are:

(a) Filing should be electronic, and searching should be on-line.
(b) As a general principle, all charges should be registrable except financial collateral. Pledges should continue to be excluded from the registration requirement.
(c) Registration should not be required in relation to overseas companies …
(d) The security created by a registrable charge should be void if not registered within the time limit.
(e) Charges should be registrable in advance of their creation (by means of priority notices along the lines of those operated by the Land Registry).

149 See www.lawcom.gov.uk/company_security.htm (last visited September 2009). However, the Law Commission's page was last updated 5 October 2005!

3 A Canadian academic's reactions to the Law Commission's proposals

Jacob Ziegel[1]

Introduction

Canadian lawyers have followed with much interest, and some puzzlement, the 35 years' efforts to reform English chattel security law. The efforts began in 1971 with the publication of the Crowther Report[2] and were resumed with the publication of the Diamond Report in 1989.[3] The Halliday Report,[4] although primarily concerned with the Scottish position, gave the issues some renewed exposure. However, a major new thrust emerged with the publication of the Law Commission's Consultation Paper No. 164 in 2002[5] followed by the Commission's Consultative Report of 2004[6] and, finally, their Final Report, which was published in August 2005.[7]

The critical question now is whether a British government will ever accept the Law Commission's recommendations and the case for fundamental reform of chattel security law based on the type of Personal Property Security Acts (PPSAs) seen in Canada and elsewhere, all of which are ultimately based on Article 9 of the US Uniform Commercial Code (UCC). If it is difficult for an English lawyer to provide an informed answer to this question, it is even more hazardous for an overseas observer. For the time being it appears as if the reform question has been shelved but it is reasonable to assume that it will recur. However, predictions over the future course

1 I am grateful for research assistance in the preparation of this chapter from a number of former University of Toronto students and, in particular, Carlin McGoogan and Scott Ollivierri. Except as otherwise indicated, this chapter describes the Canadian position as of May 2007.

2 *The Report of the Committee on Consumer Credit* (London: HMSO, 1971); Cmnd 4596, note especially, Part V.

3 *A Review of Security Interests in Property* (London: HMSO, 1989), Chairman Professor A. L. Diamond.

4 Scottish Law Commission, *Report by Working Party on Security over Moveable Property*, 1986 (the Halliday Report)

5 See Law Commission, *Registration of Security Interests: Company Charges and Property other than Land. A Consultation Paper*, Consultation Paper No. 164 (2002) (London: The Stationery Office, 2002)

6 Law Commission, *Company Security Interests. A Consultative Report.* Consultation Paper No. 176 (London: The Stationery Office, 2004); (Consultative Report).

7 See Law Commission Report No. 296 Company Security Interests (2005) Cmnd 6654 (The Final Report). For a fuller account of this Report, see the chapter by McCormack in the present volume, pp. 83–116.

of events in England are not helped by the fact that even the Law Commission's proposals involved an incremental series of reforms to be brought in over a period of time following extensive consultation and debate as to whether the reforms should apply to companies alone or also to other forms of business entity and to consumer debtors. Therefore, even if the government had decided to act on the Law Commission's recommendations we would have seen merely a first phase of reform in the Companies Act 2006 to be followed by yet more consultations and recommendations!

The Law Commission rightly noted,[8] that, beginning with the adoption of Article 9 by the American states in the 1950s and the adoption of personal property security legislation by the Canadian provinces from 1967 onwards,[9] there has developed a powerful trend in market economies, nationally and internationally, in favour of modern rational, efficient and comprehensive chattel security regimes with predictable rules. The common assumption underlying all these efforts is that secured credit, despite its many critics and sceptics, is efficient credit and that the availability of security for lenders is the necessary price for the availability of large volumes of credit to businesses and consumers.

Given the long and successful history of chattel security reform in other common law jurisdictions, it remains a puzzling question as to why England lags so much behind in the modernisation of its chattel security rules.[10] This is especially the case given the hard work put in by the Law Commission, which seems now to have been abandoned. Some have suggested it is because of the costs and uncertainty likely to be engendered by the introduction of an entirely new type of registration system for corporate securities and the adoption of new priority rules. I have not seen the costs spelled out anywhere but presumably they fall under two main heads: (a) the cost for secured creditors and their lawyers of learning an entirely new set of rules and training their staffs in the accurate use of the new perfection provisions; and (b) the cost to the British government of establishing a modern 'real time' electronically based registration system. So far as the second item is concerned, the Canadian statistics show that a personal property security registry can be a major profit centre for its operators[11] and that the initial capital costs of the equipment can be expected to be

8 See Consultation Paper 164, fn 5, para. 1.36 *et seq.*

9 Ontario was the first province to adopt personal property security (PPS) legislation. The Act was adopted in 1967, but did not become fully operational until 1976. The intervening period was used to establish a computerised central registry (the first in North America) and to allow existing chattel security registrations to be transferred to the new system.

10 England is not alone. Australian chattel security law faced similar challenges. However, the Australian position is substantially more complex because Australia, like Canada, is a federal state and has to contend with the chattel security laws of six states and two territories and the banking laws of the Commonwealth government. However, following extensive consultation and discussions it now appears as if Australia has come round to the cause of PPS reform and, unlike the UK, a new PPSA scheme is expected to come into force in 2011; see further the chapter by Fisher in the present volume, pp. 366–86.

11 The revenue generated by the Ontario Registry between 2001 and 2004 was as follows: 2001–2002: (Canadian $) $45,622,251; 2002–2003: $46,122,251; 2003–2004: $43,642,357. The revenue is not segregated but is paid into Ontario's consolidated revenue fund. Information regarding the costs of operating the registry is not available, one of the reasons being that the Companies and Personal Property Security Branches have amalgamated. However, in the writer's view, it is safe to assume that the cost of operating the registry is only a fraction of the revenue generated by the registry. Even if one assumes that the operational costs

quickly recovered. So far as the cost to solicitors and their clients of having to acquire a new set of skills is concerned, if Canadian experience is a suitable guide, even a non-specialist English solicitor should have no difficulty grasping the basic principles of an Article 9-type law. Mastering the fine details and policy implications of the new rules admittedly requires more time and effort. However, in this writer's view, the costs are likely to be moderate compared to the uncertainties and formidable complexities of the existing English chattel security rules.

I suspect however that other factors are at play in English resistance to the introduction of comprehensive reforms apart from the cost factors.[12] An obvious factor is the powerful interests of City of London law firms and their financial clients. The law firms have a huge intellectual and professional investment through their mastery of the intricacies of the existing English rules which, understandably, they may be reluctant to surrender to an entirely new and untried statutory regime. This is true even though, judging by North American experience, there is no reason to believe that the law firms' services will be any less needed in the new corporate chattel security environment than they are now.

Another ground of opposition may be the reluctance of suppliers of equipment and other durable goods, and the intermediaries financing these transactions, to abandon the privileged position of quasi-securities (hire-purchase agreements, financing leases, retention-of-title clauses, receivables financing and securitisation of receivables) and to subject them to the discipline, registration requirements and priority rules of an Article 9-type regime. A North American lawyer would respond that the transformation is for the most part painless and that the benefits of a reasonably clear and functional set of rules for quasi-securities greatly outweighs their cost. This experience also answers the complaint of some British scholars, examined in greater detail later

amount to as much as 50 per cent of revenue, it would still leave the Ministry of Consumer and Business Services (MCBS) with a very tidy annual profit. The number of registrations and of searches of the registry's records made during the above periods were as follows:

Registrations

2001–2002: 1,694,777
2002–2003: 1,912,943
2003–2004: 1,809,832

Number of searches:

2001–2002: 781,620
2002–2003: 821,844
2003–2004: 878,379

Source of statistical information: Laurinda Gorgulho, Ontario MCBS, July 2004.

12 For an examination of comparable factors in an international context involving the opposition of civilian countries to the introduction of general registration requirements for security interests in movables, see Mooney 'Extraterritorial impact of choice of law rules for non-United States debtors under Revised Uniform Commercial Code Article 9 and a new proposal for international harmonization', in (eds) Bridge and Stevens, *Cross-Border Security and Insolvency* (New York: Oxford Press, 2001), ch. 10, pp. 199–200. Professor Mooney also notes the important role of that branch of economics known as 'public choice' economics in examining economic factors influencing support or opposition by organised groups to changes in the law. For a detailed review of the history of regulation in England, see the chapter by de Lacy in the present volume, pp. 3–82. Note also the chapter by Calnan, in the present volume, pp. 162–87, which serves to demonstrate that many remain unconvinced of the case for such fundamental reform that a new PPSA would bring about.

in this chapter,[13] that the functionalism of Article 9 has been purchased at the expense of a decent respect for ownership concepts in hybrid securities.

Still another objection by English observers may be that an insufficient case has been made out for including consumer transactions in the new statutory regime and that consumers should not be encouraged or permitted to pledge household possession and, even less, their earnings, as security for a loan or line of credit. Similarly, it is argued that the financing of motor vehicles and expensive household durable goods can continue to be financed by hire-purchase and leasing agreements, as they are now. In my view, the Law Commission's Consultation Paper[14] persuasively showed the frailties of this reasoning.[15] However, logic itself may be insufficient to dislodge a mental framework and set of legal rules that have been in place for over a hundred years.

Finally, there is the element of national pride. As the home of the common law, England is more used to being an exporter of legal ideas than being a borrower of innovations from other common law jurisdictions.[16] The attitude is not unnatural and American lawyers have traditionally been even more reluctant than the British establishment to adopt foreign imports. Nevertheless, the conservatism of the legal profession contrasts unfavourably with the much greater rate of change accepted willingly by scientists as a price for expanding the frontiers of knowledge without regard to national boundaries. Greatly to its credit, it must also be noted that the Law Commission has shown no national inhibitions in citing and recommending, in many cases almost verbatim, adoption of the concepts and statutory language in Article 9 and its Canadian counterparts.

This chapter examines, from a Canadian perspective, some of the key features of the Law Commission's work and concentrates, in particular, on the Commission' Consultation Paper, Consultative Report and Draft Regulations since these were the documents which considered the case for fundamental reform of the entire system of personal property security. (See the McCormack chapter in this volume, pp. 83–116, above for a detailed treatment of the Final Report of the English Law Commission). For the time being the government has rejected all these reform proposals and the current Companies Act 2006 remains essentially the same as its 1985 predecessor in its treatment of company charge security interests. Nevertheless, it can only be a matter of time before the reform question is raised again. With this in mind this chapter offers support for the Law Commission's recommendations and, in some cases, indicates areas where the recommendations may give rise to difficulties. The areas selected for particular analysis are: (a) the notice-filing registration system;[17] (b) conflict of laws issues;[18] (c) treatment of floating charges in the new regime;[19]

13 See pp. 145–8.

14 Consultation Paper 164, Part X, fn 5, para. 10.2 *et seq.*

15 For further discussion of this issue, see pp. 150–3.

16 This reluctance to borrow is not confined to the use of overseas statutory precedents. It is also reflected in British reluctance to adopt UNCITRAL conventions and model laws and UNIDROIT-inspired initiatives in private law areas. A conspicuous example is the UK's failure to ratify the UNICITRAL International Sales Convention, now in force in 65 jurisdictions, despite the very active role played by British representatives in the drafting of the Convention.

17 See pp. 124–132.

18 See pp. 132–57.

19 See pp. 137–42.

(d) treatment of quasi-security interests;[20] (e) extension of new regime to unincorporated businesses and consumers;[21] and (f) enforcement of security interest on the debtor's default.[22] Before turning to these specific issues, there are some preliminary questions that need to be addressed first.

Analysis of key Law Commission recommendations

Some methodological issues

The Law Commission faced formidable difficulties in preparing its various Papers/ Report. The principal difficulty arose from the fact that the Law Commission's original and primary mandate had been to consider the desirability of adopting a notice-filing system for the registration of company charges. It is true the Law Commission's remit was broad enough to consider the other components of a modern chattel security system.[23] Nevertheless, the Law Commission recognised it was unlikely that the Department of Trade and Industry (DTI) (since renamed, the Department for Business, Enterprise and Regulatory Reform) would be able to gain sufficient parliamentary time to introduce more than the new registration provisions for company charges before the then expected general election of 2005 (which did in fact occur). However, in the hope that the rest of the Commission's recommendations might be considered, at least in the post-election parliamentary period, the Commission decided to add three optional parts to its Consultation Paper. These dealt respectively with quasi-securities,[24] security interests created by non-corporate debtors[25] and what, a little puzzlingly, was referred to as a restatement of security principles[26] but appears in fact to correspond to Parts II and VI of Revised Article 9 in the United States and Parts II and V in the Canadian Personal Property Security Acts.

The Law Commission's dilemma, as reflected in the 2002 Consultation Paper, was readily understandable. However, its segmented approach to the adoption of an English version of Article 9 also presented significant conceptual difficulties. The first was that it was misleading to describe the first of its recommendations as 'only' concerned with the introduction of a notice-filing system for company securities. It is clear from the Consultation Paper itself[27] (and is even clearer from the Consultative Report)[28] that the Commission envisaged the notice-filing recommendations also encompassing priority issues, though conceptually filing issues and priority issues are quite separate issues. Again, Part XI of the Consultation Paper dealing with the restatement of chattel security principles embraced two quite separate components: (a) principles governing the creation and maintenance of the security interest and general obligations of the parties; and (b) enforcement of the security interest on the

20 See pp. 142–45.
21 See pp. 148–53.
22 See pp. 153–54.
23 See Consultation Paper 164, fn 5, para. 1.16.
24 Ibid., Parts VI and VII.
25 Ibid., Parts VIII, IX and X.
26 Ibid., Part XI.
27 See Consultation Paper 164, fn 5, para. 4.118 *et seq.*
28 See Consultative Report, fn 6, para. 3.198 *et seq.*

debtor's default. Perhaps unavoidably, this fragmented approach left a misleading impression of the different parts of the Commission's recommendations and underestimated the importance of considering chattel security reform as an integrated package of interdependent provisions. Happily, many of these difficulties were resolved in both the Law Commission's excellent and comprehensive Consultative Report, and in its Final Report of 2005, where the Commission's recommendations and draft statutory Rules are presented in a format much more familiar to North American readers.

Whose chattel security model?

Once the Commission reached the conclusion that the current registration provisions for company securities were seriously deficient and inefficient, it was natural that its search for solutions should have gravitated to those common law jurisdictions that have adopted the Article 9-type model. The question, however, was: whose model? Revised Article 9 of the American Uniform Commercial Code? Ontario's Personal Property Security Act,[29] the oldest in Canada? The Saskatchewan Act,[30] which also formed the basis for the Model Act adopted by the Canadian Conference on Personal Property Security Law? The Canadian Model Act?[31] Then, too, there was the New Zealand Personal Property Securities Act 1999, which is largely based on the Saskatchewan Act but contains important deviations from it.[32] The Consultation Paper never answered this question and readers were left to draw their own conclusion from the fact that most of the overseas statutory references in the Consultation Paper were to the Saskatchewan Act and, to a lesser extent, the New Zealand Act. There is very little discussion of the history of Article 9 in the US and the provincial PPS acts in Canada and the essential differences between them. Presumably the Law Commission elected largely to adopt the Saskatchewan provisions in preference to the Article 9 provisions because the Saskatchewan drafting style is more congenial to English eyes and because Revised Article 9 was regarded as too complex for easy absorption.[33] The Saskatchewan Act apparently was preferred over the Ontario Act because the Saskatchewan Act formed the basis of the Model Canadian Act, which has been adopted in all the common law provinces and territories other than Ontario. However, this overlooks the fact that Ontario is by far the most populous

29 RSO 1990 c P-10 as amended.

30 SS 1993 c P-6.2 as amended.

31 For the complex history of the Model Act, see: Ziegel 'The new provincial chattel security regimes' (1991) 70 *Canadian Bar Review* 681, p. 696 *et seq.*; and Ziegel and Denomme, *The Ontario Personal Property Security Act. Commentary and Analysis* (Butterworths Canada, 2nd edn, 2000), pp. lxxvi–lxvii.

32 See Gedye 'A distant export: the New Zealand experience with a North American style personal property security regime' (2006) 43 *Canadian Business Law Journal* 208.

33 In the author's view, Consultation Paper No. 164 underestimated the importance and number of the changes made in Revised Article 9. The new Article 9 is much more rule-oriented than its predecessors. It also caters much more to special interests. The American law teachers with whom I have spoken find the Revised Article 9 much more difficult to teach than the old version and one suspects that the average US practitioner also has difficulties negotiating his way around the complex new provisions. For an excellent evaluation of the new Article 9 from a Canadian perspective, see Cuming and Walsh 'Revised Article 9 of the Uniform Commercial Code: implications for the Canadian Personal Property Security Act' (2000–1) 16 *Banking and Finance Law Review* 339.

and industrialised of the provinces[34] and is the home of most of Canada's major financial institutions. Ontario also accounts for 40 per cent of Canada's gross national product. Between them Ontario and Quebec account for just over 60 per cent of Canada's gross national product.[35] It seems a pity therefore that these facts did not provoke some inquiry by the Law Commission to determine why Ontario practitioners continue to prefer the Ontario Act over the Model Act and the Saskatchewan Act, although it is also true that Ontario practitioners recognise the need for further updating of the Ontario provisions.[36]

In the interests of providing readers with as detailed a scheme of how the Commission's proposal might work in practice, the Consultation Paper quoted copiously from the Saskatchewan and New Zealand precedents and much less often from Article 9 and the Ontario Act.[37] The Consultation Report carried the process a step further in that it provided the reader with a set of draft regulations incorporating the Commission's recommendations – a process that was repeated in the Final Report of 2005. This was altogether admirable and the Commission is to be strongly commended for this fine work and the great care to which both these Reports have gone to provide the reader with as comprehensive description of the legislative implications of the Commission's proposals as time would allow. Nevertheless, the reader also needs to be aware that detailed drafting of the provisions frequently involved a

34 As of July 1, 2007, Ontario's population was 12,803,900m and represented 38.9 per cent of Canada's population of 32,976,000m. The population of Saskatchewan at this time was only 996,900. See Statistics Canada, online: www.statcan.

35 For the details see Statistics Canada, online: www.statcan.ca/english/Pgdb/econ03.htm; www.statcan.ca/english/Pgdb/econ04.htm; and www.statcan.ca/english/Pgdb/econ15.htm.

36 For further discussion of these issues, see Canadian Bar Association – Ontario, *Submission to the Minister of Consumer and Commercial Relations Concerning the Personal Property Security Act* (Toronto, November 1998). Quebec comprehensively revised its law of security interests in movables in 1994 as part of the revision of the Quebec Civil Code. The new Quebec rules borrow extensively from key features of Article 9 and the provincial common law personal property security Acts, but the differences are even more important. There are also basic differences in drafting style and presentation of rules and concepts. See: Ciotola 'La reforme des sûretés sous le Code civil du Québec' in *La reforme du Code civil*, vol. III (Quebec: Presses de Université Laval, 1993), p. 303; and Louis Payette, *Les sûretés dans le Code civil du Québec*, 2nd edn (Editions du Yvon Blais, 2002). The concept of a generic security interest is recognised in the new Civil Code in the form of a revitalised *hypothèque* in movables (*hypothèque mobilière avec dépossession*). The Code also established a central electronic notice-filing system for non-possessory security interests. The main differences appear to be that hybrid security interests (e.g., conditional sales and chattel leases and sales with a right of repurchase) are not treated as security interests although they are subject to registration requirements. See Boodman and Macdonald 'How far is Article 9 of the Uniform Commercial Code exportable? A return to sources?' (1996) 27 *Canadian Business Law Journal* 249 and see also below, at the text accompanying fn's 140–41. There are also stronger restrictions or prohibitions than in the common law provinces on the availability of non-purchase-money security interests in household goods. Following earlier codal precedents, enforcement of security interests must generally proceed through the courts.

37 In fairness to the Commission, it must be noted that the Consultative Report contains a much larger number of references to Revised Article 9 and the Ontario Act than did the Consultation Paper, although they are still much smaller than the number of references to the Saskatchewan Act. The Consultative Report also recognises some serious weaknesses in the New Zealand Act, particularly in those areas where the New Zealand Act departs from the Canadian models.

policy choice between alternative models and it would have been helpful if that choice had been made explicit in a greater number of cases.

Apart from the policy choices, English readers will surely also be interested to learn how well the Canadian provincial personal property security legislation works in practice. What are its principal strengths? Its weaknesses? How much litigation has the legislation engendered? Who are the principal users of the registration system? What has been the effect of the abolition of the floating charge and its replacement by a fixed ('attached') security interest with an express or implied licence to the debtor to continue to carry on its business? The Commission rightly assumed that the 50-year tenure of Article 9 in most of the American states and the close to 20 years' experience with PPS legislation in most of the Canadian provinces was sufficient proof of the acceptability and durability of the new chattel security regimes. However, this does not provide sufficient guidance to the questions posed above and I shall endeavour to answer at least some of them in the course of this chapter.

The notice-filing registration system

Understandably, adoption of a notice filing system, in place of the cumbersome and seriously inefficient transactionally based registration requirements for company charges, forms the first part of the Law Commission's recommendations. 'Understandably', because it was the *raison d'être* of the Commission's remit from the DTI[38] and the focus of the Company Law Review Steering Group's Final Report in July 2001.[39] The adoption of a notice-filing system coupled with a central registry, in place of the complex branch registry and exacting requirements of the pre-PPSA regimes, was also the feature that attracted the overwhelming support of the commercial bar in Ontario as far back as 1964 in support of the draft PPS Act prepared by the Catzman Committee.[40] It is therefore not surprising that the great superiority of a notice-filing system also quickly recommended itself to the Law Commission. In 1964, the future availability of an electronic real-time electronic registry system was not as obvious then as its reality is now. Given its introduction in the intervening period, dispensing with transaction filing became even more compelling since transaction filing would have defeated much of the purpose of introducing electronic filing. Notice filing became even more the system of choice when online electronic filing from secured parties' and filing agents' offices became both feasible and readily affordable.

The Law Commission's Consultative Report contains a detailed description of the operation of the proposed English notice-filing system. Nevertheless, there are some significant problems that are not discussed in the report, or not adequately discussed, that warrant examination here in light of Canada's extensive experience. The problems are presented under the following headings in the discussion that follows: (a) what do you file? (b) where do you file? (c) when do you file? and (d) what are the consequences of an error in the financing statement?

38 See Consultative Report, fn 6, para. 1.16.

39 See *Modern Company Law for a Competitive Economy: Final Report URN 01/942* (London: DTI, 2001). See further Consultation Paper No. 164, fn 5, para. 1.12.

40 See further Ziegel 'The draft Ontario Personal Property Security Act' (1966) 44 *Canadian Bar Review* 104, p. 108.

What do you file?

In the North American model,[41] an original financing statement[42] has three essential components comprising (a) the debtor's name and address; (b) the secured party's name and address; and (c) a description or classification of the collateral.[43] Most of the policy issues in Canada, and the very extensive jurisprudence generated by the filing regulations, have revolved around the first and third components. So far as the debtor's name is concerned, describing it correctly becomes of critical importance if the name is the key to an effective search by a third party wishing to determine whether a debtor has given a security interest in the debtor's personal property.

So far as English corporate debtors are concerned, the Law Commission's Final Report envisages that the company will have a unique identifying number allocated to it by the registrar of companies.[44] The assumption will cease to hold true if the debtor is not a registered company[45] and will do so even more if the notice-filing system is expanded to include non-corporate debtors. The Canadian experience is that errors in identifying correctly both corporate and non-corporate debtors' names (but especially the latter) are quite common and provide a fruitful source of contention that the secured party does not have a properly perfected security interest. This in turn has raised a much litigated question whether, in the case of motor vehicle collateral and other collateral required to be identified by a serial number, a correct serial number will cure defects in the description of the debtor's name. The answer turns on the proper construction of the statutory provisions concerning the effect of errors in a financing statement on which appellate courts across Canada have reached conflicting conclusions.[46]

Description of the collateral

In Canada, the provincial PPSAs and supporting regulations distinguish between the description of the collateral necessary to satisfy the writing requirements for the

41 E.g., UCCR 9–502, OPPSA O Reg. 912 as amended.

42 The requirements for the contents of a financing change statement will vary depending on the reasons for the filing of the statement.

43 There may be other components as well depending on the particular jurisdiction. For example, the Ontario regulations require disclosure of the maturity date of the filing and, in the case of a natural debtor, the debtor's birth date. O Reg. 912 as amended, s. 3.

44 See *The Final Report*, fn 7, p. 57, para. 3.103.

45 This also raises the question which conflict of laws rule will apply to determine the validity, perfection and effect of perfection of a security interest given by a debtor. See pp. 129–132 below. Revised Article 9 introduced a new rule for the perfection of security interests in a 'registered organization', that is the organisation's place of incorporation regardless of the type of collateral involved. See Revised UCC 9–307(e) (f). 'Registered organization' is defined in UCCR 9–102(70) as an 'organization organized solely under the law of a single State or the United States and as to which the State or the United States must maintain a public record showing the organization to have been organized.' Opposition has been expressed to Canada adopting a similar rule but, in the writer's opinion, its simplicity has much to commend it. Cuming and Walsh, fn 33, p. 357 *et seq.*

46 See pp. 129–32 below.

attachment of a security interest[47] and the description required in the financing statement.[48] So far as the latter is concerned, there is a basic difference between the Ontario approach and the approach adopted in the other provinces. The Ontario regulations provide for a series of 'collateral boxes' in the financing statement, one or more of which must be ticked off by the secured party. The boxes are labelled, 'consumer goods', 'inventory', 'equipment', 'accounts' and 'other than consumer goods, inventory, equipment and accounts'. If it wishes, the secured party is also free[49] to provide a specific description of the collateral and in practice a secured party will do so if it wants to avoid having to answer queries from third parties about the collateral encompassed in a ticked-off box.[50] The Canadian model law jurisdictions, on the other hand, require a verbal description of the collateral by item, type or class as well as a specific description in the case of serial-numbered consumer goods and, for all practical purposes, serial-numbered equipment.[51]

Obviously ticking off a collateral box is much easier than having to provide an itemised list of collateral where the secured party is not claiming an 'all-asset' security interest in the debtor's collateral. The Ontario system seems to work well in practice and most commercial practitioners and secured parties in Ontario seem to prefer it over the more exacting model law requirements. It is true that searchers in Ontario may need to contact the secured party for more detailed information than is provided for in the financing statement but this is not regarded as a serious problem.[52]

47 See, e.g., OPPSA, s. 11(2)(a), 'a description of the collateral sufficient to enable it to be identified'. The Consultative Report proposes to dispense with any mandatory writing requirement for the security agreement (Consultative Report, fn 6, para. 3.75 *et seq.*) but the reasons given are unpersuasive, i.e., that it will avoid needless litigation whether there is writing and whether it is sufficient. The Canadian experience is that the security agreement is almost invariably reduced to writing where a professional secured party is involved and that problems usually only arise where the secured party is inexperienced and seeks to rely either on an oral agreement or on a reservation-of-title clause in an invoice sent out after the goods have been delivered to a buyer. Op. cit., Ziegel and Denomme, fn 31, pp. 122–3. In the writer's view, dispensing with a writing requirement will not diminish litigation but is more likely to have the opposite effect. If a creditor deems it important enough to bargain for a security interest it should also be prepared to put its claim into writing in fairness to the debtor's other creditors and to enable a liquidator or trustee in bankruptcy readily to establish the position if the debtor becomes insolvent. These important roles of the writing requirement appear to have been overlooked by the Law Commission.

48 See, e.g., O Reg. 912 as amended, s. 3(f).

49 OPPSA, s. 46(3).

50 There is an important exception to the above rule in the case of a motor vehicle classified as consumer goods. O Reg. s. 3(1)(f). In this case, the financing statement must provide a description of the vehicle and its serial number. In the case of non-consumer vehicles, the secured party is free to provide a serial number (s. 3(7)) and has an incentive to do so for vehicles classified as equipment if it wants to be able to enforce its security interest against a bona fide buyer of the vehicle. See OPPSA, s. 28(5).

51 See, e.g., BC Reg 279/90 as amended, ss. 11–13. The doubt arises in the case of equipment because s. 11(1)(c) provides that the collateral must be described in accordance with ss. 12 or 13. However, s. 13 only applies where collateral is described 'other than by serial number', so presumably s. 11(1)(c) is a drafting error.

52 It may not be a serious problem but secured creditors regard it as a nuisance to be required to answer numerous enquiries seeking particulars about the collateral actually claimed by them against the debtor's property. Accordingly the Personal Property Security Committee of the Ontario Bar Association adopted a resolution in 2006 supporting a switch by Ontario from the collateral box identification system to the itemised list system used in the Western

The Consultative Report seemed to favour an intermediate position between the Ontario collateral box system and the model law requirements. However, one cannot be sure since the alternative Canadian approaches were not discussed in the Report. The Report did however stress that both the Commissions and the respondents strongly favoured short-description requirements and the need to avoid verbal prolixity currently found in the abstracts filed under the Companies Act.[53] The Report also mentioned the possibility of resorting to tick boxes for common and easily identifiable categories.[54] However, in its Final Report the Commission changed its policy following consultation because it was feared a short description might mislead searchers as to the true ambit of the security. As the Commission noted, although 'it will add to the volume of any search results this disadvantage is outweighed by the increased accuracy and reliability of the filing'.[55] Should reform be taken up again in the future the Commission might do well to conduct an *in situ* investigation of the comparative merits of the Ontario and model law approaches with respect to collateral description requirements in financing statements.

So far as serial numbered goods are concerned, the Consultative Report adopted a nuanced position.[56] Inclusion of a unique serial number in the financing statement is always optional and failure to include the number will have different consequences. It will not affect the effectiveness of the security interest against an administrator or liquidator. Presumably this class of persons is meant to include execution creditors. If the goods are classified as equipment, a buyer or lessee will take free of the security interest if the financing statement does not include the serial number.[57] It seems that a general filing will also not be sufficient to preserve the secured party's priority over other perfected security interests. This is a more contestable position and especially so where the serial numbered equipment is still in the debtor's hands and involves goods other than motor vehicles. As a matter of policy, one might also consider drawing a distinction between a purchase-money security interest in serial-numbered goods of high unit value, where inclusion of the serial number in the financing statement would be a reasonable requirement, and a non-purchase-money all-asset security interest where requiring a serial number description of the debtor's equipment could be very burdensome.

Where do you file?

This question also has two components. The first component again involves a conflict of laws question and is this: whose law governs the validity, perfection and effects of perfection of a security interest? The Final Report[58] proposed that English law should govern the perfection requirements and the effects of perfection of security interests

Canada PPSAs. The Ontario government has not so far indicated its reaction to the resolution but, since the existing requirements stem from the OPPSA regulations, the changeover will not require an amendment to the Act.

53 See Consultative Report, fn 6, paras 3.124, 3.134 and Draft Regulation s. 47(7)(d).

54 Ibid., para. 3.125.

55 See the Final Report, fn 7, p. 58 para. 3.108; and p. 166 Draft Regulation 6.

56 See Consultative Report, fn 6, paras 3.177–3.179.

57 See Draft Regulation s. 33.4. The Draft Regulations do not address the position in the case of serial-numbered consumer goods. Presumably this was because the Consultative Report did not envisage the new chattel security regime being extended to consumer transactions in the foreseeable future.

58 See the *Final Report*, fn 7, para. 3.258 and Draft Regulation 2.

given by English registered companies regardless of where the collateral is situated. This may be a satisfactory answer if the proposed reforms were limited to the introduction of a notice-filing system for corporate debtors but will surely be inadequate if a British government later decides to adopt a comprehensive chattel security regime that will include unincorporated business debtors and, if the North American precedents are followed, consumer debtors as well. In that event, careful attention would have to be given to the question whether the chosen jurisdiction was the debtor's location or whether the answers would turn on the nature of the collateral, the character of the debtor or both. Similarly, in the case of non-mobile goods, consideration would have to be given to the need for reperfection of the security interest if the collateral was moved from one jurisdiction to another assuming the *lex situs* rule was the applicable choice of law rule governing perfection or reperfection of the security interest.[59]

The 'where do you file' non-conflicts question arises in the case of hybrid collateral (such as fixtures) and specific types of collateral (such as various types of intellectual property interests) for which specialised registries exist. The Consultative Report proposed that the specialised registries law would exclusively govern the perfection requirements in such cases.[60] The solution would not be deemed acceptable in Canada (or the US) where, at least in the case of fixtures, security interests in these types of collateral has for a long time been subject to double-registration requirements if the secured party seeks a fully perfected security interest.[61] It is significant, therefore, that in its Final Report in 2005 the Law Commission changed its mind and recommended that dual registration should take place in this type of situation[62] because 'the cost of double registration is worthwhile for the information and general peace of mind that it would bring'.[63]

When do you file?

This question too is not as simple as may appear at first sight. So far as the Canadian provisions are concerned, a financing statement must be filed in most cases to perfect

59 See further pp. 133–34 below.
60 See Consultative Report, fn 6, paras 2.48–2.51 and 2.89–3.3.342.
61 See OPPSA, ss. 34, 54 and SPPSA, s. 36, and cf. op. cit., Ziegel and Denomme, fn 31, p. 293 *et seq.* The double registration requirement for fixtures appeared already in many of the provincial pre-PPSA conditional sales acts. The early conditional sales legislation contained no special registration requirements for fixtures but treated fixtures subject to a conditional sale agreement no differently from other goods. This approach was changed when provincial courts held that, when the goods became fixtures, conditional sellers also had to comply with the real property registration requirements. The status of intellectual property security interests remains unsettled in Canada and has been the subject of extensive discussion. The position is complicated because both the federal and provincial governments have jurisdiction in the area depending on the nature of the intellectual property interest. See Duggan 'Patent security interests: costs and benefits of alternative registration regimes' (2002) 37 *Canadian Business Law Journal* 165 and cf. Law Commission of Canada, *Leveraging Knowledge Assets – Resolving Uncertainty for Security Interests in Intellectual Property* (Ottawa, 2003).
62 See The Final Report, fn 7, para. 3.41. In the case where the relevant specialist register gave a priority rule then the Law Commission proposed that that specialist registers priority rule should govern; see ibid., p. 87, para. 2.325.
63 Ibid., p. 42, para. 3.40.

a non-possessory security interest in the original collateral.[64] In most cases, a financing statement can be filed even before a security agreement has been concluded by the parties.[65] Failure to file promptly will expose the unperfected security interest to the claims of execution creditors, non-consensual lien holders, trustees in bankruptcy and other creditor representatives, and will subordinate the security interest to financing statements filed in the interim. Importantly, further reperfection requirements must be met or may arise (a) where the collateral is transferred by the debtor to another person with or without the secured party's consent; (b) where the debtor has changes his or its name;[66] (c) where the original registration period has expired;[67] and (d) where the collateral is brought into the PPSA jurisdiction by the debtor for other than transitory purposes.[68] The Draft Regulations in the Consultative Report contain provisions corresponding to situations (c) and (d)[69] but contain no provisions corresponding to situations (a) and (b). Presumably these omissions are due to an oversight. In both cases the integrity of the filing system would be undermined if the secured party were not required to file a financing change statement when it learns of the transfer of the collateral from the debtor to another party or of a change in the debtor's name.

Effect of errors in financing statements

The preceding discussion has shown, at least in the Canadian context and arguably also in the English context based on the Law Commission's proposals and their

64 Of course, possession of the collateral by the secured party, or an agent acting on its behalf, dispenses with the need for a financing statement; see OPPSA, s. 22. The Canadian Acts also provide for temporary perfection periods where it is not practicable to expect the secured party, or possible for it, to file a prompt financing statement; see, e.g., OPPSA, ss. 20(3) and 24. Note too Revised Article 9's expansion of the concept of notional control of the collateral by the secured party as equivalent to actual possession; see UCC R9–314. The control concept also plays an important role in the Consultative Report for perfection of security interests in financial collateral and proceeds of letters of credit. See Consultative Report, fn 6, Part 4; and note the Final Report, fn 7, Part 5.

65 In Ontario, the exception involves consumer goods. In their case, a financing statement cannot be filed before the security agreement is signed by the debtor; OPPSA, s. 45(2). The exception does not appear in the Model Act. The impulse for the Ontario exception is protection of consumers against unauthorised filings by secured creditors. Unlike the Consultative Report, the Ontario Act does not otherwise require the debtor's consent for the filing of a financing statement where the parties have not yet signed a security agreement but did require the secured party to forward the debtor a copy of the filed financing statement; OPPSA s. 46(6). Secured parties found this a burdensome requirement and the Ontario Bar Association PPSL Committee, above n.36, recommended that the requirement be dispensed with. After a long delay, the Ontario government implemented the recommendation in 2006. See Stat. Ont 2006, c.34, Schedule E, s.15(2); in force as of 1 August 2007.

66 For a discussion of the filing difficulties that may arise in the Ontario context from a change in the debtor's name as the result of an amalgamation of the debtor company with another company, see Gray, Denomme and Ziegel 'Perfection under a predecessor debtor name – comment on *Charter Financial Company* v. *Royal Bank of Canada*' (2005) 41 *Canadian Business Law Journal* 431.

67 For cases (a) to (c), see, e.g., OPPSA, s. 48.

68 OPPSA s. 7(2).

69 See Consultative Report, fn 6, Draft Regulations: 52(1) (renewal of filing) and 13(5) (reperfection of foreign security interest).

extension to unregistered debtor companies and unincorporated debtors, that there are numerous opportunities for a secured party to make a mistake in the completion of the financing statement and equally that a perfected security interest may become unperfected often without the secured party's fault and because of circumstances or events beyond its control. What should be the consequences and who should be entitled to complain in this situation?

So far as errors in a financing statement are concerned, the test adopted in most of the Canadian Acts is whether the error would seriously mislead a person searching the registry, not whether the error has *in fact* misled.[70] As a result, even a third party that actually knew of the unperfected security interest before its own interest arose, other than a buyer of the collateral,[71] will be entitled to take free of it.[72] The objective test has been justified on the ground that it is necessary to protect the integrity of the registry system and to avoid expensive litigation over what a complainant[73] knew or did not know beforehand about the security interest. Not surprisingly, Canadian trustees in bankruptcy and other third parties (including competing secured parties) take full advantage of the objective test and allegations that a financing statement is erroneous in a material respect or that reperfection requirements have not been met are very common.[74] It would be surprising if English insolvency administrators

70 See, e.g., SPPSA, s. 43(5). The Ontario test is more convoluted but is essentially the same. The test is whether 'a reasonable person is likely to be misled materially by the error or omission' OPPSA, s. 46(4). The Draft Regulations in the Consultative Report use a different formulation from the seriously misleading test but the result appears to be the same. Draft Regulation 51(1) provides that a financing statement is not effective if it contains a defect, irregularity, omission or error 'such that the existence of the security interest would not be discovered by a reasonable search under regulation 54'.

71 See, e.g., OPPSA, s. 20(1)(c). The other provincial acts have the same provision as does Article 9. Retention of the subjective test for buyers of the collateral has never been seriously disputed in North America and appears to rest in part on the long-standing commercial law doctrine of buyer for value without notice of the seller's defective title and in part on the reasoning that since buyers of the collateral do not need to file in order to acquire good title there is no justification for giving them the benefit of the normal perfection rules. The reasoning is not convincing since other third parties (e.g. execution creditors, trustees in bankruptcy and liquidators) can also attack an unperfected security interest even if they knew of it beforehand. See OPPSA, s. 20(1)(a)(ii) and cf. Draft Regulation 20(3).

72 In Ontario, any residual doubt was put to rest by the Ontario Court of Appeal's decision in *Lambert (Re)* (1994) 119 DLR (4th) 93. See further, op. cit., Ziegel and Denomme, fn 31, pp. 402–3.

73 Or interests represented by the complainant in the case of a creditors' representative.

74 Note however the important exception to the general rule found in OPPSA, s. 30(6). This reads:

> (6) Where a security interest that is perfected by registration becomes unperfected and is again perfected by registration, the security interest shall be deemed to have been continuously perfected from the time of first perfection except that if a person acquired rights in all or part of the collateral during the period when the security interest was unperfected, the registration shall not be effective as against the person who acquired the rights during such period.

For the history and judicial interpretation of the subsection, see op. cit., Ziegel and Denomme, fn 31, §30.5. The model law provinces do not have a comparable provision nor do the Consultative Report Draft Regulations. The closest provision is Draft Regulation 43 giving a secured party a 30-day grace period to correct the inadvertent discharge of a financing statement and to renew a lapsed filing. Note too that the New Zealand PPSA does

were not to pursue the same route in similar circumstances. In fact, in Canada the long-standing assumption is that a trustee in bankruptcy is obliged to challenge a security interest which, in his view, has not been properly perfected.

Whether an error in a financing statement is sufficiently misleading to invalidate the filing will depend: (a) on the searching facilities available under the filing system; and (b) in the case of serial-numbered goods, whether a searcher is expected to search against the serial number as well as against the debtor's name or whether it is sufficient for the challenging party to be able to show that the debtor's name was wrongly given in the financing statement and therefore that the security interest would not be disclosed in a search against the debtor's correct name.

So far as the first question is concerned, in Canada the Ontario searching facilities differ significantly from the protocol adopted in the other PPS jurisdictions. The Ontario regulations permit a specific or non-specific name search for individuals but only provide for a specific search in respect of business debtors.[75] Where the collateral include a motor vehicle a search is also possible under the vehicle's identification number, but the consequences of an error will differ depending on whether the vehicle is classified as a consumer vehicle or not. Under the Ontario system, a specific name search will only disclose a filing under exactly the same name ('exact match'); there is no margin for error.[76] A non-specific search is a little more relenting but not by very much.[77] It is well settled in Ontario that, for purposes of applying the Ontario Act, s. 46(4), a searcher is only required to make a specific name search.[78] In practice, a searcher (especially a searcher interested to test the proper perfection of the security interest) will only make a specific search if the searcher is confident he has the debtor's correct legal name.

The search facilities in the model law jurisdictions differ from the Ontario structure in the following respects. First, the requirement for the inclusion of a collateral's serial number is not confined to the serial numbers of motor vehicles[79] Second, a search against the debtor's name will or may reveal both 'exact' and 'close' matches.[80] However, what is an exact or close match depends on the algorithmic data entry and search protocol adopted by the particular provincial registry and may not correspond to what a non-technical searcher not familiar with the registry's search logic would expect to find.[81] The searcher may therefore find names in the close match list that are as close to the debtor's legal name as names on the exact list.[82] This raises a

not include trustees in bankruptcy and similar Consultative Report Editor representatives among the class of persons entitled to challenge unperfected security interests, seemingly on the ground that they are not prejudiced by the lack of perfection. The omission appears to rest on a misunderstanding of the status of Consultative Report Editor representatives in insolvency proceedings and also overlooks the common law's long-standing hostility to secret liens which has its roots in *Twyne's Case* (1601) 76 ER 809. See further, op. cit., Ziegel, fn 40, pp. 121–2.

75 Op. cit., Ziegel and Denomme, fn 31, §46.11.2.

76 Ibid., §46.12.1.

77 Ibid.

78 See, e.g., *Lambert (Re)* (1994) 119 DLR (4th) 93 (Ont C A), *per* Doherty J. A. construing the meaning of 'reasonable person' in OPPSA, s. 46(4).

79 See, e.g., SPPSA, s .2(1)(a).

80 SPPSA Regs, s. 23(1).

81 For an explanation of the coding and search procedure used in Alberta, see Cuming and Wood, *Alberta Personal Property Security Handbook*, 3rd edn (Calgary: Carswell, 1996), para. 48[2].

82 I am indebted to David Denomme for pointing this out to me. For example, under the Alberta search logic, if the debtor's correct name is 'Smith Builders (Canada) Ltd' 'Smyth

dilemma for the searcher. The searcher is presumably expected to look at all the names appearing in the exact-name column. Must he also examine all the names appearing in the close-match list? The model law regulations do not give a clear answer. So far as England is concerned, the Consultative Report envisaged searching facilities closer to the model law version than to the Ontario version but failed to provide any details. This important ambiguity in the Law Commission's intentions will need to be resolved if the reform proposals are revived in the future since it bears directly on what will be deemed to be a seriously misleading error in the financing statement.

With respect to the second question mentioned earlier (whether a reasonable searcher is free to make a name search or serial number search), the Canadian case law is deeply divided because the courts in Ontario and British Columbia have interpreted the registration rules one way and the courts in Alberta, Saskatchewan and New Brunswick in another.[83] As a result, in Ontario and British Columbia the financing statement will not be deemed to be seriously misleading so long as a serial number search would have disclosed the relevant collateral whereas in the other provinces the mistake will be fatal. The Consultative Report favoured the double-criteria approach, albeit in a nuanced way, but this is an inference rather than being stated explicitly in the Draft Regulations. The latter make it[84] clear that inclusion of the serial number in a financing statement is optional but that failure to include the number will make the security interest unenforceable against a good faith buyer and against a competing security interest.

Conflict of laws issues

Given the United Kingdom's membership of a rapidly expanding common market in Europe and the expansion of investment and trade among the European Union (EU) member states and beyond, one would have expected a commensurate growth in the amount of litigation involving cross-country security interests, particularly where the debtor has become insolvent. However, this does not seem to be true and a transatlantic observer is struck by the paucity of modern UK case law in the movables security conflicts area.[85] Assuming the few reported cases are also an accurate reflection of the practical position, it helps to explain why the Law Commission found no enthusiasm among city solicitors for the adoption of comprehensive

Partners Building Ltd' will appear as an inexact match but 'H. B. Smith Builders Ltd' will not. This is because the system will treat the first two letters H. B. as part of the access code. See op. cit., Cuming and Wood, fn 81, p. 385.

83 The cases are discussed in: op. cit., Ziegel and Denomme, fn 31, §46.11.2; Wood, 'Registration requirements and registration errors under the APPSA' (1996) 27 *Canadian Business Law Journal* 132; and Denomme 'Search again? Names, numbers and reasonable persons' (2001–2) 17 *Banking and Finance Law Review* 1. For the New Brunswick decision, see *Stevenson* v. *GMAC Leasco Ltd* (2003) 227 DLR (4th) 154.

84 Draft Regulation 47(8). Cf. Draft Regulation 54(8) listing optional criteria for searches, including (d) the collateral's unique identifying number.

85 It has been suggested to the writer that the paucity of UK case law is due to the much smaller movement of collateral supplied as a security interest between the UK and the continent. The North Sea and the English Channel are said to constitute a deterrent. The explanation is unpersuasive. For example, the existence of sea borders has not discouraged a large traffic in stolen vehicles between Canada and the West Indies. A better explanation may be the existence of different legal systems between England and the continent.

conflicts rules in the proposed chattel security regime and why the Commission opted in favour of a 'minimalist' position.[86]

This is in striking contrast with the North American experience. Litigation arising out of the removal of goods from one state to another or from one Canadian province to another province was already commonplace in the first quarter of the twentieth century and explains why both the American Uniform Conditional Sales Act, adopted in 1918, and the Canadian Uniform Conditional Sales Act, adopted in 1922, contained provisions requiring the conditional seller to reperfect his security interest if the goods were moved from the original jurisdiction to a new state or province. From the Depression era onwards, the courts in both countries increasingly had to address choice of law questions concerning the law which governed the contractual relations between the parties.[87] In the ensuing discussion, I will first summarise the current North American conflicts provisions and then describe and offer some Canadian perspectives on the Law Commission's proposals.

Canadian and revised Article 9 conflicts provisions

The current Canadian conflicts provisions are substantially identical and are based, with important variations, on the provisions in UCC 9–103 of the 1972 revised version of Article 9.[88] The essential rules are these:

1. The *lex situs* at the time of creation of the security interest governs the validity, perfection and effect of perfection in goods, other than goods classified as equipment or inventory held for lease. The *lex situs* rule also applies to a possessory security interest in documentary intangibles (namely securities, instruments, negotiable document of title, money and chattel paper).[89]
2. If the goods are intended by the debtor to be kept in a jurisdiction other than the jurisdiction where the goods were delivered, the law of the other jurisdiction will apply if the goods are taken to the other jurisdiction within 30 days of the original delivery.[90]
3. A security interest in intangibles, goods classified as equipment or inventory leased or held for lease by the debtor to others, and a non-possessory security interest in securities, instrument, negotiable document of title, money and chattel

86 See Consultative Report, fn 6, para. 3.346. Other important factors also influenced the Commission's decision and these are explained below.

87 The issues were important because, during the Depression, the Prairie provinces in Canada (Alberta, Saskatchewan and Manitoba) adopted legislation imposing severe restrictions on the seller's enforcement rights. The restrictions varied widely and this made it important for the courts to determine which law governed the seller's personal rights. See further: Ziegel 'Conditional sales and the conflict of laws' (1967) 45 *Canadian Bar Review* 284; and Goode and Ziegel *Hire-Purchase and Conditional Sale. A Comparative Survey of Commonwealth and American Law* (London: British Institute of International and Comparative Law, 1965), ch. 11.

88 Some important clarificatory, harmonising and substantive changes in the conflict-of-law provisions in the provincial Acts were recommended to the Uniform Law Conference of Canada in 2003. See R. C. C. Cuming and Tamara M. Buckwold *Reform of the Law of Secured Transactions. Report of the Working Group 2003*, pp. 25–47 (Uniform Law Conference of Canada, Proceedings 2003).

89 OPPSA, s. 5(1).

90 OPPSA, s. 6.

paper will be determined by the debtor's location at the time of the creation of the security interest.[91] For the purposes of this rule, the debtor is deemed to be located at the debtor's place of business if there is one, at the debtor's chief executive office if there is more than one place of business, and otherwise at the debtor's principal residence.[92]

4. A security interest in goods described in rule 1 above that was perfected in the first *lex situs* before the goods were brought into Ontario continues perfected in Ontario if a financing statement is registered in Ontario before the goods are brought into Ontario or if perfection occurs: (i) within 60 days after the goods are brought into Ontario; (ii) within 15 days after the day the secured party receives notice that the goods have been brought into Ontario; (iii) before the date that perfection ceases under the law of the jurisdiction in which the goods were situated at the time the security interest attached.[93] However, even if perfected under the law of the first *situs*, the non-Ontario security interest will be subordinated to the interest of a buyer or lessee who acquires the goods in Ontario as consumer goods in good faith and without knowledge of the prior security interest and before the security interest is perfected in Ontario.[94]
5. Reperfection is also required with respect to mobile goods and other collateral described in rule 3 above if the debtor changes his location to Ontario, the grace periods for reperfection being the same as under Rule 4.[95]
6. The Ontario Act, s. 8 contains rules governing the secured party's enforcement of its security interest. These rules are distinctive to Canada and have no counterpart in Article 9.

New Article 9 has introduced basic changes in the 1972 Code choice of law rules, the same rules that are still reflected in the current Canadian provisions.[96] The most important changes involve separating the law governing the perfection of a security interest from the law governing the effects of perfection or non-perfection. Perfection is governed by the law of the debtor's location, location being carefully defined in terms of the different types of debtors, while the effect of perfection is determined by the *lex situs* in the case of goods, negotiable documents of title, instruments and other intangibles. The bifurcation of the rules governing perfection and the effects of perfection was driven by the drafters' desire to simplify filing requirements for secured parties so that, where the debtor carries on business in several jurisdictions or has several residences, a financing statement will only be required to be filed at the prescribed debtor's location.

91 OPPSA, s. 7(1).
92 OPPSA, s. 7(4). Because of the difficulty of determining a corporate debtor's chief executive office for filing and searching purposes, the OBA PPSL Committee recommended earlier that the test be replaced in Ontario by the jurisdiction of incorporation or organisation of the corporation. A similar change was adopted in new Article 9. The Committee's recommendation was implemented in Stat Ont 2006, c.34, Schedule E, s. 3(2).
93 OPPSA, s. 5(2).
94 Ibid.
95 OPPSA, s. 7(2).
96 For a detailed description of the new rules, see Smith 'An introduction to Revised UCC Article 9 (1999)' in *The New Article 9. Uniform Commercial Code*, 2nd edn, pp. 48–51 (American Bar Association, Section of Business Law 2000).

Law Commission proposals

As previously explained, one of the Law Commission's reasons for not copying the North American conflicts rules was that the City of London solicitors consulted by the Commission saw no need for it and thought that, except with respect to receivables, the existing choice of law rules seemed to work quite well. The Consultative Report also advanced two other reasons.[97] The first was that the North American choice of law rules were premised on the assumption that all the relevant jurisdictions had comparable registration rules for perfection. As the Report noted, this assumption could not be made with respect to the continental European countries, most of which do not have registration requirements for non-possessory security interests. The second reason given in the Report was that the EU Insolvency Regulation[98] required the insolvency administrator to apply the *lex situs* rules to determine the validity and perfection of security given by the insolvent. The effect of this rule was that adoption by the Commission of a different choice of law rule would be a *brutum fulmen* if the debtor became insolvent.

These considerations led the Commission to propose the following 'minimalist' choice of law rules:[99]

1. The Regulations will apply to security interests created by companies registered in England and Wales over any of their personal property, wherever the property is located.
2. The Regulations will also apply to security interests created by companies registered in Scotland and foreign companies over personal property which is: (i) tangible property located in England or Wales; or (ii) other property to which English law will apply under rules of private international law for the purpose of determining questions of perfection and priority.
3. In relation to Scottish and foreign registered companies, a security interest in goods created by such a company and perfected under the law of the jurisdiction where the goods were located at the time of attachment of the security interest will remain perfected when the goods are brought to England for a period of 60 days or before perfection ceases under the prior *lex situs*, whichever is earlier.
4. However, the secured party's security interest under the preceding paragraph is subordinate to the interest of a buyer or lessee of the goods in England and Wales who acquires or leases the goods without knowledge of the foreign security interest and before the security interest is reperfected in compliance with the Regulations.

It is unfortunate that the Law Commission felt obliged to take an insular view of what would be a manageable set of conflict rules because of the general absence of registration requirements for non-possessory security interests among EU member states. This has not inhibited UNCITRAL from adopting more broadly based conflict rules in the UNCITRAL Receivables Convention[100] and in the UNCITRAL Draft

97 See Consultative Report, fn 6, para. 3.345.

98 29 May 2000 OJL 160/1, 30 June 2000.

99 See Consultative Report, fn 6, para. 3.343 *et seq*. and Draft Regulation 13. Note also The Final Report, fn 7, pp. 153–4; p. 162 Draft Regulation 2.

100 See *United Convention on the Assignment of Receivables in International Trade* (New York, 2004), chapter V. Autonomous conflict of laws rules. Art. 30. Law applicable to priority,

Model Rules for Secured Transactions.[101] Moreover, England is not alone in having to determine how much recognition to give to foreign non-possessory security interests where the law of the debtor's location has no registration requirements for perfection of the creditor's security interest. The drafters of Revised Article 9 also had to face the problem. So for a much longer period have the common law provinces in Canada in dealing with Quebec conditional sales since prior to 1994 Quebec had no registration requirements for conditional sales.[102] The issue also arises between US states and Ontario and those Canadian provinces that treat one-year plus leases as security leases where vehicles subject to such leases are brought into the province from an Article 9 state which does not adopt this characterisation. It may be tempting to treat the lessor's interest as unperfected because the US state does not require the filing of a financing statement. However, it may also be unfair because it exposes the lessor to unbargained for risks if the collateral is taken out of the state without the lessor's knowledge or consent and if the lessor's interest can be defeated not only by a bona fide purchaser in the Canadian province but also by other third-party interests.[103] In short, the suggestion that is made here is that states have to be cautious about refusing to recognise foreign security interests because the foreign jurisdiction has no registration requirements. The caveat is appropriate because the forum state may find the shoe on the other foot if it has less exacting perfection requirements with respect to its own collateral and the collateral subsequently become embroiled in extra-state litigation where the sufficiency of those perfection requirements is raised in the foreign court.

The first of the above conflicts rules proposed by the Commission is also open to the difficulty (recognised in the Consultative Report itself) that the assertion that English law applies to the secured transaction may not carry much weight in an EU jurisdiction. This will be true where an EU member state with effective control over the collateral does not recognise England's jurisdiction or if the debtor becomes insolvent and the EU's choice of law rules governing insolvencies comes into play. So far as the second of the Law Commission's proposed rules are concerned, 'tangible property' is not defined in the Consultative Report and, so far as it involves goods, it

namely 30(1). Law of assignor's location governs priority of the right of an assignee in assigned receivable over right of the competing claimant. Subsection 1 is subject to contrary priority rule in insolvency where insolvency commenced in state other than state in which assignee is located. The meaning of 'location' is explained in 'Explanatory Note by UNCITRAL Secretariat on the UN Convention, Part II.F (definition of 'location'), namely state in which the person has his place of business. If assignor or assignee has more than one place of business, the place of business is that place where the central administration of the assignor or assignee is exercised. Art. 5(h). See further Walsh 'Receivables financing and the conflict of laws: the UNCITRAL Convention on the Assignment of Receivables in International Trade' (2001) 106 *Dickson Law Review* 159.

101 See UNCITRAL. *Security Interests. Draft Legislative Guide on Secured Transactions.* Report of Working Group VI (Security Interests) on the work of its fifth session (New York, 22–5 March 2004), Ch. X. Conflict of laws. See further the chapter by Bazinas in the present volume, pp. 456–73.

102 Cf. *Bedard (Re)* (1983) 46 CBR (NS) 172 (Ont SC). (A Quebec conditional seller's interest in a Quebec-based vehicle was deemed perfected when vehicle was taken to Ontario even though Quebec had no registration requirement for perfection of the conditional seller's interest in the vehicle.)

103 This seems to be the effect of Saskatchewan's s. 7(4) deeming the foreign security interest to be unperfected in relation to any interest in the prescribed collateral acquired by a person in Saskatchewan if the extra-provincial jurisdiction does not provide for public registration of the security interest. See further, op. cit., Ziegel and Denomme, fn 31, p. 95.

is not clear how it is meant to be applied to goods which are normally used in more than one jurisdiction.[104] Similarly it is not clear how helpful it is to state that the Regulations will apply to the transaction if English law applies under the English conflict rules given the unsettled character of many of those rules. So far as the third of the above rules is concerned (goods brought into England when subject to a foreign security interest), it is not clear what the rule means in requiring the foreign security interest to have been perfected under the earlier *situs.* Draft Regulation 5(b) seems to envisage some form of public registration but the contrary construction could be argued just as persuasively given the language of Draft Regulation 23(b) dealing with the methods of perfection under Draft Regulation 13. It is also open to question whether the fourth of the proposed conflicts rules (Draft Regulation 13(6)) is not too draconian in allowing a buyer or lessee to acquire the goods in England free of the foreign security interest even though that interest has been perfected by registration or other public notice and regardless of the character of the buyer or lessee in England or the character of the goods.[105]

Treatment of floating charges

Commentators on the Commission's Consultation Paper were quick to point out the Consultation Paper's ambivalent position on the status of the floating charge under the Commission's proposals.[106] On the one hand, in addressing priorities under the proposed notice filing system it was clear that the Commission intended to retain the equitable floating charge[107] since otherwise it would not have been necessary to provide that registration of a floating charge would preclude a subsequent fixed charge from obtaining priority over the floating charge.[108] On the other hand, Part XI of the Consultation Paper, in dealing with the desirability of a restatement of chattel security principles in English law, appeared to favour Article 9's characterisation of when a security interest is deemed to attach.[109] The description was statutory in origin, did not distinguish between different types of security interests, and was incompatible with the distinctive characteristics of the floating charge.

The Commission subsequently made it clear at a public seminar held in September 2003 that it did not mean to retain the equitable floating charge in its proposals for a revised companies' charges regime and this position was confirmed in the Consultative Report.[110] In the writer's view, the Commission was right to embrace – and, it is

104 Cf. OPPSA, s. 7(1)(a)(ii).

105 Cf. OPPSA, s. 5(2), which only extends protection to an Ontario buyer or lessee who acquires the goods as consumer goods. Draft Regulation 13(6) would extend its protection to a British dealer in those goods if the dealer could show it did not actually know of the foreign security interest before making the purchase. The meaning of 'knowledge' is explained in Draft Regulation 10.

106 See: Gullifer 'Will the Law Commission sink the floating charge?' [2003] *Lloyd's Maritime and Commercial Law Quarterly* 125; and McCormack, 'The floating charge and the Law Commission Consultation Paper on Registration of Security Interests' [2003] *Insolvency Law Journal* 2.

107 And arguably also the distinction between common law and equitable fixed charges and liens

108 See the Consultation Paper, fn 5, para. 4.136.

109 Ibid., pp. 291–2.

110 See Consultative Report, fn 6, paras 2.56–2.61.

hoped, unambiguously[111] – Article 9's concept of a security interest as an exclusively statutory construct. Early Ontario judgments had difficulty grasping the radical transformation effected by the Ontario Act and sought to engraft on it some of the pre-OPPSA floating charge features.[112] The efforts only created much confusion and uncertainty and led to the adoption of explicit language in the revised Ontario Act of 1989.[113] This makes it clear that a security interest, 'including a security interest in the nature of a floating charge' attaches when the requisite elements of a security agreement, value, and the debtor acquiring rights in the collateral are satisfied unless the security agreement expressly provides for postponement of the time of attachment. In Canada, the elimination of floating charges as a separate species has had a positive effect in eliminating much of the prior litigation involving the distinction between fixed and floating charges and whether a secured party had succeeded in avoiding some of the negative consequences of a floating charge characterisation. Presumably, the same consequences would follow in England if the Law Commission's proposals were ever to be enacted into law.

Would this provide secured parties with an 'all-asset' security interest in the debtor's property with an undeserved bonanza? In the writer's view, the answer depends on one's perception of which interests presently protected by the floating charge concept deserve to be retained in a PPSA context. It is suggested that there is no economic justification for giving a subsequent secured party priority over an earlier floating charge on the ground that this result follows from the revolving or all embracing character of the collateral.[114] The result clearly does not follow and especially not when the competing secured party does not know whether the earlier security agreement requires the debtor to account for the proceeds of disposition of collateral. Similarly, there is no good reason to confer good title on a buyer of non-inventory assets from a debtor subject to a perfected all-asset security interest if the buyer would not otherwise be protected and assuming the security agreement confers no express or implied powers of disposition.

At the other end of the spectrum, if the new chattel security regime is perceived to be too generous because it leaves no free cushion of assets available on the debtor's insolvency to satisfy the claims of employees and other preferred creditors the priority

111 Ibid., para. 2.58, muddied the waters somewhat by following the clear statement in the preceding paragraph that the new charges regime would create a new type of security interest with the observation that 'under the scheme, any security agreement may permit the debtor to dispose of the collateral free of the security interest without obtaining the secured party's consent at the time'. Some readers may interpret this as a suggestion that the floating charge may be reintroduced through the back door. This surely was not the Commission's intention.

112 See: op. cit., Ziegel and Denomme, fn 31, §11.4; and Day J's judgment in *Crédit Suisse Canada* v. *1133 Yonge St Holdings Ltd.* (1996) 26 BLR(2) 83, reversed on other grounds (1999) 41 OR (3d) 632 (Ont CA), reviewing the earlier case law and the Canadian literature. OPPSA stands for Personal Property Security Act (Ontario).

113 See now OPPSA, s. 1(2)(a).

114 Purchase-money security interests are excluded from this observation and should of course continue to enjoy priority regardless of the scope of a prior security interest given by the debtor. In Canada, it is very common for all-asset security agreements to contain a clause subordinating the security interest to subsequent purchase money security interests given by the debtor. The enforceability of such subordination clauses is expressly recognised in all the Canadian PPS Acts (see, e.g., OPPSA, s. 38 and cf. the Consultative Report, fn 6, Draft Regulation 44), but their interpretation has given rise to considerable conflict when applied to particular facts. See op. cit., Ziegel and Denomme, fn 31, pp. 319–38.

adjustments could be made (as they have been made in New Zealand[115] and in some of the Canadian legislation)[116] without invoking the pre-PPSA distinction between fixed and floating charges.

There is however one important area where the Law Commission's proposals[117] failed to provide desirable clarification. This concerned the scope of the debtor's implied powers under an all-asset security interest to deal with the collateral in the course of its business. The only explicit provisions in the Canadian Acts conferring such ostensible authority on the debtor involve the disposition of *inventory* in the course of the debtor's business.[118] This is clearly too narrow to meet the exigencies of all-asset security interests. Consider the following example. A bank has an all-asset security interest in a telephone company's personal property. The company uses a fleet of vans for use by its workers in carrying on their work. The vans are traded in every two years for new vans. Will the motor vehicle dealer obtain good title to the traded-in vans even though they are subject to the bank's perfected security interest? Must the dealer obtain an express waiver from the bank? The telephone company is not in the business of selling vans so the dealer cannot rely on the 'sale in ordinary course of business' provision in the legislation.[119] Instead, the dealer may be met by the provision in the Ontario Act, s. 25(1) of (also found in the other provincial Acts) that, unless the secured party has 'expressly or impliedly authorised the dealing with the collateral' the secured party's security interest continues in the collateral and also extends to the proceeds.[120] To meet the burden of proof imposed by the subsection

115 See: Consultative Report, fn 6, para. 2.60; New Zealand Receiverships Act 1993, as amended by Receiverships Amendment Act 2001; and Gedye, Cuming and Wood *Personal Property Securities in New Zealand* (2002), Introduction, p. 10.

116 E.g., OPSSA, ss. 30(7) and (8) and SPPSA, s. 31(2). The Ontario provision provides that a security interest in an account or inventory and its proceeds is subordinate to the interest of a person who is the beneficiary of a deemed trust arising under the Ontario Employment Standard Act or under the Pension Benefits Act. However, subsec. (7) does not apply to perfected purchase-money security interest in inventory or its proceeds. See further op. cit., Ziegel and Denomme, fn 31, §30.6. The Saskatchewan section provides that a creditor who receives money or an instrument drawn or made by a debtor and delivered in payment of a debt owing by him to the creditor has priority over a security interest in the money or instrument whether or not the transferee has notice of the security interest at the time of the payment. Other model law jurisdictions have adopted the same or a similar provision. See: Bridge, Macdonald, Simmonds and Walsh 'Formalism, functionalism and understanding the law of secured transactions' (1999) 44 *McGill Law Journal* 567, para. 196; Cuming, 'Second generation personal property security legislation in Canada' (1981–2) 46 *Saskatchewan Law Review* 5, pp. 39–40. Note importantly that although the Saskatchewan section was intended to open up a cushion of free assets from an all embracing general security to enable a debtor to pay its current debts, the provision is not restricted to such cases.

117 And likewise the Canadian Acts.

118 OPPSA, s. 28(1).

119 OPPSA, s. 28(1). All the Canadian Acts have the same provision.

120 Section 25(1) reads:

> Where collateral gives rise to proceeds, the security interest therein,
> (a) continues as to the collateral, unless the secured party expressly or impliedly authorised the dealing with the collateral free of the security interest; and
> (b) extends to the proceeds.

For further commentary, see op. cit., Ziegel and Denomme, fn 31, §25.2.

the dealer would have to show that the bank had given the telephone company express or implied permission to trade in the vans or that the bank was estopped from denying that it had given its permission because the bank had stood by and allowed the trade-ins without raising objections.

Apart from the Supreme Court of Canada's leading decision in *Royal Bank of Canada* v. *Sparrow Electric Corp.*,[121] there is so far surprisingly little appellate authority in Canada on the scope of the implied authority or licence deemed to be vested in a debtor which has given an all-asset security interest in its property.[122] That case also shows the sharply divided opinions to which the question lends itself, influenced as it undoubtedly is by wider policy considerations. In *Sparrow*, the Royal Bank secured a loan to Sparrow with a general security agreement (GSA) covering all or most of Sparrow's present and after-acquired property and governed by Alberta's PPSA together with an assignment of inventory made pursuant to the federal Bank Act, s. 427.[123] Sparrow experienced financial difficulties and the Bank appointed a receiver to enforce its security. The receiver discovered that Sparrow had not been remitting its payroll deductions to Revenue Canada as required by the federal Income Tax Act, s. 153. The receiver obtained court permission to sell Sparrow's assets. An amount from the proceeds of sale equal to the amount owing to the federal government was ordered to be held in trust pending resolution of the competing claims to the money. The Bank claimed priority based on its GSA and its Bank Act security (BAS), both of which entitled it to the proceeds from the disposition of inventory. The federal government's claim was based on the Income Tax Act, s. 227, which created a deemed trust in favour of the Crown in respect of taxes deducted from wages but not remitted to the federal government.

All the members of the Supreme Court agreed: (a) that the Income Tax Act, s. 227(5) did not affect the priority of security interests given by the debtor before the deemed trust arose in favour of the Crown; and (b) that the security interests created under the Alberta PPSA and the Bank Act, s. 427 were specific security interests and not

121 [1997] 1 SCR 411.

122 One exception is *Crédit Suisse Canada* v. *1133 Yonge Street Holdings Ltd* (1998) 41 OR (3d) 632 (Ont CA), reversing on other grounds (1996) 26 BLR (2nd) 282. In *Crédit Suisse* a real estate mortgage in the bank's favour also contained an assignment of the benefit of leases in the building and of the rents payable under the leases. Paragraph 7 of the security agreement provided that 'Until notified to the contrary in writing, the Mortgagor *shall be entitled to*, and the lessee under any lease shall pay the mortgagor, all rents and other amounts then due under such lease and thereafter accruing' (author's emphasis). The Court of Appeal held that paragraph 7 meant that prior to default the debtor was absolutely entitled to retain the rents as its own and that the parties' freedom to fashion the security agreement in accordance with their wishes overrode the secured party's presumptive entitlement to proceeds under OPPSA, s. 25(1)(b). There is earlier Canadian pre-OPPSA authority on the implied powers of sale in ordinary course of a dealer or manufacturer that has given a security interest on its inventory. The leading case is *Dedrick* v. *Ashdown* (1888) 15 SCR 227; and see also Ziegel 'The legal problems of wholesale financing of durable goods in Canada' (1963) 41 *Canadian Bar Review* 54, p. 76 *et seq.*

123 SC 1991, c.46. Section 427 has a long lineage and enables banks incorporated under federal law to take a security interest in described types of collateral as regulated by the Bank Act provisions. The provisions are complex and difficult to interpret and have given rise to conflict with security interests created under provincial PPS legislation. Given the much more modern and comprehensive provincial regimes, there is a widely held belief in Canada that the federal provisions are no longer needed and should be repealed. A recommendation to this effect appears in the *CBAO Submission*, fn 36, p. 38 and Appendix C.

floating charges in the equity sense. However, the members of the court were sharply divided over the question whether the terms of the GSA, authorising Sparrow to continue to carry on its business, conferred an express or implied licence on Sparrow to use proceeds from the sale of its inventory to meet Sparrow's operating expenses, including payment of employee wages and, if there was such a licence, whether it also inured for the benefit of the Crown to the extent that Sparrow had not remitted tax deductions relating to such wages. A provision in the GSA held by the bank provided that 'until default, Debtor may, in the ordinary course of Debtor's business, sell or lease inventory and ... use Money available to Debtor (e) to pay all taxes, rates, levies, assessments and other charges of every nature which may be lawfully levied, assessed or imposed against or in respect of Debtor or Collateral as and when the same become due and payable'.

Justice Gonthier, delivering the minority opinion of three judges, gave a very broad reading to the express and implied licence conferred on Sparrow under the security agreement. In his view, the licence included Sparrow's entitlement to sell inventory to pay wages and to remit wage deductions in the course of its business, and therefore also triggered the deemed trust under the ITA, s. 227(5) in priority to the bank's GSA when Sparrow failed to remit the deductions. Moreover, the deemed trust was ambulatory in character and affected not only the receivables and monies held by Sparrow at the time of the deductions but also the proceeds of the receiver's sale of inventory at the later date. He thought this result was necessary to prevent the bank from reaping the benefit of Sparrow's non-payment of the statutory deductions and its refusing to accept the burden of Sparrow's unlawful action at the time of the receivership.

Iacobucci J, who delivered the opinion of the majority members of the Supreme Court, gave a much narrower reading to the scope of the licence conferred on Sparrow. In his view, the licence only applied where it was actually exercised *and* used simultaneously to discharge an obligation incurred through the exercise of the licence.[124] These conditions, he held, were not satisfied in the present case, first, because the receiver's sale of inventory was not connected to the exercise of the licence and, second, because it was sought to use the proceeds from that sale to satisfy an obligation to the Crown that had been incurred before the receiver's appointment. He also complained that the minority's implied licence theory would create maximum uncertainty in an area of the law where certainty was at a premium, and that the possibility was 'real' (para. 110) that the minority's view would obliterate the PPSA charge against inventory. Apart from Justice Iacobucci's criticisms, it will be noted that the minority's reading of the scope of the licence is even broader than the scope given a floating charge in equity since its effect would be felt even after the debtor had ceased to carry on business. This is unlike a floating charge whose operative effect ceases on crystallisation of the charge.[125]

Nevertheless, it seems reasonable to assume that the same division of opinion that arose in *Sparrow* would be likely to ensue under the Law Commission's proposals

124 [1997] 1 SCR 411, at para. 91ff.

125 For further discussion of the issues in *Sparrow*, see: Davis 'Priority of claims in insolvency: *Royal Bank* v. *Sparrow Electric Corp.* and its aftermath' (1997) 29 *Canadian Business Law Journal* 145; Wood, 'Revenue Canada's deemed trust extends its tentacles: *Royal Bank of Ontario* v. *Sparrow Electric Corp*' (1994–5) 10 *Banking and Finance Law Review* 429; cf. op. cit., Ziegel and Denomme, fn 31, §25.3; Ziegel 'Crown priorities, deemed trusts and floating charges; *First Vancouver Finance* v. *Minister of National Revenue*' (2002) 45 Canadian Bankruptcy Reports (4th) Series 244.

unless some attempt was made to spell out the scope of the implied licence where the debtor had given an all-asset security interest. In my view, the Commission was too optimistic in assuming that the debtor's power under the proposed new regime to dispose of inventory in the normal course of the debtor's business would be sufficient protection for third parties and that the courts would not be under great pressure to imply much broader authority even though the authority was not expressly conferred in the security agreement.

In its *Final Report* the Law Commission recommended as a temporary measure, pending further review, and work, that the distinction between a fixed and floating charge be retained.[126] The issue would then be revisited at a future date when considered along with a general review of insolvency law.[127] However, under their more modest proposals for 'immediate' reform the Commission proposed that a registered floating charge would have priority over any later registrable charge or pledge.[128] They also recommended that the Insolvency Act 1986 be amended to make clear that as against any preferential creditors and the unsecured creditors' fund a floating charge would have priority to the extent of any fixed charges over which it had priority.[129] Finally, it recommended that any charge (fixed or floating) would not have priority over a lien arising by operation of law.[130] A few other minor priority recommendations were made such as: a registered charge would take priority over the claims of execution creditors;[131] a landlord's right to distrain on goods for unpaid rent should take priority over a registered charge;[132] a registered charge would take priority over the right of a local authority to distrain for rates;[133] a transferee (other than a secured party) of property subject to a registered fixed charge would take the property subject to the charge unless the chargee had authorised the transfer;[134] a transferee of property subject to a registered floating charge would take free of the floating charge if the transfer were made in the ordinary course of the transferor's business.[135]

Treatment of quasi-security interests

The Consultative Report informed us[136] that there was substantial support among the respondents for the provisional proposal to include the sale of accounts in the proposed new securities regime but that there remained substantial opposition to the inclusion of title-retaining devices – conditional sales, leases of chattels for more than a year and consignment agreements.[137] Despite this opposition, the Consultative

126 The Final Report, fn 7, p. xi, para. 11.
127 Ibid., p. 73, para. 3.175.
128 Ibid., p. 74, para. 3.180.
129 Ibid., p. 76, para. 3.187.
130 The Final Report, fn 7, p. 76 para. 3.189.
131 Ibid, p. 80, para. 3.204.
132 Ibid., p. 81, para. 3.207.
133 Ibid., p. 61, para. 3.209.
134 Ibid., p. 83 para. 3.218.
135 Ibid., p. 84 para. 3.221.
136 See the Consultative Report, fn 6, at para. 2.85 *et seq.*
137 The Canadian PPS legislation, following Art. 9's lead, also includes an absolute assignment of chattel paper within its scope. See, e.g., OPPSA, s. 2(b). The Consultative Report did not deem it necessary to address this issue because the Commission had already concluded that there was no demand in England for treating chattel paper as a distinctive form of collateral. Ibid., para. 3.25.

Report went on to reaffirm its earlier position and recommended that quasi-securities should be included in the first stage of reform without waiting for the inclusion of unincorporated business debtors in the second stage. However, in its Final Report the Law Commission changed its mind and decided against including retention of title clauses and similar devices in the new registration scheme. This was because the main reason for making such devices registrable was to protect purchasers and it followed that the question should be discussed again in the context of the Law Commission's work on the project of the transfer of title by non-owners of goods.[138] This position only served to highlight the fragmented way in which the reform project was being handled and, perhaps, helps to explain why the UK government eventually decided against any reform of this area.

A Canadian commercial lawyer would have no difficulty endorsing the Commission's original position in wanting to see that title-retention clauses were made registrable and would be surprised to learn that there were conceptual as well as practical reasons for the opposition to the Commission's proposals. His assumption of superiority is unwarranted since the transatlantic observer would be commenting with the benefit of more than a hundred years of Canadian chattel security legislation. The following discussion is therefore divided into two parts. The first part describes the treatment of quasi-securities under pre-PPSA law in Canada and their treatment in the current PPS regimes. The second part of the discussion then addresses the practical and conceptual objections of the English critics and seeks to evaluate their persuasiveness from a Canadian perspective.

Pre-PPSA Canadian position

All the provincial PPS Acts include conditional sale agreements and absolute, as well as security, assignments of accounts and chattel paper. All the Acts, with the partial exception of the Ontario Act, also apply to commercial consignments and to leases of goods for more than a year. The inclusion of conditional sale agreements and absolute assignments of accounts never elicited any opposition for a very simple reason. Conditional sales legislation requiring registration of the conditional sale agreement as a condition of the enforceability of the agreement vis-à-vis third parties[139] has been a feature of Canadian commercial law since the late nineteenth century and was later enshrined in the Uniform Conditional Sales Act (UCSA) adopted by the Canadian Conference on Uniformity of Legislation in 1922.[140]

A general assignment of accounts, whether conditional or absolute, was also subjected to a registration requirement under the Uniform Assignment of Book Debts Act adopted by the Canadian uniformity commissioners in 1928. This initiative was triggered by a section in the Canadian Bankruptcy Act of 1919 invalidating a general

138 See The Final Report, fn 7, p. xiv, para. 21. On the issue of title conflicts, see also the chapter in the present volume by Gullifer, pp. 188–222.

139 The early Ontario legislation also treated the marking of goods with the seller's name as an acceptable alternative to registration. Somewhat puzzlingly, this feature also won the support of the Canadian uniformity of legislation conference in the 1950s in at least some contexts; see further Ziegel 'Uniformity of legislation in Canada – the conditional sales experience' (1961) 39 *Canadian Bar Review* 165, pp. 185–6.

140 See op. cit., Ziegel, fn 139.

assignment in bankruptcy unless the agreement had been registered under applicable provincial legislation.[141]

On the other hand, a lease of goods, regardless of its term and commercial consignment of goods were not subject to registration requirements and this was probably the reason why these forms of agreement were omitted from the initial Ontario Personal Property Security Act of 1967. However, it soon became clear that without effective statutory guidelines the Ontario courts would be swamped with litigation challenging financial type leases on the ground that they amounted to disguised conditional sales. Accordingly, the Uniform Personal Property Security Act sponsored by the Canadian Bar Association in 1972 (UPPSA 1972) covered a lease of goods for more than a year as well as commercial consignments.[142] The revised draft Ontario bill prepared by the Catzman Committee in 1984 included both these features but, regrettably, they were omitted by the Ontario government from the enacted bill of 1989. Efforts by the Ontario commercial bar to persuade the government to reinstate the provision for one-year plus leases have only recently proven successful.[143] In the interim, Ontario judicial decisions bridged the gap by the courts' ready willingness to find that financial leases amount to security agreements under the Act.[144]

Canadian experience with inclusion of quasi-securities

On the whole, Canadian experience with the inclusion of quasi-securities has been very favourable. Given the pre-PPSA conditional sales legislation, there was never any opposition to including conditional sales in the new legislation.[145] An absolute assignment of accounts (broadly defined in all the PPS Acts but excluding documentary intangibles) fell into the same category with one important exception. The prior assignment of book debts legislation excluded from its reach debts due at the time of

141 The provision is still in effect. See Bankruptcy and Insolvency Act, Rev Stat Can 1985, c 85 as amended, s. 94.

142 See Ziegel 'The new provincial chattel security regimes' (1991) 70 *Canadian Bar Review* 681, p. 688.

143 Stat. Ont. 2006, c.34, Sched. E, s. 2. In force as of 1 August 2007. See also Cameron, 'Ontario Personal Property Security Act – Bill 152' (2007) 45 *Canadian Business Law Journal*.

144 For the details see op. cit., Ziegel and Denomme, fn 31, pp. 57–63. The reintroduction of one year-plus leases in the Ontario Act was also strongly endorsed in the 1998 report of the CBAO PPSL Committee. See Canadian Bar Association – Ontario, *Submission to the Minister of Consumer and Commercial Relations Concerning the Personal Property Security Act* (Toronto, November 1998) ('CBAO 1998 Submission'). The Committee did not include commercial consignments in its recommendations because some members were concerned that the registration requirements would create hardship for professional artists who consign their works of art to art galleries for sale. Technically speaking, the artists might be treated as commercial consignors because they were acting in the course of a business. Nevertheless, most artists would likely be unaware of the perfection requirement and would not be well situated to comply with it if they did know of the requirement.

145 A difficulty that arose in Ontario, but which basically had nothing to do with the inclusion of conditional sale agreements in the PPS legislation, was protracted litigation over whether a secured party was entitled to recover a deficiency in the conditional sale price on repossession and sale of the collateral following the buyer's default. The Ontario courts were for a long time beguiled by a judicially crafted rule under the old conditional sales legislation holding that a seller was not entitled to recover the deficiency unless it was expressly provided for in the agreement. See op. cit., Ziegel and Denomme, fn 31, pp. 531–2.

the assignment from specified contracts. This exclusion is not retained in the PPS Acts. Similarly the Acts contain no provision comparable to old UCC Article 9–302(1)(e) dispensing with the need to file a financing statement in respect of an assignment of accounts which does not alone or with other assignments to the same assignee transfer a significant part of the outstanding accounts of the assignor.[146]

By and large Canadian financial lessors seem to have adjusted well to the inclusion of one year-plus leases in the Acts of those provinces that have adopted the requirement. In Ontario, which only adopted the requirement in December 2006, financial lessors filed anyway out of a strong sense of prudence and awareness of the proclivity of Ontario courts to equate financial leases with security leases. Part V of the provincial Acts, dealing with enforcement of security interests, does not apply to true leases. This means that in case of dispute the courts may be called upon to determine: (a) whether the deficiency clause common in financial leases is a penalty clause; and (b) how the lessor's damages are to be assessed if the deficiency clause is not enforceable.[147] However, the number of such cases has been small and suggests that Canadian lessors are not keen to litigate the issues and prefer to have their leases treated as security leases if they seek to recover a deficiency after repossession and sale of the goods.

The provisions governing commercial consignments have also attracted very little litigation in the PPS provinces that have adopted them. This may be because commercial consignments have dropped in importance as a form of inventory financing or because a non-perfecting consignor prefers to take its lumps than to throw good money after bad if a consignee becomes bankrupt before the consignor can recover the consigned goods. In any event, this writer is not aware of protests by commercial consignors of the impropriety of their being treated as deemed secured parties and requiring them to file a financing statement as a condition of the recognition of their claims.

English grounds of opposition to inclusion of quasi-securities

This leads me to consider the grounds of opposition in England to the inclusion of quasi-securities. The Consultative Report did a good job of describing the practical advantages and disadvantages of the inclusion for conditional sellers and lessors,[148] and presumably the same inventory could be drawn up for sales of accounts and commercial consignments. It is quite understandable why commercial actors whose transactions have hitherto wholly fallen outside the reach of the company charges regime should now object to being thrust into it. The answer that they are the victims of functional considerations may not cut much ice with the actors but it would strike most Canadian observers as highly persuasive. On both sides of the Atlantic, there are powerful arguments for the proposition that financing agreements serving similar

146 Draft Regulation 4(1)(d) in the English Law Commission's *Final Report*, fn 7, p. 164, excludes the assignment of a *single* account or promissory note to an assignee in full or partial satisfaction of a pre-existing indebtedness. This goes a substantial distance to meeting the objection to the over-inclusiveness of the Canadian provision but it is open for consideration whether it goes far enough.

147 For the details see: op. cit., Ziegel and Denomme, fn 31, §64.5; and *Keneric Tractor Sales* v. *Langille* [1987] 2 SCR 440.

148 See the Consultative Report, fn 6, pp. 43–48. Note also The Final Report, fn 7, pp. xiv para. 21 (title retention) and 104–115 (receivables).

purposes should be treated alike for purposes of perfection, to protect third parties, and to avoid expensive and wasteful litigation.

Nevertheless, there are respected academics (not all English academics)[149] who continue to argue that it is conceptually unsound to confuse true security interests with deemed security interests. To do so, in their minds, is to commit the cardinal sin of confusing the diametrically opposing concepts of 'I own' and 'I owe'. Because they are conceptual purists, the critics of Article 9 and its Canadian counterparts also object to a functional test being applied to the scope provisions of the Canadian and American chattel security provisions.

In my view, the objections are misplaced. Take for example the objections to treating buyers in a conditional sale agreement and lessees in financial leases as the beneficial owners of the equipment or whatever. The critics seem to view ownership concepts as abstract propositions unrelated to their practical impact and the actual terms of the agreement. About a hundred years ago, in his magisterial work on the US law of sale of goods, Samuel Williston argued that a conditional sale was merely a short form of chattel mortgage because most of the risks and benefits of ownership were with the buyer.[150] The same observation could be made about the English-style hire-purchase agreement and most financial leases.

It is true the same argument cannot be made as persuasively about commercial consignments and a sale of accounts, although much will surely turn on the terms of the agreement.[151] However, this does not dispose of the functional argument in favour of including quasi-securities in chattel security legislation – that these type of agreements create the same types of ostensible ownership problems as do true security

149 For the English critics, see in particular: Davies 'The reform of English personal property security law: functionalism and Article 9 of the Uniform Commercial Code' (2004) 24 *Legal Studies* 295; and McCormack 'Quasi securities and the Law Commission Consultation Paper on security' [2003] *Lloyds Maritime and Commercial Law Quarterly*, pp. 80–94. For a broader critique involving Canadian and Australian scholars as well as an English scholar, and examining generally the strengths and weaknesses of the Article 9 and PPSA-type functional approaches, see Bridge, Macdonald, Simmonds and Walsh 'Formalism, functionalism and understanding the law of secured transactions' (1999) 44 *McGill Law Journal* 567.

150 See: *Williston on Sales*, revised edition (Rochester, NY, Lawyers Co-operative Pub. Co., 1973–4), §579d; and cf.: Vold 'The divided property interest in conditional sales' (1959) 68 *Yale Law Journal* 839; and Goode and Ziegel, *Hire-Purchase and Conditional Sale*, ch. 14; *Conceptual analysis of Conditional Sale and Hire-Purchase Agreements* (London: BIICL, 1965). The same observation holds true of English-style hire-purchase agreements and most financial leases. Nevertheless, even in Canada, the old conceptual arguments continue to raise their heads outside the PPS realm. See, e.g., *Daimler Chrysler Financial Services (Debts) Canada Inc.* v. *Mega Pets Ltd* (2002) 212 DLR (4th) 41 (BCCA), criticised in Ziegel 'Conditional sales and superpriority Crown claims under ITA s 227' (2002) 38 *Canadian Bankruptcy Reports* 161.

151 In Canada, although securitisation of receivables has been a major activity for 20 years, there appears so far to be only one significant decision testing the characterisation of the transaction, and in that case the sale characterisation was upheld. See *Metropolitan Toronto Police and Widows and Orphans Funds* v. *Telus Communications Inc* (2003) 30 BLR (3d) 288 (Ont S C), reversed on other grounds (2005) 5 BLR (4th) 251 (Ont CA). The trial court in this case had no difficulty distinguishing on the facts between a security sale of the receivables and an absolute sale. The provincial PPS legislation was not involved and the characterisation issue arose as a question of interpretation of bonds issued by Telus to investors and of Telus' entitlement to redeem the bonds by raising funds from the securitisation of its receivables without breaching the terms of the bonds.

agreements and that third parties need just as much a mechanism for determining the true position in one case as in the other, particularly given the fine line that often separates the quasi-security from its true security counterpart. The ostensible ownership concern has deep historical roots starting with *Twyne's Case* in 1602[152] and encompassing the reputed ownership doctrine, first enacted in 1623[153] and only repealed by omission in 1986,[154] the long series of Factors Acts in England and overseas, and estoppel provisions such as those in section 25 of the English Sale of Goods Act.[155] The fact that some of these provisions and doctrines only inure for the benefit of good faith buyers does not detract from the fact that they trace their origins to a common concern and an attempt to allocate risks among competing parties.

It is also true that civil law jurisdictions such as Quebec that have recently modernised their chattel security rules,[156] and such civil law Article 9-inspired model laws as that found in the EBRD model law,[157] have either excluded conditional sales and financial leases from the scope of their provisions or subjected them to separate registration requirements.[158] However, it is not the writer's impression that maintaining conceptual purity through this segregation has simplified commercial transactions or made it easier for third parties to ascertain the status of property being offered as security. In fact, the Quebec experience points in the opposite direction.[159]

152 (1602) 3 Co Rep 306.

153 By 21 Jac 1, c19.

154 I.e., in the Insolvency Acts of 1985 and 1986. See Fletcher *The Law of Insolvency* (London: Sweet & Maxwell, 2nd edn, 1996), p. 208.

155 These provisions also appear in the Canadian provincial sale of goods acts and deal with the effect of a seller remaining in possession of the goods after they have been sold to a buyer and of a buyer being entrusted with possession of goods before title has passed to the buyer.

156 See fn 36.

157 See Ziegel 'The EBRD Model Law on secured transactions – some Canadian observations' in (eds) Basedow, Hopt and Kotz, *Festschrift fur Ulrich Drobnig zum siebzigsten Geburtstag* (Mohr Siebeck 1998), p. 209.

158 For Quebec, see op. cit., Payette, fn 36, p. 218, §686 (*ventes a tempèrament*), p. 691 (*le crédit-bail*) and p. 692 (*la vente a reméré*). Note also importantly that the Capetown Convention on International Interests in Mobile Equipment (Capetown, November 2001) covers conditional sale and leasing agreements as well as conventional security interests. See Convention, chapter I, Art. 1(j) (definition of 'debtor') and Art. 2, and see further Sir Roy Goode *Convention on International Interests in Mobile Equipment and Protocol thereto on Matters Specific to Aircraft Equipment, Official Commentary*, para. 15(1) (Unidroit, September 2002). It is significant that that the Convention, like the Quebec Civil Code, greatly complicated its treatment of security interests by insisting on distinguishing between true security interests and quasi-security interests, but at least both instruments recognised the need to treat conventional security interests and quasi-security interests alike for perfection and other purposes.

159 See *Lefebre* (*Trustee of*) (*Re*); *Tremblay* (*Trustee of*) (*Re*) (2004) 244 DLR (4th) 513 (SCC) and *Ouellet* (*Trustee*) (*Re*) (2004) 244 DLR (4th) 532 (SCC). The first of these cases involve leases of motor vehicles from motor vehicle dealers that were assigned to finance companies. The leases were not published as required under Art. 1852 of the Quebec Civil Code with the result that the leases could not be set up against third parties as provided for in Art. 241 of the Code. In the second case, the debtor bought a mobile home and automobile from a dealer under an instalment sale and the agreement was assigned to a bank. The bank failed to register the instalment sale and assignment as provided for in Art. 1749. In both cases the debtor became bankrupt and the issue was whether failure to register the agreements precluded the assignees from asserting their claims against the trustee in bankruptcy. The Supreme Court of Canada, reversing the Quebec Court of Appeal, held that the assignees

The critics also object that including quasi-securities does not resolve issues arising from the non-security aspects of the parties' relationship, such as the measurement of damages where the lessor has terminated a true lease because of the lessee's breach, or the conceptual difficulties presented by avoiding the interest of a lessor that has failed to perfect its interest in favour of the lessee's creditors and other third parties claiming under the lessee.[160] In the author's view, these and similar objections are quite unpersuasive given the fact that it is a well-known drafting technique to deem certain transactions to be what they are not by traditional standards for the purpose of achieving a broader policy goal. It is also objected that by introducing the concept of a purchase-money security interest and giving it priority status over non-purchase-money security interest, Article 9 and progenies have reintroduced the familiar conditional sale through the back door. This reasoning is surely seriously flawed. What Article 9 has done is to extract from conditional sales, and similarly from purchase-money loans, the special feature that entitles them to priority treatment vis-à-vis other secured parties. The conferment of priority has nothing to do with the locus of title (as is obvious in the case of a purchase-money loan) but everything to do with the fact that the secured party has made it possible to acquire new and identifiable assets to add to its current inventory of assets.

A still more serious flaw in the reasoning of opponents to including quasi-securities in the new company's charges regime is that they fail to explain why *any* type of non-possessory security interest given by a company should be subject to a public notice requirement. If the answer is that third parties need to know the correct position to avoid being misled in their dealings with the debtor, the opponents must explain why the ostensible ownership problem does not apply just as much to quasi-securities in common commercial use and presently not covered in the Companies Act registration scheme as it does to company charges.

Extension of new regime to unincorporated businesses and consumers

Unincorporated businesses

It has long been recognised in commercial circles in England that unincorporated businesses are badly handicapped in securing finance for their enterprises because of

were not precluded from doing so. The court reasoned that the new Quebec Civil Code carefully distinguished between the newly created movable hypothec and equipment leases and instalment sales and that, while failure to register a hypothec precluded the secured party from asserting its security interest against a trustee in bankruptcy, this was not true of equipment leases and instalment sales governed by different provisions of the Code. In the latter cases the lessor and the seller and their assignees retained title to the goods and the trustee was in no stronger position that the debtor. The trustee would only be able to impeach the non-security transactions if that right were expressly conferred on him by Code and that was not true in the present cases. The court distinguished its earlier decision in *Giffen (Re)* [1998] 1 SCR 91, in which the court had upheld the right of a trustee in British Columbia to impeach an unperfected leasing agreement between a debtor and a financial lessor, on the ground that the British Columbia Personal Property Security Act expressly included the trustee in bankruptcy among the persons against whom an unperfected security interest was unenforceable and because the BC legislation treated leases for more than a year as a security interest.

160 See *Giffen (Re)* [1998] 1 SCR 91.

the obsolete and draconian character of the Bills of Sale Acts of 1878 and 1882 which apply to security interests on existing and future personal property granted by individuals. As a result, business persons have been forced either to incorporate in order to escape the bills-of-sale restrictions and to take advantage of the much more liberal charges regime available to companies or to restrict their secured financing to title-retaining devices such as hire-purchase agreements, finance leasing and conditional sale agreements.

Not surprisingly, the Law Commission found this discriminatory treatment of unincorporated business unacceptable[161] and proposed that unincorporated business persons should be included as debtors in any new securities regime and that the proposed new rules apply alike to companies and to unincorporated businesses. The consultees apparently fully endorsed both these proposals and were anxious that if possible unincorporated business be included in the first round of legislation. However, practical difficulties and the sheer scope of the reform project meant that in its Final Report the Law Commission was obliged to limit their recommendation to registered companies and Limited Liability Partnerships.[162] The Law Commission hoped that if its recommendations, contained in the Final Report,[163] were later implemented the Commission could then review the situation with a view to applying its recommendations at a later date to unincorporated businesses and consumers. Sadly, neither of these hopes has been realized and the question of the applicability of PPSA reforms to different types of debtor/creditor will have to be addressed once again when the issue of law reform is raised.

Canadian lawyers can readily identify with the English problems in light of Canada's own antiquated bills-of-sale legislation prior to the adoption of the PPS Acts. The provincial bills-of-sale legislation was not consumer oriented and imposed no restrictions on the types of goods that might be offered as security. However, the legislation was heavily encumbered with burdensome registration, execution and affidavit requirements which made them a ready target for bankruptcy trustees if the debtor became insolvent.[164] As in England, a common solution was for the unincorporated business to incorporate as a company to take advantage of the more favourable financing and registration regimes available to companies under the English-style companies Acts or, in the provinces that had a different corporate law regime, by resorting to the corporations securities registration Acts and their simplified registration requirements.[165]

161 See: Consultation Paper No. 164, fn 5, Part IX; Consultative Report, fn 6, paras 2.70–2.81.
162 See The Final Report, fn 7, pp. 14–18, pp. 34–5 and p. 146 para. 6.2.
163 See The Final Report, fn 7, Appendix A, p. 158 *et seq.*, for the draft reform regulations proposed by the Law Commission.
164 Op. cit., Ziegel, fn 40, p. 106.
165 Before the reform of provincial companies legislation in the 1970s, about half the provinces followed the English method of incorporation by memorandum and articles of association and the other half by issuance of letters patent by a provincial authority. The letters patent corporations acts did not deal with registration of company charges. This aspect was addressed by corporation securities registration acts, legislation that, in Ontario's case, was first adopted in 1932; see op. cit., Ziegel, fn 40, p. 17. The CSRA's formal requirements were much simpler than those under the bills of sale act, the filing was valid in perpetuity, and there was a central registry office. For industry-inspired reasons, the first OPPSA excluded corporate securities from its reach. This created confusion because of a difference of judicial opinion about the definition of debenture for the purposes of the exclusion. Because of this the CSRA was repealed in 1989 and corporate securities were fully integrated in the OPPSA. See op. cit., Ziegel and Denomme, fn 31, §§2.1.3–2.3.1.

All this now belongs to Canadian legal history. None of the Canadian PPS Acts distinguishes between unincorporated and incorporated businesses, except with respect to the completion of financing statements, and the integration has given rise to no reported difficulties. It would be fair to claim that commercial lawyers old enough to remember the pre-PPSA complexities would include the integration of security interests of incorporated and unincorporated debtors as one of the great accomplishments of the PPS legislation.

Consumer debtors

As has long been recognised on both sides of the Atlantic, the treatment of consumer transactions raises a very different range of problems. The major issues here are not so much protection of creditors against undisclosed encumbrances and the determination of priorities among competing security interests as the need to protect consumers from overreaching sellers and lenders. The English Law Commission only considered the question of consumers and PPS reform in its first Consultation Paper in 2002. Time constraints and the practicalities of implementing law reform associated with the question of general reform of UK company law (since the issue of PPS reform originally arose out of the DTI Company Law Review of 1998–2001)[166] meant that the later two Papers/Reports issued by the Law Commission did not deal with this issue to any significant degree. The Consultation Paper[167] subsumed the main consumer problems under the following headings: (a) what restrictions should be imposed on the availability of consumer goods to serve as security interest? (b) should there be filing requirements to perfect a non-possessory security interest in consumer goods? (c) if there is a filing requirement, how will it affect consumer buyers of consumer goods with or without knowledge of the prior security interest. In the light of Canadian experience, a Canadian observer would suggest that these questions do not exhaust the range of issues and that, when a British Parliament is eventually ready to contemplate including consumer transactions in a new chattel security regime, there are other issues that should be addressed as well. Some of these issues will be briefly adverted to in the concluding section of this part of the chapter.

Restrictions on security interests in consumer goods[168]

The generally accepted starting point for answering this question, following the precedent of the 1882 bills-of-sale legislation, is that after-acquired goods should be wholly out of reach of a consumer security interest. The Ontario Act, following old Article 9, relaxes the prohibition slightly by exempting consumer goods acquired by the debtor within ten days after the secured party has given value.[169] The embargo

166 On the matter of the Company Law Review, see John de Lacy (ed.), *The Reform of UK Company Law* (London: Cavendish, 2002). Note in particular ch. 15 for the issue of company charge reform pre-Law Commission.

167 See generally the Consultative Paper, fn 5, p. 232, para. 10.22 *et seq.*

168 A more or less standard definition of consumer goods defines them as 'goods that are used or acquired for use primarily for personal, family or household purposes'; see OPPSA, s. 1(1) and cf. Rev. Art. 9–102(23). No definition appears in the Draft Regulations, because they are only intended for corporate debtors.

169 See OPPSA, s. 12(2)(b).

on the use of acquired-property clauses appears to be based on the premise that a consumer should be left with at least the possibility of a cushion of assets free from the secured lender's grasp. It may be suggested however that the same goal can be achieved more cleanly by disallowing non-purchase-money security interests on consumer goods exempt from execution by a judgment creditor or seizure by a trustee where the debtor has become bankrupt.[170]

Apparently the Diamond and Crowther Reports were opposed altogether[171] to allowing non-purchase-money non-possessory security interests in consumer goods, other than motor vehicles and similar high-priced items. The reasoning was that such goods have no commercial value and that a lender is more interested in the *in terrorem* effect of such security interests against a defaulting debtor than in the prospects of a meaningful realisation if the goods are seized. The Consultation Paper[172] adopted the position that the market has changed significantly over the past 25 years and that many average British income householders now owned expensive electronic and computer equipment that they should be free to use as collateral if they wished. The Report did not, therefore, endorse a blanket prohibition on the availability of existing consumer goods as collateral.

In the writer's view, the availability of consumer goods to serve as collateral cannot be divorced from other aspects of consumer credit regulation and the legitimation of the role of consumer lenders for lower and middle income borrowers. There is considerable evidence that the use of consumer credit of all types has expanded rapidly in the United Kingdom over the past 20 years[173] and that consumer loan companies and 'payday' lenders making short-term loans to low-income wage earners on the security of their next pay cheque are gaining a significant foothold. It needs also to be emphasised that the use of consumer goods as collateral for non-purchase loans is only part of a wider question of the types of collateral that should be available (or prohibited) for consumer loans. These issues were not addressed in the earlier reports and are not addressed in the Consultation Paper.

Filing (perfection) requirements and security interests in consumer goods

There is no unanimity in legislative rules among existing Article 9-type regimes with respect to this question and the Consultation Paper invited respondents' views on a series of alternative questions.[174] Section 309(1) of Revised Article 9 confers automatic perfection without filing on purchase-money security interests in consumer goods, the reasoning being that that the debtor's creditors will usually assume that consumer goods are subject to an existing lien or will in any event not look to such

170 Several of the Canadian provinces have adopted this solution. Another approach is that adopted in §522(f)(1)(B) of the US Bankruptcy Code allowing the debtor to avoid a non-purchase-money non-possessory lien in household furniture, professional books, tools of the trade and similar items excluded from the bankrupt's estate. See further Ziegel *Comparative Consumer Insolvency Regimes. A Canadian Perspective* (Oxford: Hart Publishing, 2003), pp. 25–6.

171 See Consultation Paper No. 164, fn 5, para. 10.27.

172 Ibid., paras 10.40–10.45.

173 And with it also the amount of over-indebtedness among British consumers. See op. cit., Ziegel, fn 170, ch. 5.

174 See Consultation Paper No. 164, fn 5, para. 10.50.

goods to satisfy their claims. However, the basic rule is subject to an important exception with respect to consumer goods regulated by statute or treaty as described in UCC 9–311(a). Security interests in automobiles will typically be covered in certificate of title legislation for motor vehicles.[175] It will also be noted that the automatic perfection conferred by UCC 9–309(1) does not extend to non-purchase-money security interests; those are still required to be perfected in the prescribed manner.

So far as the perfection requirements are concerned, the Canadian PPS Acts do not distinguish between consumer goods and other types of collateral; both are subject to perfection requirements. However, as will be seen, the non-Ontario Acts deal differently with the position of consumer buyers of consumer goods subject to a prior security interest. The New Zealand Act follows the Canadian Acts in requiring perfection by filing in non-possessory security interest in consumer goods.[176]

Protection of consumer buyers of consumer goods

The various common law jurisdictions also differ in their treatment of a consumer who buys consumer goods which are subject to a perfected security interest. UCC 9–320(2) protects the consumer buyer from the prior security interest if they acquire the goods for value without knowledge of the security interest and the goods are intended primarily for the buyer's personal, family or household use, *and* if the purchase is made before there has been a filing covering the goods. The Saskatchewan policy, on the other hand,[177] and that of the provinces following the Saskatchewan model, is to protect a consumer buyer or lessee of consumer goods if certain conditions are satisfied. The conditions are that the buyer or lessee acquired or leased the goods without knowledge of the prior security interest, regardless of whether the security interest had been perfected by registration, and that the purchase price does not exceed C$1,000 or, that the market value of the lease does not exceed the same amount. The Ontario Act differs from the Saskatchewan model in that it confers no special protection on consumer buyers of consumer goods except where the goods are brought into Ontario from another jurisdiction while subject to an extra-provincial perfected security interest and before the interest has been perfected in Ontario.[178]

What should we make of these diverse approaches to a common problem? In Canada, it is unusual for a secured party holding a security interest in low priced consumer goods to go to the trouble and expense of filing a financing statement, but

175 The Canadian provinces do not have certificate of title legislation for motor vehicles but rely on the PPS registries to provide interested parties with up-to-date information on outstanding consensual and non-consensual, non-possessory security interests. The information is readily available by a search against the motor vehicle's identification number. In Ontario the seller of a used motor vehicle, other than a registered motor vehicle dealer, is also required to provide the buyer with a 'used vehicle information package', which will include details of any outstanding security interests. See further, op. cit., Ziegel and Denomme, fn 31, §(43.1).

176 See Consultation Paper No. 164, fn 5, para. 10.48.

177 See SPPSA, ss. 30(3) and (4). Fixtures are excluded from the Saskatchewan provision, although there appears to be an inconsistency between subsecs 30(3) and 30(4) of the Act. The New Zealand Act follows the Saskatchewan precedent except that the upper limit of the purchase price for the protected acquisition is NZ$2,000.

178 See OPPSA, s. 5(2)(c).

this is not where the problem lies.[179] The reported Canadian cases indicate that conflict among competing claims is most likely to arise with respect to motor vehicles and other high unit items with serial numbers. This raises the question whether a consumer buyer should be protected because he is making a private purchase and the price is so modest (say, C$1,000 – approximately £400 in British currency) that it is not reasonable to expect him to make enquiries about existing liens against the goods. It is common knowledge in Canada that motor vehicles are frequently subject to a security interest and that if the buyer of a used vehicle wants to ensure that the vehicle is lien free, he should either buy from a car dealer or make a search at the provincial registry.[180] The case therefore for protecting the buyer even of a low-cost vehicle is weak.[181] It is surely stronger for the consumer buyer of other low cost used goods though even there one must worry about the incentives for skulduggery which a market overt-type rule may provide to dishonest debtors and thieves. At a minimum one would like some hard evidence of what is happening now in common law jurisdictions with a thriving consumer credit market and private trade in used consumer goods and how much of an impact current *nemo dat* rules exert either way.

Enforcement of the security interest

The drafters of Article 9 understood well that an integrated chattel security regime had to include rules for the enforcement of the security interest on a debtor's default if the goal of a functionally oriented scheme governing all the stages in the life of a security agreement was to be realised. That view was also shared by the drafters of the PPS Acts in Canada. As a result, both Article 9 and the Canadian Acts contain a separate part (Part V in the Canadian Acts, Part VI in Revised Article 9) articulating the rules for the enforcement of a security interest.

The importance of these rules needs to be emphasised. At common law and in equity the enforcement rules varied – and often varied fundamentally – depending on the nature of the security interest.[182] Frequently the legislature added glosses of its own or, in some cases (as in the case of conditional sales), adopted statutory rules substantially altering the common law regime. Quasi-securities like the conditional sale, hire-purchase agreement and financial leases greatly complicated the remedial picture because conceptually they were simply contracts entitling the creditor at common law to cancel the agreement if the debtor was in default and to sue the debtor for damages for breach.

However, it was not damages for breach of the debtor's obligations that the seller or lessor sought but the right to claim any deficiency in the price after repossession and resale of the goods or, in the case of leases, loss due to depreciation in the value

179 However, the writer was told some time ago of a University of Toronto student who bought a computer through EBay and was then required to return it to a finance company holding a perfected security interest, because the finance company was able to trace the computer by its serial number!

180 See also fn 175 above with respect to the special protection afforded buyers of used motor vehicles in Ontario.

181 Consultation Paper No.164 seems to envisage protecting the used vehicle buyer even where he knows of the prior security interest; see Consultation Paper No. 164, fn 5, para. 10.54(3). No reasons are offered for this departure from the doctrine of bona fide purchaser for value without notice.

182 See op. cit., Ziegel, fn 40, pp. 126–9.

of the chattel. This led to the introduction in North America to deficiency clauses in conditional sale agreements and depreciation clauses in leasing agreements and, in the United Kingdom, to the appearance of minimum payment clauses in hire-purchase agreements.[183] For their part, the buyer, lessor or hirer was concerned about lack of protection at common law to the seller's or lessor's right to repossess the goods and cancel the agreement for minor breaches, thereby causing debtors to lose any equity that they might have in the goods. Article 9 in the US and its Canadian counterparts sought to address these problems in a systematic way in the new chattel security regimes and on the whole did so fairly and in a balanced manner.

We are told[184] that it was only when the Law Commission had the opportunity to take a closer look at the North American models that it appreciated the real significance of the new enforcement rules and the fact that they basically applied to all security interests.[185] This epiphany made the Law Commission a much more enthusiastic supporter for an English counterpart to Part V of the Canadian PPS Acts. However, the Commission still worried whether Part V should appear in a legislative scheme which did not also include quasi-securities. The provisional conclusion was that Part V should remain in even if the government were minded to limit any immediate reforming legislation to company securities, as appeared likely at that time given the fact that a major reforming Companies Bill was in the offing following the Company Law Review. If it is not impertinent for a transatlantic observer to say so, I shared the Commission's view that half a loaf is better than none. At the same time, it seems to me most regrettable that, if quasi-securities were excluded, Part V would not exert one of its most beneficent effects – application of the same remedies to conditional sales and hire-purchase agreements and to financial leases amounting in substance to security agreements. However, by the time its Final Report was published, the Law Commission had changed track again. Feedback from the Draft Consultation Report of 2004 revealed that the draft statement of rights and remedies was 'controversial'.[186] Therefore, the Commission decided to drop the statement from its Final Report in 2005 and to consult further in the future to see if there would be much support for such a reform. Despite this provisional rejection by the Law Commission, the earlier work remains a valuable legacy and is bound to be revived if the Law Commission is given a new mandate, bearing in mind that the remedia provisions are an integral part of all the PPSA regimes in the common law world.

Law Commission deviation from North American models

In most respects Part 5 of the Draft Rules contained in the 2004 Consultative Report by the Law Commission followed the Canadian precedents closely with the exception of the following features which the Commission deemed unnecessary or objectionable:

183 See op. cit., Goode and Ziegel, fn 87, pp. 97–103.

184 See Consultative Report, fn 6, para. 2.165.

185 It must be remembered however that Art. 9 and the Canadian Acts contain separate rules for the enforcement of security interests in consumer goods. In Canada's case, these rules are often supplemented by consumer protection and other provisions found in other legislation. See op. cit., Ziegel and Denomme, fn 31, §§59.7.2, 62.4.

186 See The Final Report, fn 7, p. xiv, para. 22.

Interpretation of acceleration clauses[187]

The Canadian Acts provide that a clause in an agreement that the secured party may accelerate payment or performance by the debtor when the secured party thinks that the collateral is in jeopardy or the secured party believes itself to be insecure should be interpreted to apply only when the secured party's view is reasonable. The Consultative Report noted[188] that such clauses appeared to be uncommon in English agreements and thought in any event that an English court would import a reasonableness test to the exercise of the secured party's discretion. Since no issue of principle is at stake, I would have thought myself that no harm would have been done by retaining the Canadian provision in the Law Commission's draft.

Taking possession on anticipated default

Such a provision appears in the New Zealand Act[189] and may have been influenced by the Sales Article of the Uniform Commercial Code, s. 2–609 entitling a buyer or seller to demand adequate assurance of performance from the other party and to suspend performance of his part of the sale agreement if he has reasonable grounds for insecurity. The Law Commission initially supported such a provision when it thought that a secured party would not be able to make it part of the security agreement. However, the Commission changed its mind[190] when it became clear that the secured party would be free, after all, to look after its own interests. The author agreed with the Commission's conclusion but on somewhat different grounds. The New Zealand provision is broadly cast and would seemingly give the secured party the right to repossess the collateral on the basis of a reasonable apprehension of harm to its interests without the need for a court order even where there is sufficient time to apply for such an order, *ex parte* if necessary. In the author's view, the secured party should be obliged to secure a court order if there was sufficient time for it.

Measure of damages where a lease is ineffective because it is unperfected[191]

This unusual provision appears in the Saskatchewan Act[192] and applies to a situation where a lessor has lost its goods to a third party because the lessor failed to perfect its deemed security interest. The Law Commission thought[193] the provision was unnecessary in its own draft provisions. Again, I agreed, but I would have put the objection to the Saskatchewan provision on much broader grounds. On the assumed facts the lessor seems to be the author of its own misfortune and it is not obvious that the lessee has committed a breach of the lease (or consignment) agreement for which it should be held liable in damages. It would be open for the agreement to make the lessee absolutely responsible for the safety and inviolability of the goods while in the lessee's possession. If there were such a clause and its terms were breached, the lessor

187 See: SPPSA, s. 16, OPPSA, s. 16. Cf. op. cit., Goode and Ziegel, fn 87, p. 110 and op. cit., Ziegel and Denomme, fn 31, pp. 147–8.
188 See Consultative Report, fn 6, para. 5.103.
189 See NZPPSA, s. 109(1)(b).
190 See Consultative Report, fn 6, para. 5.105.
191 Ibid., para. 5.110.
192 See SPPSA, s. 21.
193 See Consultative Report, fn 6, para. 5.108.

would have a contractual claim for damages. This would seem a better solution than the presumption of the lessee's liability posited in the Saskatchewan Act.

An account of the distribution[194]

The issue here is whether a secured party that has seized and disposed of the collateral should be obliged to provide an accounting of the proceeds of disposition to those parties that have an interest in the goods. Both the Saskatchewan and Ontario Acts have such a provision;[195] Article 9 also has such a provision but it is restricted to consumer goods.[196] The Law Commission acknowledged[197] the usefulness of the accounting requirement in a consumer context but thought it unnecessary in a commercial environment. Nevertheless, the Law Commission's assumption can be questioned. In Canada, it is not unusual to hear creditors complaining about the difficulty of obtaining information from a repossessing secured party or private receiver. A statutory spur may, therefore, be helpful in encouraging the secured party to provide the information more readily without the debtor being obliged to seek a court order.

Reinstatement of the security agreement[198]

The Canadian Acts generally have a provision entitling the debtor to recover goods seized by the secured party on the debtor's default if the debtor makes any payment due, exclusive of the operation of an acceleration clause, and cures any other breach of the agreement for which the goods may have been seized. The Law Commission thought that this provision was inappropriate in commercial transactions and that the parties should be left free to tailor their own transactions.[199] This view makes heroic assumptions about equality of bargaining power between commercial parties which are not supported by Canadian experience. Perhaps a more persuasive answer would be that a reasonable secured party would not repossess because the debtor had missed a single payment or committed some other minor breach of the agreement. However, bad feelings or other circumstances may lead a secured party to exercise its rights to the letter of the agreement. In these circumstances it may be appropriate to throw the debtor a modest lifeline which would not significantly prejudice the secured party's interests.

Receivers[200]

Both the Ontario and Saskatchewan Acts[201] confer a power on the court to appoint a receiver to assist in the enforcement of the secured creditor's rights, and also

194 See Consultative Report, fn 6, para. 5.110
195 See: SPPSA, s. 60(3); OPPSA, s. 64.
196 See UCC Art. 9–906.
197 Ibid.
198 See Consultative Report, fn 6, para. 5.111.
199 Ibid., para. 5.114. The Report indicated that the Commission would not object to a reinstatement clause limited to consumer transactions. The OPPSA, s. 66(2) provision is limited to consumer transactions.
200 See Consultative Report, fn 6, para. 5.114.
201 See: OPPSA, s. 60, SPPSA, s. 64.

authorise the court to supervise the receiver's conduct and give directions to the receiver. These provisions were first added in the 1972 version of the UPPSA in response to widespread complaints by unsecured creditors about lack of accountability by privately appointed receivers of assets entrusted to the receiver's care.[202] Similar provisions appear in the Canada Business Corporations Act,[203] a federal measure, and in the Bankruptcy and Insolvency Act, Part XI,[204] also a federal statute. The latter provisions are of particular importance because in practice insolvency proceedings by or against the debtor frequently coincide with the appointment of a private receiver. The Law Commission, it seems,[205] was not opposed to giving the English court power to appoint a receiver as one of the enforcement remedies but it was opposed to using the new company security provisions to spell out the receiver's powers. Its reasoning was that these aspects of the receiver's functions were already fully spelled out elsewhere and that it would only lead to confusion and duplication to add new such provisions in any statement of the parties' rights and remedies in a future reformed PPS scheme. To some extent, one could make the same observation, *mutatis mutandis*, about the receivership provisions in the Canadian PPS Acts, Part V.

Other issues

Good faith and commercial reasonableness[206]

To most American lawyers and judges, and increasingly to Canadian lawyers and judges as well, the requirement that contracting parties must exercise their contractual rights and perform their contractual duties in good faith and in a commercially reasonable manner is treated as an integral feature of modern contract law. It is so treated in the Uniform Commercial Code, s. 1–203[207] with respect to all Articles of the Code and was obviously the inspiration for the Saskatchewan PPSA, s. 65(2)[208] and its counterpart in many of the other provincial Acts.[209] In England, as we know, the suggestion that good faith performance is a requirement in English contract law is still treated as heresy, so it is not surprising that the Law Commission found[210] that the North American provisions proved 'highly controversial' among consultants in informal seminars held to discuss their proposals. The Commission, for its part, thought neither of the provisions would have an 'enormous effect' on the scheme of remedies as proposed in the Consultative Report. 'Enormous' is a term of wide latitude and the critics might object that any significant degree of uncertainty is too much uncertainty. In any event, the Consultation Report did not recommend including

202 See op. cit., Ziegel and Denomme, fn 31, §60.1.
203 RSC 1985, c.44 as amended, Part IX.
204 Ibid., c.B as amended.
205 See Consultative Report, fn 6, para. 5.114 *et seq.*
206 See Consultative Report, fn 6, paras 2.172–2.182 and 5.134.
207 UCC 1–203: 'Every contract or duty within this Act imposes an obligation of good faith in its performance or enforcement.' 'Good faith' is defined for general purposes as 'honest in fact in the conduct or transaction concerned' (UCC 1–201(19)).
208 Section 65(2) reads: 'All rights, duties and obligations that arise pursuant to a security agreement, this Act or any other applicable law are to be exercised or discharged in good faith in a commercially reasonable manner.'
209 But not for the Ontario Act, which has no general good faith and commercial reasonableness provision.
210 See Consultative Report, fn 6, para. 2.172 *et seq.*

good faith as a general performance requirement and it concluded that the issue of commercial reasonableness should be dealt with in the context of specific provisions, which is the approach adopted in the Revised Article 9 of the UCC. The Commission also correctly noted that UCC 1–203 does not in fact apply to Article 9 and that Article 9 has its own elevated good faith definition[211] which apparently only applies to those Article 9 provisions expressly requiring good faith dealings.[212]

With one possible exception, there is little evidence that section 65(2) of the Model Act has had a significant impact on the case law of those Canadian provinces that have adopted the good faith and commercially reasonable conduct norms. The exception involves the treatment of 'demand payment' clauses in security agreements entitling the creditor to demand payment of the balance owing under the contract without giving the debtor a period of time within which to find the money. In England, the courts have applied the clause literally giving the debtor only sufficient time to withdraw the money from the bank or other storage facility.[213] In Canada, for the past 27 years the courts have required the creditor to give the debtor a reasonable period of time to refinance the transaction from another source, the length of the notice depending on the particular circumstances of the case. However, it is not clear from the case law whether the notice requirement is imposed as a rule of law in demand payment cases or whether it is treated as an implied term of the contract. It was treated as an implied term by the Supreme Court in *Ronald Elwyn Lister Ltd* v. *Dunlop Canada Ltd*[214] but has been treated as a rule of law in some lower court cases.[215] It is clear, however, that the Canadian courts have reached their conclusions without relying on any doctrine of good faith or the provisions of the PPS statutes.[216]

Mandatory or optional default rules?

Under this heading the Consultation Report considered the question to what extent the parties should be free to vary or exclude the provisions of Part V of the then proposed new scheme. The Commission rejected (and, in this writer's view, on very persuasive grounds) the New Zealand provision[217] allowing the parties to the security agreement to craft their own terms with respect to remedies to the extent that they did not 'relate' to the rights of third parties. As the Consultative Report noted, the New Zealand approach had been widely criticised as incompatible with the historic treatment of a mortgagee's default obligations and the mortgagor's rights of redemption and because it ignored the parties' disparate bargaining position in most secured transactions.

211 UCC 9–102(a)(43): '"Good faith" means honest in fact and the observance of reasonable commercial standards of fair dealing.'

212 See UCC 9–102, Official Comment 19, second sentence. Confusingly, the sentence goes on to suggest that the good faith obligation imposed by s 1–203 may also continue to apply in Art. 9.

213 The recent case law is collected in op. cit., Ziegel and Denomme, fn 31, p. 483, n. 17.

214 [1982] 1 SCR 726.

215 E.g., *Kavcar Investments* v. *Aetna Financial Services* (1989) 62 DLR (4th) 277 (OCA). See further op. cit., Ziegel and Denomme, fn 31, pp. 483–5.

216 In fact, in many of the cases, the PPS provisions are not referred to or the Act had not yet been adopted in the province.

217 See NZPPSA, s. 107(2) as amended by Personal Property Securities Amendment Act 2001, s. 9.

The choice therefore, as the Commission saw it, was between the oblique language of the Saskatchewan and Ontario Part V provisions allowing the parties to vary their rights and obligations if not inconsistent with the statutory provisions and following the Revised Article 9 prescription of a relatively short and clear list of rights and remedies that may not be varied. So far as the writer is aware, the Canadian approach has not given rise to practical difficulties. However, no great principle is at stake in adopting either approach and it is difficult to fault the Law Commission's preference for a more direct approach of binding rights and obligations – should the reform issue be revisited in the future.

Conclusions

It is probably safe to claim that the Company Security Interest project was the most ambitious commercial law programme initiated by the Law Commission since the Commission was created. The Commission confronted not only an intensely technical branch of the law but was also obliged to go overseas in search of suitable models to serve as a basis for its own proposals.

The Commission did its job well and expounded the issues and its own proposals with admirable clarity, fairness and thoroughness. It is sad to contemplate therefore that the Law Commission's five years of intensive labour appear to have been in vain. The reactions to the Law Commission's 2004 proposals, led by the Financial Law Committee of the City of London Law Society, were predominantly negative. Almost every significant feature of the Law Commission's proposals was opposed by some group and frequently by more than one group.[218] With a view to retrieving some valuable elements from the wreckage, the Law Commission's Final Report of August 2005 made far-reaching concessions. The Final Report proposed retaining the distinction between fixed and floating charges (at least until such time as the status of floating charges in insolvency was changed in the Enterprise Act 2002). The revised recommendations abandoned any commitment to extending the revised companies' charges regime even to quasi-securities given by companies. Similarly, the Final Report relinquished any early prospect of reforming the law of chattel security for unincorporated businesses and consumers. I have written elsewhere[219] that the Law Commission's final recommendations could not be described as amounting even to a 'mini-Article 9' type law. The recommendations did however include the adoption of a notice filing system for company charges and establishing a statutory priority scheme for such charges.

Despite the Law Commission's deep-seated concessions, the critics still were not satisfied. It now transpired there was not sufficient support even for the introduction of a notice-filing system for company charges (the cornerstone in the reform of company charges that prompted the Department of Trade and Industry's (DTI) reference to the Law Commission to begin with), only support for minor changes to the existing priority rules in the Companies Act. Not surprisingly, given the discordant voices in the legal and commercial communities, the DTI was not prepared to

218 For a summary of the objections to the Law Commission's proposals, see Beale 'The exportability of North American chattel security regimes: the fate of the English Law Commission's proposals' (2006) 43 *Canadian Business Law Journal* 178 and cf. Ziegel 'The travails of English chattel security law reform – a transatlantic view' [2006] *Lloyd's Maritime and Commercial Law Quarterly* 110.

219 See op. cit., Ziegel, fn 218, p. 119 *et seq.*

include any of the Commission's recommendations in the Companies Reform bill introduced in Parliament in 2006; nor was the bill amended in such a way prior to it becoming the Companies Act 2006.[220] We are told that there is nothing to preclude a future government from implementing the Law Commission's recommendations at a later date but this faint hope will surely not satisfy those who feel (as this writer does) that England missed a vital opportunity to reform its badly dated regime of chattel security law.

What went wrong? Elsewhere, Hugh Beale, the Law Commissioner who had carriage of the companies' securities project, has given his explanation for the negative positions of so many influential groups. I have also presumed to express some views of my own.[221] Let me quickly summarise what I perceive to be some of the salient features of the critics' position and to add some further comments of my own. First, it is said that the flexibility of the current English chattel security rules has served the commercial and financial communities well and that there is no need for the kind of basic reforms represented by an Article 9-type law. There are several difficulties about this reasoning. It totally overlooks the continuing uncertainties concerning the distinction between fixed and floating charges and the long and expensive litigation to which it has given rise over many years. It also ignores the quite arbitrary distinctions between the different types of security interests and the rules governing them. The critics have also claimed, quite incorrectly in my view, that Article 9 of the UCC and its Canadian and New Zealand counterparts constrain the parties' freedom to write their own contracts. For the most part, the opposite is true. The Ontario Act provides that that 'Except as provided by this or any other Act, a security interest is effective according to its terms between the parties to it and against third parties.'[222]

The argument is also often made that the Americans needed an Article 9-type regime to overcome the rule in *Benedict* v. *Ratner*[223] and the fetters the rule imposed on flexible and effective commercial financing. This is at best only a partial explanation for the introduction of Article 9 and in any event it never applied to Canada. In fact, the Canadian common law provinces followed the English principles of chattel security law closely before the adoption of the PPS legislation and the fixed and floating charge was a very common security device in banking financing. The dominant reason in Canada for the adoption of personal property security legislation was deep dissatisfaction with the antiquated registry systems. Article 9 was seen as providing the right conceptual structure for introducing a reformed registry system with an integrated and functionally oriented system of chattel security rules. New Zealand reached the same conclusion when it too saw the need to overhaul its badly dated registration and perfection rules.[224] Australia has also recently decided to follow the same route as New Zealand.[225] Regrettably, these important lessons were overlooked

220 See now the Companies Act 2006, ss. 860–877 (company charge provisions), which came into force on 1 October 2009; SI 2008/2860. A notable exception to this is the Companies Act 2006, s. 894 which allows the Secretary of State to make amendments to the company charge provisions of the Act. However, it remains debatable whether the power will be used to any great extent. See further the chapter by de Lacy in the present volume, p. 78.

221 See fn 218 for the relevant sources and compare the writer's conjectures in the text above and following.

222 See OPPSA, s. 9(1). Essentially the same provision appears in the other Canadian provincial PPSA s. The provision was inspired by old UCC Art. 9-201.

223 (1925) 268 US 353.

224 See op. cit., Gedye, fn 32, pp. 209–11. Note also the chapter by Brown in the present volume, pp. 328–65, for a detailed treatment of the New Zealand system.

225 See generally the chapter by Fisher in the present volume, pp. 366–86.

or misunderstood in England, so was the fact that the European Bank of Reconstruction and Development (EBRD) found (in a significantly modified version) Article 9 the appropriate vehicle for introducing a modern and reasonably functional non-possessory chattel security system for civil law systems in former state dominated economic regimes in Eastern Europe.[226]

A third factor, which seems to have received little attention in literature on chattel security law reform in England, involved the Law Commission's *modus operandi*. The point has been made to this writer by an English colleague that, given the intensely practical character of chattel security law, the Law Commission should have struck at the outset a consultative committee of outside experts to assist the Commission and to ensure that outsiders' views fed directly into the Commission's work. Such a symbiotic approach was adopted in Ontario with respect to the drafting of the Ontario PPSA[227] and was (and remains) a critical feature of the organisation of the American Law Institute and the National Conference of Commissioners on Uniform State Legislation, the two founding sponsors of the American UCC.

The final observation I would permit myself is to remark on the detached view taken by the DTI to reform of the law and practice of company charges, so atypical of the activist role played by the then Blair government in modernising other aspects of the British economy. The British government surely had, and continues to have, a direct interest in the efficient operation of the Companies Registry and in a chattel security regime that minimises transaction costs, avoids unnecessary litigation, and is accessible to all members of the business community, whether incorporated or not, and can also be used, with appropriate safeguards, in consumer transactions. The appropriate posture therefore for the DTI would have been to send a strong message to the business and commercial law communities that it supported the Law Commission's important project and hoped these two constituencies would work cooperatively with the Commission to reach a successful outcome.

At the end of the day, one cannot help feeling that the companies securities project failed because of lack of leadership at all levels – in the business and legal communities and by the Law Commission and the DTI. The loss is not just England's, important as that loss is. The loss is also that of the Commonwealth because English law and English precedents still carry great weight in other common law jurisdictions. England's failure to rationalise its chattel security law is sure also to weaken its influence in continental and overseas jurisdictions that seek to modernise their own secured transactions law and may retard the efforts of UNCITRAL[228] and other international organisations active in seeking to harmonise the rules governing international commercial transactions.

226 See Ziegel 'The EBRD Model Law on secured transactions – some Canadian observations', in (eds) Basedow, Hopt and Kotz, *Festschrift fur Ulrich Drobnig zum siebzigsten Geburtstag*, p. 209 *et seq.* (Mohr-Siebeck 1998).

227 In fact, in Ontario the actual drafting of the Ontario version of the PPSA was done by the Catzman Committee, which combined commercial law practitioners with a smattering of academics. Legislative counsel was only brought in at a later stage to assist in the drafting of the bill to ensure that it conformed to established Ontario usage.

228 On the work of UNCITRAL, see the chapter by Bazinas in the present volume, pp. 456–73.

4 What is wrong with the law of security?

Richard Calnan

Introduction

There has been much debate about the rights and wrongs of the Law Commission's proposals to effect a major overhaul of the English law of security.[1] It is not my purpose, in this chapter, to enter that debate, at least not directly. My purpose is to consider the law of security as it exists in England today and to ask how well it works in practice, and to what extent it requires reform.

My premise is that the main requirement of the law of security is that security should be capable of being created and enforced with the maximum of flexibility and certainty and the minimum of cost, delay and formality consistent with appropriate safeguards for the debtor's unsecured creditors and others dealing with the debtor. The purpose of the rest of this chapter is to consider our current law of security in the light of that requirement, to indicate the extent to which it complies with it and to propose changes where it does not.

The starting point is to explain what I mean by the expression 'the law of security'. I will limit the discussion to corporate debtors, because they are by far the most important in practice and because, although the problems of the bills-of-sale legislation are manifest, the question of the extent to which individuals (particularly consumers) should be able to create security creates its own problems which are not central to the issues raised in this chapter.

This chapter is therefore concerned with the way in which creditors of corporate debtors are able to protect themselves against the insolvency of the debtor. One way to do so is to persuade someone other than the debtor to assume liability to pay the debt. This is normally achieved in practice by means of a guarantee, an indemnity or a combination of the two. Alternatively, the creditor can obtain a proprietary interest by way of security over an asset of the debtor (or, indeed, of a third party). This is normally done by taking a mortgage, a charge or a pledge over the asset concerned. In such a case, the concern of the creditor is to ensure, first, that the security interest is effective in the debtor's insolvency, second, that it takes priority over anyone else who might obtain an interest in the asset concerned and, third, that it can be enforced in order to have the secured debt repaid.

1 The Law Commission's proposals are contained in: Consultation Paper No. 164 *Registration of Security Interests: Company Charges and Property other than Land* (London: The Stationery Office, 2002); Consultation Paper No. 176 *Company Security Interests: a Consultative Report* (London: The Stationery Office, 2004); and Report No. 296 *Company Security Interests* (London: The Stationery Office, 2005). For a critical discussion of the work of the Law Commission, see: Calnan (2004) 3 JIBFL 88; Beale (2004) 4 JIBFL 117; and Calnan (2005) 1 JIBFL 25.

The rest of this chapter is, therefore, divided into four main parts. The next section will consider the law of guarantees, a second section looks at the effectiveness of security in an insolvency, then priorities are considered, followed by enforcement. Each of these four main sections will consider how well the law works in practice and the ways in which it might be reformed. The last section will briefly draw some of the strands together.

Guarantees

The effectiveness of the law of security does not depend solely on the ability of debtors to create security interests over their assets. As important is the ability of a third party to assume liability for the debtor's obligations. Its importance in practice is largely a result of the way in which business enterprises are structured, and particularly the proliferation of companies within a group. The effect is that, although credit will frequently be granted to one member of the group (or to a small number of its members), the creditor will require guarantees from the other members of the group, in order to obtain direct access to them. In an insolvency, the creditor will want to be able to prove for the full amount of its debt in the insolvency of each group member (provided, of course, that it does not in fact recover more than the total amount owing to it). In addition, the creditor may want the ability to be able to obtain security interests over assets, not just from the debtor but from the guarantors.

In broad terms, these requirements are amply met by English law. The creditor can take a guarantee (or an indemnity, or both) and, if required, can take security for the guarantor's obligations. Alternatively, if it does not require a personal undertaking to pay, it can take a third party charge, by which a person other than the debtor creates a security interest over its assets to secure the liability of the debtor.

The main practical problem with guarantees under English law (and, indeed, in many other jurisdictions) is that, at least on the face of it, the guarantor does not obtain any real benefit commensurate with the liability which it incurs as a result of giving the guarantee. In many cases, the guarantor does obtain benefits from doing so, but they are usually indirect and difficult to value.

Most problems with guarantees result from the one-sided nature of the contract. Some are inevitable, and will always trouble the creditor in one form or another. The most obvious example is that it will always be easier to have a guarantee set aside than a principal liability. Where the guarantor is a company, the courts can use fiduciary duty concepts to enable a guarantee to be set aside if no reasonable board of directors would have considered the guarantee to be in the company's interests and the creditor knew, or ought to have been aware of, that fact.[2] This principle finds statutory recognition in the Insolvency Act 1986, s. 238 which enables the courts to set aside transactions at an undervalue entered into within two years before the guarantor went into insolvency proceedings if certain conditions are satisfied.

Where the guarantor is an individual, the application of undue influence principles can also result in the guarantee being set aside. Judges have found it very difficult to settle upon a basis for the doctrine of undue influence with which they can all agree, but there is no doubt that the nature of a guarantee makes it a prime target for an undue influence claim.[3]

These disadvantages of guarantees are inherent in their nature and, although their precise scope can be a matter for debate, they are necessary protections for those

2 See *Rolled Steel* v. *British Steel* [1986] Ch. 246.
3 See *Royal Bank of Scotland* v. *Etridge* (*No. 2*) [2002] AC 773.

who assume someone else's liability. There are, however, two aspects of the law relating to guarantees which could usefully be reformed. The first relates to the formalities required in order to enter into a guarantee, the second to the equitable protections available to guarantors. These two elements will be addressed in turn.

Formalities

Section 4 of the Statute of Frauds 1677 imposes two requirements for the creation of a guarantee – it must be in writing, or evidenced by a memorandum in writing, and it must be signed by the guarantor or its agent. Whatever the justifications there might have been for such a requirement in the seventeenth century, it cannot be justified in the twenty-first century. One of the advantages of the English law of contract is its lack of formality. Formal requirements simply make it more difficult for a court to give effect to the parties' intentions. An example of how the Statute of Frauds can subvert the parties' intentions is the recent *Actionstrength* case. [4]

In this case, A had agreed to build a factory for B, in connection with which C had agreed to provide labour to A. C alleged that it had complained to B about late payment by A and that B had entered into an oral agreement with C to persuade A to pay, failing which B would pay C itself. C sued B on the alleged oral agreement. B denied that it had made the agreement, but also applied to have the claim struck out on the basis that, even if it had, the oral agreement was a guarantee which would be unenforceable under the Statute of Frauds, s. 4. The House of Lords gave judgment for B. Although they were concerned that C's commercial expectations could have been defeated, they were bound to give effect to the Statute.

It is difficult to disagree with their Lordships' analysis, or with their conclusion that, under existing law, the claim under the guarantee failed. But, in commercial terms, it was undoubtedly the wrong decision. A contractual undertaking was ignored because it was not made in the requisite form (i.e. it was not in writing). There is no doubt that the law should protect guarantors in appropriate cases. But this should be achieved by substantive rules, such as those relating to breach of fiduciary duty and undue influence, which consider whether, in the circumstances of the case, the guarantor deserves protection. A blanket formality rule, as can be seen from the *Actionstrength* case, can work positively against the interests of justice.

In financial transactions, where guarantees are invariably in writing, the Statute of Frauds is of little practical significance, but the *Actionstrength* case shows that it can still result in injustice in non-financial cases where the requirements of commercial practice make it impracticable to record every contractual undertaking in writing. The requirement for the guarantee to be signed by the guarantor can also create practical problems, not least in international trade transactions where undertakings may still be sent by means of communication which cannot carry a signature.

In an attempt by the courts to avoid some of these problems, a distinction was developed between guarantees and indemnities which, in the words of Harman LJ in *Yeoman Credit* v. *Latter*:[5]

> seems to me a most barren controversy. It dates back, of course, to the Statute of Frauds, and has raised many hair-splitting distinctions of exactly that kind which brings the law into hatred, ridicule and contempt by the public.

4 See *Actionstrength* v. *International Glass Engineering* [2003] AC 541.
5 [1961] 1 WLR 828, p. 835.

For all these reasons, it is suggested that the Statute of Frauds should be repealed.

Guarantee protections

A further consequence of the one-sided nature of a guarantee is the various protections which the courts have developed for guarantors. Their effect is that most arrangements between the creditor and the debtor in relation to the guaranteed debt after the guarantee has been entered into will render the guarantee ineffective unless the guarantor agrees to them.

In one sense, these rules are of little importance in practice because they give way to the contrary intention of the parties, and they are invariably contracted out of in practice, at least in guarantees given in relation to financial transactions. In the words of Lord Diplock in *Moschi* v. *Lep Air Services*,[6] where there is a guarantee:

> it is open to the parties expressly to exclude or vary any of their mutual rights or obligations which would otherwise result ... Every case must depend upon the true construction of the actual words in which the promise is expressed.

It would nevertheless be useful if the underlying rules could be clarified and simplified. There is a great deal of case law, stretching back over two hundred years, some parts of which are difficult to reconcile with others. A few brief examples can demonstrate the complexity of the current law.

In the first place, as a general rule, if the creditor releases the debtor from the guaranteed liability without the guarantor's consent, that will also release the guarantor.[7] This follows from the basic principle that a guarantee constitutes a secondary liability and, if the primary liability ceases to exist, then so does the secondary liability.[8] But if the creditor does not actually release the debtor, but just agrees not to sue it[9] or expressly reserves its rights against the guarantor,[10] the liability of the guarantor may be preserved.

Rather more surprisingly, an agreement by the creditor to give time to the debtor to pay will also release the guarantor unless the guarantor consents to it.[11] There have been various explanations in the cases of why this is so, but none of them is very convincing, and it is hard to disagree with the following comment by Justice Cardozo:[12]

> The law has shaped its judgments upon the fictitious assumption that a surety, who has probably lain awake at nights for fear that payment may some day be demanded, has in truth been smarting under a repressed desire to force an unwelcome payment on a reluctant or capricious creditor.

6 [1973] AC 331, p. 349.
7 *Mahant Singh* v. *U Ba Yi* [1939] AC 601, p. 606, *per* Lord Porter.
8 *Commercial Bank of Tasmania* v. *Jones* [1893] AC 313, p. 316, *per* Lord Morris.
9 *Mallet* v. *Thompson* (1804) 5 Esp 178.
10 *Green* v. *Wynn* (1869) LR 4 Ch. App. 204.
11 See: *Mahant Singh* v. *U Ba Yi* [1939] AC 601, p. 606, *per* Lord Porter; *Samuell* v. *Howarth* (1817) 3 Mer 272.
12 See Cardozo *The Nature of Judicial Process* (New Haven: Yale University Press, 1921), pp. 153–4.

Variations of the guaranteed obligation create further difficulties. If the underlying contract has been varied, the first question is always whether the guarantor has agreed to guarantee the varied contract, or only the original one. That is, of course, a matter of construction of the guarantee. But the cases go further than that, and establish that any variation of the underlying contract will discharge the guarantor unless the nature of the alteration can only be beneficial to the guarantor.[13] In practice, this is a very difficult test for the creditor to satisfy, as can be seen in the decision of the Court of Appeal in *Holme* v. *Brunskill*.[14] In spite of the fact that the jury in that case found that the alteration to the underlying contract had not materially affected the guarantor, the court nevertheless decided that the variation did discharge the guarantor's liability.

One final example of the approach of the courts concerns the case where the creditor loses the value of other security which it was proposing to take for the secured debt. In such a case, the liability of the guarantor is reduced by the amount which would otherwise have been recovered from the security.[15]

It is impossible to do justice to the complexity of the authorities in this brief review. Suffice it to say that they contain an alarming number of different approaches to the circumstances in which the guarantor is released from liability, and the extent of that release. In some types of case (such as an agreement to give time to the debtor), any such action releases the guarantor. In others (such as variations to the underlying contract), there will generally be a release, but not if the creditor can show that the variation is necessarily beneficial to the guarantor. In a third type of case (loss of security), the guarantor is only released if it acted negligently. The effect of the arrangement also varies depending on the type of case concerned. In some cases (such as an agreement to give time to the debtor or a variation of the underlying contract), its effect is to discharge the guarantor's liability completely. In others (such as loss of security), the guarantor is only discharged to the extent that it has suffered loss.

There may well be good reasons for these elaborate distinctions, but there is much to be said for an attempt to clarify and simplify the underlying law in this area, taking into account current practice in contracting out of them. It may not be of much practical significance in relation to financial transactions, but it can be of concern in non-financial commercial transactions, where documentation is often less elaborate.

Creating security

The next sections of this chapter are concerned with the creation of proprietary rights by way of security – what is sometimes referred to as 'real' (as opposed to 'personal') security. When obtaining security over an asset, a creditor has three principal concerns. It wants to ensure that:

- the security is effective in the insolvency of the debtor;
- the security will take priority over anyone else who obtains a proprietary interest in the asset concerned; and

13 *Ankhar Pty* v. *National Westminster Finance (Australia)* (1987) 162 CLR 549, p. 559, *per* Gibbs CJ.

14 (1878) 3 QBD 495.

15 *Williams* v. *Frayne* (1937) 58 CLR 710, p. 738, *per* Dixon J.

- the security can be enforced when required, even if the debtor is in insolvency proceedings.

Advantages of the existing law

When taking security, a creditor has the choice of three methods – a pledge, a mortgage or a charge.[16] Pledges are a useful form of security in particular types of case (especially in the context of international trade transactions), but the requirement that the creditor obtains, and retains, possession of a tangible moveable asset restricts its usefulness to a relatively small number of cases.

In most cases, therefore, the creditor's choice is between a mortgage and a charge. Although there is a conceptual distinction between mortgages and charges,[17] it is rarely necessary to distinguish between them.[18] Indeed, that eminent common lawyer, Lord Justice Scrutton, once wryly remarked that, although there is a distinction between mortgages and charges, 'equity judges appear to use the terms with no such precise distinction'.[19]

This is understandable. When considering the effectiveness of a security interest against a debtor and its insolvency officer (such as a liquidator, administrator or trustee in bankruptcy), it is entirely immaterial whether the creditor has a legal mortgage, an equitable mortgage or an equitable charge. They all create a proprietary interest which is effective even when the debtor is in insolvency proceedings.[20] Indeed, the Companies Act 2006 defines a 'charge' to include a mortgage[21] and, conversely, the Law of Property Act 1925 defines a 'mortgage' to include a charge.[22] For the purpose of priority disputes between secured creditors (which are considered in the next part of this chapter) there can be an important distinction between, on the one hand, a legal mortgage and, on the other, an equitable mortgage or equitable charge. But, as far as the effectiveness of the security in the debtor's insolvency is concerned, the distinction is immaterial.

Because of their priority advantages, legal mortgages are important in practice, particularly in relation to land. But they have a limited use in relation to other types of asset. This is largely because of their inherent limitations. A legal mortgage can only be created over something which the common law regards as property. In broad

16 For a brief discussion of these types of security, see: Goode *Commercial Law* (London, Penguin, 3rd edn, 2004), ch. 22; and Bridge and Stevens (eds), *Cross-Border Security and Insolvency* (Oxford: Oxford University Press, 2001), ch. 3.

17 A mortgage requires the transfer of (legal or beneficial) title to the mortgagee as security for the discharge of an obligation (*Santley* v. *Wilde* [1899] 2 Ch 474, p. 474, *per* Lindley MR). A charge does not. It is an equitable proprietary interest created by way of security (*Re Bank of Credit and Commerce International* (*No. 8*) [1998] AC 214, p. 226 *per* Lord Hoffmann).

18 Remedies of a chargee are different from those of a mortgagee, although this is rarely of importance in practice.

19 *London County and Westminster Bank* v. *Tompkins* [1918] 1 KB 515, p. 528, a case involving legislation (since repealed) which did require the distinction to be drawn.

20 This has been the case since at least the early eighteenth century – *Godfrey* v. *Furzo (1733)* 3 P Wms 185. It has recently been reaffirmed by the House of Lords in the *Leyland Daf* case, *Buchler* v. *Talbot* [2004] 2 AC 298.

21 Companies Act 2006, s. 861(5).

22 Law of Property Act 1925, s. 205.

terms, this means that a legal mortgage can be created over land and goods but over very few types of intangible – the most notable exception being shares of companies. This is because, with a few exceptions, the common law does not recognise that intangibles, such as debts, are property which is capable of being transferred.[23] Since much of the wealth of companies is tied up in intangible assets, this is a material limitation. Even more importantly, a legal mortgage can only be created over assets which are owned by the debtor at the time the mortgage is created.[24]

It is, therefore, generally only possible to obtain a legal mortgage over land, goods or shares owned by the debtor at the time the mortgage is created. Legal mortgages over goods and shares are not particularly common in practice, certainly in comparison with the number of equitable charges over those assets. As far as goods are concerned, this is, in part, because many goods owned by a company constitute its stock-in-trade and are therefore only capable of being the subject of a floating charge; and because many items of equipment which could be the subject of a legal mortgage are, in practice, frequently leased to the debtor, rather than owned by it. With shares, the reluctance to take a legal mortgage has had more to do with the inconvenience for the creditor of becoming the registered holder of shares, and has recently been reinforced by concerns about the liability of the mortgagee for pension deficits.

In practice, therefore, the equitable charge is ubiquitous; and it is worth spending a little time considering why that is so. The main reason is that it is simple and easy to create, with a minimum of formality. In essence, there are only two requirements for the creation of an equitable charge by a corporate debtor – first, evidence that the debtor intended the charge to be created over an identifiable asset for the purpose of securing an identifiable liability and, secondly, the effecting of any necessary registration at Companies House.[25]

It is hard to overestimate the centrality of intention to the creation of a charge. In the words of Lord Macnaghten in *Tailby* v. *Official Receiver*,[26] 'The mode or form of assignment is absolutely immaterial provided the intention of the parties is clear.' The question can be stated simply: did the parties intend the creditor to have an equitable proprietary interest in the asset concerned?

Any type of asset is capable of being the subject of a charge unless it is an intangible asset which has been created by a contract which prohibits the creation of a charge,[27] or it is one of those rare types of asset which, for public policy reasons, are incapable of being the subject of a charge.[28]

Equally importantly, it was confirmed by the House of Lords in *Holroyd* v. *Marshall*[29] that, if the debtor enters into a contract to create a charge over an asset which it does not yet own, the creditor will obtain a charge over the asset once it becomes owned by the debtor, without the necessity for any further action by the debtor or the creditor.

23 *Master* v. *Miller* (1791) 4 TR 320.

24 See: *Akron Tyre Co* v. *Kitson* (1951) 82 CLR 477, p. 484, *per* Latham CJ; *Lunn* v. *Thornton* (1845) I CB 379.

25 *Re Kent & Sussex Sawmills* [1947] Ch. 177, where the first criterion was satisfied, but the second was not.

26 (1888) 13 App. Cas. 523, p. 543.

27 See *Linden Gardens Trust* v. *Lenesta Sludge Disposals* [1994] 1 AC 85.

28 Such as rights which are personal to the contracting parties: *Nokes* v. *Doncaster Amalgamated Collieries* [1940] AC 1014.

29 (1862) 10 HLC 191.

Then, in a series of cases in the 1870s,[30] it was established that a charge could be taken even over assets which were disposed of by the company in the ordinary course of its business. This was achieved by the simple expedient of implying a power for the debtor to use them until intervention by the creditor.

What is required, therefore, to create a charge is evidence of the intention of the debtor to do so, normally by the execution of a charge document by the debtor. Subject to any necessary registration at Companies House,[31] this results in the creation of a proprietary interest which is effective not only while the debtor is solvent, but also if it enters into insolvency proceedings. The effectiveness of the security in the insolvency proceedings is not prejudiced by the fact that the creditor does not have legal or beneficial title to the asset concerned or, in the case of a debt, that no notice of the charge has been given to the person liable to pay the debt.[32]

It has also been recognised that it is the substance, not the form, of the transaction which is important. This has two effects. In the first place, it is clear that any arrangement between the debtor and the creditor, the intention of which is to confer an equitable proprietary interest on the creditor by way of security, will create a charge, however the arrangement is expressed.[33] Second, a transaction which, on the face of it, is intended to transfer an outright interest to the creditor will be treated as a charge if the parties actually intended the transfer to secure the discharge of a liability.[34]

The value of this approach is that it gives the parties the ability to create security in a straightforward, simple and flexible manner. There are very few formalities and it is not necessary, as it is in some jurisdictions, to use different procedures depending on the identity of the assets being charged. It is possible for the debtor to create, in just one document, security over all of its present and future assets by means of fixed and floating charges. The advantages for the creditor are obvious, but the benefits for the debtor are equally real. If it is unable to raise finance on an unsecured basis, it will need the ability to create security and, the more straightforward the process, the quicker and cheaper it will be to create security; and this is important for the debtor because it will invariably have to pay the costs of its creation.

Although the simplicity and flexibility of the process benefits the debtor and the secured creditor concerned, it can adversely affect other persons dealing with the debtor, particularly its other creditors. The ease of creation of security makes it difficult for them to make themselves aware of the extent to which the debtor has secured its assets in favour of other creditors, and it is for this reason that the Companies Act 2006 requires most charges created by companies to be registered at Companies House, failing which, for most purposes, they will be void.[35]

In general terms, therefore, I would suggest that the current English law of security does what it ought to do. It provides a relatively simple, straightforward and flexible method for the creation of security over all the present and future assets of the debtor while providing safeguards for third parties by means of the registration system.

30 See. *Re Panama, New Zealand and Australian Royal Mail Company* (1870) LR 5 Ch. App. 318; and *Re Florence Land and Public Works Company ex parte Moor* (1878) 10 ChD 530.

31 Which is required for most mortgages or charges created by English companies (and some foreign companies) as a result of the Companies Act 2006, ss. 860 and 1052.

32 *Gorringe* v. *Irwell India Rubber and Gutta Percha Works* (1886) 34 ChD 128.

33 See: *Row* v. *Dawson* (1749) 1 Ves. Sen. 331, LC; *Brice* v. *Bannister* (1878) 3 QBD 569.

34 See: *Re Universal Management* [1983] NZLR 462, p. 470 *per* Cooke J; *Cripps* v. *Jee* (1793) 4 Bro. CC 472.

35 See Companies Act 2006, ss. 860, 861, and 874.

That is not to say that there are no problems at all. There are, for instance, some conceptual uncertainties surrounding the precise nature of a charge (particularly a floating charge) although these have not had any material impact on the practical efficacy of either type of security.[36] There are, however, two issues which, I would suggest, are in need of reform. The first relates to the distinction between fixed and floating charges, and the second to the registration system.

Disadvantages of the existing law

One of the most intractable problems which has beset English law for more than 25 years is the distinction between fixed and floating charges. Although it is relatively easy to state the test of when a charge is a floating charge (it is when the debtor can, in a commercial sense, deal with the asset concerned as if the charge did not exist), its application to the facts of any particular case involves a great deal of uncertainty; and this is supported by the evidence of the conflicting cases concerning charges over book debts decided over the last 25 years.[37] However, the reason why the distinction has to be drawn is largely because of the requirements of insolvency legislation. Were it not for the fact that insolvency legislation draws a distinction between fixed and floating charge realisations,[38] there would be very little need to draw the distinction.[39] The problem is not inherent in the nature of fixed and floating charges. It only exists because insolvency legislation requires us to draw distinctions between fixed and floating charges which have no conceptual validity or commercial purpose. The problem can be solved, but only if it is tackled in the insolvency legislation by removing the requirement for the distinction to be drawn.[40]

The other area which could usefully be reformed is the law relating to the registration of company charges. The controversy which has been occasioned by the Law Commission's proposals has rather diverted the debate from a discussion of those parts of the current registration system which are in need of reform. There are three principal issues.[41]

The first is the undesirability of having a list of those types of charge which are registrable. The list has grown incrementally over the years in a rather haphazard way, the result of which being that it is often difficult in practice to know whether a charge over a particular type of asset is, or is not, registrable.[42] Until the advent of the Financial Collateral Directive,[43] it was the general practice to register all charges created by companies, even if they were clearly not registrable (such as charges over shares) or there was doubt about their registrability (such as charges over

36 On the nature of a floating charge, see: Pennington (1960) 23 MLR 630; Ferran [1988] CLJ 213; Worthington [1994] CLJ 81 and Nolan (2004) 120 LQR 108.

37 From the decision in *Seibe Gorman* v. *Barclays Bank* [1979] 2 Lloyds Rep 142, onwards.

38 Principally as a result of the Insolvency Act 1986, ss. 245; 40, 175, 386 and Sched 6; 176A; and Sched B1, paras 70 and 99.

39 It would still be necessary to draw the distinction for the purpose of priorities between competing proprietary interests, but this is much less of an issue in practice.

40 This issue is discussed in more detail in (2004) 9 JIBFL 341.

41 For more detail, see (2001) 2 JIBFL 53.

42 The list is contained in Companies Act 2006, s. 860(7).

43 Introduced into English law by the Financial Collateral Arrangement (No. 2) Regulations 2003 (SI 2003/3226).

bank accounts). Subject to the Financial Collateral Directive, it would be far more appropriate to require the registration of *all* charges created by companies incorporated in England. Under the present law, all floating charges are registrable, as are most charges over land and goods, but fixed charges over intangibles are only registrable if they fall within certain categories, such as 'book debts'. There seems no reason for such a complicated approach. It would be far simpler if all charges were registrable unless they fell within the Financial Collateral Directive.

The second issue concerns the effect of non-registration. The existing legislation renders a charge which has not been lodged for registration within the required period void in the liquidation or administration of the debtor or against creditors with security over the same asset.[44] It does not render an unregistered charge void against subsequent purchasers of the asset concerned, nor does it prevent a secured creditor from enforcing the security before a liquidation or administration of the debtor and thereby avoiding the problem.[45] This seems unnecessarily complicated. It would be more appropriate for a charge which has not been registered in time to be void in all respects, but without prejudice to the effectiveness of the underlying secured obligation. The effect would be that, if a secured creditor had not complied with the requirements as to registration, it would have no proprietary interest in the assets of the debtor, but would continue to be able to rely on its underlying personal claim.

The third concern was the so-called *Slavenburg* registrations, but this problem has now been solved by the Companies Act 2006.[46] In certain types of case, the requirement to register a charge applied not only to companies incorporated in Great Britain, but to those incorporated outside it. This was the case if the charged property was situated in England and the company concerned had an established place of business in England at the time the charge was created. Unfortunately, the wording of the former s. 409 of the 1985 Act was such that it was held to require registration not only where the company concerned had registered under the 1985 Act, Part XXIII but also where, in fact, the company had an established place of business here, although it was not registered here.[47]

Since the test of whether a company has an established place of business is not entirely straightforward, and because lenders are unlikely to have the information necessary to make an informed judgement on the point, the practice developed that charges created by overseas companies over assets which are situated in England or might subsequently come into England were sent to the Registrar for registration, regardless of whether it was considered likely that the company had an established place of business here. In view of the penalties for failure to register, this approach was entirely understandable, but it served absolutely no useful purpose. The purpose of the requirement to register is to enable those dealing with the debtor to be able to search its register in order to establish whether its assets are encumbered. If it is neither incorporated here, nor has a registered place of business here, that purpose cannot be fulfilled, and there is no point in requiring registration in such circumstances. Happily, the government took this point on board when reforming the 1985 Companies Act and, since the Companies Act 2006 came into force in

44 See: Companies Act 2006, s. 874; *Re Monolithic Building Company* [1915] 1 Ch. 643.

45 See: *NV Slavenburg's Bank* v. *International Natural Resources* [1980] 1 WLR 1076.

46 See the text at fn 48 below for the new law on this area under the Companies Act 2006.

47 See: *NV Slavenburg's Bank* v. *International Natural Resources* [1980] 1 WLR 1076; *Re Oriel* [1986] 1 WLR 180.

October 2009, the new Act only requires registration of charges created by a foreign company if it has registered here as an overseas company at the time the charge is created.[48]

In summary, I would suggest that there is little which requires changing in relation to the creation of security under English law. On the contrary, it works very well in practice. There are, however, two areas which should be reformed. The first (which is essentially a matter of insolvency law and which is by far the more important in practice) would be to do away with the necessity to distinguish between fixed and floating charges in insolvency proceedings. The second would be to make certain relatively minor changes to the registration procedure which would enable there to be more certainty about which charges are registrable, the effect of non-registration and the extent to which overseas companies are affected by the registration requirement. The process of reform of the registration procedure has started and will continue, but it is the effect of insolvency law on floating charges which is badly in need of reform.[49]

Priorities

Although the law concerning the creation of security generally works well in practice, there can be no doubt that the law concerning the priority of security interests is much more intractable. Before looking at the issues in detail, two general observations should be made. The first is that priority issues generally arise when a debtor wrongfully, and in breach of an undertaking to a secured creditor, creates security over, or effects an outright disposal of, the asset charged to someone else. Such cases normally involve fraudulent action on the part of the debtor and there have, fortunately, been few cases in the last 50 years in which such issues have had to be resolved by the courts in the context of company security interests.[50] That is not to say that we do not need rules concerning priorities, simply that such issues are not the main concern of those taking security.

Second, and as a result, it is often extremely difficult in practice to establish the 'right' answer to a priority dispute. Because it will normally involve two innocent parties, each of whom has been duped by the debtor, there is often room for doubt as to which of the parties ought to suffer as a result. It would be naive of us to assume that we now have all the answers to issues which have perplexed judges in reported cases for more than three hundred years.

There is nevertheless no doubt that the English priority rules are detailed and complicated. For the purpose of priority issues, English law broadly divides assets into three types – land, goods and shares, and intangibles, to which it applies

48 See Companies Act 2006, s. 1052. This section gives the Secretary of State wide powers to make regulations about the registration of charges by registered overseas companies. For these purposes an 'overseas company' is a company incorporated outside the UK and s. 1052 will apply to such a company if it has registered particulars under the Companies Act; see generally Companies Act 2006, ss. 1044, 1052(6) and S.I. 2009/1917, The Overseas Companies (Execution of Documents and Registration of Charges) Regulations 2009.

49 A point driven home in a number of the chapters in Getzler and Payne (eds), *Company Charges: Spectrum and Beyond* (Oxford: Oxford University Press, 2006).

50 The most notable recent case of this type involved the dealings of Robert Maxwell; see *Macmillan* v. *Bishopsgate Investment Trust* [1995] 1 WLR 978.

different rules. These rules are also overlaid by those which regulate the priority of security interests which are registered at the asset registries (which relate to land, ships, aircraft and certain intellectual property rights).

The starting point for any discussion of priorities is the 'first in time' rule, and the main issue is therefore the extent to which that rule ought to be overridden in particular cases. It is beyond the scope of this chapter to consider these issues in detail, but it will briefly discuss the efficacy of six of the rules which are used to promote a later encumbrancer over an earlier one. These are the bona fide purchaser rule, the rule in *Dearle* v. *Hall*, the effect of registration at asset registries or at Companies House, the principle that some of these rules only apply 'if the equities are equal', the restrictions on tacking further advances and the rules concerning the priority of floating charges.

The bona fide purchaser rule

The first exception to be created was the bona fide purchaser rule, as a result of which a person who, for value, acquires a legal interest in an asset, will take the asset free from an earlier equitable interest in it of which he did not have actual or constructive notice.[51] Does this rule serve any useful purpose? Why should there be such a stark distinction between the rights of a legal, and of a beneficial, owner?

I would make four comments on this issue. In the first place, although the bona fide purchaser rule developed in relation to transactions in land, the advent of land registration has made such issues of very little importance in relation to land.[52] The principle is still relevant to fixed security over goods[53] and shares[54] and, in practice, its principal application in recent years has been in relation to security over shares. It therefore now has a relatively limited role to play. That is not to say that it should not be reformed, simply that the effect of such a reform may not be particularly material in practice.

Second, it would be unwise to alter the effect of the bona fide purchaser rule in relation to secured transactions without considering its application in the broader context of property law as a whole. The division of property rights into legal and equitable interests is fundamental to the way in which the English law of property has developed, and it cannot realistically be altered in relation to security interests in the absence of a reconsideration of this division of property rights generally.

Third, there is, I would suggest, much to be said for this division of property rights into formal legal interests and less formal equitable ones. The advantage of an equitable charge, discussed in the previous part of this chapter, is that it is simple and easy to create, with the minimum of formality, but is nevertheless effective in the debtor's insolvency. If further formal requirements are imposed in order for the creditor to be more certain of obtaining priority over other encumbrances, then so be it. The current system gives the creditor the flexibility to create the most effective security it can in the particular circumstances of the case. If it is cost-effective to do so, legal

51 See *Pilcher* v. *Rawlins* (1871) LR 7 Ch. App. 259.

52 Priority disputes in relation to registrable interests in registered land are generally decided by reference to the date of registration under the Land Registration Act 2002, ss. 48 and 29–30.

53 See *Joseph* v. *Lyons* (1884) 15 QBD 280.

54 See *Macmillan* v. *Bishopsgate Investment Trust* [1995] 1 WLR 978.

security can be taken. If not, the creditor can still obtain equitable security. This ability to meet the differing requirements of creditors in different transactions is one of the strengths of English law.

Finally, however, there is one aspect of the rule which, I would suggest, is in need of reform – the rule concerning tacking the legal estate (sometimes referred to as tacking *tabula in naufragio*). Although the basic principle is that a person acquiring a legal interest in an asset will only take free of an earlier equitable interest in that asset if, at the time he acquired the legal interest, he did not have actual or constructive notice of the equitable interest, there is an exception to this principle. As Lord Selborne LC said in *Blackwood* v. *The London Chartered Bank of Australia* (perhaps rather optimistically in the light of his opening words):[55]

> There is nothing more familiar than the doctrine of equity that a man, who has *bona fide* paid money without notice of any other title, though at the time of the payment he, as purchaser, gets nothing but an equitable title, may afterwards get in a legal title, if he can, and may hold it; though during the interval between payment and the getting in the legal title he may have had notice of some prior dealing inconsistent with the good faith of the dealing with himself.

This doctrine was originally established in relation to mortgages of land[56] and, as a result of the Law of Property Act 1925, s. 94(3) it no longer applies to them. It is nevertheless clear from the context that this section only extends to mortgages of land, and the doctrine has not, therefore, been abolished in relation to other assets to which the bona fide purchaser rule can apply – goods and shares. Indeed, the effect of the doctrine in relation to shares has recently been confirmed by Millett J in *Macmillan* v. *Bishopsgate Investment Trust*.[57]

The curious effect of the doctrine can be seen by contrasting two cases concerning security over shares – *Ireland* v. *Hart*[58] and *Dodds* v. *Hills*.[59] In each case, the debtor was the registered holder of shares in a company, which he held on trust for a third party. The debtor borrowed money from the creditor against a charge over the shares, giving the creditor a signed blank stock transfer form and the share certificate. At the time the creditor took the charge over the shares, it had no notice of the trust.

In *Ireland* v. *Hart*, the creditor completed the stock transfer form and delivered it to the company for registration but, before the board had approved the registration, the beneficiary of the trust obtained an interim injunction to prevent the creditor becoming registered. Joyce J held that the beneficiary had priority over the creditor. As between two equitable interests, the first in time took priority and, because the board had not yet approved the share transfer for registration, the creditor did not yet have legal title to the shares.

By way of contrast in the case of *Dodds* v. *Hills*, the creditor, having become aware of the trust, completed the stock transfer form and sent it, and the share certificate, to the company secretary for registration, and the shares were then registered in the creditor's name. Page Wood VC held that the creditor took priority over the

55 See (1874) LR 5 PC 92, p. 111.
56 See *Marsh* v. *Lee* (1670) 2 Ventr. 337.
57 [1995] 1 WLR 978.
58 [1902] 1Ch. 522.
59 (1865) 2H & M 424.

beneficiary because he had acquired legal title to the shares, even though he had done so after he had notice of the trust.

The crucial distinction between the two cases was that, in *Ireland* v. *Hart*, the creditor was unable to get on the company's register of members whereas, in *Dodds* v. *Hills*, he was. Priority therefore depended on the speed of action of the parties concerned once they became aware that there was a potential dispute.

I would suggest that, once a person has notice of an earlier interest, he should not be able to take action to put himself in a position to defeat the rights of the person with that earlier interest. The doctrine of tacking the legal estate was abolished in relation to land in 1925 and, it is suggested, it should also be repealed in relation to other assets. The holder of a legal interest should only be able to take priority over an earlier equitable interest if he did not have notice of that earlier equitable interest at the time he obtained the legal interest.

The rule in Dearle *v.* Hall

The rule in *Dearle* v. *Hall*[60] has caused controversy for over a hundred years. In 1893, Lord Macnaghten said 'I am inclined to think that the rule in *Dearle* v. *Hall* has on the whole produced at least as much injustice as it has prevented.'[61] But this did not stop it being extended from a rule regulating the priority of interests in trusts to the (far more important in practice) position which it now has, regulating the priority of proprietary interests in debts and other similar intangibles, such as rights under contracts.[62]

It is difficult to criticise the actual decision in *Dearle* v. *Hall*. The owner of a beneficial interest in a trust fund assigned it by way of security to A and then outright to B, in each case for valuable consideration. A had not given notice of his assignment to the trustees of the fund and, accordingly, when B made enquiries of them, he did not discover the existence of the assignment to A because the trustees were not aware of it. B did give notice of the assignment to the trustees and A subsequently gave notice to them. Plumer MR and, on appeal, Lord Lyndhurst LC each decided that B took priority over A.

Judgment was given in favour of B for two reasons. The first was based on the general proposition, which will be discussed later, that, as between two equitable interests, the first in time will only take priority 'if the equities are equal'. In this case, by failing to give notice to the trustees, A had allowed the beneficiary of the trust to be able to hold himself out as being the unencumbered owner of the beneficial interest and had therefore enabled the beneficiary to hoodwink B into thinking he had not encumbered it. This is a perfectly straightforward application of the principle that the first in time will only prevail if the equities are equal.

The second ground for the decision was that A's failure to give notice had left the beneficiary of the trust in apparent possession of the trust fund, and he could not, therefore, rely on this assignment in a dispute with B. This latter ground is rather

60 See *Dearle* v. *Hall. Loveridge* v. *Cooper* (1828) 3 Russ 1. For a detailed treatment of this rule and its application, see de Lacy 'Reflections on the ambit of the rule in *Dearle v. Hall* and the priority of personal property assignments' (1999) 28 *Anglo-American Law Review* 87 and 197.

61 See *Ward* v. *Duncombe* [1893] AC 369, p. 393.

62 This is the case in relation to statutory assignments as well as equitable ones; *Marchant* v. *Morton, Down & Co* [1901] 2 KB 892, but not transfers of shares; *Société Générale de Paris* v. *Walker* (1885) 11 App. Cas. 20.

puzzling, based, as it appears to be, on the (wholly irrelevant in this context) concept of reputed ownership in bankruptcy. Nevertheless, there is much to be said for the conclusion in the case. A had allowed the beneficiary to commit a fraud on B and should therefore rank behind B.

Subsequent cases turned the rule from an example of the principle that the first-in-time rule will not apply if the equities are not equal into an absolute rule that the first to give notice will take priority unless the later assignee was a volunteer[63] or was aware of the earlier assignment at the time he obtained his assignment.[64] The rule applies even if the later assignee made no enquiries of the trustees[65] and even if the first assignee was not negligent in failing to give notice, for instance because he was not aware of it[66] or because there was no one to whom notice could be given.[67] In *Ward* v. *Duncombe*,[68] the House of Lords decided that the rule that notice determines priority of dealings applied regardless of the conduct of the competing assignees.

In spite of the justified criticisms of the way in which the rule in *Dearle* v. *Hall* has developed, there is much to be said for the concept that the priority of assignments or charges over debts should, as a general rule, depend on the date notice is given to the person who owes the debt. Not least, this is because the person who owes the debt will get a good discharge by paying the debtor unless he has been notified of the assignment or charge.[69] Once a debt has been paid, it ceases to exist, and the priority rule recognises this fact. That is not to say that, in appropriate cases, it would not be possible for one creditor to trace the proceeds of the debt into the hands of another. But a simple rule that both priority and discharge depend on notice has much to recommend it.

The problem with the rule is that it has been carried too far. It is one thing for a subsequent assignee for value to take priority over an earlier assignee by giving notice before he becomes aware of the earlier assignment. But it does seem harsh for the earlier assignee to lose priority where the notice is given by the subsequent assignee after he is aware of the earlier assignment.[70] As with the rules concerning tacking the legal estate, I would suggest that priority should not depend on the speed of response of the parties once one or both of them becomes aware of the problem.

It is therefore suggested that it is not *Dearle* v. *Hall* which is the problem, but the way in which it has subsequently been extended. A subsequent assignee or chargee of a debt who gives notice to the person owing the debt should take priority over an earlier assignee or chargee who has not given notice only if: (a) he gave value; and (b) he was not aware of the earlier interest at the time he gave notice.

This approach would enable the bona fide purchaser rule and the rule in *Dearle* v. *Hall* to continue to be seen as complementary exceptions to the first-in-time rule. In the case of chattels and shares, a person who has gone to the trouble of obtaining a legal interest will take priority over an earlier equitable interest if he does so for value and without notice of the earlier equitable interest. In the case of debts and other similar intangibles, the bona fide purchaser rule can have no application, because the common law does not recognise the assignment of such intangibles, but the rule in

63 See *Re General Horticultural Company ex parte Whitehouse* (1886) 32 ChD 512.
64 See *Re Holmes* (1885) 29 ChD 786.
65 *Foster* v. *Cockerell* (1835) 3 Cl & Fin 456.
66 See *Re Lake, ex p. Cavendish* [1903] 1 KB 151.
67 See *Re Dallas* [1904] 2 Ch 385.
68 [1893] AC 369.
69 See *Stocks* v. *Dobson* (1853) 4 De G M&G 11.
70 See *Mutual Life Assurance Society* v. *Langley* (1886) 32 ChD 460, p. 468, *per* Cotton LJ.

Dearle v. *Hall* achieves a similar result. If the subsequent assignee takes the trouble to give notice to the person owing the debt, and he does so for value and without notice of the earlier assignment, he will take priority.

This is the existing law. The only change I would propose is that, in both types of case, the subsequent encumbrancer would only take priority where he had perfected his interest (by taking legal title or by giving notice) at a time when he did not have actual or constructive notice of the earlier interest. The problem with the current law is that such a person can obtain priority by perfecting his interest even though he is aware that someone else had already taken an interest, thereby promoting an unseemly scramble for priority when the facts get out. This would seem to be an unnecessary application of the Darwinian principle of the survival of the fittest.

In practice, even under the existing law, it is difficult for a subsequent encumbrancer to take advantage of the bona fide purchaser rule or the rule in *Dearle* v. *Hall*. Even under the existing rules, he cannot do so if, at the time he took his interest, he had actual or constructive notice of the earlier encumbrance. The advent of the registrability of many security interests in the nineteenth century has had a major effect on the issue of notice, and it is to registration that we must now turn.

Registration

English law has two registration systems, which serve different purposes – asset registries and debtor registries. The main purpose of most of the asset registries is to provide a system for the registration of the ownership of, and other dealings in, assets the value of which is such that the costs of the registration system are outweighed by the benefits which it provides. The Land Registry is the most obvious example, but there are also registries for ships, aircraft, patents and certain other types of intellectual property. The basic principle with all of these registries is that, as between two registrable dispositions (whether outright or by way of security), priority depends on the date of registration, rather than on the date of creation; and a registered disposition will take priority over a registrable, but unregistered, one.[71]

The asset registries serve a useful priority function, not least by making it easier for a person wishing to obtain an interest in a registered asset to establish whether there are any existing encumbrances over it. If that person acquires a registered interest in the asset, he will not be bound by any registrable, but unregistered, interests in that asset.

That is a desirable solution to the priority problem, but only in respect of assets of sufficient value that a person who wishes to acquire an interest in the asset would expect to have to search the register. This is the case in relation to those assets which are now the subject of asset registries but, if the principle were to be extended to other types of asset, they would need to be assets of a type which are of sufficient value that a person wishing to acquire an interest in them would expect to have to search the register. To some extent, the very creation of the register may have this effect, but it is a reason why there are limits to the extension of such registration systems to other assets.

I have one concern about the priority rules established by the asset registries. It relates to the position of a person who acquires a registered interest with notice of a registrable, but unregistered, interest. The registration systems for intellectual

71 See, for instance: Land Registration Act 2002, ss. 29, 30 and 48; Merchant Shipping Act 1995, Sched 1, para. 8; Mortgaging of Aircraft Order 1972, Art. 14.

property give the person with the unregistered interest priority in such a case.[72] In contrast, the registration systems for ships and aircraft give it to the holder of the registered interest priority;[73] and, the same seems to be the case in relation to registered land. Although the land registration system is not explicit, it seems to be generally accepted that the sanctity of the register requires the holder of the registered interest to take priority in such circumstances. But, even in the case of land, ships and aircraft, it might nevertheless be the case that the registered holder would hold its legal title to the asset on constructive trust for the person with the earlier, unregistered interest if the registered holder was aware of that interest at the time it acquired its registered interest.[74] Whether or not this is correct, I suggest that this ought to be the position, and that it should be expressed in the relevant legislation.

Subject to this qualification, the concept that the date of registration will govern the priority of registrable interests has much to recommend it where the assets concerned are of a value that makes it cost-effective to require registration and the searching of the register each time a disposition is to be made.

The other type of registration system is against the debtor rather than the asset. In the case of companies, this involves the registration of mortgages and charges over (but not pledges or outright dispositions of) most types of asset at Companies House.[75] Unlike the asset registries, registration at Companies House does not directly affect priorities.[76] The purpose of the companies register is to provide information to those dealing with the company. It is not a title registry. The registration provisions of the Companies Act do, nevertheless, have an indirect effect on priorities in two ways. The first is that a registrable, but unregistered, charge is, for most purposes, void, and will not, therefore, trouble any other person with security over the same asset.[77]

More important in practice is that the registration of a charge at Companies House may give other persons notice of that charge, and thereby prevent them from relying on the bona fide purchaser rule or, the rule in *Dearle* v. *Hall* in attempting to obtain priority over an earlier encumbrancer.[78] It is beyond the scope of this chapter to consider the issue in detail. In brief, it is suggested that the registration of a charge will only constitute notice of it to a person dealing with the debtor if either that person searched the register and thereby obtained actual notice of it or, in the circumstances of the transaction, he ought to have searched the register and, if he had, would have discovered the existence of the earlier charge.[79] In this regard, secured lenders will be expected to search the register, because that is their practice.

72 See: Patents Act 1977, s. 33; Trade Marks Act 1994, s. 25.

73 See: Merchant Shipping Act 1995, Sched 1, para. 8(1); Mortgaging of Aircraft Order 1972, Art. 14(4).

74 If the later encumbrancer had notice of the earlier encumbrance, it would be using the statutory provisions to commit a fraud; see *Rochefoucauld* v. *Boustead* [1897] 1 Ch. 196.

75 See generally Companies Act 2006, Part 25.

76 Unlike the legislation concerning the asset registries, the relevant provisions of the Companies Act make no reference to priorities.

77 See Companies Act 2006, s. 874.

78 See *Wilson* v. *Kelland* [1910] 2 Ch 306.

79 Unlike certain asset registries (e.g. under the Mortgaging of Aircraft Order 1972, Art. 13), the Companies Act provisions make no reference to registration constituting notice. It follows that a person can only obtain constructive notice of a registered charge under the normal principles, as to which see: *Barclays Bank* v. *O'Brien* [1994] 1 AC 180, pp. 195–6, *per* Lord Browne-Wilkinson; and the Law of Property Act 1925, s. 199(1).

Purchasers, however, are in a different position. In some types of case a purchaser might be expected to search the register, but not in all cases.

If that is the approach of the law, I would suggest that it is the right one. A person should not be able to rely on the bona fide purchaser rule or on the rule in *Dearle* v. *Hall* in order to take priority over an existing proprietary interest if:

(a) he knew of the existing interest (that would effectively amount to fraud); or
(b) he ought to have been aware of it (the right question to ask is not simply whether the person concerned knew, but whether a reasonable person in his position ought to have known).

There is no doubt that this approach can give rise to uncertainty in individual cases, but it does seem to be the only rule which properly weighs the competing expectations of the parties. I would, therefore, suggest that the law on constructive notice be clarified in the companies legislation so that a person who: (a) obtains a charge over an asset of the debtor; or (b) ought to have searched the register in the course of acquiring any other type of proprietary interest in the debtor's asset, will have constructive notice of the existence of charges which are on the register at the time he acquires his interest, but that no one else should have constructive notice of anything on the charges register at Companies House.

This approach would also justify one further refinement, which has been suggested by the Law Commission[80] that, as between registrable fixed charges, the first to register should take priority. On the assumption (which it is suggested is correct) that a person taking a charge over an asset from a company ought to search the register (and would, therefore, be deemed to have constructive notice of it), it is but a small step to provide expressly that the priority of registrable charges depends on the date of their registration, rather than on the date of their creation.

Are the equities equal?

The decision in *Dearle* v. *Hall* that the subsequent assignee took priority over the earlier one was largely a result of the application of the principle that, as between two equitable interests, the first in time only prevails 'if the equities are equal'. In that case, it was held that the equities were not equal because the first assignee, by not giving notice to the trustees, had allowed the beneficiary of the trust to create another assignment over the same asset. Many cases concerning dispositions of land in the nineteenth century were decided on the same principle, frequently where the first chargee had allowed the debtor to retain possession of the title deeds to the property, thereby enabling him to purport to transfer the land to someone else.[81]

There are two contradictory ideas running through these cases, the contrasting approaches of which can be illustrated by comparing the reasoning of Kindersley VC in *Rice* v. *Rice*[82] in 1853 with that of Lord Westbury LC in *Phillips* v. *Phillips*,[83] eight years later. The approach of Kindersley VC was to consider the conduct of both

80 See Law Commission Report No. 296, fn 1, paras 3.149–3.155.
81 There are many such cases; see, for example, *Farrand* v. *Yorkshire Banking Co* (1888) 40 ChD 182.
82 (1853) 2 Drew 73.
83 (1861) 4 De G F&J 208.

persons claiming priority in order to see if one had a better right to priority than the other. He said that:[84]

> In all cases of contest between persons having equitable interests the conduct of the parties and all the circumstances must be taken into consideration, in order to determine which has the better equity.

Only if the claimants cannot be distinguished on the basis of their conduct does priority of time become a relevant consideration.

The approach of Lord Westbury LC in *Philips* v. *Philips* was rather different. He said:[85]

> I take it to be a clear proposition that every conveyance of an equitable interest is an innocent conveyance, that is to say, a grant of a person entitled merely in equity passes only that which he is justly entitled to and no more.

The tension between these two ways of approaching the issue was played out in a series of cases mostly decided in the nineteenth century and most of which involved priority disputes concerning land.[86] The cases dried up in the twentieth century, and the extension of registered land has had the effect that such issues are no longer of relevance in most cases concerning land. And, paradoxically, although *Dearle* v. *Hall* was itself an example of a case where priority was given to the second assignee because the equities were not equal, later cases established that the rule that the person who gives notice first will take priority is an absolute rule, subject to just two exceptions, and that there is no room for any broader consideration of the conduct of the parties.

For these reasons, the 'equal equities' principle is now likely to be of most concern in relation to fixed security over goods and shares. In theory, a person with an equitable charge over shares might be postponed to a subsequent equitable chargee if the conduct of the first chargee was such that it had enabled the debtor to hold itself out as having the unencumbered right to the shares. This would be a particular issue in relation to shares because a charge over shares is not registrable at Companies House, and there can therefore be no question of the later chargee obtaining constructive notice of the earlier charge.

Although these principles no longer appear to have any material effect in practice, it would be helpful if they could be clarified. The best answer may well be that, having spawned the rule in *Dearle* v. *Hall*, the 'equal equities' principle can now be laid to rest except in cases where the creditor has held out the debtor as having the authority to create the interest.

Tacking further advances

Once it has been established that one charge takes priority over another, it might have been expected that its priority would extend to all obligations secured by it, regardless of when they were incurred. If, for instance, a charge is created in favour

84 (1853) 2 Drew 73 at p. 83.
85 See: (1861) 4 De G F&J 208, p. 215.
86 Compare, for instance, *Northern Counties of England Fire Insurance Company* v. *Whipp* (1884) 26 ChD 482 with *Walker* v. *Linom* [1907] 2 Ch. 104.

of A to secure all monies from time to time lent under an overdraft, and that charge ranks in priority to a charge then created in favour of B, it might be expected that A's charge will rank in priority to B's charge in respect of all monies lent by A under the overdraft, whether before or after B's charge was created.

During the eighteenth century and the first half of the nineteenth century, that was the position. In *Gordon* v. *Graham*,[87] the debtor created a mortgage in favour of A to secure present and future indebtedness and then a second mortgage in favour of B to secure a fixed amount of money. B was aware of the first mortgage. A, with knowledge of B's mortgage, continued to lend money to the debtor, and the question arose as to the priority of his security in respect of the money lent after he became aware of B's mortgage. Lord Cowper LC held that A had priority in respect of all of the money which he had lent.

Such an approach has a great deal to commend it. A's security interest was created before B's, B was aware of the terms of A's security and, once A had priority, he was therefore able to retain it.

The issue seemed to be settled but the increase of lending on overdraft in the nineteenth century led to a challenge to this principle and, in *Hopkinson* v. *Rolt*,[88] the House of Lords overruled *Gordon* v. *Graham* and decided that, in such a case, A's priority would only extend to money lent by him up to the time he received notice of B's mortgage. If he continued to lend money after he became aware of B's mortgage, then his security would rank behind money lent by B in the meantime.

The effect of *Hopkinson* v. *Rolt* is that, once the priority of a charge has been established in accordance with the principles discussed above, it is still possible for the chargee to lose his priority if he continues to lend money after he becomes aware of a subsequent charge over the same asset. There have been various attempts to justify this rule, none of which is remotely convincing. A number of refinements to the rule have been required, both in case law and in legislation.[89] It can nevertheless create material problems in practice, particularly when combined with the rule in *Clayton's* case, as can be seen by the decision of the House of Lords in *Deeley* v. *Lloyds Bank*.[90]

I would suggest that the rule in *Gordon* v. *Graham* is far preferable to that in *Hopkinson* v. *Rolt*, and that all restrictions on the tacking of further advances should be abolished. Once a person can establish that his charge has priority over another interest, that priority should extend to all obligations secured by the charge, regardless of when they are incurred. Such a rule would be both simpler and fairer than the current law.

Floating charges

The priority rules concerning floating charges are very different from those which apply to fixed charges. This follows from the very nature of a floating charge. Where the creditor has a fixed charge, the debtor is unable to dispose of it free from the charge, or create a proprietary interest over it ranking ahead of the charge, without the consent of the chargee. With a floating charge, however, the chargor is given the general prospective authority by the chargee to dispose of, or otherwise deal with, the assets which are the subject of the floating charge free from the charge until it

87 (1716) 2 Eq. Cas. Abr. 598.

88 (1861) 9 HLC 514.

89 See: *West* v. *Williams* [1899] 1Ch. 132; Law of Property Act 1925, s. 94; Land Registration Act 2002, s. 49.

90 [1912] AC 756.

crystallises.[91] It is therefore much easier to state the rules concerning the priority of floating charges than it is those relating to fixed charges. Subject to three exceptions, a floating charge will rank behind a subsequent disposition of the charged assets (whether outright or by way of security) – and it will do so simply because the debtor has the authority to create such interests in priority to the floating charge.

The most important of the three exceptions is that, where a floating charge asset is disposed of to someone who has actual or constructive notice of provision of a floating charge which prohibits the chargor from making that disposition free from the floating charge, the disponee will rank behind the floating charge.[92] In practice, such restrictions do not extend to outright dispositions (because the whole purpose of the floating charge is to enable the debtor to carry on business in the ordinary course), but floating charges almost invariably do contain restrictions on the ability of the chargor to create fixed charges. Under the current law, such a restriction is only effective if the subsequent chargee has actual or constructive notice of it.[93] Since the restriction is not a prescribed particular under the registration requirements of the Companies Act, the subsequent fixed chargee will not obtain constructive notice of it simply by the fact of its being registered. He will only obtain notice if he searches the register and finds the restriction, or becomes aware of it in some other way.

The Law Commission has suggested that the default rule should be varied so that the implied authority of the debtor under a floating charge should be limited to making outright disposals, and that it should not extend to the creation of security.[94] It would be possible for the parties to agree a variation of this default rule. Such an amendment to the law would, I suggest, be useful, and it would reflect the expectations of the parties to security transactions. If such a change were made, the default rule would be that the chargor would have the prospective general authority to dispose of its assets outright, but not the authority to create security over them unless specifically authorised to do so in the floating charge document.

The second exception is that the debtor has no authority to create a prior-ranking floating charge over substantially the same assets.[95] If the proposal described above were implemented, this exception would be subsumed in the former.

Finally, a series of cases decided in the last decade of the nineteenth century and the first decade of the twentieth century established different rules for execution creditors than apply in relation to other persons who obtain interests in the debtor's assets. This resulted from a confusion in the cases as to the precise nature of a floating charge. In principle, an execution creditor, like anyone else who obtains an interest in the assets of the debtor, should take priority over the floating charge if he obtains his interest before the floating charge crystallises. This is not the case with execution creditors. They only take priority if they complete their execution by the time the floating charge crystallises. There would seem to be no justification for having a rule for execution creditors which is different from that which applies to any other person dealing with the company, and the law could be simplified by bringing execution creditors into line with those other persons.[96]

91 See: *Re Panama, New Zealand and Australian Royal Mail Company* (1870) LR 5 Ch. App. 318; *Wheatley* v. *Silkstone and Haigh Moor Coal Co.* (1885) 29 ChD 715.

92 See *English and Scottish Mercantile Investment Company* v. *Brunton* [1892] 2 QB 700.

93 See *English and Scottish Mercantile Investment Company* v. *Brunton* [1892] 2 QB 700.

94 See Law Commission Report No. 296, fn 1, paras 3.176–3.180.

95 See: *Re Benjamin Cope & Sons* [1914] 1Ch. 800.

96 The cases are discussed in detail in Calnan 'Priorities between execution creditors and floating chargees' (1982) 10 NZULR 111.

Summary

In summary, although the existing priority rules are complex, they do not appear to be creating material problems in practice, and a series of relatively minor reforms would help to make them work better. These include:

- the abolition of the rules concerning the tacking of the legal estate to assets other than land;
- the abolition of the rule that an assignee or chargee of a debt can, by giving notice to the person who owes the debt, take priority over an earlier encumbrance where he becomes aware of the earlier encumbrance after his interest is created but before giving notice;
- the establishment of the principle that a person who acquires a registered interest will not take free of an earlier unregistered interest of which he had notice at the time he took his registered interest;
- subject to the preceding point, the ranking of charges which are registrable at Companies House by reference to the date of registration rather than the date of creation;
- the clarification of the extent to which registration at Companies House constitutes constructive notice;
- except in cases where the creditor has held out the debtor as having authority to create a prior interest, the abolition of the principle that the first-in-time rule and some of its exceptions only apply 'if the equities are equal';
- the abolition of the rules restricting the tacking of further advances;
- the establishment of a new default rule (subject to contrary agreement) that a debtor which has created a floating charge only has authority to make outright dispositions (and not to create charges) ranking ahead of the floating charge; and
- bringing the rules concerning the priority of execution creditors into line with the general priority rules concerning floating charges.

It is suggested that these changes would result in a simpler, more coherent and more practicable structure for priorities than exists at the moment, while at the same time recognising that there is much to be said for preserving the good points of our current law rather than replacing it wholesale.

Enforcement

The ability to enforce security simply and cheaply is as important to a secured creditor as its creation and priority. Security is a means to an end, not an end in itself. Its value consists in the ability of the creditor to turn the security into money in order to repay the secured obligations. The ability to enforce the security is required not only while the company is outside insolvency proceedings, but also when it is the subject of them. Because of the way in which insolvency law now deals with enforcement rights during insolvency proceedings, it is necessary to consider these issues separately – first enforcement outside insolvency proceedings, and then enforcement within insolvency proceedings.

Enforcement outside insolvency proceedings

Most security documents contain detailed provisions conferring various powers of enforcement on the secured creditor. Such provisions are, generally, effective and, in practice, secured creditors have few problems in enforcing their security outside insolvency proceedings. These provisions are crucial in practice because the underlying default rules are complicated, archaic and in need of reform.

In the absence of express provision in the security document, the creditor's powers of enforcement depend on the type of security interest which has been created. Historically, a legal mortgage gave the creditor the power to take possession of the mortgaged assets (even before default) and the power to foreclose the mortgage (i.e. to apply to the court for an order extinguishing the debtor's equity of redemption in the assets), but it had no power to sell the mortgaged assets or to appoint a receiver over them.[97] Conversely, an equitable chargee had the power to apply to the court for an order for the sale of the charged assets or for the appointment of a receiver over them, but he had no right to foreclose or to take possession of the charged property.[98] The rights of an equitable mortgagee fell between these two extremes.

Although the ability of a legal mortgagee to take possession of the mortgaged assets and to foreclose seem very powerful methods of enforcement, they were fraught with difficulty in practice, not least because of the lengthy court procedure required to foreclose and the extent of the liabilities incurred by a mortgagee which entered into possession of the mortgaged assets. Paradoxically, the more limited powers of a chargee to apply to the court for sale or receivership proved to be more valuable in practice. As a result, the practice had developed, at least by the early nineteenth century, for security documents to give creditors express powers to sell and to appoint a receiver, without the necessity to apply to the court to do so. These provisions became so widespread that they have been implied by statute since 1860,[99] and are now contained in the Law of Property Act 1925.[100]

The problem with the implied powers contained in the Law of Property Act is that there is some doubt as to their applicability to mortgaged assets other than land,[101] and they contain quite complicated provisions which are, in practice, invariably contracted out of in mortgage documents.[102] As default powers for secured creditors, they therefore leave much to be desired.

In view of the ubiquity of detailed enforcement powers in security documents, there is no pressing need to reform the law in this area, but it would nevertheless be helpful if the default powers of all secured creditors could be set out clearly in statute. The current default powers are unclear in many respects, they differ depending on the nature of the security interest concerned and the nature of the asset which is the subject of the security, they contain methods of enforcement (such as foreclosure) which are not used in practice, and the restrictions on enforcement contained in the Law of Property Act do not reflect current practice. A simplified set of default rules which would apply to all security interests over all assets and would reflect the practice in security documentation would be useful, not least because it would sweep away the necessity to consider a great deal of arcane case law which is no longer of

97 See generally: foreclosure: *Carter* v. *Wake* (1877) 4 ChD 605; possession: *Western Bank* v. *Schindler* [1977] Ch. 1, CA; no right to sell: *Cox* v. *Tool* (1855) 20 Beav 145 (although a mortgagee of goods does have an implied power of sale; *Re Morritt ex parte Official Receiver* (1886) 18 QBD 222, CA); no receivership: *Berney* v. *Sewell* (1820) 1 Jac & W 647.

98 See generally: sale: *Cox* v. *Toole* (1855) 20 Beav 145; receivership: *Berney* v. *Sewell* (1820) 1 Jac & W 647; no foreclosure: *Re Owen* [1894] 3 Ch. 220; no possession: *Vacuum Oil Co Ltd* v. *Ellis* [1914] 1 KB 693, p. 703, *per* Buckley LJ.

99 See Lord Cranworth's Act 1860.

100 Law of Property Act 1925, s. 85 *et seq.*

101 *Re Morritt ex parte Official Receiver* (1886) 18 QBD 222.

102 Particularly, the Law of Property Act 1925, s. 103.

any practical relevance. Legislation could, for instance, make it clear that any secured creditor had the power, on default, to appoint a receiver of the assets concerned, enter into possession of them or sell them. The legislation would need to make it clear that these powers could be expressly or impliedly contracted out of in any particular case, thus giving the required degree of flexibility to the parties to shape the enforcement powers to the particular context of their transaction.

Of more importance in practice are the authorities which establish the responsibilities of secured creditors and receivers when enforcing security. The cases are not easy to reconcile. Some dicta suggest that the duties of secured creditors and receivers are very limited,[103] but the preponderance of authority since the nineteenth century establishes that they do owe significant duties to the debtor and to unsecured creditors, although their primary concern is to have the secured debt repaid.[104]

The difficulty in establishing clear rules is not surprising. The courts have had to weigh the interests of the creditor and the debtor. The creditor wants to be repaid as quickly as possible. The debtor wants to ensure that full value is obtained for the charged assets. The courts have had to strike a balance between these competing interests.

The law has accordingly recognised that the powers of enforcement of a secured creditor are provided for its benefit in order to enable the secured liability to be repaid, and the creditor is therefore entitled to exercise them in its own interests, although subject to certain safeguards to protect the interests of the debtor. What this means in practice is that the creditor can enforce or decline to enforce its security when it wants to do so and in its own interests. Timing issues are in its control but, once the creditor or receiver has decided to exercise its powers, it must do so in a reasonable manner.[105]

There may be some merit in attempting to codify these principles, but experience of attempting to do so in other areas (such as the proposed codification of directors' duties) has tended to indicate that to do so may restrict the flexibility of the courts to adapt the principles to meet changing requirements. That is not to say that an attempt should not be made to codify the principles, just that a codification should be drafted in broad enough terms to enable this flexibility to continue.

Enforcement within insolvency proceedings

Until relatively recently, English law did not restrict a secured creditor's powers of enforcement if the debtor was in insolvency proceedings. Indeed, in a liquidation, it is still open to a secured creditor to enforce its security without reference to the liquidation. This is because, with one exception, to the extent that the debtor's assets are the subject of a security interest, they fall outside the scope of the assets available to be used by the liquidator to pay creditors.[106]

The introduction of the administration procedure in the Insolvency Act 1986 created the first qualification to this principle. A secured creditor is unable to enforce its security if the debtor is in administration unless it obtains the consent of the

103 See: *Kennedy* v. *De Trafford* [1896] 1 Ch 762; [1897] AC 180; *Re B Johnson & Co (Builders) Ltd* [1955] Ch. 634; *Downsview Nominees Ltd* v. *First City Corpn Ltd* [1993] AC 295.

104 *See: Farrar* v. *Farrars Ltd* (1888) 40 ChD 395; *Cuckmere Brick Co Ltd* v. *Mutual Finance Ltd* [1971] Ch 949; *Medforth* v. *Blake* [2000] Ch. 86.

105 See the cases cited in fns 103–104, above, and *Bank of Baroda* v. *Panessar* [1987] Ch. 335.

106 See: *Re David Lloyd & Co* (1877) 6 ChD 339; *Buchler* v. *Talbot* [2004] 2 AC 298. The one exception is that certain liabilities are payable in priority to the chargee out of floating charge realisations.

administrator or the permission of the court.[107] A similar moratorium applies where a 'small company' proposes to enter into a company voluntary arrangement under the Insolvency Act 2000, although this procedure is rarely used in practice. The Enterprise Act 2002 did not formally alter the position but, in practice, the restriction of administrative receivership and the consequent extension of administration brought about by that legislation will increase the number of cases in which a secured creditor is prevented from enforcing security.

It is beyond the scope of this chapter to consider these insolvency law issues in any detail. They deserve a chapter to themselves. However, it is worth making the point that most of the practical problems faced by secured creditors at present do not derive from concerns about the law of security but from developments in insolvency law over the last twenty years. The problems include:

- the ability of an administrator to prevent a secured creditor from enforcing its security when it wishes to do so (and the consequent potential for the value of the security to be reduced);
- the abolition of administrative receivership in many cases, a concept which the Cork Committee Report of 1982, described as being 'of outstanding benefit to the general public and to society as a whole';[108] and
- the proliferation of different insolvency procedures and the complication and uncertainty which results (particularly as to the circumstances in which enforcement can be by administrative receivership rather than administration).[109]

Conclusions

The purpose of this chapter has been to suggest that a successful system of security law enables security to be created as simply and cheaply as possible, with a minimum of formality and a maximum of flexibility and certainty, while at the same time protecting unsecured creditors and others who deal with the debtor. I suggest that English security law meets these objectives well and that it does so largely because of three things – a law of contract which generally gives parties the freedom to make their own bargains, a law of equity which enables proprietary interests to be created simply and with a minimum of formality, and statutory provisions which require the registration of non-possessory security.

As a result, English law of security has the following very material benefits:

- it is easy to create, without many formalities;
- it is a unified system, without the necessity to use different types of procedure for different types of asset;
- it is flexible, and gives creditors the choice of using more formal procedures or relying on the informality of an equitable charge;
- within limits, it allows the parties the freedom to vary their rights and duties by contract;
- it is concerned with the substance, rather than the form, of transactions; and
- it provides a registration system for non-possessory security which enables third parties to become aware of security which has been created.

107 See Insolvency Act 1986, Sched B1, para. 43.

108 See Insolvency Law and Practice – Report of the Review Committee (1982) Cmnd 8558 (London: HMSO, 1982), para. 495 (Chair Sir Kenneth Cork).

109 See Insolvency Act 1986, s. 72B–H.

I would therefore suggest that there is no need for any major structural change to the English law of security.

The main problem is not security law, but insolvency law. There are two issues. The first is the requirement imposed by insolvency law to distinguish between fixed and floating charges. If insolvency law were to be reformed in a way which obviated the necessity to do so, one of the main practical problems of secured lenders would be solved. The other problem of insolvency law is more intractable. It stems from legislation over the last 20 years which has limited the powers of secured creditors in an insolvency and has resulted in a proliferation of different insolvency procedures and consequent complication and uncertainty. Many of the problems have been caused by the ill-thought out provisions of the Enterprise Act 2002.

As far as security law itself is concerned, although there is no need for major structural change, there are a number of incremental changes to the system which would assist its smooth operation. I have suggested a number of these. In relation to guarantees, the Statute of Frauds should be repealed and consideration should be given to simplifying the law concerning guarantee protections. Certain adjustments to the procedure for the registration of company charges would enable the system to work more efficiently and fairly than it does at the moment. Although our current priority rules are complicated, their wholesale replacement is likely to cause as many problems as it solves, but a number of changes to our existing rules would enable them to work better. As far as enforcement of security is concerned, consideration should be given to simplifying the default powers of secured creditors.

Finally, it is appropriate to comment on the process of law reform. There were two main problems with the Law Commission's proposals of 2002 to 2005.[110] These were, first, that the Commission tried to do too much and, second, that its mandate to review the law only arose because of the proposed major overhaul of company law. What we now need is a process which will promote the gradual reform of English commercial law in a more systematic way. In some areas (the bills-of-sale legislation is an obvious example), the wholesale change of existing law is required. However, as this chapter has suggested, it is more often the case that what is needed is relatively minor incremental changes to make the system work more efficiently than it does at present. A good way of doing this would be by means of an annual commercial law reform act. English commercial law can be a very dynamic force, not least because of the flexibility of our law of contract and equity. We need to find a method of keeping it up to date without it losing that dynamism.

110 On which see fn 1 above.

5 Exceptions to the *nemo dat* rule in relation to goods and the Law Commission's proposals in the Consultative Report

Louise Gullifer

Introduction

The basic rule governing transfer of title in English law is *nemo dat quod non habet.*[1] While this is the fundamental principle, which applies to every sort of asset, it is subject to a large number of exceptions, which vary according to the asset in question. For example, the need for unrestricted and simple transfer of negotiable instruments has led to the development of the status of holder in due course, who obtains good title even from a thief. This chapter is confined to the application of the rule to goods. The exceptions to the rule in relation to goods can be criticised as being piecemeal, inconsistent and lacking in principle. However, even though imperfectly exemplified in the rules of the current law, one can detect two interconnected themes. First, an owner who holds out someone else as authorised to transfer title to his goods, is estopped from denying that authority. Second, possession is an indication of ownership, and so possession without ownership indicates 'false wealth'.[2] This is one of the main justifications for requiring the registration of security interests. However, it also arises in contexts other than where security interests are granted, for example, where goods are bailed to another person, where goods are stolen and where goods are found. English law does not allow one who acquires goods in good faith from someone in possession to take free of all previous interests. Although the rules are somewhat inconsistent, generally a person in possession of goods without the consent of the owner (for example, a thief) is not able to pass a better title than he has. A person in possession of goods[3] with the consent of the owner is sometimes, though not always, able to pass a better title than he has.

1 Literally, one cannot give what one has not got: one cannot transfer a better title than one has. This can also be expressed as 'first in time wins'; see R. M. Goode *Legal Problems of Credit and Security* (London: Sweet & Maxwell, 4th edn, 2008), p. 176.

2 See generally: R. M. Goode *The Modernisation of Personal Property Security Law* (1984) 100 MLR 234; A. L. Diamond, *A Review of Security Interests in Property* (London: HMSO, 1989) hereafter '*The Diamond Report*', ch. 17; D. Baird and T. Jackson, 'Possession and ownership: an examination of the scope of Article 9' (1983) 35 *Stanford Law Review* 175.

3 Or a document of title relating to the goods.

The exceptions to the *nemo dat* principle have been the subject of much criticism and calls for reform.[4] Part of the area is governed by the dominance of the good faith purchaser of a legal interest over an equitable interest and part by the statutory exceptions to the rule which govern transfers at law. The application of the law to absolute and security interests is inconsistent, and the statutory exceptions themselves include detailed limits which can mean that like cases are not treated alike, most notably since the statutory exceptions are located in the Sale of Goods Act 1979 and therefore generally only apply to sale transactions.[5] There have been various proposals to reform the law,[6] but little has been achieved except the abolition of the market overt rule.[7] Attempts at rationalisation have met with little success: the proposal by the Department of Trade and Industry that the innocent purchaser from someone who is in possession of the goods with their owner's consent should acquire good title[8] was heavily criticised[9] and never developed beyond the (very short) consultation document. Since many of the situations in which the exceptions to the *nemo dat* rule operate involve title retention devices, arguably the reform of the law on personal property security interests would seem an excellent opportunity to put this area of the law on a more rational footing. This was the view taken by Professor Diamond, who recommended in his Report not only the reform of the law on innocent purchasers of goods subject to security interests, but a general principle which was to apply whenever possession was given under a sale contract, a conditional sale contract, a hire-purchase agreement or a leasing contract.[10] The principle suggested was that where an owner of goods has entrusted goods to, or acquiesced in their possession by, another person who disposes of them to an innocent purchaser in the ordinary course of business, the innocent purchaser would obtain the title to which he was entitled under his contract to the full extent that the person who entrusted the goods could have bestowed.[11] However, the principle was not to extend to mere loans (or presumably other bailments, such as bailment for repair) or short-term hiring contracts. Nor did the Diamond Report consider the difficult question of whether one who gains possession through fraud or theft should be able to pass good title. The former situation has recently been considered by the House of Lords in *Shogun Finance Ltd* v. *Hudson*,[12] where the majority decided the case by application of principles of the law of contract, but which arguably throws up a problem of property rights which should be considered in the context of overall reform of the *nemo dat* exceptions.

4 See: R. M. Goode, *Commercial Law* (London, Lexis-Nexis UK, 3rd edn, 2004), p. 446; *The Diamond Report*, fn 2, ch. 13; Department of Trade and Industry: Consultation Document *Transfer of Title: Sections 21 to 26 of the Sale of Goods Act 1979* (London: DTI, 1994) hereafter '*DTI Consultation Document*'.

5 See M. Bridge, *The Sale of Goods* (Oxford: Oxford University Press, 2nd edn, 2009) p. 545.

6 Law Reform Committee, *12th Report on Transfer of Title to Chattels* (1966, Cmnd 2958); *The Diamond Report*, fn 2; *DTI Consultation Document*, fn 4.

7 Contained in the Sale of Goods Act 1979, s. 22(1), abolished by the Sale of Goods (Amendment) Act 1994.

8 *DTI Consultation Document*, fn 4.

9 See generally: (1994) 110 LQR 165; [1994] LMCLQ 322–326; (1994) 13 Tr. Law 299.

10 *The Diamond Report*, fn 2, p. 77.

11 This provision mirrors the UCC provisions in Arts 2–403, 2A-305(2) and 9–320. However, UCC Arts 2–403 and 2A-305 only apply where the person to whom the goods are entrusted is a merchant who deals in goods of that kind.

12 [2004] 1 AC 919.

Although the Law Commission's terms of reference did not include the reform of the statutory exceptions to the *nemo dat* rule, much of the actual content of the proposal made by Professor Diamond would have been included if the Commission's proposals in its *Consultative Report* of 2004[13] concerning title-retention devices[14] had been enacted. The main difference in the short term would have been that only security interests created by companies would have been covered. This, of course, would have led to great inconsistencies, but these would have not been limited to the law on transfer of title.

The inclusion of title-retention devices in the scheme proposed in the 2004 *Consultative Report* attracted little support from those practitioners and those in the finance industry who responded to the consultation. While some consultees were against including such devices in any registration scheme, others objected to the limited nature of the scheme, in that it applied only to 'quasi-security' transactions (as opposed to absolute transfers) and it applied only to financing agreements made by companies.[15] As a result, the Law Commission did not include title-retention devices in the scheme set out in its Final Report of 2005. However, it had already included a project on transfer of title in its Ninth Programme of Law Reform,[16] and as a result of the responses, it recommended that the registration and priority of title-retention devices should be reconsidered as part of, or in the light of, that project.[17] Nevertheless, the transfer of title project was not started during its Ninth Programme and in its Tenth Programme of Law Reform the Law Commission acknowledged that reform of these areas 'remain controversial'. However, in June 2008 the Law Commission stated that it would consider the case for starting the project as part of its Eleventh Programme.[18] Thus, we will have to wait and see if further action will be taken.

This chapter will explore the extent to which the Law Commission's proposals in the *Consultative Report* of 2004 would have changed the existing law and it will also address problems identified which would not have been dealt with by these proposals. It will refer to the personal property security schemes in four different jurisdictions: the US,[19] New Zealand,[20] Ontario[21] and Saskatchewan.[22] It is to be hoped that the project on transfer of title will be revisited in the near future along

13 Law Commission Consultation Paper No. 176: *Company Security Interests. A Consultative Report*; hereafter 'Consultative Report' (London: The Stationery Office, 2004). In 2005 the Law Commission published its *Final Report: Company Security Interests* (2005) Cmnd 6654; hereafter 'The Final Report'. However, the latter Report was a more modest document confined to company charge reform; see further the chapters by de Lacy and McCormack in the present volume, pp. 73–76 and pp. 96–116.

14 Such as finance leases, hire-purchase agreements, conditional sales and retention-of-title clauses.

15 See Law Commission Report No. 296 *Company Security Interests*, paras 1.60–1.66.

16 Law Com No. 293, HC 353, March 2005.

17 See Law Commission Report, fn 15, para. 1.66

18 See generally Law Commission *Tenth Programme of Reform Report 2008* (2008) HC 605, pp. 30–31, paras 4.3 and 4.4.

19 The Uniform Commercial Code (UCC), mainly Article 9 (revised) but also Articles 2 and 2A.

20 See New Zealand Personal Property Securities Act 1999 (as amended) (hereafter NZPPSA). See generally the chapter by Brown in the present volume, pp. 328–65.

21 See Ontario Personal Property Security Act 1990 (as amended) (hereafter OPPSA).

22 See Saskatchewan Personal Property Security Act 1993 (as amended) (hereafter SPPSA). The Saskatchewan Act is largely similar to the legislation in other Canadian jurisdictions except Ontario (which has some significant differences) and Quebec. The Law Commission used the SPPSA as a model for their draft legislation.

with the question of general reform of personal property security reform. Despite the fact that the work of the Law Commission is unfinished and it appears as if for the time being, at any rate, the government will not be enacting any further reforming legislation (now that the Companies Act 2006 is in force) these are areas of law which require urgent action. It is to be hoped that this chapter will demonstrate that an opportunity to reform the law has been missed and, that it will prompt further reconsideration of this area with a view to reforms being made.

Existing law: the statutory exceptions

The general rule of *nemo dat* applies both to successive legal interests and successive equitable interests.[23] Where the interests are less than absolute, for example, security interests, the rule becomes one of priority: first in time takes first. One major exception to the rule is that a legal interest acquired for value and without notice of a prior equitable interest overrides that interest.[24]

The statutory exceptions to the rule apply only to successive transfers of legal interests.[25] The mercantile agency, seller in possession and buyer in possession exceptions are all based on the principle that possession of goods[26] with consent of the person entrusting is an indication of false wealth. There are various limits to the extent to which such a possessor can pass good title to goods. These limits are unduly technical and inconsistent, particularly if all retention-of-title devices used for financing ('quasi-security interests') are seen as so similar that a rational system of law should treat them similarly. In considering the limits, it is necessary to distinguish between the two transactions referred to in the sections: first, the entrustment transaction and second the dispositive transaction.

The entrustment transaction

The sections only apply in specific situations of entrustment, which have been further refined by interpretation of the sections in the cases. Entrustment to a mercantile agent only falls within the Factors Act 1889, s. 2(1) when it is for a purpose connected with his business as a mercantile agent.[27] Section 24 of the Sale of Goods Act 1979 only applies to entrustment to a seller, and not to an owner under a contract of hire, or to a mortgagor. Section 25 only applies to entrustment to a buyer under an agreement to sell, not to a transfer of possession to a bailee under a hire-purchase agreement[28]

23 See R. M. Goode, *Legal Problems of Credit and Security*, fn 1, p. 176.

24 Ibid., p. 160. This has an important effect on priority in relation to security interests, see below.

25 It is not intended here to give a description of the statutory exceptions, which are to be found in: the Factors Act 1889, ss. 2(1), 8 and 9; the Sale of Goods Act 1979, ss. 23–25; and the Hire Purchase Act 1964, Part III. Detailed accounts can be found in: R. M. Goode *Commercial Law*, fn 4, pp. 417–46; A. G. Guest (ed.), *Benjamin's Sale of Goods* (London: Sweet & Maxwell, 7th edn, 2006), ch. 7; E. McKendrick (ed.), *Sale of Goods* (London: LLP, 2000), ch. 5; Atiyah *The Sale of Goods* (ed. J. Adams) (London: Pearson, 11th edn, 2005), ch. 21; op. cit., Bridge, fn 5, ch. 5.

26 Or a document of title relating to the goods.

27 See *Pearson* v. *Rose and Young Ltd* [1951] 1 KB 275, p. 288.

28 See *Helby* v. *Matthews* [1895] AC 471. Section 27 of the Hire Purchase Act applies to motor vehicles bailed on hire purchase.

or under a lease. Entrustment to a bailee for repair, storage or other purposes is not covered at all.

The dispositive transaction

Most sections[29] apply not only to sales by non-owners but also to pledges and other dispositions. Such a disposition is effective as if the entruster had expressly authorised it, that is, it is effective as to its terms. It is not entirely clear what is included within the term 'disposition'. Mere transfer of possession is not enough: it appears that there must be some transfer of an interest in property.[30] Thus delivery to a bailee for the purposes of sale, repair or storage is not included.[31] The question of whether a sale on retention-of-title terms is included is more difficult. Unless the full purchase price is paid, property does not pass, and so it can be argued that there is no transfer of an interest in property.

In *Re Highway Foods International*,[32] where A sold meat to B on retention-of-title terms, who sub-sold it to C, also on such terms, the court held that C did not obtain good title. It should be noted that, while the Sale of Goods Act, s. 25 applies only to delivery under 'any sale, pledge or disposition', the Factors Act, s. 9 also applies to delivery under 'any agreement for sale, pledge or other disposition'. Thus the decision in *Re Highway Foods International* was not based on the meaning of the word 'disposition', but on the argument that the effect of s. 9 is that the Factors Act, s. 2(1) applies to the transaction, and 'the effect of section 2(1) is to render the buyer's agreement for sale as valid as if it had been expressly authorised by the seller', thus in this

29 Factors Act 1889, ss. 2(1), 8 and 9; Sale of Goods Act 1979, ss. 24 and 25. The Hire Purchase Act 1964, s. 27 also refers to a 'disposition'.

30 See *Worcester Works Finance* v. *Cooden Engineering Ltd* [1972] 1 QB 210, p. 220 *per* Megaw LJ. It is unlikely that this includes creation of an equitable interest; see op. cit., Bridge, fn 5, p. 5.147

31 See generally: *Waddington & Sons* v. *Neale & Sons* (1907) 96 LT 786; *Roache* v. *Australian Mercantile Land & Finance Co. Ltd* [1966] 1 NSWLR 384 (delivery of goods to an auctioneer was not a 'disposition'); *Smith* v. *Campbell* (1911) 17 WLR 49 (Can.) (delivery of goods to a warehouse for storage not a disposition); op. cit., Bridge, fn 5, p. 5.147. Cf. *Shenstone* v. *Hilton* [1894] 2 QB 452, where a delivery to an auctioneer for the purposes of sale was said to be a 'delivery under an agreement of sale' within the Factors Act, s.9. This authority, however, is inconsistent with the later cases mentioned above decided under the Factors Act, s. 2(1) and rests upon what is now a false basis: the person delivering the goods had hired them under a hire-purchase agreement, which the court treated as an agreement to sell, relying on the decision of the Court of Appeal in *Helby* v. *Matthews* [1894] 2 QB 262, which was later overturned by the House of Lords [1895] AC 471.

32 [1995] 1 BCLC 209. The facts of the case were somewhat strange: A sold meat on retention-of-title terms to B who sub-sold it to C, also on retention-of-title terms. Neither B nor C paid anything under the sale agreements. C complained to A that a metal tag had been found in the meat. It was agreed that A would repossess the meat under its agreement with B, examine it and ensure that it was fit to eat and then resell it direct to C. C paid A directly for the meat. However, B's receiver alleged that A was not entitled to repossess the meat as title had passed to C under the Factors Act, s. 9, since B, a buyer in possession, had delivered the meat to C under an agreement to sell. The court held that since title did not pass to C under its agreement with B until full payment, s. 9 could not operate to give C title, and A was therefore entitled to repossess the meat pursuant to its agreement with B. It was, unusually, B, the buyer in possession, who argued that title had passed to C in order to claim the purchase money for itself, and it is understandable that the court felt that B's claim was unmeritorious.

case title has not passed.[33] The exact effect of this argument is not entirely clear. It can be argued that the seller (A) is therefore bound to honour B's agreement to sell, and, so long as C continues to pay the instalments due under the agreement, C is entitled to possession of the goods as against A.[34] That argument, however, would not have worked in the *Highway Foods* case itself, since under its agreement with C, B was entitled to repossess any of the goods on demand at any time before full payment.

Sales on retention-of-title terms are therefore theoretically covered by the extended wording of the Factors Act, ss. 8 and 9. Presumably the section also covers conditional sales.[35] It is, however, unlikely to cover hire-purchase agreements, since it is clear that these are not considered agreements to sell,[36] and will also not include leases. The question therefore remains whether such transactions are included in the word 'disposition'. It is clear that a hire-purchase agreement is not an agreement for a sale, nor is any property transferred until the option to purchase is exercised:[37] it is, therefore, a mere bailment, and could be said not to amount to a disposition of property.[38] However, there is considerable controversy over the closely related question of whether a lease gives the lessee a proprietary interest, or merely contractual rights.[39] It can be argued that the delivery of possession to the hirer or lessee gives him a real right,[40] and therefore there is a disposition. If this argument is correct, then the effect of the Factors Act, ss. 8 and 9 (and the Sale of Goods Act, ss. 24 and 25) would be that the hire-purchase agreement or lease was binding on the buyer (in a seller in possession case) or the seller (in a buyer in possession case) as if those persons had authorised it.[41]

Further, some dispositions only take effect if they are in the ordinary course of business of a mercantile agent dealing in goods of that kind.[42] Also, dispositions

33 *Re Highway Foods International* [1995] 1 BCLC 209, p. 214 *per* Edward Nugee QC. But the effect of s. 9 could be said to be more limited: s. 2(1) only provides that any *sale*, pledge or other disposition (not any agreement to sell, pledge or dispose) is as valid as if expressly authorised by the owner. See: op. cit., Atiyah, fn 25, p. 404; A. Tettenborn (1996) 55 CLJ 26, p. 28.

34 See Goode, *Commercial Law*, fn 4, p. 437.

35 It is not clear if consumer credit agreements would be covered. Section 9 includes equivalent wording to the Sale of Goods Act, s. 25(2). This specifically refers to the definition of a buyer in possession as not including a buyer under an agreement for the sale of goods which is a consumer credit agreement, but it might be strange to have one meaning for a buyer 'who has agreed to buy goods' and another for a (sub)-buyer 'under an agreement for sale'. However, no such wording appears in s. 8 (the seller in possession section), which also extends to a sub-buyer under an agreement for sale, and it might be even more inconsistent for ss. 8 and 9 to have different ambits.

36 See *Helby* v. *Matthews* [1895] AC 471.

37 See *Helby* v. *Matthews* [1895] AC 471.

38 Op. cit., Guest, fn 25, para. 7–064.

39 See. W. Swadling, 'The proprietary effect of a hire of goods' in N. Palmer and E. McKendrick (eds), *Interests in Goods* (London: LLP, 2nd edn, 1998); G. Watt, 'The proprietary effect of a chattel lease' (2003) 67 Conv. 62; B. McFarlane, 'Identifying property rights: a reply to Mr Watt' (2003) 67 Conv. 473.

40 See Goode *Commercial Law*, fn 4, p. 25.

41 Ibid., p. 433. See also Goode, *Hire Purchase Law and Practice* (London: Butterworths, 2nd edn, 1970), pp. 606, 607.

42 These are dispositions which trigger the exceptions in Factors Act, s. 2(1) and Sale of Goods Act, s. 25: see *Newtons of Wembley* v. *Williams* [1965] 1 QB 560.

under the Sale of Goods Act, ss. 24 and 25 require a transfer of possession to the recipient for the exceptions to operate.

The position of the recipient

The recipient only gets as good a title as the entruster had, so that if, for example, his title derived from a thief the recipient gets nothing.[43] This is sometimes called the doctrine of relative title.[44] Further, the recipient must be in good faith and without notice of the entruster's interest in the goods.

The effect of the existing law on transactions involving assets subject to security interests or quasi-security interests

The Law Commission's proposals in the *Consultative Report* would have affected the law relating to security interests and what are called 'quasi-security interests', which are title-retention devices which have the purpose of security.[45] The registration and priority provisions also were to apply to leases over one year. The purpose of this section is to examine the existing law applicable where goods which are subject to a security or quasi-security interest (including deemed security interests, such as operating leases over one year) are disposed of, either absolutely or by way of security. In the case of absolute dispositions, only the position of the disponee is examined. In certain circumstances, the secured party will have a secured claim to the proceeds of the disposition. Since this was the focus of the Law Commission's proposals, the principal focus of this discussion will be security interests or quasi-security interests created by companies, although many of the issues raised apply to interests created by non-companies as well.

Interests recognised as security interests under existing law

Pledge and lien

A pledge is created by the transfer of possession to the pledgee pursuant to an agreement to give security. Since a pledge is a legal interest, the *nemo dat* rule means that any subsequent transferee of the goods will take the goods subject to the pledge, unless an exception applies.

If a pledgee sells goods which are the subject of the pledge, this could be authorised by the power of sale under the pledge,[46] in which case the buyer takes free of the pledge. If the sale is unauthorised, the buyer will take subject to the pledge, unless the Sale of Goods Act, s. 21(2) applies, which is very unlikely. If a pledgor sells goods

43 See *National Employers' Mutual General Insurance Association Ltd* v. *Jones* [1990] AC 24

44 See: Battersby and Preston 'The concepts of "property", "title" and "owner" used in the Sale of Goods Act 1893' (1972) 35 MLR 268; Battersby, 'Reconsideration of "property" and "title" in the Sale of Goods Act' [2001] JBL 1.

45 See *Consultative Report*, fn 13, paras 2.81–84.

46 See *Burdick* v. *Sewell* (1884) 13 QBD 159.

which are the subject of a pledge, the buyer takes subject to the pledge even if he is unaware of it.[47] However, the pledgor is unlikely to be in possession of the goods, unless he has attorned to the pledgee. In this case, the pledge may have to be registered as a charge[48] but a purchaser would be very unlikely to search the register.

The position with a lien, a legal interest created by the retention of possession, is very similar to that in relation to a pledge. However, there is no automatic power of sale unless expressly agreed.

Mortgages and charges

Mortgages and charges that fall within the Companies Act 2006, s. 860 are required to be registered, and if not are unenforceable against the liquidator, administrator and creditors of the company.[49] There is no provision that unregistered charges are unenforceable against purchasers of the collateral from the company, but since purchasers usually take free from charges anyway, this is not of great practical significance. The order of priority between duly registered equitable mortgages and charges depends on date of creation, so that *nemo dat* principles apply. Although generally a later chargee will have notice of a registered earlier charge, there is an 'invisibility' period of 21 days from the date of creation of an earlier charge within which that charge can be registered and therefore take priority.[50] A later chargee taking a charge within that period may not have notice of the earlier charge even if it searches the register. A legal mortgagor will take free of an earlier equitable charge or mortgage, but not if it has notice of it.[51] Registration provides constructive notice.

Since mortgages and charges are forms of non-possessory security, it is very easy for the mortgagor or chargor to sell the goods. Often, as in the case of the floating charge or a mortgage with power to deal, there is an express or implied right to sell, in which case the buyer obtains good title.[52] Even where sale is not permitted, a buyer will usually take free of a charge or an equitable mortgage, since he acquires a legal interest for value and without notice of the equitable interest. Registration of the charge or mortgage will not usually constitute notice to the buyer, since it is only notice to those who would reasonably be expected to search the register,[53] which does

47 The buyer can only claim the goods on tendering the sum secured; see: N. Palmer & E. McKendrick *Interests in Goods*, above fn 39, p. 631; *Franklin* v. *Neate* (1844) LR 1 QB 585; *Johnson* v. *Stear* (1863) 15 CBNS 330.

48 See Law Commission Consultation paper no. 164 'Registration of Security Interests: Company Charges and Property other than Land' (LCCP), para. 4.15 n. 21 suggests that if the attornment is in writing this would requirement registration under the Companies Act 1985, s. 396(1)(c) – see now Companies Act 2006, s. 860(7)(b).

49 Companies Act 2006, s. 874.

50 See LCCP, fn 48, para. 2.37.

51 This is an application of the principle set out above.

52 The exact analysis of this process is a matter of debate. Some see it as an application of the principles of authority (*Re Castell & Brown Ltd* [1898] 1 Ch. 315, Goode *Legal Problems of Credit and Security*, fn 1, p. 196) or as an application of the principles of overreaching (R. C. Nolan 'Property in a fund' (2004) 120 LQR 108) or defeasance (S. Worthington 'Floating charges – an alternative theory' (1994) 53 CLJ 81). Much of this debate focuses on the nature of the interest created by the floating charge: there seems to be no doubt that the principles of authority apply where there is express authority, for example, where a fixed chargor sells property subject to the charge with the consent of the chargee.

53 Goode, *Legal Problems of Credit and Security*, fn 1, pp. 91–2.

not include buyers in the ordinary course of business.[54] If the buyer bought on retention-of-title terms, however, it would not obtain title until it had paid. A lessee's interest is legal and therefore would also take priority over an earlier equitable mortgage or charge, but the reversion would remain subject to the mortgage or charge.[55]

Sale of goods by a legal chattel mortgagor is less simple. The operation of the *nemo dat* rule would lead to the conclusion that the purchaser takes subject to the prior legal mortgage, unless any of the exceptions apply. The only likely exception is that in the Sale of Goods Act, s. 24 but although a mortgage involves the transfer of title to the mortgagee,[56] and can even take the form of a sale, s. 62(4) of that Act appears to prevent s. 24 applying to a mortgage.[57] Thus it seems reasonably clear that a buyer from a legal mortgagor would take the goods subject to the mortgage. As a matter of policy, it is very hard to see why there should be a different rule for those who finance by means of retention-of-title sales (and who therefore fall within s. 25 and risk losing their interest to a good faith buyer) and those who lend money on the security of a chattel mortgage. It has been argued that s. 62(4) should only apply to those provisions in the Sale of Goods Act concerning the contract between buyer and seller (the 'two-party sales issues'), and not to those provisions dealing with the transfer of title to third parties.[58] One further anomaly is that a purchaser would take subject to a legal mortgage even if it was not registered, as unregistered interests are not void as against a purchaser.[59]

Interests not recognised as security interests under the present law ('quasi-security interests')

Where goods are sold on retention-of-title terms, and then resold by the buyer in possession, either the sub-sale is authorised (in which case the sub-buyer gets good title) or, if the sub-buyer takes delivery, is in good faith and has no notice of the seller's interest, s. 25 operates to give the sub-buyer good title. If the sub-sale is also on retention-of-title terms, *Re Highway Foods* applies.[60] If the buyer bails the goods on hire-purchase

54 There is little direct authority on this point, but the equitable doctrine of constructive notice has been said to have no part in commercial transactions: *Manchester Trust* v. *Furness* [1895] 2 QB 539; *Feuer Leather Corporation* v. *Frank Johnstone & Sons* [1981] Com. LR 251. Some take a contrary view that registration is notice to all the world, see Gough *Company Charges* (London: Butterworths, 2nd edn, 1996), ch. 32, but this is hard to support, see J. de Lacy (ed.) *The Reform of United Kingdom Company Law* (London: Cavendish, 2002), ch.15.

55 This analysis depends on the view taken of the nature of a lease. If a lease gives the lessee a proprietary or possessory interest, this is clearly legal and would prevail against an earlier equitable interest. If it is a mere contractual right, then arguably it cannot bind a prior mortgagor or chargor.

56 Subject to a condition that the title to be transferred back on payment of the secured obligation.

57 That section provides: 'The provisions of this Act about contracts of sale do not apply to a transaction in the form of a contract of sale which is intended to operate by way of mortgage, pledge, charge or other security.'

58 See: Bridge *The Sale of Goods*, fn 5, p. 5.125; *The Diamond Report*, fn 2, para. 13.2.9. This would have been the effect of the Law Commission's proposals.

59 See p. 195 above.

60 See pp. 192–93 above.

terms or leases the goods to a third party, it is unclear whether the retention-of-title seller would be bound by the third party's rights under his contract.[61]

If goods are sold on retention-of-title terms, and, before the buyer takes possession, the seller resells the goods to a second buyer to whom property passes, the first buyer only has an action for damages. This is because the Sale of Goods Act, s. 24 and the Factors Act, s. 8 only apply where a seller has 'sold' goods. However, the exception to the *nemo dat* rule is not required in this case, as unless property has passed to the first buyer the seller still has good title which it can convey to the second buyer.[62]

The same analysis applies to conditional sales, hire purchase agreements and leases.

Section 25 does not apply where goods are bailed on hire-purchase terms.[63] The position, therefore, in relation to companies acquiring goods on credit, is that the company can pass good title to a sub-buyer or pledgee if it buys on retention-of-title or conditional sale terms, but not if it acquires the goods on hire-purchase terms. The distinction between the two types of contract is fine, and determining where the line lies has given rise to difficult questions of characterisation.[64] This inconsistency is hard to defend.

The position is different in relation to motor vehicles acquired on hire purchase. Under section 27 of the Hire Purchase Act 1964, where a motor vehicle is bailed on hire-purchase terms (or sold on conditional sale), a dealer purchaser from the bailee or buyer takes subject to the interest of the creditor (i.e. *nemo dat* applies) while a private purchaser takes free. Any subsequent private purchaser from the dealer purchaser also takes free of the creditor's interest.[65] The reason for this distinction is that hire-purchase or conditional sale agreements relating to motor vehicles can be registered with HPI or Experian, and dealers can be expected to search those registers.[66]

Where goods are leased to a company, whether under a finance lease or an operating lease, and the company then sells the goods, none of the exceptions to the *nemo dat* rule apply and the buyer takes subject to the lessor's interest. However, the position is very unclear when the goods are sold by the lessor. If the lessee has not yet taken possession of the goods, then it is reasonably clear that the buyer takes free from any claim by the lessee, and the lessee's only remedy is an action in damages for breach of contract against the lessor.[67] However, where possession has

61 See p. 193 above.

62 See: *Vowles* v. *Island Finances Ltd* [1940] 4 DLR 357; *Benjamin's Sale of Goods*, fn 25, para. 7–056. The seller, of course, is in breach of its contract with the first buyer.

63 See *Helby* v. *Matthews* [1895] AC 471

64 See: *Forthright Finance Ltd* v. *Carlyle Finance Ltd* [1997] 4 All ER 90; *Close Asset Finance Ltd* v. *Care Graphics Machinery Ltd* [2000] CCLR 43. Conditional sales to consumers are excluded from the ambit of s. 25, so the distinction is irrelevant in this context, although arguably the assimilation went the wrong way, since the result is that purchasers from such consumers lose all protection (see: op. cit., Atiyah, fn 25, p. 399; op. cit., McKendrick, fn 25, para. 5–080).

65 In each case the private purchaser must be in good faith and without notice of the relevant agreement.

66 It is now very easy for private purchasers to check the HPI register. the online service is relatively cheap and includes a great deal more information than just the existence of a prior hire-purchase agreement (ranging from whether the vehicle is on the Police National Register of cars reported stolen to whether the vehicle has had a registration plate change since April 1990). See www.hpicheck.com/last accessed 5.10.2009. See pp. 218–19 below. The distinction between purchases by dealers and by private buyers can now be said to be outdated, and can give rise to characterisation problems in practice; see *G. E. Capital Bank Ltd* v. *Rushton* [2005] EWCA Civ 1556.

67 See R. M. Goode *Proprietary Rights and Insolvency in Sales Transactions* (London: Sweet & Maxwell, 2nd edn, 1989), p. 7; N. Furey 'Goods leasing and insolvency' in Palmer &

already been given to the lessee, is the buyer of the goods bound by the lease? This is a question on which very different views have been expressed.[68] The situation could be said to fall totally within the law of obligations, in which case the lessee is limited to its action in contract against the lessor, and a possible action in tort against the third party, if the third party knew that it had interfered with the contract. However, if the lease gave the lessee some sort of proprietary, or possessory, interest, the *nemo dat* rule would dictate that the lessor could only sell its interest subject to that of the lessee (given that none of the exceptions apply). There are indications that the courts are moving towards recognition that a lessee has a proprietary or possessory interest,[69] but the evidence is not yet conclusive.

It remains to consider the effect of a true security interest created by the company over goods which are the subject matter of a quasi-security interest. This may either be created after the quasi-security interest, or may be a previously created interest which covers after-acquired property. Since the company does not own the goods, there is nothing to which the security interest can attach. At least in theory, any surplus value available on enforcement of the quasi-security interest belongs to the creditor, and so there can be no question of the quasi-security interest taking priority over the true security interest: the latter does not attach to the goods at all.[70]

Interests classified as security interests under the Law Commission's scheme

The Law Commission's proposals in the *Consultative Report* included as security interests all interests securing payment of an obligation, without regard to the form

McKendrick, *Interests in Goods*, fn 39, p. 787 (both deal with the related context of the lessor's insolvency).

68 Op. cit., Swadling fn 39, p. 491, maintains that a lease does not give rise to a proprietary interest, nor to a possessory interest that binds third parties owners, but is merely a contractual right which cannot be asserted against third parties. In support of this view see J. W. Harris, *Property and Justice* (Oxford: Clarendon Press, 1996), p. 59. Watt in 'The proprietary effect of a chattel lease' (2003) 67 Conv. 61, argues that Swadling is wrong, and that a lessee has an equitable proprietary interest in the goods leased. B. Macfarlane, 'Identifying proprietary right: a reply to Mr Watt' (2003) 67 Conv. 473, argues that Watt is wrong in saying that a lease gives proprietary rights, but does not express a view about the effect of the lessee's possessory interest as against a third party buyer. Others (op. cit., Goode, fn 41, pp. 35–6; Goode *Commercial Law*, fn 4, p. 55; F. H. Lawson and B. Rudden, *The Law of Property* (Oxford: Oxford University Press, 3rd edn, 2002), p. 116; J. Hill 'The proprietary character of possession' in (ed.) E. Cooke, *Modern Studies in Property Law Vol. 1 Property 2000* (Oxford: Hart, 2001); G. McMeel 'On the redundancy of the concept of bailment' [2003] LMCLQ 169) argue that a chattel lease can be enforced against a third-party buyer because it is a possessory interest.

69 See: *Bristol Airport plc* v. *Powdrill* [1990] Ch. 744 (where the Court of Appeal held that for the purposes of the Insolvency Act 1986, s. 11(3) (now Sched B1, s. 43), a lease gives a proprietary interest in a chattel); *Transag Haulage Ltd* v. *Leyland DAF Finance plc* [1994] 2 BCLC 88; *On Demand Information plc* v. *Michael Gerson (Finance) plc* [2001] 1 WLR 155 (CA) *per* Robert Walker, p. 171, approved by the HL *On Demand Information plc* v. *Michael Gerson (Finance) plc* [2003] 1 AC 368 *per* Lord Millett, para. 29 (a lessee under a chattel lease has a possessory interest in respect of which the court will give relief against forfeiture).

70 Obviously if there is a provision in the retention-of-title or hire-purchase or lease agreement for any surplus to be paid to the debtor on enforcement, then the true security interest could attach to that money at the time when it is paid, if it falls within the security agreement.

of the transaction, or the location of title.[71] Thus quasi-security interests were within the definition. Further, leases over one year and consignments were deemed to be security interests, so that the rules of priority and filing applied to them, but not the restatement of the incidents of security.[72] Following the UCC and PPSA model, the scheme had one set of priority rules which apply to all security interests, and which covered some situations of priority between security and absolute interests, but which did not cover priority conflicts between absolute interests. These fell outside the scheme and would have still been subject to the *nemo dat* rule, subject to the exceptions described above. However, in the proposed new project, the Law Commission will be able to examine the full extent of the priority rules in relation to all interests.

Priority between security interests created by the same debtor

Under the UCC, the PPSAs and also under the proposed scheme, the residual rules for priority between security interests in goods created by the same debtor are simple:

- A perfected security interest has priority over an unperfected one.
- Priority between perfected security interests depends on the date of perfection, whether by taking possession of the goods or by filing.
- Priority between unperfected security interests depends on the date of attachment.[73]
- A purchase-money security interest that is duly perfected takes priority over any previously perfected security interest (PMSI).[74]

It is in the nature of a notice-filing scheme, that the principles of the scheme override traditional *nemo dat* analysis. Let us first take the case of true security interests. An unperfected interest is ineffective against an administrator or liquidator,[75] thus the debtor company can 'pass' to its liquidator a greater interest than it has, since its interest is, apart from the provisions of the scheme, subject to the security interest. This is nothing new: exactly the same consequence flows at present from non-registration of company charges requiring registration under the Companies Act 2006, s. 860 (formerly the Companies Act 1985, s. 396). It is justified by the need to provide an incentive to register in order that the register should be a full and complete source of information, which is available to both prospective secured and unsecured creditors, and also credit agencies ('the registration argument').[76] The policy imperatives for this provision are very strong, and also justify the departure from *nemo dat* reasoning

71 See: *Consultative Report*, fn 13, para. 1.25 and appended Draft Regulations (DR) Reg. 3.

72 DRs 3(3), 8 and 9. In this the scheme followed the position under the New Zealand PPSA and all the Canadian PPSAs except Ontario. The UCC does not include leases under the Article 9 notice-filing system: priority rules relating to leases are contained in Article 2A.

73 The first three rules are contained in DR33.

74 DR 42. A PMSI is defined in DR4(1).

75 See: SPPSA, s. 20(2); OPPSA, s. 20(1)(b); UCC (revised) Art. 9–317(a)(2); DR 20(1).

76 See the discussion in M. Gedye, R. Cuming, R. Wood *Personal Property Securities in New Zealand* (Wellington: Brookers, 2002), pp. 8–10, criticising the New Zealand legislation which omits this provision, so that unregistered security interests are valid against the liquidator.

in a number of other contexts. Thus, an unperfected interest is ineffective against an execution creditor.[77] Further, an unperfected security interest loses priority to a perfected security interest created later.[78] Where both security interests are perfected, the first-to-file[79] rule means that the *nemo dat* reasoning which applies in current law will not apply. Thus despite the fact that when a second security interest is granted by a company, it can only grant an interest out of what interest it still has, if that second security interest is perfected first, it will have priority over the first security interest.[80] This rule applies irrespective of knowledge and without the application of any doctrine of constructive notice: the rules of the scheme are absolute.[81]

Second, let us take the case of quasi-security interests. Where a previously created, and filed, security interest covers goods acquired on retention-of-title terms, the retention-of-title agreement will be a PMSI and, if duly perfected, will take priority over previous security interests. The existing law reaches the same conclusion by application of the principle of *nemo dat* principles in that the debtor company never acquires any interest in the goods, and so no previous security interest can attach. Under the scheme, the retention-of-title seller is no longer seen as the owner of the goods, and will not be entitled to any surplus value.[82] A holder of a security interest which loses priority to a PMSI would therefore have a claim to the surplus.

The residual importance of *nemo dat* principles,[83] even within the scheme, can be seen by the requirement that for a security interest to attach, the debtor must have 'rights [or the power to transfer rights] in the collateral'.[84] This requirement is justified by the argument that if the debtor has no rights in the collateral, it cannot convey anything to the secured party.[85] However, the requirement of 'rights in the collateral'

77 So long as the execution creditor completes execution before perfection of the security interest: SPPSA, s. 20(1)(a); OPPSA, s. 20(1)(a)(ii); NZPPSA, s. 103; UCC (revised) Art. 9–317(a)(2); DR20(3).

78 See SPPSA, s. 35(1)(b); OPPSA, s. 20(a)(i); NZPPSA, s. 66(a); UCC (revised) Art. 9–322(a), DR33(1).

79 Or to perfect by other means.

80 This has the effect, *inter alia*, of abolishing the 21-day invisibility period which exists in current English law.

81 See, for example, in relation to the New Zealand scheme, L. Widdup and L. Mayne, *Personal Property Securities Act: a conceptual approach* (Wellington: Butterworths, 2000), p. 87. The first-to-file rule is preserved in the reduced version of the scheme proposed in the Law Commission Report, above fn 15.

82 DR65. This is the analysis employed in the PPSA and UCC jurisdictions. It was not entirely clear whether the Law Commission took this conceptual view: see *Consultative Report*, fn13, para. 2.116, although the practical results would be the same under its scheme. Some of those who responded to the consultation objected to fact that the seller would not have a right to the surplus, although this objection was chiefly made by lawyers rather than non-lawyers involved in the finance industry: see Law Commission Report, fn 15, para. 1.63.

83 Known as 'the derivative title theory' by many US and Canadian commentators.

84 See: UCC (revised) Art. 9–203; SPPSA, s. 12(2); OPPSA, s. 11(2); NZPPSA, s. 40; DR15(4) (the SPPSA, NZPPSA and OPPSA omit the section in square brackets).

85 See J. Ziegel and D. Denomme, *The Ontario Personal Property Security Act: Commentary and Analysis* (Toronto and Vancouver: Butterworths, 2nd edn, 2000), p. 125. See also *In re Emergency Beacon Corp.*, 665 F.2d 36, 40 (2d Cir. 1981) and M. Livingston, 'Certainty, efficiency and realism: rights in collateral under Article 9 of the Uniform Commercial Code' (1994) 73 NC L Rev. 115, p. 120. The requirement itself can be criticised for lack of precision, which has led US courts to use it as a way of determining priorities (e.g. between a bailor and a secured party of the bailee) rather than merely a threshold

can be satisfied by any rights over and above bare possession, including the rights of a buyer under a retention-of-title agreement and a lessee under a lease or a hire-purchase agreement,[86] and certainly does not require a full ownership interest. An argument based on *nemo dat* principles would logically lead to the conclusion that the security interest can only attach to the limited interest held by the debtor. However, it is clear from Canadian and US cases that once the requirement of 'rights in the collateral' is satisfied, the security interest attaches to the entire interest in the collateral, thus establishing (if such reasoning were to be used) an exception to the *nemo dat* principle. There are two interrelated justifications for this.

The first is that quasi-security interests are recharacterised by the scheme as security interests and are given the incidents of security. Although the nature of a security interest is not defined in the PPSA or UCC legislation it would appear that it is in the nature of an English charge;[87] since the scheme is based on the idea of a single security interest, the nature of a recharacterised quasi-security interest must be the same as that of a 'true' security interest. If this is the case, to the extent that one can justifiably talk about the location of title, title in the goods passes to the debtor who grants a security interest to the creditor.[88] When a company buys goods under a retention-of-title agreement, the company immediately obtains the entire interest in the goods, subject to the security interest of the retention-of-title seller/creditor. If the seller perfects its interest as prescribed by the scheme, it will have a PMSI which gives it priority over other secured creditors, and, apart from the possibility that other secured creditors may have an interest in any surplus, the question of what security interest can be granted to other creditors by the debtor never arises. However, when the seller/creditor fails to perfect its interest, this question arises starkly, and it is in such cases that the position set out above has been established.

In the Canadian case of *Euroclean Canada Inc.* v. *Forest Glade Investments Ltd*[89] a company gave a floating charge debenture to creditor 1, covering after-acquired

criterion; see M. Livingston, who argues that the requirement should be replaced by a scheme involving universal registration of all interests where ownership and possession are separated. Possession by the debtor, then, would be sufficient for a security interest to attach. However, it would have to be lawful possession: the holder of a security interest granted by a thief would not have priority over the true owner of the goods, thus reflecting the policy described above.

86 DR 15(7). The Law Commission's Draft Regulations made this clearer than in the other jurisdictions, where this principle is established by case law. NZPPSA, s. 40(3) is in similar terms to the DR but does not extend to leases or hire-purchase agreements. It has been argued that even naked possession (e.g. under a bailment) should be sufficient; Baird and Jackson, 'Possession and ownership: an examination of the scope of Article 9' (1983) Stanford Law Review, 175, p. 204; note also *Amfac Mortgage Corp.* v. *Arizona Mall of Tempe, Inc.*, 127 Ariz. 70, 73–4, 618 p. 2d 240, pp. 243–4 (Ariz. Ct. App. 1980).

87 See: R. C. C. Cuming 'The internationalisation of secured financing law' in (ed.) R. Cranston, *Making Commercial Law: Essays in Honour of Roy Goode* (Oxford: Clarendon Press, 1997), ch. 22; Gedye, et al., *Personal Property Securities in New Zealand*, fn 76, p. 73 and *Royal Bank of Canada* v. *Sparrow Electric Corp* [1997] 1 SCR 411.

88 See: *James Talcott. Inc.*, v. *Franklin National Bank*, 292 Minn. 277, 194 NW2d 775, 780, 10 UCC Rep. 11 (1972) M. Bridge, R. Macdonald, R. Simmons, C. Walsh, 'Formalism, functionalism and understanding the law of secured transactions' (1999) 44 McGill LJ 567. It is not clear that this was the Law Commission's view of the effect of the proposed reform see *Consultative Report*, fn 13, para. 2.116.

89 (1985) 16 DLR (4th) 289 (Ontario CA). See also *Marcel Equipment Ltd* v. *Equipements Benoit d'Amours et Fils Inc* (1995) PPSAC (2d) 31.

property, and then bought some equipment from creditor 2 under a conditional sale agreement. The debenture was registered, but the conditional sale agreement was not. The conditional vendor argued that since no payments were made under the conditional sale agreement, the company had no interest in the equipment to which the debenture holder's security interest could attach. Houlden JA held that the right to immediate possession of the equipment and the right to receive legal title upon payment of the full purchase price were sufficient 'rights in the collateral' for the security interest to attach.[90] Thus, applying the rules of the PPSA, the registered debenture took priority over the unregistered interest of the conditional vendor.[91] It was made clear that under the PPSA scheme the location of title was irrelevant, and that an authority based on the preceding law[92] supporting the conditional vendor's argument was not applicable. In the similar US case of *Morton Booth Co.* v. *Tiara Furniture, Inc.*,[93] it was made clear by the court that an argument that a buyer on retention-of-title terms had no interest in the materials to which the bank's security interest could attach could not succeed: a purchaser under retention of title was treated by UCC, Article 9 as if 'title had been transferred to the debtor and the creditor-seller had retained only a security interest in the goods'.[94]

The second justification is the registration argument discussed above; in the cases discussed an unperfected quasi-security interest loses priority to a perfected interest. Once it is established that such an interest is in fact treated as a charge, this conclusion is unremarkable and mirrors existing English law.

We must also consider the case of 'deemed' security interests. Under the current English law, and in jurisdictions where the scheme does not include a particular type of interest, a security interest granted by a debtor can only attach to the interest that debtor has in the goods.[95] Thus a lessee can only grant a security interest over its interest in the lease contract, and the owner will prevail over a secured party in relation to the leased goods once the debtor's default has triggered the owner's right to possession under the lease.[96] 'Deemed security interests' are included in the schemes for two reasons: (a) the difficulty of distinguishing them from true security interests[97] and (b) problems of ostensible ownership.[98] If such an interest is duly registered, then the *nemo dat* principle is not overridden: the lessor or consignor is protected to the

90 (1985) 16 DLR (4th) 289, pp. 298, 299.
91 Or would have done had there not been a valid subordination clause in the debenture.
92 *Rogerson Lumber Co. Ltd* v. *Four Seasons Chalet Ltd and Bank of Montreal et al.* (1980), 29 OR (2d) 193, 113 DLR (3d) 671, 36 CBR (NS) 141.
93 (1977) 564 p. 2d 210, 1977 OK 45 (Oklahoma SC).
94 564 p. 2d 210, p. 212 citing *James Talcott. Inc.*, v. *Franklin National Bank* (1972) 292 Minn. 277, 194 NW 2d 775, 780, 10 UCC Rep. 11. This is also the case in relation to leases and consignments for the purposes of security (M. Livingston, 'Certainty, efficiency and realism: rights in collateral under Article 9 of the Uniform Commercial Code') (1994) 73 NC L. Rev. 115, pp. 125–6 and the *James Talcott* case itself.
95 See op. cit., Livingston, fn 94, p. 122, n. 31. Note also *Gray* v. *Royal Bank* (1997), 12 p. PSAC (2d) 126, where the purchaser of a mobile home from a vendor who had converted it, granted a security interest in it to a creditor. The true owner of the mobile home had priority over the secured creditor, on an overt application by the court of the *nemo dat* principle.
96 UCC Art. 2A-307(1) ('a creditor of the lessee takes subject to the lease contract') 'creditor' includes secured creditor: UCC Art. 2A-103(4).
97 See: *The Diamond Report*, fn 2, ch. 9.7; *Consultative Report*, fn 13, para. 3.36.
98 See *Consultative Report*, fn 13, para. 3.31. It is, of course, possible to argue that the ostensible ownership problems are so great that all, or nearly all, situations where ownership and

extent of its own ownership interest and, since it is a PMSI, it will have priority over previously perfected security interests as well as those perfected subsequently.[99] The effect is therefore the same as under current English law. However, where the interest is not registered, the registration argument operates strongly so that *nemo dat* principles are overridden. Thus even though a lessee under a true lease has nothing more than a right to possession under the lease, it can grant a security interest which attaches to the entire interest in the goods and takes priority over the unregistered lease. In *Sprung Instant Structures Ltd* v. *Caswan Environmental Services Inc.*[100] the court at first instance held that a lessor lost priority to a bank whose security interest (in all the debtor's present and after-acquired property) was perfected by filing before the lessor filed a financing statement. Although the lessor had filed, it had filed too late to gain PMSI status, and so the priority rule applied was first to file. The Alberta Court of Appeal, in a very short judgment, reversed the decision on the grounds that the wording of the bank's charge did not cover the leased goods. Although the Court of Appeal did not explicitly overrule the first instance decision on what counted as 'rights in the collateral', it did appear to take the view that even if the bank's interest had covered the leased goods, it would only have attached to the lessee's interest. The Court of Appeal's decision has been heavily criticised as being contrary to the PPSA philosophy.[101] Further, since even true consignments are included within the UCC, Article 9 filing scheme, the UCC specifically provides that, 'for purposes of determining the rights of creditors of, and purchasers for value of goods from, a consignee ... the consignee is deemed to have rights and title to the goods identical to those the consignor had or had power to transfer':[102] a statutory exception to the *nemo dat* rule.

Priority between security interests created by a debtor and the buyer or lessee of the collateral from that debtor

Within the overseas and Law Commission schemes, the position here is totally covered by the provisions of the schemes, which provide for a basic *nemo dat* rule[103] with a large number of exceptions.

possession are split should be included within a notice-filing system. Op. cit., Livingston, fn 94, pp. 135–8.

99 The lessor will only have PMSI status if it applies with the strict time criteria for registration and notice imposed to gain such status. See: DR42; NZPPSA, ss.73–76; SPPSA, s. 34; OPPSA, s. 33.

100 [1997] 5 WWR 280, 47 Alta. L.R. (3d.) 356, 198 A.R. 41 (Alberta QB Forsyth J). See also the leading Canadian cases where the interests of lessors under unregistered leases had been held to be ineffective against trustees in bankruptcy of the lessees: *Re. International Harvester Credit Corp. of Canada Ltd* v. *Bell's Dairy Ltd (Bankrupt)*, [1986] 6 WWR 161; 50 Sask. R. 177 (CA), *Re Giffen* [1998] 1 SCR 91 [1998] 155 DLR (4th) 322 (Supreme Court of Canada).

101 Op. cit., Gedye et al., fn 76, pp. 156–7.

102 See UCC (revised) Art. 9–319. There is no equivalent provision in the DR.

103 See: DR29(1); NZPPSA, s. 45; SPPSA, s. 28(1); OPPSA, s. 25; UCC Art. 9–315(a), i.e. when collateral subject to SI is disposed of SI continues in the collateral as well as in the proceeds.

The chief exceptions to the *nemo dat* rule are as follows:

1 Where goods subject to a security interest are disposed of with the consent of the secured party[104] the security interest does not continue in the goods[105] (this is the same as the existing law).
2 A buyer or lessee [who takes possession or delivery] takes free of an unperfected security interest unless it bought or leased with knowledge of the security interest.[106]
3 A buyer or lessee of goods sold or leased in the ordinary course of business by a seller or lessee whose business normally involves selling or leasing goods of the type in question [who obtains possession of the goods] takes free of any perfected or unperfected security interest created by the seller or lessee unless the buyer or lessee knows that the sale or lease is in breach of the security agreement.[107]
4 A buyer or lessee for private purposes of goods of a low value takes free from any perfected or unperfected security interests.[108]
5 A buyer or lessee takes free from a security interest perfected by filing in goods which have a unique identifying number if they were not described by that number in the filing.[109]

How far do these provisions change current English law?

True security interests

Pledge

For a pledge to be valid, there has to be a transfer of possession to the pledgee, so there is very unlikely to be an unperfected pledge[110] and *2* will not apply. Currently a buyer or lessee from a pledgor takes subject to the pledge:[111] under the scheme exception *3* could in theory apply, but it would be unusual for a debtor to sell or lease goods which

104 Either because the security is a floating charge, or a retention-of-title sale with permission to sell, or because consent has otherwise been obtained.
105 See: DR29(1); NZPPSA, s. 45; SPPSA, s. 28(1); OPPSA, s. 25; UCC Art. 9–315(a).
106 See: DR20(4); UCC (revised) Art. 9–317(b) and (c); SPPSA, s. 20(3); OPPSA, s. 20(1)(c); NZPPSA, s. 52 (knowledge is irrelevant, but the unperfected security interest must not have been created or provided for by a transaction to which the buyer or lessee is a party). The words in square brackets do not apply in New Zealand or Saskatchewan.
107 See: DR31(3); NZPPSA, s. 53; OPPSA, s. 28; SPPSA, s. 30; UCC Art.'s 9–320, 9–321 (lessees and licensees). The words in square brackets are not included in any of the overseas jurisdictions, although see below in relation to the position in the US.
108 See: DR31(4) and (5); NZPPSA, s. 54; SPPSA, s. 30(3) and (4).
109 See: DR31(7) and (8); NZPPSA, s. 55; SPPSA, s. 30(6) and (7); OPPSA s. 28(5). This exception is considered below.
110 The scheme provides for continuous perfection if the goods are returned to the debtor for a limited purpose such as sale or loading. See generally: DR28; NZPPSA, s. 49; SPPSA, s. 26(1)(b); OPPSA, s. 24(2)(b); UCC (revised) Art. 9–312(f). A pledge of goods which remain in the possession of the debtor, but in respect of which the debtor attorns to the pledgee thus giving constructive possession, requires perfection by filing (DR24(2)) and could thus be unperfected.
111 See p. 194 above.

it had pledged, as it would not be in possession of such goods,[112] nor it is likely to be a position to enable the buyer or lessee to obtain possession.[113]

Mortgage or charge

Currently, a buyer (or lessee) from an equitable mortgagor or a chargor takes priority if it takes a legal interest without notice of the prior equitable interest. Registration is notice where the buyer would be expected to check the register, that is, where the sale is not in the ordinary course of business.[114] Under the scheme, there will be the same result where either the security interest is unregistered (exception *2*), or where exception *3* applies. One difference is that only a buyer or lessee who obtains possession will take free. At present, although delivery to a lessee would be required for it to have a possessory interest which would take priority over a prior chargee, property could pass under a contract of sale without the need for delivery if the parties intended it to pass,[115] and so a buyer could take free of a charge even if it had not yet taken delivery of the goods. This is particularly the case in relation to goods sold in bulk: a document of title may be transferred to the buyer, but it is not clear that a buyer may obtain constructive possession of the goods while they remain in the bulk.[116]

Under the scheme, in relation to goods which do not fall under exception *3* a buyer or lessee will take subject to any security interest and will be expected to check the register. This was because goods falling under exception *3* (i.e. which the debtor was in the business of selling or leasing) would usually at present be the subject of a floating charge, and so buyers or lessees would take free anyway.[117] However, charges over other types of goods (usually capital equipment) do not normally permit the sale or lease of the collateral without the express consent of the seller and it was thought that sale or lease by the debtor was sufficiently unusual for the buyer or lessee to be expected to check the register.[118] The scheme will change the operation of the current

112 Unless either of the situations listed in fn 110 above applied.

113 As required by DR31(3).

114 See fn 54 above.

115 Section 17 SGA.

116 See Gullifer 'Constructive possession after the Sale of Goods (Amendment) Act 1995 [1999] LMCLQ 93.

117 This is because the sale will be within the authority to deal expressly or impliedly given to the chargor under the floating charge. Although, under the scheme set out in the *Consultative Report*, the floating charge itself would have be abolished, it would still have been possible for the parties to agree that the debtor has permission to deal with the collateral (See *Consultative Report*, above fn 13, para. 2.58). In practice, this will not be necessary for goods falling within exception *3*. but, since existing floating charges would have been effective under the scheme, wide licenses to deal would have been likely to remain common for a considerable time. Under the more limited proposals in the Law Commission Report, above fn 15, the floating charge is retained, and only a transferee of collateral subject to a floating charge who acquired the collateral in the ordinary course of business will take free of the charge (Draft Company Security Regulations 2006 appended to the Report).

118 See *Consultative Report*, fn 13, paras 3.257–3.258. This follows the reasoning in the other jurisdictions. UCC (revised) Art. 9–320(a) provides that a buyer in ordinary course of business takes free (Art. 9–321(c) has the same provision in relation to lessees). Ordinary course of business is restricted in Art. 1–201 to a buyer or lessee from a person in the business of selling or leasing goods of that kind, and thus, although the phrase is not used in Art. 9–320(a), the subsection applies primarily to inventory collateral (see Official

law only to the extent that the boundaries of exception *3* do not coincide with the current use and definition of 'ordinary course of business'. The phrase at present has two functions: first, to determine what transactions fall within the chargor's licence to deal, and second, to determine when registration is notice to a buyer or lessee. At present, in relation to the first function, the phrase is very widely defined,[119] and will include sales of capital equipment.[120] There is no specific guidance on the definition in relation to the second function, but in other contexts the sale of capital equipment has been held to be included.[121] Under the scheme proposed in the *Consultative Report*, a sale in the 'ordinary course of business' would not have been limited to sale of inventory,[122] but its extension to sales of capital equipment could have been limited by the requirement that the debtor's business normally involves selling or leasing goods of the type in question.[123] The test was subjective: did the actual debtor sell goods of the kind in question? The Saskatchewan, New Zealand and UCC tests are also subjective.[124] Only the Ontario test is different: s. 28(1) refers to 'A buyer of goods from a seller who sells them in the ordinary course of business' and this has been interpreted as an objective test: did the sale appear to the buyer to be in the ordinary course of business of the seller, even if in fact it was not?[125] Since the purpose of the limitation is to protect buyers or lessees in transactions where they would not expect to check the register, and to facilitate commercial dealings in certain types of goods, it might be thought that an objective rather than a subjective test is appropriate.[126] In any event, the definition of 'ordinary course of business' would clearly have been narrower than under the existing law, although its exact application would have been

Comment to Art. 9–320). In relation to the New Zealand scheme (where the exception relates to goods sold or leased in the ordinary business of the seller or lessor) see op. cit., Gedye et al., fn 76, p. 221, and in relation to the Ontario scheme (again, ordinary course of business of the seller or lessor) see op. cit., Ziegel and Denomme, fn 85, p. 207.

119 *Ashborder* v. *Green Gas Power Ltd* [2004] EWHC 1517 (CH), [2004] All ER (D) 371 (Jul), para. 227. An unprecedented and exceptional transaction can still be in the ordinary course of business and permitted by a floating charge.

120 See LCCP, fn 48, para. 2.61.

121 *Stevenson* v. *Rogers* [1999] QB 1028 (sale by a fisherman of his fishing boat was held to be in the ordinary course of business and therefore subject to the implied conditions in Sale of Goods Act 1979, s. 14). The Law Commission was clear that this situation would not have been within exception *3*, unless a company regularly sold off their stocks of equipment (*Consultative Report*, fn 13, para. 3.257–8).

122 *Camco Inc.* v. *Frances Olsen Realty (1979) Ltd* (1986) 6 WWR 258, 6 PPSAC 167 (Saskatchewan CA), para. 20.

123 See *Consultative Report*, fn 13, para. 3.257–8 and DR 31(2). It would have included the sale of ex-rental stock by a hire company.

124 See: SPPSA, s. 30(2); NZPPSA, s. 53(1); op. cit., Gedye et al., fn 76, p. 226. Although the UCC (revised) Art. 9–320(1) only refers to a 'buyer in the ordinary course of business' this is defined in Art. 1–201 as limited to buyers 'from a person, other than a pawnbroker, in the business of selling goods of that kind'.

125 See: *Fairline Boats* v. *Leger* (1980) 1 PPSAC 218, *Ford Motor Credit Company of Canada* v. *Centre Motors of Brampton Ltd* (1982) 137 DLR (3d) 634, p. 644. That the difference in wording between the Ontario and Saskatchewan Acts should lead to a difference in approach is confirmed by Tallis J. A. in *Camco Inc.* v. *Frances Olson Realty (1979) Ltd* (1986) 6 p. PSAC 167, para. 25.

126 See: *Fairline Boats* v. *Leger* (1980) 1 PPSAC 218, para. 8; op. cit., Gedye et al., fn 76, p. 226, n. 33.

a question of fact in each case.[127] Purchasers and lessees of anything other than obvious inventory would have been well advised to check the register.

At present, a buyer does not take free of a legal mortgage even if it is unregistered.[128] Under the proposed scheme, this unjustifiable result would have been abolished and the position would have been as outlined above. There is a clear case for the abolition of this anomaly, which, no doubt, will be considered by the Law Commission as and when it considers this area of law.

Quasi-security interests

Currently, a buyer from a debtor who has bought or hired goods under a quasi-security agreement, will only take free from the interest of the seller, hirer or lessor (the 'creditor') if the Sale of Goods Act, s. 25 applies.[129] Section 25 applies to some quasi-security interests and not others. Under the scheme proposed in the *Consultative Report* the position (as described above) would have been exactly the same for all types of quasi-security interests (retention-of-title sales, conditional sales, hire-purchase agreements, finance leases). The uncertainties and inconsistencies discussed above would have been wiped away at a stroke. This surely must be an objective of the forthcoming Law Commission project.

Apart from this welcome change, it is worth considering how the proposed position, particularly under exceptions *2* and *3*, would have differed from the existing one. The position of the buyer (as opposed to the lessee) from the debtor will be considered first. For s. 25 to operate it is necessary that:

(a) the debtor has possession of the goods;[130]
(b) the goods[131] are delivered to the buyer;
(c) the sale is in the ordinary course of business of a mercantile agent dealing in goods of that kind; and[132]
(d) the buyer is in good faith and without notice of any lien or other right of the creditor in respect of the goods.

(a) is an indication of entrustment, and gives rise to the situation of 'false wealth'. It is the buyer who is misled by the ostensible ownership of the debtor: this, under the Sale of Goods Act, is coupled with the requirement that the debtor's possession of the goods be with the consent of the creditor. (b) can be justified by the argument that only reliance interests should be protected.[133] It can further be justified by an argument

127 As it is in the other jurisdictions; see *Fairline Boats Ltd* v. *Leger* (1980) 1 PPSAC 218, paras 12–17.
128 See p. 195 above.
129 Or, in the case of a motor vehicle, Hire Purchase Act 1964, s. 27. See generally, p. 197 above.
130 Or possession of the documents of title to the goods. The term 'document of title' is defined, for the purposes of the Factors Act and the Sale of Goods Act, in the Factors Act 1889, s. 1(4). The definition includes true documents of title (bills of lading) the possession of which gives constructive possession of the goods, and also other documents the possession of which do not give constructive possession of the goods (see op. cit., Goode, fn 67, p. 62).
131 Or a document of title is transferred.
132 See above fn 42.
133 See op. cit., Ziegel and Denomme, fn 85, p. 168 commenting on OPPSA, s. 20.

based on ostensible ownership, but this time it is the creditor which is misled.[134] The creditor, who *ex hypothesi* has prohibited resale of the goods, relies on the debtor's continued possession of the goods as evidence of the continuation of its security interest in them. If the goods are sold to a buyer who takes free of the security interest but are not delivered to that buyer, the creditor is misled. However, unless the creditor has actually acted in reliance on the debtor's continued possession (for example, by granting more credit or by refraining from taking steps to enforce its rights under the contract) it is hard to see why this should affect the priority position. The technical reason for (c) comes from the wording of s. 25, which refers to the mercantile agent exception to the *nemo dat* rule found in the Factors Act 1889, s. 2(1).[135] The requirement has been criticised.[136] It does not seem to apply to the Sale of Goods Act 1979, s. 24. It is hard to discern a rational policy reason behind it,[137] although it could be argued that that a sale in the ordinary course of business is less likely to put a sub-buyer on notice.[138] The requirement could, however, be said to be a welcome limit on the application of s. 25, which would otherwise be very wide, given the importation of the definition of consent from the Factors Act 1889, s. 2(2).[139] This issue was examined by the Law Reform Committee in 1966,[140] who recommended abolition of the requirement, but this was never implemented. This is another matter which, no doubt, the Law Commission could consider in the future. The requirement (d) that the buyer be in good faith and without notice, is implicit in the justification for the exceptions to the *nemo dat* rule: that the buyer is misled by the debtor's possession of the goods, or by a holding out that the debtor is authorised to sell the goods. If the buyer is not in good faith or is on notice, then he is not misled.

Would these requirements still have applied under the scheme proposed in the *Consultative Report*? In relation to exception 2 the Law Commission's Draft Regulations provided that the buyer would not take free of the security interest if it knew of it, which is equivalent to (d) above,[141] and also that the buyer obtain possession or

134 C. Land, 'UCC section 9–307(1) and the non-possessory buyer: is the good faith purchaser always right?' (1984) *Georgia Law Review* 123, p. 138.

135 And, on the particular facts of *Newtons of Wembley* v. *Williams* [1965] 1 QB 560), achieved a favourable result for the buyers by importing the provisions of the Factors Act 1889, s. 2(2), so that the seller's initial consent was deemed to continue beyond the date when it was in fact revoked, see op. cit., Bridge, fn 5, p. 5.159.

136 Op. cit., McKendrick, fn 25, 5–088 on the grounds that it unfairly limits the protection to sale between traders and is impossible to apply in the context of private sellers. See also: *Jeffcott* v. *Andrew Motors Ltd* [1960] NZLR721, p. 729; *Gamer's Motor Centre (Newcastle)* v. *Natwest Wholesale Australia Pty Ltd* (1987) 163 CLR 236, pp. 242–3, 252–3, 258–9; and op. cit., Atiyah, fn 25, p. 407.

137 Op. cit., Goode, fn 4, p. 437.

138 Op. cit., Guest, fn 25, para. 7–081.

139 See fn 135 above.

140 See Consultation Report, fn 6, para. 23.

141 See DR20(4)(d).This position reflects that in Canada and the US; see SPPSA, s. 20(3); OPPSA, s. 20(1)(c); UCC (revised) Art. 9–317(b)–(d). Note, however, that in none of these provisions is there a specific requirement of good faith. The position is different in New Zealand, where a buyer takes free of an unperfected security interest even if he knows of its existence (s. 52). This is to provide an incentive to register security interests, since in New Zealand, an unperfected security interest is not unenforceable against a liquidator (op. cit., Gedye et al., fn 76, p. 215; *Consultative Report*, fn 13, para. 3.172)

delivery of the goods ((b) above).[142] Does this mean that there was no requirement (a) (that the debtor be in possession of the goods)? The requirement of delivery to the buyer indicates that the debtor must at least have had the power to order delivery of the goods to the buyer, that is, at least constructive possession, although it is theoretically possible that the debtor might not have had possession at the time of the sale or lease, and only obtained it later. This does not seem at all far from the position under s. 25: that section is triggered by the delivery of the goods by the debtor to the buyer, and operates even where that delivery is effected by the creditor directly to the buyer.[143] This argument could be said to be weakened, however, as the Draft Regulations, unlike the equivalent Ontario and UCC sections, include situations where the transferee 'takes possession' as well as where it 'takes delivery'. The Saskatchewan Act and the New Zealand Acts include neither (a) or (b). It is hard to see why there should be either requirement in relation to unperfected security interests: the policy based on the registration argument is that they are unenforceable against all third parties, though not between the parties to the security agreement themselves.

In relation to exception *3*, the scheme proposed in the *Consultative Report* had no specific provision for (a), but was limited to buyers or lessees who obtain possession of the goods (a near equivalent to (b)).[144] This requirement is discussed below. The limit of the exception to goods which the debtor is in the business of selling,[145] could be said to mirror (c), but in fact is largely addressed at different facts. (c) has been interpreted as requiring a sale within business hours and at a proper place of business and in the ordinary way a mercantile agent would act.[146] It is in no way related to the actual business of the debtor: the test appears to require the court to consider the *hypothetical* position of what would have been in the ordinary course of business had the debtor been a mercantile agent dealing in goods of that kind. In relation to (d) (good faith and notice), the buyer takes free under the scheme even if he knew of the security interest, unless he knew that the sale was in breach of the security agreement under which the security interest was created.[147] There seem to be two main reasons for the difference between this provision and s. 25. First, where a security interest is registered, it is possible to find out about its existence by searching

142 See DR20(4)(c). This is also a requirement under the UCC (revised) Art. 9–317(b) and (c) and OPPSA, s. 20(1)(c), but not in Saskatchewan or New Zealand.

143 *Four Point Garage Ltd* v. *Carter* [1985] 3 All ER 12. Simon Brown J analysed the situation as being a constructive delivery by the seller to the debtor/buyer and a constructive delivery by the debtor/buyer to the sub-buyer.

144 DR31(3): 'A buyer ... of goods who obtains possession of the goods takes free of any perfected or unperfected security interest ... unless the buyer ... knows that the sale ... constitutes a breach of the security agreement under which the security interest was created.'

145 DR31(2): 'Paragraph (3) applies to goods sold by a seller ... (a) in the ordinary course of business, and (b) whose business normally involves selling ... goods of the type in question.'

146 See *Oppenheimer* v. *Attenborough & Sons* [1908] 1 KB 221, p. 230, *per* Buckley LJ (concerning the Factors Act, s. 2(1) but cited with approval in *Newtons of Wembley Ltd* v. *Williams* [1965] 1 QB 560).

147 DR31(3). This is also the position under NZPPSA, s. 53(1); OPPSA, s. 28(1) and SPPSA, s. 30(2). It is also the case under the UCC, but this result requires reading UCC 9–320(a) (which provides that a buyer in the ordinary course of business takes free, even if the security interest is perfected and the buyer knows of its existence) together with the definition of 'buyer in the ordinary course of business' in UCC Art. 1–201(9) as 'a person that buys goods in good faith, without knowledge that the sale violates the rights of another person in the goods'. Thus the UCC is closer to the Sale of Goods Act, s. 25, as it has a specific requirement that the buyer act in good faith.

the register, whereas s. 25 exists because of the picture of 'false wealth' created by the possession by the debtor. However, it is impractical for buyers in the ordinary course of business to have to search the register every time a purchase or lease is entered into. Thus the provision signals that there is no need for such buyers to make a search: no question of constructive notice arises, and the buyer takes free even if he knows or suspects that the seller may have given security interests over its inventory.[148] Second, inventory is usually covered by a floating charge or has been acquired on retention-of-title terms, which permits sale.[149] Although under the proposed scheme it would have been possible for a security agreement to provide that the debtor has a licence to deal, it would have been inconvenient if the buyer had had to concern himself with the extent of that licence. However, where a buyer actually knew that the sale is in breach of the security agreement, it would have been unfair for him to take free of the security interest.

The inclusion in the Draft Regulations of the requirement that the buyer obtain possession of the goods was welcome. There is no such requirement in the Canadian or New Zealand statutes.[150] The omission of such a requirement under the former Article 9 was much criticised; it was not even clear that the omission was deliberate.[151] It seemed anomalous that possession by the buyer was required in the former 9–301 (the buyer takes free of unperfected security interests) and not in the exception under consideration.[152] There was also the argument based on ostensible ownership.[153] In the absence of any express statutory provision, however, the courts made the scope of the exception hinge on an interpretation of 'buyer in the ordinary course of business'. The interpretation was very wide, it did not require delivery to the buyer,[154] or that title had passed to the buyer.[155] This gave very wide protection to the buyer. The justification given in the cases for this was that the secured creditor is in a better position to protect itself than the buyer.[156] However, not only is the law rendered uncertain as it is not clear at what point a buyer becomes a buyer in the

148 Op. cit., Gedye et al., fn 76, p. 224.

149 Ibid., p. 221, argues that the equivalent section in the New Zealand Act takes the place of floating charge jurisprudence.

150 Nor is it implied from any interpretation of 'buyer in the ordinary course of business'; R. Maclaren, *Secured Transactions in Personal Property in Canada* §9–02 (5) text to n. 117. See also op. cit., Ziegel and Denomme, fn 85, p. 230.

151 It was argued that the change from s. 9–2A of the Uniform Trust Receipts Act 1951 which did require delivery to a purchaser and on which Art. 9–307 (the former 'buyer of goods' section) was based must have been intentional (*Holstein* v. *Greenwich Yacht Sales, Inc.* (1979) 404 A.2d 842, p. 845, 122 RI 211, p. 216).

152 UCC Art. 9–307, now UCC (revised) Art. 9–320.

153 See: C. Land, 'UCC section 9-307(1) and the non-possessory buyer: is the good faith purchaser always right?' (1984) *Georgia Law Review* 123, pp. 25, 138; D. Baird and T. Jackson, 'Possession and ownership: an examination of the scope of Article 9' (1983) *Stanford Law Review* 175, p. 210.

154 See: *Chrysler Credit Corp.* v. *Sharp* (1968) 56 Misc.2d 261, 288 NYS2d 525; *International Harvester Credit Corp.* v. *Associates Fin. Servs. Co.* (1974) 133 Ga.App. 488, 211 s. E.2d 430; *Tanbro Fabrics Corporation* v. *Deering Milliken Inc.* (1976) 385 NYS2d 260, 39 NY2d 632, 350 NE2d 590; *Herman* v. *First Farmers State Bank* (1979) 73 Ill.App. 3d 475, 392 NE2d 344; *Holstein* v. *Greenwich Yacht Sales, Inc.* (1979) 404 A. 2d 842; *Wilson* v. *M & W Gear* (1982) 110 Ill.App. 3d 538, 442 NE2d 670 (1982).

155 See pp. 214–15 below.

156 *Chrysler Credit Corp.* v. *Sharp* (1968) 288 NYS 2d 525, p. 534; *Rex Financial Corp.* v. *Mobile Home Corp.* (1978), 580 p. 2d 8, p. 10; *Wilson* v. *M & W Gear*, 442 NE2d 670, p. 675 (secured

ordinary course of business, but the ostensible ownership argument justifies a greater degree of protection to the creditor. The position was clarified under the revised Article 9,[157] as the definition of 'buyer in the ordinary course of business' in Article 1–201(9) was amended to include 'Only a buyer that takes possession of the goods or has a right to recover the goods from the seller under Article 2 may be a buyer in ordinary course of business'.[158] The Law Commission's Draft Regulations were clearer and neater than this approach, which is also inconsistent with the Law Commission's criterion that the seller sells in the ordinary course of business rather than that the buyer is in the ordinary course of business.

Two controversies have arisen in the other jurisdictions, but seem much less likely to arise in practice if the buyer has to take possession. The first is the question of whether the debtor needs to be in possession for the exception to operate. This, of course, is a requirement under s. 25 ((a) above). There is a strong argument that this requirement is necessary to limit the *nemo dat* exception to where ostensible ownership is at its most objectionable. However, if the buyer has taken possession, in almost every case this will be at the direction of the debtor, which indicates that the debtor had at least constructive possession. It is, in any case, likely that the specific problems which arose under the former UCC would be avoided. Under the UCC, the exceptions to the *nemo dat* rule contained in Article 2 (sale of goods) are based on voidable title[159] and entrustment of possession to a merchant dealing in goods of that kind.[160] Commentators have therefore argued that the equivalent provision in Article 9 should also require entrustment to the debtor, and that the omission of a requirement in UCC 9–320[161] that the debtor be in possession of the goods was accidental.[162] However, in the absence of any express requirement, the courts interpreted the section as merely requiring that that the buyer be in 'the ordinary course of business', and whether this included possession by the debtor was a question of fact. Thus, in *Tanbro Fabrics Corporation* v. *Deering Milliken Inc.*[163] unfinished textiles were sold on retention-of-title terms by the manufacturer to a company specialising in converting the cloth. The textiles (as was usual in the trade) were stored by the manufacturer until the converter required them. The converter sold some of the textiles to Tanbro, another converter. The goods remained with the manufacturer. When the first converter developed financial difficulties, the manufacturer refused to deliver the textiles to Tanbro, relying on its security interest. Tanbro relied on exception *3*[164] and claimed to be a buyer in the ordinary course of business. The court held that, in this particular trade, the goods were sold and bought in the ordinary course of business despite the fact that the first

party could have required sight of the debtor's records to determine which goods sold but not delivered); *Herman* v. *First Farmers State Bank* (1979) 73 Ill. App. 3d 475, p. 480.

157 1999 revision.

158 See UCC Art. 1–201(9).

159 UCC Art. 2–403(1).

160 UCC Art. 2–403(2).

161 Formerly Art. 9–307(1).

162 See J. Schroeder, 'Death and transfiguration: the myth that the UCC killed "property"' (1996) *Temple Law Review* 1281, pp. 1330–2, citing Homer Kripke, 'Should Section 9–307(1) of the Uniform Commercial Code apply against a secured party in possession?' (1977) 33 Bus. Law. 153, pp. 153–62.

163 (1976) 385 NYS 2d 260.

164 UCC (old version) Art. 9–307.

converter never had possession of them. The case aroused huge controversy,[165] and courts in similar cases have refused to hold that such a sale was in the ordinary course of business.[166] The particular complaint was that it was unfair that a buyer should take free of a security interest when the goods were in the actual possession of the secured party. Arguably, this gives the buyer notice not only of the existence of the security interest (which notice is irrelevant under the Article 9 scheme) but that the sale is not authorised by the secured party.[167] In jurisdictions which provide that the buyer takes subject to the security interest when it knows that the sale is in breach of the security agreement, it can be argued that the result in *Tanbro* would not be reached.[168] In the US, the actual result in *Tanbro* has been statutorily overruled in the revised Article 9, since 9–320(e) provides that the exception does not affect a security interest in goods in the possession of the secured party.[169] However, such a specific provision is not needed if the buyer has to take possession of the goods.[170]

The second controversy concerns when a buyer becomes a protected buyer under exception *3*. The options are (1) the date of initial contract; (2) the date the goods are identified; (3) the date title passes to the purchaser; (4) the date the purchaser gets delivery; and (5) the date the purchaser accepts the goods.[171] It is clear that under the

165 See: Homer Kripke, 'Should Section 9–307(1) of the Uniform Commercial Code Apply Against a Secured Party in Possession?' (1977) 33 Bus. Law. 153, pp. 153–62; Harold F. Birnbaum, 'Section 9–307(1) of the Uniform Commercial Code versus possessory security interests – a reply to Professor Homer Kripke' (1978) 33 Bus. Law. 2607; Samuel Gottlieb, 'Section 9–307(1) and *Tanbro Fabrics*: a further response' (1978) 33 Bus. Law. 2611.

166 See: *J. Manes Co. Inc* v. *Greenwood Mills Inc.* 53 NY2d 759; 421 NE2d 840; 439 NYS2d 348; *In re Brookhaven Textiles, Inc.* 21 BR 204.

167 If UCC Art. 9–320(a) (formerly Art. 9–307(1)) is read together with the definition of 'buyer in the ordinary course of business' (Art. 1–201(9)) ('one who buys goods in good faith and without knowledge that the sale violates the rights of another') it indicates that the buyer takes subject to the security interest if it knows that the sale is in breach of the security agreement (see comment to Art. 9–320 (substantially the same for the old Article 9–307)). It is not clear why this argument was not made in the *Tanbro* case, or, conversely, why it was not argued that the sale was authorised by the secured party and thus valid under former Art. 9–306(2) (now Art. 9–315(a)(1)). See J. Schroeder, 'Death and transfiguration: the myth that the UCC killed "property"' (1996) *Temple Law Review* 1281, p. 1331, n.184.

168 See R. Maclaren, *Secured Transactions in Personal Property in Canada* §9–02 (5) text to n. 118 addressing the position in Ontario. The argument would also apply to Saskatchewan, New Zealand and to the scheme proposed in the *Consultative Report*, as well as to the US.

169 This includes constructive possession: see UCC (revised) Art. 9–313. However, merely providing that the exception does not apply when the goods are in the possession of the secured party may in itself cause difficulties, since it will require the buyer to investigate where the goods are if they are not in the possession of the debtor; see R. Cuming and C. Walsh, *Possible implications of revised UCC Article 9 for Canadian Personal Property Security Acts*, prepared for the Uniform Law Reform Commission of Canada, August 1999, paras 33 and 34 and n. 6.6. It would be simpler to provide that the goods were required to be in the possession (actual or constructive) of the debtor at the time of sale or lease.

170 It is unclear why Art. 9–320(e) was required, given the amendment of Art. 1–201(9) in the revised Article 9. Article 1–201(9) is wider than the Law Commission's Draft Regulations in that it includes situations where the buyer has the right to recover the goods, and also Art. 9–320(b) (buyers of consumer goods take free) does not appear to require the buyer to take possession.

171 See *Daniel* v. *Bank of Hayward* (1988) 144 Wis. 2d 931, p. 939; 425 N.W.2d 416, p. 419. The various difficulties discussed in the text have led the Ontario branch of the Canadian Bar Association (Submission in October 1998 to the Minister of Consumer and Commercial

scheme proposed in the *Consultative Report* a buyer would not have been protected until (4) occurs. However, the question still arises whether a buyer who has taken possession, but to whom title has not passed, is protected. Under the current law, when goods are sold under a retention-of-title agreement, and then resold under another retention-of-title agreement, no title passes to the sub-buyer under the Sale of Goods Act, s. 25 or under the Factors Act, s. 9.[172] Would the proposed scheme have changed this position? There was no complete definition of 'sale' or 'buyer' in the Draft Regulations. Under the Sale of Goods Act 1979, 'buyer' includes someone who agrees to buy goods,[173] whereas 'sale' is a transaction under which property passes.[174] Initially the latter definition prevailed in the US and Canada. In the US case of *Chrysler Corporation* v. *Adamatic Inc.*[175] the Supreme Court of Wisconsin limited the meaning of 'buyer in the ordinary course of business' to where there had been a completed sale and title had passed. Although in that case the buyer had paid substantially the whole contract price, it lost to the holder of a perfected security interest. The court took the view that the prepaying buyer (who in this case was a large company who knew well that they were financing the manufacture of these goods) could have protected itself by taking a security interest and entered into a subordination agreement with the secured creditor. However, that decision was overruled on this point by another decision of the Supreme Court of Wisconsin, *Daniel* v. *Bank of Hayward*[176] where the court rejected the use of title in the interpretation of 'buyer in the ordinary course of business' as 'unduly narrow and technical',[177] and contrary to the thrust of the UCC. In that case, where the purchasers were individual consumers, the court stressed the ability of the financier to protect itself as opposed

Relations) to recommend the following complex addition to s. 28(1) (the equivalent to DR31(3):

(1.1)(a) Subsection (1) applies whether or not:

- (i) the buyer took possession of the goods,
- (ii) the seller has been in possession of the goods at any time,
- (iii) the property in the goods passed to the buyer, or
- (iv) the seller retained or took a security interest in the goods.

(b) Despite clause (1.1)(a), subsection (1) does not apply where

- (i) the security interest given by the seller was perfected by possession and the buyer did not take possession of the goods, or
- (ii) the goods were not identified to the contract of sale.

(c) Goods are identified to the contract of sale when they are either:

- (i) identified and agreed upon by the parties at the time the contract is made, or
- (ii) marked or designated to the contract, either by the seller, or by the buyer with the seller's consent or authorization.

172 See *Re Highway Foods* [1995] 1 BCLC 209 [1995] BCC 271, and above at fn 32. However, under existing law, the disposition does take effect according to its terms, and arguably the retention-of-title buyer could continue to pay the instalments and retain possession as against the seller/creditor, unless the debtor has the right to call for possession at any time (as in *Highway Foods*).

173 Sale of Goods Act 1979, s. 61.

174 Sale of Goods Act 1979, s. 2(4). 'Sale' is contrasted with 'contract of sale'.

175 (1973) 208 NW2d 97.

176 (1988) 144 Wis. 2d 931; 425 NW 2d 416.

177 (1988) 144 Wis 2d 931, p. 943.

to the retail purchasers who were likely never to have 'heard of the Uniform Commercial Code and would not know how to go about protecting their interest'. The Canadian cases show a similar pattern. In *Royal Bank of Canada* v. *216200 Alberta*[178] the Saskatchewan Court of Appeal applied the Sale of Goods Act definition of 'sale' and required the passing of title.[179] However, in the later case of *Spittlehouse* v. *Northshore Marine Inc.*,[180] where there had been a sale on retention-of-title terms of a boat subject to a perfected security interest, the Ontario Court of Appeal approved of the reasoning in *Daniel* v. *Bank of Hayward*, and held that the definitions in the Sale of Goods Act should not apply, so that a buyer under a conditional sale who had not paid the full price and to whom delivery had not been made could be a buyer in ordinary course of business and obtain the protection of the Ontario PPSA, s. 28.[181] The overwhelming philosophy is that title is irrelevant for the purposes of the scheme, and therefore technical arguments based on title should not determine these priority questions.[182] However, one consequence of this approach seems strange. If the reason why title has not passed is because the sale is on retention-of-title terms (as in *Spittlehouse*), it is consistent with the scheme that this is viewed as a transfer of the entire interest in the goods to the buyer with the debtor obtaining merely a security interest. Thus the 'buyer' has an interest which can take priority to that of the creditor (although subject to the interest of the debtor, so that the conditions for the passing of property would eventually have to be fulfilled). But if the reason title has not passed is not that of security, it is difficult to see why the buyer should gain an interest in the goods taking priority over a secured party (creditor), since if there was no secured party and the seller (debtor) became insolvent the buyer would merely be an unsecured creditor.[183] Despite this objection, a distinction based on the function of the sale seems unworkable.[184] If *Spittlehouse* were to be followed here, this would have the effect that the concept of 'sale' under the proposed scheme would have had a different meaning from that in the Sale of Goods Act:[185] if this were to be the case, this would need to

178 (1986) 33 DLR (4th) 80.

179 It should be pointed out, however, that s. 30(1) of the Saskatchewan PPSA (now s. 30(2)) referred to a buyer of goods 'sold in the course of business', thus requiring a definition of 'sale', while the UCC Art. 9–307 (now UCC (rev) Art. 9–320) merely referred to 'a buyer in the ordinary course of business'. The Law Commission's Draft Regulations followed the Saskatchewan wording (DR31(2))

180 (1994) 114 DLR 500. Note that the Ontario PPSA also refers to a buyer of goods from a seller who *sells* in the ordinary course of business (author's emphasis).

181 This decision has been the subject of criticism; see: Cuming and Wood, *British Columbia Personal Property Security Act Handbook* (Toronto: Carswell, 4th edn, 1998), pp. 221–2; and note *Re Anderson's Engineering Ltd* (2002) BCSC 504, 33 CBR (4th) 1, 3 p. PSAC (3d) 129, 26 BLR (3d) 62, where it was held that as property had not passed to the 'buyer' pursuant to the Sale of Goods Act, s. 30 of the British Columbian Personal Property Security Act 1996 (equivalent to SPPSA, s. 30) did not apply.

182 This approach is also endorsed by commentators on NZPPSA, s. 53 (op. cit., Gedye et al., fn 76, p. 229, which suggests that otherwise there would be a distinction between a 'buyer' under a hire-purchase agreement, who would fall under s. 53 as a lessee, and a buyer under a conditional sale agreement).

183 See R. Cuming, 'Judicial development of personal property security law: the contribution of the Saskatchewan Court of Appeal' (1999) 62 Sask. L. Rev. 19, pp. 25–6.

184 Although a similar problem arises in relation to leases, see pp. 215–16 below.

185 This was the conclusion of the Ontario Court of Appeal in *Spittlehouse.*

be made clear in the legislation. The effect would be to extend considerably the protection of s. 25 beyond the current position, as set out in *Highway Foods*.

There are two other differences between the scheme proposed in the *Consultative Report* and Sale of Goods Act 1979, s. 25 which deserve comment. The first is that s. 25 requires 'delivery' to the buyer by the debtor, whereas the Draft Regulations only required that the buyer 'obtains possession'. The two concepts will generally coincide in practice, and it is clear that 'delivery' under s. 25 includes constructive delivery,[186] so the transfer of constructive possession should suffice. 'Delivery' is defined under the Sale of Goods Act 1979 as 'voluntary transfer of possession from one person to another'.[187] The Draft Regulations neither required that the transfer be by the debtor, nor that it be voluntary, so that in theory a buyer[188] who took the goods from the debtor's premises without permission could retain them free from any security interest: the secured party's position would then depend upon action being taken by the (probably insolvent) debtor.[189] The second difference was that in the Draft Regulations a buyer's protection did not arise on transfer of a document of title. This is included in s. 25, and covers cases even where such a transfer does not confer constructive possession on the transferee.[190] Even though 'possession' is likely to include constructive possession, it is unclear whether this would be applicable in relation to goods in bulk.[191] The omission of any reference to transfer of document of title in DR 31(3) probably meant that a buyer of goods in bulk would have had to take actual delivery from the bulk to be protected.

The extension of protection to a lessee from the debtor in the scheme proposed by the *Consultative Report* was also to be welcomed.[192] Further, the requirement that the lessee obtains possession made considerable sense. The position under UCC, Article 9 is the same as in relation to buyers: there is no specific provision that there must be delivery to the lessee under 9–321, but the definition of a 'lessee in the ordinary course of business' in 2A–103(u) provides that 'only a lessee that takes possession of the goods or has a right to recover the goods from the lessor under this article may be a lessee in ordinary course of business'. There is no specific provision in the Canadian or New Zealand legislation. If there were a requirement of a transfer of title to the lessee, delivery would surely be essential since, on one view, the only title acquired by a lessee is a possessory title. However, under an Article 9 or PPSA-type scheme finance leases and hire-purchase agreements are viewed as transfers of the entire interest to the lessee, with the lessor merely having a security interest, and on this view a requirement of transfer of possession is not critical, although desirable.

186 See: *Gamer's Motor Centre (Newcastle) Pty Ltd* v. *Natwest Wholesale Australia Pty Ltd* (1987) 163 CLR 236, *Forsythe International (UK) Ltd* v. *Silver Shipping Co. Ltd* [1993] 2 LLR 268. The same is true for the requirement of 'delivery' under s. 24: *Michael Gerson (Leasing) Ltd* v. *Wilkinson* [2001] QB 514.

187 Section 61(1).

188 To whom title probably need not have passed, see above.

189 It is also unclear what the debtor's remedy would be: it might well only be a personal claim for breach of contract or in conversion, which is unlikely to help the secured party.

190 Op. cit., Goode, fn 67, p. 62.

191 See L. Gullifer, 'Constructive possession after the Sale of Goods (Amendment) Act 1995' [1999] LMCLQ 93. Problems in this regard are perhaps more likely to arise in the context of a debtor owner of goods in bulk over which a creditor has a true security interest, than a quasi-security interest.

192 It is not clear whether under the present law the term 'disposition' in s. 25 includes leases; see pp. 191–92 above.

Where the lease is not for the purposes of security, there is a much stronger argument that delivery should be required, as otherwise it is difficult to see what interest the exception is protecting. A true lessee before delivery merely has a contractual right to possession, and there seems little justification for the lessee having priority over a secured party who has perfected its security interest. The requirement that the lessee obtain possession is therefore necessary in this context. It should also be noted that the protection of a lessee is that the security interest is subordinated to its limited interest[193] so that the secured party can only enforce against the lessor's reversionary interest.[194]

Priority between security interests created by someone other than the debtor and the buyer or lessee of the collateral from that debtor

In all the overseas systems, and under the scheme proposed in the *Consultative Report*, the buyer or lessee of goods sold in the ordinary course of business only takes free from security interests created by the debtor[195] and therefore takes subject to security interests created by other persons, for example, previous owners. This can arise in the following situation: B sells equipment which it is not in the business of selling to C. The equipment is subject to a perfected security interest in favour of A created by B. In these circumstances C takes subject to A's interest. C, who is in the business of selling used equipment sells the equipment to D. D takes free of any security interests created by C, but not the security interest created by B.[196]

True security interests

Here the current law does not distinguish between equitable security interests created by the debtor and those created by others, and so, in theory, the position would have changed under the scheme proposed in the *Consultative Report*. However, as mentioned above, most goods sold or leased in the ordinary course of business are subject only to floating charges, where the sale or lease is expressly permitted, and so this change would have been unlikely to have had much practical effect.

Quasi-security interests

Here the scheme mirrors the position under the Sale of Goods Act, s. 25 in that it upholds the doctrine of relative title[197] (the recipient only gets as good a title as the entruster had). Although this doctrine is most apparent where the entruster derives his title from a thief, it would also apply in the following situation: A sells to B on retention-of-title terms, prohibiting resale. B sells to C on retention-of-title terms (again prohibiting resale). Currently C does not get good title under s. 25.[198] C then sells to

193 Op. cit., Gedye et al., fn 76, p. 217 (concerning NZPPSA, s. 52).
194 See W. Lawrence, W. Henning, R. Wilson Freyermuth, *Understanding Secured Transactions* (New York: Matthew Bender, 3rd edn, 1999), p. 313.
195 See: DR31(3); UCC Art. 9–320(a); NZPPSA, s. 53(1); OPPSA, s. 28(1); SPPSA, s. 30(2).
196 This example is taken from the Official Comment to UCC Art. 9–320.
197 See materials cited in fns 42 and 43 above.
198 *Re Highway Foods* [1995] 1 BCLC 209 [1995] BCC 271.

D, not on retention-of-title terms. D would only get B's title and would not succeed if A claimed the goods, a result identical to that described above under the scheme proposed in the *Consultative Report* and the PPSA schemes. In these circumstances, both under current law and under the proposed scheme, D's only remedy is an action against C for breach of the terms implied by the Sale of Goods Act 1979, s. 12.[199] Under the UCC, it is possible that a buyer in C's position can take free of A's interest, if A acquiesces in the sale to C and this is taken as an entrusting of the goods to C, so as to trigger the exception to the *nemo dat* rule in UCC 2–403(2).[200] This could be said to be the equivalent of the Factors Act 1889, s. 2(1) but it is very unlikely that C could be said to be in possession of the goods with the consent of A, as required by that section, and so the section is unlikely to apply.[201]

In its first Consultation Paper, the Law Commission provisionally proposed that a buyer of goods in the ordinary course of business should take free of interests created by all previous owners, since even if such a buyer were to search, it could not discover security interests created by previous owners.[202] In the *Consultative Report*, however, the Law Commission upheld the relative title view set out above, on the grounds that the wider view would be a major inroad into the *nemo dat* principle, which should not be undertaken without a full review of the law of transfer of title.[203] This issue will therefore fall to be considered as part of the Law Commission's future work on transfer of title. A full review of the area can take into account the need to balance competing policy considerations: this is not best done in the context of particular kinds of interests (for example, security interests) or in the context of particular cases.[204]

In common with some of the overseas schemes, the scheme proposed in the *Consultative Report* did provide for two exceptions to the 'relative title' rule. The first was in relation to consumers who bought goods of a low value, who would have taken

199 Sale of Goods Act 1979, s. 12(1) implies a term that the seller has the right to sell the goods, and s. 12(2) implies terms that the goods are free from any encumbrance not disclosed to the buyer before the contract is made, and that the buyer will obtain quiet possession of the goods. Currently, a sale of goods acquired on retention-of-title terms where there is no permission to sell, is seen as a breach of s. 12(1) (*Butterworth* v. *Kingsway Motors* [1954] 2 All ER 694, concerning a hire-purchase agreement). Under the scheme proposed in the *Consultative Report*, it is not clear whether there would be a breach of the term implied by s. 12(1), or whether it would be more appropriate to see it as a breach of the term implied by s. 12(2), as the security interest of A could be viewed as an encumbrance (op. cit., Ziegel and Denomme, fn 85, pp. 234–5). At present the warranty of freedom from charges and encumbrances is seen as of little significance, since charges are equitable and a purchaser would take free from them (op. cit., Goode, fn 4, p. 288).

200 UCC Art. 2–403(2) 'Any entrusting of possession of goods to a merchant who deals in goods of that kind gives him power to transfer all rights of the entruster to a buyer in ordinary course of business.'

201 A contrary view (on slightly different facts) is expressed in op. cit., Ziegel and Denomme, fn 85, p. 235 in relation to the Ontario Factors Act 1990, s. 2(1), which is in identical terms to the UK Act.

202 See LCCP, above fn 48, para. 4.184. This was also the view taken in the *Diamond Report*, above fn 2, para. 13.5.4 and in the Report of the Committee on Consumer Credit (1971) Cmnd 4596 (the Crowther Report), para. 5.7.72.

203 See *Consultative Report*, above fn 13, para. 3.259.

204 For example, *Shogun Finance Ltd v Hudson* [2004] 1 AC 919.

free of any security interest, providing that they bought for value and had no knowledge of the security interest.[205] The second covered goods with a unique serial number.[206]

Goods with unique serial numbers

Problems caused by an asset having successive owners would not arise if a search could be made against the asset itself rather than against the name of the debtor. This can be done where an asset has a unique serial number, such as a motor vehicle which has a vehicle identification number (VIN).[207] The position in relation to motor vehicles at present is that hire-purchase and other financing agreements can be registered with voluntary registers such as HPI and Experian. These registers can be searched using a VIN (or the registration number of the vehicle) and reveal a great deal of information about the vehicle's history. However, registration is, in theory, voluntary (although members of HPI are contractually obliged to register) and failure to register does not render a financing agreement unenforceable, except, perhaps, against another member of HPI.[208] The current operation of the *nemo dat* rule in relation to motor vehicles is piecemeal. Private purchasers of motor vehicles take free of the interest of a financier under a hire-purchase or conditional sale agreement[209] but not of an interest under a lease, a security bill of sale or a credit sale which does not fall within the definition of conditional sale.[210] The present law has been criticised for not including these other interests,[211] for not covering dispositions of caravans, boats and motor homes,[212] for inconsistency with the other exceptions to the *nemo dat* rule[213] and for uncertainty about the nature of the title gained by a private purchaser under the Hire Purchase Act provisions.[214] Further, the rationale for the lack of protection for trade or finance purchaser is that they are able to search the HPI register: however, it is now extremely easy for a private purchaser to search the register for a relatively low fee. There are no other special provisions for assets with a unique serial number (except land, ships and aircraft, which have separate registers).

The scheme proposed in the *Consultative Report* provided that a secured party could have included the unique serial number in the financing statement, although this would not have been compulsory.[215] The effects of not including the serial number would have varied according to whether the goods were equipment or inventory. A filing in relation to equipment made without a serial number would

205 See DR31(4) and (5).
206 See DR 31(7) and (8).
207 This number is different from the vehicle's registration number, which can be changed.
208 See: *Moorgate Mercantile Co Ltd* v. *Twitchings* [1977] AC 890; *Consultative Report*, above fn 13, para. 2.93 and n. 26.
209 See Hire Purchase Act 1964, s. 27. Note p. 197 above.
210 See Hire Purchase Act 1964, s. 29(1).
211 See: *Diamond Report*, above fn 2, para.13.2.19; Law Reform Committee Twelfth Report (*Transfer of Title in Chattels*) Cmnd 2958, para. 27 and Department of Trade and Industry: Consultation Document *Transfer of Title: Sections 21 to 26 of the Sale of Goods Act 1979.*
212 See I. Davies, 'Title problems and motor vehicle financing: a call for reform' (1994) 13 INTBFL 13–15 and 28–30. HPI now have registers covering these items, see www.hpicheck.com/newfrontend/caravans-boats.jsp, last accessed 5/10/2009.
213 Op. cit., Bridge, fn 25, pp. 5.172, 5.176.
214 Op. cit., Davies, fn 212, 13–15 and 28–30.
215 See *Consultative Report*, above fn 13, para. 3.209.

have preserved validity of the security interest against a liquidator or administrator, but would not have preserved priority against other perfected security interests.[216] A buyer or lessee of equipment with a unique serial number would have taken free of any security interests of which he did not know and where the goods were not described by the unique serial number in the filing.[217] This would have applied whether the security interest was created by the debtor or a previous owner. Where the goods were inventory, a secured party would have only needed to perfect by a 'general filing' in order to preserve priority over other security interests. Usually, when inventory is sold or leased, it is in the ordinary course of business and thus the buyer or lessee would have taken free of the security interest.[218]

The Law Commission's proposals in the *Consultative Report* did not amount to a wholesale reform of the Hire Purchase Act provisions. As with all the proposals, they only related to security interests (under the extended definition in the scheme) and did not cover leases for under one year, bailments for other purposes, such as repair, or possession obtained by theft or fraud. In this area, at least, the omission in the final Report of the proposals relating to title retention devices is not to be regretted. There is an urgent need for a more general reconsideration of the exceptions to the *nemo dat* rule as regards items with unique serial numbers, since a cheap and easily accessible system of VIN registration could mean that all buyers could be expected to search, and should take subject to any registered interests.[219] Further, the proposals in the *Consultative Report* would have only applied where the debtor was a company,[220] although they would have applied to all purchasers. This would appear to have included consumer purchasers, since the price of many motor vehicles is likely to be more than the £1,000 suggested for the consumer exception.[221] However, the burden of searching which the proposals had put on all buyers and lessees is not onerous or expensive.[222] The possibility of a general system of VIN registration, maybe linking with the existing DVLC register at Cardiff, where all vehicles must be registered, is one that should be explored in detail by the Law Commission in the future.

216 See DR33(4).

217 See DR31(7) and (8).

218 See DR31(3).

219 It could also prevent the situation in *Shogun Finance Ltd* v. *Hudson* [2004] 1 AC 919 arising, since if the buyer had searched against the VIN of the car, the existence of the hire-purchase agreement would have become clear. If the buyer had then made enquiries of his seller (the rogue) it is likely that the fraud would have been exposed. Such a system would act as a deterrent to fraud and theft, by making disposal of the proceeds much more difficult. This assumes universal registration. A difficult question arises if the financier does not file against the VIN number: should it lose priority even if the hire-purchase agreement is void for mistake? This would amount to taking away ownership rights, rather than merely security rights.

220 The Law Commission in the LCCP, above fn 48, suggested that these reforms should be postponed until they could be extended to all debtors, but in the *Consultative Report*, above fn 13, it, tentatively, changed its mind (paras 2.120–2.122). There is now again an opportunity for the scheme to have general application.

221 See DR31(4) and (5).

222 The cost of a motor vehicle serial number search on the New Zealand Personal Property Register is $1 (information available on www.ppsr.govt.nz/pls/web/DBSSITEN.Main). The search is very simple to perform and takes only a few minutes. A simulated search is available at www.ppsr.govt.nz/ppsr-images/tutorial/.

Priority between interests created by debtor and those created by secured party

If A sells goods to B but retains possession, the Sale of Goods Act, s. 24 provides that a subsequent good faith buyer (C) obtains good title.[223] However, this does not apply where A sells on retention-of-title terms:[224] it is not necessary as A still has title and can pass it to C, even though A is in breach of his contract with B.[225] This is a straightforward application of the *nemo dat* principle. The same analysis would apply if the first transaction were a hire purchase agreement or a lease.[226]

What is the position if retention-of-title sales, hire-purchase agreements and (at least) finance leases were recharacterised under the scheme proposed in the *Consultative Report* as transfers of title to the debtor subject to a security interest in favour of the secured party? In the absence of an exception to the *nemo dat* principle, it would appear that C would only obtain A's security interest in the goods.[227] The most usual situation where a secured party will have possession of goods and will wish to pass good title to a purchaser, is when the secured party has taken possession after default and is seeking to realise the value under its power of sale. There are provisions in all the jurisdictions providing that, in these circumstances, a good faith purchaser takes free of the interest of the debtor, and any interests subordinate to those of the debtor and the secured party,[228] even when the procedures laid down in the legislation for giving notice to the debtor have been complied with. The Law Commission proposed to include such a provision.[229] However, it seems reasonably clear that these sections only apply after default.[230]

It would appear that in the US, such a situation can be covered by UCC 2–403(2) if leaving the secured party in possession amounts to entrustment to a merchant dealing in goods of that kind.[231] Arguably, similar situations in this country could fall under the Factors Act, s. 2(1): there is, however, the problem that the Factors Act refers to possession 'with consent of the owner', which raises the point whether a buyer under a conditional sale agreement could be said to be an 'owner'. UCC 2–403 (2)

223 Subject to the point on relative title; see p. 194 above.
224 See *Vowles* v. *Island Finances Ltd* [1940] 4 DLR 357.
225 Op. cit., Guest, fn 25, paras 7–056 and 5–004; *Wait* v. *Baker* (1848) 2 Exch. 1.
226 See p. 197 above.
227 It was specifically envisaged under the proposals that the secured party could have transferred its security interest, and no new filing will be required, although the new secured party may have wished to register its interest by filing a financing change statement (see *Consultative Report*, above fn 13, para. 3.237).
228 See: SPPSA, s. 59(14); OPPSA, s. 63(10); NZPPSA s. 115 (although it is not clear whether this covers contractual powers of sale as well as powers of sale under the Act; op. cit., Gedye et al., fn 76, pp. 408–9); UCC Art. 9–617.
229 See *Consultative Report*, above fn 13, para. 5.87, and DR62(8).
230 UCC Art. 9–617 specifically states this. The sections in the various PPSAs are in the part of those Acts specifically providing a 'Code of Rules' for enforcement of security interests.
231 *Stimson* v. *Moon* (1975) 137 Ga.App. 82, 222 s. E.2d 873 (truck left with dealer/seller after purchase amounted to entrustment by buyer). Similarly, a subsequent lessee from a lessor who has already leased the goods to a first lessee, takes subject to that first lease contract, unless the goods can be said to be entrusted to the lessor by the first lessee, the lessor deals in goods of that kind and the transaction is in the ordinary course of business; UCC Art. 2A–304 (1) and (2). A buyer from the lessor would take free in similar circumstances under UCC Art. 2–403.

sidesteps this problem by merely referring to the 'entruster' and providing that the buyer obtains 'all the rights of the entruster'.

Conclusions

The omission of the proposals in relation to title-retention devices in the Law Commission's Final Report is to be regretted, on the grounds that their inclusion led to coherence and comprehensiveness both in the registration and the priority rules. However, in relation to the statutory exceptions to the *nemo dat* rule, the opportunity for examination of the whole area is to be welcomed. There is no doubt that the scheme proposed in the *Consultative Report* would have changed the present law in relation to the statutory exceptions to the *nemo dat* rule, but would have stopped well short of a general principle of voluntary entrustment, as proposed by Professor Diamond,[232] and was not, and did not pretend to be, a wholesale review of the law of transfer of title. Instead, the scheme provided a coherent system in relation to goods subject to a security interest, based chiefly on the notion of registration as notice, so that those obtaining a subsequent interest take free of unregistered interests, and those who are not expected to search the register take free of registered interests. There would have been significant advantages in the elimination of inconsistent treatment of different types of security and quasi-security interests,[233] and also in the extension of s. 25-type protection to lessees and (probably) those buying on retention-of-title terms.[234] However, the scheme would have been limited to those situations of false wealth which were caused because of an entrustment transaction with the purpose of security (plus operating leases over one year and consignments), and further to situations where the 'debtor' was a company (although dispositive transactions involving non-companies were included). Areas completely omitted from consideration included entrustment to a mercantile agent, transfers of possession for purposes of repair or storage, as well as short-term hire agreements, void or voidable contracts of sale, and situations where a person is in possession of goods not belonging to them for an honest reason (e.g. finding) or a dishonest reason (e.g. theft). The scheme was justifiably criticised for these limitations and omissions, which were, of course, a consequence of the Law Commission's limited terms of reference.

It is to be hoped that the Law Commission will consider this whole area again in the near future. The future challenge will be to find a balance between the interests of true owners and secured parties, and bona fide buyers and lessees. Competing policy considerations, such as the deterrence of theft, the sanctity of ownership and the need for a free and efficient market in goods have to be weighed. The balance could be shifted either in favour of the true owner[235] or the bona fide purchaser.[236] Registration can help redress that balance, but universal registration is impossible, and so it will still be necessary to decide where the line is to be drawn. The task is far wider than merely dealing with security and quasi-security interests, in relation to which a registration system can be expected to operate effectively. Any future

232 See fn 2 above.

233 For example, between the treatment of a legal mortgage and an equitable mortgage or charge (see p. 207 above) and between the treatment of conditional sale, hire purchase and leases under the Sale of Goods Act, s.25.

234 See pp. 208–9.

235 Which would mean that the exceptions to the *nemo dat* rule would be narrower.

236 So that the default *nemo dat* position rarely applied.

reformed system will, however, have to dove-tail with the law relating to security interests, and wider policy considerations must not obscure the need to enable those taking security and quasi-security interests to protect their position. Even if it is decided to keep the balance roughly where it is at the moment, there is considerable imperative to eliminate the anomalies and inconsistencies in the system, many of which are discussed in this essay.[237] The project of reforming this area is of great importance, and it is to be hoped that those who had/have doubts about the need for fundamental reform and the shape it might take will welcome the opportunity to respond to a new wider and more comprehensive review.

237 Such as the inconsistent treatment of similar interests in relation to both the entrustment and the dispositive transactions; and whether the dispositive transaction includes transactions where no proprietary interest passes; the uncertainties regarding sale by a lessor; whether a sale by a non-owner should have to be in the ordinary course of business of a mercantile agent, the issues surrounding relative title and the treatment of goods with unique serial numbers.

6 Securities collateral

Joanna Benjamin

Introduction

The use of securities[1] as collateral in the financial markets may constitute one of the most economically important applications of personal property security law. London is the centre of the international financial markets. A significant proportion of securities collateral arrangements in these markets are made by companies registered in England and Wales, and/or in respect of UK collateral, and/or using documentation governed by English law. For these reasons, the proposed reform of UK law relating to company security interests is highly significant for the European financial markets.[2]

The following discussion will consider in turn: the background to the use of securities as collateral; key legal sensitivities associated with this use; operational issues raising legal risk; and legal solutions.

BACKGROUND

What are securities?

Commercial function

Securities comprise an important category of financial asset. They are created by commercial companies, government and supranational agencies and other types of institutional issuer as a means of raising capital. A significant trend in corporate finance over the last decade has been the increasing use of issues of debt securities as an alternative to bank loans. The same period has seen a very significant growth in structured finance, whereby existing financial assets are economically converted into

1 In this chapter, the term 'securities' is used to mean investment securities such as shares or bonds, or interests in them, as discussed below, pp. 223–26. This is distinct from 'security interests', which is used in this chapter to mean mortgages, pledges, charges or liens or equivalent arrangements under foreign systems of law. The term 'securities' has caused confusion, see the chapter in this volume by de Lacy, p. 33.

2 'Investment Securities, whether held directly or indirectly and whether in paper-based or dematerialised form, represent an immensely valuable form of collateral. It is therefore essential to the stability of the financial systems and the avoidance of systemic risk that the legal regime in place should, wherever possible, remove grounds for uncertainty as to the validity of security interests in financial collateral and as to the law applicable to them.' R. M. Goode, *Legal Problems of Credit and Security* (London: Sweet & Maxwell, 3rd edn, 2003), p. 210.

new securities.[3] A further development is the introduction of credit-linked notes (CLNs), in which credit derivatives are embedded within debt securities. CLNs serve to transfer credit risk from their issuer to their purchaser.[4] All of these factors serve to increase the number of securities in issue. The capital markets[5] currently comprise a significant proportion of the world's economic wealth.

Legal meaning

Securities are a type of transferable financial asset. The meaning of securities at general law[6] changes over time.[7] Originally the term meant secured debt obligations. In the eighteenth century it became the widespread practice of government agencies and commercial companies to raise capital by issuing large number of transferable debt obligations. These were known as securities because the issuer's payment obligation was secured on its assets.[8] It was long thought that the term 'securities' was confined (as its name suggests) to secured claims.[9] However, the connotation of a security interest has now been lost.[10] The term is now used more widely to include equities

3 Very broadly, structured finance involves the transfer of existing financial assets to a special purpose vehicle (SPV), and the issue by the SPV of new notes or bonds. The payment obligations under the notes or bonds are secured by the transferred assets. Structured finance transactions are generally divided into balance sheet transactions (which serve to remove the transferred assets from the balance sheet of the transferor for regulatory capital purposes) and arbitrage transactions (where the financial institution arranging the transaction seeks to profit from the excess of the income from the transferred assets – which it bought in the market prior to the transaction – over the income payable on the new securities), and may serve a range of other purposes.

Other types of transaction involving the repackaging of existing assets into new securities include depositary receipts and managed funds. See J. Benjamin, *Interests in Securities* (Oxford: Oxford University Press, 2000), ch.11.

4 'A credit linked note (CLN) is a security containing an embedded credit derivative (that is to say the credit derivative cannot be separated from the fixed income instrument). The note is linked to both the creditworthiness of the issuer and that of the underlying obligation under the credit derivative. The investor (or protection seller) will receive an increased, regular coupon payment, and will also receive the par value of the note at maturity if no credit event has occurred. If the reference asset defaults, the net amount received by the investor at maturity is reduced.' Financial Services Authority, *Cross-sector risk transfers*, www.fsa.gov.uk, May 2002, p. 11.

5 The term 'capital markets' is used to mean the sum of issues of new securities.

6 There are a number of statutory definitions. See, for example: Stock Transfer Act 1963, s. 4(1); Income and Corporation Taxes Act 1988, s. 710(2); International Development Act 2002 s. 6(3); Electricity (Miscellaneous Provisions) Act 2003, s. 1(2); and Financial Services and Markets Act 2002, s. 102A (introduced by the Prospectus Regulations (SI 2005/1433) art. 11).

7 'The word [securities] is not a term of art, but only a word of description. It is a commercial word which will vary with the history of commerce.' *Re Rayner* [1904] 1 Ch. 176, p. 185, *per* Vaughan Williams LJ.

8 *Re Smithers* [1939] Ch. 1015, pp. 1017–20, *per* Crossman J.

9 'My Lords, the normal meaning of the word "securities" is not open to doubt. The word denotes a debt or claim the payment of which is in some way secured.' *Singer* v. *Williams* [1921] AC 41, p. 49, *per* Viscount Cave. See also *British Oil Mills Co* v. *Inland Revenue Commrs* [1903] 1 KB 689, pp. 697–8, *per* Stirling LJ.

10 '[F]inally, we do not consider there is any requirement for a security to confer a proprietary interest in the fund or assets to which it relates'. Letter, Dilwyn Griffiths, HM Treasury, to Iain Saville, CRESTCo, 19 July 2000.

and other readily transferable financial investments, [11] including depositary receipts and units in managed funds. It seems likely that warrants are securities. However, it seems unlikely that futures, options and swaps are securities at general law. The term does not include cash.[12]

Certain international measures are relevant in this connection. The Financial Collateral Directive[13] does not contain a definition of securities, but its definition of 'financial instruments' very broadly equates to the general law definition of securities.[14] The Hague Convention on Securities held with an Intermediary[15] provides[16] that '"Securities" means any shares, bonds or other financial instrument or financial assets (other than cash), or any interest therein'. (This definition is very wide, but the scope of the Convention is limited by a requirement for intermediation.)[17]

11 'I am prepared to make a declaration that "securities" includes any stocks or shares or bonds by way of investment'; *Re Douglas' Will Trust, Lloyds Bank* v. *Nelson* [1959] WLR 744, p. 749, *per* Vaisey J. See also *Re Rayner* [1904] 1 Ch. 176, p. 189, *per* Romer LJ, p. 192, *per* Stirling LJ. See also *In re Gent and Easton's Contract* [1905] 1 Ch. 385.

Leading Counsel has advised (broadly) that the term is now widely used synonymously with market investments (advice obtained from CRESTCo in the context of the dematerialisation of MMIs, Richard Sykes, QC).

12 Broadly speaking, cash is taken to mean a debt claim against a deposit-taking institution, represented by a positive balance to a cash account maintained by that institution. However, money market instruments such as CDs, which are referred to as 'near cash', and all manner of cash-backed securities, are included.

13 2002/47/EC.

14 Article 2(1)(e): '"financial instruments" means shares in companies and other securities equivalent to shares in companies and bonds and other forms of debt instruments if these are negotiable on the capital market, and any other securities which are normally dealt in and which give the right to acquire any such shares, bonds or other securities by subscription, purchase or exchange or which give rise to a cash settlement (excluding instruments of payment), including units in collective investment undertakings, money market instruments and claims relating to or rights in or in respect of any of the foregoing'. A senior lawyer involved in the drafting of this definition commented that it is not entirely satisfactory, representing a compromise between member states desiring a wide definition and those desiring a narrow one; and that it compared unfavourably with the definition in the Hague Convention, discussed below.

The Directive is implemented in the UK by the Financial Collateral Arrangements (No. 2) Regulations 2003 (SI 2003/3226); article 3 of the Regulations very broadly tracks article 2(1)(e) of the Directive.

During the consultation exercise surrounding the implementation of the Directive, it was suggested that HM Treasury should extend the definition to include the types of investment specified in Part 3 of the Financial Services and Markets Act 2000 (Regulated Activities) Order 2001 (SI 2001/544). This would have included, among other things, derivatives, insurance contracts and mortgages. However, HM Treasury decided it did not have power to depart so far from the terms of the Directive, as the Regulations were made under limited powers conferred by the European Communities Act 1972.

15 See section 13.

16 In article 1.1(a)

17 This definition prima facie includes derivatives. However the application of the Convention requires intermediation. In accordance with current market practice, it would be unusual for an intermediary to agree to hold a derivatives contract as principal and trustee on behalf of a client, for the following reasons. Derivatives contracts generally involve potential liabilities as well as rights. On-exchange derivatives are in many cases concluded on principal-to-principal basis. The intermediary may be unwilling to assume the potential liabilities associated with

The Law Commission proposals for reforming the UK law relating to company security interests are discussed later in this essay. Also discussed at the point, the draft Company Securities Regulations 2006 included the term 'financial instruments', which was modelled on the drafting of the regulations implementing the Financial Collateral Directive in to the UK (although it excludes indirectly held securities). The latter are included in a wider category of 'financial assets', which also includes rights under commodity contracts. These two terms in turn support the key defined term, 'investment property'. This comprises financial instruments (i.e. directly held securities) and intermediated financial assets. As will be discussed, special perfection and priority rules apply to investment property.

A proposal for a UK Securities Statute published by the Financial Markets Law Committee (FMLC) will also be discussed. The Law Commission also looked at these issues in its Project on Investment Securities. However, the point to note is that, if and when a new Statute is drafted, the term 'securities' is not defined in a restrictive manner.[18]

Most recently drafted definitions include not only assets such as shares and bonds, but also interests in them.[19] This is because of the widespread practice of investors and collateral takers (together 'clients') of holding securities, not directly, but indirectly through intermediaries. Directly held securities and indirectly held securities will be considered in turn in the following sections.

Directly held securities

Directly held securities, or securities not held through an intermediary, are broadly categorised according to two different questions. The first question is the nature of the rights of the holder against the issuer, and the chief categories are debt and equity. The direct holder of debt securities is owed a debt by the issuer, and is generally entitled to interest and the repayment of capital at the agreed maturity date.[20] Corporate and non-corporate entities alike may issue debt securities. A very wide range of debt securities are traded in the capital markets, including treasury securities, domestic and international corporate bonds and notes (whether secured or unsecured) and money market instruments.

An equity is an ordinary share in a company. It follows that only companies can issue equities. The direct holder of an equity is a shareholder. Equities generally involve more

becoming a party to clients' derivatives contracts. In future, however, market practice may develop so that derivatives are brought within the scope of the Convention.

18 It is desirable in the interests of the financial system that the provisions of the Statute, including the 'good faith purchaser rule', should apply to a wide range of financial assets. Further, assets which are not securities at present may in the future become securities through changing market practice, and it is important that the Statute should not inhibit market innovation. For these reasons, the definition in the Hague Convention is considered a good model.

19 The draft Company Security Regulations 2006 published by the Law Commission included directly held securities and indirectly held securities in different defined terms, because different tests of control apply to each.

20 Other rights are generally provided under the terms of issue of the securities, including rights to receive information, vote and enforce restrictive covenants.

risk that debt securities.[21] However, equities offer the possibility of capital gains because increases in the value of the company are reflected in the value of the shares.[22]

The second question according to which securities are categorised, is the manner in which ownership of the securities is evidenced and transferred. The traditional categories are bearer and registered securities. A bearer security is issued in the form of a paper instrument.[23] Ownership of the security, and the right to be paid under it, are conferred by possession, and transferred by delivery (i.e. by transfer of possession).[24]

In contrast, ownership of registered securities is evidenced and transferred by registration. A registrar maintains a database known as a register on behalf of the issuer. Details of holders of the securities and of their holdings are entered on the register. A transfer is completed by amending the register to show the details of the transferee's holding.[25]

Indirectly held securities

Directly held securities have existed for hundreds of years. Since the last quarter of the twentieth century, however, the development of cross-border, electronic securities markets has affected the manner in which securities are held by clients. Today, clients commonly hold securities, not directly from the issuer, but indirectly, through one or more intermediaries.[26] The assets held by intermediaries generally comprise, not securities in traditional form, but rather intangible electronic records.[27] Further, where an intermediary holds like assets for more than one client, such assets are customarily held not separately, but pooled in a single client account. These operational changes (which render the clients' assets intermediated, intangible[28] and pooled) facilitate rapid dealings in the international securities markets.

21 Shareholders have no automatic right to income, which is paid as dividends on a discretionary basis out of available profits. Moreover, shareholders are generally entitled to the return of their capital only on the winding up of the company, and only to the extent that sufficient assets are available after the payment of all creditors.

22 Also, shareholders have voting and other rights protected by company law.

23 The issuer's promise to pay the bearer (i.e. holder) of the instrument appears on its face. By a legal fiction, the instrument constitutes the security, which is therefore treated as a tangible asset. Of course, a debt is an intangible thing, but it is deemed to be 'locked up' inside the paper instrument.

24 I.e. very broadly, physical control.

25 See *Société Générale de Paris* v. *Walker* (1895) 11 App. Cas. 20. Certificates may be issued, but these merely represent, and do not constitute, the securities.

26 Reasons for intermediation include the rise in cross-border investment (in which the use of local intermediaries is convenient) and the use of electronic settlement systems (direct participation in which may be limited).

27 In some cases, issues of securities are fully dematerialised. No paper is involved, and the securities are issued straight onto the screen. Even where paper-based securities continue to exist, these are characteristically immobilised, i.e. lodged with a depositary. The interest of investors is recorded and transferred by credits and debits to electronic accounts maintained by a settlement system, custodian or other intermediary.

28 Because the assets are pooled in the hands of intermediaries, the interest of the client or collateral taker does not attach to any physical instrument, and therefore (it is argued) constitutes an intangible.

However, the same changes take practice beyond the scope of settled law. Many rules of law relevant to the securities markets were developed in relation to traditional, paper-based practice. Their application today is in a number of respects uncertain and/or unsatisfactory. Key sensitivities are discussed below.

The importance of securities collateral

This section will discuss the importance of the use of securities as collateral for financial exposures.

Securities as attractive collateral asset class

For the holder,[29] the traditional purpose of securities is investment, i.e. the prospect of income, capital growth or both.[30] Since the 1990s, however, a very important development has been the increasing use of holdings of securities as collateral for financial exposures.[31]

In relation to listed securities,[32] official stock exchange trading prices are normally available, and this permits listed securities to be readily and reliably valued. Listed securities are generally liquid, i.e. they can be bought and sold without delay at a fair price. For these reasons they comprise an attractive class of collateral asset.[33]

For these reasons, securities are used to collateralise a wide range of financial exposures. In practice, the most sought-after form of financial collateral is cash, and in particular US dollars. However, collateral takers are not always able to insist on cash collateral, and the next choice is generally securities. Debt securities are generally more attractive as collateral than equity securities, because their market price is less volatile. Among debt securities, treasury securities, and particularly those issued by OECD sovereign government agencies, are more attractive as collateral than corporate debt securities, because of the lower risk of default. The highest demand is for US treasuries, i.e. debt securities issued by US government agencies. However, as demand for high-quality collateral often exceeds supply, increasing use is made of other forms of corporate debt securities, and even equities.

29 Securities may serve different purposes for the issuer and for the holder respectively. As has already been indicated above, for the issuer (or its sponsor), the chief purposes are raising capital and repackaging

30 Also, in relation to private companies or in corporate finance arrangements, equity securities may be held in order to control the business of the issuer.

31 Financial exposures include a right to be paid, and a right to receive delivery of financial assets. Such rights confer the prospect of payment or delivery, and therefore constitute assets. However, they also involve the risk of default, and therefore constitute exposures.

32 I.e. securities which are included in the official list of a recognised stock exchange, and admitted to trading.

33 Ready valuation assists margining (or revaluation during the term of the transaction). Liquidity facilitates immediate enforcement.

Types of exposure

Innumerable types of financial exposure may be collateralised by securities. However, the five major categories are exposures which arise in relation to: money supply operations,[34] central counterparty services,[35]

34 In money supply operations, central banks make short-term advances of cash to selected financial institutions against collateral, which generally takes the form of treasury securities. The money supply in the national economy is increased by increasing the number of such transactions, and reduced by reducing them. Thus, securities collateral is central to the supply of credit from central banks into the financial markets.

35 A very significant element in the increasing use of securities collateral in recent years is the introduction of central counterparty (CCP) services to a number of securities markets. To explain the role of a central counterparty it is necessary to provide a little background. Securities trades are concluded on securities markets (whether official markets on recognised stock exchanges, or informal 'over the counter' markets). Suppose that at 10.00 a.m. on Monday, B concludes a trade with S that B will buy 10,000 XXX shares from S for £1,000,000 and for delivery and payment on Thursday. The legal position after 10.00 a.m. on Monday and, before delivery and payment take place, is that the parties have concluded but not discharged a contract of sale and purchase. The process of making delivery against payment in order to discharge securities trading contracts is called settlement. After 10.00 a.m. on Monday and before Thursday (the settlement interval), credit exposures arise as follows. Suppose that on Tuesday the market price of 10,000 XXX shares rises to £1,100,000. B's contract now entitles her to buy the shares for less than they are currently worth. Settlement will bring her a profit, and her trade is said to be 'in the money'. Failure to settle will involve an associated loss for B. Therefore, to the extent that her trade is in the money, B has a credit exposure to S. If, conversely, the market price of 10,000 XXX shares drops below £1,000,000 during the settlement interval, S's trade will be in the money, and S will have a credit exposure to B. Because these credit exposures are equal to the potential cost of having to conclude a like contract with a third party in the event that the existing counterparty defaults, they are called 'replacement cost risk'.

Derivatives transactions are discussed in the following footnote. Because derivatives contracts remain open (i.e. unsettled) for medium or long-term intervals, they involve medium or long-term replacement cost risks. While taking collateral from a trading counterparty may mitigate these risks, a more robust measure is the use of a central counterparty. Because of the length of the exposure, the use of central counterparties has long been widespread for exchange-traded derivatives.

The normal settlement interval for UK equities and eurobonds is three business days (T+3). Until fairly recently, the markets tolerated a three-day exposure to replacement cost risk. However, in the more competitive and credit risk intolerant climate of the mid to late 1990s, more and more securities markets introduced CCP services.

A CCP is a financial institution with access to very considerable financial resources. When a trade is concluded on the market, the CCP automatically becomes a party to every trade, acting as buyer to S and seller to B. (This is usually but not always achieved by novating the original contract between S and B.) Thus, during the settlement interval, S and B bear the credit risk of the CCP, and not that of each other. Because the CCP is extremely well resourced, its use serves to upgrade the credit exposure of the market participants. Also, because it is a counterparty to every trade, it permits market participants the greatest possible netting opportunities.

If a party defaults, the CCP is still obliged to perform. If the defaulting party's trade was out of the money, performance will involve a loss for the CCP. Replacement cost risk for the whole market is therefore transferred to the CCP. This is a very significant credit exposure, and a range of measures employed to address it. One of the most important of these is securities collateral. Market participants receiving CCP services are required to post financial

derivatives,[36] securities loans and repos,[37] and intermediary

collateral, including securities collateral, in the form of initial margin and variation margin. As more and more markets introduce CCP services, the need to provide such margin is a significant factor in the pressure to consolidate the post trade infrastructure.

36 Derivatives are a type of financial transaction. The forms taken by derivatives are diverse and evolving, and there is no settled definition of a derivative. However, it is generally agreed that the chief categories of derivatives are forwards and options. Swaps are an important type of composite derivative contract. The parties to a futures contract have both the right and the obligation to make or, as the case may be, to take delivery of the reference asset at an agreed future date, against payment of an agreed price. In contrast, an option confers on one party such a right, but does not impose such an obligation.

A swap is a form of derivative transaction that is very widely used in managing financial risks, including interest rate, currency, and credit risks. Swaps also serve to create what is known as 'synthetic' structures, whereby proprietary positions in (or holdings of) financial assets are economically replicated by contractual provisions. A swap relates to income streams. An income stream is a right to receive income over a period of time; examples are rights to interest payments on outstanding debt, and to dividends on shares. The swap provides in effect for two parties to exchange differing income streams.

It is generally agreed that all derivatives share the following three characteristics. First, they are bilateral contracts. Second, performance of the obligations of the parties under the contracts is due to take place at a date (the settlement date) significantly later than the one which the contract is concluded (the contract date). Third, the positive or negative value from time to time of the contract to each party is derived from changes in the value of certain assets (or the performance of certain benchmarks or entities) which are identified in the contract (reference assets, reference benchmarks or reference entities). This third characteristic explains the term 'derivative'.

Credit risk is always associated with derivatives. For example, if A has sold a six months futures contract to B, and after one month the market price of the reference assets is £1,000,000 less than the contract price, A is in the money to the extent of £1,000,000. The futures contract is now a valuable asset for A, who bears a corresponding credit exposure to B of £1,000,000. Furthermore, this credit exposure may continue for a further five months. (It will be reduced or cease if the market moves against A, out of the money.) The medium or long term of derivatives contracts gives rise to medium-term or long-term potential credit exposures.

Derivatives contracts may be entered into on recognised exchanges, or off exchange. In order to manage credit risk, derivatives exchanges have long required their members to collateralise their derivatives obligations, using a range of financial assets including securities. Until the 1990s, it was the widespread practice for credit exposures for off exchange derivatives to be uncollateralised. Increased concern to manage credit risk led to the widespread use of credit support documentation.

37 Securities loans and repos are also important types of collateralised financial transaction. Because of similarities in the legal structure and documentation of collateral arrangements for securities loans and repos on the one hand and off exchange derivatives on the other, securities loans and repos are sometimes referred to as forms of derivatives transactions.

A securities loan is an agreement that A will, on an agreed date, deliver securities to B against the provision by B to A of financial collateral; this collateral often takes the form of other securities. There is a simultaneous agreement that, at a later date, B will redeliver equivalent (i.e. same number, same type) securities to A, against the return of equivalent collateral. The traditional function of a securities loan is to cover a B's temporary short position. A short position is an obligation to deliver assets which one does not currently hold. B might be a broker who has agreed with C that it will deliver 100,000 ABC shares on Wednesday. B does not hold ABC shares, but is expecting to receive 100,000 ABC shares

services.[38] In relation to the last type of exposure, the draft CESR/ECB standards on clearing and settlement propose to render mandatory the collateralisation of credit exposures for systemically important custodians.[39]

Generally

Thus, securities collateral has tremendous importance for the financial system. It protects the wholesale money supply and the post-trade infrastructure.[40] It supports the derivatives markets, and therefore much of the management of commercial and financial risk. Through securities lending, securities collateral supports market liquidity. Generally, securities collateral promotes the availability of credit in the economy by assisting financial institutions to manage their credit exposures. Legal risk affecting securities collateral may disturb the smooth operation of the money supply, and this explains the high level of industry and public sector commitment to law reform in this area.

from D on Wednesday. However, the delivery from D is delayed. (Settlement delays are not uncommon, particularly in cross-border transactions.) B now has a temporary short position. In order to avoid defaulting on its delivery obligations to C, B approaches A, usually an institutional investor such as a pension fund. A loans 100,000 ABC shares to B, enabling B to deliver to C. B provides XYZ shares to B as collateral for the return of the ABC shares. The delivery from D of ABC shares arrives on Friday. B delivers these shares to A, thereby closing the securities loan, whereupon A delivers equivalent XYZ shares to B.

'Repo' is an abbreviation of 'repurchase transaction', which in turn is an abbreviation of 'sale and repurchase transaction'. A repo is an agreement that A will purchase securities (usually treasuries) from B at a certain date, with a simultaneous agreement that B will repurchase equivalent securities from A at a later date (often three business days later). The traditional function of a repo is to serve as an informal alternative to a secured loan. A might be an investment bank requiring cash, and having securities available to deliver as collateral. B might be a commercial bank wishing to advance cash on a collateralised basis for profit. The purchase price serves to advance the cash; the purchased securities serve as collateral for the return of the advanced cash. The repurchase price exceeds the purchased price by a sum (the price differential) calculated in the same way as interest on a loan.

Securities loans and repos are used for a variety of other purposes, including arbitrage. See op. cit., Benjamin, fn 3, ch. 6.

38 It is not customary for investors to hold their securities directly from the issuer, but rather through intermediaries including custodians, the operators of settlement systems and/or their depositaries and nominees. Custody and settlement services routinely involve significant credit exposures to clients. Such service providers therefore normally take security interests over their client's securities (together with rights of set off in relation to cash balances).

In addition to managing routine custody and settlement exposures, a further role of securities collateral is to address intermediary exposures associated with negotiated credit facilitates. In recent years, certain custody clients have wished to exploit the potential of their custody portfolios as collateral, against which credit may be obtained. Custodian banks have therefore developed credit services such as prime brokerage. The prime broker enables its hedge fund client to raise funds against the collateral in the custody portfolio. This controversially permits very high levels of gearing or leverage.

39 *Consultative Report: Standards for Security Clearing and Settlement systems in the European Union*, CESR/ECB, 2003, standard 9.

40 I.e. clearing and settlement in the securities markets.

The legal nature of collateral arrangements

In order to understand the legal nature of collateral arrangements, it is necessary to consider briefly the difference between personal rights and property rights, and their different treatment in insolvency.

Personal and property rights in insolvency

Private law rights are divided into two categories, namely personal rights and property rights. Personal rights are rights against persons (whether natural persons[41] or legal persons[42]). Personal rights are also called claims.[43] Financial assets (including all types of debt, shares and rights under derivatives contracts) are claims. In contrast, property rights are rights in respect of assets. The most complete form of property right is ownership, or title. Other forms of property right include security interests. It is important not to confuse assets with the property rights to which assets are subject.[44]

If A owes a debt or other obligation to B, and if A becomes insolvent, B's claim may become valueless. Depending on the outcome of the insolvency proceedings, B may be paid late, in part only, or not at all. The risk for B that its claim may lose its value through A's insolvency (or other default) is called credit risk. As indicated below, the function of collateral is to address credit risk.

If A holds assets in which B has property rights, and if A becomes insolvent, the general rule is that B's property rights are not affected by A's insolvency.[45] Collateral works by giving the collateral taker property rights in the collateral assets. If the value of the collateral taker's personal rights are affected by the insolvency or other default of the collateral giver, the collateral taker may rely on its property rights instead.[46]

All collateral arrangements have these characteristics. However, the legal manner in which property rights support personal rights differs depending on the legal structure of the transaction. There are two broad categories of legal structure for collateral arrangements, namely security interests and outright collateral transfers.[47]

Security interests

A security interest confers on the collateral taker property rights in the collateral assets which generally permit the collateral taker, upon the default of the collateral giver, to sell the assets and apply the proceeds of sale to discharge the collateralised

41 I.e. human beings.

42 I.e. bodies corporate, such as limited companies and local authorities.

43 From the point of view of the person against whom personal rights arise, such rights are called obligations.

44 My home is 4 Princes Avenue. My property right in my home is a joint freehold interest. Robert also has a joint freehold interest, the bank has a legal mortgage and the neighbour has a right of way. The asset is 4 Princes Avenue, and the joint freehold interests, mortgage and right of way are property rights.

45 This is because the assets available to the liquidator for distribution to creditors are limited to the assets of the insolvent. These do not include assets held by A to the extent that such assets are subject to third-party property rights.

46 Thus collateral confers property rights which lie side by side with personal rights, in order to support them, and hence the name.

47 Arguably, a transaction originally structured as a security interest, and in respect of which a right of use has been exercised, constitutes a third type.

obligation.[48] During the transaction, the collateral giver continues to enjoy residual property rights in the collateral assets. These rights are known as the equity of redemption. The equity of redemption exists concurrently with the security interest, so that (after the creation of the security interest, and prior to its discharge or enforcement) the collateral assets are subject to the concurrent property rights of both parties. The equity of redemption permits the collateral giver, on the discharge of the collateralised obligation, to the return of the collateral assets.

The equity of redemption is important from a commercial and regulatory point of view, for the following reason. It is customary for parties to agree that the value of the collateral securities will exceed the collateralised exposure by a sum called margin. Margin is designed to protect the collateral taker from changes in the value of the collateral assets. If the exposure is of tens of millions of dollars, a margin of 3 per cent represents assets of significant value. As a property right, the equity of redemption is not generally affected by the insolvency of the collateral taker. Thus, the collateral giver does not bear credit risk in relation to margin, which (in economic effect) it owns.

'There are only four kinds of consensual security known to English law: (i) pledge; (ii) contractual lien; (iii) equitable charge; and (iv) mortgage.'[49] Pledge and lien are possessory interests,[50] and therefore rarely relevant in the electronic securities markets.

Outright collateral transfers

It was seen above that, under a security interest, the collateral giver retains the equity of redemption. In contrast, under an outright collateral transfer, the collateral giver disposes of the entirety of its interests in the collateral assets, and retains no property rights whatsoever. Naturally, the collateral giver expects to receive collateral assets upon the discharge of the collateralised obligation. However, this commercial expectation is supported by personal rather than property rights. Under the collateral agreement, the collateral taker is contractually obliged to return equivalent securities when collateralised obligation is performed, thus closing the transaction. As a personal obligation, this duty of equivalent redelivery is enforceable against the collateral taker personally, but does not attach to the collateral assets, which are delivered to the collateral taker unencumbered. It follows that the collateral taker is free to use the assets from the moment it receives them.

It was also seen above that, under a security interest, and in the event of default of the collateral giver, the normal recourse of the collateral taker is to exercise a power of sale. In contrast, with outright collateral transfer, the recourse of either party in the default of the counterparty is set off. On default, the redelivery obligation is set off against the collateralised obligation, and the excess (which should arise in favour of the collateral giver, and be equal to the agreed margin) is payable as an unsecured debt.

In practice, individual outright collateral transfer transactions are usually entered into as part of continuing programmes between the financial institutions governed by

48 Any surplus of the proceeds over the collateralised obligation must be returned to the collateral giver or its liquidator.

49 See *Re Cosslett (Contractors) Ltd* [1998] Ch. 495, p. 508F, *per* Millett LJ.

50 'A pledge and a contractual lien both depend on the delivery of possession to the creditor ... Neither a mortgage nor a charge depends on the delivery of possession. The difference between them is that a mortgage involves the transfer of legal or equitable ownership to the creditor, whereas an equitable charge does not.' *Re Cosslett (Contractors) Ltd* [1998] Ch. 495, p. 508, *per* Millett LJ.

master agreements.[51] Pursuant to the terms of these master agreements, rights of set off in respect of all outstanding transactions are exercised together, following a procedure known as close-out netting.

Comparison of structures

Both security interests and outright collateral transfers serve to collateralise credit risk, and are designed to be effective in counterparty insolvency. Both are generally balance sheet neutral and tax neutral. Both may serve significantly to reduce the regulatory capital burden associated with credit exposures. Despite these similarities, important differences remain. These differences are reduced but not eliminated by the Financial Collateral Directive.

From the point of view of the collateral giver, a security interest is generally preferable to an outright collateral transfer, for the following reason. Credit risk in respect of margin is present with an outright collateral transfer and generally[52] absent with a security interest, because of the equity of redemption as explained above.

From the point of view of the collateral taker, an outright collateral transfer is generally preferable, for the following reasons. Traditionally, security interests have often required bespoke documentation drafted by external counsel; raised possible legal sensitivities concerning perfection, particularly in cross-border situations;[53] raised possible legal uncertainties concerning priorities, particularly when multiple intermediaries are involved;[54] and in enforcement been vulnerable to insolvency freezes[55] and possible delays and formalities under certain systems of law.[56] Further, at general law, only an outright collateral transfer is clearly compatible with[57] a right of use. While the Financial Collateral Directive facilitates perfection and enforcement for transactions within its scope, and permits an enforceable right of use to be agreed in a security interest, the Directive is silent on priorities, and does not prevent an insolvency freeze from blocking the enforcement of a security interest.[58] Moreover, while a security interest over financial collateral used to be registrable[59] if it amounted to a floating charge or charge on book debts, outright collateral transfers were not. This point of difference was affected by two related developments. First, the Financial Collateral Directive removed the requirement to register collateral transactions within its scope. Second, the Law Commission's proposed reforms of the law relating to company security interests proposed to exempt many financial collateral arrangements from the need for registration, and to rationalise and simplify the law of priorities. However, for the time being, at any rate the latter proposals have not been adopted.

51 Industry standard documentation is available for the major types of transaction.
52 However, where in accordance with the Financial Collateral Directive the secured creditor has reserved, and exercised a right of use, credit risk in respect of margin is present.
53 See generally below.
54 See generally below.
55 See Insolvency Act 1986, s. 11(3)(c) (unamended) and note now the effects of the Enterprise Act 2002, s. 248 and Schedule B1.
56 See below.
57 And indeed necessarily implies.
58 A further point is that a restrictive covenant may prevent the collateral giver from granting a security interest, but not from entering into an outright collateral transfer. Of course, well-drafted contemporary restrictive covenants would prevent both.
59 See Companies Act 2006, s. 860. But see now S.I. 2003/3226 Regulation 4 which disapplies the Act to financial collateral arrangements. Note also the Banking Act 2009, s. 252.

In contrast, a range of industry standard documentation is available for outright collateral transfers, and is very widely used in practice. Outright collateral transfers of financial collateral do not generally require bespoke documentation, perfection or registration. They are not in general vulnerable to priorities disputes or enforcement delays.

There are however two legal sensitivities for outright collateral transfers, particularly in a cross-border context. These are recharacterisation risk[60] and reliance on close-out netting and set off.[61] Two developments serve to address them. First, since the 1990s, leading trade associations have dealt with these sensitivities in relation to their standard documentation through the use of legal opinions obtained from a wide range of jurisdictions. Second, the Financial Collateral Directive addresses these sensitivities for transactions within its scope.[62] For these reasons, routine outright collateral transfers are largely 'unlawyered', i.e. handled in-house without the assistance of external counsel.

Legal steps in taking collateral

From the point of view of the collateral taker, a large number of different legal steps are required to establish a reliable collateral arrangement.

Contractual and proprietary rights

For convenience, these steps can be divided into two categories, namely those necessary to establish a valid and enforceable collateral contract between the parties, and those necessary to establish and enforce effective property rights in the collateral assets pursuant to that contract.

Contractual steps

The collateral taker will wish to establish that: (i) the collateral contract is materially valid;[63] (ii) formally valid;[64] (iii) entered into with power;[65] (iv) and with authority;[66] and with all necessary authorisations;[67] and also duly executed.[68]

60 See generally below.
61 See generally below.
62 See generally below.
63 Material or essential validity means that there is nothing in the essential nature of the contract that renders it invalid, such as being contrary to public policy or (under English law) want of consideration. (Want of consideration would not be a problem for a document executed as a deed, which would not be required to be enforceable as a contract.)
64 I.e. complying with any applicable formal requirements, such as being in writing, signed or notarised. The Financial Collateral Directive removes formal requirements other than writing.
65 It must be established that a collateral giver has power (or *vires*) to enter into the agreement in accordance with its constitution.
66 I.e. the individual who executes the agreement on behalf of the collateral giver is authorised by the collateral giver to do so, and thus binds the collateral giver.
67 I.e. all necessary regulatory authorisations should have been obtained, and regulatory requirements complied with.
68 I.e. the collateral giver should have taken all necessary steps to enter into, execute and deliver the agreement.

Proprietary steps[69]

The steps outlined in the previous section serve to establish a good collateral contract. This is necessary but not sufficient for the collateral taker, who must then go on to acquire good property rights in the collateral assets in accordance with the terms of to that contract. This may[70] involve addressing: attachment;[71] perfection;[72] registration;[73] priorities;[74] beneficial ownership;[75] enforcement;[76] remittance;[77] and insolvency displacement.[78]

It will be seen from the foregoing that taking collateral can be a complex matter. Part of this complexity may be explained by reference to policy considerations.

Policy issues

Pari passu

It is generally the case that the assets of an insolvent company are insufficient to meet all debts owed by the company. A basic principle of insolvency law, known as the *pari passu* principle,[79] provides that all general creditors of the insolvent should be treated equally (i.e. paid in the same proportion).[80] However, this principle is subject to important exceptions, which significantly reduce its impact. These exceptions include rules relating to the claims of collateral takers, and of which the following is

69 For a discussion of attachment, perfection and priorities in relation to securities collateral, see op. cit., Goode, fn 2, pp. 221–5.

70 In relation to outright collateral transfers, perfection, registration and priorities are generally not relevant.

71 Attachment involves identification of the asset subject to the property right. 'Attachment denotes the creation of the security interest as between debtor and creditor. The effect of attachment is that the security interest fastens on the asset so as to give the creditor rights *in rem* against the debtor himself, though not necessarily against third parties'; op. cit., Goode, fn 2, p. 59.

72 Perfection renders an interest enforceable against third parties. Where steps are required to perfect a security interest, they generally involve an act of publicity, such as registration, notarisation or delivery. See generally, op. cit., Goode, fn 2, at p. 73.

The Financial Collateral Directive removes formal perfection requirements for transactions within its scope other than, broadly, book entry transfer.

73 There is a debate as to whether or not registration is a form of perfection, or a separate step.

74 Questions of priority arise when other third parties acquire or retain property rights in the collateral assets that compete with the interest of the secured creditor.

75 It is necessary to establish that the collateral giver either is, or is authorised by, any beneficial owner of the collateral assets.

76 In the event of default, the collateral taker wishes to be able to enforce its interests without delay or formalities.

77 Where a security interest is enforced overseas, it is necessary to establish that the proceeds of sale can be readily remitted to the collateral taker (and is not subject, for example, to exchange controls).

78 If the collateral giver is affected by insolvency at the time of the transaction or shortly thereafter, insolvency displacement rules may apply.

79 *Pari passu* is Latin for, broadly, equal footing.

80 See V. Finch, *Corporate Insolvency Law* (Cambridge: Cambridge University Press, 2002), pp. 421–9. For a contrary view, see Mokal 'Priority as pathology: the *pari passu* myth' (2001) 69 CLJ, pp. 581–621.

an extremely broad summary. Holders of fixed security interests are paid in priority to both preferential[81] and ordinary creditors. Holders of floating security are paid after preferential creditors.[82] Holders of floating security are generally paid before general creditors.[83] Further, rights of set off[84] (such as those available under outright collateral transfers) also enable creditors exercising them to be paid in priority to others. All of these exceptions serve to deplete the pool of assets available to meet the claims of general creditors, and often reduce it to nothing.

The simple point is that collateral arrangements do not reduce credit risk, but rather transfer it from collateral takers to general creditors.

Publicity

In response to the problem that collateral arrangements reduce general creditors' prospects of being paid in insolvency, company law requires that certain charges created by a company should be publicly registered. The theory is that, by examining the register of charges, potential creditors can assess the risk that, in the company's default, existing secured creditors would be paid in priority to themselves, and accordingly make their credit decisions on an informed basis. Registration requirements accord with the general principle of property law that, because property rights bind third parties, they must be public in order to be effective. Another aspect of this rule is the requirement that security interests be perfected in order to bind third parties.[85]

Systemic risk

Registration and perfection formalities are often inconvenient for collateral takers. The delays and administrative burdens associated with complying with formalities may be incompatible with the speed of dealing which characterises contemporary financial markets. The publicity may also be unwelcome. In practice, onerous formal requirements may be overlooked or deliberately omitted, thus presenting legal risk.

As indicated above, formal requirements have historically been regarded as the price of queue-jumping.[86] However, during the 1990s, a special policy case was made in favour of collateral takers in the wholesale financial markets. The importance of collateralisation to the supply of credit, and therefore to the health of the economy, was emphasised. So were the complex interdependencies between institutions participating in the financial markets. The effect of the latter is that legal risk affecting

81 Preferential creditors are now limited to contributions to occupational pension schemes, remuneration, etc., of employees, and levies on coal and steel production; Insolvency Act 1986, s. 386(1). Crown preference (in relation to income tax and VAT) was abolished by the Enterprise Act 2002, s. 251.

82 See Insolvency Act 1986, s. 175(2)(b).

83 This is subject to a general requirement that a proportion of the company's assets be set aside for general creditors; Insolvency Act 1986, s. 176A, inserted by the Enterprise Act 2002, s. 252. However, this requirement is disapplied in relation to financial collateral by the Financial Collateral Arrangements (No. 2) Regulations 2003, SI 2003/3226, Regulation 10(3).

84 See generally below.

85 See generally above.

86 I.e. escaping the status of general creditor.

institutional financial collateral arrangements might affect the financial system as a whole. These arguments paved the way for the Financial Collateral Directive.[87]

KEY LEGAL SENSITIVITIES

This section considers key legal sensitivities that arise in practice for the takers of securities collateral. It will discuss in turn sensitivities derived from: collateral giver insolvency; the terms of the collateral agreement; procedural requirements; and operational issues. The section that follows on from these topics will then consider solutions.

Collateral giver insolvency

The purpose of collateral is to address credit risk, and the chief source of credit risk is insolvency. Thus the key test of collateral is its ability to operate effectively in the insolvency of the collateral giver. Here it comes into conflict with the policy concerns outlined in above, which seek to protect general creditors. The tension between the objective of the collateral taker and these insolvency law policy concerns is the chief source of legal risk associated with securities collateral. This section will consider three areas of insolvency law: namely, insolvency set off, post-insolvency dispositions and preferences. It will also consider three aspects of standard market practice where these areas of insolvency law must be addressed: namely, close-out netting, margining and substitution. As will be seen, the implementation of the Financial Collateral Directive addresses these sensitivities for collateral arrangements within its scope.

Insolvency set off[88]

We considered above the legal nature of outright collateral transfers and saw that, if either party defaults while a transaction is outstanding, the non-defaulting party is protected by set off. Of course, the key event of default is insolvency. It is therefore essential to ensure that the default procedure is effective in insolvency.

Set off permits a debtor, who is also a creditor, to use its debt to satisfy its claim. If the debt is equal to the claim, the creditor will be in effect paid in full, even if other creditors receive nothing. Therefore insolvency law regulates the availability insolvency set off. Under English law, insolvency set off is mandatory.[89] This accords with the characterisation of England as a creditor-friendly jurisdiction. Other jurisdictions are characterised as debtor-friendly, and limit the availability of insolvency set off more closely. Within the EU, the Financial Collateral Directive addresses a number of insolvency sensitivities, including insolvency set off.[90] Outside the scope of this EU legislation, for example where a counterparty is organised in a non-EU jurisdiction, it

87 This Directive significantly improved the position of wholesale financial collateral takers, at the cost of collateral givers.

88 See During 'Setting off down a new road' (2004) 19 JIBFL, p. 349.

89 See the Insolvency Rules 1986, Rule 4.90.

90 See also: the Insolvency Regulation (1346/2000/EC); the Winding Up Directive (2001/24/EC); and the Insurance Winding Up Directive (2001/17/EC).

is important to establish whether applicable insolvency law would permit the default set-off provisions of the agreement to operate in accordance with their terms.[91] In these cases, it is generally advisable to structure the transaction as a security interest and not as an outright collateral transfer.

Even in the UK, the circumstances in which insolvency set off operates are limited.[92] The default provisions of market standard documentation are drafted with extreme care and a view to coming within these circumstances, and should generally not be amended.

Close-out netting

Market standard outright collateral transfer documents contain close-out netting provisions. These create a procedure whereby the mutual obligations of the parties are automatically and instantaneously modified after default, so as to facilitate set off. Close-out netting has the function of bringing all the exposures between the parties under the documentation conveniently within the scope of insolvency set off.

It operates in four stages. First, all outstanding transactions are accelerated.[93] Second, all non-cash obligations are converted to payment obligations.[94] Third, for multi-currency master agreements, all payment obligations in a currency other than the agreed base currency are converted to base currency.[95] Fourth, all debts are aggregated. At this stage, the parties owe and are owed a mutual debt and credit. These are set off against each other in accordance with the mandatory rules of insolvency set off in rule 4.90.

Post-insolvency disposition

Dispositions of property (including those under collateral transactions) taking place after the commencement of insolvency are, generally, void.[96] Naturally, no collateral taker would knowingly do business with an insolvent. However, two sensitivities arise. First, in some jurisdictions, zero-hour rules may have the effect of giving insolvency orders retrospective intraday effect. Second, the rule may affect not only

91 If they would not, the non-defaulting party which has applied the set-off provisions would face the risk of legal action from the counterparty's insolvency official.

92 The Insolvency Rules impose a number of criteria, including the following. The debits and credits to be set off must be mutual; this raises potential sensitivities in relation to agency and trust transactions. Rule 4.90 contemplates bilateral netting, but not multilateral netting. The latter is not effective on insolvency.

Contractual provision purporting to vary the mandatory provisions of insolvency law, including the regime for insolvency set off, are not effective: *British Eagle International Airlines Ltd* v. *Compagnie Internationale Air France* [1975] 1 WLR 758.

93 The default provisions are contained in a master agreement, under which the parties may enter into large numbers of transactions from time to time. Acceleration means that all outstanding obligations (for payment and redelivery as the case may be) become immediately performable at the moment of default.

94 An obligation to redeliver securities is converted into an obligation to pay the market value of the securities at the time of default. Detailed valuation provisions are included (to deal with difficulties such as defaults at times when markets are closed).

95 At a contractually agreed rate of exchange.

96 Insolvency Act 1986, s. 127.

the opening of the collateral transaction, but margining and substitutions made under it.

Preference rules

We have considered above the policy concern that the pool of assets available to general creditors of an insolvent should not be unfairly depleted. This same concern explains rules of insolvency displacement (often referred to in practice as 'preference rules'), which enable the insolvency official to challenge certain types of transaction entered into shortly before insolvency. Very broadly, a collateral transaction may be avoided by the liquidator if two conditions are satisfied. First, the transaction must be entered into prior to insolvency but close enough to it to fall within the statutory 'suspect period'.[97] Second, it must involve a breach of rules designed to protect general creditors against unfair depletion of the insolvent's assets, as a fraudulent preference or otherwise.[98]

Margining

As we have seen, it is customary for the parties to agree that the value of the collateral securities will exceed the value of the debt[99] by a percentage. The excess is known as margin, and a typical margin might be 3 per cent.[100] Margin may present a problem in practice as follows. During the term of the transaction, the market value of the collateral securities, and also in some cases the value of the collateralised exposure, change from time to time. Of course, these changes have the result that the actual margin differs from the agreed margin. In order to restore actual margin to the agreed margin, provision is included in the agreement for adjustments. Where there is a margin shortfall,[101] the collateral taker can make a 'margin call', requiring the collateral giver to deliver additional assets to eliminate the shortfall. Where there is a margin excess, the collateral giver may require margin to be released. This procedure is margining or marking to market and, in active markets, may take place several times a day.

The effect of this is that, at any moment during the transaction, different parts of the collateral pool may have been delivered at different times. This raises the danger under some systems of law[102] that the insolvency displacement rules may affect certain margin deliveries, even if the opening of the transactions falls outside the suspect period. Further, the risk may arise that late-received collateral may be outside

97 In the UK, for unconnected parities, this is six months: Insolvency Act, 1986 s. 240. These periods are also known as 'hardening' periods, because transactions entered into during these periods may be 'soft' or potentially avoidable.

98 See the Insolvency Act 1986, s. 238 (transactions at an undervalue); s. 239 (preferences) and s. 245 (avoidance of floating charges).

99 Or other collateralised obligation.

100 The percentage may vary depending on the identity of the counterparty and the nature of the collateral securities.

101 I.e. too little collateral.

102 The risk is not considered to be present under UK law where standard documentation is used, and/or within the scope of the Financial Collateral Directive.

the scope of insolvency set off[103] and may become weaker priority than the original collateral.[104]

Substitution

Although the collateral taker may dispose of its title to the securities, it retains an economic position in the collateral assets.[105] It will ultimately suffer a capital loss if the value of the collateral falls, and a capital gain if it rises. For these reasons,[106] it may wish to withdraw particular securities from the collateral pool during the term of the collateral transaction,[107] substituting others of equal value. Substitution procedures are included in market standard documentation.

As discussed above, margining may give rise to sensitivities concerning: insolvency displacement, insolvency set off and priorities. This is because it may result in different parts of the collateral pool being received at different times. Substitution may give rise to the same sensitivities for the same reason.

Terms of collateral agreement

The previous section considered collateral giver insolvency as a source of legal risk. A further source of legal risk may be the drafting of the collateral agreement. Two points will be considered in turn, namely recharacterisation risk and the right of use.

Recharacterisation risk

Recharacterisation risk is, broadly, the risk of the courts rejecting the legal categorisation of a transaction chosen by the parties in their contract, and substituting another. It involves a judicial assertion of legal substance over form.

Generally

The foregoing section compared security interests and outright collateral transfers. It indicated that the collateral taker generally prefers to structure its transactions as outright collateral transfers, in order to avoid a number of rules associated with security interests. These rules are inconvenient to the collateral taker, and designed to protect collateral givers and general creditors. However, the danger sometimes arises that the same policy consideration that informs the rules, may also cause courts to reject the characterisation of a transaction as an outright collateral transfer. This may bring the transaction within the scope of the rules, spelling potential disaster for the collateral taker which has not complied with them.

English law has long recognised the legitimacy of outright collateral transfers, and is slow to recharacterise them as security interests. However, English courts have

103 See Insolvency Rules 1986 (as amended), Rule 4.90(2).
104 See the discussion of priorities below, pp. 244–49.
105 This is because it has the right to receive equivalent collateral.
106 Or alternatively because the particular collateral assets are required for another transaction.
107 For example to cut a loss by selling depreciating assets, or to take a profit by selling appreciating assets at the perceived top of the market.

recharacterised purported outright collateral transfers where the transaction was a sham, or internally inconsistent.[108]

Key sensitivities

Market standard documentation used in accordance with its terms is not subject to recharacterisation risk. However recharacterisation risk may be introduced by amending key 'anti-recharacterisation' provisions,[109] or by operational steps, such as restricting the freedom of the collateral taker to deal with the collateral securities by blocking them in an account maintained by a third-party agent.[110]

The Financial Collateral Directive requires member states to recognise outright collateral transfers. Of course, this is not the same as removing recharacterisation risk completely.

Right of use

Commercial need

It is common for financial institutions which receive securities collateral under one transaction, to be obliged to deliver like securities collateral to third parties under other transactions. Because of the relative scarcity of high-quality collateral, there is tremendous commercial pressure for collateral takers to be permitted to use collateral they receive.[111]

Restriction

Of course, outright collateral transfers confer such a right of use, as explained above. However, where the collateral has been received under a security interest, the exercise of a right of use is incompatible with the equity of redemption. As it is a property right, the equity of redemption entitles the collateral giver to the return of the particular assets originally delivered, and not merely their equivalent. For this reason, at general law the collateral taker is not generally permitted to deal with the collateral assets (and thus render them unavailable for redelivery), unless the collateral giver has defaulted, and thus permitted the collateral taker to exercise a right of sale.

A body of English case law casts doubt on the contractual enforceability of right-of-use provisions included in security documentation.[112]

As will be discussed below, the Financial Collateral Directive permits right-of-use provisions in security interests to be enforceable.

108 See op. cit., Benjamin, fn 3, p. 133.

109 For example, those restricting the collateral giver from directing voting by the collateral taker.

110 This is because such arrangements suggest that the collateral giver retains residual property rights in the collateral assets; this in turn suggests an equity of redemption and therefore a security interest. For the same reason, rights of margin release and substitution that grant the collateral giver the right to require identified parts of the collateral pool to be released to it, are considered to raise potential recharacterisation risk. (See however article 2(2) of the FCD.)

111 I.e., to be permitted to use the collateral in the absence of default. Of course, security interests permit the exercise of a power of sale and sometimes foreclosure upon default.

112 See op. cit., Benjamin, fn 3, pp. 111–18.

Procedural requirements

Formalities – generally

As briefly indicated above, a number of formalities may be required under applicable systems of law for the effective establishment and enforcement of the rights of the collateral taker. These formalities may include notarisation, registration and the obtaining of a court order to exercise a power of sale. Such formalities impede the rapid operation of the international financial markets. They are addressed by the Financial Collateral Directive and the Law Commission proposals for transactions within their scope.

Registration

A formality which attracted a great deal of legal attention was registration. Under the former UK regime, certain securities collateral arrangements created by companies were registrable if they amounted to floating charges, or fixed charges over book debts. Outright collateral transfers are not registrable.[113] Uncertainty as to which purported fixed charges may be recharacterised as floating charges, and therefore avoided for want of registration, was a major source of legal risk, particularly in relation to charges over book debts.

In many cases, the operational burden and publicity involved in registration acted as a decisive disincentive. Therefore the financial community welcomed the provisions of the Financial Collateral Directive, and the Law Commission proposals, both of which seemed to reduce the operational burden, and also exempted from the requirement to register securities collateral arrangements where control is transferred. Nevertheless, although the government was quick to implement the Directive into UK law by virtue of the Financial Collateral Arrangement Regulations 2003, thereby exempting specified types of securities collateral from the registration requirement under the Companies Act, the Law Commission proposals were not adopted.

OPERATIONAL ISSUES

This section discusses legal sensitivities associated with operational issues. We have briefly considered the nature of client assets in the contemporary securities markets. We saw that such assets are characteristically intermediated, intangible and pooled. Legal sensitivities associated with each of these operational features will be considered in turn. Proposed legislative solutions are discussed later in this chapter.

Intermediation

As has been stated, in practice, clients hold their securities through one or more intermediaries. The intermediary with whom the client has a direct relationship ('the relevant intermediary') records the interest of the client by entries to accounts maintained in its books. The terms on which the intermediaries hold the assets generally protect the client from the intermediaries' credit risk. However, in the normal course

113 Unless of course they are recharacterised as registrable security interests.

the client is able to enforce its interest only against the relevant intermediary. The client is not able (in its own name) to sue the issuer or any other intermediary standing between the relevant intermediary and the issuer (each an 'upper tier intermediary').

This interesting position, whereby the client avoids intermediary credit risk but cannot enforce directly, has raised a longstanding debate as to whether the client's rights are personal or proprietary in nature. The balance of opinion is that the client enjoys a bundle of rights, comprising both personal rights against the intermediary and property rights in relation to the assets held by the intermediary for the client. For ease of reference this bundle of rights is referred to as securities entitlements[114] or interests in securities.[115] This issue is developed below. A number of practical difficulties arise, of which three are discussed below. These are: issuer set off; priorities; and choice of law.

Issuer set off

Debt securities are issued with a range of different credit ratings, reflecting differing perceived risks of issuer default. As a general rule, debt securities with poorer credit ratings pay higher rates of interest. An investor may purchase bonds with a poor credit rating in order to receive a high rate of interest, but remain concerned about issuer credit risk. One technique for managing this credit risk is through set off, as follows.

The investor who holds £10,000,000 worth of bonds incurs an equal and opposite debt to the issuer. It achieves this by entering into a swap with the issuer, under which it takes an uncollateralised out of the money position of £10,000,000. In the event that the issuer defaults on the bonds, the investor sets its debt to the issuer under the swap against the debt of the issuer to it under the bonds, and is thus paid in full.

In this structure, it is important to establish that the client's rights of set off are not affected by the intermediation of the bonds. This is a complex area of law, and because cross-border chains of intermediaries are characteristically involved, it cannot be answered in practice without reference to conflict-of-laws rules. In many cases, and under English law, the better view appears to be that the simple fact of intermediation does not affect set off, but the pooling of assets in the hands of intermediaries may.

Priorities

The intermediation of securities holdings also raises difficult questions concerning priorities.

Nature of priorities disputes

As briefly indicated above, questions of priority arise when more than one person claims property rights in the same asset, and when those rights compete with each

114 This term is used in the US UCC, Article 8.

115 This term has been used by: Professor Mooney in the US; see 'Beyond negotiability; a new model for transfer and pledge of interests in securities controlled by intermediaries' (1990) 12 *Cardozo LR* 305; op. cit., Benjamin, fn 3; and, at EU level, see *Clearing and Settlement in the European Union – the Way Forward*, Com/2004/0312.

other (i.e. the asset in not sufficient to satisfy them all). It is necessary then to determine the priority in which such claims will be met. Priorities disputes may arise in a range of different circumstances. Two in particular concern the collateral taker. The first is referred to as 'original owner claims', and the second as 'double dealing.'

Original owner claims

A danger for the collateral taker is that the collateral assets may not belong to the collateral giver, and that their use as collateral may involve breach of duty to the beneficial owner.[116] A fact pattern that, regrettably, recurs in case law is as follows. An intermediary fraudulently secures its own borrowings to a third party with client securities. The third-party advances the loan against the collateral in good faith and without notice of the fraud. In the intermediary's insolvency, the fraud is discovered, and a dispute arises between the defrauded true owners and the good faith collateral taker, both of whom claim the securities. Both litigants are innocent, and the rules governing priorities between them reflect considerations of policy rather than justice. A policy of security of title favours the client; a policy of security of transfer favours the collateral taker.

Intermediation affects the treatment of original owner claims in two related ways. The first concerns the loss of negotiable status, and the second concerns the equitable status of the client's interest.

With reference to negotiable status, markets require security of transfer and, unsurprisingly, commercial law has traditionally emphasised security of transfer over security of title. Debt securities in bearer form have traditionally enjoyed the status of negotiable instruments. The holder in due course of a negotiable instrument takes free of defects in title, and can acquire good title from a thief. However, negotiable status is not available to the intangible assets held by clients in an intermediated environment.[117]

If the client's asset is not a negotiable instrument, the question arises as to what it is. In order to establish the legal nature of the client's asset, one needs to identify the legal relationship between the intermediary and the client. The traditional characterisation is bailment. However, bailment is based on the transfer of possession of tangible assets. In relation to contemporary intangible assets, the natural characterisation is trust. On this basis, if the collateral asset is held through an intermediary under English law, the collateral taker's interest is necessarily equitable and not legal. Equally, if the fraudulent intermediary was the trustee of the defrauded client, the interest of which the client was deprived is equitable and not legal.

A rule broadly comparable to that in favour of the holder in due course of a negotiable instrument was developed by the law of equity. This provided that, where a trust beneficiary seeks to follow a trust asset into the hands of a third party, the third party can successfully defend the action if it enjoys the status of 'equity's darling'. Equity's darling means the good faith purchaser of the legal estate for value without notice of the breach of trust. In general, this rule favours security of transfer. The problem in the present context, of course, is that the interest of the collateral taker is likely to be equitable and not legal, so that it cannot enjoy the status of equity's darling. Unless another defence is available, the defrauded client will win.[118]

116 The former does not necessarily imply the latter.

117 See: Bank of England *The Future of Money Market Instruments* (November 1999) Appendix II; op. cit., Benjamin, fn 3, pp. 68–70.

118 In accordance with the principle, where the equities are equal, the first in time prevails.

Fortunately, fraud is relatively rare. However, the low level of security of transfer outlined above is unhelpful to collateral takers. The Financial Collateral Directive is silent on priorities. However, the Law Commission proposals did include good faith purchaser rules for the intermediated securities markets.

Double dealing

If fraud is rare, successive dealings in the same asset are common. An investor may (properly or improperly) grant competing interests in the same assets to a number of third parties. The collateral taker therefore wishes to ensure that its interest will, if possible, take priority over any competing interests. The existing rules of priority are complex and in some respects uncertain. The Law Commission's proposed reforms would greatly simplify the position if they were ever to be implemented.

Upper tier and lower tier claims

In relation to intermediated securities, the position is complicated by the possibility that dealings may take place at different levels in the chain of intermediation. This is best illustrated by example. Suppose that eurobonds are held by a depositary on behalf of Euroclear; Euroclear credits an interest in the bonds in favour of a participant; the participant holds this interest as sub-custodian for a global custodian; the global custodian in turn holds its interest for an investor. The investor takes a loan from a bank, which is secured by the investor's eurobond holding.

It is likely that each intermediary standing between the investor and the issuer (i.e. the depositary, Euroclear, the sub-custodian and the global custodian) has a security interest in respect of its costs and charges. While in a cross-border chain of intermediaries the legal priorities may be somewhat unclear, each intermediary has operational control that enables it to enforce its interest before the bank is paid. This problem is underestimated in practice. The FMLC's proposals for a statute would (as a matter of English law) align the legal position with the operational position, and provide that upper tier interests prevail over lower tier interests, i.e. the bank will take subject to the claims of upper tier intermediaries. Contrary provisions are not considered to be enforceable in practice.

Choice of law

One question associated with intermediation that has generated an intense debate in recent years, and indeed prompted a programme of international law reform, is the following. What system of law governs property rights in securities collateral, when that collateral is intermediated on a cross-border basis?

Proprietary questions – the need for certainty

The purpose of collateral is to protect the collateral taker against the collateral giver's credit risk by conferring property rights. Legal risk affecting those property rights may render the collateral arrangement ineffective. Different systems of domestic law have different rules for the attachment and perfection of property rights, and for competing priorities between them. It is therefore essential for the collateral taker to establish which system of law is applicable.

The need for pragmatism

The discussion in the following sections of this chapter concerns the correct choice-of-law approach for courts faced with a cross-border question concerning the collateral taker's interest in intermediated securities. This question turns on conceptual issues, including the categorisation of the question, and the legal nature of the asset. Conflict-of-laws debates in this area can be tremendously subtle. However, for the collateral taker, it is also necessary to be pragmatic. In the collateral giver's default, the collateral giver's liquidator and possibly other creditors will have a strong interest in challenging the collateral arrangements. The collateral taker may have perfected its interest in accordance with the laws of jurisdiction X, on the basis of excellent arguments that these are the applicable laws. Suppose, however, that it has not perfected in accordance with the laws of jurisdiction Y, and that there are alternative arguments that Y law is applicable. If an order of the courts of Y would be effective to dispose of the collateral assets free of the collateral taker's interest, then it is unlikely that such an order would be sought by a liquidator or competing creditors. It may not always be feasible for the collateral taker to remove this risk. It may need to assess the likelihood of such an order taking effect. Factors will include the speed with which the collateral taker is able to enforce its interest, and thereby take its assets out of the jurisdiction in question.

Choice of law: categorisation and connecting factors

The following discussion turns to the theoretical debate concerning the correct approach to choice-of-law questions of this type.

When a cross-border dispute is brought before a court, the first question for the court is whether it has jurisdiction to hear the matter. The rules concerning jurisdiction are complex, and are not considered here. Once a court has established that it has jurisdiction, it must determine which system of law it should apply.[119] For this purpose, it will identify the different questions arising in the matter. To each question, it will apply its country's choice-of-law rules.

English choice-of-law rules involve the methodology of categorisation and connecting factors. Conflict of laws questions are organised into a series of categories.[120] The court identifies the category to which a question belongs.[121] The choice-of-law rules applicable to the relevant category determine which factor in the scenario before the court serves to connect the question to a particular system of law.[122]

Interestingly, the correct categorisation of disputes concerning the collateral taker's rights in the collateral assets is itself disputed.

119 While the courts of a particular jurisdiction will in practice apply local law to most issues before it, it will apply other systems of law when its jurisdiction's choice-of-law rules so require. The court will receive expert evidence from foreign legal experts as to the provisions of foreign law. The English courts treat question of foreign law as questions of fact.

120 These are set out in leading text books, particularly L. Collins (ed.) *Dicey and Morris on the Choice of Laws* (London: Sweet & Maxwell, 13th edn, 2000), para. 1–074.

121 This is not always straightforward. Cases are won and lost on categorisation.

122 For example, if the issue is categorised as concerning the validity of a marriage, the applicable connecting factor is the law of the place where the marriage was celebrated.

Connecting factor – the governing-law approach

One argument is as follows. Securities are contractual assets. Securities collateral arrangements should therefore be categorised as assignments of contractual rights. Article 12(2) of the Rome Convention[123] provides (broadly) that the position of the assignee (or collateral taker) is governed by the governing law of the assigned asset.

There are a number of problems with this argument. The Rome Convention leaves many matters unresolved, including the question of whether or not it applies to all aspects of assignment (including proprietary aspects). It is therefore not clear that it deals with the effects of assignment on third parties.[124] Moreover, the Rome Convention applies to assignments, and the better view is that dispositions of clients' interests in securities operates by novation.[125]

Connecting factor – the lex situs *rule*

An alternative categorisation, which the author prefers, is as follows. Property questions concerning the rights of the collateral taker in the collateral assets are categorised as property rights in intangible assets. Property disputes in all types of assets, including intangibles,[126] are governed by the law of the place where the asset in question is legally located, or *lex situs.* In general, the legal location or *situs* of an intangible is the place where it is enforceable in the normal course.[127]

Application – the look-through approach

Irrespective of the categorisation, two outcomes are possible depending on how the chosen categorisation is applied. This depends on one's view of the nature of the collateral asset. One may disregard intermediation,[128]and take the collateral asset to be bonds or shares in traditional form. Alternatively, one may note the operational and legal fact that the client is able to enforce its rights only against the relevant intermediary. On this basis, one takes the collateral assets to be a bundle of rights enforceable against the relevant intermediary.

This is best illustrated by example. Suppose the collateral assets comprise a portfolio of Italian, German, Swiss and New York bonds held through an account at Euroclear. If one disregards intermediation, the governing-law approach leads us to the governing laws under which the bonds were issued (probably the laws of Italy, Germany, Switzerland and New York). Disregarding intermediation again, and assuming global bonds in physical form were issued,[129] the *lex situs* rule leads us to the laws of the places where the bonds are deposited. These will probably be London

123 The Convention on the Law Applicable to Contractual Obligations 1980, implemented in the UK by the Contracts (Applicable Law) Act 1990.

124 See the Green Paper on the Conversion of the Rome Convention of 1980 on the Law Applicable to Contractual Obligations into a Community Instrument and its Modernisation, COM (2002) 654 final, Brussels, 39

125 See op. cit., Benjamin, fn 3, ch. 3.

126 *Macmillan Inc* v. *Bishopsgate Investment Trust plc (No. 3)* [1995] 1 Ch. 747.

127 *Kwok Chi Leung Karl* v. *Commr Estate Duty* [1988] 1 WLR 1035.

128 I.e. take it to have no legal consequence.

129 This is likely the case for corporate bonds, but Treasury bonds are generally dematerialised.

and New York. In practice, either approach may be called 'the look-through approach', as one looks through or disregards the intermediaries.

The look-through approach presents two problems, one conceptual and one practical. Conceptually, it necessitates a choice between connecting factors, as governing law and *lex situs* produce different results. Practically, it results in fragmentation, with more than one system of law being applicable to an international collateral portfolio. For these reasons, the markets prefer an alternative approach, called PRIMA.

Application – PRIMA

PRIMA is an acronym, standing for the place of the relevant intermediary's account. It is a choice-of-law rule, and provides very broadly that all questions concerning the property interest of the collateral taker in the collateral assets are governed by the law of the place where the relevant intermediary maintains the account to which those assets are credited.[130] PRIMA avoids the problems of conceptual and practical difficulties associated with the look-through approach, and has the tremendous advantages of commercial convenience. In the author's view, PRIMA is consistent with English case law.[131] PRIMA is given statutory backing in a number of existing and proposed measures.

Intangible assets

The above section explained that bearer debt securities in traditional form comprised physical instruments, and that by a legal fiction the debt was identified with the paper, so that the securities were legally classified as tangible assets. The significance of this was that possessory techniques were available to collateral takers. However, as already indicated briefly, the interest of the client in the contemporary intermediated markets is intangible. Of particular concern to the collateral taker are the loss of pledge and negotiation.

In a paper-based environment, the collateral transaction could be characterised as a pledge.[132] A pledge is a strong form of security interest. It is not currently registrable, and as a legal interest may take priority over prior equities. A purported pledge over an intangible is likely to be recharacterised as a charge, which (of a floating charge, or a charge over book debts) will (under the current regime) in turn be registrable. Moreover, as an equitable interest, it will be weaker in priority then a pledge (which is a legal interest).

As discussed above, bearer debt securities in traditional form enjoyed negotiable status, and therefore security of transfer. As an intangible cannot be a negotiable instrument, the transition from paper-based to electronic practice has reduced security of transfer in the debt securities markets.

Thus, the transition from paper-based to electronic practice may raise concerns relating to priority and registration. However, these concerns would have been largely addressed by the implementation of the Law Commissions proposals.

130 Where the settlement of the collateral transaction involves debiting the account of the collateral giver and crediting another account, possibly maintained by another intermediary, in favour of the collateral taker, PRIMA applies to the latter account.

131 See op. cit., Benjamin, fn 3, ch. 7. However, the position is not beyond doubt.

132 Pledge is, broadly, delivery of possession by way of security.

Pooling

The pooling of the like assets of different clients in the hand of intermediaries is customary, and facilitates rapid dealings. However, it can be a source of risk for the client and collateral taker, because of the treatment of shortfalls.

How shortfalls arise

A shortfall arises where the securities actually held by a custodian fall short of the aggregate of client entitlements, so that the pool is insufficient to meet client claims. This is best illustrated by example. Suppose an intermediary holds 600,000 shares on behalf of its clients on a pooled basis. There is a single entry in the issuer's register, with 600,000 shares shown against the intermediary's name (together with a client designation). The intermediary itself maintains accounts showing that it holds 200,000 of these shares for each of client A, B and C. Client A concludes two trades, buying an additional 50,000 shares from Z and simultaneously selling 250,000 to Y. The intermediary settles these transactions, and its client holding in the issuer's register is reduced to 400,000. A becomes insolvent. The purchase from Z is avoided by A's liquidator as a preference. The client holding is reduced to 350,000. The result is that, because of pooling, B and C have suffered a shortfall which is attributable to A's business.

Custodians have, and are required to have, procedures in place to reduce the risk of shortfalls, and to seek to identify and address them promptly when they arise. However, the risk of shortfalls cannot be eliminated. They can arise for a range of operational reasons, including many that do not necessarily imply fault on the part of the custodian. These reasons include: the inefficiencies still associated with cross-border settlement; insolvency displacement affecting client purchases; and sub-custodian default.

In practice, a solvent intermediary may decide voluntarily to make up the shortfall. However, it will not generally be under a legal obligation to do so unless the shortfall is attributable to its breach of duty. In any event, an insolvent intermediary is unlikely to be in a position to make up shortfalls voluntarily or otherwise. The question therefore arises how the losses will be borne between B and C.

This question is relevant to collateral arrangements as follows. B may have charged its assets to a collateral taker, who has agreed to leave the collateral in B's account, and who may consequently find its collateral depleted. C may also be a collateral taker, who insisted in the collateral being transferred into its name; C also finds it collateral depleted.

Traditional rules and pro ration

The traditional rules for allocating shortfalls within a mixed fund may lead to arbitrary results,[133] or be unduly complex in practice.[134] A simpler and less arbitrary approach is for shortfalls to be borne by all participants proportionately to the size of their

133 *Devaynes* v. *Noble, Clayton's Case* (1816) 1 Mer 572. *Clayton's Case* provides for 'first in, first out', or the first debit to be attributed to the first credit.

134 The 'rolling charge' approach is discussed in *Barlow Clowes International Ltd (in liquidation)* v. *Vaughan* [1992] 4 All ER 22, p. 35, *per* Woolf LJ.

participation. This 'pro ration' was followed in *Barlow Clowes*.[135] The FMLC proposals for a UK securities statute provide for the pro ration of shortfalls in all cases.

SOLUTIONS

'Collateral is effective only if the legal mechanism by which collateral is given is robust and ensures that the lender has clear rights over the collateral, and may liquidate or retain it in the event of the default, insolvency or bankruptcy (or otherwise-defined credit event set out in the transaction documentation) of the obligor and where applicable the custodian holding the collateral.'[136] In the last decade, significant industry and public sector effort has been devoted to addressing legal risk in the use of financial assets as collateral, and this has led to a number of collateral-related law reform initiatives.

This section will consider in turn measures relating to: choice-of-law questions; securities collateral; nature of indirectly held securities; and shortfalls.

Choice-of-law measures

Our discussion has already alluded to PRIMA. Provisions supporting PRIMA are contained in the following EU legislation: the Settlement Finality Directive;[137] the Financial Collateral Directive;[138] the Insolvency Regulation;[139]and the Winding Up Directive.[140]

Of course, European directives apply only within Europe. If widely adopted, the Hague Convention on Indirectly Held Securities[141] would apply more generally. This Convention is in effect a model law which, if implemented internationally, would harmonise the choice-of-law rules for all types of dispositions of indirectly held securities (whether in collateral transactions or otherwise).

Hague develops the European model of PRIMA as follows. There are two choices of law rules, namely a primary rule and a fall-back rule. Under the primary, the relevant system of law is that chosen by the parties in the account agreement (i.e. custody agreement). This rule is known as 'party autonomy'. However, there is not complete freedom of choice. Party autonomy is subject to a 'reality test'; i.e. the contractual choice is only effective if (broadly) the custodian has a custody operation in the jurisdiction the laws of which were chosen. Thus, for example, a New York bank operating in London could choose New York law to govern property questions affecting its London clients' portfolios.

If no effective choice is made under the part-autonomy rule, the PRIMA applies as the fall-back rule. In the example given above, this would lead to English law.

135 *Barlow Clowes International Ltd (in liquidation)* v. *Vaughan* [1992] 4 All ER 22. See also *Russell Cooke Trust Ltd* v. *Prentice (No. 2)* [2003] EWHC 1206.

136 *Consultative Document, The New Basel Capital Accord* (Basel: Basel Committee on Banking Supervision, Bank for International Settlements, January 2001), p. 16.

137 Directive 98/26/EC, article 9(2).

138 Directive 2002/47/EC, article 2.

139 Regulation 1346/2000/EC, article 14.

140 Directive 2001/24/EC, articles 24 and 31.

141 See www.hcch/net.

Securities collateral

The provisions of the Hague Convention are not limited to collateral transactions. In contrast, the application of the following provisions is so limited.

Financial Collateral Directive[142]

This section will consider the Financial Collateral Directive ('the Directive'). In its 1999 Financial Services Action Plan,[143] the European Commission emphasised the importance of addressing legal risk in cross-border financial collateral arrangements, and identified the introduction of the Directive as a priority 1 action.[144] The Directive was required to be implemented in member states by the end of 2003, and is implemented in the UK by the Financial Collateral (No. 2) Regulations 2003. [145]

The Directive complements the Settlement Finality Directive and the insolvency-related Directives. It addresses the legal risk associated with financial collateral,[146] particularly that associated with the differing provisions of national insolvency laws within the EU.[147] The Directive seeks to facilitate the use of cash and securities collateral[148] in the wholesale financial markets[149] through a number of measures. These disapply *inter alia* certain provisions of insolvency law. Their overall effect is to protect the position of the collateral taker. The recitals state the objective of establishing '[a] Community regime … for the provision of securities and cash as collateral under both security interest and title transfer structures including repurchase agreements (repos). This will contribute to the integration and cost-efficiency of the financial markets as well as to the stability of the financial system in the Community …'.[150] The Directive is thus intended to facilitate the implementation of the common monetary policy.[151]

142 2002/47/EC, OJ L 168, 27/6/2002, p. 43–50. See Turing 'The EU Collateral Directive' (2002) 5 JIBFL 187.

143 *Financial Services: Implementing the Framework for Financial Markets: Action Plan*, Communication of the Commission, Com (1999) 232, 11.05.99.

144 In relation to priority 1 actions the Commission indicates 'There is broad consensus that these actions call for immediate attention. These measure are crucial to realisation of the full benefits of the euro and to ensuring the competitiveness of the Union's financial services sector and industry whilst safeguarding consumer interests', p. 21.

145 2003/3226. The first implementing regulations were withdrawn, due to a drafting defect.

146 Financial collateral comprises cash and financial instruments: see article 1(4)(a). Where a collateral arrangement relates to financial and non-financial assets alike, the position is unclear, as discussed below. Clients may be well advised to document financial collateral arrangements separately.

147 See European Parliament *Recommendation for Second Reading*, 24 April 2002, p. 6.

148 Article 1(4)(a). Member states may exclude collateral consisting of the shares of the collateral giver and comparable arrangements: article 1(4)(b). Such assets are excludable as they are directly linked to the means of production of the collateral provider.

149 Retail transactions are excluded by the criteria set out in article 1(2).

150 Recital 3.

151 Recital 12. See also *Communication from the Commission to the European Parliament*, March 2002, SEC (2002)278 final, p. 2; 'The proposed Directive seeks to resolve the main problems affecting cross-border use of collateral in wholesale financial markets. It therefore promotes integration of the European financial market and secures the full benefits of the single currency.'

The Directive seeks to achieve these aims by: removing formal requirements;[152] providing insolvency protection for collateral arrangements, close-out netting, margining and substitution;[153] confirming that the law applicable to questions of property rights and enforcement is the law of the place where account to which they are credited is maintained;[154] facilitating enforcement;[155] permitting the use of collateral by the collateral taker;[156] and addressing recharacterisation risk for outright collateral transfers.[157] These provisions are considered in turn below.

It is important to note that the scope of the Directive is slightly different depending on the legal structure of the collateral arrangement. Where collateral is provided under a security interest, there is no restriction as to the nature of the secured obligation.[158] However, where collateral is provided under an outright collateral transfer, the arrangements are covered by the Directive only if the collateralised obligation is a financial obligation.[159]

Reforms

REMOVING FORMAL REQUIREMENTS

Article 3 removes the requirement for formalities (such as execution of a deed, notarisation, advertisement, etc.)[160] for the creation, validity, perfection, enforceability or admissibility in evidence of collateral arrangements.[161] However, in order to address fraud risk,[162] the Directive does require in effect that the collateral taker should have possession or control of the collateral assets.[163] Moreover, the Directive applies only to financial collateral once it has been provided and if that provision can be evidenced in writing or in a legally equivalent manner.[164] Such evidencing must (broadly) identify the collateral assets. Identification of the relevant account is sufficient for this purpose.[165]

152 Article 3. See the UK Regulations, regulation 4.
153 Articles 7 and 8. See the UK Regulations, regulations 8 and 10.
154 Article 9. See the UK Regulations, regulation 19.
155 Article 4. See the UK Regulations, regulations 12, 13 and 14.
156 Article 5. See the UK Regulations, regulation 16.
157 Article 6. Equivalent provision was not required to be included in the UK regulations, as outright collateral transfers have long been recognised under English law.
158 See article 2(1(c).
159 See article 2(1)(b).
160 Article 4 of the original Proposal gave a non-exhaustive list of such formalities; this now appears in Recital 10.
161 Article 3(1).
162 See Recital 10.
163 Article 2(2). Provisions with equivalent effect are contained in paragraph (c) of the definition of security financial collateral arrangement, which is contained in regulation 3.
164 Articles 1(5) and 3(2). 'In this respect it should be noted that the common position aims at providing a balance between market efficiency, which is the reason behind the exclusion of formal acts, and the safety of the parties to the arrangement and third parties, thereby avoiding *inter alia* the risk of fraud.' *Statement of the Council's Reasons*, 5 March 2002, 5530/3/02 REV 3 ADD 1, p. 8. An example of evidencing which is legally equivalent to writing is the taping of telephone conversations.
165 Article 1(5). See also *Statement of the Council's Reasons*, 5 March 2002, 5530/3/02 REV 3 ADD 1, p. 6: 'The financial collateral arrangement must be evidenced in writing or in

On this basis, where interests in securities[166] are delivered as collateral, no formalities beyond book entry transfers are required.[167] For collateral transactions within its scope, the Directive removes the need to register either fixed changes over book or certain types of floating charges. (The position of floating charges is considered below.)

INSOLVENCY PROTECTION

Article 7 provides for the recognition of close-out netting provisions, ensuring that they can take effect in accordance with their terms, without formalities.[168] And notwithstanding the winding-up or reorganisation of either party;[169] or the existence of interveners.[170]

Article 8 protects collateral arrangements[171] from insolvency displacement on the basis of zero-hour rules[172] and hardening periods.[173] Protection is also provided (broadly) where the relevant insolvency event took place on the same day as the collateral arrangement, collateralised obligation or collateral delivery, provided the collateral taker did not have actual or constructive notice of it.[174] Margining and substitution provisions are protected from displacement rules that might otherwise apply on the basis of hardening periods, zero-hour rules[175] and the absence of new money.[176] However, by virtue of article 8(4), these provisions are 'without prejudice to existing ex-post judiciary safeguards, which remain necessary in the case of ill-faith and commercially unreasonable transactions'.[177]

any other legally enforceable manner provided for by the law applicable to the financial collateral arrangement, e.g. taped telephone conversations.'

166 In relation to directly held securities, see 'For the purposes of this Directive, acts required under the law of a Member State as conditions for transferring or creating a security interest on financial instruments other than book entry securities, such as an endorsement in the case of instruments to order, or recording on the issuer's register in the case of registered instruments, are not considered as formal acts.' *Statement of the Council's Reasons*, 5 March 2002, 5530/3/02 REV 3 ADD 1, p. 8.

167 The text of the Directive suggests that either crediting the assets to the account of the collateral taker, or to a special account of the collateral giver (where they are not subject to the collateral giver's control, such as escrow accounts in CREST), will be sufficient: see article 2(2).

168 Other than those agreed by the parties, such as notice: article 7(2).

169 Article 7(1)(a).

170 Article 7(1)(b). This provides that close-out netting provisions will take effect in accordance with their terms notwithstanding (*inter alia*) any purported assignment. While helpful to collateral takers, this may be unhelpful to some securitisations, which may rely on silent assignments.

171 Improving on the drafting of the original Proposal, article 8 serves to protect both the collateral contract and the delivery of assets pursuant to it.

172 Article 8(1)(a).

173 Article 8(1)(b).

174 Article 8(2).

175 Articles 8(3)(i).

176 8(3)(ii).

177 See also *Communication from the Commission to the European Parliament*, March 2002, SEC (2002)278 final, p. 4. See also *Statement of the Council's Reasons*, 5 March 2002, 5530/3/02 REV 3 ADD 1, p. 12, and Recital 16: 'this article does not prejudice the possibility of questioning the financial collateral arrangement and the provision of financial collateral

ENFORCEMENT

Article 4 provides for the collateral taker, upon the default of the collateral giver,[178] to realise securities collateral by sale, appropriation[179] or set off[180] and to realise cash collateral by set off.[181]

RIGHT OF USE[182]

Article 5 in effect protects provisions in collateral agreements conferring a right of use, even where the collateral assets have been provided under a security interest.[183] Where the collateral taker exercises this right of use, it incurs a contractual obligation (broadly) to replace the original assets with equivalent assets.[184] Upon default this replacement obligation is set off against the collateralised obligation.[185] The collateral taker's interest in such redelivered assets is protected generally,[186] and also from priority and insolvency displacement problems that might otherwise arise due to their not having formed part of the original collateral delivery.[187]

as part of the initial provision, top-up or substitution of financial collateral, under national law for *other* reasons [than the timing of the provision of the original, top-up or substitute collateral], for example where this has been done intentionally to the detriment of the other creditors (this covers *inter alia* actions based on fraud or similar avoidance rules which may apply in a prescribed period).'

178 Note that the enforcement provisions in the Directive are not reciprocal, even through the standard close-out netting provisions in outright collateral transfer arrangements are reciprocal, i.e. apply equally to collateral giver and collateral taker.

179 Appropriation is only possible if it has been agreed to by the parties, and valuation has been agreed upon: article 4(2). Member states not permitting appropriation on the date on which the Directive comes into force are not obliged to permit it pursuant to the Directive: article 4(3).

180 Article 4(1)(a).

181 Article 4(1)(b). (Interestingly, the different drafting for cash and securities collateral suggests that the Directive favours *Re Charge Card Services Ltd* [1987] 1 CH 50 over *Re BCCI (No. 8)* [1998] AC 214. See the discussion on charge backs in op. cit, Benjamin, fn 3, pp. 109,110.

182 These provisions do not alter the position that the right of use involves a credit exposure for the collateral giver, as discussed earlier.

183 Article 5(1). See also regulation 16 of the UK Regulations. (Article 5(1) improves on the drafting of the original Proposal (Article 6), which discussed the right of use but did not confer it.)

184 Article 5(2). Alternatively, the collateral arrangements may provide for automatic set off (even in the absence of default): article 5(2), second paragraph.

185 Article 5(5).

186 The drafting of article 5(4) appears obscure to the author. However, the above interpretation accords with the comments in *Statement of the Council's Reasons*, 5 March 2002, 5530/3/02 REV 3 ADD 1, p. 10. The *Communication from the Commission to the European Parliament* March 2002 SEC (2002) 278 final, pp. 7, 8 comments that 'The new paragraph 4 in Article 5 in the Common Position makes it clear that the use of collateral does not invalidate the collateral arrangement vis-à-vis third [8] parties for the reason that the collateral is not in the possession or under the control of the collateral [taker] as required in articles 1(5) and 2(2).'

187 Article 5(3). Equivalent collateral is treated as subject to the same security interest as the original collateral, and provided at the same time.

RECHARACTERISATION RISK

Article 6 requires member states to ensure that outright collateral transfer arrangements can take effect in accordance with their terms,[188] subject to default close-out netting.[189] This serves to address the risk that such arrangements might be recharacterised as security interests. However, it does not remove recharacterisation risk in all circumstances, as discussed below.

CRITERIA[190]

The Directive provides that, in order for a collateral arrangement to benefit from its provisions, each of the parties must be[191]:

- a public authority;[192]
- a public bank, i.e. a central bank, the ECB, the BIS, a multilateral development bank, the IMF or the EIB;[193]
- a financial institution subject to prudential supervision;[194]
- an infrastructure service provider, i.e. a CCP, settlement agent or clearing house;[195]
- trustees acting for bondholders or for any of the above;[196] or
- a counterparty (other than a natural person)[197] to any of the above.[198]

188 Article 6(1). This is an improvement on the drafting of the equivalent provision in the original Proposal (article 7), which in effect provided that such arrangements *would* take effect in accordance with their terms, thus appearing to prevent recharacterisation even where the arrangement was a sham, or contains provisions which are inconsistent with outright transfer. By providing that such arrangements *can* take effect in accordance with their terms, article 6 of the Directive is compatible with existing English case law, which recognises transfer of title *provided* contractual provisions reflect genuine intention of parties and nothing in arrangement inconsistent with outright transfer.

189 Article 6(2).

190 The policy reasoning behind the threshold criteria may have been as follows. The proposals significantly enhance the position of collateral takers relative to unsecured creditors, and in this respect represent an erosion of the *pari passu* principle. They could therefore not be justified if their application were general, and in particular should not apply to retail arrangements. However, between major financial institutions, the systemic benefits of addressing legal risk in collateralisation may outweigh the policy objections to eroding the *pari passu* principle.

191 Article 1(2). The original Proposal included a threshold criterion of a capital base of €100 million or gross assets of €1,000 million (article 2.4(c)); this does not appear in the Directive.

192 Article 1(2)(a).

193 Article 1(2)(b).

194 Article 1(2)(c). Unlike the original Proposal, the Directive gives a non-exhaustive list of financial institutions subject to prudential supervision including credit institutions: (i) investment firms, (ii) financial institutions, (iii) insurance undertakings, (iv) UCITS, (v) and UCITS management companies (vi).

195 Article 12(2)(c).

196 Article 1(2)(d).

197 Many fund and SPV structures are constituted as trusts and partnerships. These appear to be included.

198 Article 1(2)(e). Member states may opt out of this provision: article 1(3).

The last criterion (counterparty to any of the above) was not included in the original proposals for the Directive. This raised concerns that many economically important collateral arrangements were excluded, including the collateralisation of securities lending from pension funds[199] and collateralised swaps with special purpose vehicles in structured finance arrangements. However, the inclusion of the counterparty criterion significantly extends the scope of the Directive, in effect requiring only one institutional party, whereas the original proposal required two.

As discussed below, the UK implementing regulations provide for a wider scope. The requirement is merely that each party should be a non natural person.

POLICY ISSUES

The original proposal for the Directive was controversial, as it enhanced the position of the collateral taker at the expense of that of the collateral giver[200] and its general creditors.[201] Some commentators have argued that it represented the assertion of Anglo-Saxon (and particularly New York) legal concepts and business practices that are in many respects at odds with continental European law and practice.[202] There are indications that the drafting of the final form of the Directive has sought in some measure to respond to such concerns.[203] However, the policy case for the reforms contained in the Directive rests on the systemic importance of wholesale financial collateral arrangements.

199 It is not clear that a pension fund is subject to prudential regulation for the purposes of the threshold criteria.

200 By providing for a right of use, which (if exercised) is incompatible with the equity of redemption.

201 For example, by altering the provisions of insolvency law, and removing formal requirements that serve to render collateral arrangements public.

202 In particular, the proposal to confer a right of use on the collateral taker reflects the provisions of Article 9 of the US UCC, but cuts across established principles of some systems of continental civil law, which protect the residual rights of the collateral giver in the collateral assets.

203 In relation to the right of use, Recital 19 provides that 'This reuse however should be without prejudice to national legislation about separation of assets and unfair treatment of creditors.' This tends to suggest that member states may require that the equity of redemption be protected by the segregation of collateral, so that it is not available for use by the collateral taker. However, this theme is not picked up in the body of the Directive. In the UK, the FSA client asset rules in effect relieve collateral takers of the usual duty to segregate collateral where there is a right of use.

The original Proposal provided that enforcement must be subject to any national legal requirements for commercial reasonableness in collateral realisation or valuation (article 5(4)). In the final form of the Directive, this provision is extended to include also commercial reasonableness in the calculation of collateralised obligations, and applies not only to enforcement, but also to the right of use, and the recognition of outright transfer arrangements and close-out netting (article 4(6)). See also Recital 17.

Further, in relation to the types of collateral asset covered by the Directive, in article 1(4) 'Subparagraph (b) has been introduced to make sure that Member States may exclude from scope certain financial collateral which, although it might fall under the definition of financial instruments, is directly linked to the means of production of the collateral provider.' *Statement of the Council's Reasons*, 5 March 2002, 5530/3/02 REV 3 ADD 1, p. 5.

UK implementation

The Directive has been implemented in the UK by the UK Regulations. In general the UK Regulations reflect the terms of the Directive.[204] However, two points of particular interest arise. The first relates to scope, and the second to floating charges.

As mentioned above, the scope of the UK Regulations is somewhat wider than that of the Directive. Whereas the Directive requires each party to fall within an exhaustive list of types of institution, the UK Regulations merely require that both parties are non-natural persons.[205]

Many global custodians, settlement banks and other financial institutions operating under English law documentation in practice collateralise their credit exposures to clients by taking security interests over the pool of client securities. In most cases, the composition of that pool changes from time to time, and the client is free to remove securities from the collateral pool without the consent of the financial institution. Such freedom is the hallmark of a floating charge. Such security interests are therefore likely to be characterised as floating charges, whether or not they are described as such contractually. A floating charge is a relatively weak form of security interest. However, because the client is generally unwilling for its ability to remove assets from the collateral pool to be restricted in any way, a floating charge may be the best security available within the terms of the commercial relationship.

For these reasons, the impact of the UK Regulations on floating charges has attracted a considerable industry debate. As indicated above, there is a requirement that possession or control be transferred to the collateral taker.[206] Floating charges are included[207] 'where the financial collateral charged is delivered, transferred, held, registered or otherwise designated so as to be in the possession or under the control of the collateral-taker or a person acting on its behalf …'.[208]

Possession at common law involves the physical control of a tangible asset, and cannot relate to an intangible. Therefore the above provision predicates the possibility of control of collateral by a floating chargee. This raises the following problem. The defining characteristic of a floating charge is the collateral giver's freedom to deal with the charged assets in the ordinary course of business. Recent case law identifies the test of this characteristic as being the collateral taker's lack of control.

204 They are required to do so, as they were made under the European Communities Act 1972, s. 2(2).

205 Paragraph (d) of the definition of security financial collateral arrangement and paragraph (c) of the definition of title transfer financial collateral arrangement, both contained in article 3.

'Non-natural person' is defined in article 3 to exclude individuals but to include both bodies corporate and unincorporated associations.

206 Paragraph (c) of the definition of security financial collateral arrangement, which is contained in regulation 3. These provisions equate to article 2(2) of the Directive.

207 I.e. included in the definition of security interest, and from there into the definition of security financial collateral arrangement. See article 3.

208 Paragraph (d) of the definition of security interest contained in article 3. Paragraph (d) continues: 'any right of the collateral-provider to substitute equivalent financial collateral or withdraw excess financial collateral shall not prevent the financial collateral being in the possession or under the control of the collateral-taker'. This is equivalent to the provisions of article 2(2) of the Directive.

How then can the criteria for the application of the Directive to floating charges ever be satisfied?

It seems to the author that the answer is as follows. Different types of control may be distinguished according to two sets of distinctions. First, control may be either positive or negative. Positive control is the ability to dispose of an asset, and negative control is the ability to prevent a disposition. Second, either positive or negative control may be legal (i.e. the right to dispose or prevent disposition, as the case may be) or operational (i.e. the practical ability to dispose or prevent disposition). The test of a fixed as opposed to floating charge is understood to be negative legal control.[209] The reference to control in the UK Regulations must therefore be taken to mean either positive legal, or operational control. Thus, in relation to floating charges where the chargee has operational or legal positive control, therefore Companies Act registration requirements are not applicable,[210] and the protections under the UK regulations are also available.[211]

Positive control may be operational (i.e. the operational ability to dispose) or legal (i.e. the right to do so). Operational control will be present where for example the chargee is also the custodian. Legal control in the absence of default may be present, for example where there is a right of use.

Remaining challenges

There is no doubt that the implementation of the Directive has done much to facilitate the use of securities as collateral. However, some challenges remain, including the following.

First, important areas of legal risk are not addressed. The Directive and implementing regulations are silent on priorities. Therefore the sensitivities discussed above, stand. Also, they do not address questions of power and authority. The collateral giver therefore still needs to address these issues.

Further, the Directive and the UK Regulations do not apply to all collateral arrangements. Of course, transactions with individuals are excluded. As an EU measure, the Directive does not modify non-EU insolvency law. The insolvency-related sensitivities discussed above therefore remain in respect of non-EU collateral givers. Also, it does not remove the risk that PRIMA might be rejected by non-EU courts in relation to non-EU securities.

It is unclear whether mixed collateral arrangements (for example where a company grants security over all its assets, including financial and non-financial collateral) are included.[212] The provisions of the UK Regulations benefit 'security financial collateral arrangements' and 'title transfer financial collateral arrangements'. These are

209 See, for example. *Re Drumark Investments Ltd, IRC* v. *Agnow* [2001] UKPC 28; *Re Spectrum Plus Ltd* (*In Liquidation*) [2005] 2 AC 680.

210 See regulation 4.

211 In English legal history, recognition of floating charges by the courts was delayed because of fears about unfair prejudice to general creditors, and eventually granted on strict condition that registration should at least permit general creditors to know the risks facing them. Therefore, removal of the requirement to register a floating charge in certain circumstances involves a major change of policy.

212 The author is grateful to Martin Hughes of White & Case for this point.

each in turn defined[213] by reference to a number of criteria, including (respectively) the creation or arising of a security interest in financial collateral, and the transfer of financial collateral. It might be argued, for example, that a charge over mixed collateral does involve the creation of a security interest in financial collateral, and that the fact that security over other asset types is also created does not prevent the legislation from applying. If so, there is scope for avoidance, as one might disapply the usual formalities and insolvency restrictions applicable to security by including a small amount of cash in for example a land portfolio. However, the position is unclear, and it may be prudent to prepare separate collateral arrangements for financial and non-financial collateral respectively.

Another area of uncertainty relates to the definition of cash.[214] Financial collateral means either cash or financial instruments.[215] In turn, cash is defined[216] widely, to include 'money in any currency, credited to an account …'. It is not stated that the account must be maintained by a financial institution. The result is that current accounts between trading entities appear to be caught.

Law Commission proposals

The Law Commission published various proposals over the period 2002 to 2005 to reform the law relating to company charges.[217] The proposals were broadly based on the successful model of Article 9 of the US Uniform Commercial Code,[218] and were most welcome although the government did not implement them on the basis that there was little demand for such fundamental reforms.[219]

Nevertheless, it is important to discuss the reform proposals and, in very broad outline, the Law Commission's proposed scheme (set out in Draft Company Security Regulations at the back of their *Report* of 2005) would have: replaced the current system of registration with a new system of electronic notice filing; provided for all charges to be prima facie registrable; simplified priority rules (with the basic rule that priority follows order of filing); and included a special regime for financial collateral,[220] including securities collateral, which would be informed by the terms of the Financial Collateral Directive. Also under the proposed scheme, the new regime would ensure: registration was not required where the secured creditor taker obtained control;[221] an automatic charge would arise in favour of unpaid intermediaries who funded

213 In regulation 3.
214 Again, the author is grateful to Martin Hughes for this point.
215 Regulation 3.
216 Regulation 3.
217 See generally: Law Commission Consultation Paper's 164 *Registration of Security Interests: Company Charges and Property other than Land* (2002) and 176 *Company Security Interests: a Consultative Report* (2004); and Law Commission Report No. 296, *Company Security Interests* (2005).
218 'We have followed the UCC model because of our general policy to have a scheme that resembled the North American Models unless there was a reason to differ'; see Law Commission Report *Company Security Interests*, fn 217, p. 123, n.36.
219 The proposals still continue to generate an active debate. However, for the time being it appears as if there is little chance that they will be implemented and the Companies Act 2006 is essentially the same as its 1985 predecessor; see further on the reasons why the reform proposals were not implemented the chapter by de Lacy in the present volume, pp. 78–80.
220 See generally Law Commission Report, fn 217, Part 5, p. 196 *et seq.*
221 See Draft Regulation 36(1).

client purchases and unpaid vendors;[222] a rule in favour of good faith purchasers was also included;[223] and special priorities rules would also apply.[224]

The definition of financial collateral

For the purposes of the Law Commission's proposals for a new special regime, the definition of financial collateral involved three related terms.

The term '*financial instruments*' was defined[225] to mean directly held securities.[226] Financial instruments were subject to good faith purchaser rules.[227]

The term '*financial assets*' was widely defined[228] to include financial instruments, indirectly held securities (where the intermediary and client agree that they should

222 See Draft Regulation 37. The latter applies only to assets in physical form; see Draft Regulation 37(3).

223 See Draft Regulation 38.

224 See Draft Regulation 39.

225 '"Financial instrument" means –

(a) a share in a company or any other financial instrument equivalent to a share in a company,
(b) a bond or other form of financial instrument giving rise to or acknowledging indebtedness which is, or is of a type, dealt in or traded on financial markets, and
(c) any other financial instrument which is normally dealt in and which gives the right to acquire any such share, bond, instrument or other security by subscription, purchase or exchange or which gives rise to a cash settlement (excluding an instrument of payment)

and includes a unit of a collective investment scheme within the meaning of the Financial Services and Markets Act 2000, and eligible debt security within the meaning of the Uncertificated Securities Regulations 2001, a money market instrument, an uncertificated unit of an interest in a security as defined in the Uncertificated Securities Regulations 2001, and any right, privileges or benefits attached to or arising from any of the financial instruments included in this definition;' see Draft Regulation 41(1).

226 'In our scheme, "financial instruments" refer to directly-held securities. The draft regulations use the term "financial instruments", rather than "securities", to align the terminology of the scheme with the FCAR [Financial Collateral Arrangements (No. 2) Regulations 2003, SI 2003 No. 3226].' See Law Commission Report *Company Security Interests*, fn 217, para. 5.22.

'The definition of "financial instruments" in the regulations that we recommend in this report differs from the FCAR's definition of "financial instruments" in two respects. First, it excludes indirectly-held securities. This is because under our scheme these, together with other forms of investment property that is held on the books of an intermediary, have to be distinguished from directly-held financial instruments because the tests for control over the various types of asset differ. Indirectly-held securities are covered by the more widely defined "financial assets". Secondly, it has a provision to include depository instruments and the like held in CREST.' See Law Commission Report *Company Security Interests*, fn 217, para. 5.25.

227 See Draft Regulation 38(1) and (2).

228 '"Financial asset" means –

(a) a financial instrument,
(b) an obligation of a person or a share, participation or other interest in a person or in property or an enterprise of a person –

be treated as financial assets for this purpose) and rights under commodity contracts.[229] Financial assets would be brought within the regime where they were intermediated, as follows. Financial assets, which were held with an intermediary, were subject to the provisions for an automatic charge in favour of the intermediary;[230] subject to a good faith purchaser rule;[231] and fell within the definition of investment property, discussed below.

The term '*investment property*' was defined[232] to mean both directly held securities and financial assets held with an intermediary (including indirectly held securities and intermediated rights under commodity contracts).[233] The provisions for perfection by control; [234] and special priority rules;[235] applied to investment property (as well as cash).

Perfection by control

Under the Law Commission's proposals, the normal method for perfecting a security interest would be by filing.[236] However, under the special regime for financial collateral, security interests in investment property could be perfected by the chargee obtaining control of the collateral.[237] (This would have accorded with the provisions of the

(i) which is, or is of a type, dealt in or traded on financial markets, or
(ii) which is recognised in any area in which it is issued or dealt in as a medium for investment,

(c) any property which is held by an intermediary for another person in a securities account if the intermediary has expressly agreed with the other person that the property is to be treated as a financial asset under these Regulations, or
(d) a commodity futures contract, a commodity futures option or other similar contract;'

See Draft Regulation 41(1).

229 'Examples of financial assets that may not fall within the FCAR definitions of financial instruments or "cash", but are within our scheme if they are held through an intermediary, are rights under commodity contracts (a commodity futures, contract, a commodity futures option or a similar contract). These may be held in an account by a commodities broker or other intermediary and may be used as collateral in much the same way as other financial assets. In practice such rights normally represent a right to payment of differences and are thus roughly equivalent to "cash" held in an account, though they may not fall within the FCD.'

230 See Draft Regulation 37.

231 See Draft Regulation 38(3).

232 '"Investment property" means a financial instrument, whether certificated or uncertificated and a financial asset held with an intermediary'; see Draft Regulation 41(1).

233 'Regulation 41 defines "investment property" as … any other form of "financial asset" that is held through an intermediary. This includes rights under commodity futures contracts and options.'

(As explained above, it may be unusual in practice for derivatives contracts to be intermediated, for credit risk reasons.)

234 See Draft Regulation 36.

235 See Draft Regulation 39.

236 Unlike under the current regime, there is no 21-day limit, but a charge which has not been filed is at risk of losing priority to a later-filed charge (see Draft Regulation 24) and ineffective against a liquidator or administrator on insolvency and against execution creditors (see Draft Regulation 20).

237 See Draft Regulation 36(1)(c).

Financial Collateral Directive Regime which, as discussed above, requires the transfer of possession or control,[238] but removes registration requirements.)

The meaning of control for this purpose was determined by Draft Regulation 40.[239] Very broadly speaking, the tests of control were as follows. For physical bearer instruments, control was transferred by possession of the instrument.[240] For certificated registered securities, control was transferred by possession of the certificate or registration.[241] For paperless directly held securities, control was transferred by: CREST sponsorship arrangements;[242] transfer to an escrow balance in CREST;[243] or registration.[244] For indirectly held securities (and other indirectly held financial assets), control was transferred by: transfer to the account of the chargee;[245] binding notice of assignment to the intermediary;[246] or the use of a control agreement with the intermediary.[247] Control would be automatic where the client granted a charge in favour of the intermediary.[248] A residual rule provided for control of investment property (or cash) where the debtor was no longer able to deal with the collateral.[249] Substitution and margining rights did not prevent control.[250]

Priorities

It was indicated above that a further area of legal difficulty concerns the priorities between collateral interests and competing claims. Under the Law Commission's proposed scheme, the default or 'residual' priority rules were broadly based primarily on order of filing.[251] However, in relation to securities collateral, a system of control-based priorities was proposed. This would be consistent with the provisions for perfection by control, and, like those provisions, are designed to promote ease of transfer. [252]

238 Article 2(2) of the FCD requires the transfer of possession or control. As also discussed above, the FCD requires writing; this is picked up in the definition of control in regulation 40(1).

239 The test of control is based on negative and not positive control. See Law Commission Report *Company Securities*, fn 217, para. 5.46 *et seq.*

240 See Draft Regulation 40(2).

241 See Draft Regulation 40(3).

242 See Draft Regulation 40(4)(a). See the discussion in Law Commission Report *Company Securities*, fn 217, para. 5.73.

243 See Draft Regulation 40(4)(b).

244 See Draft Regulation's 40(4)(c) and (d).

245 See Draft Regulation 40(5)(a).

246 See Draft Regulation 40(5)(b).

247 See Draft Regulation 40(5)(c).

248 See Draft Regulation 40(6).

249 See Draft Regulation 40(9).

250 See Draft Regulation 40(11).

251 Draft Regulation 24 set out priority rules for security interests not over financial collateral (which were governed by regulation 39) or sums due under letters of credit (which were governed by Draft Regulation 26). Draft Regulation 24 also applied to sales of receivables. Draft Regulation 24 provided as follows. A registered charge took priority over an unregistered charge; (see DR 24(2)). Priority between registered charges was determined by the order of registration; (see DR 24(3)). Priority between unregistered charges was determined by order of creation; (see DR 24(4)).

252 '[T]here are exceptions to the "first in time rule" … a party who takes "control" of investment property … will gain priority over an interest perfected by filing. This is a rule designed

Draft Regulation 39 specified special priority rules for investment property and cash. These took effect subject to the good faith purchaser rules set out in Draft Regulation 38;[253] and provided as follows. A charge where the chargee had control took priority over one where the chargee did not have control.[254] Where more than one chargee had control, priority was determined by the order in which control was acquired.[255] Conflicting charges granted by an intermediary where the chargees did not have control, rank equally.[256] In other cases, the residual rules discussed above would apply.[257]

Nature of indirectly held securities

A large number of recent law reform measures (discussed above), deal with a range of different legal matters affecting securities collateral, including choice-of-law rules, formal requirements and priorities. These are important pieces of the jigsaw. However, as these measures have unfolded over the last 15 years or so, many commentators felt that a piece was missing. In order to complete the picture, and provide a coherent conceptual context for these reforms, a definition of the legal nature of the collateral asset in domestic law was required.

As indicated above, the securities markets have been affected by profound operational change in recent years. Three developments in particular (intermediation, dematerialisation and pooling) serve to facilitate rapid dealings. They also alter the legal nature of the clients' asset, taking it beyond the scope of settled law. A number of law reform measures seek to address legal risk associated with these developments.

Various domestic law measures

The US provides the most developed legislative model for the codification of this area of law.[258] In the US, the nature of the client's asset is defined in Article 8 of the Uniform Commercial Code. This was very significantly revised in 1994 to address the indirect holding system.[259] The interest of the client is a 'securities entitlement'.[260] This term is a shorthand for 'the package of rights that a person who holds a securities position through an intermediary has against that intermediary and the property held by that intermediary'. [261] A securities entitlement comprises both personal rights against the intermediary and property rights in respect of the underlying assets. These rights are enforceable by the client only against the securities intermediary, and not against the issuer or any higher tier intermediary.

to ensure the ready transferability of these types of collateral.' Hugh Beale 'Reform of the law of security – another view', BJIBFL, April 2004, 117, p. 118.

253 See Draft Regulation 39(1).

254 See Draft Regulation 39(2).

255 See Draft Regulation 39(3).

256 See Draft Regulation 39(4).

257 See Draft Regulations 39(5) and (6).

258 Not an exact model for all markets, it reflects the concerns of context in which it was drafted, namely in respect of priorities.

259 See generally Rogers 'Policy perspectives on Revised UCC Article 8' (1996) 43 UCLA L Rev 1431.

260 Securities entitlements are dealt with in Part 5 of Article 8.

261 See op. cit., Rogers, fn 259, p. 1450.

A securities entitlement confers property rights on the client, which are protected from the credit risk of the intermediary, and can be dealt with in collateral transactions and otherwise. Informal dealings are facilitated, and a high level of security of transfer provided.

Domestic legislation clarifying the nature of the client's rights in the international and electronic securities markets is also available in Belgium, Luxembourg, France and Japan, and is proposed in Canada and Switzerland.[262]

UNIDROIT project

In 2002 UNIDROIT[263] established a Study Group for the Preparation of Harmonised Substantive Rules regarding Securities Held with an Intermediary.[264] In 2005 the group published a draft convention.[265] The provisions of the draft convention related to: intermediated securities;[266] protection of innocent acquirer;[267] insolvency;[268] duties of intermediary;[269] relations with issuers of securities;[270] and collateral transactions.[271] Further work was undertaken on the Draft Convention in May 2007 before it was resolved by the Committee of Government Experts that the Convention was ready to be laid before a Diplomatic Conference. At the invitation of the Swiss Government a Diplomatic Conference was held in Geneva in September 2008 where further measures were added to the Draft Convention.

The draft convention was a tremendous achievement in the effort to achieve international harmonisation of this complex area of law. UNIDROIT held a Second Session of the Diplomatic conference to discuss the draft convention in Geneva in October 2009 where the final version of the Convention was adopted.

FMLC project

'English law, though addressing the conversion of certificated to uncertificated securities, has not yet grappled with the implications of the move from direct to indirect holdings, a move which provided the motive power for the revision in 1994 of Art. 8 of the Uniform commercial Code and has particular implications for those taking an interest in investment securities as collateral. The Financial Markets Law Committee

262 See Financial Markets Law Committee, *Issue 3 – Property Interests in Investment Securities, International Overview*, June 2004; available at www.fmlc.org.

263 The International Institute for the Unification of Private Law.

264 This forms part of the wider Study Group for the Preparation of Harmonised Substantive Rules on Transactions on Transnational and Connected Capital Markets.

265 UNIDROIT, *Preliminary draft convention on harmonised substantive rules regarding intermediated securities*, Rome, May 2005. See now the Final Convention on Substantive Rules for Intermediated Securities, October 2009, available at www.unidroit.org.

266 Chapter II.

267 Chapter III.

268 Chapter IV.

269 Chapter V.

270 Chapter VI.

271 Chapter VII. This includes articles on enforcement (22), right of use (23) and top-up or substitution (24).

is examining the issue.'[272] The Financial Markets Law Committee[273] established a working party[274] to consider property rights in indirectly held investment securities. The Statute will serve to codify an area of law that is not currently well understood. The existing provisions of English law applicable to the cross-border electronic securities markets are in general adequate. Because these rules are generally applied in a flexible and commercially sensitive manner by the judiciary, they provide a reasonably good operating environment in practice. However, the securities markets have been subject to profound operational developments in recent years, and certain corresponding legal developments would be desirable in the interests of efficiency and fairness. While the continued exercise of judicial discretion may be sufficient to address legal questions as they arise on a case-by-case basis, legislation is desirable for two reasons. First, while wholesale change is not considered appropriate, it would be helpful to clarify existing principles and their contemporary application. Second, the securities markets operate on an increasingly international basis, and measures such as the Hague Convention on Indirectly Held Securities offer opportunities for parties to select the legal regime that will apply to all aspects of their arrangements. In such an environment, different systems of commercial law compete for business. It is therefore desirable that English law should be as accessible as possible.

In July 2004 the working party published draft principles for a proposed UK securities statute clarifying this area of law.[275] It is hoped that these will provide a model for legislation, whether at the UK or EU level.

The draft principles apply where securities are held by a client through an intermediary. They define the client's rights as including personal rights against the intermediary and property rights in relation to the securities; confirm that the securities are not available to creditors of the intermediary; and provide that shortfalls will be pro rated. In accordance with the Law Commission's proposals for company charges, the draft principles permit third-party interests to be created without formalities; and provide for perfection by control; and control-based priorities. Client/issuer set off is facilitated.

There are very clear similarities between the UNIDROIT and FMLC projects. First, the two have the same subject matter, namely intermediated investment securities, with an emphasis on property issues. Second, they have the same objectives, namely the promotion of legal certainty in the international securities markets. Third, and fortunately, they have the same broad recommendations, including the following principles:

- no look through;
- insolvency ring fencing;
- account finality;
- simplified dealings;
- account-based and control-based priorities; and
- the pro ration of shortfalls.

272 See op. cit., Goode, *Legal*, fn 2, p. 210.
273 See further at www.fmlc.org.
274 Of which the author is a member.
275 See: *Property Interests in Investment Securities*, July 2004; note also – *Hague Convention on the Law Applicable to Certain Rights in Respect of Securities Held with an Intermediary*, (FMLC, paper, November 2005); available at www.fmlc.org. The FMLC have also published a response to the EU Commission consultation on harmonising the laws of April 2009; see Issue 136: *Intermediated Securities* (10 June 2009).

Both are inspired by Article 8 of the UCC; neither follows it slavishly. Thus, the projects accord in substance.

EU Legal Certainty Project

In 2004 the European Commission issued its[276] Communication on Clearing and Settlement.[277] The Communication refers to the finding of the Giovannini Reports[278] that, within the EU, the international post-trade infrastructure for securities and derivatives transactions is fragmented and inefficient;[279] and stresses the importance of a safe and efficient international clearing and settlement.[280]

An important part of the communication deals with the need for legal certainty.[281]

'The safety of any securities clearing and settlement system ultimately depends on the soundness of the legal system on which it is built.'[282] While the two Giovannini Reports identified a number of legal issues as barriers to integration,[283] some of these are addressed by existing measures.[284] However, the Commission argues, three important issues remain. In order to tackle them, the Commission established a group of experts from academia, public authorities and practising lawyers. In addition

276 A prior communication on this topic, dated 2002, is entitled 'Clearing and settlement in the European Union: main policy issues and future challenges'.

277 *Clearing and Settlement in the European Union - the Way Forward*, Com/2004/0312. The Commission mandated a group of legal experts, the Legal Certainty Group, to advise them and the Group presented its advice in August 2008; see *Second Advice of the Legal Certainty Group on Solutions to Legal Barriers related to Post-Trading within the EU*, available at http://ec.europa.eu/

278 *Report on Cross-Border Clearing and Settlement Arrangements in the European Union*, 2001 and 2003.

279 'Purely domestic clearing and settlement activities in the EU are relatively cost effective and safe. But cross-border arrangements are complex and fragmented, resulting in much higher costs, risks and inefficiencies.' European Commission, fn 278, p. 4.

'The inefficiencies of cross-border arrangements in the EU are due to a lack of global technical standards, the existence of differing business practices and inconsistent fiscal, legal and regulatory underpinnings.' European Commission, fn 278, p. 7.

280 'The creation of an integrated and efficient European capital market is one of the most important and ambitious economic projects currently under say in the European Union ... A crucial element of this framework will be the safety and efficiency of the arrangements required to finalise securities transactions ("Clearing and Settlement") ... Without efficient clearing and settlement arrangements, the ability and willingness of participants to trade in EU securities will be sub-optimal; the liquidity of financial markets will be affected and the cost of capital will be higher than it need be.' European Commission, fn 278, p. 4.

281 The Communication refers to the Legal Certainty Project; this equates to the account certainty project discussed in the Giovannini Reports.

282 European Commission, fn 278, p. 23.

283 Fragmented laws relating to conflict of laws rules, bilateral netting and the legal nature in interests in securities and record date for the purposes of corporate actions.

284 In particular, by the Settlement Finality Directive, the Financial Collateral Directive and the Hague Convention on Indirectly Held Securities. See the discussion in European Commission, fn 278, pp. 24, 25.

to considering corporate actions[285] and securities location,[286] the expert group considered interests in securities. The Legal Certainty Group presented its advice in August 2008 and following an open conference to debate it in October the Commission decided that a new legal initiative was required. As a result in April 2009 the Commission issued a consultation document "Legislation on Legal Certainty of Securities Holding and Dispositions". The consultation closed in June 2009 and we still await the final results. However, the work of the Commission will be an important factor in getting harmonisation and unity of regulation across the EU and international communities.

Law Commission project

In December 2005 the Law Commission launched its project on property interests in investment securities as part of its 9th Programme of Law Reform. 'The Law Commission's aim is to establish a set of clear legal principles covering the ownership and transfer of indirect held investment securities in the European Union. Our proposals will be designed to assist the Treasury in influencing and responding to the work of the European Commission in this area. To do so, we will be looking both at English law and at securities law in the other member states of the European Union in order to identify and resolve common aspects that are unclear or out-of-step with market practice. If progress is not made at European level, we will consider including in our Report draft legislation for England and Wales.'[287] The Law Commission finished its work in May 2008 and provided the Treasury with its advice on the way forward based on adopting the final version of the Convention that UNIDROIT is currently working on and expected to be finalised by the end of 2009.[288]

285 'Another issue that needs to be addressed concerns differences in national legal provisions affecting corporate action processing, such as discrepancies in Member States' laws as to the determination of the exact moment when a purchaser is considered to be the owner of a security, e.g. for the payment of dividends.' European Commission, fn 278, p. 26.

286 'It has been suggested that restrictions relating to the issuer's ability to choose the location of its securities act as a further barrier to Securities Settlement Systems consolidation' (26). This comment is open to two possible interpretations. It may mean that issuers should be free to choose which clearing and settlement systems should have capacity to process transactions in their securities. If so, the proposal is welcome. However, it may alternatively mean that issuers should be free to export their registers of members. This would raise a concern for direct settlement systems such as CREST. The accounts of CREST constitute the register of members of the issuer in respect of uncertificated shares. The register in respect of certificated shares is maintained by the issuer or its registrar in the traditional way. Together, these registers comprise the issuer's register of members. This arrangement is given statutory backing by the USRs, and in order for this solution to work, both parts of the register must be subject to UK law and therefore to the USRs. (Of course, these concerns relate to shares and not debt securities, which may be issued under foreign law.)

287 Law Commission, Letter to Interested Parties, 5.12.05.

288 For full details see the Law Commission website at www.lawcom.gov.uk/investment_securities.htm. Note also Law Commission *Annual Report 2008–09* (2009) HC 811 at p. 19.

Conclusions

This chapter has emphasised the economic and regulatory importance of securities collateral and the need to minimise legal risk in relation to securities collateral arrangements. It was seen that two major sources of legal risk affecting securities collateral are insolvency-related policy concerns, and the intermediation of the electronic securities markets. A number of existing and proposed law reform initiatives address legal risk from these sources. These include the reforms proposed by the Law Commission for company securities. Given that, for the present at any rate, the latter proposal has not been adopted by the government, it is now likely that any future reform measures will come from EU and international (UNCITRAL) initiatives.

However, it is important to remember that, even in a perfect legal environment, securities collateral is not a complete answer to credit risk. Collateralisation manages credit risk, but does not eliminate it. The crisis that surrounded the near collapse of the hedge fund, Long Term Capital Management (LTCM), in 1998 illustrates this. The credit exposures of major New York banks to LTCM were considered to be so significant that the failure of LTCM would have threatened the stability of the financial system. For this reason, a rescue package was organised.[289] In this context, it is salutary to remember that the credit exposures that precipitated the crises were fully collateralised.[290] The recent 'credit crunch' has served only to reinforce the point. The collapse of the sub-prime mortgage market in the US in the summer of 2007 was to have far-reaching effects on the global economy. The collateralisation of US (sub-prime) mortgages and inflated credit ratings effectively polluted the international market and led to the drying up of capital. This was to have a dramatic effect in the UK and led to a run on the Northern Rock bank[291] in September 2007 forcing the government to bail it out and later to nationalise the bank in 2008. Further intervention was also required and the Bradford and Bingley Bank was also nationalised along with the quasi-nationalisation of other leading UK banks, such as Lloyds/HBOS and RBS, the UK government becoming the major shareholder in these institutions following billions of pounds of financial support to prevent them going broke. These events graphically illustrated that although securities collateral can importantly assist effective credit risk management, it is no substitute for it. The government now recognises that more effective and wide-ranging regulation is needed and we await with interest to see what will be forthcoming.[292]

289 See generally the Report of the President's Working Group on Financial Markets, *Hedge Funds, Leverage, and the Lessons of Long-Term Capital Management*, April 1999, available at www.treas.gov/press/releases/report3097.htm.

290 Because of the size of the exposures, and the extreme market conditions in early 1998, it seemed likely that the simultaneous sale of numerous extremely large holdings of securities collateral would have precipitated systemic market failure. As one commentator memorably stated, 'You can't all get out the door at the same time'.

291 See generally: *SRM Global Master Fund LP* v. *HM Treasury* [2009] EWHC 227 (Admin) and [2009] EWCA Civ 788; National Audit Office Report *The Nationalisation of Northern Rock* (2009) HC 298.

292 See generally: *The Turner Review Report* March 2009 available at www.fsa.gov.uk. Note also *The Economist*'s Inaugural City Lecture speech by Lord Turner 'The financial crisis and the future of financial regulation' 21 January 2009; available at www.fsa.gov.uk (speeches).

7 Security over moveables in Scots law

George Gretton

Introduction

This chapter will examine the case for the introduction of a new personal property security act (PPSA) into Scottish law. My chapter will review the developments to date in this area, particularly the work of the Scottish Law Commission, and offer some thoughts on how things are likely to develop in the future. By way of introduction, it is important to note that Scots law is a mixed system. That does not mean, however, that every part of the law is mixed. Some parts of the law are, some are indistinguishable from English law and some are predominantly civilian. Property law is an example of the latter and, as always in the civilian tradition, the concept of 'property law' includes moveables as well as immoveables.[1] While the earlier Roman law had a division between law and equity – the latter being the *jus honorarium* – the later civilian tradition fused them.[2] To that fusion Scots law was an heir. There is thus no distinction between legal and equitable rights. (There is equity in the sense of *aequitas*, but that is not English equity.) Trusts, indeed, exist, but without equity: trust law runs on a predominantly civilian software, but the on-screen are much the same as for English law.[3] In the absence of a law–equity division, there is no distinction between legal and equitable security rights.

The key to a civilian system of property law is the doctrine of real rights.[4] The primary real right is ownership. The limited real rights, or, as they are called in Scots law, the subordinate real rights, form a *numerus clausus*. One of them is security, itself having certain sub-types. The ways in which ownership interacts with the subordinate

1 I am using the Scottish spelling of these words, rather than the more usual 'movable' variant.

2 In this chapter I am guilty of at least three oversimplifications. The first is to treat the division between common law and civil law as clear and unproblematic. It is not. The second, connected with the first, is that I write as if civilian systems of property law did not have doctrines that could be characterised as equitable. They do. The third, connected with the first two, is that I write as if Scots law were a pure heaven, or hell, of civilian property law. It is not, but a chapter that was fully nuanced on these points would lose in readability more than it gained in precision.

3 I have tried to explain this in 'Trusts without equity' (2000) 49 ICLQ 599. See also Kenneth Reid's chapter in J. M. Milo and J. M. Smits (eds), *Trusts in Mixed Legal Systems* (Nijmegen: Ars Aequi Libri, 2001). Although the 'onscreen' results are similar for express trusts, in the area of constructive and resulting trusts the results are far from the same.

4 Scots law follows the civilian tradition in tending to use the vernacular expression rather than *jura realia* or *jura in rem*, or (*in re*).

real rights, the ways in which the subordinate real rights interact as between themselves (for instance a usufruct[5] with a security, or two securities with each other), and the mechanisms for the creation, transfer and extinction of real rights, are regulated, in the civilian tradition, by a remarkably small set of rules. Indeed, to the common lawyer the rules may appear too simple and restrictive. For example, Lawson, perceptive as always, wrote of a 'certain intentional poverty of ideas'[6] in the civilian tradition, and the system of real rights is a good example of that. In this imperfect world, every solution has its pros and cons. Civilian property law, with all its pros and cons, is, at all events, the system that Scotland has. There is a clear concept of ownership. Ownership can always be located. When it passes, it does so at a single moment: it does not ooze across. In all property matters, ownership is always the starting point. This is the source of one difficulty that many Scots lawyers have with a PPSA system such as Article 9 of the Uniform Commercial Code in the USA. Under a PPSA, if there is a quasi-security, then the debtor is treated as owner and the creditor is treated as having a mere security interest. That may or may not be a good idea in terms of policy, but that is not the point for present purposes. The point for present purposes is that *if* that policy is to be adopted in Scotland *then*, in the Scottish system of property law, it would have to be made coherent by making the debtor the *actual* holder of the real right of ownership, while what the creditor would *actually* have would be the subordinate real right of security. The 'as if' or 'deemed to be' approach does not work well in a civilian property law system. Now, achieving that integration – the integration of PPSA policy with a civilian property law system – is not so simple. I do not suggest that it cannot be done. It can be done. But to do it would require time and skill.

One aspect of the law of real rights is the publicity principle: the principle that juridical acts relating to real rights should, as far as practicable, be public. The rationale is that third-party effect cannot be justified without publicity. While all civilian systems subscribe to this principle – as indeed the common law tradition does also in some measure – there are considerable variations between systems. For example, German law applies the publicity principle fairly strictly to rights in land, but is lax when it comes to moveables. In German law it is possible, and indeed easy, to grant security rights in both goods[7] and receivables without any sort of public act at all.[8] Scots law has traditionally applied the publicity principle rather strictly – probably more strictly than any other system of civilian property law. That is not just some more-or-less arbitrary fact, but something that enters into the very *mentalité* – to use a currently fashionable word – of the Scots lawyer.

These points are mentioned, albeit only in the most cursory manner, because they pose difficulties – not necessarily insurmountable ones – to the harmonisation of security rights in the UK. These difficulties are not mere surface difficulties: they affect rather basic issues.

5 Scots lawyers occasionally use this term, but more commonly use the curious word 'liferent' – curious because it has nothing to do with rent.

6 See F. H. Lawson *A Common Lawyer Looks at the Civil Law* (Ann Arbor: University of Michigan, 1953), p. 68.

7 This term is used as shorthand for corporeal moveables.

8 *Sicherungsübereignung* for goods and *Sicherungsabtretung* for receivables.

The Scots law of security rights: a nutshell guide

A security is a subordinate right.[9] It is constituted when it becomes real, and it becomes real by the appropriate form of publicity, such as registration. The date upon which a security becomes real is important not only for creating the right, but also as the priority point. That makes the ranking of secured creditors simple, at least in theory, especially if it is recalled that there are no complexities arising out of equitable securities. The fact that civilian property law has, built into the software, a complete, and fairly simple, set of ranking rules is also important when considering how the law of secured transactions is to develop. One driver behind possible reform in England and Wales is a sense that the rules of ranking are not clear. That driver does not exist in Scots law.[10]

In the case of land there is the 'heritable security'. There used to be various kinds of heritable security, but now there is only the boringly named 'standard security'. For goods, there is the pledge, which is possessory, and which of course exists in all legal systems, and the lien, which is also possessory. (Unlike most civilian systems, Scots law classifies the lien as a subordinate real right.) The distinction between them is that pledge is express (*ex voluntate*) while lien is tacit (*ex lege*). Non-possessory security is called hypothec.[11] Scots law has traditionally been suspicious of hypothecs, because of the difficulty of satisfying the publicity principle, and accordingly hypothecs are recognised only in certain narrowly defined cases.[12] Apart from the two hypothecs of ship mortgage and aircraft mortgages, the hypothec has limited commercial significance. However, the introduction in 1961 of the floating charge into Scots law changed everything.[13]

There are thus four kinds of true security in Scots law: heritable security, pledge, lien and hypothec. In all of them there are two real rights in the same thing; first, the debtor's real right of ownership and, second, the creditor's subordinate real right of security.

What about assets other than land and goods, such as receivables? Such rights are classified as incorporeal moveables. Security in the true sense (sometimes called proper security) is not possible over receivables and other incorporeal moveables, for in such cases the right cannot be divided between the collateral-provider (debtor) and the collateral-taker (creditor). So what has to be done is to transfer the right completely to the creditor, subject to a contractual right to a reconveyance on

9 This is the true or 'proper' security. For 'improper' security, see below.

10 This overstates the case somewhat. Ranking problems can arise. But when they do it is mainly because of poorly drafted legislation, or poorly drafted deeds. The common law, with its civilian rules, is usually clear enough.

11 What '*hypotheca*' meant precisely in Roman law is an interesting question. But the traditional view is, in Ulpian's words, that '*proprie pignus dicimus, quod ad creditorem transit, hypothecam, cum non transit nec possessio ad creditorem*' (Dig. 13.7.9.2). That is to say, hypothec means a non-possessory security. The main non-possessory security is over land, and in most legal systems the word 'hypothec' has thus come to mean such a security. But Scots law has gone the other way, and uses the term to mean non-possessory security over moveables.

12 The civilian tradition was favourable to moveable hypothecs until about the close of the eighteenth century. Scots law may pride itself on anticipating the trend. As Lord Stair writes 'our custom hath taken away express hypothecations … and of the tacit legal hypothecations hath only allowed a few' (*Institutions of the Law of Scotland* (1693), pp. 1, 13, 14).

13 By virtue of the Companies (Floating Charges) (Scotland) Act 1961. Floating charges under Scots law is discussed below.

repayment of the debt: in other words, *fiducia cum creditore*. Such a transfer of an incorporeal moveable is known as assignation in security. It is somewhat cumbersome and inconvenient because in Scots law an assignation is without effect until it is formally notified to the account debtor: such notification is called intimation.[14]

Quasi-securities are arrangements where title is vested in the creditor: arrangements such as hire purchase, retention of title in sale, and sale and lease-back. These are not proper securities since there is no division of the real rights. Hire purchase and retention of title in sale are recognised,[15] although they are not classified as security rights. Sale and lease back is recognised if it is a genuine such transaction, but not if it is not. In practice there is something of a presumption that such arrangements are not genuine; Scots law is certainly more reluctant to recognise them than is English law. The way that the non-recognition operates is that the transfer is regarded, under Scots law, as invalid. Since Scots law generally adheres to the so-called principle of abstraction, this non-recognition of the act of transfer is surprising. But in such matters Scots law switches from the abstract approach to the causal approach.[16]

Before the introduction of the floating charge, therefore, Scots law made it difficult to create security, except over land. For goods the only method was the possessory pledge, which is, of course, usually too inconvenient for commercial purposes. For receivables there was assignation in security, but once again this was inconvenient and thus not widely used. The Companies (Floating Charges) (Scotland) Act 1961 introduced the floating charge, at first without receivership, which was added by the Companies (Floating Charges and Receivers) (Scotland) Act 1972.[17] This made security easy, but only for company debtors, and with all the problems to which floating charges are subject. Moreover, the legislation that introduced the floating charge never integrated the institution into the general fabric of Scots law. But whatever the problems in law, the floating charge proved, not surprisingly, popular in practice. Most security rights in practice are either heritable securities or floating charges.

14 The above is subject to the Financial Collateral Directive, 2002/47/EC and the Financial Collateral Arrangements (No. 2) Regulations 2003, SI 2003/3226. For their interpretation in Scots law, see Gretton 'Financial collateral and the fundamentals of secured transactions' (2006) 10 *Edinburgh Law Review* 209.

15 On retention of title in sale, and indeed, other aspects of the law of security over corporeal moveables, see D. L. Carey Miller, *Corporeal Moveables in Scots Law* (Edinburgh: W Green & Son and the Scottish Universities Law Institute, 2nd edn, 2005). For the law in a comparative setting, see Eva-Maria Kieninger (ed.), *Security Rights in Movable Property in European Private* Law (Cambridge: Cambridge University Press, 2004).

16 For land, see the Conveyancing and Feudal Reform (Scotland) Act 1970, s. 9. For moveables, see the Sale of Goods Act 1979, s. 62(4). While the latter applies both sides of the border, in practice it has functioned almost as if it had a 'Scotland only' label. The reasons are complex. One is that the Act is in substance a codification of English common law, so that if s. 62(4) disapplies the Act, then either: (a) the sale is subject to the common law, and the English common law regime is similar to the Act itself, or (b) it is subject to the Bills of Sale Acts. By way of contrast, if s. 62(4) operates to disapply the Act to a sale in Scotland, the effect is to bring Scots common law into operation, and that law, based on the Roman law of sale, is different from the Act, and, among other things, requires *traditio*. (The Bills of Sale Acts do not apply in Scotland.) Moreover – and this is a key point – Scots law allows *constitutum possessorium* only in exceptional cases.

17 For some account of the unhappiness that some Scots lawyers feel about the floating charge, see David Cabrelli 'The case against the floating charge in Scotland' (2005) 9 *Edinburgh Law Review* 407.

Registration of company charges

The idea of a separate system of registration for security rights granted by companies, as opposed to other persons, is from an international perspective an usual one. Scotland did not have such a system before 1961. This did not cause problems because the rather strict application of the publicity principle meant that secret security rights were virtually impossible. When the floating charge was introduced it was decided to introduce the whole English system of registration of company charges – not only for the new floating charge, which evidently needed some sort of registration, but also for any other security right granted by a company. The rules are not precisely the same as the corresponding English provisions, but there is little substantive difference.[18] The only one worth mentioning is that the rule in the English provisions[19] requiring registration of a charge which, if granted by an individual, would come under the Bills of Sale Acts, has no equivalent in the Scottish legislation, where those Acts do not apply, and where non-possessory security of goods is generally invalid at common law. Registration is in Edinburgh rather than in Cardiff.[20] Why the system was introduced not only for floating charges but also for other charges was not explained at the time and has remained a mystery ever since. It is a feature of the system that has always been rather unpopular. There has also been a dissatisfaction with the fact that a floating charge can exist for up to 21 days without registration (the 'invisibility period'). This is a breach of the publicity principle that is particularly at odds with Scottish legal thinking. No reason for it has ever been advanced.[21]

Possible reforms: a brief history

The history of unimplemented recommendations in this area is well known. The story has been similar on both sides of the border. In 1971 the Crowther Report recommended the introduction of a new PPSA to the UK.[22] A Scottish working party was set up to consider how this might be done and this resulted in the publication of the Halliday Report in 1986.[23] The Halliday Report recommended that any PPSA should be limited to commercial transactions. The Report did a good deal of work on how a PPSA might be integrated into Scots law, but did not really complete the task. The Report looks more like a 'promising first draft' than a finished report and many important issues were left dangling. In 1989 the Diamond Report recommended reform on both sides of the border, but of course that never happened.[24]

18 The company charge registration provisions are found in the Companies Act 2006, Part 25.

19 Ibid., s. 860(7)(b).

20 Companies House in Edinburgh is not a branch of the Companies House for England and Wales, but separate, with its own Registrar. However, in practice there is a high degree of integration.

21 For a full account, see Gretton 'Registration of company charges' (2002) 6 *Edinburgh Law Review* 146.

22 See *Report of the Committee on Consumer Credit* (1971) Cmnd 4596 (the Crowther Report).

23 *Report by Working Party on Security over Moveable Property* (the Halliday Report). The Report was commissioned by the Scottish Law Commission. It was submitted in 1983 and published in 1986, by the Commission.

24 By Professor A. L. Diamond, *A Review of Security Interests in Property* (London: Department of Trade and Industry, 1989) (the Diamond Report).

In 1995 there appeared another Scottish Report, the Murray Report.[25] This recommended changes to the system of registration of company charges, and also recommended the introduction of fixed registered charges over goods and receivables. It was not implemented.

In 1998 the Scotland Act added more spice to the meal. This Act devolved legislative power to the Scottish Parliament in some areas but reserved it in others and, as a consequence, sometimes the result is rather awkward. Company law is a reserved area,[26] but the law of rights in security, including floating charges, is devolved to the Scottish Parliament. As a result of this, interpreting the limits of legislative competence is a constant source of difficulty and, in general, the approach has tended to be a cautious one: if any statable doubt exists, the matter is usually left to London. Whether the rules in the Companies Acts about the registration of company charges are subject to the legislative competence of the Scottish Parliament is one about which statable doubt exists.

It is not necessary to trace here the history of the Company Law Review, or the decision that the question of company charges would have to be looked at by the Law Commissions. Joint work by the two Commissions is not uncommon, especially in the sphere of commercial law, and it seems that the DTI at first intended to make a joint reference. But that was not what happened. Separate references were made, and in different terms. The DTI's reference to the Scottish Law Commission was:

> To examine the present scheme on the registration and priority of rights in security granted by companies and to make recommendations for its reform as it applies to (a) companies having their registered office in Scotland wherever the assets are located; (b) security granted under Scots law by oversea companies and companies having their registered office in England and Wales.

Unlike the reference to the English Law Commission, there was no mention of quasi-securities, and no mention of securities granted by debtors other than companies. Why were there separate references in substantially different terms? In 2001/2002 the DTI had its foot on the accelerator. Draft legislation was requested at top speed. That is not how it happened, but that was the plan. Rapid preparation of comprehensive – and radical – legislation for Scotland was out of the question, for two reasons. One was that the Scottish Law Commission, being smaller than its London counterpart, finds it harder to take up a new project at short notice. The other is that the sort of reform contemplated, though undoubtedly a great change for English law, would have been an even greater change for Scots law, while at the same time being (arguably) less needed. It is worth quoting at some length from the Scottish Law Commission's 2002 Discussion Paper:

> Existing models of notice filing presuppose Anglo-American property law and turn on distinctions between creation, attachment and perfection which are unknown in Scots law or in other systems drawn from the Germanic stream of the civil law tradition.[27] A system of notice filing suited to English property law could

25 *Security over Moveable Property* (London: Department of Trade and Industry, 1994) (the Murray Report).

26 See the Scotland Act 1998, s. 29(2)(b) and Schedule 5 Part II Head C1.

27 The Commission adds a perceptive footnote: 'The distinction between attachment and perfection is more readily compatible with the Romanistic branch of the civil law tradition.

not readily be modified or adapted to accommodate the very different structures and concepts of Scots property law. While it would no doubt be possible, with patience and care, to devise some form of notice filing suitable for Scotland the task would be a substantial one which would require to address, among others, the familiar but unsolved issue of a non-possessory security over moveables, and the creation of such a form of notice filing cannot sensibly be considered in the context of corporate debtors alone. In any event the case for notice filing is likely to be weaker in Scotland than in England and Wales. In Scotland publicity and priority are already substantially secured by other means, the latter by the straightforward principle that real rights rank in order of creation (*prior tempore potior jure*). And there would be a natural hesitation in adopting a system which puts pressure on two of the principles (sufficiency and accuracy) identified earlier as central to the registration of securities. The whole question, however, is too complex for detailed discussion here, and no view is expressed. The issue of notice filing is one to which this Commission, or some other body, may wish to return in the future. We would merely add that if, as is tentatively suggested below, registration of company securities is restricted to floating charges, the way would be open for the later introduction, if thought desirable, of a uniform system of notice filing applying to both corporate and noncorporate debtors.[28]

The Scottish Law Commission's report of 2004

The Scottish Law Commission's provisional recommendations attracted wide support, in both the business and legal communities, and their Final Report, which appeared in September 2004,[29] therefore followed the general line of those recommendations. The main ones were as follows.

(a) The special regime for the registration of company charges, as found in the then Part XII of the Companies Act 1985, should be abolished. Security rights, other than the floating charge, should be created according to the general law: the fact that the debtor is a company should make no difference.
(b) What is now the Register of Charges – i.e. a part of the Companies Register – should be abolished, and replaced by a new Register of Floating Charges. This would not be administered by the Scottish Registrar of Companies, but by the Keeper of the Registers. The 'Keeper', as he is always called, is a person whose position goes back some centuries and who administers a number of Scottish registers.
(c) Floating charges should come into existence on registration, and not before.[30] Thus the 21-day 'invisibility period' would disappear.
(d) The priority rules should be simplified, in that floating charges should rank from the date of registration, subject to certain qualifications.

Indeed the only civil law jurisdictions to have introduced notice filing are Quebec and Louisiana.' The term 'Romanistic' is here used to mean the French branch. As to property law, Scotland belongs to the Germanic branch.

28 See Scottish Law Commission Discussion Paper No. 121: *Discussion Paper on Registration of Rights in Security by Companies* (2002), paras 1.28 and 1.29 (footnotes omitted). In quoting this I am not quoting myself: I did not become a Commissioner until 2006.

29 See *Report on Registration of Rights in Security by Companies* (Scottish Law Commission Report No. 197, 2004).

30 Though there would be an 'advance notice' option.

(e) The charging document itself should be registered, and not merely 'particulars' as under the current law.

(f) These rules should apply to any floating charge, as far as assets in Scotland are concerned, regardless of whether the company was Scottish or not. Thus, a floating charge created by an English company or a non-UK company would have full effect over assets in Scotland only if the charge had been registered in Edinburgh.[31] This recommendation is not to be found expressly stated in the draft bill which was appended to the Final Report, because it was considered to be implicit in the draft provision stating, in unqualified terms, that the effect of a floating charge would depend on its registration in the new register. However, in view of its limited remit, the Law Commission did not make any recommendations for further reforms of the floating charge.

The Commission did not rule out the idea of a new PPSA, but it made clear that there would be considerable obstacles in the way. While to a large extent the fundamental policies and objectives are the same on both sides of the border the Scottish Law Commission noted that:

> common aims cannot always be achieved by common means. In this area of company law, as in few others, a full harmonisation of rules seems unattainable. There is nothing surprising about this. Registration of rights in security granted by companies is perhaps more a part of the law of rights in security than of company law. At any rate the rules of registration cannot be separated from the underlying law of property, and that underlying law is radically different in the two jurisdictions.[32]

The Scottish Act

The Scottish Law Commission's Report could in practice not be implemented without support in both Westminster and Holyrood. The law relating to floating charges is devolved but, as has already been mentioned, some uncertainty exists as to whether the rules in the Companies Acts about the registration of company charges are reserved or devolved. As a matter of caution, therefore, implementation of the Law Commission's recommendations had to be twofold. Remarkably, that twofold support was obtained – or rather, it was obtained in Edinburgh and partially obtained in London. In Scotland the result was the passing of the Bankruptcy and Diligence etc. (Scotland) Act 2007. This Act establishes the new Register of Floating Charges, provides that a floating charge is not created until registered in that register, and generally consolidates, with some changes, the provisions about floating charges from the Companies Act 1985.[33]

The idea of abolishing registration of security (i.e. company charges) in the Companies Register was, in the end, not supported by the DTI. Instead, a halfway house emerged, applying both sides of the border, whereby Westminster legislation would provide that when a security is registered in another register (a 'special' register) then that would amount to deemed registration for the purposes of the Companies Acts,

31 For the cross-border issues, see below.

32 See *Discussion Paper on Registration of Rights in Security by Companies*, above fn 28, para. 1.25.

33 The Companies Act 2006 did not repeal Part XVIII of the Companies Act 1985, which has provisions about floating charges for Scots law. Part XVIII is repealed by the 2007 Act.

with information being supplied by the special register to the Registrar of Companies.[34] This provision requires orders to activate it, and the expectation in Scotland is that an order bringing it into force in relation to the Scottish special registers will be regarded as a priority.

Why does Scotland hesitate about a new PPSA?

Apart from the time that would be needed to develop a PPSA suitable for Scotland, why was Scotland hesitant about following the lead given by the Law Commission? I cannot speak for Scotland, but it is productive to offer some tentative thoughts on the matter, some have already been mentioned.

Dislike of limping rights

In the first place, there is the difficulty that the attachment–perfection distinction, which seems to be essential to schemes based on Article 9 of the Uniform Commercial Code (UCC), is unknown to Scots law. In Scots law the idea of a property right that is effective 'as between the parties' is not one that fits in with Scottish general property law. Real rights either exist or do not exist. If real rights do exist, then, in principle, they are effective *erga omnes*. Indeed, the rule that an unregistered charge is 'void against' certain parties but good against others,[35] is still something that Scots lawyers cannot really understand, despite the fact that it is now more than four decades after this law was first introduced to Scotland.[36] Some might argue that this is due to a defective understanding in Scotland. However, the alternative explanation is that a 'void against' formula does not fit in well with a system which does not normally allow property rights to 'limp'; i.e. property rights that are valid in some respects but not in others. By way of contrast, a rule that protects a buyer in good faith, such as the Sale of Goods Act 1979, s. 25 does not give rise to limping rights: first one person is the owner and then another and that ends the matter. Any 'good against' or 'void against' formula, however, does give rise to limping property rights.

Nevertheless, one must not make too much of this point. Most or all civilian systems do have limping rights to some extent.[37] That is also true of Scots law. However, limping rights are awkward because of the complexities they give rise to, and the feeling is that they should be admitted only if a strong case is made for them. It is noteworthy that the EBRD Model Law on Secured Transactions, which, although inspired by UCC Article 9 (and was developed for use in the transition economies of the former Soviet bloc) does not use the attachment–perfection distinction.[38] One wonders whether it is in truth a necessary one, or, indeed, one which is wise to use in the context of modern European convergence. At all events, it is a distinction that is problematic for Scots law.

34 See Companies Act 2006, s. 893. This section came into force on October 1 2009 by virtue of SI 2008/2860.

35 See: the former Companies Act 1985, s. 395 (England and Wales) and s. 410 (Scotland); and now Companies Act 2006, s. 874 (England and Wales) and s. 889 (Scotland).

36 By the Companies (Floating Charges) (Scotland) Act 1961.

37 Cf. the *relative Unwirksamkeit* of German law, and the *non-opposabilité* of French law.

38 The EBRD has published this in print form, and it is also available on its website: http://www.ebrd.com/. It will also be found in Joseph J. Norton and Mads Andenas (eds), *Emerging Financial Markets and Secured Transactions* (London: Kluwer, 1998).

The need to locate ownership

In a civilian system of property law, ownership is an unambiguous and primary conception. Common lawyers deconstruct ownership as a 'bundle of rights' and it may well be that in the common law systems that is correct but, in the civil law, ownership is not a bundle of rights.[39] Rights can be subtracted from ownership, of course, but what remains is always precisely the same in its nature, albeit the less valuable as the more is subtracted; what remains is ownership. That civil lawyers do not see ownership as a bundle of rights is not due to a failure of analysis, but because common lawyers and civil lawyers are not starting off with the same concepts. The Scottish conception of ownership is the civil law conception.[40] In the civil law there is always, at one point in time, one right of ownership.[41] When that right of ownership passes, it does so instantaneously. Rights other than ownership are either subordinate real rights or personal rights. This logic does not easily fit in with a PPSA approach.

The UCC says that 'the retention or reservation of title by a seller of goods notwithstanding shipment or delivery to the buyer ... is limited in effect to a reservation of a security interest'.[42] What does this provision mean to a civilian? One interpretation would be that the buyer becomes owner, and the seller has a limited real right. If that is correct, however, it means that the seller has ceased to be the owner even though there was no *animus transferendi dominii*. Equally it means that the buyer has become the owner without an *animus acquirendi dominii*. Well, that is possible – statutes can do anything, almost. However, one would want to think rather carefully before accepting a statutory provision of this sort. Note that it does not merely visit the sanction of nullity upon a juridical act of which it disapproves. That is common: the law often fires bursts of grape-shot-nullity into the tangled masses of human transactions. The provision quoted, however, appears to go further than that.

Nevertheless, one could question if the provision really does mean this? If we go back to the definitions, then we see that the UCC defines 'security interest' as 'an interest in personal property or fixtures which secures payment or performance of an obligation'.[43] That could mean ownership itself, for ownership is itself an 'interest' that can be used to 'secure[s] payment or performance of an obligation'. This is what is sometimes known in the civilian tradition as security ownership.[44] Therefore, 'security interest' might mean a limited real right, namely the real right of security, but it might also mean the real right of ownership, employed for a certain purpose.

Nor is that all. The UCC also says that 'except as otherwise provided with respect to consignments or sales of accounts, chattel paper, payment intangibles or promissory notes, the provisions of this article with regard to rights and obligations apply whether title to collateral is in the secured party or the debtor'.[45] That indicates that

39 Ownership has, indeed, traditionally been thought of as involving the *jus utendi*, the *jus abutendi* and the *jus fruendi* (or in short *usus*, *abusus* and *fructus*), a mode of thought that nowadays survives more in some systems (e.g. France) than others. But this does not characterise ownership as a bundle of three rights; rather, it sees it as a unity with three facets

40 This paragraph jumps over deep crevasses. For instance, the French description of limited real rights as *démembrements* could be used to challenge the account given in the text. A full treatment of this subject would be out of place here.

41 Which may, of course, be shared, as when two people buy something together – ownership *pro indiviso*.

42 See UCC Art. 1-201 (35). See also UCC Art. 2-401.

43 See UCC Art. 1-201 (35).

44 *Propriété à titre de garantie*, or, in the neat German term, *Sicherungseigentum*.

45 See UCC Art. 9-202.

in, for instance, retention of title in a sale of goods transaction, the seller way well indeed be the owner.

'Security interest' turns out to be (from a civilian perspective) elusive. The policy of the UCC is this: 'In title finance, the title is functionally a security interest. So the law should characterise it as such.' That could be done either by converting it into a limited real right, or by keeping it as ownership but strictly as security ownership. When one puts the text of the UCC under a magnifying glass, it is unclear which of these is happening. However, that criticism is perhaps itself a culture-bound criticism. In a system where ownership is conceptualised as a bundle of rights, the sorts of issues being canvassed above perhaps do not matter and perhaps do not even make sense.[46] Civil lawyers are, it might be said, obsessed by the question of who has which real rights at each moment. Anglo-American lawyers are not so obsessed. Having established that the philosophy of the UCC is functionalism, for the Anglo-American lawyer the story is ended. The civil lawyer may well be prepared to accept the functionalism, but wishes to make it run on a different operating system. It is unfortunate that scepticism about UCC Article 9 has often been misconstrued as a distrust of functionalism. That may come into it, but a functionalist philosophy, however enthusiastically embraced, still needs technical implementation.

The publicity principle

The publicity principle is the principle that rights having third-party effects ought to be public. It is not confined to property law, though it is most closely associated with that area of law. Different systems adhere to it with varying degrees of fidelity. As has already been mentioned, one would have expected that German law would adhere strictly, but in fact to does not. Americans, imbued with the spirit of Article 9, are always shocked by the German law of secured transactions and, in my view, rightly shocked. Scots law has long been a stickler for the publicity principle. It introduced a deeds registration system as far back as 1617,[47] so that real rights in land were in the public domain. The sanction for non-registration was nullity – not nullity as to the personal right, but nullity as to the real right.[48] The law of security rights has always required publicity. Attempts have been made time and time again to circumvent that requirement, but on the whole without success. It has already been noted that attempts to create quasi-hypothecs by sale and lease-back transactions have been repeatedly struck down by the Scottish courts. Retention of title has been upheld, but that is a special case, because no attempt is being made to create a real right without publicity. Hire purchase has a statutory foundation.

Perhaps the major breach in the publicity principle, as applied to security rights, has been *Tay Valley Joinery Ltd* v. *CF Financial Services Ltd*, which held that a security right over receivables can be effected by secret act between debtor and creditor, by the use of a trust.[49] The decision remains controversial. However, there seems to be a general agreement that, while *Tay Valley* itself may have been wrongly decided, the

46 An outsider cannot, however, wonder whether US attitudes are entirely consistent. While adhering to the 'bundle of rights' theory, US lawyers also speak of 'title' in a way that has close similarities with the civilian *dominium*.

47 See Registration Act 1617.

48 An attempt to persuade the House of Lords to overturn this principle was made in *Burnett's Tr.* v. *Grainger*, 2004 SC (HL) 19, but without success. Had the decision gone the other way, the Scottish Parliament would perhaps have legislated to reinstate the law.

49 1987 SLT 207, 1987 SCLR 117.

law does make it too difficult to constitute security over receivables, and the Scottish Law Commission is considering the issue with a view to possible reforms.[50]

A concern with the notice-filing system is that while it does comply with the publicity principle, the compliance is at the minimal level. Under the notice-file system, third parties know merely that: a security right may or may not have been constituted, and that if it has not, then it may or may not hereafter be constituted, in favour of a named person, and that this security, if it exists, or if it will exist, is or will be over some class of assets – a class that may be stated extremely broadly, such as 'all receivables'. Such a system may warn a third party but it scarcely informs them of anything of substance (unlike the deeds registration system). This is a perfectly possible model but it is one that a Scots lawyer naturally feels a little less comfortable with than a lawyer from a common law background. In Scotland deeds relating to land have been recorded since 1617. The recording is normally of the complete deed,[51] and the register has always been open to the public. That practice is one that has made a deep impression. Scots lawyers are so publicity minded that important legal documents are often publicly registered even if the law does not require it. There also exists in Edinburgh a register whose function is notarial.[52] This register contains all sorts of deeds, such as contracts, trusts and testaments. Registration in that register is optional, but common. The point is made to illustrate the deep differences of outlook between English and Scottish lawyers. To the Scots lawyer minimal registration is a difficult system to accept. Indeed, Scots lawyers have always been puzzled that the Companies Act 2006 requires registration merely of 'particulars' instead of the whole deed.[53]

The philosophy of facilitation

Part of the underlying philosophy of the UCC and PPSA systems is that the law should make it easy for security rights to be created. The law should not put obstacles in the way of commerce – its role should be to facilitate.

This philosophy has plenty of support in Scotland as it does in England, but there are also some doubts. The American legal scholar Lynn LoPucki remarks that 'security is an agreement between A and B that C takes nothing'.[54] Security benefits debtor and creditor, but the loser is the unsecured creditor. Unsecured creditors have no lobby, and so their voice is seldom heard.[55] It may be that no tears need to be shed for the unsecured creditors, and that if they suffer it is for the greater good of commerce. But even on that view there are sceptics who argue that secured finance is no more efficient than unsecured finance or equity finance, and even that secured finance may lead to an efficiency by the unbargained-for externalisation of risk. This is not the place to explore such issues[56] but, it is probably fair to say, in Scotland the view that the policy of the law should be to encourage the use of secured credit is not an uncontested one.

50 As the French have done with the *loi Dailly* (1981, now consolidated as L.313–23 *et seq.* of the *Code monétaire et financier*). The Scots law of assignation, or cession, seems to have been borrowed from France in the late mediaeval period, and the two continue to resemble each other.

51 Since the Land Registration (Scotland) Act 1979 this is no longer true as such. But this is a detail which need not be entered into here.

52 This goes by the curious name of the Books of Council and Session.

53 See generally Companies Act 2006, s. 860(1) (England), s. 878(1) (Scotland).

54 'The unsecured creditor's bargain' (1994) 80 *Virginia Law Review* 1887, p. 1899.

55 But see Enterprise Act 2002 at Part 10 for a limited exception to this.

56 For a survey of the law-and-economics aspects, see G. McCormack *Secured Credit under English and American Law* (Cambridge: Cambridge University Press, 2004), ch. 1.

Less need to restate the priority system

In Scots law the priority system for security rights is fairly straightforward. Indeed, it is so straightforward that it is sometimes difficult to think up good examination questions, unless one brings in floating charges. The Scottish floating charge is essentially an English animal and the complexities and uncertainties that surround its ranking are rather shocking to a perhaps too easily shocked Scottish legal mind. The Bankruptcy and Diligence (Scotland) Act 2007 has brought about some simplification, but difficulties remain. In English law there is an understandable pressure for the general law relating to priorities to be rationalised and restated. However, that pressure does not exist in Scotland.

Lack of evidence of demand for change

A few years ago the Scottish Executive commissioned a report on whether small and medium-sized enterprises and their institutional lenders felt that the existing system of security was unsatisfactory.[57] The answer, which some might find surprising, was that there was little pressure for change.

Private international law

English private international law is prepared to accord extra-territorial effect to equitable security rights. For example, in *Re Anchor Lines*[58] the question arose as to the effect of a floating charge granted by an English company in relation to assets in Scotland. The Chancery Division held that the security was good, even though at that time Scots law did not have the floating charge. That was in 1937. In 1961 the floating charge was introduced and, on the whole, since then the private international law problems between England and Scotland have not been great. A floating charge registered in Edinburgh is recognised in England and Wales, and the converse is equally true. Problems can arise for other English equitable securities, but have seldom done so. Difficulties are usually masked by the fact that the right of an English liquidator, receiver, administrator or trustee in bankruptcy to realise assets in Scotland is accepted. Once the asset is realised, the proceeds can then be distributed on the basis that the equitable security is to be regarded as valid: this is the approach underlying *Re Anchor Lines*.

The 2007 Act provides that a floating charge is not valid unless registered in the Register of Floating Charges. This measure represents a substantial change from a private international law standpoint. It means that if an English company grants a floating charge, and the charge is duly registered in Cardiff, but is not also registered in Edinburgh, that charge will be regarded as invalid by the Scottish courts; although it will presumably be regarded as valid by the English courts (on the basis of *Re Anchor Lines*). Such a floating charge will thus be in the same position as other English equitable securities over Scottish assets. To illustrate some potential future problems I give below a few case examples set ten years in the future. In all of these cases the

57 See Report: *Business Finance and Security over Moveable Property* (Edinburgh: Scottish Executive Central Research Unit, 2002). The Report was submitted to the Scottish Justice Department.

58 [1937] Ch. 483. For a valuable study of this area, see C. Bispeng, 'The classification of floating charges in international private law' 2002 *Juridical Review* 195.

basic facts are the same: ABC Ltd, an English company, grants a floating charge to a bank, the charge is registered in Cardiff but not in Edinburgh. The company later gets into financial difficulties and an administrator is appointed. The company owns property with a Scottish *situs*.

Case (1)

There are no third-party rights affecting the property. The administrator sells the property and pays the proceeds to the bank. Even although Scots law does not recognise the charge, nevertheless the charge has worked. (It is difficult to see how the administrator's power of sale could be questioned.)

Case (2)

Before the administrator was appointed, ABC Ltd borrowed money from DEF Ltd and, in security of the loan, granted a security over the property to DEF Ltd. This security was created in accordance with Scots law. In relation to DEF's security, the floating charge is invalid. The administrator now wishes to sell the property, but will, it seems, find that he cannot give a purchaser an unencumbered title unless DEF Ltd is paid.

Case (3)

Instead of being granted a security, DEF Ltd attaches the property for an unpaid debt. Here the result would seem to be the same as in the previous case.

Case (4)

DEF Ltd has taken a floating charge. This charge is registered in the Register of Floating Charges in Edinburgh. As far as Scots law is concerned, this is the only valid floating charge. But in this case it is not easy to see how DEF Ltd's priority is enforceable.

Other cross-border problems might also arise. For example, take Case (1) above and vary it, so that the floating charge is registered in Cardiff three years before it is registered in Edinburgh, and that its registration in Edinburgh is followed six months later by liquidation. Now consider the impact of the Insolvency Act 1986, s. 245. That section says that a floating charge that is created less than two years before winding up may (depending on the circumstances) be invalid. In this, as the previous cases, the answer may vary according to whether the court that determines the issue is English or Scottish. In the case where the issue is decided by an English court (*Re Anchor Lines*) the court is likely to be prepared to apply English law extraterritorially. However, a Scottish court is likely to refuse to accord extraterritorial effect on a security that is invalid under Scots law.

Of course, such issues will not arise if the floating charge has been registered in Edinburgh. How common that will be remains to be seen. If, at the time the charge is granted, the company has no Scottish assets, but later acquires them, it would always be possible to register the charge in Edinburgh at that stage. There is no time limit for the registration of floating charges: the rule is simply that, as far as Scots law is concerned, they are not created until registration is made.

Conclusions

The Scottish Law Commission did not reject a PPSA approach. It merely said:

(a) that there exist serious obstacles in Scots law to the adoption of such an approach; and
(b) that within the time-frame prescribed by the DTI, and within the resources available to the Commission, it was not possible to develop a PPSA that could include Scotland.

In the meantime it has announced a review of security interests in receivables and other incorporeal moveables.[59] The Commission also acknowledged that 'the difficulty in creating an effective fixed security over receivables in Scotland places Scottish businesses at a competitive disadvantage …'.[60] However, this review will not take place until the Commission has finished its work on land registration in Scotland and it follows that there will be a delay of at least a few years before workable reform proposals are forthcoming.[61] On the wider question of whether a GB-wide or UK-wide PPSA is a real possibility within the foreseeable future remains uncertain. One political issue is that the law of security rights is, for the most part, devolved, but that is less of a hurdle than might be supposed. If legislation were passed at Westminster for England and Wales, dovetailing legislation for Scotland could be passed at Holyrood. Alternatively, a single bill, with appropriate special provisions for Scotland, could be passed at Westminster on the basis of a Sewel Motion.[62] However, the fact remains that the real issue here is the fact that Scots lawyers are hesitant about a PPSA, for the reasons that I have tried to explain.

In theory it might be possible to evolve a system that would be acceptable on both sides of the border. For example, as has already been mentioned, it is not clear that the attachment–perfection distinction, which Scots lawyers are unenthusiastic about, is really an essential part of a PPSA. But to develop such a system would not be easy, and it is understandable that in the circumstances the attempt has not been made. It might perhaps be that if such a system were established in England and Wales and proved successful, Scotland, might wish to join in, as Louisiana eventually did in relation to the United States UCC Article 9.[63] It might be that events at a European level will eventually take over in this area.[64] However, for the moment at least the gap between England and Scotland, which before 1961 was wide, and which even since 1961 has been a significant one, will not disappear. The tectonic forces of the European Union may be pushing the systems of Europe closer together, but the more local tectonic forces resulting from devolution are perhaps pushing the other way.

59 See Scottish Law Commission Report No. 198 (2005) *Seventh Programme of Law Reform* (Edinburgh: The Stationery Office, 2005).
60 Ibid., p. 20, para. 2.38.
61 Ibid., p. 19 para. 2.31.
62 This is a system that has emerged whereby Westminster Parliament will legislate on a devolved matter if the Scottish Parliament has so consented by means of a resolution in the latter. Sewel motions are quite common in practice.
63 An analogy can also be made with the floating charge which was common in England since the 1870s but, which required the Act of 1961 to introduce the concept into Scots law.
64 On European developments note also the chapter by Drobnig in the present volume, pp. 444–55.

8 Security interests in intellectual property

*Jacqueline Lipton**

Introduction: intellectual property as security for a loan

Increasingly over recent years, even decades now, intellectual property has come to the fore as comprising a variety of valuable business assets in many industries, and is thus potentially a subject for secured financing transactions. In the United States with its highly evolved film and television, music and computer software industries, all heavily reliant on intellectual property rights (notably copyright), legal and practical issues relating to the use of these assets as loan collateral have taken on particular significance. Governments in other jurisdictions have also started coming to grips with the various legal and practical issues inherent in attempts to utilise such rights in this context. In 2001, for example, the Law Commission of Canada hosted a major international conference to consider federal reform of Canadian secured finance law to better accommodate securities over intellectual property.[1]

The issue of how best to deal with the legal and practical issues arising from attempts to utilise intellectual property as loan collateral has also emerged in debates about reforming the personal property security system in the United Kingdom. In its Consultation Paper 164 on the reform of security interests in personal property,[2] the English Law Commission specifically referred to the issue of security interests in intellectual property.[3] One of the most notable references to intellectual property in

* The author would like to thank Alanna Arnold for her valuable research assistance.

1 Law Commission of Canada, Leveraging Knowledge Assets Security Interests in Intellectual Property, University of Western Ontario, 16–17 November 2001. This culminated in the publication of a set of conference papers as a book: Howard Knopf (ed.), *Security Interests in Intellectual Property* (Carswell: Canada, 2003). For the ongoing status of the project, see: Law Commission of Canada, *Federal Security Interests/Security Interests in Intellectual Property*, available at http://www.lcc.gc.ca/en/themes/er/fsi/fsi_main.asp.

2 *Registration of Security Interests: Company Charges and Property other than Land* (London: The Stationery Office, 2002), available at http://www.lawcom.gov.uk/files/cp164.pdf; hereinafter Consultation Paper 164.

3 See Consultation Paper 164, above fn 2, at paras 4.199–4.211, 5.123, 8.39. The Scottish Law Commission also reported on this area; see Scots Law Commission Report No. 197: *Company Security Interests* (2004) HC 1003 (Edinburgh: The Stationery Office, 2004), available at http://www.scotlawcom.gov.uk; prior to this Report, the Scots Law Commission published Discussion Paper No. 121 Registration of Rights in Security by Companies (October 2002) hereinafter, Discussion Paper 121. See in particular Discussion Paper 121, paras. 4.14–4.17, suggesting a general principle that security interests in incorporeal intellectual property assets that are registrable outside the companies register should not be required to be registered with the Registrar of Companies.

that paper was the suggestion that any new personal property securities register adopted in the United Kingdom should exclude registration of charges over assets that have their own specialist registers.[4] This would have included a number of intellectual property assets, such as patents, registered trade marks and registered designs.[5] However, this recommendation was later reversed by the Law Commission in its *Final Report* of July 2005.[6] Instead the Commission recommended that charges over these assets should be included on both the specialist registers and on a new form of Company Security Register described in the Report.[7] However, the priority rules from the relevant specialist register(s) would be applied to charges over those assets.[8] This recommendation is considered in more detail below.

The aim of this essay is first, to describe the basic features of the various forms of intellectual property that might be utilised as loan collateral. The discussion then turns to an examination of the most obvious legal, conceptual and practical difficulties inherent in utilising intellectual property as loan collateral regardless of the form of registration system in place for personal property securities in a given jurisdiction. The 'dual registration' issue described above is also considered. The recommendations set out in the Law Commission's *Final Report* would likely be a way of resolving dual registration confusions if they were to be later adopted in the United Kingdom. However, there are many other issues that cannot be resolved through a registration system and require further legal and/or commercial consideration. Although, at the present time, it appears as if the Law Commission's proposals will not be implemented, this chapter will analyse many of the issues that are in need of reform and it will, therefore, provide a useful service in offering pointers as to the future course the law should take if, and when, the reform question comes up again.

The nature of intellectual property

Defining intellectual property

In order to discuss the use of intellectual property as loan collateral, it is first necessary to have some understanding of the term in a practical sense. Commercial lawyers and lenders engaged in secured financing transactions are often not overly familiar with the nuances of this term. The following discussion attempts to unpack some of the connotations of the phrase 'intellectual property' as applied in modern commercial practice.

As a stand-alone term, 'intellectual property' is difficult to pin down with any certainty as it covers such a broad array of intangible assets and potentially also various forms of 'quasi property' such as trade secrets/confidential information and Internet domain names.[9] It is also very easy to confuse an intellectual property right,

4 See Consultation Paper 164, above fn 2, para. 4.211.
5 Ibid., para. 5.123(1).
6 *Company Security Interests* (London: The Stationery Office, 2005), available at http://www.lawcom.gov.uk; hereinafter Final Report 296.
7 See Final Report 296, above fn 6, para. 3.231.
8 Ibid., para. 3.235.
9 These items are not unequivocally regarded as 'property' but are often included in discussions of intellectual property in relevant texts. See, for example, Cornish, W. R. and Llewelyn, D., *Intellectual Property: Patents, Copyrights, Trade Marks and Allied Rights* (London: Thomson, 5th edn, 2003); Ricketson, M. and Richardson, M., *Intellectual Property: Cases, Materials and Commentary* (Sydney: Butterworths, 2nd edn, 1998), Bouchoux, D., *Intellectual Property: the Law of Trade Marks, Copyrights, Patents and Trade Secrets* (USA: West, 2000).

such as copyright, with an intangible asset in which such a right might 'reside', such as a computer program. A computer program may, in fact, embody a number of different intellectual property rights, such as one or more patented algorithms,[10] lines of code that attract copyright protection as a 'literary work',[11] and perhaps even copyright in a graphical user interface,[12] which is what a computer user sees as a graphical display when he runs the program.

An additional conceptual difficulty about intellectual property rights to those unfamiliar with them is that the different intellectual property rights are significantly different in nature and scope; for example, copyright only protects the right holder against unauthorised activities involving *copying or reproduction* of the relevant work,[13] whereas a patent protects an inventor against virtually any unauthorised exploitation of a patented invention,[14] provided that the patent is valid.[15]

Akindemowo has attempted to explain the idea of 'intellectual property' in terms of its modern-day usage as follows:

> The term 'intellectual property' used contemporarily refers to the fruit of human intellectual endeavour and is now understood to encompass both literary or artistic creations and industrial property. Strictly speaking the term intellectual property refers not to the intellectual output in the form of an idea or particular expression *per se*, but to those limited aspects of the output that are protected by specific rights.[16]

Here, Akindemowo has identified both the broad range of interests encompassed by intellectual property laws in the modern world, and the fact that it is only certain aspects of human endeavour that are protected by intellectual property rights. In fact, intellectual property rights can be even more wide-ranging and confusing than this description suggests. The various sub-categories of intellectual property have expanded and developed in the information age to the extent that some of them seem to be potentially as broad and amorphous as the above description of intellectual property itself. Speaking of copyright law in the late twentieth century, Ricketson and Richardson noted that:

> Originally formulated as a law for the protection of literary endeavour, copyright is now the 'broad church' of intellectual property law, encompassing within

10 Different jurisdictions have, in fact, taken various views on the patentability of different kinds of algorithms at different times. The European Patent Convention currently excludes mathematical algorithms from patentability. Article 52(2)(a) excludes patentability of 'mathematical methods' which is basically another way of describing a certain type of algorithm. For a more detailed, although somewhat dated, description of patenting algorithms, at least in the computer software context, see Swinson, 'Copyright or patent or both: an algorithmic approach to computer software protection' (1991) 5 *Harvard Journal of Law and Technology* 145.

11 For example, the Copyright, Designs and Patents Act 1988, s. 3(1)(b) defines a 'literary work' for copyright purposes as including a 'computer program'. The Copyright 1968 (Australia) acknowledges a computer program as a literary work for copyright purposes: see, for example, s. 44E.

12 See discussion in op. cit., Swinson, fn 10, pp. 202–9.

13 See, for example, the Copyright, Designs and Patents Act 1988, ss.16–27.

14 See, for example, the Patents Act 1977, s. 60.

15 On validity of patents in the United Kingdom, see op. cit., Cornish, fn 9, ch. 5.

16 See Olujoke Akindemowo, *Information Technology Law in Australia* (Sydney: LBC, 1999), p. 138.

> it all manner of productions, from the humble railway timetable to the computer program. Large and important industries such as publishing, film, sound recordings, and computer software, to mention only a few, have their basis in copyright law, and copyright issues have frequently been the subject of public debate in recent years.[17]

Initially important to increasingly industrialised economies in the late nineteenth to early twentieth centuries, intellectual property has grown and adapted to economic changes in the societies it serves. As western societies have moved from an industrial to an information economy, a move that is now itself changing direction and expanding throughout jurisdictions, such as China and India,[18] new forms of intellectual property have been developed to take account of the shifting asset bases of many businesses. These moves can be rapid, and law reform efforts to accommodate and support these rights can take place equally quickly. The inherent vagueness and fluidity surrounding the nature and scope of intellectual property rights is in itself a significant problem for commercial lenders who are often unfamiliar with relevant rights in the best of circumstances. This difficulty is exacerbated in times of great economic change and uncertainty about the nature of many forms of intellectual property rights.

In order to better understand intellectual property from a loan financier's point of view, the following sections attempt to break down intellectual property into different categories, identifying those that are potentially the easiest to deal with in a secured financing context as a matter of law. However, even those categories that are easiest to deal with in a legal sense do carry inherent practical and commercial risks as loan collateral. These are also identified below.

The following discussion breaks intellectual property down into three categories: (a) traditional statutory forms of intellectual property; (b) newer *sui generis* statutory forms of intellectual property; and (c) forms of intellectual 'quasi-property' that tend to be created by common law and/or commercial practice rather than through legislation. These may be more risky to deal with commercially because of their less clear status as legal 'property'. They include things like confidential information/trade secrets and Internet domain names.

Traditional forms of statutory intellectual property

When most people think of intellectual property, three traditional sub-categories of the term come to mind: copyrights, patents and registered trade marks. Historically, these are the forms of intellectual property that have existed for the longest time and they are the forms with which commercial practitioners are generally the most familiar. Together, they protect much of what is identified by Akindemowo as coming within the ambit of the term 'intellectual property': that is, literary and artistic creations and industrial property. These are largely covered by copyright and patent law, while trade mark law protects commercial designations/source identifiers.

17 See Sam Ricketson and Megan Richardson, *Intellectual Property: Cases, Materials and Commentary* (Sydney: Butterworths, 2nd edn, 1998), p. 55.

18 See, for example, information at: www.indiachina.org/home.htm for details of trade developments in India and China; www.expresspharmapulse.com/ for details on India's growing pharmaceuticals/biotech industry; www.expresspharmapulse.com/ for details of developments in various industries, including e-commerce throughout Asia.

Although these three interests have a common law genesis, and to a greater or lesser extent, each of them has current common law counterparts,[19] they are now basically created/supported by statute in most jurisdictions. In the United Kingdom, the relevant legislation is: (a) the Copyright, Designs and Patents Act 1988 (the CDPA) for copyrights; (b) the Patents Act 1977 for patents; and (3) the Trade Marks Act 1994 for registered trade marks.

There are various other less 'mainstream' statutory intellectual property rights in the United Kingdom, such as various forms of design rights, plant breeders rights and database rights. These are discussed in the following section. Many of them can be extremely valuable in commerce and are good candidates as loan collateral. However, to the extent that they are created/protected through legislation, most of them have arisen subsequently to copyrights, patents and trade marks. Further, most of them borrow features from the copyright, patent and/or trade mark legislative regimes so it is worth first considering the more mainstream intellectual property rights and then moving to a consideration of the other statutory intellectual property rights.

Copyrights

As noted by Ricketson and Richardson,[20] copyrights were developed with the aim of protecting literary and artistic creations against unauthorised reproduction. The basis of copyright law today remains pretty much unchanged, although the scope of works that might attract copyright protection has increased over the years, as also observed by Ricketson and Richardson. A brief glance at the opening provisions of the CDPA affirms this fact. Under this statute, which reflects the copyright legislation in many other jurisdictions, copyright is extended to original literary, dramatic, musical and artistic works.[21] Copyright may also be asserted in sound recordings,[22] films,[23] broadcasts,[24] cable programmes[25] and the typographical arrangement of published editions.[26] Most of these categories of copyright works have extensive sub-categories, some of which are spelled out in the relevant legislation; for example, 'literary works' are defined as including compilations,[27] computer programs[28] and databases,[29] while 'artistic works' include photographs,[30] sculptures,[31] collages[32] and architectural

19 For example, most jurisdictions support both registered and unregistered trade marks, although unregistered trade marks tend to be protected by common law torts in the areas of passing off, unfair competition, misleading and deceptive conduct, etc. The law of confidential information/trade secrets supports common law/equitable actions in most jurisdictions to protect many secret processes and methods that might be protected by patent law if the right-holder were prepared to forego the secrecy.
20 Op. cit., Ricketson and Richardson, fn 17.
21 See CDPA, s. 1(a).
22 See CDPA, s. 1(1)(b).
23 See CDPA, s. 1(1)(b).
24 See CDPA, s. 1(1)(b).
25 See CDPA, s. 1(1)(b).
26 See CDPA, s. 1(1)(c).
27 See CDPA, s. 3(1)(a).
28 See CDPA, s. 3(1)(b).
29 See CDPA, s. 3(1)(d).
30 See CDPA, s. 4(1)(a).
31 See CDPA, s. 4(1)(a).
32 See CDPA, s. 4(1)(a).

works.[33] Copyrights generally last for the duration of the author's life plus 70 years.[34] They protect the author against unauthorised reproductions and distributions of the copyright work,[35] subject to certain defences, notably a group of activities generally classed as 'fair dealing' in the United Kingdom.[36] Fair dealing activities include things like reproducing portions of a work for research and private study purposes[37] or for criticism, review and news-reporting purposes.[38]

It is important to appreciate that copyrights in most jurisdictions, including the United Kingdom, are not registrable. The prevailing view on copyrights at the international level is that those who create should be rewarded per se for their creations by the grant of a copyright without being required to go to the time and expense of registering the relevant interest.[39] However, the United States, which is obviously a jurisdiction of major commercial significance involving copyrights, does have a specific copyright register distinct from Article 9, and copyrights generally are registered in the United States, particularly when they are utilised in commerce.[40]

This fact becomes important when considering the registration of security interests in copyright in a comparative context. In the United Kingdom, there is no potential 'dual registration' issue regarding a security interest in a copyright as there is no possibility of the interest being registered under the CDPA, there being no copyright register in the United Kingdom. However, in the United States, security interests in copyrights are often registered under the federal copyright register.[41] This has caused practical inconsistencies when lenders are unsure whether such interests should be registered under the federal register or the relevant state personal property securities register. The two forms of registers operate differently[42] and there is often a much greater time lag in attempting to register such an interest in the federal copyright register.[43]

33 See CDPA, s. 4(1)(b).
34 See CDPA, s. 12(2).
35 See CDPA, s. 16.
36 Similar defences in the United States are generally described as involving 'fair use'. See 17 USC § 107, Sheldon Halpern, Craig Nard and Kenneth Port, *Fundamentals of United States Intellectual Property Law: Copyright, Patent and Trade mark* (The Hague: Kluwer, 1999), pp. 112–31.
37 CDPA, s. 29.
38 CDPA, s.30.
39 Op. cit., Cornish, fn 9, para. 10–32 (Berne Convention conceives copyright as property flowing 'naturally' and without formality from the act of creation).
40 Op. cit., Halpern, fn 36, p. 44.
41 See: Bender, *Secured Transactions Under the Uniform Commercial Code* (Matthew Bender & Co, 2003), §§ 25.08[3][d] & [4]; *In re Peregrine Entertainment Ltd*, 116 BR 194, 11 UCC Rep Serv 2d 1025 (CD Cal 1990); Ronald Mann and Jane Winn, *Electronic Commerce* (New York: Aspen, 2002), pp. 501–14.
42 For example, the copyright register has historically been asset-indexed while the Article 9 personal property securities registers have been debtor-indexed.
43 Presently, according to the Copyright Office, if the applicant's submission is in order, a certificate of registration will be sent within approximately four to five months of submission: see 'I've mailed my application, fee and copy of my work to the Copyright Office. Now what?' US Copyright Office, available at www.copyright.gov/help/faq/faq-what.html. However, all mail currently sent to the US Copyright Office is being screened off-site prior to being delivered to the Copyright Office, thereby, adding three to five days to the delivery time and, thus, to the effective date of registration of the work. 'Delivery of mail to the US Copyright Office,' US Copyright Office, available at http://www.copyright.gov/mail.html. Contrarily, according to others, it usually takes 8–9 months to obtain a registration, unless

Where copyrights tend to be most relevant in secured financing is often in the context of businesses connected with the film and television industry, the music industry, the publishing industry and computer software production. These industries generate valuable copyrights which may be utilised as loan collateral. Attempts to utilise such copyrights as loan collateral raise certain legal and practical difficulties which are addressed below.

Patents

Patents create intellectual property rights in inventions that are new, involve an 'inventive step' and are capable of industrial application as contemplated in the Patents Act 1977.[44] The standards for patentability are high and patent applications are subject to scrutiny at the relevant patent office prior to a patent being granted.[45] Certain classes of inventions are specifically excluded from the patents system as non-patentable subject matter. These reflect the requirements of the European Patent Convention[46] to exclude from patentability: (a) discoveries, scientific theories and mathematical methods;[47] (b) literary, dramatic, musical or artistic works and other aesthetic creations;[48] (c) schemes, rules and methods for performing a mental act, playing a game or doing business;[49] (d) computer programs;[50] (e) the presentation of

an extra fee of $500 is paid to expedite the application, in which case a response is received within 10 days to 3 weeks. See, e.g., Stephen E. Feldman, 'Questions and answers about copyright,' found at http://www.jewelersresource.com/Business/Studio/Copyright.html.

44 See Patents Act 1977, ss. 1(1), 2, 3 and 4.

45 Pursuant to the European Patent Convention (EPC), the European Patent Office, set up in Munich with a branch at The Hague, grants European patents, upon application by the inventor or his successor in title, for a period of 20 years from the date of filing: see EPC Arts 58 and 63. A patent application may be filed in Munich, The Hague, or at the legally recognised central industrial property office or other competent authority of a Contracting State: see EPC Arts 65 and 75. The grant of a European patent may be requested for one or more of the (currently) over 20 Contracting States, which must be designated in the request for the grant: see EPC, Art. 79. Each copy of the patent application must, upon request of a Contracting State, be provided in the Contracting State's official language: see EPC, Art. 65. A European patent has the effect, in each of the enumerated Contracting State(s), of and is subject to the same conditions and laws as a national patent granted by that State, unless otherwise provided in the Convention: see EPC Arts 2 and 74. The protection afforded a European patent applicant, from the date of its publication under the EPC, Art. 93 are provided in Article 64, which includes the same rights as would be conferred by a national patent granted in each Contracting State. Any infringement of a patent is dealt with by national law: see EPC, Art. 64. Further, a Contracting State may extend the term of the European patent, under the same conditions as those applying to national patents. The full text of the European Patent Convention may be found at http://www.european-patent-office.org/legal/epc/. For an overview of the European Patent process, see Simon Mounteney, 'European Patent Office update,' available at http://thomsonderwent.com/ipmatters/euroiss/8199808/epodone.pdf.

46 See Convention on the Grant of European Patents, 5 October 1973. The subject matter patentability requirements of the Convention are set out in Articles 52 and 53: the Convention is available at: http://www.european-patent-office.org/legal/epc/e/ma1.html.

47 See Patents Act 1977, s. 1(2)(a).

48 See Patents Act 1977, s. 1(2)(b).

49 See Patents Act 1977, s. 1(2)(c).

50 See Patents Act 1977, s. 1(2)(c).

information;[51] (f) inventions the publication or exploitation of which would be generally expected to encourage offensive, immoral or antisocial behaviour;[52] and (g) inventions of animal or plant varieties or any essentially biological processes for the production of animals or plants.[53]

Most of these exclusions are self-explanatory. They relate to items that are covered by other intellectual property rights in an attempt to avoid overlap between the different intellectual property schemes; for example, it seems more appropriate for literary, dramatic, musical and artistic works to be protected by copyright than patent. Some of the exclusions relate to items that are best kept in the public domain as a matter of public policy; for example, it is regarded as inappropriate to 'propertise' basic scientific theories.

Two exclusions from patentability that may be particularly relevant to a consideration of secured finance practice are the exclusions of computer programs and plant/animal varieties from the patent regime in the United Kingdom and, in fact, throughout most of Europe. While computer code is protected as a 'literary work' under copyright law in most jurisdictions, copyright has certain shortcomings in this context. In particular, there are methods in practice for creating a competing computer program that functions similarly to the original without literally copying the underlying computer code.[54] Thus, a competitor can usurp the fruits of an original software producer's labours without technically committing a copyright infringement. As a result, some jurisdictions have proved to be more comfortable than others with the idea of extending patents to software-related inventions, at least in certain situations.[55] Software-related inventions are, in fact, patented through the European Patent Office, if drafted appropriately.[56] Thus, despite the wording of the Patents Act, it is important not to discount the possibility of patent rights in software, or a software-related invention, as a potential source of loan collateral.

Animal and plant varieties are another interesting exclusion from patentability in this age of advances in biotechnological research that often require significant funding. Associated with this exclusion is that of potentially immoral or offensive inventions, or inventions contrary to public morality. This exclusion may also have significant impact on the ability to commercialise biotechnological inventions if they are considered contrary to public morality. Genetically modified animals and crops may be implicated by this exclusion as well as by the more specific exclusion of animal and plant varieties from patentability.[57]

51 See Patents Act 1977, s. 1(2)(d).
52 See Patents Act 1977, s. 1(3)(a).
53 See Patents Act 1977, s. 1(3)(b).
54 As computer code can be expressed in a variety of different ways, but still perform substantially the same function, copyright protection can be of limited use. Copying function without literal expression has, in fact, become a standard practice in the computer software industry where 'clean room' copying has become commonplace. In 'clean room' copying, there are two teams of programmers from a competitor to the author of the original code. The first team ascertains the functionality of the program and describes it to the second team without reference to the literal code. Then, the second team writes new code to perform the same functions. See Hollaar, L. *Legal Protection of Digital Information: Chapter 2 (Copyright of Computer Programs)*, available at http://www.digital-law-online.com/lpdi1.0/treatise27.html.
55 Mark Lemley, Peter Menell, Robert Merges and Pamela Samuelson, *Software and Internet Law* (New York: Aspen, 2nd edn, 2003), p. 149.
56 Op. cit., Cornish, fn 9, paras 19-26–19-32.
57 Op. cit., Cornish, fn 9, paras 5-76–5-83.

If costly and potentially lucrative biotechnological innovations are unpatentable, it is arguably much more difficult to utilise them as security for a loan. It is possible that such inventions could be protected by trade secrecy. However, as the following discussion demonstrates, trade secrets are a risky and difficult form of loan collateral because of their legal nature and quasi-proprietary status.[58] Such innovations are unlikely to attract any other form of intellectual property protection that might be utilised as loan collateral other than possibly biotechnological developments relating to plant varieties. These might be potential subjects of the *sui generis* plant breeder's right that is created by the Plant Varieties Act 1997. This right is examined below.

In general, patent rights endure for a period of 20 years following the date of filing the patent application.[59] They provide much more powerful rights than copyright, as they protect the right holder against any unauthorised exploitation of the patented invention, not just unauthorised reproduction or distribution. Patents, once granted, are published on the patents register. The patentee enjoys the exclusive grant of patent rights for the duration of the patent term, after which time the invention passes into the public domain. This is regarded as the 'social bargain' for the grant of the patent. The inventor is given a limited period within which he has the exclusive right to exploit commercially the patent in return for disclosing his invention to the public and, ultimately, releasing the invention into the public domain. For this reason, in some contexts, inventors prefer to protect the fruits of their intellectual labours through trade secrecy/confidentiality. If they can effectively keep the relevant information secret, they can maintain their commercial advantage often for much longer periods than the maximum term of patent protection.[60]

Although patents sound like very powerful intellectual property rights in practice and thus, perhaps, ideal candidates for a secured financing transaction, there are a significant number of commercial risks inherent in utilising patents as loan collateral. These are taken up in detail below. However, to summarise a few of the risks relating to patents per se, it is important to remember that the grant of a patent does not guarantee its validity. A competitor can always challenge the grant of a patent, and this often occurs as a counter-suit in a patent infringement action.[61] Thus, what appears at first to be a potentially valuable security may, in fact, turn out to be a costly legal liability.

The 20-year duration of a patent can also be a trap for unwary financiers. It is important to ensure that there is still sufficient legal 'life' left in the patent for the desired financing transaction. Engaging in a five-year financing transaction in the nineteenth year of patent that is unlikely to be renewed is a mistake that should be avoided. It should also be kept in mind that the fact that a patent term extends for 20 years does not necessarily mean that the commercial 'shelf life' of the relevant invention will match its legal life. Some inventions, notably software-related inventions, have a realistic commercial life span of much fewer than 20 years, so it is important for financiers to conduct due diligence exercises with respect to patent valuation prior to engaging in a financing transaction. The same is true for software copyrights.

Another general point to bear in mind about patents in the United Kingdom is that the Patents Act contains a compulsory licensing provision for patents. Section 48 allows persons other than the patentee to apply for a compulsory licence of a patent on grounds that the patent is not being worked effectively by the patentee. Although the

58 See Lipton, J., *Security Over Intangible Property* (Sydney: LBC, 2000), pp. 172, 185–7.
59 See Patents Act 1977, s. 25(1).
60 Op. cit., Lipton, fn 58, p. 170.
61 See Patents Act 1977, s. 72.

Act contemplates that royalties should be paid to the patentee on the grant of such a compulsory licence,[62] the existence of the compulsory licensing regime potentially does affect the level of control a patentee might exercise over his or her invention. As such, the commercial value of a patent in the hands of the patentee and, therefore, in the hands of a loan financier may be adversely affected.

Trade marks

Trade marks are the other major form of intellectual property right that can be very valuable and, in some circumstances, may be useful as security for a loan. The registered trade mark system was originally derived from common law tortious actions relating to passing off/misleading and deceptive conduct in commerce, particularly conduct that potentially confused consumers about the source of a particular good or service.[63] The registered trade mark system allows a business to register a mark that it uses in commerce to differentiate its products and/or services from those of its competitors. Section 1(1) of the Trade Marks Act 1994 defines a 'trade mark' as 'any sign capable of being represented graphically which is capable of distinguishing goods or services of one undertaking from those of other undertakings'. The section goes on to state that a trade mark may consist of words, designs, letters, numerals, or the shape of goods or their packaging.

As with patents, the grant and registration of a trade mark does not guarantee its validity. There are a variety of reasons why a trade mark may be removed from the register. If a registered trade mark is confusingly similar to someone else's earlier trade mark, and it is registered for goods or services similar to those for which the earlier mark is registered, the earlier mark holder may challenge the registration.[64] A mark can also be invalidated if it was registered in bad faith.[65] It might further be removed from the register for non-use,[66] or if the mark becomes the 'generic' name in a particular trade for all goods or services of a particular description.[67]

In terms of duration, a registered trade mark can last indefinitely provided that its validity/registrability is not successfully challenged and that the registration is renewed in accordance with the provisions of the Trade Marks Act every 10 years.[68] Thus, in terms of potential duration and value, trade marks can be very valuable business assets. One might therefore think that they would be ideal candidates as security for a loan. However, as with the other forms of intellectual property, there are significant risks in utilising trade marks as loan collateral.

Other than any potential concerns about ongoing validity that may be raised about a particular mark, it is important to remember that a trade mark is a source identifier. As such, its registration can only be maintained by a business validly using it as such with respect to particular goods and/or services. In essence, it is valuable in the hands of its owner, but may well be of limited value to anyone else. Thus, although a financier may be able to obtain, and to register, effective security over a trade mark, the financier may have very little recourse to the trade mark on default by the

62 See Patents Act 1977, s. 50(1)(b).
63 Op. cit., Cornish, fn 9, paras 15-04–15-07.
64 See Trade Marks Act 1994, s. 47(2).
65 See Trade Marks Act 1994, s. 47(4).
66 See Trade Marks Act 1994, ss. 46(1)(a) and (b).
67 See Trade Marks Act 1994, s. 46(1)(c).
68 See Trade Marks Act 1994, ss. 42 and 43.

security provider. There may well be no market for the trade mark in the event of a foreclosure on the security and commensurate attempt to sell the security provider's assets. As the following discussion demonstrates, this problem is not necessarily limited to trade marks as loan collateral. However, trade marks, by their very nature, especially lend themselves to this difficulty.

It is also important to realise that other valuable forms of source identifier exist in the modern world outside of the registered trade mark system. The common law still protects unregistered trade marks under tortious actions, such as passing off. In fact, the Trade Marks Act, s. 2(2) of specifically states that the registered trade mark system is not intended to affect the law of passing off. The sub-section also acknowledges the existence of unregistered trade marks and states that no actions lie under the Trade Marks Act to protect an unregistered mark.

The modern commercial world also boasts new forms of source identifiers that are technically outside the registered trade mark system unless they happen to infringe a registered trade mark. The obvious examples are Internet domain names[69] and meta-tags.[70] The United States has gone further than any other jurisdiction in suggesting that Internet domain names are, in fact, a new form of intellectual property akin to trade marks.[71] The Anti-Cybersquatting Consumer Protection Act of 1999 added several new provisions to the federal trade marks legislation in the United States. One of these provisions contemplated *in rem* proceedings against an Internet domain name in the event that an *in personam* defendant could not be located in a dispute over registration of a domain name.[72] However, the legislation stops short of actually defining a domain name as a trade mark per se. The legal nature of Internet domain names and their potential status as a new form of intellectual property is considered in more detail below. For present purposes, it is important to appreciate that registered trade marks are not the only valuable source identifiers utilised in business. Their value may be affected by new forms of source identifiers that potentially encroach into their markets.[73]

Sui generis *forms of statutory intellectual property*

While the above discussion has focused on the three traditional pillars of intellectual property law, this section focuses on some of the more unusual forms of *statutory*

69 An Internet domain name is basically an alpha-numeric/mnemonic/plain English expression connected to a numeric Internet Protocol (IP) address by a domain name registration authority such as VeriSign. For further information, see: http://www.verisign.com.

70 Metatags are self-selected keywords embedded in web pages in Hypertext Markup Language (HTML). These metatags are invisible to users but can be read by search engines to direct people to relevant web pages. See Raymond Ku, Michelle Farber and Arthur Cockfield *Cyberspace Law: Cases and Materials* (New York: Aspen, 2002), p. 318.

71 For a discussion of the 'proprietariness' or otherwise of Internet domain names, see Chander, 'The new, new property' (2003) 81 *Texas Law Review* 715.

72 See discussion in op. cit., Ku et al., fn 70, pp. 77–81.

73 For example, if a registered trade mark holder is forced to battle with a holder of a confusingly similar Internet domain name, this may affect the value of the trade mark holder's mark and overall business in a number of ways. The mark's value may be diluted by the Internet domain name. The owner of the relevant website and Internet address may be drawing custom away from the trade mark holder's business. Further, the costs of dispute resolution, which may or may not include litigation on a local or cross-border scale, will likely impact on the value of the business of the trade mark holder.

intellectual property right. These include registered designs, database rights, plant breeder's rights and rights in digital circuit layouts/semiconductor topographies. They are all created by statute as legal personal property rights, and are generally modelled, at least to some extent, on the more mainstream statutory intellectual property rights described above.

Design rights

It is questionable whether design rights properly belong in this category of intellectual property rights or in the earlier category of more mainstream intellectual property rights. Design rights are not *sui generis* rights in the same sense as database rights, plant breeders' rights or circuit layout rights. This is because design rights are not rights in a specific type of asset. They are a more 'generic' class of intellectual property right, somewhat akin to copyrights and patents. However, they are arguably a more confusing and less mainstream type of intellectual property right than patents, copyrights and trade marks, and so have been included here. In many ways, they operate as a 'gap filler' between these three more fundamental rights, comprising elements of all three. They are like copyrights to the extent that they protect 'artistic' aspects of industrial items. Registered designs, at least, are like patents to the extent that they provide exclusive rights to utilise a design for a set period of time.[74] Designs can also function somewhat like source identifiers in a similar way that trade marks operate in commerce. This is because registered designs have to be perceptible by the human eye[75] and may well, in some ways, serve to attract custom/identify source to the extent that they visually appeal to potential consumers of an article.

The United Kingdom has different classes of design rights under each of the Registered Designs Act 1949 and the CDPA. The more traditional form of design right exists under the former scheme and relates to features of shape, configuration, pattern or ornament applied to an article by an industrial process which can be judged by the eye.[76] There is also an unregisterable 'original design' right created by the CDPA, s. 213. This right relates to any aspect of the shape or configuration of an article, and covers some designs that would be excluded from registration under the Registered Designs Act. In contrast to the registered design right, the 'original design' right can cover designs that are not perceptible by the human eye,[77] and designs that are not 'novel' as required by registered designs law.[78] The intricacies of designs law are beyond the scope of this chapter. However, if a security provider seeks to utilise a design right as security for a loan, it is important for a lender to ensure that that person is the registered owner of a registered design right, or a valid owner of an unregistrable design right in an original design under the CDPA. Each of these rights is a personal property right.[79]

A registered design endures for an initial five-year period[80] that is extendable on application to the registrar.[81] The rights given by registration are set out in the

74 See Registered Designs Act 1949, s. 8.
75 See Registered Designs Act 1949, s. 1(1).
76 See Registered Designs Act 1949, s. 1(1).
77 See discussion in op. cit., Cornish, fn 9, para. 14-37.
78 See discussion in op. cit., Cornish, fn 9, para. 14-38.
79 See Registered Designs Act 1949, s. 2(1); CDPA, ss. 213(1), 215(1).
80 See Registered Designs Act 1949, s. 8(1).
81 See Registered Designs Act 1949, s. 8(2).

Registered Designs Act, s. 7. They basically comprise the exclusive rights to make or import for sale or hire, or to use in trade or business, an article in respect of which the design is registered.[82] Like patents and trade marks, registration of a design right does not guarantee its validity and its registration may be revoked on application of a person claiming that the design was improperly registered for various reasons set out in the Registered Designs Act, s. 11. Registered design rights are also subject to a compulsory licensing scheme in the United Kingdom, again much like patents.[83] All of these factors may affect the validity and/or value of a registered design in the hands of the right holder, and may therefore affect a decision to accept a registered design as security for a loan.

Original design rights under the CDPA endure for a period between 10 and 15 years depending on when articles made to the design are first made available for sale or hire.[84] Like copyrights, these design rights protect the interests of the right-holder only with respect to copying and commercial distribution of a design.[85] There is also a compulsory licensing system for these design rights that comes into effect in the last five years of a design right.[86] Again, this might affect the value and utility of such a right as security for a loan, depending on the circumstances.

Plant breeders' rights

Plant breeders' rights (PBRs) are an example of a truly *sui generis* intellectual property right created by statute. In the United Kingdom, the relevant legislation is the Plant Varieties Act 1997. This statute creates *sui generis* intellectual property rights in new varieties of plants as defined in s. 1(3). To qualify for a PBR, the relevant plant variety must be distinct, uniform, stable and new, as contemplated in s. 4(2).[87] The rights granted to the holder of a PBR are set out in s. 6(1). They include the ability to prevent anyone from engaging in a number of commercial activities with respect to the propagating material of a protected plant variety without authorisation.

The restricted activities include unauthorised selling, marketing, exporting, importing, stocking for commercial purposes and producing or reproducing relevant material.[88] There are exceptions for private and non-commercial activities, experimental activities and activities conducted for the purpose of breeding another plant variety.[89] PBRs are registrable and generally endure for 25 years, although rights in potatoes, trees and vines endure for 30 years.[90] As with patents and registered designs, there is a compulsory licensing regime for PBRs in the United Kingdom.[91]

Although these rights may seem somewhat unusual to those unfamiliar with industries involved in creating plant varieties, many potentially lucrative businesses engage in such activities. In many jurisdictions, vineyards/wineries are a good

82 See Registered Designs Act 1949, s. 7(1).
83 See Registered Designs Act 1949, s. 10.
84 See s. 216.
85 See ss. 226–227.
86 See s. 237(1).
87 These criteria are described in greater detail in Part I of Schedule 2 to the Plant Varieties Act 1997.
88 See Plant Varieties Act 1997, s. 6(1).
89 See Plant Varieties Act 1997, s. 8.
90 See Plant Varieties Act 1997, s. 11(1).
91 See Plant Varieties Act 1997, s. 17.

example of an industry heavily reliant on PBRs. They often develop vine varieties that are protected by PBRs, particularly in jurisdictions where patent protection is unavailable for plant varieties. These PBRs can be useful security for loan financing in developing such businesses.

Database right and semiconductor topographies design right

The final *sui generis* statutory intellectual property rights for consideration here are the 'database right' and the rights in semiconductor topographies, each created by regulations made under the CDPA. In the case of semiconductor topographies, the relevant regulations are the Design Right (Semiconductor Topographies) Regulations of 1989 (the Semiconductor Regulations)[92] and in the case of 'database rights', the relevant regulations are the Copyright and Rights in Databases Regulations of 1997 (the Database Regulations).[93]

The Semiconductor Topographies Regulations basically create a form of the unregistrable original design right created by the CDPA, s. 213. The main difference is that this design right subsists in a 'semiconductor topography'.[94] This is fundamentally a scheme that extends the existing original design right to computer chips/ electronic circuit layouts. The features of the design right in a semiconductor topography are very similar to those of the standard original design right, including the 10- to 15-year duration depending on when the relevant semiconductor topography was first made available in commerce.

The database right created under the Database Regulations is a little different. It reflects the implementation by the United Kingdom of the EU Database Directive.[95] The Database Regulations create a new *sui generis* intellectual property right in a database or compilation of information which may not be sufficiently original in the selection or arrangement of its contents to attract copyright protection.[96] The database right will protect a database if there has been a substantial investment in obtaining, verifying, or presenting the contents of the database.[97] Sufficiently 'original' databases will be protected by copyright law as 'literary works'.[98] Thus, the main difference between protection of a database under the copyright and database schemes is that copyright law requires some minimal level of originality or creativity to grant protection to a database, whereas the database right is granted on the basis of effort and/or resources put into the creation of a database. It is often difficult in practice to draw this line.

The leading American case on copyrighting databases/compilations has held that a white pages telephone book is not copyrightable because an alphabetical listing of telephone numbers is not sufficiently original to attract copyright protection.[99] However, in that case, the Supreme Court suggested that the originality requirements

92 SI 1989 No. 1100.
93 SI 1997 No. 3032.
94 See Semiconductor Topographies Regulations, reg. 2.
95 Directive 96/9/EC of the European Parliament and of the Council of 11 March 1996 on the Legal Protection of Databases.
96 See CDPA, ss. 1(1), 3A(2).
97 See Database Regulations, reg. 13(1).
98 See CDPA, ss. 1(1)(a), 3(1)(d).
99 See *Feist Publications Inc,* v. *Rural Telephone Service Co* (1991) 449 US 340, pp. 362–3.

for copyright protection in a database are fairly low level.[100] The database simply has to be more original than a basic alphabetical listing. A subsequent federal court decision in Australia considered the same issue and held that a white pages telephone book is copyrightable under Australian law.[101] Thus, the question of what databases are sufficiently original to attract copyright protection is very murky throughout most of the world. In any event, under the legislative scheme in the United Kingdom, it is possible for the same database to attract both copyright and 'database right' protection.[102] Databases can be very valuable business assets in a number of industries and, as such, may well be offered as security for a loan. Thus, it is important for financiers to understand the various intellectual property rights that may subsist in a database.[103]

Like copyright, database rights are not registrable in the United Kingdom. A database right is intended to last for 15 years from the date of completion of the database or the end of the calendar year in which the database was first made available to the public.[104] However, because database rights can be extended as a result of making successive additions, deletions and/or alterations to a relevant database,[105] a database right can effectively last indefinitely provided that it is regularly updated.[106] Unlike copyright which focuses on reproduction and dissemination of copyrighted material, database rights prevent the unauthorised extraction and/or reutilisation of database contents.[107] Exceptions are granted for lawful users of a database right that has been made available to the public for purposes of illustration for teaching or research, provided the purposes are not commercial in nature.[108]

Colloquial and common law intellectual property

The final class of intellectual property financiers need to be aware of is a group of interests that I have tentatively identified as 'colloquial and common law' intellectual property. This is a somewhat miscellaneous category involving valuable products of the human mind that are not the subject of clear statutory property rights. The category includes 'generic' rights created under the common law and/or equity such as rights in trade secrets/confidential information and unregistered trade marks. Also included are specific valuable assets that are not intellectual property rights per se, although they may comprise, contain and/or coincide with various intellectual property rights. These are often referred to *colloquially* as 'intellectual property', when this

100 See *Feist Publications Inc,* v. *Rural Telephone Service Co,* 449 US 340, pp. 358–9.
101 See *Telstra Corporation Limited* v. *Desktop Marketing Systems Pty Ltd,* FCA 612 (2001), available at http://www.austlii.edu.au/au/cases/cth/federal_ct/2001/612.html. This decision was unsuccessfully appealed to the full Federal Court and an application for special leave to appeal to the High Court was rejected in 2003.
102 See Database Regulations, reg. 13(2).
103 For a more detailed examination of the various different intellectual property interests that may exist in a database and strategies for dealing with them in the secured finance context, see Lipton 'Security interests in electronic databases' (2001) 9 *International Journal of Law and Information Technology* 65.
104 See Database Regulations, reg. 17(1) & (2).
105 See Database Regulations, reg. 17(3).
106 Ian Lloyd, *Legal Aspects of the Information Society* (London: Butterworths, 2000), pp. 189–90, Mark Davison, *The Legal Protection of Databases* (Cambridge: Cambridge University Press, 2003), pp. 92–3.
107 See Database Regulations, reg. 16.
108 See Database Regulations, reg. 20.

appellation is not, strictly speaking, correct. They are rather assets that may comprise one or more intellectual property rights. An example is an Internet domain name. Domain names are not necessarily trade marks but may act as source identifiers and often will coincide with one or more trade marks.[109]

The main point to make about these types of quasi-intellectual property is that they tend to be risky forms of loan collateral for a financier to rely on. This is because of their equivocal legal status as well as some of the practical difficulties in dealing with them as security for a loan that are detailed in the following discussion. Where a business boasts mainly these classes of valuable assets and seeks loan finance, the best type of security for a financier to employ is probably a general floating charge, along with personal securities such as guarantees from directors and perhaps fixed securities over the directors' personal assets where possible.

Intellectual property as security for a loan: some potential pitfalls

Legal/conceptual issues

This section considers some of the main problems that financiers may face in utilising intellectual property as security for a loan. It is divided into three sections: (a) legal/conceptual issues; (b) commercial problems; and (c) issues related to registration. A move from the current secured finance system in the United Kingdom to a system such as that suggested in the Law Commission's Final Report on *Company Security Interests* of 2005 might resolve some of these issues, notably the dual registration problem. However, amending the system in this way will likely only have a limited impact on the difficulties financiers currently face in utilising intellectual property as loan collateral.

In terms of legal/conceptual issues inherent in attempts to utilise intellectual property as security for a loan, one of the most salient problems is whether a particular intellectual asset classifies as 'property' at law. Most of the existing forms of security transaction in the United Kingdom rely on manipulating legal and/or equitable proprietary interests in loan collateral. Legal mortgages require an assignment of legal title to the relevant property, while equitable mortgages and charges are premised on the existence of equitable interests in personal property.[110]

As noted above, all of the forms of intellectual property created by statute are unequivocally classes of personal property. This is made expressly clear in the statutes creating the relevant intellectual property rights.[111] However, the common law/colloquial forms of intellectual property discussed above are more problematic. It is not accepted as a matter of common law that valuable assets like trade secrets/confidential information and unregistered trade marks are forms of legal property. They may

109 A domain name may correspond with a registered trade mark, or it may in fact become an unregistered/common law mark if it develops significant goodwill in the 'customer recognition' sense. However, the registration of a domain name per se does not automatically give the registrant trade mark rights in it, unless it is also registered as a trade mark at the same time.

110 Craig Wappett and David Allan *Securities Over Personal Property* (Sydney: Butterworths, 1999), p. 6.

111 See: Patents Act 1977, s. 30(1); Registered Designs Act 1949, s. 2(1); Copyright, Designs and Patents Act 1988, s. 90(1); Trade Marks Act 1994, ss. 2(1), 24(1); Plant Varieties Act 1997, s. 12; Copyright and Rights in Databases Regulations 1997, reg. 13(1).

well be protected by various causes of action, including breach of contract,[112] the equitable action for breach of confidence,[113] the common law action for passing off,[114] etc. However, describing them as property and attempting to assign legal and/or equitable property interests in them to financiers is probably beyond the formal reality of the situation. As noted above, there is no problem with taking a general floating charge supported by personal securities given by directors in respect of companies that rely mainly on these types of assets for their value. However, it may be difficult to deal with these items directly as subjects of a security transaction.

Where the valuable assets in question are things like computer software and electronic databases, it may be possible to take security over copyrights and other intellectual property rights subsisting within those assets. However, it is important to recognise that it makes little conceptual sense to take a legal or equitable mortgage or charge over computer software per se as distinct from, say, the copyright in the software. This is because the software per se is not a form of legal property right. This is one area where a north-American style security system, such as that found in Article 9 of the Uniform Commercial Code in the United States, may be helpful. As the focus in that system is not on *forms* of security transaction, but rather on transactions that *function* as security, there may be fewer conceptual problems with taking security over an asset like a trade secret or computer software program.

Another legal/conceptual problem with intellectual property, particularly intellectual property created by statute, is its 'legal life'. Many of the classes of valuable statutory intellectual property have legislated expiration dates, such as the 20-year legal life of a patent. Additionally, many intellectual property rights can be invalidated subsequent to the initial grant of the right; such as when a trade mark is challenged for becoming 'generic'.[115] This is a different question from loss of *commercial* value. Any asset, including intellectual property, can lose its commercial value for a number of reasons including changes in a relevant market for the particular asset. Physical assets obviously do not have automatic expiration dates on their existence like some intellectual property. These expiration dates, coupled with the possibility of invalidation of the relevant right, can pose great risks for a financier. A lender may believe there is a valuable asset securing a loan only to find the very existence of the asset brought into question. The issue of specific difficulties for financiers relating to the *commercial* life of intellectual assets is taken up in the following section. The problem of the limited legal life of an intellectual asset will persist regardless of the secured finance laws in place in a particular jurisdiction.

Commercial problems

Outside the legal/conceptual issues identified above, a number of significant commercial/practical issues arise in attempts to use various classes of intellectual property as loan collateral. Most of these problems will persist regardless of the registration system in place for security interests in intellectual property. The most salient practical problems may be classed into three categories: (a) ascertaining ownership

112 Op. cit., Cornish, fn 9, para. 8-06–8-07 (historical relevance of contract law to the action for breach of confidence).

113 Ibid., ch. 8.

114 Ibid., paras 16–01 - 16–47.

115 Op. cit., Cornish, fn 9, paras 17-4–17-75.

of relevant intellectual property rights; (b) value of intellectual property rights; and (c) international/cross-border issues.

Ascertaining ownership of intellectual property

Ascertaining ownership of intellectual property rights may be more difficult than it first appears. For one thing, not all intellectual property rights are registrable. Copyrights, for instance, come into existence as soon as a relevant work is 'fixed' in a tangible form.[116] Copyrights can also be assigned from one person/business to another, and other interests can be created in them such as licences and securities. In order for a lender to ascertain who is the owner of what rights in a copyright work, it is necessary to undertake a variety of due diligence exercises.[117] These can be time consuming and expensive. The lender needs to establish whether the costs of such an exercise are justified in terms of the importance of relying on the copyright as collateral in any given transaction.

Even registrable intellectual property rights raise potential problems in terms of effectively ascertaining ownership. The registration of patents and trade marks does not guarantee their validity. Patent and trade mark registration can always be challenged on a variety of grounds. The same rings true of other less 'mainstream' registrable intellectual property rights such as PBRs. Obviously, this problem is not confined to intellectual property. In some contexts, it might also be difficult effectively to ascertain the ownership of tangible property that might be offered as loan collateral. However, it is probably fair to say that intellectual property generally raises greater risks in this area because of the number of people who might potentially contest the validity of a particular intellectual property right; for example, competitors in a relevant field.[118]

Value of intellectual property rights

In terms of commercial value, intellectual property rights raise significant risks that are not inherent, or at least not to the same extent, in much tangible personal property that might be offered as loan collateral. For one thing, it can be notoriously difficult to value intellectual property from an accounting point of view.[119] Some intellectual property only flourishes in the hands of its creator(s) and some intellectual property is very specific to a particular market. This may also be true to a certain extent of physical assets. Certain plant and equipment may be very specific to a particular industry, and may have limited commercial value outside that industry.

116 Op. cit., Cornish, fn 9, paras 10-33–10-34.

117 These might include requiring as much documentation as available from the security provider in relation to the development and ownership of the copyright work, and searching as many relevant intellectual property and securities registers as possible, particularly in relation to a business with a copyright that may be utilised in more than one jurisdiction in commerce. Op. cit., Wappett, fn 110, pp. 151–2.

118 Good examples in the patent context are seen in the American cases of: *State Street Bank & Trust Co* v. *Signature Financial Group, Inc*, 149 F 3d 1368 (Fed Cir, 1998) and *Amazon.com, Inc* v. *Barnesandnoble.com, Inc*, 73 F Supp 2d 1228 (WD Wash 1999); 239 F 3d 1343 (Fed Cir 2001).

119 On approaches to valuation of intellectual property, see Smith 'Business, economic and valuation issues', ch. 8, in Howard Knopf (ed.), *Security Interests in Intellectual Property* (Thomson/Carswell, 2002).

However, this probably does not arise to the same extent as it does with intellectual property. If an intellectual asset has limited, or no, value outside the business providing security, it will be of limited use as loan collateral if the financier is concerned with the possibility of a default sale.

The limited commercial 'shelf life' of an intellectual asset can raise similar problems. Intellectual property rights in computer software arguably retain commercial value for a much shorter period than their strict legal duration. Whereas a computer software manufacturer may assert copyright in a program for the programmer's life plus 70 years,[120] the actual commercial value will likely be somewhere between 18 months and three years. Thus, a financier should not be lulled into a false sense of security (no pun intended!) by the suggestion that a software copyright endures for many years. In actual fact, it may be worthless as a matter of commercial practice in a considerably shorter time than the legal duration of the copyright.

Other issues to bear in mind when dealing with interests in computer software as collateral include the necessity of the lender being physically able to access the software on a default sale. This may mean that the lender has to ensure it has access rights over any physical media in which the software is stored.[121] Further, because software tends to be an incrementally developing industry, it is important that a financier takes security over the relevant rights in future iterations of software that is being utilised as collateral. There is little point in being able to assert rights only in the first generation of a software product that has now moved on to its sixth generation where there is no residual market for the first generation.

Another potential problem for financiers that relates to the value of intellectual property is the possibility, in certain situations, of a competitor of the security provider 'designing around'[122] a patent or reverse engineering a copyrighted asset[123] and going into competition with the security provider. This can significantly lessen the value of the initial intellectual asset in the hands of the security provider if the competing product encroaches into the security provider's market. An obvious example occurs in the computer software business where a security provider may be asserting copyright in a particular piece of software. There are a variety of reverse engineering techniques that involve the creation of a new software product that functions similarly, or even identically, to the original product without literally copying the source code of the original program.[124] Thus, there is commercial competition without any copyright infringement.

Even where there is a potential for patent or copyright infringement by a competitor, a lender probably wants to avoid a situation where its security provider has to bring infringement proceedings against a competitor to the extent that this can be avoided.[125] This kind of situation might well impact on the financial position of the

120 See CDPA, s. 12.

121 See: op. cit., Lipton, fn 58, p. 196; Pollard 'Aspects of lenders' security over computer software copyright' (1995) 6 *Australian Intellectual Property Journal* 80, pp. 82–83.

122 It is possible for a competitor of a patentee to 'design around' a patent by creating a functionally similar invention without technically infringing the terms of the invention as claimed in the patent. See op. cit., Lipton, fn 58, p. 184.

123 As noted above, a variety of techniques are developing in the software context to copy the functionality of a software program without literally copying the underlying copyrighted source code. See fn 54 above.

124 See fn 54 above and the main text thereat.

125 A financier will likely also want to avoid a situation where the security provider might be infringing someone else's intellectual property rights. This can also adversely affect the value

security provider and, possibly, ultimately on the lender's position, particularly if the validity of the relevant intellectual property right is called into question in the relevant proceedings.

Some writers have suggested that in these kinds of situations, lenders should ensure that they have a legal mortgage, rather than an equitable security, over the relevant intellectual property so the lender can take more control of any proceedings that might impact on the value of the security.[126] This would also enable the lender to obtain the benefit of any remedy granted by a court in its own name, which could be particularly valuable in a situation where a security provider has gone into default. There are, however, downsides to a legal mortgage in this context, involving a legal assignment of the relevant intellectual property to the lender and a licence-back to the security provider. For one thing, this arrangement involves putting the ultimate responsibility on the lender for other incidents of legal ownership of the intellectual property such as maintaining registration formalities of a registered trade mark.[127]

International/cross-border issues

Another issue for lenders to bear in mind in relation to intellectual property is that it has international dimensions unlike physical assets. Although intellectual property is generally a matter of relatively well harmonised national laws,[128] there is still a cross-border/international dimension to it, particularly in an increasingly globalised business community. This certainly has the potential to create headaches for anyone, including a financier, attempting to protect and assert legal or equitable interests in relevant assets.

It is probably no longer sufficient for a security provider to simply grant a security to a lender over the local form of many types of intellectual assets. Lenders increasingly have to look at the international picture. Does anyone else hold a similar copyright/trade mark/patent in another jurisdiction that could impact on the value of the security provider's business? If not, should the lender insist that the security provider register relevant copyright[129]/trade mark/patent rights in other jurisdictions to

of the security if the security provider has to go to the expense of defending an action or paying a settlement to another intellectual property owner. If such a dispute results in the loss of the intellectual property to the security provider, or its continued use on payment of significant licensing fees, this can have major adverse flow-on effects to the lender.

126 In the context of security over copyrights, see, for example, John Swinson 'Security interests in intellectual property in Australia', in Howard Knopf (ed.), *Security Interests in Intellectual Property* (Canada: Carswell, 2003), p. 393 (talking about taking a legal mortgage over a patent to obtain greater control over the patent).

127 With a trade mark as security, there is the associated risk that a situation where the lender was the legal title holder would create a risk that the mark in question would be held to be invalid for non-use because the lender *per se* has no intention of using the mark in the manner contemplated by the trade marks legislation. For an analysis of these risks in Australia, see op. cit., Lipton, fn 58, pp. 110–11.

128 The international harmonisation of intellectual property law is largely coordinated through international bodies such as the World Intellectual Property Organization (WIPO) and the World Trade Organization (WTO). A number of international treaties on intellectual property are administered by these bodies. For a full list of international intellectual property treaties administered by WIPO, see http://www.wipo.org/treaties/en/index.html.

129 Some jurisdictions, such as the United States, do have copyright registers and it is important for lenders to be aware of this when contemplating the use of copyright as loan collateral.

protect its commercial assets in the home jurisdiction and/or in the event that it chooses to expand to other jurisdictions? Trade marks and Internet domain names, in particular, have the potential to be used globally, as do many digital assets that can be shared online such as digital music products, digital video products, digital databases, software, etc.

Financiers considering these types of intellectual assets as loan collateral should formulate an appropriate set of due diligence exercises prior to extending funds to a borrower to ensure that their securities will be adequately protected in the global context.[130] Again, it will be an open question whether the costs of undertaking these due diligence exercises are justified by the benefits of the specific intellectual property security to the financier.

Dual registration

One of the more obvious problems when thinking about personal property security law reform and intellectual property is the issue of registration of relevant security interests. As noted above, a number of intellectual property systems include specialist registers for certain legal and equitable interests in the property in question. Historically, these registers, such as the patents and trade marks registers and the designs register, have been asset-indexed and have attempted to create a relatively comprehensive record of legal and equitable interests in the relevant property right.

In the United Kingdom, security interests over personalty have predominantly been registered as corporate charges under the companies legislation.[131] The corporate charges register is debtor-indexed, and generally requires registration of charges over the mainstream forms of intellectual property. Section 860(7)(i) of the Companies Act 2006 currently requires registration of a charge on intellectual property which is defined as including patents, trade marks, registered designs, copyright and design rights, as well as any licences in respect of any such rights.[132]

This obviously raises the potential for 'dual registration'. On which register should a lender lodge its security interest over an asset such as a patent or trade mark, or indeed a registered design right or PBR? If the relevant intellectual property statute conflicts on priority questions with the corporate charges law, which system should govern a priority dispute between chargees? The dual registration issue does not arise for security interests over intellectual property for which there is no specialist register – copyrights, database rights and original design rights under the CDPA in the United Kingdom. Securities over these assets presumably can only be registered under the Companies Act, and priority questions between chargees would be determined under that legislation.

Although the dual registration issue has caused some confusion in the United States,[133] there has been no significant litigation on the issue in other jurisdictions that

130 Such procedures could involve detailed checks of business records relating to the ownership and value of the relevant intellectual property, and searches of any applicable securities and/or intellectual property registers in relevant jurisdictions.

131 See generally, Companies Act 2006, ss. 860 and 861.

132 See Companies Act 2006, ss. 860(7)(i) and 861(4). Note also Law Commission Consultation Paper 164, above fn 2, p. 29.

133 While the *Peregrine* case (*In re Peregrine Entertainment Ltd*, 116 BR 194, 11 UCC Rep Serv 2d 1025 (CD Cal 1990)) suggests that securities over copyright in the United States should be registered on the federal copyright register, other American courts have held that securities

have considered amending, or that have amended, their personal property securities laws in line with the American model in recent years.[134] The Law Commission proposal suggested avoiding the problem by effectively requiring all charges over intellectual property to be registered as corporate charges[135] alongside any registration that may be required under a specialist intellectual property register.[136] However, where an intellectual property statute sets out a scheme for governing priorities in charges over the relevant asset, that scheme will govern those issues.[137] Patents and registered designs are the obvious examples here.[138] If the Law Commission's proposals were ever to be implemented, then this scheme would be likely to remove any potential 'dual registration' problems that could otherwise arise in Britain in relation to company securities over intellectual property.

Conclusions

Despite the Law Commission proposals, there are still a myriad of legal and commercial reasons why relying on intellectual property as security for loans can be more difficult, and more risky, for financiers than dealing with more 'traditional' assets as security. The decision for a financier as to whether to engage in a transaction involving the use of intellectual property as loan collateral is much more likely to revolve around commercial costs and risks inherent in the transaction than around the precise nature of the legal system put in place to deal with personal property security transactions. The system proposed by the Law Commission may help to make securities over intellectual property less complex in a strictly formal sense. However, despite the fact that the government has shown no desire to implement the Commission's proposals, the fact remains that this is generally the least of a financier's worries when dealing with intellectual property in a secured financing context.

At the end of the day, the major issues facing lenders considering utilising intellectual property as security for a loan will not be resolved, even in small part, by an overhaul of the personal property securities system. These issues require moves to educate lenders about the legal and commercial nature of intellectual assets, and the due diligence measures that need to be put in place when employing them as loan collateral. It may be that the most cost effective way to deal with any intellectual asset is in the context of a more general security interest, like the floating charge in current finance practice, supported by personal guarantees given by appropriate company officers.

Alternatively, it may be more cost-effective to the economy as a whole if businesses with a predominantly 'intellectual' asset base seek financing from venture

over trade marks and patents, other than securities created by assignment of title, should be registered under state Article 9 registers; see: *Moldo* v. *Matsco, Inc* (*In re Cybernetic Services, Inc*), 252 F 3d 1039 (9th Cir June 6, 2001) on registration of securities over patents; *In re Together Development Corporation*, 227 BR 439 (Bankr. D. Mass. 1998) on the registration of securities over trade marks.

134 Obvious examples of such jurisdictions are Australia, New Zealand and Canada, as well as the United Kingdom. As noted above, the Canadian Law Commission has recently considered the issue: see fn 1 above.

135 In fact, all charges would be registrable unless specifically excluded under the proposed system: see Final Report 296, above fn 6, para. 2.3(6).

136 Ibid., para. 3.41.

137 Ibid., para. 3.235.

138 Ibid., para. 3.233.

capitalists rather than loan financiers. Venture capitalists are likely to take significant proprietary interests in the business as a whole, including relevant intellectual assets. Further, they are set up to manage the risks inherent in their financing portfolios in a way that is probably superior to many banks and other traditional debt financing institutions in this context. In fact, this is what has happened throughout many major trading jurisdictions in practice. It should also be noted that traditional debt financiers mainly need to understand security over intellectual property in the context of larger financing transactions in which the security over intellectual property is not the major part of the overall security package provided to the lender, but is only a small proportion of the security provided. If this is the case, lenders will have to think carefully about how much cost and effort to undertake in order to effectively secure the relevant intellectual property. Once again, it will probably not much matter to lenders in this context what legal system is in place for personal property securities, other than to the extent it simplifies the formal aspects of their overall security transaction. Thus, it is probably sensible for any future law reform initiatives to focus, as they have in the past, on utilising other types of assets as security, and to make some clear and consistent incidental provisions about how different forms of intellectual property should be treated as loan collateral, specifically in terms of where relevant securities should appropriately be registered.

9 Technology-based small firms and the commodification of intellectual property rights

Iwan Davies

Introduction

Intellectual Property (IP) is 'property' in the sense that it can be bought, sold, licensed or traded in the same way as any other form of property.[1] The value of such assets relative to physical and financial assets has increased considerably over the last 30 years and such rights often comprise the foundation for market dominance, as well as continuing profitability for leading companies. As such, the commercial exploitation of IP rights is pivotal to the development of many enterprises.

There exists a tension in the present legal position between, on the one hand, an intellectual property legal regime where the focus is to reward endeavour by protecting, through monopolistic rights, the originator of the IP and, on the other hand, a credit finance law which is concerned to provide a framework for conducting transactions that establishes an effective security regime for creditors with clear priority and enforcement rules following default. In particular, this phenomenon can be illustrated in the context of the financing of technology-based small firms because firstly, their value is often linked to their longer-term growth potential derived from scientific knowledge and their IP; second, they lack tangible assets which may be used as collateral; lastly, their products have little track record and may be subject to high rates of obsolescence.[2] In view of these characteristics, the risks for traditional finance is both high and problematical.[3]

The proper goals for an effective credit and security regime in IP will be elaborated in this chapter and the business financing context of, especially, technology-based small firms will be specifically discussed. Historically, IP has rarely been used

1 In England and Wales, the principal statutes are: Patents Act 1977; Trade Marks Act 1994; Registered Designs Act 1949; and the Copyright Designs and Patents Act 1988. Compare rights such as passing off or breach of confidential information which are essentially procedural in nature and are, as such, 'weaker rights' than the IP rights which arise under the intellectual property statutes.

2 See Bank of England Report, *Financing of Technology-Based Small Firms* (2001).

3 See generally Cosh and Hughes (eds), *Enterprise Britain: Growth, Innovation and Public Policy in the Small and Medium Enterprise Sector* (Cambridge: ESRC Centre for Business Research, 1998); Whincop (ed.), *Bridging the Entrepreneurial Financing Gap* (2001).

as security for debt financing[4] and, where it has been used, this has been in addition to security taken over intangible assets almost as a catch-all security provision with little acknowledgement being given to the value of the IP. Financing is traditionally provided by way of a combination of fixed charges over a business' tangible assets and a floating charge over all of the business' assets. Evaluation of IP as specific collateral has not generally occurred.

If companies with high ratios of intangible assets cannot raise finance by using their IP, they will be disadvantaged in terms of their ability to invest. The recent otherwise far-ranging *Gowers Review of Intellectual Property*[5] did not tackle this problem. In this chapter we shall consider the availability of IP as collateral in the context of the lending criteria adopted by financiers. This has implications for the reform of English personal property security law.

Business finance and technology-based small firms

At the outset in the development of a business, financing may be provided internally by the entrepreneur himself and other immediate backers.[6] By definition, there will be a limit to the financial leverage of such an individual which will be linked to his personal wealth and the value of his available assets including, perhaps, the home. Another form of internal financing is the granting of equity by way of a share issue which has the effect of splintering the ownership of the company. The issue here relates to a judgement by the investors as to the future prospects of the company and this will be linked to a view of the turnover and forecast turnover of the company. In the case of small- and medium-sized enterprises (SMEs), the number of such owners will be small, not least because the value of the company and the shares that can be issued are necessarily limited. If a finance gap is to be avoided, external finance will eventually be necessary[7] and this has been recognised by government with policies including investment subsidies,[8] 'public' venture capital,[9] fiscal incentives

4 See Bezant, 'The use of IP as security for debt finance' (1998) 1 *Journal of Knowledge Management* 237.

5 *Gowers Review of Intellectual Property* (December 2006).

6 Firms will usually use internal sources of finance before seeking external funding. See Cosh and Hughes 'Size, financial structure and profitability: UK companies in the 1980s' in Hughes and Storey (eds), *Finance and the Small Firm* (1994). This is sometimes referred to as the 'pecking order' hypothesis.

7 See Bank of England Report *Finance for Small Firms*, Eighth Report (2001). SMEs have in recent years become less dependent on external finance – only 40 per cent of SMEs sought external finance between 1997–1999 compared with 65 per cent in 1987–1990, while micro-businesses are the least reliant with only 30 per cent seeking external finance between 1997–1999; see para. 3.1 of the Report.

8 There are many examples, including the Small Firms Merit Award for Research and Technology; the Enterprise Fund; the Enterprise Management Incentives; University Challenge.

9 Government and European initiatives abound to promote venture capital-style investments, for example, Venture Capital Trusts. There are also fiscal incentives to encourage corporate venturing. For example, the Corporate Venturing Scheme allows investor companies to obtain corporation tax relief; defer tax on any gains made on corporate shareholding under the scheme; claim tax relief against income for capital losses (net of corporation tax relief) on disposal of shares. For a discussion see Bank of England Report, above fn 7, paras 4.50–4.64.

promoting R&D investment,[10] legal regimes designed to encourage innovation, of which IP rights are the most important[11] and, more recently, recommendations in respect of the role of the Patent Office in promoting IP.[12]

The role of equity finance in the development of technology-based small firms is potentially significant. In this respect, a general distinction should be drawn between private and public equity finance: Formal private equity is available from banks, special investment schemes and venture capital firms, while the informal market includes investments through business angels, that is, high net worth individuals willing to risk capital in smaller unquoted companies. A characteristic of venture capital or private equity finance is the fact that the venture capitalist will become an equity partner and will look to the longer term success of the business for a return on capital.[13] The proportion of external finance for SMEs accounted for by private equity is nonetheless small.[14] This reflects the fact that external equity is often perceived to be costly while for private equity, firms demand relatively high returns to offset the high level of risk involved – often including a 30–40 per cent equity stake and a seat on the board, as well as a management role.[15]

Formal private equity in start-up and early-stage companies can be regarded as a proxy of the finance available for small firms and, as we have seen, this is small. It may be that informal venture capital through business angels[16] can fill an equity gap, as they can provide, in return for an equity stake, both capital and also management expertise.[17] Potentially, this source of funding is very significant for small technological-based SMEs and a survey conducted in 2002 of business angels activity showed that three-quarters of business angels made investments averaging less than £50,000 while 40 per cent averaged less than £20,000 per investment.[18] Their ability to do this reflects a lower cost base and perhaps different aspirations. The problem

10 Tax credits are available for investments in R&D and these were introduced for SMEs in Schedule 20 to the Finance Act 2000. Similar relief was extended under Schedule 12 of the Finance Act 2002 to larger companies. The relief enables a business to write off immediately the whole of its capital spending on R&D against its trading profits.

11 See, for example, the Patents Act 2004 which in amending the 1977 Patents Act seeks to improve the patent legal framework, especially in respect of the enforcement of patent rights.

12 See Gowers Review, above fn 5.

13 The investment typically lasts for between three and seven years and the equity partner will bring, in addition to finance, expertise and experience.

14 From 1991–2000 only 3 per cent of external finance for SMEs was accounted for by private equity. See Bank of England Report, above fn 7, para. 4.4. The amounts available fluctuate greatly from year to year.

15 See Poutziouris, Cittenden and Michaelas *The Financial Development of Smaller Private and Public SMEs* (1999), Manchester Business School.

16 The conventional definition is that they are high net worth, non-institutional private equity investors, that is, they have the desire and have sufficient net worth to enable them to invest part of their wealth into risk-high return entrepreneurial ventures in return for a share of voting control, income and ultimately capital gain.

17 Angels vary in the way that they have an involvement in the investment. Active angels closely monitor the firm they invest in while passive angels provide money but rarely monitor the firm closely. They are usually part of an informal network led by active angels who perform the due diligence, syndicate the deal and manage the investments. See Acs and Prowse, 'Angel investors and the Angel Capital Electronic Network', ch. 3, in Whincop (ed.), *Bridging the Entrepreneurial Financing* Gap (2001).

18 See C2 Ventures, *InvestorPulse UK Angel Attitude Survey* (2003).

here is that most business angels wish to remain anonymous so it is difficult to measure the impact of this source of finance, although surveys have consistently shown that in terms of investments made in start-up and early-stage finance, the informal market is on a par with the formal market in the provision of such funds.[19]

Growing numbers of business angels networks are developing[20] and there is also some evidence of business angels and venture capitalists working together, including co-investing and sequential investing.[21] In this respect, a careful distinction should be drawn with corporate venturing, as this is a relationship between a larger and an independent smaller company 'in which both contribute financial, management or technical resources, sharing risks and rewards equally for mutual growth'.[22] The larger company may take a direct equity stake in the smaller company and in return has access to new ideas and skills and also potential attractive returns on new technologies.[23] A large corporate investor may be in a better position to assess the viability of an investment than perhaps a venture capitalist because it will be operating in the same market as the investee company which can then in some way mitigate the information asymmetries that can undermine the provision of finance to small companies.

Turning to the issue of public equity, the substantial fixed costs associated with flotation makes this an uneconomic option for SMEs, other than those with strong growth potential.[24] At the same time, as we have discussed, only comparatively modest sums are allocated by private equity by way of early-stage finance. In large measure this reflects the complexities of due diligence for technology projects[25] and this expresses itself in high information and transaction costs.

The identity of the financier will change as the amount financed rises and this is often linked to the stage of the development of the business.[26] During the early growth of a technology-based SME following the completion of development of IP, the demands for financing will include the need to fund market penetration and also

19 It has been estimated that the UK has nearly 18,000 actual and potential business angels investing annually approximately £500m. See Mason and Harrison 'Public policy in the development of the informal venture capital market', in Cowling (ed.), *Industrial Policy in Europe* (1999). See also *Sources of Business Angel Capital 1999/2000*, Survey of the British Venture Capital Association (2000).

20 See www.busangels.co.uk.

21 In their survey of angel activity, C2 Ventures, above fn 18, showed that approximately 55 per cent of business angels expressed a preference for risk-sharing when making investments but only around 25 per cent had actually done so. There are some successful angel syndicates, notably, Archangel and the Great Eastern Investment Forum.

22 See CBI Report, *Connecting Companies: Using Corporate Venturing For Growth* (1999).

23 The investee company obtains new risk capital and benefits from new technical and management expertise, as well as being able to take advantage of established marketing and distributions channels.

24 Capital markets will provide financing for smaller quoted companies. Second-tier markets have also emerged which provide smaller companies with access to public equity at an earlier stage than would otherwise be the case. Essentially, the UK has a three tier capital market structure – an Official List, the Alternative Investment Market with less onerous admission and trading requirements and also an off-market trading facility, PLUS Markets formerly known as OFEX.

25 The complexities of due diligence for high-technology projects requires an experienced venture capital team, but investors find it difficult to identify such teams.

26 The commonly accepted stages range from conception to development through to growth and maturity. For a general discussion, see Bezant 'The use of IP as security for debt finance' (1998) 1 *Journal of Knowledge Management* 237.

the need for working capital. Since the original investors will have absorbed the development risk and will have produced a product with a proven market potential, additional equity funding may therefore be restricted and debt financing will be needed to continue investment in research and development. However, the SME may still have a limited ability to service the debt and what is being sought is low-cost financing over a longer time to reflect the timescale necessary for the IP to reach its potential. The availability of debt financing at this stage may be crucial to the survival of the enterprise.

In the absence of further equity finance, the narrow issue revolves around the extent to which this gap can be bridged by debt finance which of course is predicated upon the ability of the SME to borrow money. In this respect, it is often the case that technologically based small firms have few tangible assets to offer as security, although at the same time they may have originated significant actual or potential IP. The extent to which debt finance is available for such small firms in the absence of formal collateral will now be examined.

The dilemma of credit and security and technology-based small firms

Debt finance is not equity capital. While asset realisation through repossession is the nature of such financing, this is the default scenario.[27] In practice, the credit stream will be based on the cash flow projections for the business and the ability of the SME from these to service the debt. The availability of such finance for SMEs has been the subject of government initiatives and the determining factors in lending decisions have been the object of Bank of England consideration.[28] It would appear that the major factors involved in the lending decision revolve around the business plan and the projections set out. At the same time, an assessment of the management team in terms of risk profile, including credit history, evidence of repayment capacity is made and in the case of start-ups, the applicant's willingness to invest in the business is considered by financiers to be essential.

There is evidence that significant levels of lending is available to SMEs on unsecured terms.[29] The major explanation for this is that, in small loans, the transaction costs involved are high, relative to the value of the loan,[30] while the availability of

27 There has been a change in the culture of dealing with corporate crises which has been recast by legislative changes brought about in the Enterprise Act 2002. This is discussed below. The emphasis is upon managing risk rather than mere debt collection although this approach is mainly focused on the largest companies. Significantly, ss. 1–2 and Scheds 1–2 of the Insolvency Act 2000 provide a 28-day moratorium to 'small' and 'eligible' companies when directors propose a company voluntary arrangement which protects them from winding-up petitions, administration applications, administrative receiverships and steps to enforce security. See: Finch 'The recasting of insolvency law' (2005) 68 MLR 713; Finch, 'Doctoring in the shadows of insolvency' [2005] JBL 690.

28 See Bank of England Report, *Finance for Small Firms*, Ninth Report (2002), paras 2.23–2.34.

29 In the USA, 40 per cent of debt issued to small businesses is unsecured. See, for example, Booth 'Contract costs, bank loans and the cross-monitoring hypothesis' (1992) 31 J Fin Econ 25. For a general discussion on unsecured debt within the UK, see Tudela and Young, 'The distribution of unsecured debt in the United Kingdom: survey evidence' *Bank of England Quarterly Bulletin*, winter 2003.

30 In the Bank of England Report Survey, above fn 28, para. 2.28, the availability of security was considered to be an important factor in lending to established businesses than start-up

credit is such, particularly credit card lending, that the taking of a security interest will not, in any event, inhibit the borrower's ability to obtain additional funds.[31] In addition, technological advances have provided mechanisms which enhance the information available to financiers in making lending decisions which in turn have lowered the general riskiness of loans. In fact, the development of credit and behaviour scoring systems have reduced the banks' reliance on collateral.

Scorecards are used for credit applications up to £100,000.[32] At the bottom end for small loans, the score is the primary decision maker but at the upper end it provides an aid to the lending decision. The use of scorecards and the confidence in the system is such that some banks are more willing to make smaller loans on an unsecured basis and there is evidence that lending up to £35,000 is likely to be unsecured.[33] Credit scoring actually enhances the attractiveness of unsecured lending because it provides an absolute reduction in the riskiness of small business lending, that is, the credit underwriting process is more sophisticated and less costly to administer than a non-automated system which requires investigations of assertions made and considerable experience is necessary for lending officers in making such decisions.

Despite the general availability of unsecured credit, the significance of security for financially distressed SMEs should not be underestimated. In an influential study conducted by Franks and Sussman,[34] the typical profile which emerged of an SME in financial difficulty was that there was one main bank lender[35] which held a fixed or floating charge, or both, over all or part of the firm's assets. As a secured creditor, the bank stands at the head of the queue to recover from the proceeds of the disposal of the secured asset what it is owed upon the insolvency of the debtor. It follows that the bank will exercise considerable control rights[36] in the event of insolvency and, historically, this was the case given that the bank as holder of a floating charge could appoint an administrative receiver.[37] Because of these control rights, Franks and Sussman found that banks employed sophisticated 'intensive care' processes for such firms in financial difficulties by being referred to their respective rescue unit. A large proportion[38] emerged from the rescue unit and either they were turned around or

because it was stated the former tend to borrow larger amounts and that security was usually required against larger loans of £25,000 or more.

31 In the USA, for example, credit cards provide the primary source of working capital for 5 per cent of small businesses. See Oppenheim, 'Bank financing up, loans from relatives down' [1997] *American Banker* 5. By using credit cards it is possible for a business to avoid the need to grant security to secure business debt.

32 See Bank of England Report *Finance for Small Firms*, Tenth Report (2003), para. 4.22.

33 See Smallbone and Deakins, *Ethnic Minority Businesses in the UK: Access to Finance and Business Support* (2003).

34 See Franks and Sussman, *The Cycle of Corporate Distress, Rescue and Dissolution: a Study of Small and Medium Sized UK Companies* (2002).

35 This is also borne out in the US literature. See, for example, Baird 'Security interests reconsidered' (1994) 80 Virginia LR 2249, p. 2263.

36 Security gives creditors access to managerial information and a right in certain circumstances to be represented on the board.

37 The Enterprise Act 2002 has replaced administrative receivership with administration as the process for dealing with financially distressed companies. This has changed the culture of the approach taken to insolvency. See op. cit., Finch, above fn 27.

38 The Survey by Franks and Sussman, above fn 34, identified that approximately 75 per cent emerged from the rescue units and avoided formal insolvency procedures. The remaining 25 per cent entered some form of insolvency, usually administrative receivership.

they would repay the outstanding debt by finding, for example, alternative banking sources. Typically, the bank would use its control rights as a secured creditor through leverage by forcing distressed firms to undergo restructuring and sometimes to replace their management.[39]

The ratio of security value and the interest charged was the least significant of all the hypotheses tested in the work conducted by Franks and Sussman, that is, offering security did not lead to a reduction or increase in the interest rates charged. This is not surprising as larger financially strong companies do not have an incentive to offer secured credit[40] because the financial strength of creditworthy companies leave little room for secured credit to enhance the attractiveness of a financing transaction.[41] While in the rescue unit the bank debt was secured, this was not a result of a 'bargain' with the bank in return for a lower interest rate: it was a precondition for being able to borrow at all. As the Bank of England has pointed out:[42] 'Ready access to finance when needed is often a more compelling consideration for small firms than is actual cost.' At the same time, the Bank of England Report noted that debt financing for small firms depends upon the value of the assets which could be given as security.

It would appear that a determining factor in the decision to lend is the availability of security, especially in the case of new companies with no established track record.[43] Small firms are most likely to fail and produce the least asset recovery value and this is a pattern which can be clearly seen during the last 10-year period.[44] Their overrepresentation in the statistics demonstrates the importance of the availability of security and this is especially the case when companies are facing a 'credit crunch', or 'liquidity crisis'. The effective creation of security interests in IP may therefore be of great importance to the survival of technology-based small firms with otherwise few tangible assets to offer as security.[45]

39 As a result of this tension, Franks and Sussman, above fn 34, found that rebanking often occurred. In respect of one of the banks surveyed, when customers entered their rescue unit they frequently terminated their relationship and banked elsewhere. Significantly, the bank charged lower interest to their customers than other banks with lower levels of rebanking.

40 The alleged advantage of lowering interest rate with security does not apply to financially strong firms because the issue of probable default is not a concern. See Mann 'Explaining the pattern of secured credit' (1997) 110 Harv LR 625.

41 See Lasfer, 'Debt structure, agency costs and firm's size: an empirical investigation' (24 November 1999) available at http://www.business.city.ac.uk/af/wopapers/mez/debtStructure.pdf. This is a study of all companies quoted on the London Stock Exchange 1984–1996 which showed that secured debt is negatively related to firm size. Indeed, the proportion of small companies' debt that is secured is three times (61 per cent) of that seen with larger companies (17 per cent).

42 Bank of England Report, *Finance For Small Firms*, Sixth Report (1999), p. 25.

43 See Bank of England Report, *Finance for Small Firms* Ninth Report (2002), para. 2.32.

44 Association of Business Recovery Professionals Tenth Report *Corporate Insolvency in the UK: a Decade of Change* (2002), p. 9.

45 SMEs generally report problems in raising finance. The ability to use IP as security might remove a major barrier to growth. See Hall 'Lack of finance as a constraint on the expansion of small innovatory firms', in Barber, Metcalf and Porteous (eds), *Barriers to Growth in Small Firms* (1989), pp. 39–57.

IP assets as collateral for technology-based small firms

Patents, trademarks and designs are registrable rights under the IP statutes which are fully transferable to third parties and are property rights in the sense that they are owned and are exclusive and binding against third parties.[46] This is the effect of registration. However, there is a conceptual difficulty underlying all three IP registration statutes, in that they seek to be both non-compulsory, as well as compulsory registration schemes. While the common law environment is that a legal interest binds the world, nevertheless, neither the Patents Act 1977 nor the Trade Marks Act 1994 establish a compulsory system of registration. As a result, legal interests are treated as equitable interests since they have no effect against a subsequent interest holder who does not have actual notice of their existence.[47] Actual knowledge gleaned outside of the registration process binds a potential lender. Significant evidential problems emerge and in this regard the registered intellectual property schemes could be likened to pre-1925 (unregistered) land schemes.[48]

At least in the case of registered IP there is a notice mechanism for equitable mortgages and charges and a process for creating security interests. This is obviously more problematical in the case of a non-registered right, such as copyright,[49] or a database right, because the financier who holds a legal title to the right under a legal mortgage has no mechanism of putting others on notice of the financier's interest through public registration. Of course, it may be possible to include publicly on a piece of art (in respect of a copyright or a database right) that the IP in question is subject to a security interest but this is not a commercial solution as it could give the wrong impression as to the financial means of the originator of the work of art. Furthermore, in the case of database rights, there is no means of registering any form of mortgage or charge under the Companies Act 2006 because while sections 860(7)(i) and 861(4) provide for registration,[50] this only extends to certain forms of IP.

In the context of creating effective security interests in IP assets, a priority dilemma can emerge between the companies charges register and the registers created under the IP statutes. If a charge is registered on the companies charge register and not on the relevant IP register, then it follows that this register will show that the patent, trademark or design right, is unencumbered. While the onus is upon the financier to search the registers, if this is not achieved, then apparently binding charges could be void in a companies context for failure to register in either register.[51] This is now

46 See: Patents Act 1977, s. 30; Trade Marks Act 1994, s. 24; Registered Designs Act 1949, s. 19. For a discussion, see the chapter by Lipton in the present volume, pp. 285–307.

47 See Townend *Using Intellectual Property as Security* (1996).

48 See Townend, op. cit., fn. 47 at p. 24.

49 An important recommendation arising out of the *Gowers Review*, above fn 5, is Recommendation 14a which envisages the establishment of a voluntary register of copyright. The purpose is not to link validity with registration but rather to facilitate the identification of copyright holders, especially 'orphan works', i.e. where users are unable to locate and seek permission to use works within the copyright period such as films.

50 For a general discussion, see the chapter by Lipton in the present volume, pp. 285–307.

51 For a discussion on the consequences of non-registration see Law Commission Consultation Paper 164 *Registration of Security Interests: Company Charges and Property other than Land* (London: The Stationery Office, 2002), paras 2.26–28.

expressly anticipated in the reforms set out in the Law Commission Report[52] where registration in the companies security register is necessary if a charge is to be effective in the debtor's insolvency, irrespective of whether the charge is also registered in the relevant IP register.[53] There is no constructive notice doctrine included in the reform proposals on the basis that the priority rule is that of notice filing and the first-to-file principle. Thus, registration in the specialist IP register is not constructive notice for the purpose of interfering with the priority regime in the company security register. Nevertheless, the priority rules which operate within the context of the specialist registries remain, and indeed will prevail over the general rule that priority is determined from the date of filing.[54] In effect, while it is necessary to register in the company's security register to preserve priority on insolvency, priority in respect of conflicting interests will be governed by the priority rules over such assets set out in the specialist register.[55]

In the case of an unregistered security interest in the relevant specialist IP register, the narrow issue is whether registration at the company charges registry is notice for the purpose of priority within that register. It is unlikely that registration at the companies registry will be notice for the purposes of the Patents Act 1977, since s. 33(1)(c) of that Act refers to knowledge, that is, where the subsequent interest holder 'did not know of the earlier transaction or event'. The Trade Marks Act 1994 provides that a later transaction will have priority over an earlier one if the party to the later transaction is ignorant of the earlier one.[56] The problem is that the Patents Act and the Trade Marks Act refer to actual notice being sufficient unless the interest is registered. Does this mean that unless the subsequent interest holder can be shown to have known about the previous interest he will not be bound by it? If so, constructive notice may be relevant in the sense that the subsequent interest holder should be deemed to have notice of a charge on the companies register where this must be registrable to have effect against third parties.[57] Interestingly, the Registered Designs Act 1949 does not even specifically refer to priority and, in this context, it would appear that the normal common law rules will apply, so that a party will be deemed to have constructive notice if the earlier transaction is validly registered under the relevant Companies Act.

It is absurd to refer to the need to protect unregistered equitable and legal interests by reference to an actual notice doctrine, since registration under the Patents Act and Trade Marks Act do not offer complete protection for potential creditors. The Acts omit to refer to actual or constructive knowledge per se, they simply refer to the fact that unless the interest is registered, only actual notice is sufficient. As such, the current

52 See Law Commission Report No. 296 *Company Security Interests*, Cm 6654 (London: The Stationery Office, 2005).

53 Ibid., paras 3.41, 3.231.

54 Ibid., para. 3.235.

55 See proposed Model Law Commission Company Security Regulations, above fn 52, p. 186, Regulation 25(1) (conflict with transactions registered in specialist registers).

56 See Trade Marks Act 1994, s. 25(3).

57 Compare negative pledge clauses which forbid the company to create any charge that will rank ahead of, or *pari passu* with, the floating charge. Such clauses are not registrable under the Companies Act, and even if particulars of it are included in the registration, subsequent creditors will not have constructive notice of it because the doctrine of constructive notice applies only to those items which must be registered. See Goode, *Commercial Law* (London: Penguin Books, 3rd edn, 2004), pp. 664–6 and contrast with de Lacy (ed.), *The Reform of United Kingdom Company Law* (London: Cavendish Publishing, 2003), pp. 369–80.

IP registries are concerned with documenting the conferral of rights, the identity of the original owner and all the assignees in the case of patents, trademarks and design rights and essentially were designed for transaction filing. Moreover, while the registration systems are ownership based, they do not necessarily show all ownership, for example, assignments do not have to be filed. The registration process is also flawed because while the patent system describes the rights that are claimed, trade mark registration does not describe the actual use made of the mark and non-use can lead to invalidity. At the same time, there is no official copyright register. The legal position is, therefore, highly problematical as the existing law does not facilitate the transfer of interests in IP and the exploitation of those interests. This brings into focus the issue of reform and specifically the treatment of IP assets in the debate over the reform of English personal property security law.

The ideology of the reform of personal property security law in England

Article 9 of the Uniform Commercial Code has significantly influenced the debate over the reform of personal property security law in England and Wales.[58] The draftsmen of Article 9 were concerned to expand the pool of assets available for security interests to attach[59] through the recognition of the floating lien, accompanied by a first to file priority rule and a notice-filing mechanism. In this regard, it is doubtful whether

58 In 1971, the proposed Lending and Security Act, suggested by the Crowther Committee, *Report on Consumer Credit* Cmnd 4596 (1971), leaned very heavily on Article 9. In addition, the Scottish Law Commission's Working Paper on *Security over Moveable Property* (1986), the Halliday Report, as well as the DTI Paper prepared by Professor Diamond, *A Review of Security Interests in Property* (1989) drew on the Crowther Report. The Diamond Report recommended that the law should be reformed by the introduction of a new law of security and the creation of a notice-filing system. The Halliday Report, while recommending the establishment of a register of security interests with notice filing, was more selective in its drawing on the Crowther Report and, in particular, avoided recommendations that would introduce alien concepts into Scots law. The Law Commission Consultation Paper, *Registration of Security Interests: Company Charges and Property other than Land* No. 164 (2002) in recommending the introduction of a new law on security interests drew heavily on Article 9 of the UCC and similar personal property security interests legal regimes. This was also the case in respect of the Law Commission Consultation Report, *Company Security Interests* No. 176 (2004). For a general review of the history of law reform in England, see the chapter by de Lacy in the present volume, pp. 43–80.

59 A distinction is drawn under Article 9 between the enforceability of the security interest *inter se* and as against third parties. An agreement which creates or provides for a security interest, together with 'attachment' of the security interest, are all that is required. Normally, three conditions have to be fulfilled for attachment to occur, namely, the parties must *intend* attachment; value must be given; the debtor must have rights in the collateral. In order to obtain priority as against *third parties* on the other hand, it is necessary to 'perfect' the security interest. This occurs when the security interest has attached and all the steps required for perfection have been completed, which means either possession or registration of a financing statement. See UCC, Art. 9–203(1). For a general overview see Davies 'The reform of personal property security law: can Article 9 of the US Uniform Commercial Code be a precedent?' (1988) 37 ICLQ 465.

any previous security statute has so warmly embraced the after-acquired property interest.[60]

The Article 9-type filing system promotes information exchange and acts as a 'bulletin board' by providing credit information to interested parties.[61] This is achieved through the search mechanism which reveals potential interests of prior secured parties so as to provoke inquiry. Without access to the filed financing statement, the potential creditor would only be able to rely on the representation of the debtor.[62] At the same time, the first-to-file priority rule provides the necessary incentive to use the filing system because it allows the creditor to stake a claim. Article 9 is a pure 'race statute' in which a subsequent creditor with notice will nonetheless prevail in verifying its claim based upon the fact of fixing priority by first public filing.

The most recent revision of Article 9,[63] which was implemented in 2001,[64] represents an expanded restatement of the law of personal property security. Article 9 has now been comprehensively reorganised, rewritten, renumbered and is an expanded restatement of the US law of personal property security. Not surprisingly, the new Article 9 (R9) was drafted by people who were moulded by the old Article 9[65] and, indeed, they took the concepts further by making it easier for financiers to create and perfect security interests in the various contexts in which secured financing is used.[66]

In the revision process of Article 9, the question of whether secured credit is efficient in an economic sense had little impact on the debate for reform. In large measure, this was because the whole efficiency debate was presented as a puzzle[67]

60 Article 9-204(1) of the UCC envisages that 'a security agreement may provide that any or all obligations covered by the security agreement are to be secured by after-acquired collateral' while Article 9-204(3) provides that 'Obligations ... may include future advances ...'.

61 See Alces 'Abolish the Article 9 filing system' (1995) 79 *Minnesota LR* 679.

62 If priority was dependent on the parties' own records for the determination of priority, this would give an incentive to competing creditors to manipulate their agreements and advance the relevant dates. See McDonnell, 'The floating lienor as good faith purchaser' (1977) 50 S *Cal LR* 129.

63 There is a Permanent Editorial Board of the UCC which includes representatives from the NCCUSL and ALI which meets twice a year to deal with problems of interpretation of the UCC and makes recommendations for revision to the NCCUSL and ALI. An earlier revision of the UCC was completed in 1972.

64 The revised Article 9 is referred to as R9. It came into force in July 2001 and has been adopted in all the states in the US, including Louisiana. The text can be found at http://www.accusl.org.

65 The Working Study Group consisted of 3 legal academics and 13 lawyers, the majority being senior counsel for asset financiers.

66 See Schwartz and Scott 'The political economy of private legislatures' (1995) 143 University of *Pennsylvania LR* 595.

67 Compare Scott 'The truth about secured financing' (1997) 82 *Cornell LR* 1436, p. 1437: '[T]he continuing publication of succeeding generations of articles exploring the topic has yielded precious little in the way of an emerging scholarly consensus about the nature and function of secured credit. Put simply, we still do not have a theory of finance that explains why firms sometimes (but now always) issue secured debt rather than unsecured debt or equity. Moreover (and because of the lack of any plausible general theory), we lack any persuasive empirical data to predict whether, in a particular case, a later security-financed project will generate sufficient returns to offset any reduction in the value (that is the bankruptcy share) of prior unsecured claims.'

as distinct from a demonstration of inefficiency.[68] There are limitations in the efficiency debate, not least because a zero-sum argument fails to address considerations of fairness and distribution on insolvency. While at first sight the recognition of security interests appears to be inconsistent with the *pari passu* principle of distribution, in practice, all this means is that creditors within a particular class must be treated equally within the particular distribution regime.[69] In effect, the distributional consequences of a secured credit regime are the major determinant in the setting of sound policy.[70]

The new Article 9 (R9) facilitates security interests in deposit accounts, expands the financier's automatic claims to proceeds of collateral, permits filing against a corporate debtor in its state of incorporation, even though the collateral assets are located in other jurisdictions, and also assists the securitisation of rights to payment.[71] Attempts made to make significant amendments in terms of approach to the reform process of Article 9 were unsuccessful. Thus, when consumer groups, for example, pressed for reform of Article 9, the eventual compromise between consumer groups on the one hand and industry representatives on the other was to leave matters where they were in terms of the original Article 9.[72]

R9 facilitates the taking of security and has expanded the pool of assets available on collateral, for example, by making it possible for formerly non-assignable rights[73] to be the subject of attachment and perfection, thereby facilitating credit. In this regard, R9 will have material distributional effects in bankruptcy, that is, secured claims will reach more of the assets in bankruptcy and the pool of free, unencumbered assets will shrink.[74] To deal with this distributional balance problem, it was

68 See White 'The politics of Article 9: work and play in Revising Article 9' (1994) 80 VA LR 2089. For a discussion on the secured credit debate from an English point of view see McCormack 'The priority of secured credit: an Anglo-American Perspective' [2003] JBL 389.

69 The reference here is to preferential claims on insolvency. In England, under Sched 6 of the Insolvency Act 1986, these fell into two main categories, namely, tax and employee claims. The Enterprise Act 2002 abolishes Crown Preference so that s. 251 deletes from the preferential debts list debts due to the Inland Revenue, debts due to HM Revenue & Customs and also social security contributions. Employee preference remains the justification being their inequality of bargaining power and consequently they may lose out in their employer's insolvency.

70 This matter was not considered by the Law Commission in their recent review of company security interests.

71 This is not to say that Article 9 is a wholly complete Code. For example, while bankruptcy cases will probably involve Article 9 issues, the substance of bankruptcy law is in the 1978 Bankruptcy Code. See Harris and Mooney 'Revised Article 9 and the Bankruptcy Code: policy and impact' (2001) 9 Amer Bank Inst LR 85.

72 While consumers are affected by some of Article 9's provisions, in particular the remedial regime, the difficulty was effective representation of their interests. Consumers suffered from agency costs in their legal representation or alternatively had to rely on self-appointed agents to guard their interest. See generally Janger 'Predicting when the Uniform Law process will fail' (1998) 83 Iowa LR 569, referring to some early success by the US Consumers Union 'in softening the effect of Article 9's remedial scheme on consumers' but this did not carry through to the final version.

73 Article 9-408.

74 See Warren 'The anti-bankruptcy act: Revised Article 9 and bankruptcy' (2001) 9 Am Banks Inst LR 3.

suggested that there should be a carve-out of the debtor's assets[75] requiring the trustee in bankruptcy to set aside 20 per cent of the proceeds of sale[76] of the collateral to pay the claim of unsecured creditors.[77] Perhaps, reflecting the domination of the banking interest group element in the private legislative process,[78] it is significant that this proposal was not examined closely by the reviewers as part of the revision process of Article 9.[79]

The objections to the carve-out proposals in the US were made on the basis that they constituted a partial subordination of the secured debt regime, creating an economic disincentive that would cause many potential lenders to refuse to make loans to debtors, thereby restricting the pool of credit available.[80] Such an approach is not sustainable because secured credit in the US already operates in a world of partial priority.[81] Under the US Bankruptcy Code, most notably Chapter 11 which deals with corporate reorganisation proceedings, restrictions are imposed on the enforcement of security interests, potentially compromising their value because over time the value of the collateral may fluctuate.[82] The voluntary petition filed by the corporate debtor in corporate reorganisation proceedings brings about a moratorium on enforcement proceedings against both the debtor and its property and allows the company board to remain in control during the reorganisation.[83]

In 1982, the Cork Committee Report on Insolvency Law and Practice in England recommended that 10 per cent of floating charge realisation should be set aside for distribution to unsecured creditors.[84] This proposal which effectively reduced some of the priority that secured creditors enjoyed, was opposed by lenders[85] and the Insolvency Bill that resulted from the Cork Report did not include this provision.[86]

75 This was rejected by the Drafting Committee of Article 9. See McDonnell 'Is revised Article 9 a little greedy?' (1999) 104 *Commercial Law Journal* 241.

76 This proposal was modelled on Bebchuck and Fried 'The uneasy case for the priority of secured claims in bankruptcy' (1996) 105 *Yale LJ* 857.

77 It has been argued that the R9 process was a 'headlong rush to enlarge every scintilla of priority for secured creditors'. See Warren, 'Making policy with imperfect information: the Article 9 full priority debate' (1997) 82 *Cornell LR* 1373.

78 Banks and other US financial institutions continuously pressed for more effective and comprehensive security rights rather than weaker ones. The R9 process has been described as a 'secured creditors' grab' entrenching wealth in the hands of banks, insurance companies and finance companies. See Klee 'Barbarians at the trough: riposte in defense of the warren carve-out proposal' (1997) 82 *Cornell LR* 1466.

79 Op. cit., Janger, fn 72 above.

80 See Harris and Mooney, 'Measuring the social costs and benefits and identifying the victims of subordinating security interests in bankruptcy' (1998) 82 *Cornell LR* 1349.

81 Op. cit., Bebchuck and Fried, fn 76 above.

82 See Baird and Jackson, 'Corporate reorganisations and the treatment of diverse ownership interests: a comment on adequate protection of secured creditors in bankruptcy' (1984) 51 Univ Chic LR 97.

83 In this sense, the US Bankruptcy Code has been described as being 'pro-debtor'. See DTI *Review of Company Rescue and Business Reconstruction Mechanism* (2000) at pp. 38–41.

84 (1982) Cmnd 8558.

85 Banks saw this measure as interfering with their contractual freedom and property rights and that the scope and size of the percentage fund could increase over time.

86 The then Conservative Government considered that the proposal would hinder business in tying up money in special trust accounts that would require policing.

Twenty years later, the Enterprise Act 2002 provides[87] that a percentage of floating charge realisation should be set aside for the benefit of unsecured creditors[88] which operates once claims secured by a fixed charge, or preferential debts in respect of the same property, have been discharged.[89] This is part of a series of measures aimed at balancing the respective rights of secured and unsecured creditors, the thrust of the Act being to redress the balance of bankruptcy law in England which was considered to be pro-creditor, especially in its use of administrative receivership proceedings. The fixed fraction benefits all unsecured creditors. Such an approach is in stark contrast to that seen under Article 9 with its statutory bias towards secured creditors. Curiously, the DTI, which sponsored the Enterprise Bill and eventual Act, did not consult with the Law Commission on this approach, even though the Law Commission had begun its work on the reform of company charges and security interests law.[90]

The new emphasis of administration under the Enterprise Act 2002 is upon rescuing the company as a going concern. The theory underlying this is the concept of the 'going concern surplus', that is, preserving the value of a firm which is more than the liquidation value of its discrete assets.[91] In practice, firms in financial distress are unlikely to have a substantial going-concern surplus because most firms do not depend upon assets that are custom-made for its operation. However, this may be significant in the context of firms with intangible assets which are firm-specific, such as know-how, as part of the knowledge capital of a firm and its IP assets. Even so, the legislation does not require the administrator to rescue the firm where the creditor's interests dictate a maximisation of realisation strategy.[92]

87 Section 252 which inserts a new s. 176A into the Insolvency Act 1986. The percentage is set down by statutory instrument see S.I. 2003/2097. Holders of existing floating charges are not subject to the requirement to make a proportion of their recoveries available for unsecured creditors. They enjoy a considerable short-term benefit in that they will enjoy an immediate benefit from the abolition of Crown preference.

88 It is unlikely that the restriction on the floating charge priority can be construed as a breach of the Human Rights Act 1998 on the basis of a breach of Article 1 of the Convention that it unjustifiably interferes with the property rights of secured creditors since the provision itself is designed to protect the interests of third parties and legislatures are given a wide discretion in determining public interest safeguards under the Convention. See op. cit., McCormack, fn 68 above, pp. 417–18.

89 The provision does not apply if the company's net property is less than the prescribed minimum and the liquidator, administrator or receiver considers that the cost of making a distribution to unsecured creditors is disproportionate when compared with the benefits.

90 Remarks made by the senior Law Commissioner in charge of the Security Interests Project, Professor Hugh Beale, QC, delivering the Lord Morris of Borth y Gest lecture at Swansea on 29 April 2004.

91 For a discussion, see: Bebchuck 'A new approach to corporate reorganizations' (1988) 101 Harv LR 775; Baird 'Bankruptcy's uncontested axioms' (1998) 108 Yale LJ 573; Adler and Ayres 'A dilution mechanism for valuing corporations in bankruptcy' (2001) 111 Yale LJ 83.

92 Section 3(3) to Sched B1 of the Insolvency Act 1986 requires the administrator to attempt to achieve objective (a), when he thinks that this is not reasonably practicable or that the creditors as a whole would be better off under objective (b). The administrator's conduct is open to challenge under paras 74 and 75 of Schedule B1. See Frisby 'In search of a rescue regime: the Enterprise Act 2002' (2004) 67 MLR 247.

Intellectual property as economic assets: the challenge of reform

As has been pointed out, many SMEs lack the capital structure to make the law of corporate reorganisation at all relevant, that is, they will not have institutional debt. Typically, 'start up' companies will rely upon equity investments and loans from insiders, such as the entrepreneur and his family while most external financing comes from venture capital as the enterprise progresses. Venture capital contracts specifically set out when (in terms of company performance) control shifts to the venture capitalists and often the venture capitalists will select the management team and can change this when the firm does not meet specified targets. In the case of an SME 'start-up', the expertise in the IP will rest with the entrepreneur who has set up the firm. Often, the only question for the outside investor is how long to continue to develop the product before giving up. It is at this point that the ability of the originator to raise capital on the security of its IP asset will be significant.

There is a conceptual gulf between the current IP registers and an Article 9 regime. This can be conveniently illustrated in their respective treatment of filing and priority issues. Section 33(3) of the Patents Act 1977 (as amended) requires that certain types of transaction are registered, namely, an assignment of the patent or application for a patent; a mortgage of the patent or application or the grant of a security over it; the grant or assignment of a licence or sub-licence. Registration is necessary for two reasons: first, registration defeats earlier transactions that have not been registered (that is, it is proof of title); second, the subsequent proprietor of the patent or an exclusive licensee may be compromised in terms of a claim for damages or an account of profits for any infringement of an unregistered patent.[93] As such, the existing registration process is a form of transaction filing and contemplates individual discrete filings as additional IP assignments are made. It follows that problems will arise in respect of future interests.

Under current legislation, there is no mechanism available to take security over after-acquired property such as pure future patents over which no registration application has been made. The underlying rationale for the present English position is that what is made public is the actual transaction in which the parties transferred an interest in IP. This is in stark contrast to an Article 9 type of system where a single financing statement is sufficient to perfect multiple security interests between the same debtor and creditor. The case for a notice-filing mechanism that embraces IP rights and patents in particular is that financing tends to be ongoing and fluid, particularly in the case of SMEs. In the situation of ongoing finance, a transactional approach involves more expense than notice filing because this will involve multiple registration at, for example, the specialist patent register. This expense falls on the borrower and decreases the value of patents for financing purposes. A direct advantage of moving to an Article 9 regime is that this will reduce transactional and searching costs, while the filing of security interests would become simpler and cheaper and less numerous because of the shift from transaction to notice filing. Clearly, it would be necessary for the patent security interest to be registrable against the originator and not only the patent number because if there was a requirement for registration only against a patent number this could not be accommodated under an Article 9 type of regime with rules dealing with perfection of security interests in after-acquired property.

93 See Patents Act 1977 (as amended), s. 68.

A first-to-file system requiring recordation by *all* transferees would represent a major change from the present legal position. The current system makes notice outcomes determinative and in a contest between A and B, if A is earlier in point of time but has not registered his mortgage, B if he takes for value and without notice will prevail against A. This is unsatisfactory because a debtor may be fully expected to grant a security interest in the same property to several creditors: their concern is not that only one can assert a claim, but rather the order in which they can assert their claims. We need better rules for establishing priorities than those provided under the current statutory framework. Requiring recordation by all transferees through a first-to-file principle would accomplish this.

The Law Commission's approach in its Report of 2005 to maintain the specialist IP registers and that the determination of the validity of registered charges should be governed by the rules of that register,[94] effectively undermines the benefits of an Article 9 type of regime in the context of IP assets. As a matter of logic, IP as a form of personal property should be governed by the new approach. In the US, it is now clear[95] that copyrights, trademarks and patents all fall specifically within the definition of 'general intangibles' to which R9 provides the means for perfecting security interests.[96] Under the specialist IP registers in England there are sketchy priority rules which are in stark contrast to the detailed, specific priority rules seen in R9. The retention of the specialist registers, while at the same time applying the new regime to copyright and some design rights, would in fact create a problem of two conceptually different filing systems in respect of various IP assets with an uncertain interrelationship. This brings into focus the extent to which the proposed reform will actually promote dispute avoidance and dispute resolution because two different filing systems, one transaction and one notice filing, will co-exist. The simplicity and effectiveness of the priority rules is compromised by this approach.

Notice filing fixes the priority point and provides the incentive to register. The registration schemes which exist under the IP statutes are mainly concerned with the creation of IP rights and not those security interests which arise by way of subsequent dealings with IP as assets. Actual knowledge binds a potential lender and since registration under the relevant statute is not compulsory in the sense that it provides the means of perfecting a security interest, the creation of a valid security interest over registered IP is technically difficult to achieve under the current law. Thus, interests which exist outside the register are binding upon a subsequent purchaser or lender who has notice of that interest, for example, in the case of an equitable interest, a notice made on the certificate of registration, the document creating the licence or the assignment. In the light of this, the process of due diligence for lenders regarding the security of registered IP assets can both be lengthy and costly in terms of the

94 See Law Commission Report No. 296, above fn 52, paras 3.234–3.235.

95 See UCC R9–106.

96 Problems arise in the USA in respect of the state and federal competency dilemma and there have been several proposals to change the law in the USA to seek to resolve the federal versus state issue in IP security law matters. See Driza 'Perfecting Security Interests in Intellectual Property' (2000) 98 *Illinois Bar Journal* 162. For a brief discussion see the chapter by Lipton in the present volume, pp. 285–307. Similarly, in Canada, there is an overlap between federal and provincial law. The Federal Patent Act (RSC 1985) requires the registration of patent assignments and exclusive patent licences. The Act is in conflict with provincial PPSA's because the Patent Act priority rules revolve around registration in the Patent Act registry, whereas under the PPSA's priority turns on registration in the appropriate provincial PPSA register.

professional fees associated with the scrutiny of all the relevant documentation. This is particularly the case with legal interests which 'are binding against the whole world' and are not always visible on the face of the register. For example, assignments of IP are rights which are created outside of the registration mechanism and will not therefore always be visible on the register. Extreme care is needed in the case of financiers who seek to have priority by way of a security interest in registered IP. By retaining the issue of actual notice within the priority regime, as is the case under the specialist IP registers, circular priority problems will persist.

A search of the specialist IP register may not even reveal all the binding interests in the IP. The reason for this is that the certified copies of the entries on an IP register provide only a snapshot of the register at a particular time. There is no grace period whereby the certified copy guarantees the position. The problem is further compounded by the fact that there is no time limit within which the registration of security interests must take place.[97] In theory, there may be a number of registrable interests which could find themselves placed on the register after the snapshot has been provided and which crucially would enjoy priority. Furthermore, unlike the electronic 'real time' process of registration seen in modern personal property registries, in the case of the current IP registries there will be some delay before the interest is registered. As such, invisibility or blind spots are inherent in the current IP registration system. Effectively, financiers are required to take a leap of faith[98] in financing registered IP assets, that is, they are exposed to the commercial risks of fraudulent or the careless creation of double security and many financiers will consider this to be unacceptable to a lending decision predicated upon the assumption of a valid security interest rather than lending on an unsecured basis.

To retain the priority regime in respect of securities over assets for which there is already a specialist register such as IP rights from any new personal property securities regime is deeply flawed. This is antithetical to the purpose of a modern personal property security regime modelled on an Article 9 type system which seeks to harmonise and streamline transactions involving security over personalty. The adoption of the Law Commission approach would make the legal treatment of security interests in IP assets appear to be haphazard and in the case of the current IP registries could severely compromise the situation where, for example, a lender takes not only a security over a patent or trademark but also the income stream generated by that asset. Lenders would continue to have different sets of registers to contend with and different priority regimes in respect of various categories of IP assets. What is required is a single register of security interests in IP.[99]

97 Registration is necessary in terms of bringing action for an infringement and tardy registration is to a certain extent punished by the availability of bringing actions for such infringement. See, for example, the Patents Act 1977 (as amended), s. 68.

98 In a survey of technology-based SMEs in Wales, the length of time taken to register a security interest with a relevant specialist IP register could, it emerged, take up to three months. See Davies *Financing of Welsh SMEs and the Commodification of IP Rights* (2004), p. 69.

99 This does not mean that the IP statutes should be unified because the function of IP rights in terms of the categories of IP is different. For example, while patents and trade marks are concerned with originality and validity of the IP and the release of the monopoly right so created and its use in the industrial or commercial environment, copyright looks to the automatic creation of rights for all those who produce original works so as to protect creativity.

The creation of a notice-filing mechanism in the context of a single register of security interests should not be regarded as a panacea. This is because of the nature of intellectual property which gives the owner the right to exclude others from making, using or selling the invention as defined, for example, in a patent claim. Essentially, it is a bundle of personal property rights that may be subdivided.[100] The owner may choose to exploit it directly by selling it or, alternatively, the owner may exploit it indirectly by transferring some of the bundle of rights by way of an assignment or licence. An assignment consists of a transfer of all or an individual part of a title in, for example, a patent and the assignee substantially stands in the shoes of the grantor. Unlike assignment, a licence does not represent a transfer of any property interest in the patent – it represents a promise by the owner not to sue another who but for the licence would be an infringer of the patent and, as such, is a sharing of rights rather than a transfer. Essentially, a licence is a personal right that cannot be transferred in the absence of a provision permitting sub-licensing.[101]

The line between an assignment and a licence becomes fuzzy when a licence is exclusive, that is, where there is a promise by the licensor not to licence others to use the invention. Any comprehensive reform of English personal property security law in respect of intellectual property assets would require the adoption of a careful differentiating approach to the legal treatment of assignments and exclusive licences, especially since a central feature of an Article 9 type of regime is the development of a generic unitary concept of the security interest and the specific rejection of formalism in security transactions.[102]

The problem with functionalism is that it cannot distinguish meaningfully between different transactions, that is, analyse, classify and compare transactions and the consequences that flow from each.[103] The reform of English personal property law can only be achieved within the context of property transfer law with its underlying baseline concepts, that is, the conceptual framework will be older than the statute itself. A distinction must be drawn between extinguishment and priority disputes. In the case of the former, the issues go to rights of ownership whereas in the case of priority disputes there are completing security interests in the same asset which may be resolved either through a subordination agreement or through clear priority rules. The differentiation between extinguishment and priority disputes can be illustrated in the context of the rights and obligations of the parties in the assignment or licensing of IP carried out in the ordinary course of business. In many ways this is analogous to the sale or a disposition of tangibles. Thus, in the context of licensing in the ordinary course of business, the appropriate balance between the rights and obligations of all the parties will be based upon the implied authority of the licensor to deal with his own property, even if there is a restriction by a creditor of the licensor to

100 See: Kruse *Rights to Property* (1939); Penner 'The "bundle of rights" picture of property' (1996) 43 *UCLA Law Review* 711.

101 Under R9-408 the licensor in the US can prohibit or require consent for transfer by the licensee of the IP license.

102 Under an Article 9 regime, the list of financing arrangements to which notice filing applies relates to all functionally equivalent security devices which are referred to as 'quasi-security interests'.

103 The unitary concept of 'security interest' is too wide-ranging in that 'true' ownership interests are included within the regulatory framework, thereby threatening the principle of normal usage of language in legislative draftsmanship. See Davies 'The reform of English personal property security law: functionalism and Article 9 of the Uniform Commercial Code' (2004) 24 *Legal Studies* 295.

deal with his IP right, for example, because the IP asset is worth more to the creditor if unencumbered by any interest acquired by a transferee. By leaving the licensor in control of the IP asset, he is deemed to have implied authority to deal with it in the ordinary course of business, since it is from the proceeds of disposition that the mortgagee expects the outstanding obligation to be repaid.[104] Alternatively, an estoppel argument is pertinent, that is, the secured party gives every appearance to both the debtor and subsequent licensees of permitting the debtor to freely deal with the asset.[105]

It is important to distinguish between extinguishment and priority disputes because otherwise, in any reform of English personal property law, there is the danger of applying the wrong law.[106] Extinguishment disputes go to rights of ownership, whereas a priority dispute arises where there are competing security interests in the same asset which can be resolved either through a subordination agreement or through clear priority rules. Such an approach is fundamental to the conceptual scope and structure of any new reform in England and Wales which does not seek, Llewellyn-like,[107] to unseat and expunge title as the first rule of property law.

Conclusions

The growth of high-technology businesses entails going through cycles, from early conception, where internal and informal financing may be sufficient, through to more formal investors and venture capitalists, who provide capital during the early and further growth stages of such businesses. Debt financing becomes increasingly necessary as enterprises mature and, in this respect, a determining factor in the decision to lend will be the availability of security. If finance gaps are to be avoided, it will become necessary for financiers, as a matter of due diligence, to evaluate the IP assets of, especially, technology-based small firms. However, the structural uncertainty in the law relating to the use of IP as collateral for the purpose of raising debt finance has meant that enterprises are being unnecessarily impeded in their ability to raise capital. There is an under-utilisation of IP as collateral for debt financing which may impact upon the survival of technology-based firms where their assets principally comprise of their IP.

To embed an effective credit and security regime in IP assets, it is necessary first, to provide clear rules which can facilitate future planning and, second, to establish a system that minimises the costs and risks in taking a security interest in IP assets.[108] In contrast to this ideal, the current English legal position is deeply flawed. The existing IP registry systems are designed for transaction filing, so actual knowledge gleaned outside of the registration will bind third parties, which in turn leads to

104 See generally, Adams and Takach 'Insecure transactions: deficiencies in the treatment of technology licenses in commercial transactions involving secured debt or bankruptcy' (2000) 33 Can Bus LJ 321.

105 Under R9-321 of the UCC, a non-exclusive licensee in the ordinary course of business takes free of a security interest created by the licensor, even if the licensee had knowledge of the security interest.

106 Compare Weinberg and Woodward 'Easing transfer and security interest transactions in intellectual property: an agenda for reform' (1990/91) 79 Kentucky LJ 61.

107 See Llewellyn 'Through title to contract and a bit beyond' (1938) 15 NYULQ 159.

108 Compare Nimmer and Krauthaus, 'Secured financing and information property rights' (1987) 2 High Technology LJ 195.

significant evidential problems. At the same time, the existing IP statutes are not geared to deal with interests in after-acquired property.

Creators of IP usually go on to create more IP which can enhance or replace the IP originally secured. The revised Article 9 clearly contemplates after-acquired property in IP through the notice-filing mechanism. No detailed description is required and a financing statement covers after-acquired property automatically. However, the US position is not wholly ideal, mainly because of the overlap between state and federal laws and, in addition, under R9 the PMSI is specifically restricted to sellers and lenders who enable the debtor to acquire rights in goods or in software that is or will be embedded in goods but is not available to financiers of an IP right. Such an approach is anomalous and echoes the needs of an historic economy based upon manufacturing of goods, as distinct from the requirements of a modern knowledge-driven economy.

The current legal position is deficient in terms of the length of time that can be taken to register a security interest with the specialist IP register, together with the lack of grace period between applying for the registration of a security interest and the actual registration taking place. The Law Commission did not adequately deal with the credit and security challenge associated with the commodification of IP as assets. It may be that the cultural divide between existing intellectual property law, which is concerned to protect, through monopolistic rights, the owner of an intellectual property asset, and a credit finance law, which is concerned with distributing rights and obligations, can only be overcome by the emergence of a completely new body of commercial finance law[109] capable of supporting the development and exploitation of IP as economic assets by technology-based firms.

109 See Davies 'Secured financing of intellectual property assets and the reform of English personal property security law' (2006) 26 OJLS 559.

10 The New Zealand Personal Property Securities Act 1999

David Brown[1]

Introduction

In 1989 the New Zealand Law Commission's Advisory Committee wrote:

> The Committee believes that the introduction of a Personal Property Securities Act in New Zealand, based on the Canadian and United States models, and consistent with major reforms now being recommended in the United Kingdom by Professor Diamond, will mean that New Zealand will not only provide a lead in the adoption of standardised procedures between Australia and New Zealand but also play a significant role in harmonisation between the Australasian jurisdictions and their major trading partners in Canada, the United States and the United Kingdom.[2]

It is gratifying for a small country to boast that this seems near to proving true. The Committee no doubt hoped it would eventuate sooner than 1999, but equally slow progress in Australia[3] and the United Kingdom[4] meant that the New Zealand Personal Property Securities Register was the first of these systems to become effective. Indeed, in November 2002 the millionth financing statement was registered, and by April 2003 the millionth search had been made.[5] The positive side to the delay has been that New Zealand had the opportunity to learn from North America's 'second generation' PPSA legislation,[6] and utilised technological advances

1 I am grateful to Tom Telfer, Associate Professor, University of Western Ontario, for comment on an earlier draft, particularly on recent New Zealand and Canadian developments.

2 See *A Personal Property Securities Act for New Zealand*, NZLC R8 (Wellington: Law Commission, 1989), pp. 8–9.

3 See fn 56 below. The draft Personal Property Securities Bill 2008 was referred to the Senate Standing Committee on Legal and Constitutional Affairs on 13 November 2008.

4 See now Law Commission of England and Wales, *Company Security Interests*, Law Commission Report No. 296 (London: The Stationery Office, August 2005). Despite the lengthy period of consultation and the work of the Law Commission, the Companies Act 2006 (Part 25) has retained the existing provisions for the registration of company charges. For general treatment of the English position see, in particular, the chapters by de Lacy (pp. 3–82) and McCormack (pp. 83–116) in the present volume.

5 Statistics provided by the Ministry of Economic Development Contact Centre.

6 See: Cuming, 'Second generation personal property security legislation in Canada' 46 *Saskatchewan Law Review* 5; Ziegel, 'The new personal property security legislation' [1986] *Lloyds Maritime and Commercial Law Quarterly* 160.

to become the first online register.[7] The government has claimed that it is the cheapest and most effective securities register of its kind in the world. Search and filing fees are significantly lower than in North American systems, but effectiveness is difficult to define or measure.

It is nine years since the passing of the Act, although it did not take effect until 1 May 2002.[8] Even before then, the legislation was amended, and significant amendments have been made since.[9] Some are not simply rectification of teething troubles, but involve policy decisions and significant drafting matters which should have been anticipated. There have been five Court of Appeal cases to date, and a substantial number of High Court cases, some of which are discussed in more detail later in this article.[10]

The PPSA was modelled largely on two Canadian provinces' legislation, and the New Zealand government was assisted by the advice of Canadian jurists. The features of Article 9 based systems are detailed in the English Law Commission's Consultation Paper[11] and elsewhere in this book, so the limited purpose of this chapter is to highlight the background to the New Zealand version, the extent to which key features differ from those in other jurisdictions, and point to actual or potential areas of controversy or uncertainty in order that those considering similar systems in the UK or elsewhere may be assisted.

A brief background to New Zealand commercial law

New Zealand has a unitary system of government. In this respect it has an advantage; much of the Canadian PPSA litigation has concerned conflicts between Federal and provincial jurisdiction or law. In addition, New Zealand has a unicameral Parliament, and the relative volume and speed of legislation has sometimes occasioned comment from overseas visitors. However, speed is a mixed blessing, and despite its years in gestation, the PPSA was swiftly delivered, and a less than leisurely repentance has followed in the form of amendments and criticisms.

7 It is recommended that readers consult the Register online at www.ppsr.govt.nz.

8 See PPSA Commencement Order 2002, SR 2002/60. The Act came into force on 1 May 2002, as did the PPSA Amendment Act 2001, the PPS Regulations 2001 and Receiverships Amendment Act 2001.

9 See: Distress and Replevin Amendment Act 2004; Personal Property Securities Amendment Act 2004; Receiverships Amendment Act 2005. Note also Companies Amendment Act 2006, First Schedule (incorporating new Schedule 7 Companies Act 1997 setting out the order and detail of preferential debts), and see Second Schedule, consequential amendments to Receiverships Act 1993, s. 30 (receiver's obligation to pay preferential claims).

10 The Court of Appeal cases are: *Graham and Gibson* v. *Portacom* [2004] 2 NZLR 528 (priority of a perfected debenture over an unperfected indefinite lease of portable buildings which fell within PPSA 1999, s. 16(b)(i)); *New Zealand Bloodstock Ltd* v. *Waller* [2006] 3 NZLR 620 (CA); *Agnew* v. *Pardington* [2006] 2 NZLR 520; *Dunphy and Shephard* v. *Sleepyhead Manufacturing Company Ltd* [2007] 3 NZLR 602; *Simpson* v. *Shephard and Dunphy* (*as Liquidators of Service Foods Manawatu Ltd*) (*In rec and liq*) [2007] 2 NZLR 130.

11 Law Commission of England and Wales, *Registration of Security Interests: Company Charges and Property other than Land* Consultation Paper No. 164. (London: The Stationery Office, June 2002). See now Law Commission of England and Wales, *Company Security Interests*, Law Commission Report No. 296 (London: The Stationery Office, August 2005) both available at http://www.lawcom.gov.uk.

New Zealand's population is dispersed, and separated into two main islands. An online register has the advantage over different physical registries located in larger cities and towns, and was one of the main reasons why calls for reform were made.

The structure of New Zealand's commercial law is based on English law, the received law on colonisation.[12] As with Canada, major pieces of commercial legislation were largely modelled on their English precursors. The relevant ones here included the Insolvency Act 1967 (based on the old English Bankruptcy Act 1914),[13] the Bills of Sale Act and its subsequent Amendment Acts. The registration of company charges under the Companies Act 1993 was not dissimilar to the English Companies Act 1985. As can be seen from *Agnew* v. *CIR*,[14] New Zealand law as to floating charges and other equitable concepts was originally based on English and other Commonwealth precedents.

In Real Property, the Torrens-based system of registration of title[15] works well, and online conveyancing was introduced in 1998.[16]

The pool of commercial lawyers and expert officials is inevitably smaller than one would find in Canada, the UK or the US. For that reason as well as the precedent value, overseas advice in designing the PPSA was crucial.

Problems with the pre-PPSA law

The major piece of relevant legislation prior to the introduction of the PPSA in New Zealand was the Chattels Transfer Act 1924, based on the English Bills of Sale Act 1854.

Riesenfeld[17] traces the history of legislation, showing how English amendments were grafted onto New Zealand law, sometimes one pace behind the English amendments.[18] A particular New Zealand feature extended to mortgages of future wool, whale oil and bone, stock and growing crops, and harekeke, a type of flax distinct from European varieties. More important, the Act extended to instruments by way of bailment, so that (subject to the list of exempted agreements), conditional sale agreements, hire purchase agreements and equipment leases were within the registration system; in that respect, the registration of personal property security in New Zealand has always been more comprehensive than in England.

12 See English Laws Act 1851, s. 1; see now Imperial Laws Application Act 1988.

13 An Insolvency Act 2006 has recently been passed which modernises some aspects of bankruptcy law, but still replicates many of the 1967 Act provisions.

14 [2001] 2 AC 710. See also *Supercool Refrigeration* v. *Hoverd Industries Ltd* [1994] 3 NZLR 300, which was discussed by Lord Millett in *Agnew*.

15 See generally Land Transfer Act 1952. The New Zealand Law Commission has, however, recently initiated a major review of the Act, the first since its enactment; see Review of the Land Transfer Act 1952, Issues Paper 10 (Wellington: NZLC, October 2008).

16 See: Land Transfer (Automation) Amendment Act 1998; Land Transfer (Computer Registers and Electronic Lodgement) Amendment Act 2002; Land Transfer Regulations 2002. Online conveyancing became compulsory from 1 July 2008.

17 See Riesenfeld 'The quagmire of chattels securities in New Zealand' (Legal Research Foundation, Occasional Pamphlet No. 4, 1970), p. 6.

18 For a complete overview of the legislation, see Garrow and Fenton, *Law of Personal Property in New Zealand* (Wellington: Butterworths, 1998), ch. 8; see also Cain, 'The Chattels Transfer Act, oddments and oddities' (1959) *New Zealand Law Journal* 87 and 167.

The 1924 Act provided that 'instruments' could be registered, failing which they would be avoidable by an assignee for creditors, the Official Assignee, sheriffs or bailiffs, and in some circumstances, by a bona fide purchaser or mortgagee. The Act was primarily designed to register chattel mortgages, although the definition of 'instrument' was crucial, in particular the exclusion of 'customary hire purchase agreements' and 'customary chattels', the latter of which were gradually extended, to a range of items that became 'customarily' the subject of hire purchase agreements.[19] The original justification was that it would be too costly for retailers to register, but given that the exclusion covered motor vehicles and many other large items, this drew a 'coach and horses', or more literally a car, through the Act.

Furthermore, it was not entirely clear whether any, and if so what, consequences would follow from non-registration of non-customary hire purchase agreements.[20]

In 1895 book and other debts were made registrable,[21] and in 1919 mortgages or charges granted and registered under the Companies Act were added to the exceptions.[22] The Companies Act 1903, following the English approach, provided that a mortgage or charge created or evidenced by an instrument which, if executed by an individual, would require registration as a bill of sale, would require registration within 21 days, with the same consequences of non-registration as in England. Since then, the Companies Acts have reflected the English categories of registrable charges. However, the exclusion from the CTA of debentures, charges or mortgages created by companies, continued to sit uncomfortably with the specific categories of registrable charge under the companies legislation, so some specific charges over after-acquired property, unless amounting to floating charges, did not require registration under either regime.[23]

Since the actual instrument had to be registered, registration constituted notice of its contents as well as its existence.[24] Unlike the Companies Act, unregistered instruments were void against a bona fide purchaser for valuable consideration without express notice, and in respect of bona fide dealings by auctioneers, agents or dealers in the ordinary course of business.

However, the consequences of non-registration depended on uncertain concepts such as 'apparent possession', and lapse of registration after five years[25] was a trap for the unwary. In addition to registration, non-compliance with other requirements[26] would render the instrument ineffectual against the same persons as in the case of

19 So much so that at one point it was thought that two-thirds of chattel dealings that would otherwise require registration were exempted through the operation of s. 57 of the Act; see op. cit., Cain, fn 18.

20 Law Commission Preliminary Paper No. 6 *Reform of Personal Property Securities Law* (NZLC: Wellington, 1998), pp. 30–2.

21 Other than those secured on land.

22 As a consequence of *Carncross* v. *Wilson's Motor Supplies Ltd* [1924] NZLR 32, the 1924 Act removed the requirement for actual registration, so that mortgages or charges registrable under the Companies Act were excluded from the Chattels Transfer Act regime, even if not actually registered with the Registrar of Companies.

23 See McLauchlan 'Corporate personal property secured transactions' (1978) *New Zealand Law Journal* 137.

24 Chattels Transfer Act 1924, s. 4(1); *Official Assignee* v. *Westpac Banking Corporation* [1990] 3 NZLR 545, p. 547, *per* Somers J.

25 Subject to renewal in time.

26 Such as the need for a detailed inventory.

non-registration; but in other cases, for example as to details of stock, it would do so only against certain of those persons.[27]

Despite its complexity and anomalies, the major criticism of the Act related to its decentralised nature. The actual instrument, or a true copy, had to be filed in the Court in the provincial district within which the chattels were situated at the time of making the instrument, within 21 days.[28] New Zealand was divided into 11 Districts, some having more than one Registry. It was sometimes necessary to use agents in up to 11 towns or cities to effect a comprehensive search. Such a system could only be effective in earlier days when travel and relocation were less frequent.

In addition, the Law Commission described the formalities of registration as 'unnecessarily elaborate', pointing out[29] that a certificate had to follow the form in the First Schedule.

Turning to company charges, registration within 21 days was mandatory (unlike the CTA) and non-registration also rendered registrable charges ineffective against creditors, liquidators or the Official Assignee.[30] Registration was originally effected by filing a copy of the instrument at the office of the District Registrar of Companies where the company records were lodged. There was originally no exchange of information, so agents would be required in the 12 different districts. Company charges also had to be registered on the company's own register of charges;[31] some would have to be registered there which did not require registration at the Companies Office.

The same problems of categorising types of charge and collateral, and the category defined by reference to registration under the Bills of Sale Act, existed as in the English legislation.

Registration under the CTA afforded priority, unlike the position under the Companies Act 1955. However, where a charge was registered under the Companies Act[32] the CTA deemed this to be notice of the existence, and of the contents, of the charge, as far as it related to chattels.[33] In the case of companies one had to search the Land Titles Register in respect of dealings with land; the latter of course is a priority-based register of title.

Motor Vehicle Securities Act 1989

Due to public concern about unwary purchasers having cars repossessed by sellers' finance companies, the Justice Department embarked on reform of motor vehicle security law at the same time as the Law Commission was reigniting the issue of Article 9 based reform. Indeed, it appears that the two agencies did not

27 See: op. cit., Garrow and Fenton, fn 18, p. 467; op cit., Cain, fn 18.
28 A High Court order for rectification would be required in event of failure to register in time.
29 See fn 19 above, p. 28.
30 The Official Assignee is the state official that is appointed as trustee-in-bankruptcy in all cases. There are no private trustees in bankruptcy.
31 See Companies Act 1955, s. 110.
32 Or Industrial and Provident Societies Act 1908.
33 Charges falling under the Industrial and Provident Societies Amendment Act 1952, ss. 16–24 were excluded from the definition of 'instrument' under the CTA.

initially realise that both issues were being separately pursued.[34] Even when they did, they resolved to continue, notwithstanding that this added a third track of registration.

The 1989 Act was avowedly a consumer protection measure[35] although it did provide for priority rules between competing owners or security interest holders. It established a separate central registry. For the first time, telephone searches were possible, and later, online searches. Motor vehicle security instruments no longer fell within the Chattels Transfer Act. The Act was designed to give protection to consumers, both from dealers, and from others by providing a simple centralised register which the public would be expected to check, although how far people buying cars privately would do so was questionable. Many people wrongly assume that the State system of vehicle registration and consequent licensing on transfer of a car amounts to ownership, or a certificate of ownership. Having said that, the most numerous problems then caused by chattels security law were caused by fraudulent sales of motor vehicles, and this legislation certainly assisted in reducing that. The Act did also introduce the concept of 'security interest' into legislation, and was consistent with legislation introduced in most Australian states.

One important difference from previous registers was that non-registration did not render a security interest in a motor vehicle void against creditors, the Official Assignee or liquidators.

Motor vehicle hire purchase agreements ceased to be 'customary' as under the CTA, so became registrable. Where a company granted security, registration under the Companies Act would still be required. Consumers would take clear title from licensed motor dealers, but in the case of other purchasers, hire purchasers or lessees, they would only take free if without notice, registration being deemed notice under the Act. It was held that a fixed charge on a motor vehicle would not be void for non-registration under the Companies Act, because it was registrable under the MVSA, irrespective of whether it was actually registered.[36] If, on the other hand, it was a floating charge, it would not be registrable under the MVSA, so would be void.

Ships

The Ship Registration Act 1992 provides for registration of mortgages and transfers of title to ships,[37] and the Chattels Transfer Act excluded transfers or assignments of ships registered under Part A of the New Zealand Register of Ships.[38] A mortgage of a Part A registered ship may be registered and will give priority over earlier interests even where there is notice.[39] Failure to register affects priority. Where the debtor is a company, the ship mortgage might have had to be registered at the Companies Office,

34 See McLauchlan, 'Motor vehicle securities: the quagmire deepens' (1989) *New Zealand Law Journal* 211.

35 See generally, Garrow and Fenton, above fn 18, at Chapter 7.

36 See *Green* v. *Meltzer* (1993)6 NZCLC 68, 393 (CA).

37 Although note that it is not a system of title by registration, see op. cit., Garrow and Fenton, fn 18, p. 619.

38 The compulsory registration part, which generally applies where the ship exceeds 24 metres register length, though see: *Keybank National Association* v. *The Ship 'Blaze'*, 9/2/07, HC Auckland, Baragwanath J, CIV 2006-404-2266, and the text to fn 151 below.

39 See s. 40.

depending on whether or not the ship was a registered ship, or capable of registration, under the Ship Registration Act.[40] Further, as between the Chattels Transfer Act and the Ship Registration Act, there was room for uncertainty in that transfers of Part A registered ships were excluded from the definition of 'instrument' in the CTA. It was unclear if this extended to mortgages, but more so with regard to charges.

History of law reform proposals

The history of reform can be traced to 1965, when the Legal Research Foundation began a study, completed in 1970.[41] At the same time, similar work began on an Article 9 based approach in Ontario, the first Canadian province to enact such legislation.

The report, while recommending immediate amendments,[42] favoured a centralised register for all chattel securities. A member of the Advisory Committee, Steve Riesenfeld, then visiting lecturer at Auckland, described the law as a 'quagmire'[43] and stated:

> the law as presently existing bristles with inconsistencies, contradictory or outmoded policies, and haunting obscurities[44]

In 1982, in isolation from the debate on a comprehensive personal property security system, and apparently without the input of its the Law Reform Committee,[45] the Justice Department introduced a Bill amending Part IV of the Companies Act 1955, which deals with registration of company charges. In 1984 a ministerial working party considered changes to that regime, again in isolation from the broader subject.

Soon after its establishment,[46] in its fifth preliminary paper, the Law Commission tackled company law reform generally, and it became clear that the Commission would have to include the subject of personal property security law when considering Part IV of the Companies Act. Parallels with the current situation in the UK are clear, though it remains to be seen whether the ultimate outcome will be the same.

In 1987, Professor John Farrar, then Dean of the University of Canterbury, and Mark O'Regan, then a partner in Chapman Tripp Sheffield Young, were invited by the Law Commission to visit North America.[47] They submitted a report[48] which was favourably received by the legal profession.

40 See s. 103(1)(a) Companies Act (now repealed).
41 In 1968 the Tariff and Development Board produced a report on Instalment Credit Trading which mentioned the possibility of reform along Article 9 lines.
42 See 'Reform of the law as to chattels securities' (Legal Research Foundation, Occasional Paper No. 2, Auckland, 1970). These were that changes should be made to the Chattels Transfer Act to facilitate financing of dealers' stock-in-trade so that it would not be necessary for dealers to incorporate in order to seek lending secured by a floating charge, and that customary hire-purchase agreements should not be exempt from registration.
43 See 'The quagmire of chattels security in New Zealand' (Legal Research Foundation Occasional Pamphlet No. 4, Auckland, 1970).
44 See fn 40 above, p. 15.
45 See McLauchlan, 'Contract and commercial law reform' (1984) 11 *New Zealand Universities Law Review* 37, p. 51.
46 The Law Commission was established in 1985.
47 They visited Michigan and Illinois in the USA, and Ontario, Saskatchewan and British Colombia in Canada and met (*inter alia*) with Professors Ron Cuming QC and Jacob Ziegel.
48 See LCPP 6, above fn 20.

In Canada, a draft PPSA was released by the British Colombian government. The New Zealand Law Commission commented that the pre-PPSA law there was quite similar. As appendices to its Preliminary Paper No. 6 the Law Commission attached the Saskatchewan and British Colombia models. Both were drafted largely by Professor Ron Cuming, QC.[49] The Law Commission appointed an Advisory Committee[50] which had the assistance of Professor Cuming.[51]

In 1989 the Law Commission produced a report accompanied by a draft Bill.[52]

In two areas, upon which the Advisory Committee were divided, the Commission stated that the matters should be deferred, namely the question of the effect of non-registration on insolvency, and the question of remedies. In relation to the former, the Commission noted that there was to be a review of insolvency law[53] and in relation to the latter, this was a matter for consumer legislation. As regards insolvency, the Advisory Committee noted that 'consistency between these reform initiatives is essential and they should proceed together'.

The Committee emphasised that interim reform of company charges alone should not be countenanced. In view of the parallels with the recent debate in the UK, it may be worth commenting that perhaps the New Zealand situation was more urgent, the 'quagmire' arguably being deeper than it presently is in the UK. The 1993 Companies Act was passed on the basis that there would be a PPSA, but when that did not happen, it was necessary to pass the Companies (Registration of Charges) Act 1993 to prolong the prior scheme for registration of company charges.[54] Nevertheless, the New Zealand situation shows that any attempt to deal separately with company charges is problematic, and runs the risk that comprehensive reform will be pushed to the political back-burner.

This sense of urgency was followed by a period of inactivity. The reasons given were the pending insolvency law review, lack of official time until completion of company law reform, and the need to work in step with Australia. Since the 1990s, Australian discussion of the possibility of a personal property securities register has taken into account developments in New Zealand, for example the Australian Law Reform Committee report in May 1993, and the Attorney-General's report in 1995, having explicit regard to the Memorandum of Understanding on Harmonisation of Business between Australia and New Zealand. Recent initiatives under the Closer Economic Relations link with Australia suggest that we may be moving towards a

49 The report recommended certain amendments to the Sale of Goods Act 1980 to deal with problems stemming from the *nemo dat* rule, though these could be effected without waiting for a PPSA.

50 Which included Professor Farrar, as well as members of the New Zealand Law Society's Contract and Commercial Law reform committee. Note that one current member of the new Supreme Court (Blanchard J) and one current member of the Court of Appeal (O'Regan J), was on that Committee.

51 Moreover, both the separate New Zealand texts on the PPSA are co-authored by Canadians: Gedye, Cuming and Wood *Personal Property Securities in New Zealand* (Wellington: Brookers, 2002) (hereafter 'Gedye et al.') and Widdup and Mayne, *PPSA – a Conceputal Approach* (Butterworths, 2000). Linda Widdup was a Saskatchewan solicitor.

52 See Law Commission Report No. 8 *Personal Property Security Law* (Wellington: NZLC R8, 1989).

53 Which has led to legislation in 2006, see fn 13 above.

54 When the re-registration period expired in 1997, and there was still no PPSA, it was necessary to extend the company charge system once more.

single market; competition, securities and insolvency law are moving closer towards harmonisation,[55] and a PPS regime for Australia looks imminent at the time of writing, with the publication of a draft Bill and discussion paper.[56]

Returning to the situation in New Zealand, at about the same time as the Law Commission's draft Bill was produced, the Motor Vehicle Securities Act 1989 was passed.[57]

In the mid-1990s, the decision to proceed with the Law Commission's proposals was made by a National government.[58] In August 1996 the Ministry of Commerce[59] circulated to interested stakeholders its Preliminary Thinking on PPS law reform. The PPS Bill was passed in October 1999, by the new Labour government.

Thus the concept of an Article 9 system for New Zealand had been first mooted in 1965, and given substance in 1989. It was 10 years before it was enacted, and a further two and a half years before it came into effect. One would have thought that, especially given the Canadian precedents and advice, this was sufficient time to get it right. However, arguably the government, having made the policy decision, then rushed the matter. Certainly the legislative changes that have already been compelled, and others still in the pipeline or which should be made, suggest that mistakes have been made, though it is not clear that lack of time is the only reason.

Key issues and influences for New Zealand

The Act was modelled on North American statutes, and the concepts of security interests, attachment, perfection, notice filing or purchase money security interests are now well understood,[60] and amply explored in the Diamond Report[61] and in the English Law Commission's Consultation Paper and Final Report.[62] Furthermore, where decisions had to be made as to the scope of the New Zealand Act, for example as to the treatment of leases[63] and commercial consignments, or non-consensual

55 See the Review of the Memorandum of Understanding between the government of New Zealand and the government of Australia on Co-ordination of Business Law, Ministry of Economic Development, Wellington, and Australian Treasury, Canberra (February 2006), available at http://www.med.govt.nz/templates/MultipageDocumentTOC_17202.aspx, last accessed 29 December 2006.

56 See http://ag.gov.au/pps (last accessed 10 December 2008). The draft Personal Property Securities Bill was referred to the Senate Standing Committee on Legal and Constitutional Affairs on 13 November 2008. For the Australian position, see generally the chapter by Fisher in the present volume, pp. 366–86.

57 See above, pp. 332–3.

58 Cabinet approval in principle was given in December 1995.

59 Preliminary Thinking on Personal Property Securities Law Reform, 24 July 1996 (released to the author under Official Information Act 1982). The Ministry of Commerce took over responsibility for commercial law and policy from the Ministry of Justice in 1995.

60 I do not mean to suggest that they are uncontroversial, see for example, Catherine Walsh, 'Super priority for asset acquisition financing in secured transactions law: formalism or functionalism', in Worthington (ed.), *Commercial Law and Commercial Practice* (Oxford and Portland: Hart, 2003), ch.16.

61 *A Review of Security Interests in Property* (London: HMSO, 1989).

62 See fn 11 above.

63 See *Graham and Gibson* v. *Portacom* [2004] 2 NZLR 528, discussed, below, p. 359.

security, New Zealand largely adopted the Canadian approaches, and detailed differences between the jurisdictions are the subject of comment in the English Law Commission's Consultation Paper. The discussion here is, therefore, confined to the most important departures from the Canadian approach, controversial issues, or those more relevant in New Zealand.

By the time of the Bill, the Ministry had identified four 'controversial' issues.[64] The first was the issue of motor vehicles, and second, the effect of non-registration on insolvency of the debtor. These two issues are dealt with in detail below.

The other two issues identified by the Ministry deserve brief mention. During the 1990s there had been a number of failures of agricultural businesses, particularly meat processors, where suppliers found that they had ineffective reservation of title clauses. Farming groups regarded the proposed PPSA as diluting their rights, since they argued that individual farmers did not have the bargaining power to stipulate for effective retention of title clauses, even if these could now be registered and extend to accessions and commingled goods. Their main argument was that the purchase money security interest should be automatically conferred, rather than left to contractual arrangement. This was rejected, because it was thought that farmers may be able to negotiate through their industrial associations, and, second, because the problems of farmers were thought best left to the insolvency law review. It is suggested that this was the right approach and the PPSA was not the appropriate forum for giving special rights to farming suppliers, even if this were desirable.

Lastly, Treasury and financial organisations were concerned about the extension of the Act to investment securities, as it was felt that this could be detrimental to the smooth running of exchanges and real-time settlement systems. The provisions of the Act were designed to take into account these concerns, so that although the Act does extend to investment securities, there are special priority rules, so that a purchaser of an investment security has priority over a perfected security interest[65] where the purchaser gave value, and acquired the investment security without knowledge of the security interest and took possession of it. This recognises that it would not be practicable or appropriate for searches of the Register. There is a wide meaning of 'purchaser',[66] and the definition of knowledge differs from the general definition in s. 19. Thus, a purchaser will only have knowledge if she knows that the transaction violates the terms of the security agreement and the investment security was acquired in the ordinary course of the debtor's business.[67] However, the definition of 'investment security' has been criticised as potentially too wide and inaccurate in terms of overlap with other definitions such as 'accounts receivable'.[68] Although the Example given for the definition is 'shares in a listed company', the definition is not confined to such securities.

64 Personal Property Securities Bill: Approval for Introduction – Cabinet Paper dated 13 November 1998, obtained under Official Information Act 1982.

65 It is therefore recognised that perfection through 'possession', as defined in s. 18, and extending to recording of the security interest or investment security by a clearing house or securities depository, or issuer, or a nominee if held by a nominee, is more appropriate than registration for this type of collateral. Listed companies in New Zealand do not usually issue share certificates; see Companies Act 1993, s. 95(2).

66 See PPSA, s. 16.

67 See PPSA, s. 97(2).

68 See Gedye et al., fn 51, p. 58.

Effect of non-registration

The Law Commission's Advisory Committee was divided on whether failure to perfect by registration should invalidate a security interest against creditors, liquidators or the Official Assignee. The Chattels Transfer Act 1924 made unregistered charges void against certain persons[69] as did the Companies Act 1955.[70] The Motor Vehicle Securities Bill, then before Parliament, did not have that effect. Since the Committee was almost evenly divided, it was felt preferable to follow the precedent set by the Bill. It was also stated that it was best to leave this matter to the insolvency law review.[71]

However, the Law Commission and others mentioned policy arguments for not following the North American approach.[72] It was said that in practice, only two parties may be misled by non-registration, a prospective creditor who normally took first ranking security, and unsecured creditors who would either not care whether there was security in place, or would assume that there was anyway. As for the first category, it was said that filing of a financing statement would protect such secured creditors against unperfected security interests. Prospective buyers and lessees were protected unless they had actual knowledge. The priorities between perfected security interests, and purchasers and lessees, were in any event governed by specific provisions in the draft Bill.

Implicit in these brief remarks was the view that unregistered security interests do not mislead any individual or group, and that in any event this was a matter for insolvency law. However, neither the recent Companies Amendment Act 2006, nor the insolvency law review papers that preceded it, contains any discussion or provision on this issue.[73] Second, that stance does not explain why the Committee, and the Act, departed from the existing effects of non-registration in the two major pieces of legislation that it replaced, the Chattels Transfer Act and the Companies Act. Surely the status quo in 1988 should have been preferred, though the passing of the Motor Vehicle Securities Act 1989 shifted the ground.

Furthermore, the consumer protection purpose of the motor vehicle legislation was very different from the purposes of the CTA, Companies Act and the PPSA, so to adopt the approach in the 1989 Act simply because it was the latest example would be too simplistic.

The question of the effect of non-registration was not one of the 21 issues circulated for consultation by the Ministry in August 1996,[74] so one could conclude that a policy decision had already been made to follow the Motor Vehicle Securities Act precedent.

The principal arguments in favour of the approach taken by the Law Commission, and in the Act, have been made by Donald Dugdale, a member of the Advisory Committee, and later a Law Commissioner.[75] He stated that the reason why earlier

69 The detailed rules have been mentioned above, pp. 330–32.
70 See s. 103(2).
71 Above fn 51, pp. 3, 114–15.
72 Above fn 51, pp. 114–15.
73 Although it would be preferable to not having any legislation, one can see that the natural home for a clause on the effect of non-registration under the PPSA is not actually in insolvency legislation, but by direct amendment to the PPSA.
74 See fn 56 above.
75 Legal Research Foundation symposium, 18 August 1998; note also 'The proposed PPSA' [1998] *New Zealand Law Journal* 268.

legislation had invalidated unregistered charges was to protect creditors from secret liens, but that in 1967 the reputed ownership provision in bankruptcy was removed. Since there had never been such provision in relation to companies, this meant that preservation of the policy against 'secret liens' no longer had any basis. Dugdale argued that in the case of individuals, credit was no longer granted on the basis of apparent ownership, and in the case of companies, the function of disclosure of a company's financial position is best left to other legislation.[76]

Dugdale conceded that the US and Canadian legislation was expressly premised on the policy against secret liens, in relation to both companies and individuals.[77] He responded to the arguments put forward by Professor Goode.[78] These arguments were: first, the common law disliked secret liens; second, the registration provisions helped to curb fabrication or antedating of security agreements on the eve of winding up; third, unsecured creditors have an inchoate interest in the company's property on winding up; fourth, some unsecured creditors may have extended credit due to lack of registration, but it would be expensive and impracticable for the liquidator to investigate each creditor's claim to ascertain the creditor's state of mind at the time, and lastly, there is a public notice function as well as a perfection function, and the avoidance provision is a powerful inducement to comply with the law.

Dugdale's response was that first, the secret lien argument only applied while the doctrine of reputed ownership governed. Second, there was no problem, at least in New Zealand, with fabrication or ante-dating of security agreements. Third, any argument that unsecured creditors had an inchoate interest was consequential. The fourth point was a repetition of the apparent ownership point. Lastly, since the repeal of the reputed ownership provisions, and given that the new legislation, as with the Chattels Transfer Act, did not require registration let alone impose any criminal sanctions, it was hard to see why there should be a mandatory inducement for creditors to perfect.

However, Ziegel[79] has argued that New Zealand's failure to include such provision is based on a 'serious misinterpretation' of the historical position. Ziegel cites two historical strands. The first is the line of authority from *Twyne's Case*[80] that regarded secret bills of sale as presumptively fraudulent on creditors. Second is the related line of legislation beginning with the Bills of Sale Act 1854, which was adopted as the basis of the avoidance provision for companies. Third, the reputed ownership rule, pointing out that England only abolished this in 1985. Ziegel conceded that little reliance is placed on appearances, but that did not mean that unsecured creditors were not concerned with whether debtors had given security. Creditors rely on credit agencies who search registers. In addition, he argued that there is a 'psychological' aversion to secret non-possessory security interests which in part derives from the *pari passu* principle, and in part derives from concerns about fraudulent preferences.

76 Such as the accounting requirements of the Financial Reporting Act 1993.

77 Citing the British Columbia Law Reform Commission *Report on Debtor/Creditor Relations* (1995), p. 135, Official Comment on Article 9-301, para. 9.

78 See *Principles of Corporate Insolvency Law*, 2nd edn (London: Sweet & Maxwell, 1997), pp. 420–1; see also Goode 'The modernisation of personal property security law' (1984) 100 LQR 234, p. 238.

79 See 'Canadian perspectives on the New Zealand Chattel Securities Act' (2001) 7 New Zealand Business Law Quarterly 118, pp. 121–2; see also Ziegel 'Personal property security and bankruptcy: there is no war' (1993) 72 *Canadian Bar Review* 44, p. 48.

80 (1601) 3 Co. Rep. 80b, 76 ER 809.

At the least one can state that there is no conceptually clear basis for unperfected security interests to be avoided against liquidators, creditors or the Official Assignee.[81] The doctrine of reputed ownership has been expressly repealed, and antecedent transactions, including fraudulent ones, are specifically dealt with in insolvency legislation.[82] However, those in favour of the avoidance rule place more emphasis on the publicity function of the register. While some of this function was related to the policy against secret liens, Dugdale and the New Zealand government have ignored the width and importance of the policy. There was no evidence cited by the Advisory Committee, or by Dugdale, to suggest that *no* creditors rely on the fact or absence of registration. Individual creditors or their agents may well do so. The North American legislation makes it clear that publicity, as well as priority, is an express purpose there. Further, inducement to register will assist insolvency practitioners and others to ascertain who *is* a secured creditor, and the extent to which there are multiple security interests.[83] Backdating of security interests could be innocent or dishonest, but the fact is that it will be harder for officeholders to ascertain the exact date of creation of security interests which they may wish to challenge, and this may encourage more dishonest backdating.

Furthermore, whatever view one holds as to the advantages or otherwise of secured credit, the effect of PPSA legislation is to strengthen the position of secured creditors. The legislation extends the scope of security interests by the in-substance definition of security interest, as well as automatically extending to proceeds, accessions and commingled goods, and no longer requiring registration of actual instruments. Creditors whose proprietary claims may have been debateable or ineffective in the absence of registration in the past, will merely have to file a financing statement in respect of each borrower with whom they deal, and the cost of doing so is extremely low.[84] In addition the PPSA makes an unregistered interest invalid against execution creditors,[85] so they are placed in a better position too.[86]

It is widely acknowledged that the *pari passu* principle has been eroded, not only by the introduction of quasi-security devices but by the extension of the statutory list of preferential creditors.[87] In England this has now been ameliorated by the abolition of Crown preference and the retention of a prescribed portion of realisations for

81 But see de Lacy 'Reflections on the ambit and reform of Part 12 of the Companies Act 1985 and the doctrine of constructive notice', in J de Lacy (ed.), *The Reform of UK Company Law* (London: Cavendish, 2002), pp. 355–65 for a justification for avoidance under the UK Companies Act in this situation; see also A. Duggan and J. Ziegel 'Justice Iacobucci and the Canadian law of deemed trusts and chattel security' (2007) 57 UTLJ 228 for a defence of the Canadian regime. Note also the Law Commission of England and Wales, *Company Security Interests*, above fn 10, p. 51, fn 115, where the issue is relegated to a footnote and the sole justification given is that credit rating agencies consult the register, as do others upon whom unsecured creditors may rely.

82 See: Companies Act 1993, ss. 292–299; Insolvency Act 2006, ss. 194–216; Property Law Act, 2007, ss. 344–350.

83 See fn 51 above, p. 9.

84 For a useful article on the effect of the New Zealand PPSA on retention-of-title claims, see Brown and Sampson 'Retention of title under New Zealand's PPSA' (2002) 17 *Journal of International Banking Law*, pp. 102–9.

85 See s. 103 and note below, p. 358.

86 See McLauchlan, 'Unperfected security interests under the PPSA' [1999] NZLJ 55.

87 See: Finch, *Corporate Insolvency Law* (Cambridge: Cambridge University Press, 2002), chs 13 and 14; Mokal *Corporate Insolvency Law, Theory and Application* (Oxford: Oxford University Press, 2005), p. 96.

unsecured creditors.[88] Despite recommendations by the New Zealand Law Commission that the Crown's categories of preferential debts be reduced, and despite this having some support in government, the Treasury appears to have won the battle. The opposition National party voted against the recent package of insolvency law reforms, including the introduction of the voluntary administration regime, expressly because of the failure to remove Crown priority.[89] In addition, the preferential status of employees has recently been strengthened by an increased threshold and a future index linking, as well as extending priority to contractual redundancy pay.[90]

Therefore the least that can be done is for secured creditors to have to take the simple step of registration.[91] After all, this can be done cheaply and on the internet. There is no need to make registration mandatory, still less to have criminal sanctions, but a powerful inducement should be that non-registration will render the security ineffective against the liquidator or Official Assignee, as well as execution creditors.

Ultimately, the Act did not make unregistered security interests void on insolvency, and this crucial distinction from the Canadian position seems to have been overlooked in the Law Commission of England and Wales's Consultation Paper when discussing the effect of non-registration.[92]

The failure to include such an avoidance provision on insolvency may have consequences for the operation of other aspects of the PPSA. First, liquidators and the Official Assignee will inevitably seek to challenge some security interests, aside from antecedent transactions. There are two principal avenues where the litigation might occur. First, s. 36 requires the debtor to sign or assent in writing, so that oral non-possessory security agreements are not enforceable against third parties. The Official Assignee on bankruptcy would be a third party but there was until recently some doubt as to whether a liquidator is a third party in this context. Since a company's assets, unlike those of an insolvent individual, do not vest in the insolvency practitioner,[93] the better view is that the liquidator is not a third party, but the agent of the company. The Court of Appeal has recently upheld an emphatic High Court judgment on this point under s. 36 in *Dunphy* v. *Sleepyhead Manufacturing Company Ltd*.[94]

The other avenue relates to whether the financing statement is 'seriously misleading'. Only where a defect in a financing statement is seriously misleading will it be ineffective. The New Zealand PPSA has sought to clarify doubts by providing that a statement may be seriously misleading notwithstanding that nobody is shown to have

88 Sections 251 and 252 Enterprise Act 2002 (the latter inserting new section 176A Insolvency Act 1986 so that a 'prescribed part' of floating charge realisations (see Insolvency Act 1986 (Prescribed Part) Order 2003, SI 2003 No. 2097), be retained for unsecured creditors in relation to new floating charges).

89 See 29 (Weekly) New Zealand Parliamentary Debates, Insolvency Law Reform Bill (Part 8) 24 October 2006, p. 6051. See also Insolvency Law Reform Bill 2006 No. 14-2, Commentary, p. 16 (Minority Report of Commerce Select Committee members).

90 Companies Act Amendment Act 2004, s. 4, see now Schedule 7 Companies Act 1993, para. 1(2) inserted by First Schedule, Companies Amendment Act 2006.

91 This view was put forward by Professor McLauchlan in a response to Dugdale, see fn 86 above.

92 See fn 11 above, p. 96, para. 4.120; but this distinction was recognised in its Final Report, see fn 78 above.

93 See *Ayerst* v. *C & K (Construction) Ltd* [1976] AC 167.

94 [2007] 3 NZLR 602 (CA); for the High Court, see *Re King Robb Ltd (In Liquidation)* (2006) 2 NZCCLR 959.

been actually misled;[95] in other words an objective test, which seems to be the outcome of the later Canadian cases.[96] New Zealand has not opted for technology that allows similar, rather than exact, match searching, but does have the possibility for 'wild card' searches.[97] One suspects that there is still much room for litigation on this subject and on the precise meaning of the objective test.[98]

In the only case to date on the subject, *Simpson* v. *New Zealand Associated Refrigerated Food Distributors Ltd* [99] the High Court took a practical view of what was described as an 'overly broad' description of collateral, namely 'all present and after-acquired property' in what would otherwise, in a pre-PPSA environment, have been a traditional retention of title agreement extending to proceeds. Receivers of a purchaser challenged the enforceability of the security agreement. The court held that notwithstanding that the description did not specify any goods,[100] the purpose of the 'seriously misleading' provisions was to prevent a searcher being unable to find a financing statement due to an error in the debtor's name or the collateral's serial number.[101] Although s. 36(1)(b)(i) required an adequate description of the collateral by item or kind, it did not prescribe what constituted an 'adequate description' of the collateral. That was dealt with in s. 150 in a non-exhaustive manner. It was obvious from the terms of trade in this case that in practice, despite the broad description, the security would be confined to goods, and such proceeds of goods as could be appropriately traced. The Court of Appeal agreed, stressing that it was the security agreement that defined the security, notwithstanding a broad description in the financing statement. The Court also emphasised that the policy was that online registration was supposed to be a simple machinery, and that the debtor could always issue a notice to modify the description if it objected to an overly broad description of the collateral.[102] Nevertheless, they did suggest[103] that it was 'best practice' for the description of the collateral in the financing statement to reflect accurately that in the security agreement. To do otherwise, whilst not necessarily ineffective as a form of notice to searchers, was counter-productive and inefficient.

The Canadian litigation in this area has often arisen from challenges by trustees in bankruptcy trying to set aside financing statements, and the courts have been

95 See ss. 149–51.

96 *Kelln (Trustee)* v. *Strasbourg Credit Union Ltd* (1992) 89 DLR (4th) 427(Sask Court of Appeal); *Re Lambert* (1994) 119 DLR (4th) 93 (Ont Court of Appeal); *Gold Key Pontiac Buick (1984) Ltd* v. *BDO Dunwoody Ltd* (2000) 189 DLR (4th) 668 (BCCA). See also *GMAC Leasco Ltd Moncton Motor Home & Sales Inc.* (*Trustee of*) (2003) 227 DLR (4th) 154 (NBCA).

97 For the nuances of the New Zealand search system, and its improvements upon the Canadian systems, see Gedye et al., fn 51 above, p. 490 *et seq.* Gedye has made the point (Legal Research Foundation Symposium, 18 August 1998) that it is partly the state of technology that determines what is 'seriously misleading'.

98 For discussion of the Canadian cases, see Cuming, 'Judicial treatment of the Saskatchewan PPSA', (1986–7) 51 *Saskatchewan Law Review* 129, pp. 135–45.

99 [2007] 2 NZLR 130 (CA); (2006) 9 NZCLC 263, 979(HC), Goddard J.

100 Regulation 8 of the Personal Property Securities Regulations 2001 states that all collateral must be assigned to the category of either (a) goods or (b) all present and after-acquired security and only in the former case does it state that a further description must be provided.

101 See PPSA, s. 150.

102 See ss. 162–167.

103 Para. 34.

reluctant to give a windfall to unsecured creditors.[104] The absence of an avoidance provision may influence the frequency of challenges in New Zealand, and the approach which courts take. One would also hope that the technology will in the near future allow similar-match searching. Given that the PPSR is self-financing, a software upgrade should be considered, thereby reducing the extent to which technology is dictating legal outcomes.

Remedies

The Law Commission stated that the issue of whether or not to include remedies had divided its Advisory Committee.[105] It clearly viewed its draft Bill as concerned with priorities,[106] and that remedies were a matter that should be dealt with separately. However, more experienced counsel prevailed, and the North American precedents were followed by the time the government's Bill came to be drafted, the enforcement provisions now being contained in Part 9 of the PPSA.

> Conceptually the arguments in favour of inclusion of default remedies are that since the Act regulates priorities between security interest holders and third parties, it would be incomplete if the form of security interest was to dictate what remedies were available at common law, or other statutes. In addition, minimum default remedies do potentially provide some certainty and protection for consumers and creditors with inadequate bargaining power relative to secured creditors. Furthermore, it can be said that the PPSA brings forth a statutory security interest, and if no remedies provisions are included, it would be contentious as to what they should be in the absence of provision in the security agreement.[107]

As discussed in more detail later, the Property Law Act 2007 cures a defect by amending s. 109 so as to extend the remedies to secured parties other than those having priority over all others.[108]

Having said that, Part 9 is far from a comprehensive code.[109] Much of the regulation of security interests in consumer goods is regulated by the Credit Repossession Act 1997, which was amended in 1999 to largely confine it to consumer goods so that there was a clear divide between enforcement of security interests in consumer goods and others covered by the PPSA.[110] Largely this has been achieved, though leases

104 See Gedye et al, above fn 51, p. 472.

105 See fn 50 above, p. 3; note also Farrar 'New Zealand considers a PPSA' (1990) 16 *Canadian Business Law Journal* 328.

106 See, for example, the Law Commission's submission on the Bill, February 1999, describing the Act as a 'machinery' statute, submission released to the author under the Official Information Act 1982.

107 See: Ziegel, 'Canadian perspectives on the New Zealand Chattel Securities Act' (2001) 7 *New Zealand Business Law Quarterly* 118, p. 123; Telfer, 'Enforcement of security interests under the Personal Property Securities Act 1999' (2000) 6 *New Zealand Business Law Quarterly*, pp. 192–207.

108 Schedule 7 Property Law Act 2007, 'Consequential amendments', s. 109 PPSA 1999; see below, p. 345.

109 See *Agnew & Waller* v. *Pardington* [2006]2 NZLR 520, p. 524, *per* Glazebrook J.

110 See PPSA, s. 105(a).

over one year are not covered by the 1997 Act, and there has been no attempt to deal with this by confining the exception to leases which are in substance security interests; to do so would, however, re-introduce the difficulties of deciding which leases are 'true leases', which the PPSA sensibly avoids.

In addition, the legislation on consumer credit and hire purchase continues to be relevant.[111] Under Part 5 of the Credit Contracts and Consumer Finance Act 2003, the court can re-open credit contracts where there has been oppressive conduct, either in the terms or in the manner of enforcement. 'Oppressive' is further defined as 'oppressive, harsh, unjustly burdensome, unconscionable, or in breach of reasonable standards of commercial practice'.[112] The definition of 'credit contracts' in that Act would apply to most PPSA security agreements, yet the latter are also subject to the slightly differently worded duty in s. 25 of the PPSA which provides that 'all rights, duties or obligations that arise under a security agreement ... must be exercised or discharged in good faith and in accordance with reasonable standards of commercial practice'.[113]

Furthermore, while provisions of the Property Law Act 1952 concerning the remedies of mortgagees were largely mirrored by Part 9 remedies, there were still problems where the definitions in the 1952 Act were not aligned with the PPSA terminology.[114] To some extent, this has been rectified by amendments in the Property Law Act 2007, which came into force on 1 January 2008.[115]

Reflecting the fact that the inclusion of Part 9 was a late addition, it was no doubt a compromise that many of the provisions can be contracted out of,[116] but surprisingly, these include important rights for a debtor to receive a statement of account, receive notice of sale of collateral, to recover a surplus or to redeem collateral, and the limited right to have the security agreement reinstated.[117] While the Credit Repossession Act 1997 protects consumers, it is unfortunate that the policy of the PPSA to subject all in-substance security interests to the same regime is undermined by allowing contracting out. There is no particular method of contracting out laid down so it is a contractual matter, and it will be interesting to see what approach the courts take. They may take the view that since consumers are otherwise protected, even implied contracting out may be permitted. A 'bright line' between protection for consumers in the Credit Repossession Act 1997, and the ability for non-consumer parties to contract out may have been intended, but there are uncertainties surrounding the scope of the 1997 Act. Given that the remedies contained in Part 9 are the standard minimum remedies, to be found in all North American models, there seems little need to permit extensive contracting out, and

111 The Consumer Credit Act 1981 and Hire Purchase Act 1971 were repealed and merged into one Credit Contracts and Consumer Finance Act 2003, most of which came into force on 1 April 2005. The new Act strengthens consumer protection and enables the Commerce Commission to take action on behalf of individual consumers.

112 See Credit Contracts and Consumer Finance Act 2003, s. 7 ('credit contracts') and s. 118 ('oppressive').

113 See *Houston* v. *ANZ*, Heath J, HC Auckland, 9/12/04, CIV 2004-440-6932.

114 See Part VIIA PLA 1952. Note also Gedye et al., fn 51 above, p. 38.

115 See sections 152–154 Property Law Act 2007 for order of distribution of income by mortgagee in possession, and s185 (application of proceeds of sale). The Property Law Act is supplementary to the PPSA, and in case of conflict, the latter applies (s. 78 PLA).

116 See s. 107.

117 The section originally permitted contracting out of any provision that did not relate to the rights of third parties but this was submitted to be too uncertain, so was amended (PPS Amendment Act 2001, s. 9) to produce a list of sections.

larger secured creditors are inevitably going to pursue harsher terms. Fortunately, it is not possible to contract out of the underlying duty to act in good faith and in accordance with general standards of commercial practice, which also applies to remedies.[118]

Furthermore, the situation was complicated by the strange limitation which existed until 2007 in s. 109 wherein, in the case of taking possession and selling collateral where the debtor is in default, or the collateral is at risk as there defined, the remedy was expressly confined to 'a secured party with priority over all other secured parties'. This meant on its face that subordinated security interest holders could not avail themselves of the remedy provided, which would be a startling departure from the prior legal position, especially if Part 9 was interpreted as overriding or replacing any contractual enforcement rights. If this literal interpretation were adopted, a subordinate creditor would have to appoint a receiver as agent of the debtor, since Part 9 does not govern receivership.

It appears that the drafters were attempting to ensure that subordinated security interest holders could not 'steal a march' on a prior interest holder, but s. 109 went beyond that objective, which arguably was unnecessary anyway.[119] In any event the parties can contract out of this section.

The 'significant and justified criticism' of this by Gedye and others was noted by the High Court in *NZ Bloodstock* v. *Jenkins*,[120] and Parliament has now rectified the situation by amendment in the recent Property Law Act 2007, simply removing the words 'with priority over all other secured parties' from s.109(1) PPSA.[121]

Receivership

As originally drafted, the PPSA stated that Part 9 did not limit the rights, powers and obligations of a receiver, and that in the event of inconsistencies between Part 9 and the 1993 Act, the latter would prevail.[122] It is now made clearer that Part 9 does not apply to a receiver.[123] Since receivership will continue to coexist with Part 9 it was clearly felt that the Receiverships Act provided its own code. While the 1993 Act has largely worked well, the drafters were also conscious of the impending review of insolvency law.[124]

Part 9 contains similar, although less onerous, reporting and other duties to those in the Receiverships Act. Receivers who are appointed expressly as agents of the secured creditor pursuant to a power in the security agreement, are outside the scope of the Receiverships Act and are subject to Part 9.[125]

118 See s. 25, and note the text to fn 99 above. The 'good faith' standard is one of honesty; see *Houston* v. *ANZ*, Heath J, HC Auckland, 9/12/04, CIV 2004-440-6932. Indeed, subsection (2) makes it clear that mere knowledge will not negate good faith.

119 See Gedye et al., fn 51 above, pp. 394–6.

120 19/4/07, HC Auckland, Winkelmann J, CIV 2004 404 5795

121 See Sched 7, Property Law Act 2007, Consequential Amendments, PPSA 1999, s. 109(1).

122 See PPSA, s. 106 as amended by Personal Property Securities Amendment Act 2001, s. 8.

123 Within the meaning of the Receiverships Act, s. 2(1)

124 Although there is nothing in that review or the subsequent Companies Amendment Act 2006 which directly affects receivers' powers and duties in this connection, see fn 12 above.

125 See Receiverships Act 1993, s. 2(1). Such an appointor may also be subject to the Property Law Act 2007, see s. 9(1), (3) Receiverships Act 1993, s. 119 Property Law Act 2007.

Further problems remain, despite the legislative intention that receivership would be wholly governed by the 1993 Act.[126]

Section 30A of the Receiverships Act was added to bring the situation on a sale of secured collateral by a receiver into line with the approach taken under the PPSA. Section 115 PPSA provides for this in relation to collateral sold by a secured party using the remedies in s. 109 PPSA. It was intended to ensure that third party purchasers take free of subordinate security interests.

However, since Part 9 does not now apply to receiverships falling under the 1993 Act, the effect of s. 30A seemed to be that subordinate interests in collateral sold by a receiver are extinguished, but without the corresponding protection for subordinated security interest holders that is found in the PPSA, namely the transfer of their security interests into an interest in the surplus proceeds of sale.[127] Section 117 states clearly who should be paid and in what order of priority where there is a surplus after satisfying the security holder who has sold the property. There was no clear statement in the Receiverships Act 1993, other than s. 30[128] in relation to preferential claims.[129] A receiver is under a duty, owed to anyone interested in the secured property, to obtain the best price reasonably obtainable[130] but this does not impose a duty to distribute in any order of priority. Section 30A prejudiced the position of secured creditors in a receivership, and left the receiver exposed to competing priority claims to a surplus.

Having been brought to the attention of the government by this author and others, corrective legislation was eventually passed.[131] However, before this legislation was even drafted, the error had led to practical problems in a number of cases, one of which came before the court. At first instance,[132] the judge concluded that s. 30A was clear and unambiguous, and even though he was made aware of the Bill before Parliament which was expressly intended to correct this error, he felt himself obliged to hold that Parliament in 1999 must have expressly intended to alter the previous order of distribution of a surplus. Fortunately, the Court of Appeal[133] took a more realistic approach to the situation in a judgment given a week after the passing of the corrective legislation. The court accepted that the purpose of s. 30A was to mirror s. 115 PPSA and thereby provide clear title to any purchaser, but that Parliament had omitted to carry over an equivalent of s. 117, which preserves the subordinate security holders' interests in the proceeds. The court found that it was possible, and more consistent with the context and purpose of Parliament in 1999, and with previous common law, to interpret s. 30A as confined to *subsequent* security interests. Thus the situation is now clarified by the double protection of the Court of Appeal decision and the corrective legislation.

126 The Receiverships Act, s. 2 was amended to harmonise with PPSA terminology, 'accounts receivable', 'inventory', 'new value', 'proceeds' and 'Purchase Money Security Interest'; see Receiverships Act Amendment Act 2001 (effective 1 May 2002).

127 See PPSA, s. 117.

128 S. 30(2) has recently been amended to make the order of payment out of accounts receivable and inventory expressly clear, see Companies Amendment Act 2006, Schedule 2.

129 There is some support for the view that the Receiverships Act 1993 reflects equitable principles rather than being a complete code, see: *Parsons* v. *Graham & Gibson*, unreported, High Court, 13/12/02, XP 601/IM-01; *National Bank* v. *DFC* [1990] 3 NZLR 257(CA).

130 See Receiverships Act 1993, s. 19.

131 See Receiverships Amendment Act 2005.

132 *Agnew & Waller* v. *Pardington* (2005) 9 NZCLC 263,830, Williams J.

133 Unreported, 22 December 2005, CA 109/05.

Structure, style and scope of legislation

The Law Commission's draft legislation was 57 sections, the two Canadian precedents being 74 and 78 sections, and the final New Zealand statute contains 201 sections. Various provisions have been broken up into separate sections rather than subsections, and the other reason for the length is the inclusion of Part I described below.

The name of the Act is worthy of remark, in that the use of 'Securities' is in contrast to the singular in Canadian statutes, and is the same word as is used in New Zealand legislation on securities[134] in its traditional sense of shares and other debt obligations. Although this was pointed out by North American commentators,[135] the government chose to follow the precedent in the Motor Vehicle Securities Act 1989.[136] Given that the Act is about security interests, the short titles of this and the 1989 Act seem confusing and inaccurate.

Part I is intended only as a guide to the subsequent Parts, and contains no substantive provisions.[137] The intention was that this would be a layperson's guide to complex commercial legislation. However, the Long Title provides a fuller description of its purpose and broad content than the purported synopsis in s. 4. In addition, the Act contains a Table of Contents giving the Part and Section headings, and much of the information in Part I simply duplicates this. Part I does not appear to use language any different from the other Parts, so to the extent that laypersons consult the Act, they are unlikely to be greatly assisted by this innovative approach. Furthermore, they may actually be misled by Part I; Gedye et al. give several examples of where Part I has, in the attempt to be succinct, omitted crucial information.[138]

While one is in favour of use of plain English in legislative drafting, complex aspects will be the subject of legal advice, and to the extent that consumers and small businesses need to examine the Act, the Ministry could issue guides to the Act without having to muddy the legislative content in this way.[139] The purported attempts to make the legislation 'user-friendly' are in marked contrast to the limited steps and resources devoted to informing the public about the new register, as discussed below.[140]

The other unusual approach is the use of examples throughout the Act. Section 21 states that every example is part of the Act. This serves to emphasise that unlike Part I, which is expressed to be only a guide, or marginal notes, which are relevant in cases of ambiguity only, the Examples can be used as an aid to interpretation. However, it then states that an example is only illustrative of the provision to which

134 Principally the Securities Act 1978 and Amendment Acts, administered by the Securities Commission.

135 Memorandum dated 6 August 1996 from Professor Cuming to Ministry of Commerce, released to the author under Official Information Act 1982; Memorandum from Harry Sigman, Attorney, Los Angeles dated 12 August 1996 to Ministry of Commerce, obtained under OIA.

136 The Law Commission Preliminary Paper No. 6, above fn 20, used the singular 'security' (1988) but, by 1989, Report No. 8 had moved to the plural.

137 See s. 3 which states that it is 'only a guide'.

138 See Gedye et al, fn 51 above, at pp. 33–42; note particularly the commentary on ss. 7, 8, 9, 11 and 12.

139 Various guides to the Register and registration process are available on the website, www.ppsr.govt.nz though with a disclaimer.

140 See fn 151 below and the main text thereat.

it relates, and does not limit the provision. Furthermore, if there are inconsistencies between the example and the provision, the provision prevails. Section 21 is likely to become relevant since a number of the examples have been found to be incorrect, and in any event do not deal with more complex scenarios that may arise.[141]

Scope of the Act

Crops

Article 9 contained special provisions regarding security over crops, if harvested more than one year after execution, to prevent long-term arrangements involving crops as security, because they should be treated as interests in land.[142] The Law Commission stated that the one-year limitation prevented coercive arrangements being made by creditors for long-term financing of orchards or vineyards.[143] However, the one-year limitation was not incorporated into the PPSA, so that in this respect, crops were not treated differently from any other asset. Despite the special importance of agriculture to the New Zealand economy there is also no super priority for crop financiers as in some Canadian provinces.[144]

Section 51 PPSA now provides that a 'security interest in crops'[145] means in crops while growing, and afterwards when cut or separated from the soil, and for the latter purposes, it does not matter whether the crops are removed for storage from the land where they were grown. There is a suggestion that this may limit the extent to which effective priority may be given for security over crops which are not growing at the time of the agreement. While on the one hand, after-acquired property may be the subject of security under the PPSA,[146] s. 51 seems to provide that there is no security interest in crops until they are growing.

In this respect, New Zealand has departed from the Canadian approach and followed that under the Chattels Transfer Act.[147] It is provided that a security interest in crops does not prejudicially affect the rights of a lessor or mortgagee of land on which the crops are growing if those rights existed when the security interest was created and the lessor or mortgagee has not consented in writing to the creation of the security interest.[148] This suggests that land titles protected under the Land Transfer Act 1952, which confers indefeasibility of title on registered interest holders,[149] will not be affected by subsequent security interests in crops on that land. Conversely, a perfected

141 See: Ziegel, fn 79 above, p. 121, n.9; Gedye et al, fn 51 above, p. 23, commenting on the example in section 55.
142 This largely reflects the position under the Chattels Transfer Act, s. 36.
143 See fn 51 above, p. 134.
144 Gedye et al., fn 51 above, p. 212.
145 Trees are excluded.
146 See s. 40.
147 Saskatchewan PPSA, s. 37 generally gives priority to the security interest in the crops over the interest in the land, save where a person acquires a registered interest for value in the land while the crops are growing crops, or to the extent of an advance under a registered mortgage made without fraud, or where the mortgagee obtains an order for sale or foreclosure without fraud, in both cases before the interest in the crops is perfected by registration.
148 See PPSA, s. 100.
149 See LTA 1952, s. 62.

security interest in crops will not be extinguished or prejudicially affected by a subsequent sale, lease, mortgage or other encumbrance of or upon the land on which the crops are growing.[150] Provided s. 101 is read as subject to s. 100, so that mortgagees are free to exercise their powers of sale or lease, for example, this seems straightforward enough.[151] This interaction between the land title regime and chattels security registration existed under the previous Chattels Transfer Act, and whilst theoretically the removal of the one year limitation might give cause for concern, the definition of 'security interest in crops' in s. 51, combined with the priority in s. 100, means that the holder of the interest in land will prevail over a creditor whose security is over frequently planted or replanted crops.[152] Nevertheless, the principle of indefeasibility under the Land Transfer Act lies at its heart, and in the absence of express harmonisation in relation to crops, this may prove to be an area for litigation in future.[153] It may have been thought that the CTA provisions were clear, so should be incorporated. However, this is an example of where reasoning should have been explicit as to why there was departure from the Canadian models.

Ships

As set out above,[154] ship mortgages are subject to registration in some circumstances under the Ship Registration Act 1992. Those which fall for mandatory registration under Part A of the Register of Ships were intended to be excluded from the PPS regime; broadly that is those over 24 metres which are New Zealand owned. However, the position of pleasure craft and other vessels which do not have to be registered under the 1992 Act, and smaller vessels, for which registration is voluntary, was obscure, partly because exclusion from the PPSA scheme is by reference to 'transfer, assignment mortgage or assignment of a mortgage' of ships over 24 metres, or shares in such ships, rather than by specific reference to those required to be registered under Part A of the 1992 Act.[155] This issue has recently been explored in *KeyBank National Association* v. *The Ship 'Blaze'*, where there was a US mortgage over an ocean-going yacht under 24 metres. Although the US mortgage was properly registered both in the US and in terms of the Ship Registration Act, a purchaser of the vessel, which by then was located in New Zealand, registered a financing statement under the PPSA, and only after that did the US mortgagee register under the PPSA. The purchaser argued that the US mortgage had no effect and that its registration under the PPSA prevailed, since s. 23 of the PPSA had only excluded vessels over 24 metres from the PPSA registration regime, thereby impliedly including those under 24 metres within its scope. Baragwanath J held that Parliament could not have intended to repeal the Ship Registration Act by a side-wind (in respect of vessels

150 See PPSA, s. 101.

151 See Gedye et al., fn 51 above, at pp. 365–6. This should have been made clear, but is the only sensible interpretation of the two provisions, and this was the view of the old law taken by the Law Commission PP No. 6, above fn 20, p. 34.

152 See Gedye et al., above fn 51, pp. 365–6.

153 Although the PPSR is a register of security interests in non-land, the definition of 'land' in the Land Transfer Act 1952 can include crops, so that there is potential for conflicting securities under both regimes.

154 See pp. 333–34.

155 See s. 23(e)(xi). See now *See KeyBank National Association* v. *The Ship 'Blaze'* [2007] 2 NZLR 271

under 24 metres) and that in addition, the principle of comity should apply to give effect to the valid US mortgage. The alternative construction would have invalidated 19 per cent of securities on ships under Part A of the ship register.

Fixtures[156]

Although the Act contains provisions about accessions and commingled goods,[157] it curiously omits any provision about fixtures, unlike the North American statutes upon which the Act, and the accessions and commingled goods provisions, were largely modelled. The Law Commission's draft expressly rejected the North American model which allows those with purchase money security interests in chattels to retain priority over interests in the land. The Law Commission[158] stated that this did not reflect New Zealand construction financing methods, and was not appropriate to a Torrens land title system, and that the Canadian provisions had been frequently amended and were uncertain. They proposed a Schedule consisting of chattels which would become attached to the land, which only had one item in it, office partitions. The effect of this would be that in all other cases, the security interest would become extinguished on the item becoming a fixture to the land. Ziegel points out[159] that the Advisory Committee seemed to misunderstand the history of the Canadian legislation, and also failed to realise that the Western provinces have Torrens title too.

Whatever the criticisms of the Canadian provisions, to omit any provisions regarding fixtures, thereby leaving the way open to difficult issues of priority between chattel lenders and those with interests in the land, seems undesirable, allowing common law disputes to resurface. It appears that the drafters intended that all security interests in chattels would be extinguished on their becoming common law fixtures.[160]

Consumer protection

In drafting Article 9 in the United States, the most controversial question was whether or not to have consumer protection provisions.[161] It was decided to deal with consumer protection in separate legislation.[162]

The Law Commission's Paper No 6 favoured leaving consumer protection to separate legislation, provided that this gave adequate protection, though it did note that in many provisions, the Canadian statutes provided consumer exceptions.[163]

156 See S. Baas 'Fixtures under the Personal Property Securities Act: what New Zealand doesn't know it's missing' (2000–01) 19 NZ Univ Law Review 403.
157 See ss. 78–86.
158 See Gedye et al., above fn 51, at p. 132.
159 See Ziegel, above fn 79.
160 See MED Summary of Policy Settings, 26 August 1998, obtained under Official Information Act 1982.
161 Gilmore, *Security Interests in Personal Property* (Boston, Little Brown and Company, 1965), vol. 1, p. 293.
162 Though there are some provisions protecting consumer goods transactions, for example Art. 9-505(1).
163 For example, purchase of consumer goods, PMSI's re consumer goods see LCCP R8, above fn 50, at pp. 82–3.

The PPSA has made the position of purchasers who were consumers stronger, since they could easily check an electronic national register, and it covers motor vehicles as well as other chattels.

In New Zealand, in addition to the priority rules laid down in the PPSA, the Consumer Guarantees Act provides remedies against the supplier where consumers have purchased goods subject to an undisclosed security.[164]

The Motor Vehicle Dealers Act 1975 provided for consumer protection when buying from licensed dealers. A Fidelity Fund existed, which has recently been abolished[165] because honest dealers were cross-subsidising rogue dealers. Section 15 of the Motor Vehicle Sales Act 2003 provides that motor vehicle traders regulated by that Act must display on a used vehicle a statement of the effect of s. 58 PPSA.

In addition, other consumer protection legislation relevant to personal property security has already been mentioned in discussing remedies.

The Credit Repossession Act 1997 replaced the repossession rules in the Hire Purchase Act and Chattels Transfer Act, and also covered security interests in motor vehicles. The Act governs requirements for default pre-possession and post-possession notices to the debtor, protection regarding entry onto premises, duties regarding sale or disposal of collateral and providing statements of account.[166]

However, the 1997 Act covered 'instruments by way of security' under the CTA, and security interests in motor vehicles. The Act therefore prolonged distinctions between different types of functional security, and was criticised.[167] In an attempt to bring the 1997 Act into line with Part 9 of the PPSA, the Credit (Repossession) Amendment Act 1999 came into force on the same day as the PPSA.[168] It narrows the scope of the 1997 Act to certain consumer goods only, using the definition in the PPSA. However, it excludes various types of dealing that consumers would not be expected to make.[169]

The general policy of the PPSA is that consumer protection is not a primary purpose of the legislation, but since there are special provisions regarding priorities, the low value threshold, and motor vehicles, it is not quite accurate to say that the PPSA does not have a purpose of protecting consumers, at least as regards priorities of buyers and lessees.

Small goods exception

In the United States, it is not necessary to take steps to perfect security interests in consumer goods at low value; they are deemed perfected in order not to clog the register. This approach was considered[170] but ultimately rejected in New Zealand.

164 See Tokeley, *Consumer Law in New Zealand* (Butterworths, Wellington, 2000) at p. 119.
165 See Motor Vehicle Sales Act 2003, which came into force on 15 December 2003, ss. 158–162. The Act repeals the 1975 Act.
166 See further Tokeley, above fn 164, at pp. 235–42.
167 See McLauchlan 'Some Comments on the Credit (Repossession) Act 1997 (1998) 4 New Zealand Business Law Quarterly 156.
168 The commencement date being 1 May 2002; see Credit (Repossession) Amendment Act Commencement Order 2002.
169 See CRA, s. 3 (as amended).
170 See Ministry of Commerce Preliminary Thinking, above fn 59, at p. 39.

The PPSA makes a distinction between consumer goods that have a value not exceeding $2,000 at the time of attachment. First, they are defined as goods that are used or acquired for use primarily for personal, domestic or household purposes.[171] While this is the standard definition in the North American statutes, Tokeley points out that the Consumer Guarantees Act uses an objective test, requiring goods to be 'ordinarily' so used.[172] The definition of consumer goods is relevant in the PPSA for several purposes in the Act.[173]

The $2,000 threshold was a compromise. Some groups such as the Consumers Association were in favour of exempting all consumer goods, irrespective of knowledge of the security interest. Others favoured a lower or higher threshold. Retailers wished to retain the right to pursue goods under that threshold where the goods were on-sold by the original purchaser. Provided the value is reviewed periodically, this seems like a sensible compromise in order to keep smaller domestic goods and appliances off the register. The decision to include the threshold value in the statute, rather than in delegated legislation, means that it is in theory more accessible to consumers and others, but makes it slightly harder to alter it for inflationary effects, though New Zealand seems to be having Business Law Reform Bills annually. Where consumer goods are below the threshold at the time the security interest attached, buyers[174] or lessees automatically take them free of any security interest provided they gave value and had no knowledge of the security interest.[175]

In the case of goods over that threshold, or non-consumer goods, buyers or lessees of goods sold in the ordinary course of business of the seller or lessor, will be free of security interests created by the seller or lessor provided there was no knowledge that it amounted to a breach of a term of the security agreement.[176] This reflects the position prior to the PPSA and prevents the need for buyers or lessees to search the register.

The 'ordinary course of business of the seller' will be best left to be determined in accordance with North American precedents using the same phrase;[177] the use of the phrase in other New Zealand contexts would not be applicable, not least because the phrase in other contexts was not confined, as it is in the PPSA, to 'the seller's business'.[178] In a recent High Court case, *Orix New Zealand Ltd* v. *Milne*[179] the Court found that the question of whether a party was a 'seller' was not directly answered in the PPSA itself, so that the broad definition in the Sale of Goods Act 1908 would apply – thus there was no requirement that the seller had to be the owner of the goods so

171 See s. 16.
172 See fn 153 above, at p. 126.
173 See, for example, s. 55, though this has limited application.
174 'Purchaser' is defined in the Act broadly, whereas buyer, used here, is not defined, and is thus confined to sales.
175 See s. 54.
176 See s. 53, and note *Orix New Zealand Ltd* v. *Milne* [2007] 3 NZLR 637.
177 See: *Camco* v. *Frances Olsen Realty* [1986] 6 WWR 258 (Sask. CA); *Royal Bank of Canada* v. *216200 Alberta Ltd* (1986), 33 DLR (4th) 80 (Sask. CA).
178 The phrase has been used in the context of the floating charge, see *Reynolds Bros. (Motor) Pty Ltd* v. *Esanda Ltd* (1983) 8 ACLR 422, and in Companies Act, s. 292 (transactions having preferential effect). However, the former seems irrelevant now that the floating charge itself is irrelevant, and in the latter it is (a) not confined to the seller's ordinary course of business and (b) in any event has now been removed due to proving uncertain, Companies Amendment Act 2006, s. 27, amending Companies Act 1993, s. 292.
179 [2007] 3 NZLR 637.

that, for example, an agent could fall within the definition.[180] On this aspect the Court found that the analysis was consistent with the Canadian approach.[181] The more crucial question was whether the seller was selling in the ordinary course of its business. Here, the High Court said that there was a two-stage test. First, what was the business of the seller? Secondly, was the sale made in the ordinary course of that business? Here the Court also looked to Canadian authorities for guidance, though in the circumstances everything pointed to a normal and mainstream trade transaction; the fact that sales were not frequent and were only a small part of the seller's business had been held in Canada to not be decisive against an ordinary course conclusion.[182]

Purchases from persons other than sellers in the ordinary course of business will take free of security interests if they are unperfected, unless the unperfected security interest was created or provided for by a transaction to which the buyer or lessee is a party.[183] This is different from the position in Canada, where buyers or lessees also have to show that they are without knowledge of the security interest. Since unperfected security interests are still enforceable on insolvency in New Zealand, this provision is the most important incentive for registration of security interests.

Motor vehicles

In the case of motor vehicles, original drafts of the Bill proposed that they should be treated the same as other chattels, but it was then realised that this would dilute the protection that consumers had where they purchased from licensed dealers. Under the initial proposal purchasers would only take free of security interests, perfected or otherwise, created by the dealer from whom they purchased. However the Act as finally passed covers all security interests, so that the consumer takes free provided that any security interest was not provided for in a transaction to which the consumer is a party, or was disclosed to the buyer in writing before the transaction was completed.[184] Tokeley points out that given that this was intended to preserve the existing protection for buyers and lessees from dealers under the MVSA, it is odd to note that the definition of 'consumer' for s. 58's purposes is narrower than that in the MVSA, since it excludes all manufacturers, wholesalers and finance companies, not just those in the motor trade.[185]

However, the combination of the protection for consumer buyers or lessees in Part 5 of the PPSA, and the special protection in s. 58, means that consumer buyers of motor vehicles are in a privileged position over those in relation to other assets, since they do not need to search the register when buying from a licensed dealer, though this will not guarantee them title to the vehicle.[186]

180 See s. 2, 'a person who sells or agrees to sell goods'.
181 *Royal Bank of Canada* v. *216200 Alberta Ltd* (1086)33 DLR (4th) 80 (Sask CA).
182 Note particularly: *Camco Inc* v. *Frances Olson Realty (1979) Ltd* [1986] WWR 258 (Sask CA); *Royal Bank of Canada* (1986) 33 DLR (4th) 80 and *Alberta Pacific Leasing Inc* v. *Petro Equipment Sales (1995)* 10 PPSAC (2d) 69 (Alta QB).
183 See s. 52.
184 See s. 58.
185 See: Tokeley, above fn 164, p. 127; and PPSA, s. 57.
186 The Consumer Guarantees Act 1993 will provide a guarantee as to title in some circumstances.

Publicity to consumers

Despite the existence of the low value threshold, and the attempt to separate consumer protection in the amended Credit Repossession Act, the PPSA does affect consumers.

Prior to the Bill it was agreed that publicity would be required.[187] There was a certain amount of publicity in the main newspapers at the time of the register going live, but most of it was targeted at secured creditors, their advisers, and motor vehicle dealers, rather than at consumers. The government has stated that PPSR communications were relatively low cost.[188]

Given that the government was altering the protections of consumers in relation to motor vehicle sales, which represent by far the largest transactions on the register, more targeted publicity and resources should have been expended on explaining the law. If the government thought that the matter could be left to consumer representatives, the main association, the Consumers' Association, does not appear to have publicised the matter to its members.[189]

As argued above, the effect of a PPSA is to practically strengthen the position of secured creditors and extend the scope of secured creditors, all for the cheap price of registration of a financing statement. When adopting such a regime, the least that can be done is to ensure that the impact on others, particularly those with no or limited access to professional advice, is understood. However, it is fair to acknowledge that since the launch of the Register, the government, through its website and telephone helplines, has provided far more information and assistance to consumers and users of the register than it did at the time of the commencement of the Register. This now includes the ability for mobile phone users to search for security interests in the case of motor vehicles, called TXTB4UBUY.[190]

Fixed and floating charges

It was recognised as inevitable that the categories of fixed and floating charges could not effectively be continued. As in Canada, while parties may continue to use these labels, what matters is that a statutory security interest can attach in respect of after-acquired assets, and the concept of crystallisation is now redundant.[191] Section 17(3) of the Act states, for the avoidance of doubt, that the Act applies to a range of security devices including, expressly, the fixed charge and floating charge.

Nevertheless, as the *Agnew* case shows,[192] the consequences of a charge being categorised as fixed or floating, was extremely significant in relation to the

187 Cabinet Economic Committee minutes 25 February 1998, released to the author under Official Information Act 1982; Cabinet note of 23 November 1998 CAB(98)M 44/2.

188 See fn 4 above.

189 The monthly magazine, *Consumer*, does not reveal any mention of the PPSA around May 2002 when the register went live, though a short feature about a boat sale was run in October 2003, available at http://www.consumer.org.nz/newsitem.asp?category=News&docid=1681&topic=New%20property%20register.

190 www.ppsr.govt.nz, last accessed 11 December 2008.

191 See: Wood 'The floating charge in Canada' (1989) 27 *Alberta Law Review* 191; op. cit., Widdup and Mayne, fn 51, pp. 206–8.

192 [2001] 2 AC 710.

pre-PPSA regime.[193] The PPSA sought to preserve the existing priorities but through the new terminology. Schedule 1 of the PPSA attempted to amend the Seventh Schedule of the Companies Act 1993, which sets out the priority list of preferential creditors, to take account of the terminology of the PPSA regime, and to do so after the High Court's decision in *CIR* v. *Agnew*[194] which was later overturned on appeal to the Court of Appeal and the Privy Council.[195] There were problems with the first attempt at preserving the priorities without using the old language, so the Commerce Select Committee[196] recommended that preferential creditors have priority over 'assets which the parties intended could be sold or disposed of in the ordinary course of business'. That too was rightly regarded as too uncertain, since it would have thrown the law back onto the floating charge concept, and it was necessary to amend the relevant provisions again before the PPSA came into force.[197]

The personal insolvency regime was originally left untouched in 1999, so that s. 104 Insolvency Act 1967, which provided for priority creditors on bankruptcy, was not amended to reflect the terminology of the PPSA, though this was rectified in the recent Insolvency Act 2006.[198]

The concepts of accounts receivable and inventory as defined in the Act, are used to describe the category of traditional floating charge assets (stock-in-trade, work in progress, book debts and other monetary sums). However, under the PPSA the security interest automatically extends to the proceeds, so that the proceeds of inventory, for example, will include accounts receivable that fall under a security over inventory.

'Purchase money security interests' over accounts receivable and inventory are excluded from the category of assets which will be subordinated to preferential claims. This is because retention of title clauses and other interests where in-substance security is being given in order to facilitate purchase of the asset, are 'purchase money security interests', yet prior to the PPSA these interests would have been proprietary or possessory interests which had priority over chargeholders and over preferential claims.

The PPSA also addresses the position of 'sales' of accounts receivable, as on factoring, and ensures that notwithstanding that such transactions are deemed to make the acquirer the holder of a security interest, the assignees' pre-PPSA priority over preferential creditors will be preserved.

A potential stalemate situation was identified. The receiver of the holder of a security interest which is not a PMSI or sale of accounts receivable, must pay preferential creditors, but the holders of a PMSI or assignee of accounts receivable for new value (such as a factor), will also have priority over preferential creditors; under the

193 The New Zealand provisions are contained in Companies Act 1993, s. 312 and Seventh Schedule (as amended by Companies Amendment Act 2006, First Schedule); Insolvency Act 2006, ss. 274–81.

194 [1999] 19 NZTC 15,151 (Fisher J).

195 See fn 168 above; for the Court of Appeal, see [2000] 1 NZLR 223.

196 Appendices to the Journal of the House of Representatives, Select Committee Reports, No. 251–2, p. 45e.

197 See Receiverships Amendment Act 2001, PPSA (Amendment) Act 2001 (effective from 1 May 2002). The Act affected the priority for preferential creditors in the Companies Act (s. 312, Seventh Schedule), s. 30 Receiverships Act 1993, and similar regimes in Corporations (Investigation and Management) Act 1989, s. 51 and Industrial and Provident Societies Amendment Act 1952, s. 13(1).

198 See Insolvency 2006, s. 275.

PPSA, the latter will not necessarily have priority over the holder of the general security interest under and in respect of which a receiver was appointed, so there is a conflict between the receiver's duty to pay preferential creditors and the PPSA which in some circumstances, will accord priority to the holder of the general security interest.[199] Notwithstanding this, as originally worded the receiver under a general security agreement that is not a PMSI or sale of accounts receivable, had a statutory duty to pay preferential creditors out of realisations of inventory and accounts receivable,[200] whatever the priority position between that security agreement and others under the PPSA itself. This was described as a 'serious flaw' in the preferential creditor provisions.[201] The recent Companies Amendment Act 2006 attempts to cure the circularity problem by clarifying that the obligation to pay preferential creditors ahead of security interests over accounts receivable and inventory does not apply to a PMSI *that has been perfected* at the time the debtor, or another person at the request of the debtor, obtains possession of the collateral, whichever is earlier.[202]

Chattels subject to distraint

Another area where the legislation attempted to preserve the existing situation, but found it difficult to do so without making substantive amendments and policy decisions, is the priority between a landlord and a secured creditor.

The Distress and Replevin Act 1908 until recently still governed a landlord's right to distrain for rent. This could only be done over the goods of the tenant or person in possession, but s. 4 provided that chattels the property of the tenant over which the tenant has given an instrument under the Chattels Transfer Act 1924 are deemed chattels of the tenant. It will be recalled that company charges were not 'instruments' under the CTA. When the PPSA was passed, no express amendment was made to the 1908 Act to reflect the repeal of the CTA. Clause 38 of the Business Law Reform Bill 2003 proposed to repeal s. 4 of the 1908 Act and substitute the following:

(a) This section applies to chattels subject to a security interest that are the property of any tenant or person in possession of any messuages or lands.
(b) All chattels to which this section applies are deemed, for the purposes of distress for rent, to be the property of the tenant or person in possession of the messuages or lands if the chattels are found in or on the messuages or lands in respect of which the rent is due at the time the distraint was made.
(c) In this section, security interest has the same meaning as in section 17 of the Personal Property Securities Act 1999.

The apparent purpose of this clause would appear to be to do the minimum to alter the language of the 1908 Act so as to reflect the concept of security interests under the PPSA. However, this seemed to cancel out the effect of *Metropolitan Life Assurance*

199 See further Gedye et al, above fn 51, p. 22.
200 Under Receiverships Act 1993, s. 30.
201 See Gedye, 'The structure of New Zealand's "new" priority debts regime' [2003] 9 *New Zealand Business Law Quarterly* 220.
202 See Companies Amendment Act 2006, First Schedule (inserting new Schedule 7 Companies Act 1993), clause 2(1)(b)(i)(B)(C), and see Personal Property Securities Act 1999, s. 74.

Co v. *Essere*,[203] since *Essere* was based on the exception for company charges from the definition of 'instrument' under the Chattels Transfer Act, which is now no longer relevant. Therefore, the Distress and Replevin Amendment Act 2004[204] takes the approach of deeming certain chattels not to be the property of the tenant, which it was thought were chattels the security over which would have formerly given secured creditors priority over landlords, namely chattels charged to a company or incorporated society, or security over any motor vehicles.

The *Essere* decision was a confusing decision, in which the Court of Appeal construed previous piecemeal amendments to the Chattels Transfer Act, and also attempted to gauge the policy behind the 1908 Act. It resulted in the situation whereby chattels charged by individual tenants were deemed available for distraint, but not those subject to a fixed charge in favour of a company. It was strongly arguable that the original 2003 proposal was justifiably in keeping with the policy of the PPSA to remove distinctions according to the form of security interests, even if this would have had the effect of altering the priority which banks had over landlords in respect of company charges post-*Essere*. However aside from lobbying by the banks and their advisers, s. 22 of the Interpretation Act 1999 gave rise to the possibility that by repealing the Chattels Transfer Act, the PPSA impliedly replaced the reference to instruments registrable under the CTA into the Distress and Replevin Act 1908, with the concept of security interest under the PPSA, which would have the effect of giving landlords priority over company charges. Whatever the government chose to do would alter the balance between landlords and security interest holders.

Nevertheless, s. 4(1) of the 1908 Act, even with the amendment, still left room for confusion, since it seems to beg the question as to whether chattels subject to a security interest are the 'property of any tenant'. Fortunately, the Property Law Act 2007 has now abolished the landlord's continuing remedy of distress for rent for all distraint completed after 1 January 2008.[205]

Factors

The Personal Property Securities Amendment Act 2004[206] inserted a new s. 75A into the PPSA in order to deal as a matter of policy with priorities between factors and trade suppliers. It states that a non-proceeds security interest in accounts receivable that is given for new value has priority over a PMSI in the account receivable as proceeds for inventory if a financing statement relating to the security interest in the accounts receivable is registered before the PMSI is perfected or before a financing statement in relation to it is registered.

As one of the exceptions to the general first-in-time rule in s. 66, a PMSI holder could obtain priority over prior perfected security interests, and where accounts receivable are proceeds of inventory, factors could lose priority to PMSIs even where registered after registration of the factors' security interest.[207] Effective lobbying by the factoring industry attempted to restore the previous situation where generally, factors would have obtained priority over ineffective retention of title clauses. The government acknowledged that there had been submissions at either

203 [1991] 3 NZLR 170 (CA).
204 See s. 3, substituting new s. 4 Distress and Replevin Act 1908.
205 See Property Law Act 2007, s. 265.
206 See s. 15.
207 See s. 74.

end of the spectrum, but that in particular there had been an inability in some situations for factors to obtain priority, and that this was diminishing an important source of working capital; the resulting clause was an attempt to achieve a balance between these views. It seems to be the solution proposed by the Law Commission in its draft Bill[208] and reflects the situation in many Canadian PPSAs.

This need for a policy decision, even after the Act had been passed, shows that a PPSA is not just a mechanical means of regulating priorities, but that some hard choices will need to be made, preferably with evidence as to the relative costs and benefits of according priority to one particular type of credit over others.

Execution creditors

Despite an unperfected security interest not being ineffective against a liquidator or the Official Assignee, an exception is made for execution creditors, who are given priority over unperfected security interests. Section 103 states that the interest of an execution creditor in any collateral has priority over any security interest in the same collateral, if the latter is not perfected at the time of execution.[209]

This policy decision was probably made on the basis that execution creditors could be separately identified as creditors who had expended time and money on pursuing a debtor, so that their otherwise wasted costs were relatively harder to bear than in the case of other unsecured creditors represented by the liquidator or Official Assignee. Nevertheless, problems still remain with this provision, because of the interaction with insolvency law. Section 251 of the Companies Act [210] provides that an execution creditor who has not completed execution by sale prior to the commencement of liquidation, will have to disgorge the effects of seizure to the insolvent estate. However, given that the PPSA does not render an unperfected security interest ineffective against the liquidator or Official Assignee, the effect is that the secured creditor will be able to claim the relevant assets. This seems to suggest an unresolved conflict between two policy decisions taken in the PPSA.

Approach of the courts

There have now been a handful of significant PPSA cases at both Court of Appeal and High Court level raising or clarifying interpretation issues.[211] As a result it can be said generally that the courts have had no difficulty embracing the concept and purpose of the PPSA.

208 See fn 52 above, at p. 129, clause 27(5).

209 Section 18 Personal Property Securities Amendment Act 2004 inserts s. 103(1A) to the effect that the time of execution is the time of seizure, if applicable, or in the case of a charging or garnishee order, the time of making the order. The meaning of time of execution was uncertain, and it would not have been appropriate to follow precedents such as Companies Act 1993, s. 251 which refers to completion of execution on sale of the collateral, since that would allow perfection of an unperfected security interest before sale. However, the Bill now makes it clear that seizure is the appropriate time, but also that 'execution creditor' extends to enforcement by charging or garnishee orders, to cover collateral which is not capable of being 'seized'.

210 See also Insolvency Act 2006, s. 108.

211 There have been about eight cases before the High Court and/or Court of Appeal, though only the most important are mentioned in this article.

In the first case before the High Court, *Graham* v. *Portacom New Zealand Ltd*,[212] receivers appointed by a debenture holder which had perfected its all-embracing security agreement by registration under the Act, applied for directions as to whether they had power to sell portable cabins which had been leased to the company debtor by Portacom, which had failed to register its security interest. Section 17(1)(b) PPSA provides that security interests include a lease for a term of more than one year, whether or not it secured payment or performance of an obligation. Section 40(1) provides that a security interest attaches to collateral when value is given by the secured party and the debtor has rights in the collateral. Subsection (3) provides that for those purposes, a debtor has rights in leased goods no later than when it obtains possession of the goods. It was argued for Portacom that the debtor only had a possessory interest in the goods, and therefore could not confer any right on the debenture holder, through the receiver, to sell the buildings.

In rejecting this view, the court followed the approach of the Supreme Court of Canada in *Re Giffen*,[213] emphasising that concepts of security interest and the rights of the parties under it were no longer dependent on traditional questions of title. The Supreme Court took the view that the PPSA deemed the lessee to have a proprietary interest, at least for priority purposes. Thus Rodney Hansen J held that the debtor lessee's rights in the portable cabins were, as against its secured creditors, not merely possessory, but proprietary rights which gave it the ability to grant security in the buildings themselves, not just its leasehold interest in them. He went on to find that this deemed proprietary right was an 'asset' within the terms of the debenture.

This receptive approach to the new concepts and purpose of the Act was continued in *Agnew & Waller* v. *New Zealand Bloodstock*.[214] In this case a company, SH Lock, took a debenture over the assets of the debtor and registered a security interest on the day the PPSA came into effect. The debtor had entered into a 'lease to purchase' agreement with NZ Bloodstock in respect of a horse called 'Generous', which, for eponymous reasons, earned considerable amounts in stud fees, including in England. A later agreement extended the term of the lease arrangement, and NZ Bloodstock assigned the benefit of the agreement to NZBF. The agreement was not registered under the PPSA. In early July 2004 NZ Bloodstock repossessed the horse due to default, and two weeks later SH Lock appointed receivers, who claimed entitlement to the stallion and stud fees. Since this was the case of one registered and one unregistered security interest, the prima facie result was straightforward, SH Lock being entitled to the horse by being first to perfect.[215] However, as in *Portacom*, it was argued that the horse, being merely leased to the debtor, did not fall within 'property' charged in the debenture. Allan J at first instance, drawing support from *Portacom*, held that the broad approach to 'assets' taken there, applied to the word 'property' in this debenture. In both cases the debtor's interest in a lease fell within the term, having economic value. In this case, Allan J rejected an argument that the debenture was drafted under the 'old regime', for example referring to floating charges, so that the parties could not have intended the leasehold interest in the horse to be included within the security agreement, and the '*nemo dat*' rule would have excluded it prior

212 [2004] 2 NZLR 528.

213 (1998) 155 DLR (4th) 332, see also Bridge et al., 'Form, functionalism and understanding the law of secured transactions' (1999) 44 McGill LJ 567.

214 [2005] 2 NZLR 549(HC); [2006] 3 NZLR 629 (CA).

215 See PPSA, s. 66.

to the PPSA. However, in November 1999 they would have been well aware that the Act was pending.

Second, it was argued that in this case, unlike *Portacom*, the lessor had retaken possession of the goods and purportedly terminated the lease, at which point, it was argued, possession and ownership was merged. However, Allan J rejected this argument too, stating that NZ Bloodstock had not perfected its security interest, either by registration or by possession. Retaking possession was expressly excluded from that latter concept.[216] An argument based on certain Canadian authorities,[217] to the effect that where the lessor's interest had merged with its ownership interest, the PPSA priority rules between security interests had no relevance, was eventually rejected. Citing an academic reference to Rodney Hansen J's characterisation of the statutory proprietary basis of the debtor's lease in *Portacom*,[218] Allan J commented:

> The fact that NZBF may have legal title to Generous is simply irrelevant in a situation where as here, NZBF holds an unperfected security interest and is in competition with a party with a perfected security interest. The lessor's interest in the collateral takes or cedes priority as the case may be according to the Act's priority rules, not according to the dictates of the common law relating to legal title. It is the lessee who is to be treated as owner of the goods for registration and priority purposes, and not the lessor. Although the lessee does not itself hold legal title to Generous, it is nevertheless capable of passing good title to the leased assets, despite the fact that it has no absolute contractual right to require title itself. That is further spelt out in s24, which appears to have no counterpart in the Canadian legislation ...
>
> To those unfamiliar with the Act, this conclusion may be surprising, and perhaps difficult to accept. After all, prior to the ... Act, there could be no doubt that NZBF would have been entitled to priority over SH Lock, simply by reason of its title to Generous. But the result is a reflection of the extent to which the registration regime introduced by the Act has altered long-established priority principles grounded in notions of legal title. Irrespective of title, it is paramount that security interests be the subject of registration if priority is to be preserved.

The majority of the Court of Appeal[219] endorsed this approach, citing extracts from the English Law Commission's Consultation Paper[220] and its later Report[221] in their preference for a broad approach to characterisation of security interests under the New Zealand PPSA, ss. 17 and 36. William Young J, dissenting, stated the debenture was drafted in terms of the pre-PPSA regime, and that if Parliament had expressly intended to statutorily inflate pre-PPSA rights of security holders so that they obtained security interests greater than the rights of those conferring them, Parliament would have used explicit language. He regarded the debtor as having the same rights in Generous prior to the PPSA as it did after it's coming into force. The difference between the majority and minority turned on interpretation of s. 40,

216 See s. 41(b)(ii).

217 See: *Sprung Instant Structures Ltd* v. *Caswan Environmental Services Inc* [1997] WWR 280; *Bodnard* v. *Capital Office Systems Inc* (1992)3 PPSAC(2d) 71; *Re Glencoe Express Inc* (1992) 3 PPSAC (2d) 239.

218 See Gedye (2004) 10 NZBLQ 203, p. 206.

219 [2006] 3 NZLR 629.

220 See Report No. 164 'Registration of Security Interests: Company Charges and Property other than Land (2002), paras 7.12, 7.13, 7.18.

221 Report No. 176 Company Security Interests (2004), paras 3.31–3.32.

the majority regarding the debtor as having acquired 'rights in goods' to which the security could attach under s. 40(3). William Young J took the view that since the giving of value had pre-dated the coming into force of the PPSA, s. 40 could not have any application. Moreover, the majority's view was that (absent any express dealing with the point in transitional provisions) there should be no difference between a security agreement executed prior to 1 May 2002,[222] and one executed after that date as respects attachment of after-acquired property. Therefore, whether further value was given by the debenture holder after that date was irrelevant, since its security had already attached when funds were advanced prior to 1 May, and was perfected on 1 May. It is suggested that the majority's approach is preferable, especially given that a number of security agreements drafted in pre-PPSA terms will survive for many years, and in any event it would expose ownership-based security interests such as retention of title to a high degree of uncertainty. The majority approach, and that in the High Court decisions, shows that it is possible to apply pre-PPSA contractual documents, in a manner consistent with the substance-based, broad approach supported by cases such as *Re Giffen*.[223]

Broad meaning of 'security interest'

The above decisions emphasise that a 'substance over form' inherent in the legislation itself[224] has been reflected in the early Court of Appeal decisions.[225] The Court of Appeal in *Shephard and Dunphy* v. *Sleepyhead* also took the opportunity to clarify how the lack of conceptual and terminological harmonisation between the Companies Act 1993 and the PPSA could be resolved. Although there were significant amendments to the 1993 Act brought about, as a result of the review of insolvency law, by the Companies Amendment Act 2006, the government elected, in that review process, to retain the Companies Act language of 'charge'.[226] The Court concluded that although a 'security interest' is defined in the Companies Act as someone holding a charge, and 'charge' is defined in s. 2 of that Act as 'a right or interest in relation to property *owned* by a company, by virtue of which a creditor of the company is entitled to claim payment in priority to creditors', 'owned' in this context must be read in a manner consistent with the PPSA. Therefore in the context of retention of title, the goods were 'owned' by the buyer for PPSA purposes even though title was retained by the seller under the Sale of Goods Act. Thus, Sleepyhead was entitled to be paid by the liquidator in priority to unsecured creditors under the Companies Act. This was consistent with the interpretation given by the Court in its earlier decisions on the ability of chattel lessees to create security interests for PPSA purposes.[227] This decision attempted to avoid the consequences of the persistence of form over substance in the Companies Act definitions of 'charge' and 'secured creditor'.

222 The date when the PPSA came into force; see fn 8 above.
223 (1998) 155 DLR (4th) 332.
224 See s. 17.
225 See also *Simpson* v. *Shephard and Dunphy* (*Liquidators of Service Foods Manawatu Ltd*) [2007] 2 NZLR 130, discussed at p. 341 above.
226 There may have been other consequences for company law of removing the language of 'charge' and replacing it with 'security interest' in PPSA terms, for example in terms of harmonisation with the voluntary administration provisions of Australian law, where the 'charge' is still used, absent a PPSA regime to date there.
227 See: *Graham* v. *Portacom NZ Ltd* [2004] 2 NZLR 528; *Waller* v. *NZ Bloodstock Ltd* [2006] 3 NZLR 629.

There have been a number of High Court decisions, particularly concerning retention of title clauses, where this broad approach has been upheld, illustrating that the New Zealand courts have been generally remarkably alert to the need to adapt to the new paradigm and embrace Canadian jurisprudence.

In a number of retention of title cases, the High Court has followed[228] the approach taken by the Court of Appeal and commentators[229] to the effect that concepts of title and ownership are not decisive of the scope of security interests. Thus conditional sale agreements and retention of title clauses are within s. 17. In one such case,[230] it has been stressed that although the definition governs consensually arising security interests, there is no requirement that possession by the debtor be consensual.

However, the most recent High Court case does suggest that ultimately, it is impossible to remove uncertainty and reconcile the discordant old and new concepts and terminology without legislative intervention. In a further two judgments arising out of the Service Foods Manawatu receivership and liquidation, Dobson J[231] had to deal with the issue of the value of the purchase money security interest and thus the distribution of monies held by the receivers where a retention of title claimant claimed an interest in stock in priority to a bank's general security agreement. The case is interesting as it deals with some of the factual issues which traditionally arose in a supplier attempting to establish a retention-of-title claim, for example identification of stock unpaid for. In this particular case, while Dobson J said that the PPSA had not made any difference to the contractual relationship, so that it would normally be for the supplier to prove that remaining stock in hand was unpaid for, in this case there was a running account type of dealing, so the normal inference would have been that earlier stock supplied would be paid for first, i.e the rule in *Clayton's Case*.[232] The receiver argued that there would have to be a 'ruling off' of the indebtedness as at the date of perfection of the PMSI so that subsequent payments would have to be applied to fresh liabilities incurred thereafter. This was because s. 293 Companies Act 1993 provided for 'voidable charges', which could be avoided if created within one year prior to liquidation, but with the proviso in subsection (4) that 'nothing in subsection (1) applies to a charge given by a company that secures the unpaid purchase price of property, whether or not the charge is given over that property, if the instrument creating the charge is executed not later than 30 days after the sale of the property.

> (1) For the purposes of … subsection (4), where any charge was given by the company within the specified period ... all payments received by the grantee of the charge after it was given shall be deemed to have been appropriated so far as may be necessary–
>
> (b) towards payment of the actual price or value of property sold by the grantee to the company on or after the giving of the charge.'

228 See: *JS Brooksbank & Co* v. *EXFTX Ltd*, HC Auckland, 21/11/07, Stevens J, CIV 2006-404-5693; *Segard Masurel (NZ) Ltd* v. *Nicol and others*, HC Auckland, 9/10/07, Cooper J, CIV 2007-404-3603.

229 See, for example, Gedye, 'What's yours is mine: attachment of security interests to third party assets' (2004) 10 NZBLQ 203.

230 *JS Brooksbank & Co* v. *EXFTX Ltd (in rec and liq)*, 21/11/07, HC Auckland, Stevens J, CIV 2006-404-5963.

231 HC Wellington, CIV 2007-485-1563, 28/4/08.

232 (1816) MER 529.

Thus this provision, insofar as it affects charges given by the company over its assets, would apply within the one-year period. However, under pre-PPSA law of course, the retention of title clause was not a charge given by the company, and not over assets of the company; rather it was retention of title by the supplier.

Nevertheless, the dicta in *Dunphy* v. *Sleepyhead Manufacturing* discussed above,[233] states that for the purposes of the PPSA the debtor can be said to be an owner for the purposes of conferring a security interest, and in the context of a retention of title claim this approach is consistent with the earlier cases of *Graham* v. *Portacom* and *Waller* v. *NZ Bloodstock Ltd.*[234] Therefore, the goods in the possession of Service Foods in this case are 'owned' for the purposes of conferring the security interest on the supplier. In *Dunphy* the Court of Appeal concluded that the security interest in that case was a 'charge' for the purposes of the Companies Act as it entitled the supplier to claim payment in priority to unsecured creditors within s. 2(1) of that Act. In the instant case, Dobson J stated that: 'once this extended definition applies for any purposes under the Companies Act, consistency required it to apply for all purposes, including section 293'. He also stated that he had real reservations about this but applied it in the interests of commercial certainty. The unsatisfactory consequences for holders of retention of title clauses and other PMSIs identified by Dobson J were that:

> it will likely mean that amounts outstanding in an existing supply relationship at the time a PMSI is taken can only be recovered after there has been full payment for goods supplied after the PMSI is perfected, if the purchaser becomes insolvent within one year of the security. Suppliers in the same situation may be forced to stipulate for a PMSI from the very outset of a trading relationship. Where there is a history of unsecured supplies, suppliers will have to devise other strategies to recover, or secure payment of, the debt outstanding at the time a PMSI is put in place.

However, in a later judgment,[235] this earlier judgment was recalled and this issue (inter alia) was reopened. Dobson J decided that s. 293 had no application in a case between two secured creditors. Counsel for the receivers argued that the supplier was an unsecured creditor in relation to the pre-perfection goods unpaid for, so that it was not strictly a priority issue between two secured creditors. Of course, s. 293 provides that charges falling within it are 'voidable' at the instance of the liquidator, and the liquidator has to issue a notice to set aside such a charge to the extent that it is voidable.[236] Therefore strictly speaking, although Service Foods was in liquidation, the issue between the receivers and the retention of title claimant did not strictly engage s. 293. However, the point was well made in the first judgment that s. 293, following the dicta of the Court of Appeal in *Shephard and Dunphy* v. *Sleepyhead*, does now extend to retention of title claims and other security interests within the PPSA. In a contest between a liquidator and a ROT claimant, the point made in the first judgment is a valid one. Moreover, while suppliers and their advisers may not have appreciated these consequences, it is not so clear that this result is so unfair. It recognises the reality that these contractual arrangements formerly acknowledged as quasi-security despite the seller retaining ownership in contract law, have always been security devices designed to

233 [2007] 3 NZLR 602, CA, discussed above, p. 341.
234 See fn 215 above.
235 *NZARFD Ltd* v. *Simpson and Walton*, HC Wellington, 20/6/08, CIV 2007-485-1563.
236 See Companies Act 1993, s. 294.

give the supplier a lawful advantage over other unsecured creditors. If the law against voidable charges already deals with 'purchase money charges', why should it treat PMSIs any differently? The objective of such provisions is to reverse security taken other than for true new value, and it is entirely consistent that this should apply to retention of title clauses. Whilst the registration system has meant that retention of title clauses and other PMSIs still need perfecting on the register, there are other advantages of the PPSA regime for retention of title clauses, given that there is a statutory security over proceeds, and provisions governing commingling.[237]

Conclusions

Though the New Zealand PPSA was a long time in development, once commenced, the legislative process was unduly expeditious, and this led to immediate and subsequent amendments. There continue to be legislative problems, many of which are detailed matters that have been and will continue to be interpreted by the courts, but others are more fundamental, such as the effect on insolvency, and the interaction with other legislation.

In providing salutary lessons for adoption of PPSA regimes elsewhere, a holistic approach is strongly urged. It might be politically hard to achieve, particularly in bureaucratic regimes, but in the long term, comprehensive reform is preferable. For example, insolvency, other creditors' remedies, and both non-corporate and corporate security over personal property, all need addressing at the same time, along with a careful scrutiny of other statutes upon which the regime will impact. The New Zealand experience shows that a PPSA regime is not simply a mechanistic registration system, but will throw up hard policy choices to be made on priorities between different interest-groups; – it is better that such choices are made in an informed and consultative process than at a very late stage by a Parliamentary draftsperson or civil servant.

Second, if the PPSA is primarily to be a facilitative statute, with consumer protection provisions dealt with in other legislation, it needs to be very clear where the lines are drawn. In any event, though default remedies should be included, it has to be recognised that they do have a different impact on consumers, so that it is impossible to completely separate commercial and consumer debtors into different statutory regimes. Where consumers are affected, they should not be forgotten, as they are a diverse and poorly represented group.

If following models in other jurisdictions, as Ziegel points out, there have to be good reasons for departing from them on the detail then the question needs to be asked whether the situation is really different locally, or whether lobbying by interest groups is attempting to preserve common law positions that are no longer credible?

In New Zealand, the position of factors, landlords' right of distress, circular priorities, and preservation of the status quo regarding subordination of (former) floating charge realisations to preferential creditors, all resulted from trying to make new terminology fit, or to adjust to take account of different groups' vested positions. Issues remain in terms of harmonisation with retained concepts of 'charge' in the Companies Act. It is an impossible task to adapt new terminology and concepts in order to reflect completely the previous common law position; sometimes substantive changes will have to be made. The history of the New Zealand experience to date also suggests that, though the system is an improvement on the previous

237 See Brown and Sampson, fn 84 above.

patchwork of common law and registration systems, personal property securities legislation cannot be drafted in isolation from underlying personal and corporate legislation concerning credit and insolvency. If the latter position is not followed then there will be inefficiencies, litigation costs and commercial uncertainty, which the new registration system was designed to remove.

Nevertheless, one hesitates to be too negative. The express objectives of the government were to simplify the law, reduce transaction and agency costs associated with unregistered securities, and remove arbitrary consequences stemming from conceptual distinctions.[238] So for there is no reason to think that these are not being largely achieved.

In the matter of detail, and relationship to other legislation, New Zealand should have paid more attention to eminent overseas advisers and precedents. Nevertheless, the adjustments made in the North American regimes suggest that a certain amount of subsequent legislative amendment will be inevitable. There is always a temptation to expect a new statutory code to deal with every situation, but judicial interpretation can sometimes avoid the need for legislative amendment. Use of North American concepts, and in many cases whole sections from Canadian statutes, should mean that there is plenty of judicial precedent and already we are starting to see a welcome absorption of overseas Commonwealth case law into our commercial and PPSA jurisprudence.[239] The adoption by Australia[240] of the New Zealand model of PPSA reform will further enhance this process.

238 From Cabinet Committee on Enterprise, Industry and Environment (CIE/95/M42/9), minutes of 13 December 1995 (released under Official Information Act 1982).

239 The first example of this, *Graham and Gibson* v. *Portacom* [2004] 2 NZLR 528, draws on Canadian case law, see also. *Service Foods Manawatu Ltd* (*in rec & liq*) v. *NZ Associated Refrigerated Food Distributors Ltd* (2006) 9 NZCLC 263, 979; *Harvestpro Logging Ltd* v. *Cordyline Holdings Ltd*, 3/10/06, HC, Auckland, Doogue AJ, CIV 2006-404-3107. However, the Court of Appeal has sounded a note of caution that the New Zealand legislation is not wholly identical to any one Canadian jurisdiction, see *NZ Bloodstock Ltd* v. *Waller & Agnew* [2005] 2 NZLR 549, p. 550.

240 See Australia's PPS Bill 2009 (Cwth), passed by the House of Representatives on 16 September 2009 and expected to become a full Act later in 2009. However the new PPS Act 2009 is not expected to come into force until 2011.

11 Personal property security law reform in Australia

History, influences, themes and the future

Simon Fisher

Introduction

The enactment of the Companies Act 2006 in the UK signalled, for the time being at any rate, a conclusive rejection by the UK government of the case for personal property security (PPS) law reform. In Australia however, the prospects for reform of this area of law have never been brighter and it now appears highly likely that we will see enacted a new Personal Property Securities Act which is expected to come into force in 2011. This chapter has three essential objectives. The first is to provide a short history of reform initiatives and attempts in the area of PPS law (or secured transactions law) in Australia. The second is to identify and map the most important international and domestic influences on Australian personal property security law reform. The third objective is to identify and explore some of the key themes in personal property security law reform in Australia. Given that Australia is now likely to enact a new Act in this area, UK readers might find this material of considerable interest if, as seems likely, the subject of reform is raised again in the near future.

If one looks at the meaning of 'security interest' at common law, then the scheme developed by Lord Jauncey is a good starting point. He stated:

> A right in security is a right over property given by a debtor to a creditor whereby the latter in the event of the debtor's failure, acquires priority over the property against the general body of creditors of the debtor. It is of the essence of a right in security that a debtor possesses in relation to the property a right which he can transfer to the creditor, which right must be retransferred to him upon payment of the debt.[1]

This statement describing the essential nature of a security interest can be broken down into the following classification scheme by which a security interest is:

(a) a right over property;
(b) given or ceded by the debtor over the debtor's property in favour of the creditor;
(c) it is activated by a breach of a contract, duty or other obligation owed by the debtor to the creditor;

1 See *Armour* v. *Thyssen Edelstahlwerke AG* [1991] 2 AC 339, p. 354F–G.

(d) the creditor acquires priority over the secured property of the debtor as against the general (or unsecured) creditors of the debtor; and
(e) the security right is defeasible – the creditor's rights over the debtor's property can be annulled if the debtor performs the duty owed to the creditor.[2]

This classification represents an atomisation of security for general law purposes and helps to demarcate security from other property and obligatory relationships.[3]

At a more general level McCormack has stated[4] that any modern secured transactions law must be founded upon the following five critical elements:

(a) the security right must adhere to the essential qualities of a property right (right in *rem*);
(b) the law should provide for the granting of security in the widest possible range of circumstances;
(c) the existence of a security right over property must be effectively publicised;
(d) there should be a rapid and cost-effective means of recovering the debt from the secured asset; and
(e) the cost of creating, maintaining and exercising the right should be kept at a reasonable level.

These five elements represent what might be termed as the critical design features and goals of a modern secured transactions law. There is no conceptual incompatibility between these two accounts of security provided above.

Personal property securities are securities over personal property interests.[5] It is not intended in this chapter to enter into (never mind resolve) the debate whether securities represent an example of numerus clausus.[6] The focus of this chapter is on non-possessory personal property securities, not on possessory personal property securities.[7] In short this chapter will argue that Australia should now enact a new Personal Property Security Act that adopts a substance over form approach in the characterisation, operation and consequences of personal property securities. The PPS Bill brought out by the Attorney General of Australia's Department and introduced into the Federal Parliament in June 2009[8] is the model that should be followed, subject to amendment brought about following consultations and the normal legislative process. If Australia does this, then its secured transaction law will be in alignment with international best practice. This will have the added benefit of

2 See generally: Fisher *Commercial and Personal Property Law* (Sydney: Butterworths, 1997), para. [8.2]; Goode *Legal Problems of Credit and Security* (3rd edn, London: Sweet & Maxwell, 2003), pp. 11–12.
3 See Ali, *The Law of Secured Finance: an International Survey of Security Interests over Personal Property* (Oxford: Oxford University Press, 2002), ch. 2, for explanations of security interests.
4 See McCormack 'Personal property security law reform in England and Canada' [2002] JBL 113, p. 116.
5 See, generally, op. cit., Fisher, fn 2, chs 1 and 2 and the material cited there.
6 For examples of this debate, see the chapter by de Lacy in the present volume, pp. 27–37.
7 For a review of the general law on possessory personal property securities (namely the pledge and lien), see op. cit., Fisher, fn 2, ch 6.
8 Available at www.ag.gov.au. The PPS Bill 2009, which should be passed by the end of the year, contains 343 clauses and is one of the best pieces of such legislation seen so far.

harmonising Australia's secured transactions law with that of New Zealand,[9] which will help to achieve a raft of uniform trans-Tasman business laws.

A history of personal property security reform in Australia

The reform of Australia's laws on PPS must be based on clear defects in the operation of the current laws. Furthermore, any legislative reform must have the capacity or propensity to cure the particular defects identified. With this in mind, it is useful to look briefly at the current state of play concerning PPS law in Australia with a view to demonstrating why reform is necessary.

Commentators approach the topic of security over personalty by lamenting the current state of law in this area.[10] Gillooly writes:[11]

> The law in Australia relating to securities over personalty is in a confused and uncertain state. Under the current regime, the legal position of security holders is determined by reference to a patchwork of State and Federal legislation, superimposed on a fabric of often outmoded principles or case law. The rights and liabilities of the debtor and third parties vis a vis the secured creditor, are largely dependent upon the form of the security transaction rather then its substance. The availability of statutory procedures for the registration of security interests and the consequences of failing to utilise such procedures vary with a medley of factors including: the type of property over which the security is given; the jurisdiction within which that property is located; the legal nature of the security giver; and the mould in which the security agreement is cast.

It would seem incontrovertible that PPS law in Australia is in a chaotic state. An eminent Australia commentator, the late Professor David Allan, has described PPS law in Australia as a 'multiple and complex system of state and federal laws and procedures'.[12] A similar type of claim about the complexity and anomalous state of some aspects of PPS law has been made in the UK where that state of the law is much the same as in Australia.[13] The parlous state of the law in Australia could not continue and the modern process of reforming the law began in the 1990s. Various law commissions started the process off and this was quickly followed by private sector and academic initiatives, before the government took the law reform project onboard.

The modern reform movement can usefully be divided into two phases, each of which are now considered in turn.

9 On which, see the chapter by Brown in the present volume, pp. 328–65.

10 See op. cit., Fisher, fn 2, ch 8; Fisher '*Romalpa* clauses as security interests: problems, pitfalls and solutions' [1993] JIBFL, pp. 74–9; 119–26.

11 See Gillooly 'Introduction' in Gillooly (ed.) *Securities over Personalty* (Sydney: Federation Press, 1994), p. xix.

12 See Allan, Quirk, Martin 'Chairman's Introduction' (2002) 14 *Bond Law Review* 8, p. 8.

13 See: Goode 'The modernisation of personal property security law' (1984) 100 LQR 234; Bridge 'Form, substance and innovation in personal property security law' [1992] JBL 1. However, not all commentators think that the UK needs a new PPSA type of system; see generally the chapters by McCormack (pp. 83–116) and Calnan (pp. 162–87) in the present volume.

The first phase of reform

The first phase of reform began in 1992 and ended in 2002, encompassing five main developments:

(a) In 1992 the Australian Law Reform Commission (ALRC) and the Law Commission of New South Wales (NSW) issued a joint discussion paper entitled 'Personal Property Securities'[14] which was followed, in August 1993, by ALRC *Interim Report No. 64* 'Personal Property Securities'.

(b) In August 1992 the Victorian Law Reform Commission and the Queensland Law Reform Commission issued a joint discussion paper 'Personal Property Securities Law: A Blueprint for Reform'. This discussion paper proposed wholesale reform to Australian law, but it differed in key policy respects from the joint proposals of the ALRC and NSW Law Commission in (a) above.

(c) The initiatives in (a) and (b) above were followed by a further discussion paper 'Personal Property Securities – A National Approach' issued by the Commonwealth Attorney General's Department (Business Law Division) in January 1995, which invited comments and submissions from the public on a range of proposals to reform the law.

(d) In December 1995 a Personal Property Security Law Reform Workshop was held at Bond University and developed a plan of action embracing several measures to make law reform a reality. These measures included convening a taskforce to confirm, estimate and promote the benefits of PPS law reform for Australia in 1996. A second taskforce was established in 1997 to deal with any measures that state governments might propose. The 1995 Workshop identified the following objectives as needed in any reform measures that might be brought in at a later date.

- a legal regime that is uniform throughout Australia;
- a single legal regime for the regulation of priorities – both as between security interest holders, and as between security interest holders and other claimants to the debtor's property;
- a single national system of registration for personal property securities;
- a functional definition of personal property securities (i.e. a definition which covers anything which functions as a security over personal property, with the possibility of specific exclusions or inclusions to be considered);
- a system which applies to all types of personal property and all types of debtors;
- a legal regime where priorities depend on the date of registration and not on notice (actual or constructive);
- a legal regime which accommodates, in substance, Australia's floating charge subject only to the objective of determining priority by the date of registration; and
- a legal regime which recognises the implications for a system of personal property security priorities of the legal issues addressed in Article 9 of the US Uniform Commercial Code and its Canadian counterparts, in particular the enforceability of security agreements and remedies upon default.

14 See: ALRC Discussion Paper No. 52; NSW Law Reform Commission Discussion Paper No. 29 (1992).

The above were the accepted benchmarks for the future reform project and any future proposals would have to be judged against them.

(e) In April 2002 Bond University held another Workshop on personal property security law reform. At this workshop a new draft Personal Property Security Act was revealed for discussion that had been developed after several years' work by a Committee of the Banking and Financial Services Law Association of Australia and New Zealand and of the Financial Services Committee of the Business Law Section of the Law Council of Australia.[15]

This completed the first phase of the law reform and in 2002 it remained speculative as to whether or not the reform project would be taken any further and be adopted by state and national governments. Fortunately, as the second phase, discussed below, reveals, any fears that law reform would falter, as happened in the UK, were to prove groundless.

The second phase of law reform

The second phase of law reform began in April 2006 when the State Committee of Attorney Generals (SCAG) issued an options paper[16] which canvassed the general case for reforming PPS law and the shape such reform might take. In order to promote this work the Commonwealth Attorney General sponsored public seminars in all mainland state capitals with more than 300 people attending. Such was the success of this measure that in August 2006 the Australian government announced that it now supported harmonisation and rationalisation of the law in this area.[17]

Following widespread acceptance throughout Australia that fundamental reform was now needed SCAG then effectively took over the reform project. The Work of SCAG in propelling PPS reform from idea to reality cannot be underestimated and the next stage of the reform process came in the form of four separate discussion papers:

Discussion Paper 1

In November 2006[18] SCAG issued its first discussion paper entitled 'Review of the Law of Personal Property Securities: Discussion Paper; Registration and Search Issues'. This paper canvassed the general reform question but expanded into the specific issues relating to a new registration system. It was clear from the tone of this paper that the reform project was on track and this was later confirmed by the papers that followed.

Discussion Paper 2

In March 2007 a second paper was issued by SCAG: 'Review of the Law of Personal Property Securities: Discussion Paper 2; Extinguishment, Priorities, Conflict of Laws,

15 See further Allan (2002) 14 *Bond Law Review* 1.

16 The paper was 'Review of the Law of Personal Property Securities', comments sought by 2 June 2006.

17 See 'Review of the Law of Personal Property Securities: Discussion Paper 3, Possessory Security Interests' (SCAG, Australia, April 2007), p. 5, para. 36; available at www.ag.gov.au.

18 The closing date for responses to this paper was 9 February 2007.

Enforcement, Insolvency'. By the time this paper was published, reform was firmly on the agenda, as the paper stated:

> it is proposed that Australia should adopt the New Zealand model as the basis for reform except where good cause can be shown for departing from it.[19]

Discussion Paper 3

In April 2007[20] a third paper was published: 'Review of the Law of Personal Property Securities: Discussion Paper 3; Possessory Security Interests'. This paper concerned security interests over investment property, negotiable instruments, chattel papers, accounts and liens. Taken together, the three discussion papers covered most of the main topics that needed to be dealt with if workable reforms were to be introduced at a later date.

By the summer of 2007 a comprehensive scheme of PPS reform was under way. The reform process was fully transparent and open to full public/interest group participation. Following due consideration of all the responses to the three discussion papers, on 16 May 2008 the Australian Attorney General[21] was able to publish a new draft Personal Property Security Bill for public consultation.[22] Once again, in the spirit of openness and accountability that has characterised the Australian reform project, full publicity was given to the Bill and the public were encouraged to give their views. As part of the consultation process a number of public seminars were held to promote the Bill and encourage comment. Most of these seminars were held in the week beginning 26 May 2008 at Sydney, Melbourne, Perth and Brisbane. A further seminar was later held on 3 July 2008 in Adelaide.

As a result of all this consultation, by August 2008 SCAG was able to move onto the more technical side of the reform project and published its Fourth Discussion Paper: 'Review of the Law of Personal Property Securities: Discussion Paper; Regulations to be made under a new Personal Property Security Act'.[23] As its name suggests, this paper covered the technical aspects of a new Act and the regulations that would need to be brought in to ensure that the new Act worked in practice.

It can be seen from the above that Australia has taken the question of reforming its laws in this area very seriously. Given that Australia is made up of both national (Commonwealth) and local (state) governments it is remarkable that such unity of purpose has been achieved in such a relatively short period of time. Crucial to this harmony has been the fact that the government has been prepared to put resources into the reform project. In contrast to the UK,[24] government support was aided by

19 See Discussion Paper 2, p. 13, para. 56.

20 Responses to this paper were for 18 June 2007.

21 Robert McClelland MP.

22 The closing date for responses to this Bill was 5 August 2008. The Bill is an impressive and comprehensive document stretching to 307 draft sections. Professor Duggan has commented on the proposed new PPS Bill: 'The proposed Australian reforms are superior in a number of respects to Article 9-type laws in other jurisdictions'; see *Submission to Senate Legal and Constitutional Affairs Committee Inquiry into the PPS Bill 2008* available at www.aph.gov.au.

23 Comments to be received by 17 October 2008.

24 For the UK position and various views thereon see the chapters in this volume by de Lacy (pp. 3–82), McCormack (pp. 83–116), Calnan (pp. 162–87) and Ziegel (pp. 117–61).

the fact that most people in Australia supported the case for reform and the introduction of a new PPS law. This support can only have been encouraged by the experience of our neighbour New Zealand which had implemented a new Personal Property Security Act in 1999.[25] It is interesting to note that, contrary to what happened in the UK, the Australian legal[26] and financial communities fully embraced reform. This support was key to gaining government approval for the reform project.[27]

The rationale and purpose of the new reform Bill can been explained under the following five principles:[28]

(a) adopting a functional approach to secured lending over personal property;
(b) establishing a comprehensive orderly set of rules based on a system of alerts;
(c) providing adequate protection to certain classes of people – primarily consumers;
(d) managing transition; and
(e) encouraging parties to manage risk.

So far the reform project had been propelled by SCAG. However, if the proposals were ever to achieve legislative force, then government action was needed. Given the federal nature of the Australian state, the legislative process itself could be seen as an impediment to reform. Australia is made up of six individual states (New South Wales; Victoria; Queensland; Western Australia; South Australia and Tasmania) two self-governing internal territories (Capital Territory and the Northern Territory), an internal non-self-governing territory (Jarvis Bay Territory) and seven external territories.[29] The six states mentioned were federated under the Commonwealth of Australia under enabling legislation enacted by the UK Parliament in 1900.[30] However, legislative power in Australia is shared between the Commonwealth and the states and, in particular, this applies to legislative competence in respect of commercial matters generally and personal property securities in particular.[31] Therefore, in order that a

25 On which, see the chapter in this volume by Brown, pp. 328–65.

26 See the chapter in this volume by Calnan, pp. 162–87, for a typical approach by an English City practitioner to the question of PPS reform. Note also the chapter in this volume by de Lacy at p. 79 fn. 581 and the main text thereat.

27 'Throughout the 1990s a core of legal practitioners and banking and finance representatives maintained a spirited campaign for personal property security reform'; Sandra Henderson-Kelly, Senior Legal Officer, Australian Attorney General's Department, Paper 'Personal Property Securities Law – An Update' 16 September 2008, paper given to Law Society of New South Wales CLC Conference, p. 1 para. 6; available at www.ag.gov.au/pps/papers.

28 See Sandra Henderson-Kelly's Paper, above fn 27, p. 2, para. 10.

29 For a more detailed history see I. Stewart 'Structure of the Australian legal system' in G. Moens and R. Biddot (eds), *The Convergence of Legal Systems in the 21st Century: an Australian Approach* (Brisbane: Australian Institute of Comparative Law/Copyright Publishing Co. Pty Ltd, 2002), pp. 181–208.

30 See the Constitution of the Commonwealth of Australia Act 1900 (UK), s. 9. The Australian Constitution was 'repatriated' by the Australia Act 1986 (Commonwealth) and the Australia Act 1986 (UK). See generally: O'Brien 'The Australia Acts' in Ellinghaus, Bradbrook and Duggan (eds), *The Emergence of Australian Law* (Sydney: Butterworths, 1989), pp. 337–54.

31 For example, company charges are regulated by federal statute, Corporations Act 2001, at Chapter 2K, while most other forms of securities beside company charges are governed by state law.

new fully national scheme of reformed PPS law could operate uniformly throughout Australia cooperation at both national and state level is a prerequisite.[32]

Fortunately, constitutional issues have not caused any problems to the reform project. In October 2008 the Australian Federal government met with the state and territory governments and agreement was reached on how reform should be taken forward. Rather than each state legislating on its own version, or versions, of a PPS Act, instead the states have agreed to refer legislative power on this area to the Commonwealth Parliament under the Commonwealth of Australia Constitution, s. 51 (xxxvii).[33] This agreement was reached in the landmark Personal Property Security Agreement, signed on 2 October 2008 by all states and territories and the Commonwealth. By virtue of this agreement it was now anticipated that we would see by the end of 2009 a new Personal Property Security Act which was expected to apply uniformly throughout Australia from May 2010.

The PPS Law Agreement was the most significant step forward so far in the quest for law reform in this area and, for the first time, fundamental reform came within our grasp. Under the Agreement the Commonwealth will enact legislation reforming PPS law and establish a new national system of regulation.[34] The Commonwealth Parliament will have power to amend any new Act following consultation with the states and territories.[35] The states and territories will later repeal any existing legislation that might inhibit the operation and establishment of the new Act as the main source of regulation in this area.[36] There are minor exceptions in terms of having a truly national system of PPS law, for example, security interests over fixtures and water rights will not be subject to the new Act.[37] Any new Personal Property Security Act will be reviewed 'no later than 5 years after the commencement of the national system'.[38] The Personal Property Security Bill of May 2008 would form the basis of any future scheme, subject to amendments brought about by the consultation process and normal process of legislative enactment. The Bill was introduced into the Federal Parliament in November 2008 and referred to the Senate Standing Committee on Legal and Constitutional Affairs for inquiry and report. The Senate Standing Committee reported back in March 2009 commenting favourably on the Bill but recommended that further work and consultation was necessary before it could be enacted and it also recommended that the potential commencement date be put back until May 2011 to allow for this to take place.[39] The Federal Attorney General's Department accepted most of the Committee's Report and a new revised PPS Bill 2009 was then introduced into the

32 For discussion of the constitutional issues pre-phase 2 reform see: Rose 'Uniform personal property security legislation for Australia – constitutional issues' (2002) 14 *Bond Law Review* 26; Hetherington 'The constitutional mechanism for personal property security legislation in Australia: a comment on the constitutional issues' (2002) 14 *Bond Law Review* 55.

33 The self-governing territories are not party to the referral but have signed the national agreement and so will be caught by the new personal property security regime when finally enacted in 2009. This process was used to achieve a single national corporate law in the shape of the Corporations Act 2001 (Commonwealth).

34 See PPS Law Agreement Recitals, Clause 3.

35 See PPS Law Agreement, Clause 4.

36 See generally PPS Law Agreement, Clause 3.1.

37 See generally, PPS Law Agreement, Clause 3.2.

38 See PPS Law Agreement, Part 6.

39 The Senate Report is available at www.ag.gov.au/pps/papers. See also the Report of 20 August 2009 discussed above in the main text.

House of Representatives on 24 June 2009. The Bill was then passed on to the Senate Legal and Constitutional Affairs Committee for Report. On 2 July the Council of Australian Governments agreed that any new PPS Act should not come into force until May 2011 to allow adequate time for the commercial community to adopt to the new regime. The Senate Committee reported back to Parliament on 20 August recommending in their Report that the PPS Bill be passed subject to minor points. The Bill is currently still going through the Parliamentary process but it now appears certain that it will become an Act before the end of 2009, however the new PPS Act will not come into force until 2011.

It can be seen from the above discussion that law reform in Australia is now at an advanced stage and it is now likely that Australia will join the 'club'[40] of nations enjoying a functional system of security interest regulation.

Influences on PPS reform in Australia

As law reform is now at an advanced stage in Australia, it is useful to put this reform into an international context and consider some of the more salient forces that have aided the reform process.

Globalisation

There can be no doubt that one of the 'buzzwords' or additions to the argot of the marketplace, particularly in the international business marketplace is 'globalisation'.[41] Globalisation has been defined by one commentator as:

> Globalisation refers to the multiplicity or linkages and interconnections between the states and the societies which make up the present world system. It describes the process by which events, decisions and activities in one part of the world come to have significant consequences for individuals and communities in quite distant parts of the globe. Globalisation has two distinct phenomena: scope (or stretching) and intensity (or deepening). On the one hand, it defines a set of processes which embrace most of the globe or which operate worldwide; the concept therefore has a spatial connotation ... On the other hand, it also implies an intensification of the levels of interaction, interconnectedness or interdependence between the states and societies which constitute the world community. Accordingly, alongside the stretching goes a deepening of global process.[42]

It is well recognised that globalisation has several dimensions, including economic, political, cultural and ideological.[43] In their masterly study of global business regulation,

40 E.g. USA, Canada, New Zealand.

41 See generally Fisher 'Commercial law in a global context: current influences and the future for Australia' in A. Mugasha *Perspectives on Commercial Law* (Sydney: Prospect Publishing Ltd, 1999), ch 10.

42 See A. McGrew 'Conceptualising global politics' in A. McGrew and P. Lewis (eds), *Global Politics: Globalisation and the Nation State*, cited by J. Dunning 'The role of FDI in a globalising economy', in G. Green and T. Brewer (eds), *Investment in Asia and the Pacific Rim* (New York: Oceana Publications, 1995), p. 44.

43 For an analysis of these dimensions to globalisation see M. Steger *Globalisation: a Very Short Introduction* (Oxford: Oxford University Press, 2003), chs 3–6.

Braithwaite and Drahos[44] identified three distinct kinds of globalisation, namely, the globalisation of firms, of markets and of regulation. In Australia the *Financial Inquiry Final Report* (the Wallis Report) conducted in relation to the Australian financial system identified the globalisation dimension to the Australian financial markets in these terms:

> As a result of the liberalisation of trade and capital flows, Australian financial markets have become increasingly global over the last decade and are now characterised by a relatively high degree of integration with international markets. Australian businesses and markets have responded in four ways: fund raising by corporations and institutions is becoming increasingly global; foreign inwards and outwards investment are both growing; trading is becoming more international; and the location decisions of many financial services corporations reflect an increasingly international perspective.[45]

Secured transactions law operates interstitially with trade and capital flows which, as stated above, form part of the globalisation phenomenon. Therefore, a tentative claim can be made that some kind of connection exists between secured transactions law and globalisation. The link between the secured transactions law and globalisation that can be identified is that globalisation is propelling momentum towards a common conceptual framework for secured transactions law that rests upon the dominant substance over form paradigm.

Golding has referred to globalisation in these terms:

> 'Globalisation' is said to mean the end of national politics, which will be replaced by exchange in a totally free global market for goods, services and ideas.[46]

Whether Golding endorses this view, or is simply reporting it, is of no great moment here, but the interesting point embodied in this view is the reference to the global market for ideas. The movement of commercial ideas is essential to international commercial law and practice and when good ideas are adopted by market participants, the result is improvements in business-to-business relations or in business-to-consumer relations. An illustration of this phenomenon at work is the growth of the 'due diligence' practice in the acquisition and disposal of business assets. Whatever its origin, the term 'due diligence' has entered the commercial law lexicon and is now entrenched as a feature of the commercial legal landscape.[47] Other cross-border travellers include the concepts of 'lender liability'[48] and 'truth in lending'.[49] Article 9 of the US UCC has also become a potent symbol of the forces driving change in global secured transactions law.[50] If we focus on globalisation simply as an abstract phenomenon, we are apt to lose sight of exactly what its impact is in a business sense.

44 See Braithwaite and Drahos *Global Business Regulation* (Cambridge: Cambridge University Press, 2000), p. 7.

45 See Report: *Financial System Inquiry Final Report* (Commonwealth of Australia, Canberra, March 1997), section 4.3.

46 See Golding 'Globalisation, national sovereignty and the harmonisation of laws' [1998] Uniform Law Review 435, p. 437.

47 See generally W. Duncan and S. Travers *Due Diligence* (Sydney: LBC Information Services, 1995).

48 See generally J. O'Donnovan *Lender Liability* (Sydney: LBC Information Services, 2000).

49 There is a Truth in Lending statute in the US; see 15 USC s. 1601 *et seq.*

50 See Simmonds 'Getting Article 9: an introduction to a Panel's Papers on Secured Transactions Law In Australia', in A. Mugasha (ed.), above fn 41, pp. 77–8.

Steger describes the economic dimensions of globalisation as the intensification and stretching of economic interrelations across the globe. Some of these economic interrelations include the liberalisation of financial transactions which proceed hand in glove with the intensification of financial trading. So in the train of these developments in the intensification and stretching of economic interrelations has come the quest for a common global platform for secured transactions law. The process of globalisation is particularly relevant to PPS law reform and commentators have gone as far to describe secured lending as situated within globalisation.[51]

The commercial sector and 'seamless' business borders

Another influence that deserves particular mention when considering PPS law reform is the quest by the business community for 'seamless' business borders.[52] As Meyer has remarked, 'commerce knows no state borders'.[53] By this is meant that any firm that seeks to do business on a cross-border basis is faced with negotiating and performing transactions crossing national legal and political boundaries. It is trite to observe that the legal conditions in the country from which the transaction originates and in the country where the transaction is performed (the host country) will not necessarily be the same. The same comment applies, with appropriate modifications, to countries such as Australia where there are multiple jurisdictions within one polity. To level the playing field,[54] the business community has a desire for as much uniformity in the context and operation of business laws as is possible to achieve, so that it is as if there is a seamless transition from one country to another (or, within Australia, when it comes to inter-state and state-to-territory trade and commerce). The impulse for seamless business borders is economic. Again, to quote Meyer:

> The commonly accepted hypothesis is that the economy expands if more credit is available and uniform rules facilitate this effect. Transaction costs are minimised if parties in different states can rely on a known body of law when entering into a transaction and resolution of problems between the parties becomes easier if the outcome of litigation in whatever jurisdiction is reasonably predictable and uniform.[55]

The ideal of a seamless business sector is utopian, but it can be operationalised and achieved in part through transnational PPS law reform. The result should be seamless business transactions that integrate adequately and smoothly with the allied business task of extending and securing credit. From an internal perspective within Australia, it is a federation comprising separate jurisdictions.[56] Each jurisdiction has its own law-making competence. Firms face different frameworks for giving and

51 See: Duggan 'Globalisation of secured lending law: Australian developments' (2001) 12 *Journal of Banking and Finance Law and Practice* 85; Allan 'Uniform PPS legislation for Australia: introduction to the Workshop on PPS Law Reform' (2002) 14 *Bond Law Review* 1, p. 4.

52 See op. cit., Fisher, fn 41, pp. 109–36 and 115–16.

53 See K. Meyer 'Purchase monies security interests under Revised Article 9 of the UCC' in I. Davies (ed.), *Security Interests in Mobile Equipment* (Aldershot: Ashgate/Dartmouth, 2002), pp. 251–90, especially p. 253.

54 Leebrom describes this phrase as the 'metaphoric symbol of fairness'; see Leebrom 'Claims for harmonisation: a theoretical framework' (1996) 27 *Canadian Business Law Journal* 63, p. 64.

55 See op. cit., Meyer, fn 53.

56 See generally pp. 372–73 above.

taking security over personal property in each of those jurisdictions in Australia,[57] with the exception of the regime for consumer credit (or retail credit) where there is a unified regime in place[58] that governs security over consumer goods as part of a broader regulatory regime governing consumer credit. Indeed, there is now firm evidence that the Australian courts are beginning to accept the need for a more functionalist approach when deciding cases, especially in relation to the ambit of the term 'security interest'.[59] When Australia does implement a new PPS Act, then the task of extension by the finance sector of credit to the business sector will be facilitated by seamless business borders. Seamless business borders, in turn, constitute an important element of the globalisation of markets.

Another tool that has been used within Australia to achieve the free movement of workers (including professionals) is the mutual recognition scheme.[60] The mutual recognition scheme is underpinned by the notion that markets in a federation such as Australia are really national, as opposed to state based or territory based, and so impediments to the free movement of goods and services across internal borders should be removed as far as possible by enhancing the mobility of labour, and removing unjustified impediments to the free movement of goods. This scheme is part of a broader process of microeconomic reform that has been under way in Australia since the 1980s. The scheme has its principal purpose of promoting the goal of freedom of movement of goods and service providers in a national market in Australia.[61] The scheme provides for the free cross-border movement of goods[62] and mutual recognition of occupations.[63] The relevance of the mutual recognition scheme is that it shows that microeconomic reforms of close interest to the business sector can be translated into policy and legally operable rules that are designed to secure an improvement in the conditions under which business takes place.

Accordingly, examples exist within Australia of the partial implementation of measures that respond to the drive towards seamless business borders on the part of the commercial community. These examples demonstrate that the current PPS law reform project fits comfortably within the quest for seamless business borders.

Good commercial laws follow good commercial practice

The saying 'good commercial laws follow good commercial practice' is a well-known saying with judicial sanction.[64] It is not possible to elevate this saying into a

57 This refers to the complex and not always compatible Commonwealth and state legislative regimes dealing with personal property securities. See further C. Wappett and D. Allan *Securities over Personal Property* (Sydney: Butterworths, 1999), ch. 2.

58 Each Australian jurisdiction has enacted the Consumer Credit Code. See generally D. McGill and L. Willmott *Annotated Consumer Credit Code* (Sydney: LBC Information Services, 1999).

59 See *General Motors Acceptance Corp.* v. *Southbank Traders* [2007] HCA 10 (A retention-of-title clause is a security interest for the purposes of Chattel Securities Act 1987 (Vic) which contains a statutory definition; see s. 3).

60 See Mutual Recognition Act 1992 (Commonwealth). For further details see Carroll 'Mutual Recognition: Origins and Implementation' (1995) 54 *Australian Journal of Public Administration* 35.

61 See Mutual Recognition Act 1992, s. 3

62 See Mutual Recognition Act 1992, Part 2.

63 See Mutual Recognition Act 1992, Part 3.

64 See *Commercial Factors Ltd* v. *Maxwell Printing Ltd* [1994] NZLR 724, p. 727, *per* Hammond J.

hard-and-fast rule of commercial law; rather, it is inspirational, not normative in nature. It is not a canon of law but a canon of prudence or a desirable canon of policy, much like legal maxims that are organising legal principles instead of principles or rules whose infraction sound a cause of action. Assuming the maxim exposes an idea that commands general acceptance among commercial lawyers, what are some of the implications of this maxim? First, it suggests, self-evidently, that commercial laws need to be underpinned by sound business practices. Second, the corollary is true; bad business practices lead to bad commercial laws, unless bad business practices are corrected by good commercial laws. In the context of PPS law reform, Professor Goode has pointed out[65] that the desire for a 'quiet life' or 'better the devil you know' should not stand in the way of reform 'not simply because bad commercial law militates against business efficiency but also because the law should be just and should be seen to be just'. Essentially, maintenance of the status quo should not stand in the way of principled commercial law reform. Third, this commercial maxim implies that the key members, or stakeholders, of the commercial community need to be involved actively in the process of commercial law reform if they wish to secure laws that facilitate business instead of impede commerce.[66] Fourth, the task of lawyers who speak into the process of commercial law reform is to ensure that legal policy makers and legislators hear the message of sensible and measured law reform that is in step with developments in the market place. Fifth, the maxim concentrates the commercial mind on the fact that good commercial practices that should follow good commercial laws are those informed by benchmarking against best international practice, rather than relying on the lowest common denominator. Institutions, such as the International Chamber of Commerce can play an important role in creating and stabilising best international business practices.[67] Sixth, and building on the previous point, the ability of Australian commercial lawyers, having the ability to marry different legal cultures to synthesise, change or improve commercial practices via the supply of legal services. Seventh, the maxim underscores judicial deference to positive or, beneficial, business practices. This suggests a partnership or alliance between the judiciary and the commercial community concerning the rejuvenation of business practices and the adoption of innovative business techniques by the commercial community. Eighth, one of the perennial problems in commercial law is the impact of technology on commercial transactions and the need for adaption of the law concerning commercial transactions and the institutions of commercial law. Finally, the maxim underscores the truism that there is no place for complacency in the reform of commercial law for those who fail to act to protect their own interests in securing the passage of better business laws. Taken together, these operative background factors suggest that the practice of a functional definition of security interest that is becoming the dominant model internationally should be adopted in Australia in a new PPS Act. The PPS Bill 2009 does follow best practice in this respect.[68]

65 See op. cit., Goode, fn 13, pp. 246 and 251.

66 Some commentators prefer to see the commercial community as a driver of commercial law reform; see Arden 'Time for an English commercial code?' [1997] CLJ 516, p. 535.

67 On the role of the ICC, see Cattaui 'Harmonising commercial law: keeping pace with business' in I. Fletcher, L. Mistelis and M. Cremona (eds) *Foundations and Perspectives of International Trade* (London: Sweet & Maxwell, 2001), pp. 36–42.

68 See PPS Bill 2009, s. 12.

Transnational commercial law

The expression 'transnational commercial law' is gaining currency in the scholastic literature.[69] Transnational commercial law operates as a subset of a broader overarching conception of the transnationality of law. Goode defines transnational law as 'the totality of principles and rules, whether customary, conventional, contractual or derived from any other source, which are common to a number of legal systems'.[70] It is possible to consider secured transactions law as part of the framework of transnational commercial law, especially in the light of contemporary initiatives for the cross-border harmonisation of secured transactions law. In particular, one of the key principles of modern secured transactions law is the functional, not conceptual, approach to defining security agreements and interests, ultimately modelled on Article 9 of the UCC in the USA. The Article 9 approach has become the triumphant model of secured transactions law in developed and transition economies.[71] The principle of substance not form has become one of the principles of secured transactions law that transcends national boundaries and accordingly, it forms part of a transnational commercial law.[72]

Australia-New Zealand Harmonisation of Business Laws Memorandum of Understanding

Another significant feature that helped with the reform project were the already close business relationships between Australia and New Zealand. The Memorandum of Understanding on Harmonisation of Business Law between the two countries signed in 1988 symbolises the close ties that the countries enjoy.[73] Under the Memorandum, both governments have committed themselves to harmonise their business laws so that trans-Tasman trade can take place between both countries with broadly similar (that is comparable) business laws. Although the Memorandum did not specifically mention the harmonisation of PPS law, its practical impact has been to focus attention on both countries respective business laws and a common search for agreement.

More important than this spirit of cooperation was the passage in 1999 of the New Zealand PPS Act.[74] This Act has been in force since 1 May 2002 and has been generally well received by the business community. There can be no doubt that this was a key development in the Australian PPS reform adventure. For the first time, law

69 See, for example, C. Schmitthoff *Commercial Law in a Changing Economic Climate* (London: Sweet & Maxwell, 2nd ed, 1981); Goode 'Usage and its reception in transnational commercial law' in J. Ziegel (ed.), *New Developments in International Commercial and Consumer Law* (Oxford: Hart Publishing, 1998), pp. 3–36.

70 See Goode's essay in op. cit., Ziegel, fn 69, pp. 3–36.

71 See p. 375, fn 50 above.

72 See Draft Consultation PPS Bill 2009, s. 12 for this approach in an Australian context.

73 See also the Australia New Zealand Closer Economic Relations Trade Agreement (ANZCERTA) which came into force on 1 January 1983 and has been amended many times since.

74 The Act came about following the publication of the New Zealand Law Commission Report *A Personal Property Securities Act for New Zealand* Law Commission Report No. 8 (Wellington, Law Commission, 1989). For a general discussion of the New Zealand Act, see the chapter by Brown in the present volume, pp. 328–65.

reform passed from abstract idea into commercial reality. It is no coincidence that the Australian reform project has fully taken off since New Zealand led the way.

Transnational initiatives concerning PPS interests

Some parallel initiatives may have exerted 'gravitational pull'[75] on the development of PPS law reform in Australia. These initiatives fall into two clusters, namely transnational secured transaction law harmonisation and, second, the Corporate Economic Reform Program in Australia. The first cluster of initiatives is closely connected to PPS law reform in Australia. The second initiative is one that is localised to Australia but, which has important ramifications for the institutions of the Australian economy.

The first cluster of initiatives as a group relates to transnational secured transaction law harmonisation. Where laws are harmonised between two or more jurisdictions the underlying process is that the laws are not made identical in each of the jurisdictions but, they are brought generally into line so that it can be said that there are equivalencies in the content of the laws as between the different jurisdictions.[76] An example of this can be found in the European Union where the European Commission issues Directives to member states but leaves each member state to decide on the form or method of implementing the relevant directive into their national law. The first initiative to take note of is the Model Law on Secured Transactions prepared by the European Bank for Reconstruction and Development (EBRD) in April 1994.[77] This Model Law can provide the basis for states to enact secured transaction laws that mimic or, less slavishly, implement, the principles enshrined in the EBRD model. The second initiative is the product of the Final Act of a Diplomatic Conference to adopt the Convention on International Interests in Mobile Equipment and the Protocol to the Convention on International Interest in Mobile Equipment on Matters Specific to Aircraft Equipment held in Cape Town in 2001. The latter came under the joint auspices of the International Institute for the Unification of Private Law (UNIDROIT) and the International Civil Aviation Organisation (ICAO).[78] The movement for transnational secured transaction law harmonisation is shaped by a desire for clearer and more efficient PPS laws which has its genesis in the significant legislative reforms accomplished in the USA (see Article 9 of the UCC) and also in Canada (where its PPS laws have been markedly influenced by Article 9, although there are substantive differences between the schemes). The early Australian

75 The metaphor is borrowed from *Akins* v. *Abigroup Ltd.* (1998) 43 NSWLR 539, pp. 547–8, *per* Mason P.

76 In practice harmonisation can be a complex process. Geiger has divided harmonisation into two types, harmonisation by commonality and harmonisation by reciprocity. The former embraces the modification or replacement of domestic rules with substantially similar rules as those of other jurisdictions, while the latter involves the deference by the host jurisdiction to the laws or standards of other jurisdictions; see Geiger 'The Case For Harmonisation of the Securities Disclosure Rules in the Global Market' [1997] *Columbia Business Law Review* 241 at p. 298.

77 Available at www.ebrd.org. Note also the essay by McCormack in this volume at pp. 112–14.

78 For a discussion of these two instruments, see: Cuming 'The characterisation of interests and transactions under the Convention on International Interests in Mobile Equipment, 2001'; Stanford 'From Ottawa to Cape Town: Unidroit's role in the modernisation of the law governing leasing and the taking of security', chs 10 and 11 in op. cit., Davies (2002), fn 53.

responses to Article 9 showed a heavy imprint of the North American approach to reform and adopted the 'substance not form' approach to the characterisation of PPS. This was also taken up in the more recent, and ongoing, law reform project but the New Zealand scheme was now the main driver (albeit that that scheme was itself derived from Article 9).[79] When Australia finally implements a new PPS Act the end product will have conceptual similarities with similar laws applying in the USA, Canada and New Zealand but each of these countries' laws will not be the same. What harmonisation will accomplish is equivalence rather than identical laws.

Domestic Australian business law reforms

Some domestic Australian business law reforms have also acted as a driver to PPS law reform. In 1997 the Australian government launched the Corporate Law Economic Reform Programme (CLERP).[80] This programme has involved a fundamental review of key areas of regulation which affect business and investment activity. The objective of CLERP is to ensure that business regulation is consistent with promoting a strong and vibrant economy and provides a framework which assists in adapting to change. One of the claims made under the rubric of CLERP is that a fundamental review of Australia's corporate law is needed 'otherwise the complexity and rigidity of Australia's current business laws will place a costly compliance burden on business in Australia'.[81] It has been said that the CLERP reform program amounts to the 'Americanisation'[82] of Australian corporate law and this observation is also applicable to PPS law reform. In parallel with CLERP, the Australian government, and state and territory governments, have been conducting a review, under the framework of the National Competition Policy, of all legislation that has an effect on competition in most markets in Australia.[83] Pursuant to this review of legislation, the Australian Treasury is undertaking a review of the Bills of Exchange Act 1909 (Commonwealth).[84] These reform initiatives indicate the willingness of governments in Australia to assess the suitability and effectiveness of some business laws and to reform business laws when reform is needed. The current PPS law reform project has a good pedigree.

Commonwealth regulation of PPS interests and intellectual property interests

There is already some Commonwealth regulation of PPS interests in the shape of legislation that touches and concerns these interests as a by-product of broader non-PPS specific legislation and regulatory regimes. Commonwealth legislation dealing

79 See generally pp. 370–74, above.

80 See generally at www.treasury.gov.au for the work and reform papers from CLERP.

81 See Commonwealth of Australia CLERP document *CLERP: Policy Framework*; available at www.treasury.gov.au.

82 See von Nessen, 'The Amercianisation of Australian Corporate Law' (1999) 26 *Syracuse Journal of International Law and Commerce*, pp. 239–66.

83 See the National Competition Council, *Legislation Review Compendium*; available at www.ncc.gov.au.

84 See Working Group of Officials *National Competition Policy Review of the Bills of Exchange Act 1909*; available at www.treasury.gov.au.

with PPS includes: the Trade Marks Act 1995; the Designs Act 1996; the Life Insurance Act 1995; the Shipping Registration Act 1981 and the Air Navigation Act 1920. Intellectual property (IP) laws enacted by the Commonwealth also provide for the recognition of some types of PPS interests that are peculiar to intellectual property. These laws also regulate the recognition and grant of securities in respect of IP. Accordingly, there is already Commonwealth laws regulating some forms of PPIs and PPS interests. Seen from this angle there does not appear to be anything revolutionary in the current PPS reform project and the fact that Commonwealth legislation will be the ultimate outcome.

Summary

The above discussion has presented a broad survey of some of the critical background forces that have shaped PPS reform in Australia. Although these critical forces are disparate in nature and effect, the key propositions that emerge from this survey can be stated as follows:

(a) The economic drivers of globalisation as well as the effects of globalisation on individual markets and market participants suggests that a modernised PPS law in Australia based on a functional definition of security will assist the integration of the Australian capital markets with global capital markets. Allied to the norms of globalisation is the quest by the business community for seamless business borders.
(b) Transnational commercial law has adopted the functional definition of security and has clearly had a positive influence on the law reform project.
(c) The Memorandum of Understanding on the Harmonisation of Business Law between the governments of Australia and New Zealand has been one of the main drivers for trans-Tasman business laws with New Zealand, taking into account the New Zealand PPS Act 1999.
(d) Australian governments must take into account the significant international dimensions when reforming PPS law. When the new law comes into effect in 2011 it should be in accordance with best international practice.

Themes relating to PPS reform in Australia

There are three main key themes associated with PPS law reform, namely:

(a) reconceptualising security interests;
(b) user-initiated reform; and
(c) PPS reform implementation/reform fatigue.

These three key themes will now be addressed in turn.

Reconceptualisation of security interests

PPS law reform in Australia will require the reconceptualisation of security interests. The most obvious change will be a shift away from narrow legal conceptualisation of security interests to the functional definition and operation of security interest.[85]

85 See PPS Bill 2009, s. 12 for this approach.

On its face, this dichotomy sets up the debate between conceptualism and pragmatism in the definition and nature of securities over personal property. Conceptual thinking and classification of PPS is unavoidable under the contemporary Australian law in this area. Pragmatism (or, in the present context, functionalism) on one level of analysis, is already at the heart of the nature and definition of PPS. Pragmatism has also crept into other aspects of the contest between legal concepts and legal policy in commercial law. This can be clearly seen in the case of *Morris* v. *Rayner Enterprises Inc.*,[86] which involved the issue whether a charge-back is conceptually possible or, conceptually impossible.[87] A charge-back arises where a depositor of money with a bank purports to charge the deposit to the bank by way of security (either for the depositor's indebtedness under a separate contact or, on behalf of a third-party's indebtedness, in which case it is a surety-like security). Charge-backs, although common in commercial practice in England but, less so in Australia, have created much controversy since the case of *Re Charge Card Services Ltd*,[88] decided in 1986.[89] Charge-backs represent a species of functional but not conceptual security interests. The case of *Morris* v. *Rayner Enterprises Inc.*[90] indicates a limited triumph of pragmatism over conceptualism in a discrete area of commercial law. Whether this case presages the extension of the business credit market is another matter altogether. The absence of the wholesale abandonment of conceptualism may indicate that pragmatism is not yet the triumphant model in commercial law.

The ultimate model of all PPS law systems is Article 9 of the US Uniform Commercial Code (UCC). Article 9 provides a very clear example of the use of substance instead of form in its description of the types of security transactions that are caught by the Article 9 regime. Article 9-102(1) states:

> Except as otherwise provided in Section 9-104 on excluded transactions, this Article applies:
>
> (a) to any transaction (regardless of form) which is intended to create a security interest in personal property or fixtures including goods, documents, instruments, general intangibles, chattel paper or accounts; and also
> (b) to any sale of accounts or chattel paper.

The current Australian PPS Bill 2009, s. 12 states a 'security interest':

> means an interest in relation to personal property provided for by a transaction that, in substance, secures payment or performance of an obligation (without regard to the form of the transaction or the identity of the person who has title to the property).

86 [1997] UKHL 44.

87 Charge-backs illustrate neatly the tension between legal concepts and legal policy. The case of *Morris* v. *Rayner Enterprises Inc.* has its critics, most notably Professor Goode; see generally: Goode *Commercial Law in the Next Millennium: the Hamlyn Lectures* (London: Sweet & Maxwell, 1998), pp. 68–71; Goode 'Casenote' (1998) 114 LQR 8. Note also G. McCormack *Secured Credit under English and American Law* (Cambridge: Cambridge University Press, 2004), pp. 249–62.

88 [1987] Ch. 150.

89 See generally: op. cit., Goode, fn 87; P. Ali *The Law of Secured Finance: an International Survey of Security Interests over Personal Property* (Oxford: Oxford University Press, 2002), paras 9.05–9.26.

90 [1997] UKHL 44.

McCormack states, in connection with this type of functional definition of security interest, that 'certain legal philosophers may assert that ambiguity is inherent in legislation in that there are penumbras of uncertainty'.[91] This much may be conceded as a general proposition but, by the same token, this does not militate against PPS reform. Other commentators contend that reforms will produce greater certainty.[92]

In addition to the basic Article 9 concept of a 'security interest' that is created by means of a 'security agreement', the Australian commercial legal landscape will feature the reformed triumvirate of attachment,[93] perfection[94] and priority[95] when the new scheme comes into force in 2011. Professor Goode is probably the leading exponent in the Anglo-Australian sphere of systematising the process which the law has identified as creating effective securities. Goode has atomised this process into three distinct steps:[96]

(a) Attachment – this denotes the creation of the security interest between the creditor and the debtor. It is concerned only with relations between these parties.
(b) Perfection – the taking of additional steps prescribed by a creditor or other interested party to give public notice of the security interests in order to bind third parties. The purpose and function of perfection of a security interest is to diffuse awareness or notice of the security interest from the private realm of the debtor–creditor relationship to the world at large.
(c) Priority – the legal regime which declares the ranking of the security interest in relation to rival claims to the debtor's property.

Attachment itself is a legal phenomenon which is part of a continuum of legal phenomena which govern the recognition, enforcement and effects of securities. Attachment is the primary step in creating an effective security interest at general law and it is followed by the secondary and tertiary steps of perfection and priority respectively.[97] Now that PPS law reform is at an advanced stage in Australia, the commercial community and its legal advisers will need to understand quickly the new conceptual framework as described above.

User-initiated reform

As has already been noted, PPS law reform has been driven by the commercial sector and embraced by government agencies. In Australia, some of the key players involved in the quest for PPS law reform have included the banks and financial institutions and also consumers of credit (including corporate borrowers and consumer debtors).[98] These are the users who will have to shoulder the administrative and financial burden when PPS law reform is implemented in 2011. These users are also those whose interests are diametrically opposed at times when it comes to granting and undertaking

91 See McCormack 'PPS law reform in England and Canada' [2002] JBL 113, p. 121.
92 See Allan, Quirk and Martin 'Final report – Workshop on PPS Law Reform' (2002) 14 *Bond Law Review* 8, p. 16.
93 See PPS Bill 2009, s. 19 and at Part 4.
94 See PPS Bill 2009, s. 21 and Part 4.
95 See PPS Bill 2009, s. 54 and Part 2.6.
96 See Goode *Commercial Law* (3rd edn, London: Penguin Books, 2004), p. 624.
97 See generally, Fisher *Commercial and Personal Property Law* (Sydney: Butterworths, 1997), para. [6.25].
98 For details see op. cit., Allan, fn 92, pp. 12–15.

security over personal property. In short, the stakeholders affected by the revised PPS regime are supportive of it in principle. One of the reasons why the UK government did not accept the Diamond Report[99] and the Law Commission abandoned plans for a new PPS regime in the UK was the perception that there was no major stakeholder group pressing for fundamental reforms.[100] Given the history of PPS law reform in the UK[101] it is a clear case of the dangers of reform fatigue setting in.[102]

PPS law reform implementation/reform fatigue

Although the case for PPS law reform is now universally accepted in Australia and the reform project is at an advanced stage, law reform in this area has been a long drawn-out process effectively starting for our purposes in 1992.[103] This can be contrasted with the UK experience where reform has been on the agenda for nearly 40 years.[104] The reasons for delay stem from the complexity and fundamental conceptual change involved in moving over from the present formalistic system of our security law to the PPS scheme based on Article 9. The switch from the present system will also catch many more transactions due to the expanded concept of 'security interest' based on a functional classification.[105] Security registrants will also have to pay registration fees and these can be expected to, in part at any rate, fund the roll-out and continuing operation of the PPS registration scheme. However, this should benefit the legal profession as there will be additional work involved particularly associated with documentary and systems redesign, client education and possible post-PPSA litigation. Linked to this, and also responsible for the delays in reaching PPS reform implementation, is 'reform fatigue'.

Reform fatigue results when distinct community groups are affected by reforms that have binding effect and which compel compliance to the extent that affected groups become overburdened by reforms and resistant to change such that they are reluctant to commit the finances and resources necessary to secure reform. Reform fatigue therefore, makes it difficult to secure the passage of the legislation necessary to implement fundamental reform. Fortunately in Australia, although it seemed that reform fatigue might be significant in preventing the development of PPS reform these fears were overcome in the second phase of reform post-2006.[106] In the UK 'reform fatigue' in the legal profession appears to have a veto on any reform project in this area.

Conclusions

This chapter has shown that it is now time for Australia to enact a new reformed PPSA. It now appears a certainty that this will happen and, from May 2011 onwards, Australia will be a full member of the international club of countries with a functional

99 *A Review of Security Interests in Property* (London: HMSO, 1989), by Professor A. L. Diamond.
100 See: op. cit., McCormack, fn 91, p. 115.
101 On which, see generally the chapter by de Lacy in this volume, pp. 3–82.
102 See p. 385 below for reform fatigue.
103 See generally at p. 369 above.
104 The process began with the publication of the Crowther Report in 1971; see pp. 47–55 in this volume.
105 See PPS Bill 2009, s. 12.
106 See generally at p. 370 above.

system of PPS law. This will also harmonise Australia's secured transactions law with that of New Zealand which will also help to secure further uniform trans-Tasman business laws. PPS reform will also deliver benefits to the key stakeholder groups affected by its implementation. Even taking into account the costs associated with the adoption of the new PPSA scheme in the long term Australia can only benefit from proven law reforms. It is ironic that it now appears as if Australia will become a case study in law reform to the UK when, inevitably, the subject of PPS reform comes up again.[107] It is to be hoped that after the PPSA comes into force in 2011 Australia will, indeed, become a positive role model for scholars interested in law reform and the process of implementation.

107 Past PPS law reform initiatives in the UK include: the Crowther Report 1971; the Diamond Report 1989; DTI *Consultation Paper* 1994 and the work of the English Law Commission 2002–2005; see pp. 43–76 in this volume.

12 Personal property security interests in Singapore

Yock Lin Tan

Introduction

The transformation of Singapore from an entrepot economy verging on a monopoly into a modern diversified economy has been nothing short of dramatic. In a relatively short span of 30 or so years, the economy has broadened and deepened and the per capita income has come to rival some of the most advanced economies in the world.[1]

There are no studies to reveal the extent to which secured credit mechanisms have contributed to this spectacular performance, only arguments that they must have had an impact. It is possible to suggest that no such structural transformation as occurred in the Singapore economy could have taken place without a concomitant structural change in credit provision.[2] The entrepot system characteristic of the Singapore economy throughout the early and mid-1900s and up to the 1960s was based on a sophisticated commercial network which could circulate or distribute goods cheaply.[3] Cheap financing was as crucial as availability of cheap storage and warehousing facilities but in all likelihood, intimate knowledge of one's trading partners and intimate relations leading to short unsecured loans served in place of security. There is certainly little evidence in the banking statistics that the entrepot economy was underpinned by sophisticated secured credit mechanisms.[4] On the other hand, from what we know of the immigrant Singaporean's ethic and mentality, it would not be surprising if most of the largest businesses were more or less self-financing by choice.

It was probably only between the 1970s and the 1990s, when an export-oriented manufacturing base evolved, that secured financing became important in Singapore.[5]

1 For some good albeit dated accounts, see Lim Chong Yah 'Singapore's economic development: retrospect and prospect' in P. Chen (ed.), *Singapore: Development Policies and Trends* (Oxford: Oxford University Press, 1983), ch. 4; K. Bercuson (ed.), *Singapore: a Case Study in Rapid Development* (Washington, DC: IMF, 1995).

2 See Goode 'The changing nature of security rights' in J. Norton and M. Andenas (eds), *Emerging Financial Markets and Secured Transactions* (London: Kluwer Law International, 1998), p. 1 who states that the World Bank makes a sound security a precondition for world bank lending to developing countries.

3 The first phase in Singapore's industrialisation which occurred between 1959 and 1965 involved the pursuit of import-substitution policies. See van Elkan 'Singapore's development strategy' in op., cit., Bercuson (ed.), fn 1, ch. III.

4 Such as field warehousing.

5 Provision of services shares in some of these features although the range may be wider. That is to say that some services partake more of the nature of trade while others require more medium and long term financing. There is evidence that small businesses relied on a number

Manufacturing at least theoretically involves risks which financiers cannot well manage without recourse to secured credit; among other things the greater distance between lender and borrower, and hence the information asymmetry as between them makes it difficult for intimate knowledge to serve as dispensation of security.[6] Although in the first days of its development, manufacturing was largely financed through foreign direct investments in selected key sectors and in critical turn-key projects, the industry has today acquired characteristics typical of other advanced economies, namely a high volume of secured inventory financing at various manufacturing levels and for a time in the 1970s and 1980s a high volume of secured consumer financing.[7]

Whatever may be the importance of secured credit, or lack of it in the past, there are numerous views endorsing the importance of secured credit for the future.[8] Economists studying its role in the modern economy affirm that secured creditors demand security in order to protect against the higher risks of liquidation and non-payment while borrowers benefit from the interest rate reduction associated with the use of secured debt. Significantly, an expanded role for secured credit is envisaged for several reasons. First, secured credit is no longer the poor man's hope. Second, it is no longer driven solely by the objective of protection against insolvency by maximising prospects of recovery as against other creditors. Third, for some creditors, secured financing could repress the debtor's temptation to substitute risky assets for low risk assets. This is because an unsecured loan may easily be diverted into another employment unlike most secured loans which are necessarily dedicated. Fourth, for others, it could repress the equity owner's temptation to under-invest, shying away from contributing new capital which would only benefit bondholders. Fifth, some economists maintain that secured financing is a cost-efficient way to signal a firm's creditworthiness to the market in the face of information asymmetries between lenders and borrowers. This is a considerable advantage when speed of transaction is vital and credit investigations would be an impediment. Sixth, secured credit financing is increasingly employed with a view to exercising control over the deployment of the asset which is secured or even the management of the debtor.[9]

of informal credit devices including the illegal tontine and that the informal credit market stayed pretty liquid. Companies in the finance industry seemed to use less secured financing than those in the other service sectors.

6 Some other peculiarities which favour secured lending are start-up costs which are typically large and, correspondingly, start-up investments take a while to gestate and yield returns and cash flows and mismatches are likely particularly when there are unseasonal fluctuations.

7 The statistics firmly show a strong and steady growth in purchases of moderate to huge ticket items; although more recently aggressive promotion by banks has resulted in a shift from secured financing to unsecured credit card payments for the purchase of smaller items such as television sets and household appliances. Credit card companies of course rely on their self-generated credit payment histories.

8 Cf. R. Edwards 'Native title: dead capital' [2003] SJLS 80, p. 113 who argues that lenders typically look to the borrower's ability to pay rather than to the security. Op. cit., Goode, fn 2, mentions two new developments which will raise the importance of secured financing; privatisation and hence the need to take security when before it was unnecessary, and the risk of greater volatility stemming from interdependence of world markets.

9 Including control over realisation of asset. Some banks insist on security for facilities not as an end but as means to ensure disclosure and consultation at critical junctures of an investment. Some banks 'use their control rights to encourage or force financially distressed firms to undergo restructuring'. This point is highlighted in G. McCormack *Secured Credit under*

To be sure, such recent investigations as have been published in Singapore are inconclusive as to the extent to which secured financing benefits lenders and borrowers.[10] In an interesting study,[11] Chen, Yeo and Ho reported that there was a significant negative relation between firm size and use of secured loans; firms with higher volatility of earnings, larger amount of loan financing, and higher marketability of assets tended to use more secured loans. Higher-quality firms, however, did not seem to use secured loans to signal their creditworthiness to the market while firms in the finance industry and large firms also relied more on unsecured financing. This study unfortunately does not tell us about the relationship between secured financing and personal guarantees which are frequently insisted on as additional security in Singapore;[12] as a result, we are unable to say whether the law is skewed towards personal security and therefore inefficient. Further, secured lending and unsecured lending are obviously linked 'in that large numbers of small unsecured loans can be bundled to form the security for larger loans'.[13] This means that there should have been a cross-sectional study of lending and borrowing behaviour across the sectors but the report is silent on this matter. Still further, it must be asked whether there is differentiation between corporate and non-corporate borrowers. As equity and debt are interchangeable at the margin for corporate borrowers, differences in borrowing behaviour as between the two categories of debtors cannot be ruled out.

However, even if the precise determinants of secured credit are uncertain, studies of this nature consistently indicate that, all things equal, the decision to offer security is made only when security is economically efficient.[14] It is obvious that the law cannot ignore economic efficiency, which is of primary concern in reform. To the extent the law promotes economic efficiency, it would also be protecting legitimate expectations.[15] There are complications of course. Economic efficiency is not the only consideration of fairness and between two equally efficient outcomes, has nothing further to say, leaving the choice to be made in terms of what is just or right, not

English and American Law (Cambridge: Cambridge University Press, 2004), p. 10; note see also at pp. 7–11. It should be noted that there is no central credit reference agency to turn to for credit information and so far as banks are concerned, banking secrecy rules prohibit the sharing of credit information. This means that each lender must generate its own advance warning system capable of detecting early signs of credit difficulties.

10 See e.g. Shupak 'Solving the puzzle of secured transactions' (1989) 41 *Rutgers Law Review* 1067.

11 'The determinants of debt maturity: the case of bank financing in Singapore' (1999) 12 Review of Quantitative Finance and Accounting, pp. 341–50.

12 See in the case of hire-purchase agreements: *Ho Yew Weng Alan James* v. *Poh Eng Weng Mark t/a SG Vehicles Trading* [1997] SGHC 179; *Ng Beng Lai* v. *Ong Ee Beng Bernard* [2002] SGDC 202.

13 H. Fleisig 'Economic functions of security in a market economy: the changing nature of security rights' in op. cit., Norton and Andenas (eds), fn 2, p. 21.

14 Critics say banks charge whatever interest rate they can get away with; but surely not for long, if the market is competitive. It can be supposed that generally, commercial people who must maximise profits will not do anything that is inefficient. Recognition that the law must promote efficiency appears in remarks that 'the law has to be moulded and developed to meet the commercial developments which are taking place': *Karflex Ltd* v. *Poole* [1933] 2 KB 251, p. 264 *per* Goddard J. See also Lord Hoffmann in *Re Bank of Credit and Commerce International SA (No. 8)* [1998] AC 214, p. 228.

15 Yet the importance of economic efficiency was not always given its due regard; thus, the charge over the chargor's indebtedness was considered a legal impossibility in *Re Charge Card Services* [1987] Ch. 157 though economically efficient. Note that the decision was reversed in *Re Bank of Credit and Commerce International SA (No. 8)* [1998] AC 214.

what is merely efficient. For instance, unsecured financing and secured financing are efficient in their own right and under certain outcomes;[16] but when the borrower can no longer cease to function, it is not obvious that in all cases it will be just to unsecured creditors to let the secured creditors prevail, though that could be efficient.[17] Thus, there are laws which recognise that the tension between efficiency and justifiability may not be capable of being resolved in a market economy by the protagonists themselves without a fresh imposition of law which intervenes in favour of continuation and rescue.[18] Efficiency must also give way to the right of free determination. Whether or not recognition of a right will produce an efficient outcome, the law must not tolerate any abuse of this right of determination. One may or may not agree with their validity, but arguments for strengthening the floating charge by recognising the negative pledge, so as to ensure that the original property is not abusively dissipated and replaced by property subject to paramount interests, are rights-based arguments.

It is this continual tension between efficiency and right which has revealed two opposed schools of thought within the legal and commercial community in Singapore with respect to reform of the law of personal property security interests. The first sees nothing fundamentally wrong with the existing law and little that is wrong which cannot be righted by incremental reform.[19] The second advocates thorough, overhaul-like reform along the lines of Article 9 of the Uniform Commercial Code (UCC). The debate in Singapore however is of recent currency.[20] Strong economic ties to the United States notwithstanding, interest in Article 9 is fairly novel. It is traceable to a Law Reform Committee initiative in 1996; and in turn to an English initiative in 1989.[21] For a while, it seemed that Article 9 protagonists found a champion in the Law Reform Committee. Although the Committee's remit was pretty narrow (i.e. to modernise the Bills of Sale Act),[22] the Committee found it neither logical nor expedient to confine reform to the archaic statute of the nineteenth century. It was

16 Op. cit., Fleisig, fn 13, pp. 18–19 explains that while the underlying characteristics are similar namely asymmetric information, moral hazard and adverse selection, 'these combine to produce the main characteristics of loan markets that reach extreme levels in the transitional and other developing countries: high interest rates, small loans and credit rationing'. He adds, p. 21, that 'both systems occupy important places in lending'.

17 Thus, the debate about whether secured credit is economically efficient has focused on its effect on insolvency and here it is obvious from the inconclusiveness of the debate that there are conflicting considerations of fairness.

18 This may be because being involuntary creditors they could not have participated in the credit decisions of the debtor or being consensual creditors they would be hampered from reaching an efficient credit decision by the free rider phenomenon.

19 By way of improvements to the existing registration systems. See also R. Cranston 'Credit security and debt recovery: law's role in reform in Asia and the Pacific' in op. cit Norton and Andenas (eds), fn 2, whose view, p. 235, is that: '[Article 9] is not a model for the region; the best approach would seem to be to improve existing systems of registration for transactions concerning land, motor vehicles and company charges.'

20 This can be contrasted with the position in England where the debate has been raging since the publication of the Crowther Report in 1971; see generally the chapter by de Lacy in this volume, pp. 43–80. For historical debate on the situation in England, note also: op. cit., McCormack, fn 9; Bridge 'How far is Article 9 exportable? The English experience' (1996) 27 Can Bus LJ 196.

21 A. Diamond *A Review of Security Interests in Property* (London: HMSO, 1989) which contains a review of the charges registration system. See also I. Davies 'The reform of English personal property security law' (1990) 32 Mal L Rev 88.

22 Cap 24, 1985 Rev Edn.

persuaded that the way forward was to adopt comprehensive legislation along the lines of Article 9 of the UCC. Nothing came out of this initiative eventually; though there was fairly unreserved acceptance that reform would be beneficial, industry inertia, fear of the unknown and the lack of urgency of reform in the wake of the Asian crisis in 1997 are thought to explain the drifting away of the proposals to adopt the article. It seems however that reformative interest has revived more recently when the Company Legislation and Regulatory Framework Committee alluded to the possible advantages of converting to legislation based on Article 9.[23] Article 9 evidently has continued to attract its share of supporters who praise it as representing 'the most modernised, rational and comprehensive system of security interests in the present world'[24] and imply it is worthy to be imitated all over the world.

This essay will charter the law of personal property security in Singapore and seek to assess whether Article 9 offers a way forward which should be adopted. At the time of writing it remains speculative as to whether or not such fundamental reform is a possibility in the immediate future. However, whatever the chances of reform taking place in the immediate future it is, nevertheless, a productive exercise to charter some of the implications were such reform to be undertaken. It will be submitted that Singapore is worthy of such reform and the economy would ultimately benefit, as other common law states have, from undertaking a new modernised personal property security regime.

Existing law versus Article 9

The question whether adoption of reform modelled on Article 9 will be an advance on the law in Singapore requires a comparative evaluation of the general law and Article 9.[25] This evaluation in the present view must be conducted with special reference to the multitasked use to which secured financing is now put, transcending creditor protection on debtor insolvency. It will become apparent that the role of quasi-security interests[26] is a critical factor in this evaluation. These are very well suited to the multifaceted functions demanded nowadays of security interests as they are informal, easily erected and dismantled, less invasive and more fluid, making them popular also with the judiciary, who are naturally hesitant about recognising new full-blown security rights for fear of prejudicing third parties.[27]

No comprehensive definition

The most obvious contrast is between Article 9's singular definition of security interest[28] and the general law's casuistry. In relation to personal property, the

23 See *Report of the Company Legislation and Regulatory Framework Committee* (October 2002), ch. 2, para. 4.1.2 echoing the Company Law Review Steering Group in *Modern Company Law for a Competitive Economy: Final Report Vol. 1* (London: DTI, July 2001), p. 247; although the Committee advised caution for the time being, para. 4.1.3.

24 *Study on Security Interests* in *UNCITRAL Yearbook* (1977), vol. 8, p. 171, s. 2.6.2.3.

25 It is interesting that U. Drobnig 'A comparative introduction to security over movables and intangibles' in op. cit., Norton and Andenas (eds), fn 2, pp. 6–13 identifies five basic issues: unitary security interest or multiple security interests, formal requirements, registration, the fluctuating collateral (including global security) and enforcement.

26 See, pp. 392, 398–99.

27 See, p. 398.

28 Until the 1998 revisions, Art. 1-201(37) UCC defined security interest as 'an interest in personal property or fixtures which secures payment or performance of an obligation'.

common law proceeded largely in terms of possessory rights, protected by the torts of conversion, detinue and trespass.[29] The chattel mortgage was less developed; because of the frauds which the non-possessory chattel mortgage renders possible, the recognition of it came only after it was subjected to a publicity or registration scheme. This was what the Bills of Sale Act[30] established.

Ironically perhaps, the legislature having invented the nearly all encompassing security bill of sale, which covered every conceivable form of non-possessory chattel mortgage, the common law then virtually abandoned it in the ensuing years. By the mid-twentieth century, it was permitting financiers to offer a variety of so-called quasi-security interests which left the Bills of Sale Act a virtually impotent piece of legislation. Chief among these quasi-security devices were the hire purchase, sale with title retention, the security or financing lease, the sale and repurchase and the consignment of tangible property.[31] More recently, there has evolved a similarly impressive range of devices in relation to intangible property such as the negative pledge coupled to a floating charge, the subordination agreement, to name a few. These like the earlier-mentioned interests serve as security in some fashion[32] although they do not amount to a grant of a proprietary interest or right of appropriation of property enforceable against third parties.

On the equity side, the charge was brilliantly conceived as a right of appropriation of property, although conferring neither possession nor ownership, unlike the equitable mortgage.[33] A further innovation on the basic concept produced the floating charge[34] which has the honour of being the single most important device in inventory financing in today's commercial world.

This brief outline is still an accurate description of the law of Singapore. There is yet no uniform doctrine by which common law and equitable ideas of what is security can be gathered together; hence no comprehensive definition which will embrace devices which perform the economic function of security but which are not structured as a legal or equitable grant of proprietary rights to the creditor.[35]

This was to be determined according to substance and not form, without regard to where the title resided: Art. 9-202. The text of Art. 9 approved in 1998 no longer contains a definition of security interest but it is not thought that this has altered the general conceptual approach of the article. Art. 9-202 remains unaltered.

29 Hence, the pledge and the lien.

30 Cap 24, 1985 Rev Ed. The Act was amended slightly in 1993.

31 A Malaysian judge, Edgar Joseph J, in *Sungei Way Leasing Sdn Bhd* v. *Sena Land Development Sdn Bhd* [1989] 3 MLJ 37 remarked that *Romalpa* clauses were commonplace in commercial contracts.

32 Unlike the hire purchase or retention of title cases, these are not rights over property. Strictly therefore, they are not quasi-security interests in property. See in the case of rights of set-off, *Electro Magnetic (S) Ltd* v. *Development Bank of Singapore Ltd* [1994] 1 SLR 734.

33 See: *Re Bond Worth Ltd* [1980] Ch. 228, p. 250; *Swiss Bank Corp* v. *Lloyds Bank Ltd* [1982] AC 584, p. 595.

34 From second half of the nineteenth century: see *National Westminster plc* v. *Spectrum Plus Ltd* [2004] EWCA Civ 670, para. 2; note also [2005] UKHL 41.

35 In Singapore no court has yet attempted a comprehensive definition. Cf. *Re Paramount Airways Ltd* [1990] BCC 130, p. 149, *per* Browne-Wilkinson VC and *Bristol Airport plc* v. *Powdrill* [1990] Ch. 744, p. 760, *per* Browne-Wilkinson VC. See also *Flightline Ltd* v. *Edwards* [2003] 1 WLR 1200, p. 1212 for a discussion of 'procedural securities'.

Persistence of equity and common law

The lack of a comprehensive definition of security in general and the persistence of two streams of security interests in particular continue to divide both advocates and detractors of the general law. Some have praised the resultant flexibility which they say accommodates very different risk profiles, creditworthiness, security objectives, and characteristics of collateral or security.[36] Without hesitation, they add that the fundamental distinction between possessory and non-possessory security interests adds to the flexibility already inherent in the distinction between common law and equitable security interests.

However, detractors criticise the complexities of the flexible law. They point out that the law does not divide neatly between possessory and non-possessory security interests but admits some which do not fit the apparently simple taxonomy. Documentary intangibles are an obvious misfit. Whereas intangible property is generally incapable of possession, as a special rule, documents of title to tangible property or to payment of money, distinguished from tokens of authority, are deemed to be capable of possession, actual or constructive. It results immediately that a deposit of documents of title may be an equitable mortgage or a pledge or a charge.[37] Nothing but a careful scrutiny of the documentation will unravel the complexity with which the courts in Singapore have grappled with greater or lesser conviction. In each case, the possibility that some other person may be in constructive possession by attornment makes it a question of fact fraught with extreme difficulty.

With judicial recognition of a pledge of general intangibles,[38] the same complex exercise is now engaged when the security is a general intangible. In *Re City Securities Pte*[39] the High Court denied that the parties had created a pledge of securities, though they had also used the language of pledge in their security documentation.[40] This was because there was no delivery of the shares and there could not be a pledge without delivery.[41] It seemed that if the shares had been delivered, the court would still have denied that a pledge of the shares had been created.[42] This was because the court was

36 According to a rough and popular rule of thumb, common law possessory interests serve the short-term financing needs of people without a credit history while the fixed charge accommodates variable longer term financing needs involving greater risks.

37 But an equitable mortgage by deposit of documents of title to goods is impossible. Such deposit is simply a pledge.

38 Some nineteenth-century cases alluded to the possibility of a pledge over shares; see: *Colonial Bank* v. *Cady* (1890) 15 App. Cas. 267; *Carter* v. *Wake* (1877) 4 Ch. D. 605.

39 [1990] SLR 468.

40 The court distinguished *Askrigg Pty Ltd* v. *Student Guild of the Curtin University of Technology* (1989) 18 NSWLR 738 where the security agreement contemplated and stated that the specified bills were pledged and held on behalf of the investor and the bills were put into a packet designated for the investor and kept there for him. Those facts constituted an attornment whereby the property passed into the constructive possession of the investor, as pledgee. See also *Dresdner Bank Aktiengesellschaft* v. *Ho Mun-Tuke Don* [1993] 1 SLR 114.

41 The essential features of the letters of hypothecation issued by City Securities Pte were substantially similar to those issued by Lin Securities (Pte) which the court had the occasion to consider in the case *Re Lin Securities (Pte)* [1988] SLR 340. Many of the arguments canvassed in the present proceeding were also canvassed in *Re Lin Securities (Pte)*. In effect, the present hearing gave the court an opportunity to review the decision made in that earlier case.

42 Chao Hick Tin JC said that he doubted whether shares as opposed to bearer bonds could be pledged. City Securities Pte (City) had at diverse dates obtained loans, advances

doubtful whether a pledge of securities was legally possible. A couple of years later, however, doubts about whether shares may be pledged appear to have melted away. In *Chase Manhattan Bank NA* v. *Wong Tui Sun*,[43] the decisions both in the court below[44] and in the Court of Appeal (which upheld the decision of the lower court) 'were based on a construction of the memorandum of agreement setting out the arrangements rather than a categorical dismissal of the possibility that a pledge could be created over registered securities'.[45] The result is that the pledge is no longer possible only in respect of documentary intangibles.[46] This is not to say that a pledge of general intangibles stands on the same footing as a pledge of documentary intangibles. But the practical effect is exactly that they do since while a pledge of share certificates does not confer on the pledgee the rights attaching to the shares, and therefore no interest in the shares passes thereby, it seems conversion will lie for wrongful interference with the pledgee's possession.[47] Here practice has clearly forced the hand of theory.

or credit facilities from the 18 defendant banks. As security for the facilities obtained, City executed in favour of each of the first 17 defendants a letter of hypothecation whereby it charged to each bank all stocks and shares held by it in the course of its business, which were more particularly listed out in daily certificates. Each lender would receive a daily certificate describing the stocks, shares and bonds which were a continuing security for the lender. The borrower was entitled in all respects to deal with the same. The lender should have a pledge on the securities deposited with City. In some cases, City was obliged to keep the securities in safe deposit boxes and separate fire-proof cabinets. But it appears that this obligation was left unfulfilled. The court held that the letters of hypothecation created floating charges and not pledges, essentially because there was merely a contract to create a pledge which was never at the material times carried into effect. There were merely unconsummated rights of possession which did not amount to an act of delivery constituting possession.

43 [1993] 1 SLR 1.

44 *Re EG Tan and Co (Pte)* [1991] 3 MLJ 301. In fact, the High Court cited *Colonial Bank* v. *Cady* (1890) 15 App. Cas. 267 and *Carter* v. *Wake* (1877) 4 Ch. D. 605 as supporting the proposition that a pledge of shares is legally possible.

45 As the High Court in *Pacrim Investments Pte Ltd* v. *Tan Mui Keow Claire* [2005] 1 SLR 141 explains, para. [14]. The Court of Appeal in that case had to decide whether certain arrangements made between a stock broking company and one of its bankers created a pledge of the shares (which did not require registration pursuant to s. 131 of the Companies Act) or an equitable mortgage which, for want of registration under the Companies Act, was void against the liquidator and creditors of the company.

46 The idea of a lien over securities in the sense referring to the physical paper evidencing the rights concerned is uncontroversial. See *PD Manufacturing International Pte Ltd* v. *ING Bank NV* [1999] SGHC 236. Referring to clause 15 which affected 'any funds and chattels including securities and other valuables deposited with the bank in safe custody', the court said that it could give rise to a common law lien which is dependent for its existence on possession. The court agreed that such a lien was not a charge to which s. 131 of the Companies Act applied but immediately observed that not all liens were dependent on possession. The court added that the security interest in clause 15 would certainly include a possessory lien over the documents representing the securities but might extend to rights over the interests in the securities represented by the documents.

47 See *Pacrim Investments Pte Ltd* v. *Tan Mui Keow Claire* [2005] 1 SLR 141 reversed on other grounds [2008] 2 SLR 898 where the Court of Appeal agreed with counsel that a 'pledge' of registered securities accompanied by duly signed transfers is an equitable mortgage. It is said that the courts incline to find an equitable mortgage from a deposit of marketable securities. See also *Harrold* v. *Plenty* [1901] 2 Ch. 314. In another case, *JB Jeyaretnam* v. *Law Society of Singapore* [1988] 3 MLJ 425, the PC thought it clear that a cheque given for no consideration

While some general intangibles are in law capable of possession in some sense, without a true possessory interest arising, not all possessory interests, the cases seem to go on to say, are necessarily destroyed by loss of possession. In other words, not all possessory liens are entirely possessory in character. The heresy, to some, comes from Malaysia, through the Federal Court decision in the case of *Asia Commercial Finance (M) Bhd* v. *JB Precision Moulding Industries Sdn Bhd*.[48] In this case a security deposit in relation to a leasing agreement was held to be a contractual lien, despite the absence of possession of the deposit by the creditor. While a direct holding of a similar nature is yet to be found in Singapore, there is no lack of literature on the Malaysian decision. It is evident that the Malaysian case has excited interest and has been closely analysed and examined. For example, Lee Eng Beng[49] admits only a very limited scope for non-possessory contractual liens outside negotiable instruments,[50] and maintains further that as a general rule a lien cannot be created over the purported lienee's indebtedness to the lienor.[51] However, Adrian Wong[52] argues that the parties in the Malaysian case created a contingent debt and not a present consensual charge; the debt materialising only upon fulfilment of the leasing agreement. Wong's construction of the parties' agreement as creating a contingent debt signifying an intention to create an interest by way of security after default in payment by the borrower seems unlikely and unreal. On the other hand, Lee's point does not fully explain why although the contractual lien and the non-possessory vendor's or purchaser's lien are evidently comparable in function,[53] they should produce a difference in result.[54]

The real difficulty is that a contractual lien without possession is a secret interest.[55] Such a lien may do less damage in relation to negotiable instruments because the element of negotiability will minimise the element of surprise and render it of little effect so far as the third party holder in due course is concerned. But where *nemo dat* is the yardstick of security of title, innocent purchasers would be prejudiced by an

was simply no reified chose but see the immensely interesting and entertaining exchange of views in its wake, namely K. Shanmugam 'Transfer of property in relation to cheques – *JB Jeyaretnam* v. *The Law Society of Singapore*' [1989]1 MLJ xli and P Jeyaretnam 'A matter of principle: the rights of the donor drawer of a cheque' [1989] 2 MLJ xxxiii.

48 [1996] 2 MLJ 1.

49 'Security deposit arrangements in insolvency' (1996) 8 SAcLJ 458, p. 463.

50 *George Barker Ltd* v. *Eynon* [1974] 1 WLR 462 and *Re Coslett (Contractors) Ltd* [1998] Ch. 495 seem to suggest that the contractual lien is necessarily possessory.

51 See Lord Hope of Craighead in *National Westminster Bank plc* v. *Spectrum Plus* [2005] UKHL 41, para. 60: 'A banker has a general lien over all bills, notes and negotiable instruments belonging to the customer which his customer may have deposited with him in security of the customer's indebtedness to the bank. But a lien is a right to retain possession of property that belongs to someone else, and the banker has no lien over funds which, when deposited in its account by the customer, become his own property. Moreover the relationship is one where, if the account is in credit, the banker is indebted to his customer. So it was a misuse of the word lien to say that the bank could assert a right of that kind over the proceeds.'

52 'An Introduction to Liens in Commercial Transactions' (1999) 20 Sing L Rev 134, p. 152 *et seq.*

53 Though not in origin; the former being consensual and the latter an imposition of law.

54 This is the equitable lien. An equitable lien in the context of sale of goods is excluded by the Sale of Goods Act, s. 41 as in England. See also: *Re Crossman, Salaman* v. *Crossman* [1939] 2 All ER 530; *Re Nanwa Gold Mines Ltd, Ballantyne* v. *Nanwa Gold Mines Ltd* [1955] 1 WLR 1080.

55 And so it has elsewhere been construed as a bill of sale, as in *Coburn* v. *Collins* (1888) 35 Ch. D. 373.

interest of which there was no prior indication. To accept that a non-possessory contractual lien, a legal and not an equitable interest, is legally possible is to say that it will prevail over even the innocent purchaser ignorant of its existence.[56]

Is flexibility desirable?

The need for flexibility in secured financing goes without saying. As an external economy, Singapore needs to offer external investors and financiers at least the entire range of devices with which they are familiar, not less.[57] However, flexibility comes at a price. While party autonomy is advanced if parties are free to tailor their transaction to suit their peculiar interests and circumstances, the same flexibility may become an instrument of litigation and oppression, catching third parties by surprise. The trade-off between flexibility as between the parties and fairness to third parties is presently struck in terms of the numerus clausus principle with its abhorrence of secret and indeterminate interests.[58] It may be difficult to form a precise estimate of the trade-off between flexibility and fairness to third parties and determine the degree of flexibility which is optimal. Nevertheless, we can prove that the Article 9 strikes a better balance than the numerus clausus principle.

Assuming first that flexibility is desirable in itself without qualification, a question foremost in law reform must be whether conversion to a scheme modelled on Article 9 would result in loss of flexibility without significant gains in predictability for third parties. There is sometimes a hasty impression that such an approach to personal property security interests would be vastly inferior in achieving flexible solutions. This impression is false.

While Article 9 relies on a common functional concept of security, it does not alter the features and attributes of the security agreement or the rights and obligations between the parties to it. Thus, a sale with retention of title does not cease to be a sale; and questions of the passing of property to a third party are still to be answered from the law of sale.[59] Again, under Article 9 an outright sale of general intangibles does not merge into an assignment for security; in fact, the former is outside the scope of Article 9.[60] When Article 9 does obliterate a distinction, it is for limited purposes, usually for the purposes of requiring public notice to be given and the determination of priorities. Therefore, the distinction between an outright sale of book debts (what Article 9 refers to as accounts)[61] and an assignment of book debts

56 If the fear of hidden interests is the reason that the contractual lien must be suppressed, then it would cease to be dangerous to recognise the contractual lien if a way could be devised to furnish public notice of the otherwise hidden interest.

57 There is no evidence of a duality with the external side reliant on secured credit and the domestic side on intimate control.

58 For a discussion of the principle, see W. Swadling 'Property: general principles' in Birks (ed.), *English Private Law* (Oxford: Oxford University Press, 2004), vol. 1, ch. 4, pp. 206–9 and 211. In the present view, the policy against hidden interests is embraced by the principle.

59 Cf. R. Cuming 'Internationalisation of secured financing law' in R. Cranston (ed.), *Making Commercial Law: Essays in Honour of Roy Goode* (Oxford: Clarendon Press, 1997), pp. 522–3.

60 The term 'general intangibles' embraces all that is not picked up by the other categories of personal property dealt with by the article.

61 Which is not for the purpose of collection only or in full or partial satisfaction of a pre-existing indebtedness or part of a sale of the business out of which the accounts arose.

for security is removed for these purposes only.[62] Despite the obliteration of the distinction, the former retains all the attributes and incidents of a sale. The assignee in the former case consequently does not account to the assignor for any surplus but retains the surplus as the owner of the receivables.[63]

To conclude anything serious about Article 9's impact on flexibility, we need to be very clear that it is flexibility in practice that is critical. Flexibility is not a virtue when it is more the product of the historical divide between common law and equity than practical convenience or expedience or principle. With respect to receivables financing, for instance, it could be, and has been, argued that there appears to be no reason to maintain both the mortgage and charge over receivables. One (the mortgage) confers title while the other (the charge) a mere right of appropriation on default. However, the difference between them in effect is very subtle and it almost diminishes to nothing in practice because the charge will, in the vast majority of cases, confer an express power to appoint a receiver.[64]

Further, it must not be overlooked that a concept of security interests based on a grant of a proprietary interest, or right of appropriation of property, has inherent limitations, which are absent under an economic or practical view of the matter. One such limitation is that 'it is not possible in law to have a legal estate in a chattel'.[65] Strictly therefore, you cannot have a lease of chattel – it is only a contract to give possession or a bailment and, hence, you cannot have a lease as security interest. In recent years, another limitation was in currency for a while: namely, the impossibility of a chargor creating a charge over his own indebtedness. This limitation on common law flexibility as applied to bank accounts created a stir in Singapore when it was announced in *Re Charge Card Services Ltd*.[66] It had the effect of invalidating a commercially expedient device whereby a bank could obtain a security interest in deposits held by its customer. A bank making a loan to a customer can obtain security by requiring the customer to make a deposit and providing for contractual rights of set-off or combining accounts. It can make the deposit a flawed asset by imposing contractual limitations on the right to withdraw. However, although only the charge could improve the priority of the depositary, a charge over one's own indebtedness

62 See: *Tancred* v. *Delagoa Bay and East African Railway* (1889) 23 QB 39; *Hughes* v. *Pump House Hotel Co Ltd* [1902] 2 KB 190. Note also *Business Computers Ltd* v. *Anglo-African Leasing Ltd* [1977] 2 All ER 741, [1977] 1 WLR 578. There are other differences between an absolute assignment of book debts and an assignment by way of security. The debtor is obliged to pay the assignee who gives him notice but not the chargee and there are also differences regarding rights of set-off. The reason for bringing both within an Article 9-type scheme is that it is very difficult to distinguish between them and sufficiently important to forestall disputes about proper classification.

63 One may not always agree with the way these obliterations are done. For instance, the Australian and New Zealand Law Reform Commissions did not agree that operating leases should be excluded from an Article 9-type scheme. See now the Personal Property Security Act 1999 of New Zealand. The exclusion of operating leases under Article 9 is one of the most litigated issues in the US and there may be practical wisdom in including operating leases within the list of security interests which are perfected by filing.

64 See F. Oditah *Legal Aspects of Receivables Financing* (London: Sweet & Maxwell, 1991), p. 96.

65 See W. Swadling 'The proprietary effects of a hire of goods' in Palmer and McKendrick (eds), *Interests in Goods* (London: LLP, 2nd edn, 1998), ch. 20.

66 [1987] Ch. 150.

was held to be impossible in *Re Charge Card Services Ltd.*[67] In Singapore, the effect of this decision was quickly reversed by legislation.[68] It is apparent that under an economic view of security interest such limitations which are a curb on common law flexibility would have been inconsequential.

There is a paradox in common law flexibility worth mentioning. While the common law is flexible in its core application, it encounters serious difficulties in coming to terms with quasi-security interests. Its inability, or refusal, to admit them into the class of proprietary security interests means that the flexibility which these offer must be enjoyed by financiers and credit providers outside the established proprietary framework. One effect has been evident. Quasi-security interests are a frequent source of litigation because they are very difficult to separate from established security interests.[69] Of the *Romalpa* clause,[70] a Malaysian judge has not without cause said: 'their effectiveness is subject to satisfactory negotiation of a combination of technical aspects of the law of sale of goods, bailments, trusts, mortgages and tracing'.[71] *Romalpa* sellers quickly realise as a result that only litigation will demonstrate whether their title in the goods has carried over to the proceeds of sale of those goods.[72]

The refusal of the general law to recognise quasi-security interests as proprietary in nature follows from its adherence to the numerus clausus principle. This principle which works by inclusion has the rationale of admitting a limited number of proprietary interests in order to avoid fraud, confusion and surprise, hence achieving fairness to third parties.[73] But as the development of the chattel mortgage testifies to, the dreaded fraud, confusion and surprise disappear if there is a way to bring the interest to public notice. Thus, the suspicion of secret liens and hidden legal interests which led to the common law rejection of chattel mortgages was dispelled when the Bills of Sale Act prescribed a way to give public notice of the chattel mortgage.[74] Article 9 operates with the same effect of giving public notice and arguably achieves greater efficiency consistent with protection of third parties than the numerus clausus principle. Intrinsically conservative and directed at maintaining the status quo, the numerus clausus principle cannot easily accommodate the development of novel security interests. Paradoxically, Article 9's flexibility is superior, not inferior to the

67 Admittedly, the full impact of this is only felt on insolvency and may be neutralised by the generous insolvency set-off rules. This has led to observations that the true impact of the decision lies in the context of cross-border insolvency. The decision invalidating the charge back would in a cross-border context leave the bank at the mercy of narrower insolvency set-off rules common in civil law systems.

68 See s. 13 of the Civil Law Act (Cap 43, 1994 Rev Ed) introduced in 1993.

69 On the difficulties of separating a sale of receivables from a charge over them, see: *Lloyds and Scottish Finance* v. *Cyril Lord Carpet Sales* [1992] BCLC 609; *Welsh Development Agency* v. *Export Finance Co Ltd* [1990] BCC 393. On the difficulties of separating a sale and repurchase from a collaterised loan, see: Tjio 'When is an Elephant a Bird' (2006) 18 SAcLJ473, discussing *Cheah Geok Tuan* v. *Lie Khin Sin* [2006] 1 SLR 340.

70 The *Romalpa* case has been followed in *Gebrueder Buehler AG* v. *Chi Man Kong Peter* [1986] SLR 344. The Malaysian HC reached a result similar to the *Romalpa* case in *Au Yong Kun Ming* v. *Tractors Malaysia Bhd* [1997] 5 MLJ 168.

71 *Sungei Way Leasing Sdn Bhd* v. *Sena Land Development Sdn Bhd* [1989] 3 MLJ 37.

72 See: *Re Bond Worth Ltd* [1980] Ch. 228; *Stroud Architectural Services Ltd* v. *John Laing Construction Ltd* (1993) 35 Con LR 135. See also *Hendy Lennox (Industrial Engines) Ltd* v. *Grahame Puttick Ltd* [1984] 1 WLR 485; *Re Andrabell Ltd* [1984] 3 All ER 407. Cf. *Associated Alloys Pty Ltd* v. *CAN 001 452 106 Pty Ltd* (2000) 202 CLR 588.

73 See W. Swadling 'Property: general principles' in Birks (ed.), fn 58, ch. 4, pp. 206–9.

74 See pp. 424–26.

general law's; for instance, as already alluded to, Article 9 produces greater flexibility in relation to contractual liens as it easily allows the contractual lien an expanded role in secured financing.[75] In relation to *Romalpa* clauses, Victor Yeo has argued both the pros and cons of a registration system which embraces retention of title.[76] Yeo concluded that it would simply mean giving priority to the prior floating chargee thereby worsening the position of the *Romalpa* seller who under the existing law prevails over the floating chargee.[77] This conclusion would not be true of a system modelled on Article 9, since it would give priority to the *Romalpa* seller under its super-priority rules.[78]

The advantage of greater efficiency which Article 9 brings to the law is not unqualified. While it correctly argues that quasi-security interests should be treated like security interests for the purposes of notice and priorities, it does not always furnish convincing solutions to the difficulties of distinguishing between them. The difficulties of distinguishing a sale from a lease-back[79] and an outright sale of receivables and an assignment by way of security[80] are well known. It seems sometimes that one can as likely get it wrong as right when called upon to classify them. However, the important point is that this problem of definition is not unique to Article 9 – it is there whether or not we adopt Article 9 – and cannot be reason to reject reform modelled on Article 9. Leases, for instance, can be true operating leases or security leases and the problem of classification is sometimes cited as argument against reform modelled on Article 9. This argument is valid only if it is right to ignore quasi-security interests altogether in any reform of the law. If the view is that they must be included, and the choice is between reform modelled on Article 9 and reform based on the present charges registration system, the fact that there are difficulties in identifying quasi-security interests is a matter of indifference. They will be present whichever system is adopted.

With respect to structured or hierarchical secured financing, the greater flexibility of Article 9 which results from its abandoning the proprietary concept of security interest is especially evident. Contrary to theory, documents which are not documentary intangibles play a significant security function in Singapore; as was seen in such cases as *Re City Securities Pte.*[81] It is also instructive to consider another case for a utilisation unique to Singapore. In *PP* v. *Koh Beng Oon*,[82] customers who placed an order for a motor car were required to pay a booking fee and a COE (certificate of entitlement) deposit. Those who did not make full payment were required to deposit either the log-card or the Preferential Additional Registration Fee certificate for their existing vehicle with the car dealer, pursuant to a signed form, which stated that they pledged their vehicle document as part payment for the COE deposit. The dealer undertook to secure the COE for its customers, either by bidding for it on its own or through an agent. Under the COE bidding system, 50 per cent of the bid amount

75 Among local legal scholars, this fear of secret liens is very often the submerged argument. See Tan Cheng Han 'The negative pledge as a security device' [1996] SJLS 415, p. 417. While acknowledging that the negative pledge does not satisfy the definition of security interest, Professor Tan accepts that it functions as a security interest

76 Yeo 'Visiting an old friend – the *Romalpa* clause' (1997) 9 SAcLJ 250.

77 See Yeo, fn 76, at p 273.

78 Cf. G. McCormack 'Reforming the law of security interests: national and international perspectives' [2003] SJLS 1, p. 25.

79 See *Orion Finance Ltd* v. *Crown Financial Management Ltd* [1996] BCC 612 commenting on *Re George Lightfield Ltd* [1933] Ch. 1.

80 Cf. the Malaysian case of *Public Finance Bhd* v. *Scotch Leasing Sdn Bhd* [1996] 2 MLJ 369.

81 [1990] SLR 468.

82 [2000] 1 SLR 276.

was deducted from the applicant's bank account as a deposit for the bid application. In order to finance the difference between this amount and the COE deposit received from its customers, the dealer obtained a COE financing facility from financiers in respect of customers who needed COE bidding, pledging the documents as security. It is significant that the court had no hesitation or difficulty in accepting that the vehicle documents had been pledged and that there were no restrictions against a sub-pledge; even though the documents were not documents of title. In fact, the pledge could only be a pledge for a contingent debt. Yet the court was prepared to place rationale above technical law, saying that 'the underlying rationale for security interests such as pledges, as well as liens and mortgages, is to facilitate commerce, and if a pledge for a contingent debt can serve a useful commercial purpose, and there is no denying its utility in the COE bidding context for both Auto Asia and their customers, there seems no reason to unduly confine the pledge to being a security device for existing debts'.[83]

The appeal to economic efficiency was fully justified. Reified choses circulate in high volumes, making it expedient and convenient from the economic point of view that they should be capable of fictional transfer of possession. It is the same with documents which prove rights in property or to use property and, indeed, those which prove a security interest such as hire purchase agreements or lease agreements. If the courts in Singapore have approved a pledge of uncertificated securities as well as rights of use of a motor car, contrary to strict theory, there is nothing to stop them extending the same concession for the sake of commerce to documents which merely prove a security interest. Even so, the resultant flexibility compares poorly with Article 9's idea of chattel paper, which is more logical, pragmatic and flexible. Article 9-102(11) defines chattel paper as a record or records that evidence both a monetary obligation and a security interest in specific goods.[84] By a symbol, the evidence of the claim is taken as the claim and rendered capable of transfer of possession by delivery. This categorisation at once brings chattel paper within the filing requirements as well as immediately making it possible to take possession of such intangibles. Article 9 thereby promotes their use in financing and affords the flexibility that the secured creditor may also choose to file in the alternative to secure protection in those cases where possession is lost or not taken.[85]

Will attachment and perfection engender more difficulties?

On the creation of a security interest, Singapore lawyers will have reason to be doubtful whether Article 9 would be useful or confusing. The primary inspiration for the notion of attachment in Article 9 stemmed from the need to accommodate

83 The pledge is also widely used in floor stock financing of used cars. The dealer pledges the log book and a copy of the transfer form bearing the signature of the current registered owner to the financier as security. If the borrower defaults, the financier will fill in its own name on the transfer form and obtain legal ownership to the vehicle. 'The car dealer usually does not transfer the ownership to its name'; see *Lim Woon Cheng Anthony* v. *PP* [1998] 1 SLR 14.

84 Art. 9-102(31) defines 'electronic chattel paper' to mean 'chattel paper evidenced by a record or records consisting of information stored in an electronic medium' while Art. 9-102(78) defines 'tangible chattel paper' to mean 'chattel paper evidenced by a record or records consisting of information that is inscribed on a tangible medium'.

85 Positively it facilitates re-financing credits extended to hirers under hire purchase and buyers under conditional sale agreements.

after-acquired and future property. According to Article 9-203, an interest attaches as soon as the parties have agreed that it attaches so long as value is given and the debtor has acquired rights in the property subject to a security agreement. Attachment means the same as creation when rights are intended to come immediately into effect over property which is in existence. When however goods materialise at some future date, we cannot suppose that there is still perfect equivalence or exact correspondence between creation and attachment.[86] A security interest in after-acquired or future goods is created at the time of the security contract in the sense that equity, assuming consideration is provided for the agreement, deems or looks upon that as done which ought to be done.[87] Until the goods materialise, there is immediately an interest in equity capable of binding third parties who are not bona fide purchasers for value without notice. Ultimately, however, because specific enforceability is discretionary, it does not always follow that this binding effect will be produced. This is unlike attachment which is automatic, being defined to operate immediately the rights are acquired, independently of the equitable maxim which is in fact discarded. Thus, attachment takes the discretion out; although the goods have not yet materialised when there are inconsistent dealings in the security by the debtor, once they do materialise, the attachment relates back to the time of the security contract, giving the secured creditor who first attaches the goods legal rights against another who deals later with the debtor.

Further, equity only blends the obligation and property; it does not create a new interest where none before existed. So Kelvin Low writes: 'It is axiomatic by the terms of the maxim that specific enforceability by itself does not create an equitable proprietary interest. A further condition, indeed a precondition, to the effectiveness of the maxim to create property rights is that that the eventual performance of the relevant obligation will create property rights recognised by the common law.'[88] On the orthodox view, creation is more restrictive than attachment in the Article 9 sense inasmuch as a security interest can attach in future goods (in the Article 9 sense) whether or not that security interest matches some interest already known to law in accordance with the numerus clausus principle. One should, of course, be careful not to overstate this difference in Singapore. In *Golden Village Multiplex Pte Ltd* v. *Marina Centre Holdings Pte Ltd*,[89] the Court of Appeal, affirming the High Court, held that the doctrine of *Walsh* v. *Lonsdale* would apply to create a lease in equity even if strict specific performance was not available, provided equity would intervene by an order of an injunction to prevent a breach of contract. The court applied the equitable maxim even though the parties had agreed that the lease to be executed was not to be in a form registrable under the Land Titles Act.[90] Thus, to some extent, the notion of creation already begins to relax the requirement of existence of a known interest in property. Be that as it may, attachment as defined by Article 9 removes the rule of presumed intention, that where an interest is intended to be created in one

86 In the case of accounts receivables, attachment occurs when the debts come into existence. The general law regards the agreement as a contract to assign future debts. As the debts materialise, there is an equitable assignment of each present debt.

87 *Tailby* v. *Official Receiver* (1888) 12 App. Cas. 523.

88 Citing Meagher, Gummow and Lehane, *Equity: Doctrines and Remedies* (Chatswood: NSW, Butterworths, 4th edn, 2002), p. 69; see *Annual Review of Singapore Cases [2002] Equity and Trust* (Singapore: SAL, 2003), ch. 12, para. 12.6.

89 [2002] 1 SLR 333.

90 See also *Bristol Airport Plc* v. *Powdrill* [1990] Ch. 744.

way, which is an invalid mode, the courts will not spell out a valid mode from the invalid mode.[91] Article 9 emphasises the agreement to create rather than the mode of transfer, necessarily so because it embraces quasi-security interests in which there is no grant of proprietary rights to the creditor. As long therefore as there is a written agreement to create a security interest, and the other requirements of attachment are met, it will not matter whether the debtor employed an invalid mode of transfer or a valid mode. Thus, under an Article 9-inspired system a failed transfer of trust for the purposes of security would be effective and be treated as if it were a declaration of trust by the debtor.[92] To avoid this result, the debtor will have to get the creditor to agree to postpone attachment by an explicit agreement, which Article 9-203(2) allows, making the mode critical.[93]

Some of these differences may be overlooked as a result of incorporation of Professor Sir Roy Goode's terminology of attachment which has found its way into the local case law. Goode meant to stress the acquisition of rights in the property. In this sense of attaching to property, the terminology usefully differentiates a security contract from a contract to create future security.[94] Attachment in this sense was approved in *Asiatic Enterprises (Pte) Ltd* v. *United Overseas Bank Ltd*[95] when the court, giving clause 10 its ordinary and natural construction, held that it gave the United Overseas Bank a right or entitlement at some future date, upon the occurrence of any of the events of default, by unilateral action on its part to assert or to impose a security on the property of Asiatic. Singapore lawyers may not fully appreciate that this was using attachment in a different sense from Article 9.

The notion of perfection as implemented in Article 9 is perhaps hardly more familiar to lawyers in Singapore.[96] The notion of perfection in general law is understood and employed in the constituent sense. Amplifying the meaning of creation, it stresses that an interest which is purportedly created at law for value may merely exist as an agreement to create the interest (in the eyes of equity) until it is perfected at law by compliance with some legal requirement as to the mode of transfer or

91 See: *Milroy* v. *Lord* (1862) 4 de GF and J 264; *Richards* v. *Delbridge* (1874) LR 18 Eq 11. Note also the relaxation in *Pennington* v. *Waine* [2002] 1 WLR 2075 and *Jaffa* v. *Taylor Gallery Ltd*, Times Law Report 21 March 1990.

92 For a discussion of stamp duty implications, see H. Tjio 'Factoring and stamp duty in Singapore and Malaysia: *Arab-Malaysian Merchant Bank Bhd* v. *Boustead Trading (1985) Sdn Bhd*' [1994] SJLS 183.

93 The Canadian courts do not accept that merely using the terminology of floating charge has the effect of postponing the time of attachment to time of actual materialisation of property. See *Canadian Imperial Bank of Commerce* v. *Otto Timm Enterprises Ltd* (1995) 130 DLR (4th) 91.

94 '[A]ttachment does not take place unless the conditions for attachment specified in the security agreement have been fulfilled. This does not, however, imply that the parties may, consistently with the equitable rules for creation of a security interest by agreement, stipulate any event they choose as producing attachment. On the contrary, where the designated event is a mere contingency – an event which may or may not occur – then unless the contingency is simply the debtor's acquisition of an interest in the asset the agreement will not by itself be effective to create a security interest, even on the occurrence of the contingency': *Legal Problems of Credit and Security* (London: Sweet & Maxwell, 3rd edn, 2003), p. 65.

95 [2000] 1 SLR 300.

96 Although it appears that American precedents are used. See Art. 9-308 which states that a security interest is perfected when it has attached and when all the steps required for its perfection under any provision of the article have been complied with.

constitution.[97] A classic example of lack of perfection occurs when there is a voluntary transfer of shares which does not comply with the legally accepted or prescribed mode; ordinarily the transfer is not perfected until the shares are registered in the company's register in the name of the transferee.[98] However, although the transfer is voluntary, there may nevertheless be an earlier stage in which the gift is perfected in equity if the transferor has done everything that is necessary and in his power to do to make the gift.[99] Put another way, the creation of an interest is ineffective in law unless the interest is also perfected, except where the creation is effective in equity either because equity deems that as done which ought to be done or considers the creation perfected in equity. There is no hiatus between the coming into being of proprietary rights and the enforceability of these rights against third parties. The moment the rights come into existence, they are by virtue of their in rem nature already binding as much between the parties as on third parties including those who are later legal interest holders who are not bona fide purchasers for value without notice, if the rights are equitable. Again, the terminology of perfection which Professor Sir Roy Goode has employed (i.e. the sense in which perfection gives notice to third parties) was approved in *Ng Wei Teck Michael* v. *Oversea-Chinese Banking Corp.*[100] This however is perfection in a different sense from Article 9.

Singapore lawyers may not immediately appreciate that perfection as used in Article 9 does not correspond to perfection as understood in the general law or in the more limited sense which Professor Sir Roy Goode has employed it. Perfection in Article 9 means enforceability against third parties and is distinguished from enforceability as between parties to the security agreement. Although not invariably so, the state of perfection is achieved by taking a further act – in the case of non-possessory interests, this is the act of filing – to perfect the interest which has attached.[101] There is almost a clear gap between attachment the effects of which are confined to the parties themselves and perfection which is effective against third parties. The only situation in which security rights which have attached but have been left unperfected are enforceable against third parties who are unsecured creditors occurs when the debtor is solvent.[102]

In some respects, the notions of attachment and perfection (in particular, the notions of temporary and alternative perfection) improve the protection currently

97 Thus, where the purported voluntary transfer amounts to an incomplete instrument, it is said to be an imperfect gift of which a court of equity will not compel perfection; see *Macedo* v. *Beatrice Stroud* [1922] 2 AC 330.

98 The courts speak of the perfection of all documentation in this sense; see *Industrial and Commercial Bank Ltd* v. *Banco Ambrosiano Veneto SpA* [2003] 1 SLR 221, para. 86.

99 See: *Re Rose, Midland Bank Executor and Trustee Co Ltd* [1949] Ch. 78; *Re Rose, Rose* v. *Inland Revenue Comrs* [1952] Ch. 499. Note also *Pennington* v. *Waine* [2002] 1 WLR 2075.

100 [1998] 2 SLR 1, para. 34. See Goode *Principles of Corporate Insolvency Law* (London, Sweet & Maxwell, 2nd edn, 1997), p. 422: 'It should be borne in mind that registration is purely a perfection requirement designed to give notice to third parties; it is not a condition of validity of the charge, which remains fully enforceable against the company prior to winding up or administration.' It therefore follows that the security must remain unrealised at the time the liquidator is appointed.

101 Where after-acquired property is concerned, attachment will occur after filing and thus perfection will occur and by relation back be deemed to have occurred as at the time of filing. See *Re Smith* (1971) 326 F Supp 1311.

102 Article 9 in effect gives the grantee of a security interest a choice. He can leave things pretty much as they were in contract and choose when he will confer third party rights on himself.

afforded to possessory interests. Possessory interests are ineffective once possession is lost[103] and in cases where possession of goods has to be given up, some other device such as a trust receipt has to be employed in order to ensure that the secured creditor retains the security interest in the goods.[104] Article 9's answer is that perfection will continue for 20 days upon consensual parting of possession for trade purposes, which is a simpler mechanism of protection.[105] The article additionally allows dual or alternative perfection; by possession as well as by filing.[106] A simple filing notice will therefore serve to protect the secured creditor from losing out to another secured creditor, without the fuss of a trust receipt.

Would there be serious difficulties in comprehending the new concepts of attachment and perfection which Article 9-type reform would entail? One envisages that there would be some confusion at first and that certain established modes of reasoning would have to be abandoned but not that the difficulties could not be overcome. Additional difficulties will arise because the separation between attachment and perfection is not intuitive and as will be seen, experience gained with existing registration systems may not be fully helpful.[107] To guard against complications, it would be necessary to clarify that these notions are replacement concepts. Otherwise, it might erroneously be argued that third parties have nevertheless pending filing obtained rights by estoppel or other means under general law.

Purchasers of absolute interest

Where absolute dealings in secured property are concerned, it is difficult to discern what policy should be adopted. For example, Goode has written disapprovingly of the unsatisfactory patchwork of legislative provisions detailing the exceptions to the *nemo dat* rule. The latter have given rise to grave interpretation problems, often resolved at a highly technical level.[108] The inadequate legislation may well be reflecting uncertainties in policy as to how the balance should be struck.[109] Speaking in a similar context, Denning LJ (as he then was) once referred to the conflict between the two principles which hold sway, one favouring security of absolute title and the other, security of transaction.[110] These remarks are equally pertinent in the context of property subject to security interests. Should the law favour keeping articles of commerce

103 In the case of a lien, when the lienee voluntarily parts with possession: *Sweet* v. *Pym* (1800) 1 East 4.

104 See *North Western Bank Ltd* v. *Poynter, Son and Macdonalds* [1895] AC 56.

105 Art. 9-312(f). The enumerated purposes are ultimate sale or exchange, loading, unloading, storing, shipping, trans-shipping, manufacturing, processing, or otherwise dealing with them in a manner preliminary to their sale or exchange.

106 Art. 9-312(a) which states that 'A security interest in chattel paper, negotiable documents, instruments, or investment property may be perfected by filing.' And Art. 9-313(a) which states that 'Except as otherwise provided in subsection (b), a secured party may perfect a security interest in negotiable documents, instruments, money or tangible chattel paper by taking possession of the collateral …'.

107 See pp. 432–433.

108 See *Commercial Law* (London: LexisNexis, 3rd edn, 2004), p. 446.

109 The famous dictum of Ashhurst J. in *Lickbarrow* v. *Mason* (1787) 2 TR 63, p. 70, namely 'wherever one of two innocent persons must suffer by the acts of a third, he who has enabled such third person to occasion the loss must sustain it', is not very revealing.

110 See *Bishopsgate Motor Finance Corp Ltd* v. *Transport Brakes Ltd* [1949] 1 KB 322, pp. 336–7.

in general circulation or should it protect the security title? The problem lies in a non-inventory chattel which is disposed of in breach of the security agreement. While the security interest holder could have little means of discovering an intended breach of a security agreement, the third party could be ignorant of any breach of the security agreement, as the breach is likely to have been concealed from him. The policy probably tilts in favour of the third party; since if tracing into the sale proceeds is readily available, the security holder has recourse against the proceeds of the property subject to security whereas the third party could only sue for damages for breach or restitution of the price. But how should this be done? Professor McCormack has attempted to show that there is a rough sort of equivalence here and what is achievable under Article 9 is achievable under the common law.[111] Both are equally solicitous of third party dealings. This observation requires some elaboration and obliges us to look more closely at absolute dealings under common law and equity.

Under general law, the enforcement of a security interest against third party purchasers is complex.[112] Depending on whether the interest is created at law or in equity, the third party's notice or lack of notice will be material.[113] Legal protection is absolute and the lack of notice is immaterial save when a *nemo dat* exception applies. In fact, the *nemo dat* exceptions are quite narrow. The buyer and seller in possession exceptions are of limited scope because although not confined to second sales, they presuppose the first transaction is a sale, as opposed to the creation of security interest.[114] If the first transaction is not a sale but a hire purchase, neither the seller in possession nor the buyer in possession exception will apply;[115] in Singapore there is no equivalence of the Hire Purchase Act 1964, s. 27(3) which extends the *nemo dat* exception to the hire purchase.[116] The same is true of the lease as a quasi-security interest; the good faith and without notice purchaser will not secure a better title because the *nemo dat* exceptions will not be available.[117] That leaves only

111 See fn 9 above, pp. 105–8.

112 This question arises with respect to non-consensual dealings with the third party.

113 We should further notice that dealings in the possessory security interest are inhibited because with loss of possession, there is loss of enforceability through loss of the possessory title. In the case of negotiable instruments, so long as the pledgee keeps the instrument in possession, no competing dealing can occur. It is impossible to create a non-possessory security interest in a negotiable instrument because once possession is given up, the holder in due course will always take free of his security interest. Negotiable documents of title receive the same treatment; 'pledge thus became the only available security device for documents as it was for negotiable instruments'.

114 Typical cases involve *Romalpa* clauses. The sub-buyer takes free of the seller's retained title. See *Re Highway Foods* [1995] 1 BCLC 209. The second transaction may be a pledge and ss. 2, 8 and 9 of the Factors Act (Cap 386, 1994 Rev Ed) may then be applied to validate the pledge.

115 *Helby* v. *Matthews* [1895] AC 471.

116 See *Chua Heng (Motors) Pte Ltd* v. *Lim Soon Huat Ernst* [2004] SGDC where the hirer left the car with the dealer in a situation short of default for the dealer to sell on his behalf. See also *Gunasegeran s/o Pavadaisamy* v. *PP* [1997] 3 SLR 969 which shows that the only deterrent measures are criminal prosecutions for forgery and cheating.

117 See A. Hicks 'Reservation of title; a pious hope' [1985] MLR 63 at n. 23 who refers to competition between the *Romalpa* seller and the financier pledgee of the buyer. See also *R Esmerian Inc* v. *Ghassan Fahkreddin* [1996] SGHC 7 affirmed in *Diamond Centre Pte Ltd* v. *R Esmerian Inc* [1996] 3 SLR 377.

the agency and estoppel exceptions the scope of which is pretty narrow in such cases.[118]

Equitable protection is a matter of good conscience and the purchaser in good faith without notice has the trump card. Equitable charges, or interests, are enforceable against the buyer or transferee who is not a bona fide legal purchaser for value without notice. More importantly, the doctrine of constructive notice is not applicable.[119] A buyer will not take free if he knows that the goods are subject to an equitable security interest. If in fact the sale is in breach of some duty or restriction against selling involving or not involving consent to the sale, it necessarily follows that the buyer who is aware of the breach will not take free of the security interest.[120]

In the case of pure intangibles, the general rule is that a person taking a chose in action from a person who has not a valid title has no better right to it as against the true owner than the person from whom he has taken it.[121] The Malaysian and Singapore courts hold that this is the law even though the person is a bona fide legal purchaser or mortgagee for value without notice of the true ownership.[122] The Malaysian courts however go further in saying that no *nemo dat* exception has been imported from the law of the sale of goods and '[n]o known statute has modified debts or book debts effectively to interfere with the application of the *nemo dat* rule to them'.[123] The Court of Appeal in Singapore, in *Pan-Electric Industries Ltd*

118 See *Pan-Electric Industries Ltd (in liquidation)* v. *Oversea-Chinese Banking Corp Ltd* [1994] 3 SLR 695. In the case of legal interests which are short of ownership, liability in conversion is strict and so also lack of notice is immaterial. Where the second transaction is a sale, the *nemo dat* exceptions contained in ss. 24 and 25 of the Sale of Goods Act (Cap 393, 1999 Rev. Ed.) will seldom apply. In the case of a legal charge, the chargee simply enforces it against the third party. That leaves only the estoppel exception; but the law hesitates to find an estoppel merely from delivery. See *Biggs* v. *Evans* [1894] 1 QB 88.

119 *Feuer Leather Corporation* v. *Frank Johnstone and Sons* [1981] Com LR 252 affirmed [1983] Com LR 12. See also *Cowan de Groot Properties Ltd* v. *Eagle Trust plc* [1992] 4 All ER 700; *Macmillan Inc* v. *Bishopsgate Investment Trust plc (No. 3)* [1995] 1 WLR 978. Lindley LJ in *Manchester Trust* v. *Furness* [1895] 2 QB 539, p. 545 said: 'As regards the extension of the equitable doctrines of constructive notice to commercial transactions, the courts have always set their faces resolutely against it. The equitable doctrines of constructive notice are common enough in dealing with land and estates with which the Court is familiar; but there have been repeated protests against the introduction into commercial transactions of anything like an extension of those doctrines, and the protest is founded on perfect good sense. In dealing with estates in land title is everything, and it can be leisurely investigated; in commercial transactions possession is everything, and there is no time to investigate title; and if we were to extend the doctrine of constructive notice to commercial transactions we should be doing infinite mischief and paralysing the trade of the country.'

120 But notice of breach is unnecessary; notice of the existence of an equitable interest is sufficient. Note that there is no further knowing receipt or knowing assistance liability for there is no fiduciary or trust relationship to be protected.

121 See *Pan-Electric Industries Ltd (in liquidation)* v. *Oversea-Chinese Bank Corp Ltd* [1994] 3 SLR 695, para. 26.

122 See *Public Finance Ltd* v. *Scotch Leasing Sdn Bhd (in receivership) (Perwira Habib Bank Malaysia, intervener)* [1996] 2 MLJ 369. Note also *Pan-Electric Industries Ltd (in liquidation)* v. *Oversea-Chinese Bank Corp Ltd* [1994] 3 SLR 69, para. 26.

123 In other words, there is no known statute which protects a subsequent bona fide buyer of a book debt for value without notice.

(*in liquidation*) v. *Oversea-Chinese Bank Corp Ltd*,[124] expressed a different view: 'Whilst we would wherever possible adhere to the basic principles of the law of personal property, we will equally apply the doctrine of estoppel as an exception to the *nemo dat* rule if the facts so warrant.'[125]

The general law prescribes three models for the determination of priorities as between the security interest holder and the purchaser, depending on whether the property concerned is a common law tangible, an equitable tangible, or intangible: namely, *nemo dat* with exceptions, doctrine of good faith purchase without notice, and *nemo dat* with no or very limited exceptions.

Article 9 strikes a different note by drawing an innovative line between purchases of inventory and non-ordinary course purchases.[126] It sees less need to favour the purchaser of non-inventory property. In the case of non-inventory purchases, the fact of good faith and notice is crucial. However, the good faith purchaser of inventory is protected regardless of notice of security interest, for the sake of commerce. If he has notice of the breach of security agreement, nothing will save him. This is perfectly fair and commercially workable since it is open to a purchaser to adopt a position of ignorance and to refrain from asking whether the property he wishes to buy is or is not encumbered. Further, the article extends, to the non-negotiable instrument or document, a degree of protection not available under general law because it protects the good faith legal purchaser in the ordinary course.

These differences between Article 9 and the general law in Singapore are not merely cosmetic or remedial and cannot be underestimated. Article 9 is significantly more solicitous of third party dealings than the general law. However, there has admittedly been little litigation under the general law involving good faith buyers of inventory from dealers or manufacturers. This is despite the fact that the hire purchase is now the preferred mode of financing the commercial purchase of heavy equipment, which in the absence of a *nemo dat* exception protecting the purchaser from the hirer in possession, would seem to be a fertile source of litigation.[127] The surprising paucity of litigation could indicate that dealers and manufacturers and finance houses think it bad form to pursue innocent purchasers but, writing off their loss, choose to 'redouble their control' on the hirers or dealers who are left. If so, in practice, the system appears to cope only because of financier or lender largesse. But whether it is more efficient to let the innocent purchaser be, or to hold him responsible for the loss, or to leave it to lenders to decide when they are able to overawe innocent purchasers and induce them to hand over the purchased articles, it is hard to be unimpressed by the fact that inventory sales are rightly given greater protection than non-inventory sales. With respect to high volume sales of assets in dematerialised or immobilised form, this differential protection is incontrovertible and may even be essential policy.

124 [1994] 3 SLR 695.

125 Para. 28. The decision appears to be supported by *Colonial Bank* v. *Cady* (1890) 15 App. Cas. 267.

126 Still, it must be stated that the position was arrived at after a series of preceding legislative changes, reversing the common law position as declared by the courts. See G. Gilmore *Security Interests in Personal Property* (Boston: Little, Brown, 1965), p. 684.

127 See *Public Finance Ltd* v. *Scotch Leasing Sdn Bhd* (*in receivership*) (*Perwira Habib Bank Malaysia, int ervener*) [1996] 2 MLJ 369. Note also *Colonel Lim Poh Weng* v. *Probo Pacific Leasing Pte Ltd* [1993] 3 SLR 662.

Priorities among security interests

It could be argued that the contest between a secured creditor and a third party purchaser, although loosely described as a problem of priorities, is more a problem of overreaching with loss of priority as a consequence. Property and priority conflicts involve conflicting security interests which are valid and of the same order.[128] At the heart of priority conflicts in this narrower sense lies an economic function of great importance. It is the possibility of ranking security interests among themselves that will exploit the full value of the security. Efficient use of collateral cannot be achieved without creating a market in collateral as well. If a borrower has inefficiently provided collateral it is the marketability of it that will restore its efficient use. This argues for clear rules, at least as an ideal, to be employed not just when the debtor is insolvent, but when the debtor or creditor esteems it is more efficient to offer further security.[129] In fact, there are always two important issues in any assessment of a priorities law. One is the more static one as to rankings of security interests, including the possibilities of reversals of priorities by party autonomy and statutory imposition. The other is the ability of the law to respond decisively to novel priority conflicts. The inescapable fact is that new novel priority conflicts will arise and the rules must be capable of predicting their disposition with reasonable accuracy.

Priority conflicts in Singapore have thus far tended to be fairly narrow and confined to three or four areas. Disputes are particularly common in shipping cases. They have resulted in the ranking of the repairer's lien ahead of the salvor's claim,[130] but on account of the greater public interest,[131] after Central Provident Funds (CPF) claims,[132] and port dues.[133] The pre-eminence of the lien was strikingly affirmed when the court refused to preclude the lien holder from further re-arresting the ship and enforcing his lien, after final judgment.[134] Frankly, these cases only tell us half the story. They merely hint at the need for a different approach towards priorities when the subject property is more an enterprise than a passive asset. Consistent with the value of the ship as a going concern, which is of decisive importance, the lien is pre-eminent among private security interests because it preserves the value of the ship. Even so, this priority cannot be fixed rigidly. The cases just described do not say this. Nevertheless, although clear Singapore authority is lacking, one can suppose that

128 There is some recognition of this in Singapore. In *Salim Anthony* v. *Sumitomo Corp Capital Asia Pte Ltd* [2004] 3 SLR 331 an interesting question of conflict between rights of the subrogee and assignee did not require to be determined because the assignment could not be binding in the absence of a valid notice. The purported notice was not clear and unconditional. The question of whether security rights are validly created or transmitted is not a priorities question.

129 Op. cit., Davies, fn 21, accepts this as a primary rationale for Art. 9, citing Baird and Jackson 'Information, uncertainty and the transfer of property' (1984) 13 *Journal of Legal Studies* 299.

130 See: *Alexander G Tsavliris and Sons Maritime Co* v. *Keppel Corp Ltd* [1995] 2 SLR 113; *The Honey I* [1987] 1 SLR 282.

131 Although it could be argued that the first is bottomed on inequality of bargaining power while the second on absence of equal opportunity to assess the risk of loss on insolvency.

132 See *Sinwa (Singapore) Pte Ltd* v. *Owners of the Ship or Vessel 'Hurst' Ex 'Grigory Petrenko'* [1999] 1 SLR 237.

133 See '*The Felicie*'; *Bombay Trading Co (Pte) Ltd* v. *Owners of the Vessel* '*Felicie*' (*Marmaestra Companhia Naviera SA, Interveners*) [1992] 1 SLR 175.

134 See *The Daien Maru No. 18* [1985] 2 MLJ 90. Note also David Chong Gek San 'The spectre of re-arrest of a vessel' [1986] MLR 102.

as with the Admiralty and Appellate Courts, the courts here will adopt a broad discretionary approach to priorities of security interests in ships, ranking them by reference to considerations of equity, public policy and commercial expediency, with the ultimate aim of doing that which is just in the circumstance of each case.[135] Since Article 9 predicates fixed priorities, with no judicial discretion to alter them, any reform modelled on Article 9 must leave out priorities in ships and respect the need for separate consideration of these priorities.

Another security device has figured actively in the Singapore case law and literature on priorities, [136] namely the floating charge.[137] The courts, in agreement with the English courts, resolve the tension between the fixed charge and floating charge by giving priority to the fixed charge unless the fixed chargee has actual notice of a negative pledge binding on the owner when he takes the charge.[138] Content with this explanation, legal scholars have debated the question whether registration of the particulars of the negative pledge on the public register of charges will count as notice. However, there has yet to be a definitive judicial pronouncement since this point was left open in *Kay Hian & Co (Pte)* v. *Jon Phua Ooi Yong.*[139] Nevertheless, one thing argues well for the floating chargee. The fact is that the floating chargee can easily be abused by the debtor who makes ill-considered asset shifts and the negative pledge can provide some check against abuse provided it is suitably notified to the public.[140]

Tacking is not a common source of disputes[141] which seems odd in the context of construction loans where it should be commonplace.[142] Under a doctrine of tacking,[143] a prior chargee may gain in priority over a subsequent secured creditor if

135 See *The Ruta* [2000] 1 WLR 2068.

136 In the case of *PD Manufacturing International Pte Ltd* v. *ING Bank NV* [1999] SGHC 236 it was recognised that a floating charge containing a negative pledge clause can, by giving notice, block attempts by the debtor to enter into new security agreements.

137 As in England, its importance in Singapore commercial life should not be underestimated, to use the language of Lord Millett in *Agnew* v. *Commissioner of Inland Revenue* [2001] 2 AC 710, p. 718. See further op. cit., Tan Cheng Han, fn 75.

138 Following *Wheatley* v. *Silkstone and Haigh Motor Coal Co* (1885) 29 Ch. D. 715.

139 [1989] 1 MLJ 284.

140 *Dresdner Bank* v. *Ho Man-Tuke Don* [1993] 1 SLR 114. Both the High Court and Court of Appeal came to the same conclusion that the parties had created a floating charge since the shares charged were ambulatory and shifting in nature and City had the liberty to trade. Singapore may have been 'spared the abundance of litigation concerned with charges over receivables'; see op. cit., McCormack, fn 9, p. 20.

141 For tacking by a mortgagee of land, see T. Menon 'Tacking further advances in Singapore' (1974) 16 Mal L Rev 260 and see s. 70 Land Titles Act (Cap 157, 2004 Rev. Ed.).

142 See *Chung Khiaw Bank Ltd* v. *Four Seas Communications Bank Ltd* [1965] 2 MLJ 74.

143 Known as the rule in *Hopkinson* v. *Rolt* (1861) 9 HLC 514. See also *Bradford Banking Co* v. *Briggs* (1886) 12 App. Cas. 29 where, as regards moneys which became due from the shareholder to the defendant company after notice of the deposit of the share certificates with the bank, the defendant company could not claim priority over advances made by the bank after such notice. The rule is that: 'a first mortgagee, whose mortgage was taken to cover what was then due and also future advances within a fixed amount, could not claim to be repaid such advances in priority to a second mortgagee, of whose mortgage he had notice at the time when he made them.' The second case also shows that 'the notice to the defendant company of the deposit of the share certificates with the bank was not a notice of a trust within the meaning of s. 30 of the Companies Act, 1862; and that the bank by giving notice of the deposit did not seek to affect the defendant company with notice of a

an arrangement has been made to that effect with the secured creditor; if the prior chargee had no notice at the time of further advance; and if he is obliged to make further advances.[144] The dearth of cases and the use of the floating charge even when future advances are clearly anticipated (i.e. the expanded use of the floating charge) suggest that the doctrine has proved to be too restrictive to provide adequate protection for the furnisher of ongoing lines of credit.

With respect to intangibles, the famous rule in *Dearle* v. *Hall*[145] which modifies the normal equitable first in time rule has surfaced only a few times. The rule makes priority turn on time of giving notice instead of time of creation;[146] thus, a later assignee will defeat an earlier assignee if he gives prior notice to the debtor and is without notice, actual, imputed or constructive, of the earlier assignment. Legal scholars in Singapore have asked whether this rule applies to unit trusts, in respect of each purchase and sale which is an assignment of pre-existing interests.[147] Another question which has been raised elsewhere is whether the equitable tracing creditor can be defeated by an assignee of the sale proceeds. This has not gone unnoticed in Singapore. For the view that the equitable title holder is not so defeated,[148] the reason is given that before the assignment can take place, the interest, if equitable, in the sale proceeds has already vested in the seller. Similar reasoning commended itself to the Malaysian Federal Court in the case of *Public Finance Ltd* v. *Scotch Leasing Sdn Bhd* (*in receivership*) (*Perwira Habib Bank Malaysia, intervener*)[149] where it was held that the leasing company could not assign in equity to the debenture holder something which the leasing company did not already own or have, and the *nemo dat* rule applied.[150] This is an application of the *scintilla temporis* rule but, Professor Sir Roy Goode has disagreed with this[151] contending that the assignee will have priority if he is the first to give notice. Goode bases his contention on the fact that an equitable tracing creditor, who leaves the assignor in apparent ownership of the receivables, loses priority to the receivables financier who acquires them in good faith, for value and without notice.

trust, but only to affect the defendant company in their capacity as traders with notice of the interest of the bank.' There is no equivalent of s. 94 of the Law of Property Act 1925 of England and Wales.

144 A secured creditor who must disburse his loan in successive stages wishes to ensure that he is protected from diversion of funds and that the mortgagee's security does not become encumbered by liens or retention of title devices. Tacking helps him to achieve both objectives. Section 70 of the Land Titles Act which has altered the rule of tacking is confined to land.

145 (1823–28) 3 Russ 1. The rule applies to both equitable and legal assignments; see *E Pfeiffer Weinkellerei GmbH and Co* v. *Arbuthnot Factors Ltd* [1988] 1 WLR 150. For a detailed treatment of the rule, see de Lacy 'Reflections on the ambit of the rule in *Dearle* v. *Hall* and the priority of personal property assignments' (1999) 28 Anglo-American L Rev 87 and 197.

146 See *Public Finance Ltd* v. *Scotch Leasing Sdn Bhd* (*in receivership*) (*Perwira Habib Bank Malaysia, intervener*) [1996] 2 MLJ 369.

147 See: H. Tjio 'The regulation of unit trusts and trustees' powers to invest in them' [1999] SJLS 148, p. 178 and K. Sin *The Legal Nature of Unit Trust* (Oxford: Clarendon Press, 1997), pp. 322–5.

148 See D. McLauchlan 'Priorities – equitable tracing rights and assignment of book debts' (1980) 96 LQR 90, p. 91.

149 [1996] 2 MLJ 369.

150 See also op. cit., Davies, fn 21.

151 See *Legal Problems of Credit and Security* (London: Sweet & Maxwell, 2nd edn, 1988), p. 121.

The difficulties which the law as described poses for non-notification financing are, of course, well-known. First, it is tedious and seriously inconvenient to give notice each time expectant receivables are realised. Second, notice given before the expectant receivables come into existence to a possible or future receivables debtor is ineffective and an assignee of expectant receivables is in danger of being defeated by a later assignee who gives notice to the actual receivables debtor after the receivables have come into existence.[152] There is probably a good reason for the dearth of Singapore case law despite the inconvenience which the rule poses for non-notification financing. In the case of corporate debtors, registration under the Companies Act 'will disable the rule in *Dearle* v. *Hall*'[153] since future book debts are registrable and registration will constitute notice to subsequent chargees and prevent them from obtaining priority by giving notice to receivables debtors despite the absence of notification.

Subordination agreements are not unknown in the literature and in practice,[154] and in the case law, a related question, 'Can the rule in *Hopkinson* v. *Rolt*[155] be excluded?' has been subject to judicial decision. In *Chung Khiaw Bank Ltd* v. *Four Seas Communications Bank Ltd*,[156] the court answered the question in the negative, refusing to uphold a provision in the articles of association expressly providing that the lien which the company had over its issued shares was to have priority in respect of a debt incurred after notice of a previous mortgage to another person.[157] The court explained:

> [T]he articles of association of a company constitute a contract only so far as concerns the company and the members as members of the company. If therefore the company chooses to enter into normal commercial relations with its members it cannot rely on the articles to exempt it from ordinary rules of justice. In other words, the articles do not apply to such business transactions between the company in its capacity as a trader and its members as are capable of being transacted between the company and non-members, such as lending money on security; and the articles cannot interfere with the application of principles of equity to the equitable interests of non-members.[158]

The article in question which gave the lien priority was therefore ineffective against the mortgagee. This reasoning was far wider than the determination of the case necessitated since it would have been sufficient to hold that the mortgagee had not agreed and could not have agreed in the absence of notice of the lien clause to subordinate its interest to that of the bank. In all likelihood, the case does not

152 *Webster* v. *Webster* (1862) 31 Beav 393; *Johnson* v. *Cox* (1880) 16 ChD 571.
153 (1823–28) 3 Russ 1. See also text at pp. 432–33.
154 Tan Cheng Han 'Debt subordination' [1993] SJLS 491, p. 492, remarked that it has been observed between parent company and bank granting a loan to its subsidiary.
155 (1861) 9 HLC 514.
156 [1965] 2 MLJ 74.
157 The court preferred the view of Lord Blackburn in *Bradford Banking Co* v. *Briggs* (1886) 12 App. Cas. 29, that 's. 30 of the Companies Act, 1862, did not give the defendant company the power to disregard the ordinary rules of justice which included the rule in *Hopkinson* v. *Rolt*. He held that the legislature was competent to enact that a trading company should have the right to disregard the ordinary rules of justice thereby implying that a trading company cannot, without statutory authority, give itself such a right in its articles.'
158 [1965] 2 MLJ 65, p. 77.

propound the exclusion of subordination agreements and legal writers in Singapore would appear to have assumed that this is so.[159] Article 9-316 of course plainly declares that nothing in it prevents subordination by agreement by any person entitled to priority.[160]

The general law is open to criticism because it does not let security transfers stand apart but instead applies the same principles governing priorities in a conflict of security interest and absolute interest to a conflict of security interest and security interest.[161] The point that is overlooked is that the *nemo dat* principle should not continue to overshadow the way successive security interests are created over the same property. The principle restricts the needs of successive secured creditors; it is over-protective of the first title which it assumes is exhaustive of the secured rights in the property and therefore creates extremely limited opportunities for a second and third creditor. The possessory security interest is clearly exclusive and exhaustive while the non-possessory security interest in relation to tangible property was made exclusive and exhaustive. This has resulted in a proliferation or multiplication of quasi-security interests which not only serve to break the strangle-hold of the floating charge but are also the only way of introducing an additional layer of secured creditors. Undermining the simplicity of the dichotomy of possessory and non-possessory, it has driven a wedge between them.[162]

The doctrine of good faith purchaser without notice likewise requires modification when applied to the problems of prioritising security interests. Where there is a legal owner charged with ultimate responsibility for another's equitable property (which is the paradigm case for it) the doctrine arguably strikes a fair balance between competing proprietary rights. However, as has been seen it responds inadequately to the ease with which the floating charge may be destroyed by asset shifts.[163] With respect to choses in action, the doctrine is premised on keeping hidden equitable interests off the transaction record so far as is consistent with good faith. But these premises are irrelevant where several hidden equitable dealings are in competition. In partial recognition of this, the rule in *Dearle* v. *Hall*[164] replaces the principle of good faith

159 See Tan Cheng Han, fn 154. See also the English cases such as: *Re Maxwell Communications Corp (No 2)* [1993] 1 WLR 1402 and *Re British and Commonwealth Holdings plc (No 3)* [1992] 1 WLR 672.

160 See *Joo Yee Construction Ltd* v. *Diethelm Industries Pte Ltd* [1990] 2 MLJ 66. But it seems that there are two schools of thought about whether subordination agreements should trump the *pari passu* principle which is an equalising principle and results in creditors being paid pro rata. Upon liquidation of an insolvent company (whether voluntary or compulsory), subject to the rights of preferential creditors and also secured creditors, if any, its property must be applied in settlement of its liabilities *pari passu*, and any contract made by the company which provided for a distribution of any of its property for the benefit of one or more of its unsecured creditors which ran counter to or sought to vary this rule was contrary to public policy, and the law as regards distribution of the insolvent`s property under the insolvency legislation must prevail.

161 See *Northern Counties Fire Insurance* v. *Whipp* (1884) 26 Ch. D. 482 in which the pledgee was subordinated in priority to the subsequent equitable chargee either because he was party to the fraud by which the equity was created or he had given another power to deal with the property and dealt in excess of his authority.

162 Unlike the common law, equity tolerates the creation of similar interests in the same thing and relies on knowledge principally to sort them out.

163 See text at p. 409.

164 (1823–28) 3 Russ 1.

with a principle of first notice; avoiding the more flexible and wide ranging examination of the equities under the first in time rule, both of which are complex and time consuming.[165] Even so, the rule does not go far enough, as the question of priorities as between equitable tracing creditor and receivables financier holder indicates. Both the argument favouring the equitable tracing creditor and that favouring the equitable assignee are good[166] but neither seems more attractive than the other on intrinsic merits. The former does not promote the market for receivables while the latter inhibits the market for retention titles.[167] The correct rule should approach both security interests on an equal footing but that is impossible as the rule stands. If the creation of a market in security interests is a policy of first importance, the *nemo dat* principle and the doctrine of good faith purchaser without notice are both inconvenient. Neither will be more efficient than Article 9 which is essentially the rule in *Dearle* v. *Hall* engrafted with a requirement of public notice, shorn of the requirement of private notice to the debtor.[168]

The point just made concerning the conflict between the equitable tracing creditor and receivables financier is only one aspect of a much wider problem of first importance in reform. Professor Drobnig has written: 'By allowing retention of title but restricting it essentially to the goods sold, trade credit is primarily restricted to the first phase of the business cycle. By allowing the assignment of accounts receivable, sometimes even on conditions privileging banks, but disallowing non-possessory security, banks are largely confined to the final stage of the business cycle. By thus dividing the spheres of accessible collateral, conflicts between sellers' security rights and banks' security rights are largely avoided.'[169] As long as the priority rules remain as uncertain as they are, this artificiality is just as well.

The simplicity of Article 9 priorities is striking when compared with the uncertain and bewildering combinations in which common law and equity vie for pride of place. Priorities under Article 9 depend solely and exclusively on date of filing. The rule is the simplest possible: he who is first to file is the first in time. This simplicity is deceptive because it comes with fundamental changes, reflecting the policy of creating a market in security interests. Thus, Article 9 reverses the law of tacking

165 Admittedly, it is usually stated that the rationale is either that giving notice is tantamount to taking possession or that it prevents fraud. This is not to say that the rule is otherwise satisfactory. For criticisms of the rule, see F. Oditah 'Priorities: equitable versus legal assignments of book debts' (1989) 9 OJLS 521.

166 See p. 410.

167 See Oditah's critique of Goode's argument (in fn 64, p. 151); because the tracing creditor is disadvantaged as there is no registration for retention rights.

168 Admittedly, commentators who are warranted experts have not presented the quasi-security interest as a critique of inadequate priorities. There are only a few cases. We have at least one case showing the recourse to quasi-security interests as an escape from a negative pledge. In *Thai Chee Ken* v. *Banque Paribas* [1992] 2 SLR 848 the attempt based on a sale and repurchase succeeded. The performance bond is very popular but oddly enough there have been few priority fights between the lender of a construction loan who is an assignee of the payments due under the construction contract and the surety who provides the performance bond and has rights of subrogation against the payments as they fall due. This could be due to the coincidence of lender and surety in practice, which is a little remarkable when we compare with the US practice.

169 See 'A comparative introduction to security over movables and intangibles' in op. cit., Norton and M Andenas (eds), fn 2, pp. 10–11.

as well as making knowledge immaterial. Priority of the first to file is retained in respect of any further advance for which provision has been made,[170] even if made with the knowledge that a second party has made a prior advance secured by a perfected security interest in the same collateral.[171] In fact, the advances do not have to be of the same class as the original and, as some have argued, do not even need to flow out of any commitment to future advances.[172] The effect of Article 9 on floating charges is particularly well documented.[173] Prior to adoption of Article 9, the notion of a floating lien was contrary to the policy that a free cushion of assets should be available for the protection of the debtor and its unsecured creditors.[174] Article 9 rejecting that policy on the ground that it was ineffective introduced the idea of a floating lien as a fixed charge with a licence to deal.[175] It did this not by prescribing expressly for instatement of the floating lien but by ensuring that a security interest could cover after-acquired property, future advances,[176] and proceeds,[177] by overruling the Supreme Court decision in *Benedict* v. *Ratner*,[178] and by providing that a simple filing statement would be effective to cover after-acquired property and future advances.[179]

So far as concerns the floating charge in Singapore, a change-over to reform along the lines of Article 9 would not just be a make-over. Debates about the limits of the negative pledge would cease to be anything other than academic. Under Article 9, the first floating chargee does not need a negative pledge to gain in priority because he will always be first in time if he is first to file and generally speaking will never lose out to a second chargee, even with respect to future advances which he makes after the second charge is notified.[180] Other differences are more significant. Professor McCormack, writing on the implications of reform along Article 9 in Singapore, takes the view that the effect would be to assimilate the distinction between floating and fixed charge[181] and reform would hence require consequential adjustments

170 See *Coin-O-Matic Service Co.* v. *Rhode Island Hospital Trust Co.* 3 UCC Rep 1112 (1966).
171 Art. 9-323. See also *Re Smith* (1971) 326 F Supp 1311. Cf. the common law rule in *Hopkinson* v. *Rolt* (1861) 9 HLC 514 that 'notice of an intervening security interest terminates the ability of a secured party to make further advances' with superior priority.
172 See op. cit., McCormack, fn 9, pp. 82–4.
173 For an English perspective, see op. cit., McCormack, fn 9, pp. 108–12.
174 See Art. 9-204 Comment 2.
175 See op. cit., McCormack, fn 9, p. 110. Note also *Royal Bank of Canada* v. *Sparrow Electric Corp* (1997) 143 DLR (4th) 385.
176 See Art. 9-204.
177 See Art. 9-315(a) and (c).
178 (1925) 268 US 353. Art. 9-205 overrules it by stating that 'A security interest is not invalid or fraudulent against creditors solely because: (1) the debtor has the right or ability to: (A) use, commingle or dispose of all or part of the collateral … (B) collect, compromise, enforce or otherwise deal with collateral; (C) accept the return of collateral or make repossessions; or (D) use, commingle or dispose of proceeds; or (2) the secured party fails to require the debtor to account for proceeds or replace collateral.'
179 A simple description of the collateral as 'all inventory now owned or hereafter acquired' or 'all accounts receivables now or hereafter arising' will do it. See Arts 9-108 and 9-504.
180 However, parties may continue to use the negative pledge to avail themselves of the protection of disclosure and prior approval where this is appropriate. The bare contractual negative pledge is irrelevant as it is not an interest in property.
181 Echoing the view of the Supreme Court of Canada in *Royal Bank of Canada* v. *Sparrow Electric Corp* (1997) 143 DLR (4th) 385.

preserving the differential effects of a floating charge on preferential debts and judicial management, among other things.[182] It may be doubted whether the assimilation produced by Article 9 goes so far since there is nothing to preclude a secured creditor if he so wishes from creating a fixed charge by confining his agreement to present collateral and the present advance. Given the ease with which the floating lien is created and the ready protection it is afforded under Article 9, creditors may in practice be motivated to abandon the fixed charge for the floating charge especially when the latter can be created by a simple reference in the security documentation to after-acquired property. However, as long as the fixed charge and floating charge continue to receive differential treatment on insolvency,[183] and no one presently suggests that they should not, there would be reason to differentiate between them. Consequential adjustments to the insolvency law would not be necessary. It would only be necessary to decide whether a fixed charge, for example over proceeds, has been granted[184] or whether a floating charge has been converted to a fixed charge. The reason for the last point is that under a system modelled on Article 9, there should be no difficulty in converting a floating charge to a fixed charge,[185] since no fresh filing would be necessary and no prejudice occasioned to those persons such as involuntary creditors and employees for the protection of whom preferential treatment is accorded.

It is worth emphasising that differential creation and conversion of security interests would be possible under a system modelled on Article 9. Just as it would be possible for a security interest in inventory or accounts to be vested in one creditor and a security interest in their proceeds in another, so also would it be possible to convert one but not the other into a fixed charge. A recent line of cases at the highest level, namely, *Agnew* v. *Commissioner of Inland Revenue*[186] and *Spectrum* v. *National Westminster Bank*,[187] has considered the differential creation of a fixed charge over receivables and a floating charge over the proceeds to be purely academic. In practice, it is difficult to see of what utility the differential creation would be to a secured lender since to Lord Millett 'an assignment of a debt which does not carry with it the right to the proceeds is a worthless security'.[188] A fixed charge over receivables accordingly entails payment of the proceeds into a blocked account. The coupling of a fixed charge over receivables with a floating charge over the proceeds is virtually impossible; and such a so-called fixed charge is in truth a floating charge. Despite Lord Millett's practical logic, there is commercial sense in allowing the financial debtor free use of the proceeds in a bank account – these are the debtor's inventory – so long as the debtor is an ongoing concern. Once the debtor ceases to be solvent, however, the creditor benefits from the fact that he has a fixed charge over receivables, even if his right to trace the proceeds may not rank ahead of preferential creditors.[189] The refusal to

182 See op. cit., McCormack, fn 78, pp. 22–3.
183 A fixed charge on debts ranks ahead of certain preferential creditors in Singapore just as in England. See ss. 226 and 328 Companies Act. See also *Re Permanent Houses Ltd* [1988] BCLC 563. Notable examples of preferential creditors include the Central Provident Fund and unpaid employees.
184 Cf. *Canadian Imperial Bank of Commerce* v. *Otto Timm Enterprises Ltd* (1995) 130 DLR (4th) 91.
185 Cf. *Dresdner Bank AG* v. *Ho Man-Tuke Don* [1993] 1 SLR 114.
186 [2001] 2 AC 710.
187 [2005] UKHL 41.
188 [2001] 2 AC 710, para. 46.
189 See p. 410, 413.

tolerate differential security interests in the original collateral and its proceeds – and it follows its substitutes or exchange product – may lie elsewhere than in practical inutility. In the present view, it is the fear of prejudicing third parties which explains the decision. As the fixed charge over bank accounts is not registrable under the charges registration system, there is danger that third parties may deal with the account to their prejudice.[190] The insistence on payment of the proceeds into a blocked account is a call for a demonstration of control for the sake of avoiding prejudice to third parties.

On a sober assessment, while Article 9 satisfies the requirement of a precise calculus of priorities which discards considerations of good faith and notice,[191] the legal advance which it represents may be more modest. The formulation of a grand calculus of priorities is constantly challenged by new developments and Article 9's attractiveness must be considered in the light of its ability to cope with and adapt to new economic and commercial realities satisfactorily. When Gilmore wrote his seminal book, he frankly admitted the deficiencies or gap in Article 9 in relation to executory contract rights but he thought that Article 9 would cope pretty well with developments in that field.[192] Experience has shown that Gilmore was not extravagant in his optimism. The reason seems to be that a system which is rational and simple in framework will be more adaptable than one that is a complex patchwork of rules which are operated by those with accumulated experience.

The arguments for reform must, for the sake of completeness, take full account of that marvellous invention of Article 9, the super-priority purchase money security interest, as well as its prohibition of anti-assignment devices.[193] Super-priority is conferred on the secured lender who injects new capital in the debtor's business. This is fleshed out in turn and the precise degree of super-priority turns on whether the security for the fresh capital is in inventory or capital equipment. Despite Gilmore's demonstration for the United States, the super-priority which is achieved under general law would not be nascent in reform modelled on Article 9. It is anticipated in the priority which is attached to the fixed charge which is subsequent to the floating charge, perhaps only distantly since no fresh value need be given for the fixed charge to earn this priority. It has an affinity with retention of title clauses,[194] whether or not title is retained in inventory or capital equipment. In both instances, the requirement of fresh capital injection is missing from the general law. In the words of the Supreme Court of Malaysia:

> our research into the authorities shows that, neither in England nor in Australia, is there any policy for the protection of the holder of the purchase money security interest; instead, the approach adopted by the courts there in resolving the dispute, is a technical one, everything depending upon whether the equitable rights of the holder of the purchase money security interest, be he mortgagee or chargee under the contract to make the loan advance, attaches to the property

190 In relation to the floating charge, the prejudice is small since it is implicit that third parties can deal with the subject of the floating charge.
191 Cf. *Re Howard's Appliance Corp* (1989) 874 F2d 88 which employs notions of constructive trust to defeat the strict priority rules.
192 See fn 126 above, ch. 41.
193 See Arts 9-406 to 9-409.
194 Under a 'simple' or 'current account' clause.

before the borrower company concerned acquires the legal ownership of it on completion of the purchase.[195]

There is also an element of super-priority in other manifestations of the *scintilla temporis* principle but the purchase money security interest (PMSI) of Article 9 is very attractive in comparison with the *scintilla temporis* principle which is overly technical. It avoids giving the prior general security holder a windfall increase through the new funds injected by another.[196] It serves to facilitate the survival of the debtor as an ongoing concern.[197] This argument is economic in nature: the idea of the purchase money security interest is efficient. It may save the debtor without detracting from the assets available to existing secured creditors. It is true that the idea differentiates between money and non-monetary assets; but any anachronism is superficial. Money unlinked to particular assets for the purposes of paying salaries and wages may seem to be just as essential to the debtor as an ongoing concern[198] but a security interest in the debtor's existing asset is not privileged as a super-prior security interest. There is no real injection of fresh funds. A loan of this nature only has the effect of a fresh injection of funds if secured by a personal guarantee or by assets of another. In that event, super-priority is irrelevant; the creditor simply looks to the guarantor or to the security of the third party. Also missing from the common law's inchoate notion of super-priority is any differentiation regarding types of assets. Under Article 9, the rules of super-priority are less favourable to the new inventory financier because he must notify existing perfected financiers before the debtor receives possession.[199] The capital financier however gains this super-priority by simply perfecting within 20 days of the debtor receiving possession. This difference purports to reflect the greater need to equip existing general secured creditors such as floating chargees with such information as is necessary to make a proper decision regarding future advances.[200] The same need is lacking in the case of creditors financing capital equipment who are very unlikely to have obliged themselves to make future advances in respect of the same security. The super-priority given to the chattel paper financier deserves a brief mention. Article 9-330(b) gives among other things the purchaser for new value of chattel paper a better priority than the general secured creditor who claims the proceeds of inventory. On one view, the favour accorded to the financier who lends against chattel paper is unwarranted.[201]

As for the prohibition against anti-assignment provisions in relation to accounts and general intangibles, this is clearly part of the general policy to create a market in securities. Adoption of this policy would be a fairly sharp departure from the common

195 See *United Malayan Banking Corp* v. *Aluminex (M) Sdn Bhd* [1993] 3 MLJ 587, p. 603, *per* Edgar Joseph SCJ. For the position of the PMSI in England, see de Lacy 'The purchase money security interest: a company charge conundrum?' [1991] LMCLQ 531.

196 See op. cit., Goode, fn 94, p. 191.

197 Admittedly, the reasons usually given to support the PMSI are that it does not prejudice existing secured creditors and may even benefit them, that any other rule could result in an unjustified windfall for the general prior secured creditor, and that the general prior secured creditor should not be permitted to monopolise the assets of the debtor. See also Law Commission Consultation Paper No. 164 *Registration of Security Interests: Company Charges and Property other than Land* (London: The Stationery Office, 2002), para. 4.159.

198 See Gough *Company Charges* (London: Butterworths, 2nd edn, 1996), p. 436.

199 Note that a PMSI in consumer goods is automatically perfected.

200 See Art. 9-324 Official Comment.

201 See op. cit., McCormack, fn 78, p. 27.

law which upholds anti-assignment clauses;[202] it is very unlikely that the leading English case was a decision on absolute assignments only and not security assignments.[203]

Possessory interests and priorities

It is useful at this point to briefly canvass the innovations Article 9 has brought about to priorities in relation to possessory interests. The basic idea that possessory security interests require no notification and define their own priority is simple enough. By the very act of taking possession, the secured creditor gives notice of his interest and, whilst the thing is in his possession, it would seem virtually impossible for the debtor to strike a fresh security interest over the property. To this simple idea, the decision in *Lloyds Bank* v. *Bank of America*[204] introduced a serious qualification. There it was held that if a pledgor who was otherwise a mercantile agent had possession with the pledgee's consent and re-pledged the pledged goods, the second pledge had priority over the first.[205] Another development has also put a serious qualification on this, namely constructive possession which is instantaneous. While the law still denies that the pledgor can be the pledgee's agent to take possession, it accepts situations falling short of that which give the pledgor constructive possession which is instantaneous.[206] These propositions imply that it is no longer entirely true that possession gives effective notice. The person seemingly in possession may not be in possession because another may have constructive possession and with instantaneous constructive possession his possession will alter without another being any the wiser. For such situations, perfection by filing as an alternative and temporary perfection for loss and other temporary purposes which was earlier mentioned[207] would confer distinct advantages, quite apart from savings achieved on the greater costs of segregating goods and posting signs.

Proceeds of collateral

Article 9 inspired reform will also require a significant shift in thinking about proceeds and substitutions from dealing with the original secured property. For a long time the distinction between common law tracing and tracing in equity was obscure. However, the common law position has recently been clarified[208] and, perhaps, it is not premature to say that common law tracing into the sale proceeds is not in doubt these days.[209] In light of this, it would not be possible to claim for Article 9 a simpler approach which avoids the complexities of the common law and equity divide. Nor is

202 *Linden Gardens Trust Ltd* v. *Lenesta Sludge Disposals Ltd* [1994] 1 AC 85. Cf *Pacrim Investments Pte Ltd* v. *Tan Mui Keow* [2008] 2 SLR 898. However, this principle is increasingly being eroded; see *Don King Productions Inc* v. *Warren* [2000] Ch. 291.

203 See *Mississippi Bank* v. *Nickles and Wells Construction Co* 421 So 2d 1056 (1982) on the latter point.

204 [1938] 2 KB 147.

205 In accordance with s. 2 of the Factors Act 1889. The Singapore equivalent is the Factors Act (Cap 386, 1994 Rev. Ed.).

206 See *Michael Gerson (Leasing) Ltd* v. *Wilkinson* [2001] QB 514.

207 See p. 404.

208 *Foskett* v. *McKeown* [2001] 1 AC 102 followed by the Court of Appeal in *Caltong (Australia) Pty Ltd (fka Tong Tien See Holding (Australia) Pty Ltd)* v. *Tong Tien See Construction Pte Ltd (in liquidation)* [2002] 3 SLR 241.

209 See *Trustee of the Property of FC Jones and Sons* v. *Jones* [1997] Ch. 159.

there any doubt nowadays that the common law recognises the security holder's right to trace his security interest in identifiable proceeds; so that as Professor Sir Roy Goode says, security in an asset carries through to its proceeds.[210] The problem is that the dangers of ostensible ownership are equally present with respect to proceeds of sale when they are used for the provision of security. To the person dealing with the debtor in respect of the proceeds, the tracing creditor is hidden from view and so, Article 9 gives priority to the secured creditor, only if he has perfected it by his filed statement; otherwise the interest in the proceeds becomes unperfected after a lapse of time. Tracing from inventory to account receivables under the general law should not be problematic since there is already authority that a security interest in the land is one in the fruits of the land.[211] But the difficulty is the same; the tracing creditor is hidden from view, as was seen earlier in connection with the conflict between the tracing creditor and receivables financier. Tracing from an equipment lease is impossible. On the orthodox view, the lease of personal property is merely a contract and does not result in a grant of an interest in property. It follows that the rentals cannot be proceeds of the lease. Similarly, tracing to the right to compensation for loss of the security due to fault or wrongful act of a third party or even the actual fruits of compensation seems impossible. The law of tracing, however generously understood, has not gone this far. In all these instances, however, efficiency arguments support total equivalence of security, proceeds, exchange product and lost value. '[The] security-holder must be protected against diminutions in the value of the security that arise not only from sale, but also from other events or transactions that damage the security.'[212] Any information asymmetry as between secured lenders in relation to its transformation detracts from the proper evaluation of the promise to pay. It factors in circumstances outside the control of the lender, perhaps entirely within the control of the borrower, making it difficult for the lender to undertake a true assessment of the risks of attaching the proceeds.

Judged by these criteria, Article 9 in many respects promotes structured secured financing more effectively. It steers away from insisting on fundamental incompatibility between a fixed security and freedom to dispose of the charged asset in the course of business. It presses the distinction between proceeds or realisation of a receivable

210 Thus, where a vessel subject to a possessory lien was arrested and sold at the instance of a third party, the right of the holder of the possessory lien was preserved by transferring the lien holder's rights from the vessel to the proceeds of sale; see '*The Dwima I*'; *Pan-United Shipyard Pte Ltd* v. *Owners of the Ship or Vessel 'Dwima I'* (*First Leasing* (*Panama*) *SA, first interveners*) [1996] 2 SLR 670. Note also: *The Tergeste* [1903] P 26; *The Gaupen* (1925) 22 LlLR 57. Cf. *The Ally* [1952] 2 Lloyd's Rep 427. The equitable chargee obtains a proprietary interest in the property (see *Bland* v. *Ingrams Estates Ltd* [2001] 1 WLR 1638, p. 1645) sufficient to give the mortgagee a proprietary interest in property which represents the property originally mortgaged following completion of an unauthorised disposition by the mortgagor.

211 Thus if a mortgagor grants security over a lease and he then surrenders the lease and takes a new lease, the mortgagee has a security interest in the new lease: *Hughes* v. *Howard* (1858) 25 Beav 575. Where a mortgagor renews a lease the mortgagee obtains a security interest in the new lease without express mention in the mortgage deed; *Leigh* v. *Burnett* (1885) 29 Ch. D. 231. In all these cases, the mortgagee is entitled to the fruits of the mortgaged property; see generally W. Clark (ed.), *Fisher and Lightwood's Law of Mortgage* (London: Butterworths, 11th edn, 2002), pp. 84–90. See also *Buhr* v. *Barclays Bank plc* [2001] EWCA Civ 1223.

212 *McGonigle* v. *Combs* (1992) 968 F2d 810, p. 828.

and the receivable itself to its conclusion.[213] The security holder's interest automatically continues in identifiable proceeds; thus, the secured creditor who has the receivable as security is entitled to the proceeds or realisation of the receivable.[214] But that does not guarantee priority in title. Similarly, a financier who has taken possession of equipment leases may not necessarily gain priority in the underlying equipment itself. Priorities depend on how these interests are perfected by their holder. The upshot is that the secured financier will need to file a notice of his security interest in the receivables as well as a notice of his security interest in the proceeds if he desires priority on all fronts. There are qualifications of course. If the proceeds are cash proceeds and the security interest in inventory is perfected, the state of perfection in the original collateral is automatically transmitted to the proceeds.[215] In most other cases, there is a 21-day-automatic-perfection rule; after 21 days the security interest will lapse unless the creditor perfects a new security interest in them.[216]

Overriding technicalities, Article 9 also offers a solution to the problem that a chargee is probably not under general law entitled to trace to the proceeds of sale in the hands of the chargor.

At this point a somewhat more obscure effect of Article 9 deserves a brief mention. Article 9's economic definition of security interest and hence also its definition of proceeds extends to quasi-security interests. Under general law, it remains controversial whether an attempt to extend the security interest to proceeds will succeed in a retention-of-title case.[217] Under Article 9-315(2), a security interest continues in any identifiable proceeds;[218] since retention of title creates a security interest the interest continues in the proceeds to the extent of the debtor's indebtedness. This could be a welcome improvement in Singapore, obviating the need to produce carefully drafted clauses which purport to ensure that the seller's ownership of goods continues in the proceeds of those goods by making the buyer the seller's fiduciary to account for those proceeds to the seller.[219]

Fixtures

Finally, there is the question of the priority of security interests in relation to fixtures. Fixtures are not straightforwardly substitutes nor are they accessions. The relative immobility of real property, the rigidity of the real property market, the high threshold of entry into that market – all bear on the solution the common law has devised, which is to give all that is annexed to or incorporated in the land to the landowner

213 Despite unsatisfactory case law to the contrary, the Permanent Editorial Board for the UCC takes the view that rentals under an equipment lease are proceeds within the meaning of Art. 9-306(1).

214 Art. 9-102(64)(A) defines proceeds to mean 'whatever is received upon the sale, exchange, license, collection or other disposition of collateral or proceeds'.

215 Art. 9-315(d)(2). Indeed, regardless of whether the security interest in the original collateral remains perfected.

216 See Art. 9-315(e).

217 See: *Re Bond Worth Ltd* [1980] Ch. 228; *Compaq Computer Ltd* v. *Abercorn Group Ltd* [1991] BCC 484. For a detailed treatment of *Romalpa* theory, see de Lacy '*Romalpa* theory and practice under retention of title in the sale of goods' (1995) 24 Anglo-American L Rev 327.

218 Here the rules of equity are incorporated but no further. See *Universal CIT Credit Corp* v. *Farmers Bank* (1973) 358 F Supp 317.

219 See p. 398.

and therefore his financier. It is possible to speculate that the industrialisation of Singapore did not accentuate the competition between personal property security holder and mortgagee only because much of this industrialisation occurred originally on land leased from the state agency and not private landowners. A pro-personal property bias could have suited the industrialisation policies better as it would encourage secured financing of equipment to be installed in land which being state land was mostly unmortgaged land. Given however the pro-land starting point, a sensitive approach to fixtures was necessary. It was not lacking in Singapore, for the test was, and remains, a mixed question of law and fact, depending upon the intention with which the so-called fixtures must be taken to have been incorporated, to be discovered having regard to the degree of annexation and the object of annexation.[220] Ready availability of self-help afforded a partial answer. Typically the lender could reserve a right to enter the land to remove the so-called fixture and the courts have been lenient about what is or is not detachable without destruction. *Gebrueder Buehler AG* v. *Chi Man Kwong Peter*[221] was a case which showed all too clearly the limitations of self-help. Relying on a retention-of-title clause, Gebrueder Buehler claimed that the machinery supplied by them to ACO belonged to them. It was held at first instance that the machinery supplied had become part of the land and therefore Grebrueder Buehler had lost their title to the machinery. The fact that Gebrueder Buehler had armed themselves with the right to enter the land and sever the machinery from the land was of no avail. The Court of Appeal held that as the mortgagee had entered into possession under its security, the previous owner was no longer entitled to sever and remove chattels which were attached to the premises. The mortgagee's entry into possession would also have terminated any licence to sever the fixtures implied from the mortgagee having left the mortgagor in possession of the land. The self-help accordingly is only valuable before the mortgagee enters into possession, which means that in practice the supplier of fixtures must decide either to act prematurely or not act at all. Further, in that case, the moneys which were used to buy the machinery were not drawn from the loans provided by the mortgagee and in many cases in practice, they will not be. The decision that title to the fixtures was lost upon annexation to the land, argues Francis Tseng, resulted in a windfall for the mortgagee.[222]

Some consolation is now offered to the fixtures supplier by the House of Lords *obiter dictum* that where there is a right to remove, the *Romalpa* financier of the equipment has an equitable interest and the question whether the prior or subsequent legal mortgagee is bound depends on notice and in any other case, on whether the equities predominate in favour of one or the other.[223] The Singapore courts are expected to follow this *obiter dictum*. The concept of trade fixtures affords some form of mitigation. In *BP Refinery Singapore Pte Ltd* v. *Amazon Group Ltd*[224] it was held that a tenant had as against his landlord a right to remove the fixtures it annexed to the land for the purposes of his trade (i.e. a fixture which is recognised as a trade fixture and which is annexed to the land by a tenant for the purposes of his trade). During or at the expiration of the tenancy the title to the tenant's fixtures did not vest in the owner

220 *Material Trading Pte Ltd* v. *DBS Finance Ltd* [1988] SLR 293.
221 [1988] 2 MLJ 69.
222 'The *Romalpa* prayer unheard – *Gebrueder Buehler AG* v. *Chi Man Kwong Peter*' (1988) 10 SAcLJ 124. The argument is not conclusive as the mortgagee who came in afterwards could have provided a larger loan on the basis of the value of the fixtures annexed to the land.
223 *See Melluish* (*Inspector of Taxes*) v. *BMI Ltd* (*No 3*) [1996] 1 AC 454.
224 [1999] 1 SLR 315.

of the land until and unless the tenancy had terminated and the fixtures had not been removed. The court boldly pronounced this logical extension of the reasoning in *Saint* v. *Pilley*.[225] It seems clear, however, from the earlier case that the *Romalpa* seller who retains title to trade fixtures supplied to a tenant will not prevail over the mortgagee of the landlord, if the latter has entered into possession.[226]

This can be contrasted with Article 9-334(d) which gives the fixture financier priority if: the security interest is a PMSI; the interest of the financier of the land arises before the goods become fixtures; the security interest is perfected by a fixture filing before the goods become fixtures or within 20 days thereafter; and the debtor has an interest of record in the land or is in possession.[227] This pro-personal property bias seems necessary in Singapore even though virtually all land is registered land and it might be thought that the register already affords adequate notification of the mortgagee's interest. The point is that the land may be unencumbered when the equipment is first installed in it but becomes encumbered afterwards. The present law thus gives the mortgagee priority even though he came in afterwards and could be justified if the mortgagee has provided a larger mortgage loan based on the added value of the fixtures. Nevertheless, the additional loan value is more likely to reflect the fire cost sale of the fixtures rather than the added value of the land as an ongoing enterprise. The result is overestimation of the mortgagee's contributions to the debtor's business. Reform modelled on Article 9-334 would remove the favour presently accorded to the financier of real property and place the two lenders, fixtures supplier and mortgagee, on an even footing. There could of course be a problem of unfairness if the fixture financier was given the right to force a sale of the land in order to apply the proceeds of sale to its claim. To forestall that problem, the former Article 9-313 obliged him to repossess the fixtures, on reimbursing the landowner for physical damage to the land.[228] There would also be a problem when land is to be developed with funds provided by a construction lender. Such a lender is akin to the purchase-money lender; without his injection of funds, the fixture supplier would not in the first place be in a position to do business with the debtor. Under pressure from the real estate bar, Article 9-334(h) has in fact been amended to give super-priority to the construction mortgage in enumerated situations.[229] It would not be hard to justify the same result given the modern emphasis in Singapore on rejuvenation and reconstruction of old industrial properties.

Registration

I have taken a long time to come to registration, and perhaps a word of apology is appropriate because some preliminary remarks are necessary before we can

225 (1875) LR 10 Exch 137.

226 Indeed, whether or not the mortgagee has entered into possession, according to op. cit., Clark (ed.), fn 211, p. 84.

227 Art. 9-334(e) adds that a perfected security interest in fixtures has priority over a conflicting interest of the financier of land among other things if the debtor has an interest of record or is in possession of the real property and the security interest is perfected before the interest of the financier or owner is of record; or if the fixtures are readily removable in the prescribed sense and the security interest is perfected before the goods become fixtures.

228 The present Art. 9-604(b) provides for alternative enforcement under real property law.

229 See para. (d).

approach it with some hope of ascertaining its real significance. The most conspicuous feature the observer will note is the absence of security interest legislation of similar breadth, covering chattel mortgage, factors' lien, trust receipt or conditional sale, in some major jurisdictions. Frankly, the legislation was of uneven importance. Even in the United States, the chattel mortgage proved inferior as an inventory financing device and legislation was necessary to avoid the apparently logical difficulty that a regular power to sell would be inconsistent with the mortgagee's interest.[230] In any case, trust receipts under the Uniform Trust Receipts Act subsequently 'took over the field of financing'. In these registration statutes, there was always something a little more than providing for public notice of the security interest of concern, namely some policy to promote a market for them. It could be that the lack of a similar policy dissipated the pressure for comparable legislation in Singapore. Consequently, there is little experience here with registration systems apart from the systems established by the Bills of Sale Act[231] and the Companies Act[232] and certain very specialised shipping and aircraft registers;[233] so that avoidance of a plurality of registers is not a strong argument for reform modelled on Article 9.

Again by way of preliminary observation, when considering Article 9 as a public notification scheme, it is important to appreciate that the problem of short-changing other secured lenders is only one aspect of the larger problem of secured credit and should not, as it has sometimes been, be presented as the essence of the article. The problem we are told is that the debtor in possession appears to be the owner and can easily mislead another into lending him on the same security of another. Registration therefore was originally a fraud prevention exercise. Indeed, modern arguments about the merits of Article 9 still centre on the ease with which fraud may be perpetrated. For instance, it has been argued that there is no need to require registration of possessory security interests because possession is in another, not the debtor, and no third party should be misled by any notion of ostensible ownership on the part of the debtor. Arguments such as these while valid overlook the importance of allowing a secured creditor to set up this want of publicity against another who has neglected to provide it. They also overlook the need to provide as much information about the security as is possible in an impersonal, readily accessible manner and for the sake of business efficacy. In the case of structured or hierarchical financing, another lender may already know that the property is encumbered but may desire the information in order to estimate the profitability of purchasing all previous security interests as well. Registration here serves also to display the debtor's credit history, indicate equity dilution if any and may be necessary to the evaluation of the financial health of the debtor as a whole, if for instance the debtor has permitted recourse to executory contract rights so as to avoid creating an obligation which will show on the parent company's balance sheet.

These considerations, of course, affect the design of the system of public notification. For instance, should the system register transactions or, intention to transact?[234]

230 Cf. *Re Morritt* (1886) 18 QBD 222, p. 233.

231 See fn 22 above.

232 Cap 50, 1994 Rev. Ed.

233 For a case on the effect of non-registration of a shipping mortgage, see *The Jarguh Sawit; Navigation Maritime Bulgare* v. *Owners of the Ship or Vessel 'Jarguh Sawit'* [1995] 3 SLR 840.

234 Part 5 of Art. 9 requires notice filing rather than transaction filing. Containing the barest of details about the financing transaction entered into or intended to be entered into, the notice envisages that further inquiries may be made of the secured party, at the debtor's

Will extended registration hamper the speed of transactions? Should the particulars to be notified be limited or unlimited? Nevertheless, these questions are beyond the scope of our present enquiry. What is more important is to elicit from our experience with existing registers lessons or insights as to what is feasible and what is not.

The Bills of Sale Act

Of the two general statutes providing for registration of security interests the Bills of Sale Act[235] is far older than the other, the Companies Act. Though copied extensively from the English Bills of Sale Acts, the former Act is not entirely and in every respect the same as the English Acts.[236] In objective, however, there is no material distinction between them. The Singapore Act shares the objects of the English Acts, namely to prevent false credit being given to people allowed to remain in possession of goods which apparently are theirs, the ownership of which they have parted with, and to prevent needy persons being entrapped into signing complicated documents which they might often be unable to comprehend and so being subjected by their creditors to the enforcement of harsh and unreasonable provisions.[237] The first object nowadays seems exaggerated. But its legacy has survived. The mortgage without the taking of possession was seen as suspicious and a fraudulent conveyance; the writing was imposed to safeguard against this concern. 'Judicial attitudes derived from this tradition naturally dictated the result that the statutes which established filing systems should be strictly construed against the mortgagees who sought to take advantage of them.'[238]

It is interesting to chart the course of Singapore as well as Malaysian case law on the first statute.[239] The bill of sale was employed for the financing of fixed as well as working capital. In one case, the bill of sale was given in relation to a cart and a pair of bullocks, being presumably the prime movers of the cart.[240] There was some sophistication in the employment of the bill of sale. In one case, the grantor of a bill of sale was indebted to the grantee for rent who was pressing him for payment, and the grantee thought a bill of sale more satisfactory than the mere right to distrain; perhaps because he charged interest on the arrears of rent which could not be distrained for.[241] In another nineteenth-century case, a bill of sale was given in respect of two billiard tables but was void as the judgment debtor had no property and was not the true owner of the chattels at the time he granted the bill of sale.[242] In another

request. See also Art. 9-210 which compels disclosure by the secured party in prescribed situations.

235 See fn 22 above.

236 The Bills of Sale Act differs from its English version in that it invalidates bills of sale given in consideration of a pre-existing debt.

237 See *Halsbury's Laws of England* (London: Butterworths, 4th edn, 2002), vol. 4(1), para. 612.

238 As a first principle, the Bills of Sale Acts are nowhere designed to interfere with the ordinary transactions of trade and commerce; see *Re Winkelmann and Lubkin Ltd* (1921) 14 SSLR 19.

239 Leaving out the cases which raise problems peculiar to Malaysia such as the problem of movable houses; see *Harnam Singh* v. *K V. Sambavisam* [1954] 1 MLJ 251.

240 See: *Annamalai Chetty* v. *Kader Tamby* [1885–1890] 4 Ky 620; [1890] 3 SLJ 53. Note also *K Muthukaruppan* v. *VPR Nagapa Chetty* [1922] 1 FMSLR 97.

241 See *Re Rebeiro's Bill of Sale* [1892] 2 SSLR 1.

242 See *Singapore Gas Co* v. *SC Hodges* [1888] 1 SLJ 24.

case, a bill of sale of stock-in-trade was given by way of security for the payment of money.[243] It seems from all this that lay persons were able to operate a very technical piece of legislation and further utilise it in all aspects of their businesses.

With reference to the second object of consumer protection, the heavy protectionist complexion of the Bills of Sale Act did not seem very congruent with the more informal needs of the time. The local Bills of Sale Ordinance 1886 however exceeded even the already stringent requirements of the English Act of 1882. A local bill of sale was like an English bill of sale void if it was not made in the form set forth in the schedule. However, the schedule of the local Ordinance did not give the latitude allowed by the English form in several respects. At first, the courts enforced the forms strictly, though reluctantly. In one case it was held with obvious reluctance that a bill of sale was void as it failed to provide, as required by the local Ordinance, the abode and occupation of the grantor and every attesting witness. As the grantor and his witnesses were Europeans and Eurasians, it was impossible that these facts in so small a place as Penang were unknown.[244] The impossibility of an acceleration clause was insisted on in another case, also with a hint of reluctance.[245] There, a Bill of Sale which provided that 'in case of default of payment of any one instalment [secured thereby] the whole amount remaining unpaid should become immediately due and payable' was held to be void under the Bills of Sale Ordinance 12 of 1886, s. 8 as not being in the form set forth in the Schedule to the Ordinance.[246]

Little by little, however, the judicial vigilance softened[247] and, despite the greater stringency of the local legislation, the courts began to adopt the test suggested in *Sharp* v. *McHenry*,[248] which was to inquire whether anyone could be misled or any wrong or damage be caused by this mistake?[249] A rule of substantial compliance thus emerged. In accordance with this rule, the omission to include the agreed amount of interest payable monthly in the instalment set out in the Bill of Sale, was held to be 'a variance from the statutory form calculated reasonably to deceive those for whose benefit the statutory form is provided'. The variance was material and the Bill of Sale was void as being not in substantial accordance with the statutory precedent.[250]

243 See *Re Estate of Lim Kong Chuan decd* [1898–1890] 5 SSLR 70.

244 See *Duval* v. *Scully* [1885–1890] 4 Ky 120.

245 See *Jamalsah* v. *Vershat* [1895–1890] 4 Ky 471. Note also *KAKM Narayanan Chetty* v. *Amat bin Na'aris* [1922] 1 FMSLR 368.

246 See also: *Official Assignee* v. *Koh Kam Neo* (1898), 5 SSLR 70; *Aroonasallam Chetty* v. *Tay Heng Lee* (1906) 10 SSLR 92. In the interesting Malaysian case of *Santa Singh s/o Lehna Singh* v. *Santa Singah s/o Meya Singh* [1939] 1 MLJ 324 it was held that the offsprings of certain buffaloes were not included in the bill of sale which contained a reference to the buffaloes in the schedule because these offsprings were not there set out and clearly described.

247 It is interesting that a Malaysian court attributed this to passage of the Interpretation Act 1947 of Malaya which provided in one place for the disregard of slight deviations not affecting the substance or calculated to mislead. See *Jackson* v. *Co Ltd* v. *Song Song; Jagat Singh and Co* [1954] 1 MLJ 238.

248 (1887) 38 Ch. D 427.

249 See *RMS Sinniah* v. *RMS Muttiah* [1923] FMSLR 21.

250 See also *Re Estate of Lim Kong Chuan decd* [1898–1890] 5 SSLR 70) where a bill of sale of chattels (stock in trade) given by way of security for the payment of money, by which the grantor purported to assign the chattels 'as administratrix' was not made 'in the form' given in the schedule to the Bills of Sale Ordinance 1886, and was therefore made void by s. 8 of that Ordinance.

In these circumstances, it is hardly surprising that businesses in Singapore began avoiding the security bill of sale like the plague.[251] This is not a misleading proposition. References to the security bill of sale in the modern reported cases are not uncommon. But they are of two kinds. In the first group of cases, when they appear, it is because some mistake has occurred. About the mid-1960s, for instance, when the hire purchase was still a fairly new concept to the legal profession, a mistake occurred in the way an extension of the original loan was to be secured and in *Tan Tien Choy* v. *Kiaw Aik Hang*,[252] the Federal Court sitting in Singapore decided that though the second agreement was structured as a hire purchase agreement it was void as an unregistered bill of sale.[253] Such instances are now rare. Of course, counsel is always tempted to take the bill of sale point and there have been one or two recent cases in which counsel faintly contended in a preliminary way that what was called a lease was in fact a bill of sale, only to drop the contention at trial.[254] These things are evidence that the legal profession has acquired experience in dealing with such quasi-security interests as the hire purchase[255] and lease[256] and are unlikely these days to run foul of the Bills of Sale Act. In the second group of cases, and the cases here overwhelmingly surpass the cases first-mentioned, the hire purchase is employed as a cloak for an illegal moneylending transaction.[257] Paradoxically perhaps, this also demonstrates avoidance of the Bills of Sale Act. Upon the whole, it is fair to say that the Bills of Sale Act has failed in its first objective notably because it adopted incorrectly the second objective.

The Companies Act

Modelled on the English company charges registration system established in 1900, sections 131 to 133 of the Companies Act[258] adopt the same enumeration technique as the Bills of Sale Act: producing a 'limited category of enumerated charges'.[259]

251 For some cases on the absolute bill of sale, see: *Guan Chong Cocoa manufacturer Sdn Bhd* v. *Pratiwi Shipping SA* [2003] 1 SLR 157; *BP Refinery Singapore Pte Ltd* v. *Amazon Group Ltd* [1999] 1 SLR 315.

252 [1965–68] SLR 40.

253 See *Polsky* v. *S and A Services* [1951] 1 All ER 185 applied in *United Investment and Finance Ltd* v. *Abdul Rahman* [1965–1968] SLR 446.

254 See: *Tan Chin Kim Sawmill and Factory Sdn Bhd* v. *Lindeteves-Jacoberg (M) Sdn Bhd* [1982] 1 MLJ 18; *Quah Poh Hoe Peter* v. *Probo Pacific Leasing Pte Ltd* [1993] 1 SLR 14.

255 See also: *Chew Kong Huat* v. *Ricwill (Singapore) Pte Ltd* [2000] 1 SLR 385; *Singapura Building Society* v. *Chua Yew Seng* [1997] SGHC 16; *Singapura Building Society* v. *Djie Sui Thjiang* [1996] SGHC 211; *Hong Leong Finance Ltd* v. *Farmco (S) Pte Ltd* [1993] 1 SLR 348.

256 See *Tunas Pte Ltd* v. *Flexi Van Leasing Inc* [1993] SGHC 183. Note also *Baby@Bathma* v. *Mutharasa* [2003] SGHC 257.

257 The hire-purchase agreement which is a sham to disguise a moneylending transaction is struck down as unregistered bill of sale as in *BSNC Leasing Sdn Bhd* v. *Sabah Shipyard Sdn Bhd* [2000] 2 MLJ 70. For a similar Singapore case, see *United Investment and Finance Ltd* v. *Abdul Rahman* [1965–1968] SLR 446. Cf. *Tong Bee Finance Co Ltd* v. *Sunland Monstreal (S) Pte Ltd* [1988] SLR 18.

258 See fn 232 above.

259 To be registered under the Companies Act within 30 days after creation of the charge: (a) a charge to secure the issue of any debentures; (b) a charge on the uncalled share capital of a company; (c) a charge on shares of a subsidiary of a company which are owned by the company; (d) a charge or an assignment created or evidenced by an instrument which if

The scheme has been well described as a registration scheme as opposed to a filing scheme. What is registered is a done thing, albeit there is no requirement to submit the original instrument of charge.

Unlike the Bills of Sale Act, the charges registration system has a more limited object but an overreaching modus, as will be shown. It operates by incentive; for the creditor who does not register his charge is penalised as against the liquidator and creditors, secured and unsecured.[260] This follows from the effect of s. 131 that a registrable but unregistered charge is 'void against the liquidator[261] and any creditor of the company'. The reference to any creditor is not further qualified by any phrase such as 'in the event of liquidation' but it has been held that in the context 'any creditor' means a creditor who has acquired a proprietary right to or an interest in the subject matter of the unregistered charge.[262] In *Ng Wei Teck Michael* v. *Oversea-Chinese Bank Corp Ltd*,[263] the Court of Appeal so held, before then proceeding to hold that an unsecured creditor qualifies as such creditor on the presentation of a petition to wind up, for then he becomes a beneficial owner under a statutory trust. Such unsecured creditors are in the nature of cestuis que trust with beneficial interests extending to all the company's property; however the unregistered but registrable charge is not void as against any creditor, secured or unsecured, unless a petition to wind up has been presented. The reasoning for giving the expression a narrower meaning is that in the absence of liquidation no unsecured creditor may intervene in the disposition by the debtor of its own assets. The reasoning is not fully convincing. While this is a fundamental tenet of property law, it is a little circular to rely on it; for it presupposes that s. 131 was not intended to change this state or condition of things. The reasoning has also not satisfied some commentators. It would have been sufficient, argued Professor Tan Cheng Han (without recognising that the unsecured creditors are cestuis que trust) for the court to hold that until the appointment of a liquidator, an unsecured creditor has *locus standi* to intervene in the decision to extend time for registration.[264]

Two consequences flowing from the decision indicate that the unsecured creditor is over-protected. First, once a winding-up petition is made, the trust may arise to the detriment of another secured creditor who has registered its charge. Suppose a floating charge is unregistered. It will be void as against the unsecured creditors and secured creditors alike on a winding-up petition being made. As the interest of the unsecured creditors is one under a trust, it may conflict with the interests of other secured creditors who might otherwise seem to have impregnable charges.

executed by an individual would require registration as a bill of sale; (e) a charge on land wherever situate or any interest therein; (f) a charge on book debts of the company; (g) a floating charge on the undertaking or property of a company; (h) a charge on calls made but not paid; (i) a charge on a ship or aircraft or any share in a ship or aircraft; and (j) a charge on goodwill, on a patent or licence under a patent, on a trade mark or on a copyright or a licence under a copyright.

260 Thus, the registrable but unregistered charge is enforceable against the debtor; see *Re Ehrmann Bros Ltd* [1906] 2 Ch. 697.

261 As at the time of appointment. See *Ng Wei Teck Michael* v. *Oversea-Chinese Bank Corp Ltd* [1998] 2 SLR 1; followed in the Malaysian case of *Arab Malaysian Merchant Bank Bhd* v. *Orient Apparel Bhd* [2002] 1 MLJ 89.

262 Cf. s. 395 Companies Act 1985 (UK). Note also *Re Telomatic Ltd* [1994] 1 BCLC 90, p. 95.

263 [1998] 2 SLR 1.

264 See 'Unregistered charges and unsecured creditors' (1998) 114 LQR 565. Note also Lee Eng Beng (1998) 10 SAcLJ 241.

The equitable interest under the trust will usually be inferior to an earlier registered charge; but if the equities are not equal it may trump the earlier interest. The result is that the secured creditor's position may be worse under the charges registration system. Second, there is therefore a period from the lodgement of a petition to wind-up to the appointment of the liquidator during which the secured creditor's failure to register its charge is possibly fatal and abridgment of time unlikely. In terms of providing information on which lenders can act or make rational decisions, the favour shown to unsecured creditors who are unlikely to have relied on the register during this window of time is unwarranted.[265]

It may be that these incongruencies explain Yong Pung How CJ's enlightening remarks in *Thai Chee Ken* v. *Banque Paribas*[266] which indicate that the courts will not intervene to fill any lacuna in the registration law but will respect the forms of arrangements where they are of a different substance chosen by the parties in the consciousness that new financing arrangements are constantly developing. The danger is that if courts force new arrangements into the legal mould of the registration law, they may be 'strapped by precedents based on arrangements which are outmoded in topicality'.[267] This danger is very real if the courts are not fully certain that the system is coherent and rationally discriminating.

As a further example of the system's lack of coherence, there is an obvious lacuna in the omission of a fixed charge over marketable securities.[268] A floating charge over marketable securities is registrable but not a fixed charge. It may be that in practice, a fixed charge would be unattractive and would be avoided. But still there is no logic in including one but excluding the other; so that the only safe rule would be to insist on taking possession of the share certificates if anything with the effect of a fixed charge is intended. This problem is mitigated in the case of scriptless securities. Section 130N of the Companies Act makes it clear that only a fixed charge may be created and requires the chargee to be a depositor. Further s. 130 voids a second fixed charge. Thus, any intended second lender would soon enough discover that his charge cannot be created from the rejection of his application to be a depositor. The scriptless system is however not a publicity system; the information is only available once an application is made but not before. Incidentally, in *Dresdner Bank AG* v. *Ho Mun-Tuke Don*[269] an attempt to take advantage of the omission of the fixed charge over marketable securities was rebuffed. The contention was that upon crystallisation the floating charge became a fixed charge which did not require registration and was hence not void against the liquidator. The Court of Appeal held that crystallisation did not alter the fact that the charge was created as a floating charge. The resulting fixed charge arose from the original floating charge and was in effect the same security affecting the same assets. As the original floating charge was void by reason of non-registration of the charge, it remained void even after crystallisation.

265 But *Re Yolland, Husson and Birkett Ltd* [1908] 1 Ch. 152, p. 156 is silent on this distinction.

266 [1993] 2 SLR 609.

267 [1993] 2 SLR 609, para. 14. It was held that a sale and repurchase agreement did not have to be registered under s. 131(3)(c) of the Companies Act.

268 There is little doubt that the proposition in *Re Sugar Properties (Derisley Wood) Ltd* [1988] BCLC 146 represents the law in Singapore. Unlike in England, charges over shares in a subsidiary company owned by the chargor are registrable; see Companies Act, s. 131(3)(c).

269 [1993] 1 SLR 114.

Difficulties have also arisen, as illustrated by the *Asiatic Enterprises' case*,[270] in connection with extension of the meaning of 'charge' to an agreement to give or create a charge. The courts have apparently not reached a firm view on whether the extended definition applies to the charges registration system. In that case, the Court of Appeal held that a clause entitling the lender as equitable chargee to attach the outstandings to any property of the borrower created not a floating charge but a contingent agreement to create a charge; and that accordingly there was no present security interest in respect of a certain parcel of land which was generally contemplated within the agreement. Further, it was held that the mere lodgement of a caveat in respect of that land did not create any interest that was registrable. It would seem that the maxim, equity looks upon that as done which ought to be done, will not operate here.[271] There was no discussion of the effect of the extended definition of charge in the Court of Appeal presumably because the agreement itself had not been registered and discussion would have been academic.[272] As Lee Eng Beng has pointed out, the decision makes sense as an attempt to avoid surprising creditors with hidden security interests.[273] He argues however that a floating charge characterisation would have been furnished a fairer outcome in that case. Victor Yeo disagrees.[274] It is not hard to understand why he sees little need to strain the language of the parties forcing it into the floating charge mould. The agreement would be registrable in view of the extended definition of charge and as the creditor should have registered the agreement to create a charge over land, the defendant creditor should pay for its omission in fairness to other creditors. In fact, the proposed solution is not so easy. The agreement in that case was arguably not sufficiently certain and it would not be right to bring every agreement to create a charge, however vague, within the charges registration system which contemplates a charge of some exactitude.

Reference may also be made to *Asia Commercial Finance* v. *JB Precision Moulding Industries* which was mentioned earlier. The criticisms which this case has attracted rest on the fact that the security interest in the company's deposit account was hidden from view and apt to take other intended secured creditors by surprise. Had the case arisen after 1993 there would have been no difficulty for the lien would have been registrable as a charge over a bank account under the amended provisions of the Malaysian Companies Act. Similar amendments have not been enacted in Singapore and as in England, the question whether a charge over a bank account is registrable or not remains uncertain.

With respect to liens, the register leaves out liens arising by operation of law. This is despite the fact that the real issue is not whether the lien is imposed by law, as opposed to being consensual, but, rather, whether the interest is possessory or non-possessory in nature. This distinction seems to be what legal writers in Singapore

270 See *Asiatic Enterprise (Pte) Ltd* v. *United Overseas Bank Ltd* [2000] 1 SLR 300.

271 See: *Williams* v. *Burlington Investments Ltd* (1977) 121 Sol Jo 424; *Re Gregory Love and Co* [1916] Ch. 203.

272 Cf. the High Court in *United Overseas Bank Ltd* v. *Asiatic Enterprises (S) Pte Ltd* [1999] 4 SLR 226 which took the view that the extended definition applied to the charges registration system.

273 See Lee 'Invisible and springing security interests in corporate insolvency law' [2000] 12 SAcLJ 210.

274 See Yeo 'No security for unsecured creditor – *The Asiatic Enterprises (Pte) Ltd* v. *United Overseas Bank Ltd*' [2000] 12 SAcLJ 218. See also Tan 'Springing Security Interests and Registration' (2001) 13 SAcLJ451.

are hinting at in their comments and criticisms of the decision in the case of *Asia Commercial Finance* v. *JB Precision Moulding Industries*.[275] To maintain a consistent policy, liens which are non-possessory in nature and could be the subject of contract should also be registrable.[276] There are, of course, practical reasons for keeping charges arising by operation of law off the register. It has been argued that liens arise by operation of law in many situations 'where it would be impractical to require the creditor to contract for security before undertaking the relevant transaction' and 'where it is necessary for the protection of the weaker party and for the sake of encouraging the business or activity in the interests of the general community'.[277] To this may be added the argument that as such liens may be presumed to be known to all and are consistent with preservation of the property,[278] any prejudice to third parties resulting from their omission from the register would be slight. Yet these arguments are not conclusive. Take the case of the vendor's lien, which is an equitable non-possessory lien. It is not registrable because it arises by operation of law, out of the relationship of the parties and not out of express contract.[279] The lien is also effective when the contract is made and continues even after possession and title are transferred to the purchaser, remaining until the vendor receives the price payable before or at the time of completion.[280] That being the case, one can imagine a creditor surprised by the existence of a hidden vendor's lien and incurring a prejudice that is non-negligible. It is not possible to justify this result in any of the terms mentioned above and the same reasons given for including the *Romalpa* clause, which is consensual, within the charges registration system also apply to the vendor's lien which is imposed by operation of law.[281] The English experience with respect to the lien on sub-freights is useful – there are liens and there are liens. Some liens, like the liens on sub-freights, simply do not bind third parties[282] and should not be included in any charge registration system. What is now needed is a more careful analysis of what liens should be included and what excluded.

The cases highlighted above indicate that the charge registration system is dogged by a lack of coherence because the policy against hidden interests is not consistently

275 [1996] 2 MLJ 1.

276 There is a view that an equitable lien created *inter partes* by written agreement is registrable if created by an individual under the Bills of Sale Acts and if created by a company, under the Companies Act. If created by enforceable agreement other than in writing it will be avoided as against an individual by the Bills of Sale Acts, but will still require registration under the CA if created by a company. See Gleeson *Personal Property Law* (London: FT Law and Tax, 1997), p. 269. Charges arising by operation of law are not registrable; see *London and Cheshire Co Ltd* v. *Laplagrene Property Co Ltd* [1971] 1 Ch. 499.

277 See de Lacy 'Reflections on the ambit and reform of Part 12 of the Companies Act 1985 and the doctrine of constructive notice' in de Lacy (ed.) *The Reform of United Kingdom Company Law* (London: Cavendish Publishing, 2002), p. 337.

278 With respect to contractual liens, some are registrable as charges on book debts. See *Re Welsh Irish Ferries Ltd* [1986] Ch. 471. With respect to pledges, Parker LJ in *Re Hardwick, ex p Hubbard* (1886) 17 QBD 690, p. 854 doubted whether a pledge created by constructive delivery by attornment would be outside the registration requirement.

279 See *Re Welsh Irish Ferries Ltd* [1986] Ch. 471.

280 *Re Caveat No. CV/21366D Lodged by Lim Saw Hak* [1996] 2 SLR 196.

281 Cf. the Bills of Sale Act which creates an exception for liens over trading stock transferred in the ordinary course of trade; see *Re Young, Hamilton and Co, ex p Carter* [1905] 2 KB 772.

282 See *Agnew* v. *Commissioner of Inland Revenue* [2001] 2 AC 710, pp. 727–8. See also F. Oditah 'Judicial nature of a lien on sub-freights' [1989] LMCLQ 191.

maintained in the companies register.[283] Unlike the Bills of Sale Act, which was established due to a fear of fraud by a non-owner remaining in possession of goods, the charges system was established purely to give notice to general creditors.[284] The main objectives of the company charges register were: to provide intended creditors with ready means of checking on the borrower's financial affairs as well as secured creditors with ready means of protecting their interests.[285] That being the case, the system should not have stopped at a closed list of registrable charges and, whilst it was not essential to require all security interests to be registered, it should have given the holders of security interests an option to register for the purposes of giving notice. Instead, the Companies Act directs the rejection of applications to register charges that are not listed.[286] Security interest holders are then left to devise their own peculiar, and often more costly, ways of giving notice to third parties.

Further, unsecured creditors are over-protected by the Companies Act because the *pari passu* principle is extended in operation to the time a petition to wind up the company is presented. Under Article 9 however, the filing of a petition to wind-up only produces the effect that the trustee in bankruptcy is a judgment or lien creditor who has attached or levied execution on the collateral. The priority of an unperfected security interest is never defeated as against an unsecured creditor save to this extent.[287]

As to the protection of registered secured creditors, mention has just been made of some omissions which are indefensible. Earlier, mention was made of the difficulties posed by quasi-security interests. It has been observed that the list of registrable charges which the registration system employs draws a line between instruments typically of interest to secured creditors and instruments typically of interest to buyers.[288] If this is indeed so, it still cannot explain why the quasi-security interests are left out, for they have ceased to be typically of interest to buyers.[289] The limited nature of the charges register was of course deliberate. It was thought wrong to embrace all charges, thereby imposing 'impossible duties which could damage commercial transactions by, for example, preventing people from taking certain types of charge which are currently common'.[290] In other words, privacy is important

283 The discussion has left out the point made by Professor Ellinger 'Absolute assignments of company book debts – is registration required?' [2004] SJLS 547 concerning the effect of s. 104 introduced by the Bankruptcy Act 1995.

284 Unlike the Bills of Sale Act. See *The Manchester, Sheffield and Lincolnshire Ry Co* v. *The North Central Wagon Co* (1888) 13 App. Cas. 554.

285 See *The Manchester, Sheffield and Lincolnshire Ry Co* v. *The North Central Wagon Co* (1888) 13 App. Cas. 554.

286 Of course where there is doubt whether a charge is an enumerated charge, the prudent course is to register it since no harm is done and some good may be achieved if it is in fact not a registrable charge.

287 Arts 9-301(1)(b) and 9-301(3).

288 McCormack therefore argues that the trade purchaser is unaffected by the system; see *The Registration of Company Charges* (London: Sweet & Maxwell, 1994), pp. 141–4.

289 The question whether *Romalpa* devices are registrable depends on whether they would be bills of sale if granted by an individual. *Reeves* v. *Barlow* (1884) 12 QBD 436 suggests that simple retention devices are not registrable. The English courts do not accept that they are exceptions in the sense of being transfers of goods in the ordinary course of trade; see *Ian Chisholm Textiles Ltd* v. *Griffiths* [1994] BCC 96.

290 See *Official Reports Standing Committee D (Companies Bill)*, 10th Sitting (20 June 1989), p. 404, as cited in de Lacy 'Reflections on the ambit and reform of Part 12 of the Companies Act

and the law should not compel a company to forego its privacy by reason only that it needs a secured loan or that it wishes to make a secured loan of a quasi-nature. Frankly, this argument for the exclusion of some charges which are common in any trade or calling, is hard to comprehend. The desire for privacy could have been catered for by giving the secured creditor an option not to register and allowing the holder of the unregistered charge to prime the unsecured creditor.

Registration and priorities

The protection of secured creditors under the charges registration system is surprisingly incomplete. This is because the system was never intended to affect priorities. Despite its conspicuous silence on priorities, the system has shifted to focus on priorities between charges and absolute proprietary interests. Gough has explained, that the absence of priorities from the registration system was countered by a judicial invention of the most complex order, namely the doctrine of constructive notice, 'a product of both the statutory and non-statutory elements',[291] but this intervention established 'only a partial and incomplete priority system'.[292] Registering a charge is said to attract the doctrine of constructive notice but the doctrine is entirely judge-made. This in turn, has attracted severe criticism for creating uncertainty in the law, for it is unclear how wide the doctrine of constructive notice operates. Gough has identified the absence of a clear-cut policy approach as the reason for this uncertainty. He concludes by saying that '[u]tilising concepts of constructive notice is the most confusing and least efficient means of regulating priorities'.[293] One may add that making a system of priorities turn on nice questions of good faith and bad faith is another recipe for uncertainty; especially when interests are rapidly created and re-created.

A particular question which has arisen in Singapore is whether the register can be employed as a means to give notice of quasi-security interests.[294] The view that while the negative pledge is not a registrable particular, notice can still be given by registering this detail on the register, is still only tentative.[295] Under this view, a subsequent specific chargee is not fixed with notice of a restrictive clause merely because the previous floating charge is registered. Constructive notice is rejected. 'A restrictive clause [is] effective to retain priority for the floating charge only if the subsequent

1985 and the doctrine of constructive notice' in de Lacy (ed.), *The Reform of United Kingdom Company Law*, fn 272, p. 339, n. 48.

291 See fn 198 above, p. 900.

292 See fn 198 above, p. 901.

293 See fn 198 above, p. 835.

294 Such as the negative pledge and subordination agreements. Consideration of the negative pledge and subordination agreements has focused on the doctrine of notice and the decision in *Siebe Gorman and Co Ltd* v. *Barclays Bank Ltd* [1979] 2 Lloyd's Rep 142 where the negative pledge was ineffective to preserve priority for the prior specific charge against a subsequent absolute assignment of book debts. That case has been overruled by the House of Lords in *National Westminster Bank Ltd* v. *Spectrum Plus Ltd* [2005] UKHL 41 on the ground that the charge there could not be a specific charge when the chargor was free to draw on the proceeds of the book debts. Note that the register gives constructive notice of registered charges per se.

295 See: Tan Cheng Han, fn 75; *Kay Hian* v. *Jon Phua* [1989] 1 MLJ 284. Note also *Fire Nymph Products Ltd* v. *The Heating Centre Pty Ltd* (1992) 7 ACSR 365. Cf. *United Malayan Banking Corp* v. *Alumninex Sdn Bhd* [1993] 3 MLJ 587 which is to the contrary.

adverse party had actual notice of the restriction at the time that his interest was taken.'[296] Against this, it has been argued that the notice which the register effects is notice of existence of the type of charge and not of its contents.[297] One may also make the more fundamental point that the register was never intended to become a way of establishing the existence of particular rights. Adoption of reform based on Article 9 would certainly alter significantly the way we have hitherto thought about the priority of company charges. For example, it would make notions of equity and fairness immaterial in priority conflicts,[298] thereby enhancing commercial certainty. The complexities of the negative pledge would become history.

Insolvency

Needless to say, consideration of the charges registration system is incomplete without some observations on the impact of reform on the rights of the liquidator or trustee in bankruptcy. There are three types of insolvency proceedings under Singapore law: (a) a scheme of arrangement under the Companies Act, s. 210; (b) a petition for the liquidation of the company under Part X of the Act; and (c) a petition for judicial management under Part VIIIA of the Act. The first two administrative procedures do not alter the fundamental tenet that security interests are outside the bankrupt's estate; but that in the case of deficiency the secured creditor and unsecured creditor are treated alike.[299] Thus, s. 210 of the Act empowers a company to propose a compromise or arrangement with its creditors subject to the sanction of the court[300] but the pendency of such a scheme has no automatic effect on security enforcement.[301] Similarly, the presentation of a winding up petition does not in any way take away a secured creditor's right to deal with its security. It is only the presentation of a petition for the judicial management of the company that brings into effect an automatic statutory prohibition on the taking of any steps for the enforcement of security rights and other rights which have the function but which may not

296 Mere knowledge does not necessarily fix the subsequent chargee with constructive notice; see: *Re Valletort Sanitary Steam Laundry Co Ltd* [1903] 2 Ch. 654; *Re Standard Rotary Machine Co* (1906) 95 LT 829.

297 The difference is in the burden of proof; because the burden of proof of the defence of bona fide purchaser without notice is on the purchaser.

298 Notions of equity are only relevant under UCC Art. 1-103 to the extent they are not displaced and there is no question that the priority rules displace these notions. An example is *Citizens State Bank* v. *Peoples Bank* (1985) 475 NE 2d 325 where a secured creditor who had represented to another his intention to abandon his security interest was estopped from asserting priority in the collateral as against the representee creditor.

299 The fundamental tenet is that the secured creditor's rights stand *de hors* the bankruptcy or liquidation of the debtor. These are rights of preference. Here surprisingly, the courts maintain an economic perspective, and not a purely legal one. The Malaysian High Court held in *M Hashimi bin Ibrahim* v. *Asia Commercial Finance* [2001] 4 MLJ 67 that the financier to a hire purchase is a secured creditor. The Malaysian Federal Court in *Asia Commercial Finance* v. *JB Precision Moulding Industries* [1996] 2 MLJ 1 held that a lessor with a security deposit is a secured creditor.

300 Section 210 is *in pari materia* with s. 895 of the UK Companies Act 2006 and s. 411 of the Australian Corporations Law.

301 However, s. 210(10) makes provision for a court order restraining further proceedings in any action or proceedings against the company once a scheme has been proposed. Secured creditors are not obliged to consent to a scheme of arrangement under s. 210.

have the form of security subject to the leave of court.[302] Unlike the provisions establishing the charges registration system, there is abundant recognition of the importance of quasi-security interests as a source of trade credit and of the fact that the quasi-security interest may decisively affect the chances of keeping the debtor out of bankruptcy or insolvency. Generally, with the prior approval of the court, and for the purposes of the judicial management,[303] the judicial manager may exercise his dispositive powers, overriding the wishes of any creditor who has rights which function as security in the property to be disposed of.[304] To ensure that the company will have every opportunity to survive, the judicial manager is further empowered to dispose of, or otherwise exercise his powers in relation to, any property of the company which is subject to a floating charge as if the property were not subject to the security.[305]

Adoption of Article 9 should not alter the effects of the seller's right of stoppage in transit.[306] It could however introduce some changes to the insolvency law. Under the present law, while charges which are registrable but not registered are void against the liquidator,[307] they are enforceable against the judicial manager. If reform modelled on Article 9 is introduced, such security interests as are unperfected will not be void against liquidator and judicial manager alike but will be subordinate to the interest of the liquidator and judicial manager, whether or not he knows of the interest.[308] This difference is not large, but it may surprise the unwary. Suppose that the buyer has yet to pay for goods he has bought but that he has also given a floating charge over inventory. On the buyer's insolvency, the unpaid seller's right of stoppage will prevail over an unperfected floating charge. The unperfected floating charge is not however void and if the seller has released its right of stoppage or has been paid from sources other than the proceeds of the goods, it may be enforced against the liquidator.

Will reform modelled on Article 9 break new ground in the law on transaction avoidance, particularly in relation to pre-existing floating charges? It is not thought that there would be any enlargement or reduction of the possibilities of striking down

302 The judicial management provisions are virtually the same as the English administration provisions under the UK Insolvency Act 1986.

303 Stated generally, these are (a) the survival of the company or the whole or part of its undertaking as a going concern; (b) the approval of a scheme of arrangement; or (c) a more advantageous realisation of the company's assets than would be effected on a winding up.

304 The security interest is transmitted to the proceeds of sale of the secured property.

305 For this purpose, a right of set-off is not a floating charge; see *Electro Magnetic (S) Ltd* v. *Development Bank of Singapore Ltd* [1994] 1 SLR 734.

306 Nor the rule stated in *Ng Wei Teck Michael* v. *Oversea-Chinese Bank Corp Ltd* [1998] 2 SLR 1 that the unsecured creditor becomes an interest holder under a trust upon lodgement of a winding-up petition.

307 The position has been clarified in *Ng Wei Teck Michael* v. *Oversea-Chinese Bank Corp Ltd* [1998] 2 SLR 1. On the presentation of a winding-up petition, an unsecured creditor acquires sufficient interest in the subject matter of the unregistered charge so as to qualify as a 'creditor' for the purposes of s. 131(1).

308 See Art. 9-301(3) which says that the trustee in bankruptcy is a lien creditor from the moment the petition is filed and Art. 9-301(1)(b) which says that the lien creditor has rights preferable to the unperfected security interest. In the case of Chapter 11 bankruptcy, the debtor in possession is given all the powers of a trustee in bankruptcy: Bankruptcy Code 11 USC Art.'s 1107(a), 1203.

a secured loan with a preferential effect.[309] The issue whether a pre-petition floating charge is a 'suspect' transaction is strictly independent of Article 9 for it falls to be determined in accordance with the bankruptcy or insolvency laws. Nevertheless, in the United States it was found necessary to dove-tail the Article 9 provisions as to when perfection occurred and the bankruptcy laws because the latter provided that a transfer for preference did not occur until perfection.[310] The bankruptcy laws as they then stood could be read to invalidate the floating lien as being a preference in respect of any after-acquired property perfected as the property actually materialised within four months of bankruptcy. Notwithstanding the courts invariably glossed over the 'so far perfected' language of the laws,[311] the Bankruptcy Code now contains clarificatory changes, resulting for instance, in a new exception that a perfected floating lien over inventory or receivables will prevail save where the creditor improves his position within 90 days of bankruptcy.[312] A voidable improvement occurs if the amount of the secured debt at the time of petition exceeds the amount at 90 days before bankruptcy and if there is prejudice to unsecured creditors. Otherwise, a floating lien (over equipment) for instance will be tested by the general rule of materialisation, namely that a transfer is not made until the property has actually materialised. A floating lien which is not given to secure an enabling loan or where the after-acquired property is not merely substitute equipment or proceeds of equipment may be preferential; all of which are instances in which the debtor's estate is not depleted but the security interest shifts to another item before bankruptcy. As the bankruptcy and insolvency laws of Singapore do not employ the language of perfection, strictly, the problem which arose in the United States is avoided. Under the Companies Act, s. 330 the floating charge created within 6 months of the commencement of winding up is invalid except to the extent that fresh advances are given or unless it is proved that the debtor was solvent when it granted the charge.[313]

Uniform remedies?

In spite of the many advantages of Article 9, the case for Article 9-based reform is not conclusive. If the criticisms which have been made of the charges registration system can be addressed without converting to a system modelled on Article 9, the more modest way forward would be right. Protagonists for reform along Article 9 lines naturally argue that Article 9 establishes an integral system to create and promote a market for security interests. If this is also the correct policy for Singapore, it would be desirable to go all the way rather than stop short in timidity. However, a cut and paste approach could be disastrous. A final assessment of what I regard as the crux of the case for Article 9 will be attempted in the conclusion. Be that as it may, some aspects of Article 9 are in any case clearly dispensable, namely, those that

309 See: *Dean* v. *Davis* 242 US 438 (1917); *Re American Properties Inc* 14 BR 637 (1981); and *Re Health Gourmet Inc* 29 BR 673 (1983) discussed in B. Clark *The Law of Secured Transactions under the UCC* (Boston: Warren, Gorham and Lamont, 1993), para. 6.03.

310 The notorious Art. 60(a)(2) of the Bankruptcy Act 1898.

311 See *Rosenberg* v. *Rudnick* 262 F Supp 635 (1967). Cf. *Re Tempco Business Services* 3 Bankr Ct Dec 416 (1977) discussed in op. cit., Clark, fn 309, para. 6.03[5][a].

312 Bankruptcy Code s. 547c(5).

313 See also Lee Eng Beng 'The avoidance provisions of the Bankruptcy Act 1995 and their application to companies' [1995] SJLS 597.

pertain to remedies; but they are briefly dealt with here for the sake of completeness. It was pointed out almost at the outset that the flexibility of the law is important to allow parties room to structure the transaction according to their respective risk averseness or proclivity, costs of funds and other circumstances. Flexibility of remedies is as vital. It must satisfy the divergent needs of creditors and debtors and accommodate their respective risk averseness or proclivity, costs of enforcement and convertibility (i.e. the rate at which the creditor can turn the property into money).[314] As no secured creditor can anticipate in advance which remedy will most advance his interests unless he can foresee the actual circumstances which will arise, the law ought to and does allow him nearly complete choice of remedies (with freedom to agree on non-recourse or exclusion of remedies) and hold that the remedies are cumulative (almost always, at any rate).[315]

Not all of the flexibility in remedies which the general law affords is justifiable other than as an accident or incident of the historical distinction between law and equity. There are some outstanding examples of this. Thus, a pledgee can sell under a power of sale but only a mortgagee can foreclose.[316] The reason is the legal one that the pledgee has no title in the goods upon which to foreclose. On economic grounds, this difference is unjustifiable. Again, the lienee has no power of sale[317] and of course no power to foreclose.[318] This absence of a power of sale or of foreclosure might be justified on the basis that the costs of repairs and other services rendered will normally be small in comparison with the value of the article; and that in these circumstances, it would be unfair to permit the creditor to sell or to foreclose on the security. These bases, however, are doubtful because if the costs of repairs and other services rendered are relatively small in comparison with the value of the security, redemption should seldom be a problem; but in those cases where they are, the creditor should have the power to sell or foreclose on the security (instead of incurring storage fees at his own expense). Examples from the law as to mode of sale reinforce the lack of coherence. It is said that a pawnee must sell by public auction and a private sale is denied but a mortgagee by deed may sell by auction or by private contract.[319] Such complexities detract from the real question which is whether the best price or true market value has been obtained, and the real solution which is that secured parties should be free to adopt such mode of realisation of the security as will yield the best price or true market value. Article 9-based reform would have the merit of simplifying matters. Just as its concept of security interest is an economic one, so the solutions it offers are essentially more economic than technically legal. But Article 9-based reform would not be essential.

As a practical matter there is no danger that a uniform approach towards the power of sale would merge a sale and security agreement under one rubric. The surplus arising after exercise of the power of sale will never go to the security holder whether the interest is a security or quasi-security interest. There is already ample recognition of this principle. Thus, a seller who sells after the buyer breaches his contract of sale

314 *United Overseas Bank Ltd* v. *Promotion and Sales Centre Pte Ltd* (*Central Provident Fund and Anor, Claimants* [1996] 1 SLR 374) was a rare instance of a secured creditor preferring to enforce its personal remedies. That proved to be a costly decision.

315 See *China and South Sea Bank Ltd* v. *Tan Soon Gin* (*alias George Tan*) [1990] 1 AC 536, p. 545.

316 In fact, an equitable mortgagee of personalty has no power of sale apart from statute.

317 See *Larner* v. *Fawcett* [1950] 2 All ER 727. He must apply to court for an order for sale or an order to apply the income in reduction of the debt owing unless he has a statutory or customary right to sell.

318 Because there is no equity of redemption. For this same reason, a chargee cannot foreclose.

319 Goods subject to a bill of sale must be sold by auction: Bills of Sale Act, s. 9.

under which the seller retains title has the right to the surplus but not if the buyer does not breach his contract but the seller exercises his power to resell.[320] In a factoring arrangement, the factor is still entitled to the surplus generated when the account is paid off.[321] These are clear principles of English law but the Singapore case of *United Malayan Banking Ltd* v. *Lim Kang Seng*,[322] shows the courts' commitment to the same principle. In 1985, the plaintiff bank granted banking facilities to a company to be utilised in purchasing inventory. Later, the company agreed to give possession of the inventory financed by the bank to the bank to be released to any purchaser against payment. In an action against the guarantors, it was held that the pertinent documentation showed that the inventory financed by the bank was all along regarded as security rather than as the bank's absolute property. Accordingly, the bank was not obliged to give the company an immediate credit for the value of the goods either when it first took possession of the goods or when the arrangement came to an end. This case would not be decided any differently under a system based on Article 9.[323]

Another point must still be considered and it relates to the duty of care owed by a secured party when exercising the power of sale. According to the Privy Council in *China and South Sea Bank Ltd* v. *Tan Soo Gin*, 'the creditor must decide in his own interest if and when he should sell'.[324] The secured creditor must be guilty of bad faith before he can be made liable for any decline in value of the property but he is not guilty of bad faith simply because he delays the timing of the sale because he is busy or for some other reason personal to himself. On the other hand, the decision in *Roberto Building Material Pte Ltd* v. *OCBC Ltd* appears to put some fetters on the discretion as to when to sell.[325] In *How Seen Ghee* v. *Development Bank of Singapore Ltd*[326] the court also applied an objective assessment which bordered on the commercial reasonableness test of Article 9. Frankly, it seems that the difficulties are more practical than academic. The question is almost entirely one of fact to be appreciated in the circumstances of the case. It is unlikely therefore that adoption of the Article 9 formula would be essential. According to Article 9-610(b), 'every aspect of a disposition of collateral, including the method, manner, time and place and other terms, must be commercially reasonable. If commercially reasonable, a secured party may dispose of collateral by public or private proceedings, by one or more contracts, as a unit or in parcels, and at any time and place and on any terms.' Professor McCormack considers that '[s]uch provisions are worth considering in a statutory enactment of a

320 *Clough Martin Ltd* v. *Mill* [1985] 1 WLR 111 at p. 118 *per* Robert Goff LJ (as he then was).

321 See the opinion of the UCC Permanent Editorial Board Commentary No. 14. See also Reiley 'The Article 9 revision process', p. 274.

322 [1994] 2 SLR 787.

323 Apart from the power of sale, there are other differences which can with profit be assimilated. One of these pertains to the duty to mitigate. In repossession, when the repossessed goods are to be sold, analysis of the duties incumbent on the owner proceeds in terms of the duty to mitigate the owner's loss. In hire purchase cases, not governed by the Hire Purchase Act, it has to be argued that since the hirer is entitled to mitigate, the selling owner's act of selling is a mitigation on behalf of the hirer and therefore he must act reasonably and responsibly in doing so; see *Hong Leong Finance Bhd* v. *Lee Cheng Heng* [1987] 2 MLJ 266, p. 267.

324 [1990] 1 AC 536, p. 545.

325 [2003] 2 SLR 237 affd [2003] 3 SLR 217. The court relied on *Medforth* v. *Blake* [2000] Ch. 86.

326 [1994] 1 SLR 526. Woe 'Duties of a Mortgagee and a Receiver: Whether Singapore should or should not follow English Law' (2008) 20 SAcLJ559 approves of the decision and argues the unconflicted mortgagee exercising his power of sale must take into account the debtor's interest.

secured creditor's remedies'.[327] But it is important to appreciate that this part (now known as Part 6) of Article 9 dealing with and universalising remedies Part 6 was rendered necessary because the various state legislatures had intervened in this respect, producing a patchwork of solutions. The Uniform Conditional Sales Act in an attempt to regularise matters had also established a legislative model of detailed statutory regulation which was inappropriate. It 'devolved' to Part 6 to re-establish a 'loosely organized, informal, any-thing-goes type of foreclosure pattern, subject to ultimate judicial supervision and control'.[328] With respect, Gilmore was right to say that if the business of working out default rights had been left entirely to the courts there was little reason to doubt that Part 6 would have been unnecessary.[329]

The important point underlying much of the above discussion is that self-help is the critical remedy in secured financing. The importance of self-help in secured financing is unquestionable since enforcement costs are lowest when recourse to self-help remedies is possible and expeditious realisation of the security may be vital if the debt is to be recouped with minimal loss. Recourse to judicial remedies may be too late in many instances. Article 9 will certainly advance the policy supportive of self-help since it holds to that as a key principle. However, the case law is malleable and already the power of sale without recourse to court is increasingly imposed on the parties. Adoption of Article 9 is therefore not indispensable in this respect. Further, Article 9 will not remove or eliminate the most serious limitation on self-help, which is that possession must be regained without illegality. That the creditor's ability to take possession of the security is a pre-condition of self-help is not in any doubt since the power of sale cannot in reality be exercised without the secured creditor first taking possession.[330] The difficulty then is: if the secured creditor is not in possession of the property, should his right to regain possession be unqualified?[331] Here a tension is encountered. The right to take possession without judicial proceedings is limited to situations where the owner[332] or the receiver under a debenture creating a fixed and floating charge[333] can take possession without hindrance from the debtor. It appears

327 See op. cit., McCormack, fn 9, p. 35.

328 See op. cit., Clark, fn 309 above, para. 6.03[5][a].

329 See fn 126 above, vol. II, p. 1182.

330 Repossession is usually with a view to sale and the power of sale is derived from ownership. In the case of a lease of equipment, and repossession, see: *SAL Leasing (Pte) Ltd* v. *Hendmaylex Pte Ltd* [1987] SLR 308; *IBM Singapore Pte Ltd* v. *UNIG Pte Ltd* [2003] SGHC 71. Note that the secured creditor does not have to exercise his power of sale following default by the debtor but more often than not will take possession of the security.

331 Possession after default may be of two kinds. If the secured creditor is already in possession, the question is: Should there be a difference between possession before default which is what a pledgee has and possession after default which admittedly is for a different purpose?

332 A court order is necessary for exercise of the legal mortgagee's power of sale only if the mortgagor refuses to give up possession of the land voluntarily. A court order is necessary for the exercise of the equitable mortgagee's power of sale. See also the extension of the receivership remedy to the hire purchase in *Harrick Engineering Pte Ltd* v. *Singapore Finance Pte Ltd* [1998] 1 SLR 197. So there is no evidence that the device is not 'used on the personal property side'.

333 However the onus is on the lender to ensure that the debenture was validly given and that the power to appoint a receiver has validly arisen, failing which the lender and the purported receiver will be liable in damages to the borrower.

from the case law that repossession is commonly troublesome[334] – there is even on the business side a certain amount of hide-and-seek[335] – and the courts appraise each case as it arises. However, while Article 9 is right to say about this tension that re-possession must not occasion a breach of the peace,[336] it cannot introduce any greater clarity that might clinch the case for embracing remedies within the reform.

Case for Article 9 more broadly

The preceding explanations and comments, though lengthy, must of necessity represent a limited treatment of this vast and rich subject and all that can be hoped for here is that the points raised have served to paint a reasonable picture of the prospects for law reform in Singapore. This volume of essays itself is testimony that the claims of efficiency and fairness, which Article 9 represents, are not to be dismissed lightly but merit serious consideration. Taking the general themes together, the following are the main arguments why Article 9 seems to be eminently exportable to and transplantable in Singapore.

Article 9's comprehensiveness

The idea of a code on security interests is attractive. To be able to find the entire law compendiously stated in a code, is attractive for legal practitioners and economic and financial advisers, not forgetting the businessmen they advise. This is not a slight advantage, even when we acknowledge that lawyers, let alone businessmen, will need a commentary in order to make sense of some of the provisions of Article 9. The common law works because specialist lawyers operate it but this – what Gilmore called 'the painfully acquired expertise of the specialists'[337] – comes at a price. Gilmore wrote optimistically of a mutation after Article 9: the specialists would be left behind and the amateurs would take over. This has not materialised and may not ever materialise. But then again, we must take this in perspective. The US secured credit business is huge and constantly evolving, dashing hopes of the kind of familiarity which conveyancing now enjoys among lay persons.

Article 9's responsiveness to changes

This is seldom highlighted in the reform proposals but the success of a scheme especially one as comprehensive as Article 9 depends crucially on its adaptability and its responsiveness to changes. Has Article 9 created obstacles or barriers to credit creation on its home ground? The evidence suggests that the article is no worse than the law as to registration of charges and may be better in this respect. Mention was made earlier of security assignments of executory contract rights. These emerged as a result of the economic conditions after World War II. Gilmore writes that '[t]he financing of government procurement contracts during World War II probably

334 An illegal seizure is actionable in trespass; see *Gladys Nugawela* v. *Soon Teck Finance Co* [1960] 1 MLJ 302.
335 See the Malaysian case of *Tay Kian Hock (t/a Hock Yen Co)* v. *Kewangan Bersatu Bhd* [2002] 4 MLJ 411.
336 See Art. 9-609(b)(2).
337 Op. cit., Gilmore, fn 126, p. 1079.

furnished the major stimulus for the spread of the device into other industries'.[338] The important point therefore is that at the time when Article 9 was in draft, the security assignment of executory contract rights was relatively new and the drafters had not the benefit of any pre-existing case law solution that could be replicated in statutory language. The drafters of the 1962 Article 9 tentatively inserted a category of contract rights recognising their potential utility as collateral.[339] They dealt as comprehensively as they could with the special risks posed by taking security in executory contract rights in what was then Article 9-318. Since then, the article has had to be amended to incorporate additional provisions, among which are Articles 9-406 to 9-409. These changes however do not speak negatively of the article's responsiveness to change. They were part of a fundamental change of policy in favour of creating and promoting a market in executory contract rights by prohibiting all anti-assignment clauses which is now an all-embracing policy covering security assignments of accounts, chattel paper, payment intangibles, promissory notes, leasehold and reversionary interests, health-care-insurance receivables and letter-of-credit rights, among other things.

Some of the more recent changes to Article 9 may also be noticed, although it is too soon to evaluate their success or failure. Article 9 – 314 now allows security rights in investment property, deposit accounts, letter-of-credit rights or electronic chattel paper to be perfected by control of the collateral. Professor McCormack gives a clear account of these latest revisions to Article 9 which implement the recommendations of the UCC Permanent Editorial Board Study Group.[340] In what he describes as a 'fairly radical' departure from the principle of perfection by filing, a security interest in deposit accounts as original collateral is perfected only by control. In fact, it attaches as soon as there is control so that there is some similarity between a possessory interest and a security interest in a bank deposit. The use of control as a response contrasts nicely with the developments in the general law in relation to creating security interests in securities and deposit accounts. Three devices may be employed: the trust, the charge or the flawed asset arrangement (contract).[341] One's first impression is that perfection by control is more suited to the fluctuating character of many of these rights and more accommodating of movements in them. This is because control simply means that the bank is obliged by its customer to honour the secured creditor's instructions instead of the customer's. Control in this sense is readily imposed and withdrawn unlike for instance a fixed charge created by way of a blocked account with its greater degree of permanence.

Article 9's flexibility

There is little doubt that a simplistic scheme will do more harm than good. A good scheme is simple in its basic structures, so that its logic and framework assumptions are easily comprehended, but at the same time, providing building units for more complex and hierarchical structures, whether on the trade side or finance side. Article 9 appears to satisfy these requirements.

338 See op. cit., Gilmore, fn 126, p. 1077.

339 Then Art. 9-106 which defined contract right to mean 'any right to payment under a contract not yet earned by performance and not evidenced by an instrument or chattel paper'.

340 See op. cit., McCormack, fn 9, pp. 27–30.

341 See op. cit., Lee Eng Beng, fn 49.

Article 9's adoption in some common law jurisdictions, notably the states of Canada and New Zealand

This is an argument for adoption in Singapore. It proves the exportability of Article 9 outside of its native soil but it does not of course prove that the Singapore legislation should follow either the Canadian or the New Zealand personal property security legislation.

Despite these not inconsiderable advantages, adoption will not be easy for several reasons.

Inertia

This is widely seen as the obstacle to reform, not because reform is not meritorious but because holders of quasi-security interests think themselves well and adequately protected and are apprehensive about incurring new costs of filing.[342] Loss of privacy may be a concern in some quarters. Banks on the other hand are not troubled by the complexities of the existing law and while acknowledging that Article 9 has strong merits, may see no reason to change. They have after all invested in expertise and have acclimatised themselves, as it were, to these complexities.[343] The real question is one going beyond vested interests: will reform modelled on Article 9 open up the financial and capital markets to new entrants who do not have resources to invest in such expertise? Nevertheless, there is a valid, if exaggerated, argument that the ideas which have painstakingly been built up would be overthrown only to have the process recommenced if the new ideas took their place.

Article 9's complexity

This means relearning and perhaps costly mistakes in the learning curve. First, there is no doubt that there will be attempts to engraft the old learning on the new, as in *International Harvester Credit Corp* v. *American National Bank*[344] where a party attempted to devise equitable responses to dealings with perfected interests. Then there is the complexity that is due to inability to forecast and provide for all contingencies. This complexity depends on whether there will be an incentive to avoid the article. Double complexity is a particularly invidious obstacle to reform. If there is no perfection, and the resolution of the dispute between the parties has to be thrown back to the existing law, the legal adviser will have to learn a new thing without being able to discard the old. To Article 9's credit, experience shows that this will not likely happen.

In addressing the objection based on complexity, perspective is necessary. Article 9 is complex – which system of law which has to cope with an industry running into trillions of dollars is not? – but the complexity is diffused because of the experience which can be appropriated by Singapore at the relatively cheap price of a set of United States law reports and commentaries. Secondly, any system of registration whether it is inclusionary such as the charges registration system or 'exclusionary'

342 See J. Ziegel 'Canadian perspectives on how far is Article 9 exportable?' (1996) 27 Can Bus LJ 226, p. 231.
343 See op. cit., Bridge, fn 20, p. 221.
344 (1974) 296 So 2d 32.

such as Article 9, will not be spared from being the subject of litigation when new instruments of secured credit are evolved. Prima facie, the first is more predictable since it requires the legal adviser to determine simply whether some instrument is a charge and hence included. The social costs are high. The burden to add to the list of inclusions is on the legislature; until then such instruments as should be included but have been omitted will continue to produce unfairness on discriminate creditors. Further, the pain of any incorrect characterisation will be felt, as the *Romalpa* cases well show. The second system seems less predictable because the test is an economic one. Basically if an interest in personal property is not excluded, it may or may not be a security interest and this may become a source of litigation just as the exclusion itself may become a source of litigation.[345] The social costs however are lighter.

The question of complexity is an important practical consideration. The legal profession in Singapore must constantly adapt transactions and forms devised elsewhere to suit local conditions and terms. These demands have led to serious lapses. During 1999, for instance, US$575m worth of structured real estate transactions was completed in the domestic markets. Although intended to be asset securitisations, it is now generally accepted that these deals were not asset securitisations but a form of secured structured financing.[346] The transactions incorporated a simplified master lease structure but did not incorporate key aspects commonly expected in an asset securitisation such as reserve fund for liquidity, capital expenditures, insurance, property management expenses, taxes, extended tail period required for property liquidation in case of refinancing difficulties. Under an inclusionary system, one can simply see that the transactions would not be charges. Under an Article 9 system, failure to perfect would be fatal. Nevertheless, the real practical issue is whether the requirement of perfection is an imposition that is costly. There is nothing in Article 9 to preclude 'protective' filing even if the transaction is not one of security, for the avoidance of doubt or simply to throw the burden of proof on to the party who says otherwise. Provided then that filing is not too costly, the legal adviser has a simple aphorism for his clients who are troubled by complexity: 'When in doubt, file.'

Conclusions

It remains to be seen whether Singapore will adopt reform along the lines of Article 9. Given recent experience in New Zealand and Australia there is now a greater impetus towards reform. The easy option would be to patch-up the existing system with piece-meal reform such as may well happen in England now that the 'radical' proposals of the Law Commission have not been followed. However, the fact is that Article 9 advances a policy to create and promote a market for security interests and the real question is whether that policy should be adopted. One cannot, with confidence, state that this policy will be clearly embraced and preferred in a country which continues to emphasise savings and self-discipline before credit and adventure.[347] The fact is that the Asian crisis has left its marks. The economic miracle of Singapore

345 See the experience with leases as reviewed in op. cit., Clark, fn 309, para. 1.05.

346 Cf. the CapitaMall Trust REIT of 2002.

347 In 1988, the domestic savings largely the compulsory savings held by the CPF was almost equal to the foreign reserves. In that year, domestic savings rate was nearly 42 per cent. See generally K.-P Wong 'Saving, capital and capital formation' in C.-Y. Lim and P. Lloyd (eds), *Singapore: Resources and Growth* (Singapore: Oxford University Press, 1986), ch. 3; A. Husain 'Determinants of Private Saving in Singapore', in op. cit., Bercuson (ed.), fn 1, ch. VII.

was almost derailed and only the very substantial savings – officially described as reserves – built up in the expansive years, staved off serious fundamental damage to the economy. What the experience has shown is that a seemingly strong economy has remained frail and vulnerable to external forces; the domestic market is still unable to support and sustain the expansion of industry; and perhaps surprisingly, the economy is critically dependent not only on the prosperity of the country's major trading partners, the US and Japan and increasingly China, but also South East Asia. Without the re-assuring buffer of a domestic market, and exposed to the frailties and vulnerabilities of her immediate neighbours, a policy which favours savings, and the self-imposed discipline it fosters, offers the only buffer against excess or deficiency. This lesson will not be forgotten given the relatively recent nature of the Asian crisis. Article 9 represents a fundamental change to this policy and, for that reason, may not now seem so attractive.

At the same time, the Singaporean business ethic and mentality outside a small circle of powerful home-grown businesses may not have shifted radically from commitment to thrift and self-financing as a virtue. Unlike the capitalist development of Japan which was driven by a few enormous companies, Singapore's economic progress was and remains government-charted and government-driven.[348] This government dominance reflected among other things in cheap unsecured financial support for new and more speculative business ventures further diffuses pressures to reform.[349]

348 See generally L. Seah 'Public enterprise and economic development', in P. Chen (ed.), *Singapore: Development Policies and Trends* (Oxford: Oxford University Press, 1983), ch.6.

349 Cf. The Report of Economic Review Committee *New Challenges, Fresh Goals – Towards a Dynamic Global City* (Singapore: MTI, 2003).

13 Basic issues of European rules on security in movables

Ulrich Drobnig

Introduction

The discussion which is currently taking place in the UK on a new regime for security interests over movable assets, especially the work of the English Law Commission,[1] is of great interest to all commercial lawyers in Europe (and other continents as well) who are interested in the modernisation of their domestic systems of security instruments. Over the past two centuries most European countries have developed in a haphazard, piecemeal way sets of rules to deal with a new phenomenon of overriding importance, namely non-possessory security interests. The growing demand for the supply of credit to entrepreneurs and enterprises made it obvious that the traditional possessory pledge, which had until then served as the main form of security interest, was no longer sufficient to satisfy the need for adequate security. Economic actors could no longer utilise the pledge since it meant turning over their productive assets such as plant and machinery which they needed to retain in order to produce goods for public consumption. Without the ability to produce, no revenue/profits could be created and, therefore, no repayments of debt could be made. Therefore, it became imperative for borrowers and lenders alike to be able to obtain effective new forms of non-possessory security interests. The modern industrialised economy as we now know it was founded, at least in part, on the success of the new forms of security interest that have materialised in recent years.

As a result of these developments almost all European countries have now recognised (whether it be via legislation or judicial development) non-possessory security. In this chapter I will charter some of the developments in the recognition of non-possessory security throughout Europe and offer views on how things should develop. In short I will argue that it is now time for fundamental reform with a view to a new and unified European regime.

Diversity of legal instruments for non-possessory security in Europe

It would be impossible and, for our purposes, also unnecessary for this chapter to present an extensive discussion on the present situation in continental Europe; that

1 See generally: English Law Commission: *Company Security Interests* (2005) Law Commission Report No. 296 (The Final Report); *Registration of Security Interests: Company Charges and Property other than Land* (2002) Consultation Paper No. 164; *Company Security Interests: a Consultative Report* (2004) Consultation Paper No. 176; all available at www.lawcom.gov.uk. For an overview of the work of the Law Commission see the essay by de Lacy in this volume at pp. 63–76 above.

would require a book or two.[2] The purpose of the following highly selective survey is more modest: it is merely intended to convey a general idea of the divergences existing in the more important continental member states of the European Union (EU). In this respect important topics for analysis are the legal sources for security rights and the general attitude of member states towards security. Also important are the substantive aspects concerning the regulation of security rights, such as publicity, global security and the status of security in the event of the debtor's insolvency.

Sources of regulation

Since most continental countries adhere to the principle of a numerus clausus of proprietary rights, legislation is the most important and, strictly speaking, the only legitimate source of rules on proprietary security rights.[3] Over the past 200 years, since the Code Napoléon of 1804, all the civil codes of continental Europe have regulated pledges. Nevertheless, with the exception of the most recent European code, the Dutch Civil Code of 1992,[4] all the codes enacted in the nineteenth and twentieth centuries dealt only with the possessory pledge. Rules relating to non-possessory pledges could only be found in special statutes, enacted in the course of time, usually on the impetus of special pressure groups. As a result rules relating to non-possessory pledges have tended to have a very narrow scope of application, often dealing only with a specific, small item, such as security for the purchase price of motor vehicles, or of machinery, or security for credit to farmers.

Of particular interest are the approaches of France and Spain which illustrate two extremes of approach in dealing with non-possessory security. In France more than a dozen special statutes have been enacted over the past 140 years, mostly with a terminology of their own and special regimes for publicity. Some of these statutes dealt with purchase money security (for the acquisition of industrial installations or of motor vehicles or generally with retention of title), but most deal with security for general credits, such as the financing of small enterprises, oil supplies, the production of films, agricultural activities, security in 'professional' claims (receivables), etc.[5] At the other

2 A useful general survey is offered by P. R. Wood *Comparative Law of Security Interests and Title Finance* (London: Sweet & Maxwell, 2nd edn, 2007). Note also Campbell (ed.), *International Secured Transactions* (New York, 2003), 2 vols, loose-leaf.

3 The American term 'security interest' as used in Article 9 of the Uniform Commercial Code (UCC) is not used by continental legislators, nor by legal writers. An 'interest' is not regarded as equivalent to a fully-fledged right.

4 See Book 3 of the Dutch Civil Code 1992 which contains rules on both the possessory and the non-possessory pledge; note arts 3:236–3:259.

5 A broad survey of the relevant French rules is given by M. Gdanski 'Taking security in France' in M. Bridge and R. Stevens (eds), *Cross-Border Security and Insolvency* (Oxford: Oxford University Press, 2001), pp. 59–89. Most of the special statutes were integrated in 2002 into two 'new' codes: the new version of the Commercial Code (cf. Code de commerce (2002) arts: L 142-1– 42-5 and 143-1–143-15 (enterprise mortgage); L 522-24–522-37 (warehouse receipts); L 523-1–523-15 (hotel equipment); L 524-1–524-21 (oil stockpiles); L 525-1–525-20 (industrial and commercial equipment); L 621-122 (retention of title). And a new Code monétaire et financier: arts L 313-7–313-11 (leasing); L 313-23–313-29 (assignment and pledge of commercial receivables); and L 431-4–431-6 (financial instruments, especially securities)). Some statutes were integrated into other codes, such as the Rural Code, the Film Code, etc.

A subsequent reform of 2006 has achieved slight additional consolidation by collecting all generally used forms of security into the Civil Code, i.e. retention of title and the non-possessory pledge on motor vehicles (Code civil arts 2351–2353, and arts 2367–2372). For commercial security providers, a new special form was created, the pledge of stock (Code de

extreme is a Spanish statute of 1954 on chattel mortgages and non-possessory pledges which integrates most instruments of non-possessory security.[6] By way of contrast, in both Germany and Austria, although the numerus clausus was recognised as a general principle, the regulatory regimes for non-possessory security were developed almost exclusively by the courts. Due to the lack of legislative intervention in these countries, the courts were left with a free hand in developing the rules relating to what became known in England as 'quasi-security'.[7] In Germany, the courts went particularly far since they did not even attempt to introduce substitute forms of publicity, as was done in Austria. The effects achieved may be illustrated by referring to purchase money security over movables. Here the retention of title to secure the purchase price could be extended horizontally into the buyer's claim for the purchase price against a sub-buyer[8] or into the buyer's products manufactured from the assets (i.e. goods) bought on credit. In both cases, title to future assets of the buyer is conveyed to the seller. The circle of secured claims could be extended even further beyond the claim for the purchase price to include all other claims of the seller against the buyer.[9] In addition, the security transfer of ownership and the security assignment of claims were widely admitted in Germany and used regularly for securing credit granted by banks and other credit institutions. These devices are not confined to the corporate sector and are also available to private parties and consumers.[10] However, it is important to note that the word 'security' is here used merely to distinguish these forms of transfer from absolute transfers, under English law they would be referred to as merely quasi-security interests.

In Austria the German approach has only been followed in relation to simple retention-of-title clauses. If an Austrian seller seeks to extend his title-retention interest to cover proceeds or to other claims against his debtor, then he will have to observe certain rules devised by the courts, providing for limited publicity, such as an entry in the related commercial books.

General approach to security rights

Wood has produced[11] a 'Global Law Map' which charters the attitude of individual countries to security the world over. In relation to Europe, Wood has identified four different approaches to security regulation:

(a) Very friendly to security ('favours security'). In this category he places the United Kingdom, Ireland (and an unidentifiable island in the Baltic).

commerce arts L 527-1–art L 527-11). Rules on proprietary security can now be found in three major codes, the Civil Code, the Commercial Code and the Monetary and Financial Code.

6 See Ley de Hipoteca Mobiliaria y Prenda sin Desplazamiento de Posesión of 16 December 1954 (BOE no 352 of 18 December). However, apart from ship mortgages, retention of title is also (partly) regulated by a special statute.

7 I.e. a contractual arrangement whereby the creditor manipulates title so as to give himself recourse to an asset in the event of his debtor's default, but that arrangement does not operate as a real security i.e. a mortgage, charge, pledge or lien. See further on quasi-security, the chapter by de Lacy in this volume, pp. 4–8.

8 This is achieved by the buyer's assignment to the seller of its future claim for the purchase price against the sub-buyer.

9 This is the equivalent to the English all-sums retention-of-title clause; see *Armour* v. *Thyssen Edelstahlwerke AG* [1991] 2 AC 339.

10 For further treatment, see B. Jaekel 'Outlines of security interests under German law' in op. cit., Bridge and Stevens (eds), fn 5, pp. 91–119.

11 See Phillip Wood *Global Law Maps. World Financial Law* (London: Sweet & Maxwell, 2003), p. 30.

(b) Quite friendly to security ('favourable to security'). In this category he places Scandinavia, Germany and the Netherlands.
(c) Neutral to security ('limits on security'). In this category he places Austria, Belgium, Italy, Spain and Portugal.
(d) Rather hostile to security ('quite unfavourable to security'). In this category he places France.

Although one can generally agree with this division, which produces a useful guide to European approaches to security, two qualifications are needed relative to this endorsement. First, in respect of Germany, I would respectfully disagree with the classification. Germany is roughly in the same category as the United Kingdom in that it clearly favours security, in some respects even more so than English law.[12] Second, the classification of France as hostile to security is dated and seems to be based on an earlier state of French law, it does not seem to reflect the present legal reality. It should be noted, though, that in a recently published version, Wood has introduced a different, more convincing categorisation along the lines of topic-related families of legal systems.[13]

It is necessary to go beyond these general qualifications and focus on three specific aspects of security regulation, namely: publicity; global security; and finally, the status of security in the event of the debtor's insolvency.

Publicity

Where non-possessory security rights have been introduced by statute, the relevant legislation almost always provides for some form of publicity, usually by registration,[14] with the notable exception of transactions involving retention of title. However, most of these registers are not centralised, as in England,[15] but decentralised and under the control of various local or regional administrative authorities. The only major exception to this is Spain. In Spain there is a consolidated text on non-possessory security and, correspondingly, a central registry.

Registration for non-possessory security rights is generally required and justified as a means of publicising what would otherwise be a private act. The classic possessory pledge never had this problem since possession was at all times vested with the creditor and, therefore, the other creditors of the debtor (i.e. the pledgor) could never be misled by the false appearance of wealth that the debtor would otherwise possess. Since publicity is directed towards third parties, it engenders a division between the effects of security rights *inter partes* on the one hand, which is independent of registration; and the effects vis-à-vis third parties, on the other hand, which depends upon registration. Since proprietary rights are generally defined as being effective against all the world, strictly speaking, registration ought to be understood as constitutive of a real right.[16]

As far as the effects of registration are concerned, one doubtful point is the repercussion upon transferees of the encumbered assets. Under the general approach of civil

12 For example in respect of extended retention-of-title clauses.
13 See op. cit., Wood, fn 2, p. 472.
14 A recent remarkable exception is the new version of the Luxembourg Law on Fiduciary Transactions of 27 July 2004, which expressly covers fiduciary security transactions but does not require registration; see article 8 of the Law on Fiduciary Transactions.
15 See: Companies Act 2006, Part 25 in respect of company security interests; Bills of Sale Acts 1878–1890 in respect of non-company security assignments.
16 This is otherwise known as the need for perfection.

law countries, a transferee may acquire full ownership free from any encumbrance, provided either the transferor has a power of disposition or there is transfer of possession to the transferee and the latter is in good faith with respect to the non-existence of encumbrances. The question whether registration can destroy this good faith is not regulated in many states and, where there is some form of regulation there appear to be different approaches adopted by various national courts.

In countries without registration systems where the courts 'invented' non-possessory security rights and where case law still governs there is not the means to publicise security via public registration. The courts could not institute registries when they recognised non-possessory security and, while the legislature might have intervened, this did not happen. This approach is primarily seen in Germany and Austria. Nevertheless, it also applies in part in the Netherlands which, by virtue of its Civil Code of 1992, introduced a new so-called 'silent' non-possessory pledge. The latter non-possessory pledge requires an official 'dating' of the security agreement, unless this is contained in a notarial instrument.[17]

Although the absence of public registers for non-possessory security can be problematic as far as third parties are concerned, it can be justified by the fact that all the instruments of proprietary security created by case law were based upon title. The transfer of title in movables as such does not require registration. As far as retention of title is concerned, registration is not required in almost all continental member states – even in those which require registration for other non-possessory security. One exception is found in Italy for a reservation of title in machines[18] and generally in Spain; in France registration is optional (and if done facilitates the seller's position in the event of the buyer's insolvency).[19]

How have secured creditors generally, and sellers with retention of title in particular, fared in countries without registration systems? Does not the general doctrine of good faith acquisition facilitate loss of the collateral by dispositions of a rogue seller, especially one in financial straits? The German courts have mastered this risk of loss by strongly increasing the requirements for a finding of good faith, at least among merchants. Merchants are expected to know that nowadays most items of major equipment are bought on credit and that the purchased items serve as security. Because of this, transferees have to discharge a high burden in order to prove their good faith.[20] In short, publicity by registration is replaced by a presumption of constructive knowledge of the security right. Nevertheless, it is true to say that the rate of litigation in cases of the buyers' bankruptcies is very high and as a result at least some of the initial saving of cost and time due to non-registration is later lost in litigating with the insolvency administrator.

Global security

A direct instrument of global security – to some degree an equivalent of a comprehensive English floating charge – is the continental enterprise mortgage which is recognised in five European countries – although with remarkable variations.

17 See Dutch Civil Code 1992, article 3:237.

18 See Codice civile article 1524 (2).

19 See Code de commerce (2008) art. L 624–10 – a seller under retention of title is dispensed from proving his title if it has been registered.

20 See F. Quack, *Münchener Kommentar zum Bürgerlichen Gesetzbuch* vol. VI (München: Beck, 3rd edn, 1997) s. 932 no. 35 with case references.

Two types of enterprise mortgage exist, namely the small enterprise mortgage and the big enterprise mortgage. They are distinguished by the amount of the debtor's property that can be subjected to a security. France and Belgium have favoured 'small' enterprise mortgages. In France for example, the collateral is limited to the commercial name and sign, the good will, the lease contract, the equipment and furniture and the intellectual property rights,[21] whereas inventory is excluded for the benefit of unsecured creditors. In Belgium they have been conscious of the same issue but have allowed debtors to encumber up to 50 per cent of the value of the inventory.[22] In Sweden and Finland the so called 'big' enterprise mortgages were introduced in 1984. The scope of these mortgages was unrestricted when they were first introduced; however, bad experiences recently induced both countries to restrict these mortgages to 55 per cent and 50 per cent, respectively, of the value of the encumbered enterprise assets. A parallel can be seen in the UK where measures have recently been taken to reduce the scope of the floating charge.[23]

The status of security in the debtor's insolvency

The acid test of security is, of course, its status and effectiveness in the event of the debtor's insolvency. It is unfortunate that the issue of insolvency was outside the terms of the English Law Commission's review of company security interests.[24] The essence of all real or 'genuine' security rights is that the creditor can only look to the subject matter of the security to realise the debt and no more.[25] After realising the asset, any surplus arising after the debt has been paid, goes to the debtor's insolvency administrator.

However, the situation is different for quasi-security or, more generally, for all security based upon title. Here the creditor having retained title or being the transferee of title is entitled, under general insolvency law, to separate 'its' assets from the insolvent's estate. This also means that the creditor has the right to dispose of these assets as he pleases and to retain all proceeds from any disposition. In continental Europe, this appears to be the general rule for the retention of title. To be more precise, for the simple retention of title, i.e. securing the purchase price of the specific asset in the bankrupt estate. While France extends this basic rule to the claim for the purchase price arising from a sub-sale by the first buyer,[26] Germany regards any extension of the retention of title beyond the basic, i.e. the simple retention, into proceeds or products as equivalent to a mere security right. Therefore, the proceeds resulting from any extensions of the retention of title become part of the insolvent's estate, the secured creditor being only entitled to preferred satisfaction.[27]

An even stronger diminution has been imposed, first by the German courts and now confirmed by the legislature, upon security transfers of title. They are treated in insolvency like mere security rights.[28]

21 See Code de commerce (2002) art. L 142-2.
22 See Law of 25 October 1919 on charging an enterprise, discounting and the charging of a bill, art. 2(2).
23 See generally Enterprise Act 2002, Part 10.
24 See Law Commission Consultation Paper No. 176 *Company Security Interests*, above fn 1, para. 2.60.
25 In England this is known as the equity of redemption.
26 See Code de commerce (2008) art. L 624-18 first sentence.
27 See Insolvency Code of 1999, s. 51 no. 1.
28 See Insolvency Code 1999, s. 51 no. 1.

The case for a European harmonisation of security rights

The preceding discussion has given the reader a general survey of the major divergences between the various national regimes in Europe in relation to non-possessory security. The question now arises as to whether the diverse treatment of security rights by member states is compatible with one of the major goals of the EU, that is, to constitute an internal market. There appear to be two major impediments to a single internal market in relation to security rights, namely a lack of equality in economic conditions and, second, the problem of transfers of encumbered moveable goods between member states.

Equality of economic conditions

The starting point for raising doubts about compatibility with the internal market is a purely economic consideration. It is a commercial truism that the price for credit (i.e. the interest rate charged for the advance of credit) is to no small measure influenced by the quality of any security right the debtor is able to give to his creditor in order to secure the repayment of that credit. On this basis it has been argued that if legal factors such as the diversities of the various national regimes for security rights create an economic imbalance between the member countries, the EU should step in to redress the imbalance by way of harmonisation of the diverging laws.[29]

However, this argument has its limitations. It is true that it is one of the main objectives of the EU to harmonise the national legal rules, insofar as it is necessary for the functioning of the internal market;[30] and in undertaking this task, the Community is to strive at abolishing inequalities.[31] However, for actions that are outside the exclusive legislative jurisdiction of the Community, the latter can only act, according to the principle of subsidiarity, if, and insofar as, the envisaged purposes cannot be achieved at member state level.[32] This latter condition is certainly not met since each member state is free to adapt its national rules on security rights as it sees fit.

The intra-European transborder movement of encumbered assets

More relevant for the proper functioning of the internal market is the issue of the international mobility of the assets which are subject to security rights. The proper functioning of the internal market requires that there be no obstacles to, *inter alia*, the free movement of goods and capital among member states.[33]

Unfortunately, at the present time there is no universal free movement of goods between member states where those goods are subject to security rights. This is not due to different conflict-of-laws rules. On the contrary, all member states recognise the basic conflicts rule of the *lex rei sitae* (or the *lex situs*). Unfortunately, it is precisely the faithful application of this uniformly adopted rule that contributes to this unsatisfactory result. The *lex situs* conflicts rule means that in any case where encumbered assets cross

29 See, for example, S. Sanchez Lorenzo *Garantías reales en el comercio internacional* (Madrid: Editorial Civitas, 1993), pp. 257–64.
30 See Treaty of Amsterdam, Article 3(1)(h).
31 See Treaty of Amsterdam, Article 3(2).
32 See Treaty of Amsterdam, Article 5(2).
33 See Treaty of Amsterdam, Article 3(1)(c).

state borders, two national regimes are successively called upon to govern. In the first place it is the law of the country from where the goods come (the country of exportation, E); but, after having crossed the border to the country of importation (I), it is the law of I which governs proprietary rights in the imported goods. If, under the law of E, a valid security right has been created, it depends upon the law of I whether it is willing to recognise and give effect to the proprietary security right created in E.

Case law experience demonstrates that the willingness of a state to recognise security depends upon the security regime of that importing state. If this state has a narrow security regime, e.g. by demanding an officially dated security agreement (France, Italy and Spain) or registration of the security right (such as France in many cases and Spain or England in certain cases), security rights, although validly created in another member state, will not be recognised unless they comply with the substantive and formal requirements of import state I. This means that security rights created in a member state with a liberal security system are very often denied recognition in an importing state with a strict regime. This is particularly the experience of German exporters.[34] On the other hand, the more liberal the security regime of the importing state, the easier and more generous is the recognition of imported security rights.[35]

These divergent results are achieved despite the fact that the terms of the relevant conflicts rule directing the application of the *lex situs*, are identical. This shows that it is not the conflicts rule that causes these divergent results. Rather, it is the diversity of the national provisions which creates the obstacles to the proper functioning of the internal market in this field.

It follows, therefore, that the EU has jurisdiction to remove these obstacles to the proper functioning of the internal market.[36] The EU has exercised this jurisdiction on one occasion when it enacted Article 4 of the Late Payments Directive. That provision requires the mutual recognition of retention of title in goods validly encumbered in one member state which are later brought into another member state.[37] It is true, though, that this provision takes the form of a conflicts rule, since today all member states recognise that simple retentions of title are effective in the buyer's insolvency.[38]

Whatever form a future rule may take, commercial practice in the intra-European border-crossing trade urgently requires a new and uniform remedy to promote

34 See the author's survey in von Bar and Drobnig (ed.), *The Interaction of Contract Law and Tort and Property Law in Europe* (Munich: Sellier European Law Publishers, 2004), pp. 342–9 covering case law in Austria, Denmark, France, Germany, Italy, the Netherlands, Spain, Sweden and the UK. See, for example the position in: France: Cass civ 3 May 1973, Clunet 1974, 74; Cass civ 8 July 1969, Clunet 1970, 916; Cass req 24 May 1933, S. 1935.I.257. Insofar as these decisions affected retention of title transactions, they are no longer relevant since French recognition of the effectiveness of such devices in the buyer's insolvency by virtue of the Insolvency Act 1985 and subsequent liberalisations of this regime. Italy: Cass 21 June 1974, n 1860, Rivista di diritto internazionale privato e processuale 1975, 773. Spain: Provincial Appellate Court Barcelona 13 Sept 1989, Revista Española de Derecho Internacional 1990 I 644; Provincial Appellate Court Castellón 7 July 1997, Revista Española de Derecho Internacional 1998 I 318.

35 See, for example: Germany: BGH 20 March 1963, BGHZ [official collection] 39, 173, 174 ss., IPRspr. 1962/63 no. 60; BGH 2 Feb. 1966, BGHZ 45, 95, IPRspr. 1966/67 no. 54. UK: *Armour* v. *Thyssen Edelstahlwerke AG* [1991] AC 339 (HL).

36 This follows from the Treaty of Amsterdam, Articles 3(1)(c) and 5(2).

37 See Directive 2000/35/EC of 29 June 2000 on combating late payment in commercial transactions, OJ 2000 L 200, 35.

38 Belgium was the last member state to recognise the effect of a retention of title in the buyer's insolvency; see Bankruptcy Act 1997, Article 101(2); note also Article 108.

certainty of outcome in security transactions.[39] If and where security is sought in these transactions, at present exporters are exposed to a depressing choice: either to obtain expensive and time-consuming legal advice relative to the situation in the country of importation – or to ignore the potential risk and hope that all will go well. Neither of these alternatives complies with what a merchant should expect from a true internal market.

A growing recognition of this problem has led a group of European-minded lawyers to start work on generating proposals to remedy this situation.

Basic issues of European rules on security in movables

It is now desirable that there should be uniform rules operating throughout Europe for security in movables, especially where they involve export via intra-European border-crossing commerce. Work on this issue has started only recently by the Hamburg Sub-Group.[40] The first step the Sub-Group took was to obtain a survey of the legal situation in all the 15 old member states. The Sub-Group has just finished the second and more difficult phase – to consider possible solutions on a European level.

Although the work of the Sub-Group is not yet quite finished,[41] it is appropriate to convey some of the first fruits of their preliminary thinking on this issue.

A comprehensive security right

The only way to overcome the diverse forms of security found in EU states and the discrepancies between these forms, is to adopt the American approach found in Article 9 of the Uniform Commercial Code (UCC). The situation in present-day Europe closely resembles that with which the drafters of the American uniform model code were confronted in the middle of the twentieth century, with different regulations for security interests operating throughout the US states at that time. To solve this problem, commercial interests in the US promoted a uniform law on personal property security assignments which was then adopted by the various states that make up the US Article 9 of the UCC was drafted by distilling the essential ideas underlying all the different forms of security that had been developed by the individual states, ranging from the chattel mortgage, conditional sale and receivables financing to the trust receipt and factoring.

We now see a similar situation and face the same challenge in Europe. However, in Europe the problems are on a much greater scale in view of:

(a) the greater degree of substantive and formal differences between the legal regimes for proprietary security rights in the member states;

39 This was the clearly prevailing view of stakeholders, as reported in op. cit., von Bar and Drobnig, fn 34, paras 527–9.

40 This work is being undertaken by a subgroup based in Hamburg of the Study Group for a European Civil Code directed by Professor von Bar in Osnabrück.

41 The rules elaborated by the Working Group constitute Book IX of the Common Frame of Reference, cf. C. von Bar, E. Clive and H. Schulte-Nölke (eds.), *Principles, Definitions and Model Rules of European Private Law. Draft Common Frame of Reference.* Outline Edition (München: Sellier European Law Publishers 2009) at pp. 447–99.

(b) the divergences also in the related fields of law, especially the legal regimes of general property, contract, executions and insolvency;
(c) linguistic and consequent terminological divergences.

While a comprehensive unitary security right ought to be the starting point, one should not be dogmatic and exclude any deviation from or variation of it. One exception that comes to mind, because of its great economic importance, is security for purchase money credit.

Special role of purchase-money security

One major doubt relating to a new unified approach concerns security for purchase money advances by creditors. The typical forms of this security are based upon title, for example retention of title by sellers under a contract for the sale of goods, or hire-purchase or finance leasing. The Americans and their followers in Canada and New Zealand converted retention of title into the grant of a security interest by the buyer in the sold goods, ownership of which, for security purposes, was considered as passing to the buyer upon delivery to him. Under this approach, retention of title is downgraded to the status of a non-possessory security interest rather than an ownership right based on the seller's title.[42] Likewise, finance leasing, or even leasing generally, is for most purposes treated as a security right.

Under our new scheme of recognising purchase money security no change in the present situation is involved regarding the position of the seller and the purchaser. The seller remains the owner of the goods sold until full payment of the purchase price. At the same time, a useful clarification and simplification of the purchaser's legal situation is achieved. The purchaser is now effectively treated as the conditional future owner of the goods and this allows him to grant security over those goods, although this security will be of second rank (i.e. subject to the seller's title). The buyer's execution and insolvency creditors also benefit because they can more easily enforce their (secondary) rights against the purchased goods.

Regarding the position of the seller in the event of the buyer's insolvency care has to be taken to preserve the seller's status. Under current law, subject to the insolvency administrator's right to perform the sales contract by payment of the outstanding purchase price, the seller as owner is free to reclaim the goods. The seller is also free, in most countries, to dispose of the goods and keep the full purchase price. In most cases such sellers are merchants dealing in this type of goods and as a result are more competent to resell and achieve a better price in reselling the goods than the insolvency administrator would be.

Since hire-purchase and financial leasing perform the same functions as retention of title under a sales contract, all these acquisition finance devices should be treated according to the same rules.

For reasons of economic policy, the special position of these kinds of acquisition financers should be retained under a new system. Trade credit is an important alternative or at least supplement to bank credit. It is vital that the seller's and the equivalent financers' privileged position in the buyer's insolvency be retained and purchase money security not be treated and relegated to the status of ordinary security.

For the same reasons, conflicts between security for purchase money and that for bank credit should be resolved in favour of the holder of the purchase money security. If the proceeds of goods sold under retention of title are receivables which

42 See generally UCC Article 9-107.

had already been assigned in advance by the buyer/debtor to his bank, the seller under a prolonged retention of title extended to the buyer's proceeds resulting from a resale by this buyer against a second buyer should prevail, even though the security assignment to him is later in time. This is the current practice in German courts and is today no longer controversial – although the academic reasons for this result are not easy to adduce.[43]

Enterprise mortgage

The enterprise mortgage, including its English variation, the floating charge, is difficult to justify because in its original, unabridged form it tends to give total control over the debtor's estate to the secured creditor. It is significant that in all countries which originally had allowed coverage of all assets by security interests recent reforms have been enacted to curb, and limit, the ambit of such security.[44] In that reduced form the instrument may appear to be acceptable, since it may play a useful role as an instrument securing a continuous stream of credit covering the changing assets of a going concern. Nevertheless, we have come to the conclusion that its disadvantages and risks are greater than its utility. Moreover, the same results can easily be achieved by recourse to the ordinary means of security. We allow all kinds of assets to be encumbered, present as well as future ones. Under this approach there does not seem to be any need to have recourse to an enterprise mortgage, and even less to the peculiar form of a 'floating charge' with all its practical problems of proper delimitation from a fixed charge.

Publicity

The continental member states are evenly divided between advocates and sceptics of publicity. Most countries that have legislated on security rights have only accepted non-possessory security forms upon condition of some form of publicity – as a substitute for the debtor's dispossession of the pledged assets in a possessory pledge. However, there have been major exceptions to this principle, especially for security instruments based upon the creditor's title, such as the retention of title.

On the other hand, modern forms of registration using electronic techniques have greatly facilitated access to the registers, both for the parties of a security agreement and for third parties. Electronic registration and electronic searches of such registers have become possible. These new techniques can drastically reduce the delay and cost of registration and of searching. Therefore, most people now accept that registration is the way forward in promoting a unified and objective system regulating security. In keeping with the European character and purpose of our proposed substantive rules we would propose a central electronic European register. In this, no documents can be filed but merely a notice on the creation of a security right with the obligation of the registered creditor to reply to queries concerning the existence and extent of its security right.

43 See further P. Buelow *Recht der Kreditsicherheiten* (Heidelberg: C F Mueller, 7th edn, 2007), nos 1649–1673. For a UK treatment of the purchase money security interest, see de Lacy 'The purchase money security interest: a company charge conundrum?' [1991] Lloyd's Maritime and Commercial Law Quarterly 531.

44 See above, pp. 448–49.

Conclusions

This chapter has surveyed some of the major divergences among the different national systems of security rights over movables in Europe. The different treatment of security rights has had a negative impact on the European internal market, especially in the context of export sales. This leads us to conclude that it is now necessary to create a new unified regime of security rights in movables, whether tangible or intangible throughout Europe. This is the only way to overcome the present divergences among the existing national regimes' regulation of non-possessory security rights.

However, in order to strengthen the intra-European cross-border trade in equipment and merchandise, it is also necessary to establish a unified regime of security rights for financing the acquisition of such goods by sellers and lessors. Security for acquisition financing must in some respects differ from the aforementioned general European security regime since sellers grant acquisition credits in the interest of promoting their sales. Because of this, sellers usually do not charge interest or, where they do, it is at a lesser rate of interest than that of the main financial institutions. European level recognition of retention-of-title devices in cross-border transactions indicates that European law makers have recognised the special function and position of security for acquisition financing. These considerations also apply to acquisition by means of financial leasing.

Finally, in view of the special economic and legal aspects of security for acquisition financing and the widespread practice of demanding payment 30 days after delivery of the purchased goods, these instruments should enjoy a grace period of 35 days for registration. Of course, the unregistered seller or its financer is subject to the increased risk of an unauthorised disposition by the buyer or indeed, of the buyer's insolvency.

It is to be hoped that it will not be too long before we see fundamental reform throughout Europe to produce a unified regime. In the meantime, we should look for progress at member state level. The law of non-possessory security is in need of reform in almost all relevant aspects. In the UK it is most unfortunate that it appears as if fundamental reform of non-possessory security rights will not be forthcoming, in the immediate future at any rate. The passage of the Companies Act 2006, Part 25 governing company charge security interests seems to represent the end of the reform process started by the English Law Commission in 2002. It is most unfortunate that the work of the Law Commission in its first paper of 2002[45] was not taken forward. It may well be that in order for the UK to see fundamental reforms to this area European-inspired measures will become the ultimate driver that gains acceptance.[46]

45 See Consultation Paper No. 164, above fn 1, p. 5 para. 1.16 where the Law Commission's terms of reference are stated in the widest form such that one might reasonably have thought (at that time) that fundamental reform measures would have been forthcoming. Unfortunately, this was not to be case and its Final Report, above fn 1, of 2005 was a rather limited document whose limited recommendations in respect of the reform of company charges were not adopted by the government when passing the Companies Act 2006. However, although the Law Commission were disappointed that the government did not adopt their recommendations, they have not given up hope that they might be adopted in the future; see Law Commission *Annual Report 2008–09* (2009) HC 811 at p. 64 para A50.

46 See also House of Lords European Union Committee Report *European Contract Law: the Draft Common Frame of Reference* 12th Report of Session 2008–09 (2009) HL Paper 95.

14 Key objectives and fundamental policies of the UNCITRAL Legislative Guide on Secured Transactions

*Spiros Bazinas**

Introduction

The UNCITRAL Legislative Guide on Secured Transactions (the 'Guide') was prepared by the United Nations Commission on International Trade Law ('UNCITRAL' or the 'Commission').[1]

The Guide contains commentary and legislative recommendations on all issues that need to be addressed in a modern law on security rights in all types of movable asset, tangible or intangible (including goods, equipment inventory, receivables,[2]

* The views expressed in this chapter are the personal views of the author and do not reflect the views of the United Nations or UNCITRAL. This paper is based on an article published in International Secured Transactions, Oceana Publications, Inc., Dobbs Ferry, NY, 2009.

1 For a brief description of UNCITRAL and its work, see http://www.uncitral.org/en-index.htm. Professionals both in the private and the public sector who are not familiar with UNCITRAL and its work find it often strange that a UN body, a subsidiary of the UN General Assembly, is involved in the unification and harmonisation of the law of international trade. The explanation is simple. Economic development is the other side of peace and stability (presumably, the main mission of the UN), and unification, harmonisation or modernisation of the law of international trade is a corner stone (a necessary but not sufficient condition) of economic development. One should also keep in mind that the law of international trade is broadly understood to include both national and international law, both civil and commercial law, both substantive and private international law and even public law to the extent that it covers arbitration (which is part of civil procedure law) and public procurement of goods and services. With this mandate, UNCITRAL plays a key role in the efforts of the UN to promote the rule of law (see GA resolution 62/70 of 6 December 2007 on the rule of law at the national and international levels).

2 The treatment of receivables in the Guide is consistent with the United Nations Convention on the Assignment of Receivables in International Trade (New York, 2001). For a discussion of the Convention, see Spiros V. Bazinas, 'International Receivables', in *Secured Finance Transactions, Key Assets and Emerging Markets* (Consulting Editor: Paul U. Ali, 2007, Globe Business Publishing Ltd). For a comparison of the Convention, the Unidroit Convention on International Factoring (Ottawa, 1988), the Principles of European Contract Law and the Unidroit Principles of International Commercial Contracts, see Claudia Rudolf, *Einheitsrecht für Internationale Forderungsabtretungen*, Mohr Siebeck, Tübingen, 2006. For a comparative law discussion of the issue of the third-party effectiveness of an assignment of receivables, see Stephan Bode, *Die Wirksamkeit einer Forderungsübertragung gegenüber Dritten*, Peter Lang, Frankfurt am Main, 2007.

letters of credit, bank accounts, negotiable instruments, negotiable documents and intellectual property).

The Guide does not deal with security rights in high-value mobile equipment, such as aircraft, railway rolling stock, space objects and ships, insofar as such assets are covered in other national law or international agreement (see recommendation 4, subparagraph (a)). Furthermore, it does not deal with intellectual property to the extent of any inconsistency with intellectual property law (see recommendation 4, subparagraph (b)). However, with respect to security rights in intellectual property, UNCITRAL is preparing an asset-specific supplement to the Guide.[3]

Finally, the Guide does not deal with securities, payment rights arising under financial contracts governed by netting agreements other than receivables owed on the termination of all outstanding transactions, and payment rights arising under foreign exchange transactions (see recommendation 4, subparagraphs (c) and (d)). It should also be noted that the Guide does not deal with security rights in immovable property, but applies to security rights in attachments to immovable property and may affect immovable property to the extent that the treatment of a security right in a receivable secured by a mortgage may affect the treatment of rights in the immovable property that is subject to the mortgage (see recommendation 5).

The notion of 'security right' includes all types of right created by agreement to secure payment or other performance of an obligation, regardless of the form of the transaction or the terminology used by the parties and thus includes assignments of receivables for security purposes, retention-of-title rights and financial lease rights.[4] Security rights may secure all types of obligation, present or future, determined or determinable, including fluctuating obligations and obligations described in a generic way. They may encumber specific assets or all of the assets of a grantor, present and future, including a changing pool of assets. Security rights may be created or acquired by any legal or natural person, including a consumer. However, rights of consumers under consumer-protection law cannot be affected (see recommendation 2).[5]

Following the approach of the United Nations Convention on the Assignment of Receivables in International Trade (the 'Receivables Convention'), the Guide addresses to some extent issues relating to outright transfers of receivables although they are not secured transactions. The Guide also addresses applicable law issues, as well as the treatment of security rights in the case of insolvency in a comprehensive way consistent with the UNCITRAL Legislative Guide on Insolvency Law (the 'UNCITRAL Insolvency Guide').[6]

The Guide follows a modern approach to secured transactions that can be described as integrated and functional approach, relying on a notice-based public registry for third-party and priority effects, and is reflected in several national and international texts on security interests in movable assets.[7] In this way, the Guide

3 See http://www.uncitral.org/uncitral/en/commission/working_groups/6Security_Interests.html.

4 The Guide uses the term 'security right' rather than the term 'security interest' as it is clearer and closer to the term used in other languages (e.g. droit des sûretés).The priority chapter deals with all possible priority conflicts between a security right and the right of a competing claimant whether created by agreement, operation of law or a court decision.

5 The electronic copy of the Guide is available at http://www.uncitral.org/pdf/english/texts/security-lg/e/final-final.clean.01-07-09.pdf. It is expected that the paper copy will become available in October 2009.

6 See http://www.uncitral.org/uncitral/en/uncitral_texts/insolvency/2004Guide.html.

7 See pp. 458–60 and pp. 463–64.

becomes the basic text to be referred to in the modernisation and harmonisation efforts relating to secured transactions law.[8] This essay will discuss briefly the structure of the Guide and the background of the Guide respectively and also discusses the key objectives and the fundamental policies of the Guide.[9] Finally the essay contains some preliminary conclusions about the potential impact of the Guide on the modernisation and harmonisation of secured transactions law.

Structure of the Guide

The Guide contains an introduction (with terminology, examples of financing practices covered in the Guide, and a discussion of the key objectives and the fundamental policies of the Guide, as well as of ways in which the Guide could be implemented). It also contains twelve chapters (scope; creation; third-party effectiveness; the registry system; priority; rights and obligations of the parties; rights and obligations of third-party obligors; enforcement; acquisition financing; conflict of laws; transition and insolvency) with commentary and recommendations. In addition, it contains in annex I the terminology and a consolidated set of the recommendations.

Both the commentary and the recommendations contain a general part and an asset-specific part. The general part applies to all types of asset generally, while the asset-specific part modifies the general part with respect to specific types of asset. Thus, each state can use the parts of the Guide that it needs most without necessarily having to adopt both the general and all the asset-specific recommendations of the Guide in their entirety.

The commentary discusses various workable approaches and their comparable advantages and disadvantages and explains the recommendations, which are very detailed and specifically deal with each issue to be addressed in a secured transactions law. As a result, the Guide combines the certainty of the recommendations with the flexibility of the commentary, and can be thus used by states with different legal systems and at different levels of economic development. To link the general key objectives with the specific recommendations, the Guide contains in the introduction a discussion of the fundamental policies of an effective and efficient secured transactions law.

The Guide recommends a functional approach to secured transactions, which was originally taken in Article 9 of the Uniform Commercial Code.[10] At the same time, the Guide builds on several other national laws, draft laws or reports, such as the Canadian Personal Property Security Acts[11] and the law of Quebec,[12] the recent secured transactions law of New Zealand,[13] the current draft secured transactions law

8 For the inevitability of the modernisation of secured transactions laws, see Boris Kozolchyk and John M. Wilson, *The Organization of American States Model Inter-American Law on Secured Transactions* (http://www.natlaw.com/seminar/doc13.pdf).

9 For a discussion of key policy issues of the Guide, see Spiros V. Bazinas, *Security interests in bank accounts under the UNCITRAL draft Legislative Guide on Secured Transactions, Insolvency and Restrucuring International*, Vol. 1, No. 1, May 2007, pp. 19–28.

10 Discussed in the main text below.

11 For example, for the Ontario PPSA, see http://www.e-laws.gov.on.ca/html/statutes/english/elaws_statutes_90p10_e.htm.

12 See http://www.justice.gouv.qc.ca/English/sujets/glossaire/code-civil-a.htm.

13 See http://www.legislation.govt.nz/act/public/1999/0126/latest/DLM45900.html.

of Australia,[14] and the report of the English Law Commission on Company Security Interests.[15]

Most importantly, the Guide builds on uniform laws prepared by UNCITRAL and other international organisations, such as the Unidroit Convention on International Factoring,[16] the Model Law on Secured Transactions, completed by the European Bank for Reconstruction and Development ('EBRD') in 1994;[17] the EBRD 'Core principles for a secured transactions law', completed in 1997;[18] the Organization for the Harmonization of Business Law in Africa's Uniform Act Organizing Securities, prepared in 1997;[19] the studies on insolvency and secured transactions law reform in Asia, and the Guide to Movables Registries, prepared by ADB;[20] the Receivables Convention, adopted in 2001;[21] the Convention on International Interests in Mobile Equipment, adopted in 2001, and the relevant protocols thereto;[22] the Organization of American States (OAS) Model Inter-American Law on Secured Transactions, prepared in 2002;[23] the UNCITRAL Insolvency Guide, completed in 2004;[24] the Convention on the Law Applicable to Certain Rights in Respect of Securities Held with an Intermediary, adopted by the Hague Conference on Private International Law in 2002 (the 'Hague Securities Convention');[25] and the Unidroit draft convention on substantive rules regarding intermediated securities.[26]

As the functional approach to secured transactions supported by a notice-filing system is a common theme in most modern secured transactions laws, the assertion that the Guide is a direct descendant of Article 9 of the Uniform Commercial Code[27] or that the Guide has been unduly influenced by American law[28] underestimates the impact of all these texts on comparative secured transactions law in general and, therefore, on the Guide in particular. In addition, such assertions underestimate the trends in the modernisation and harmonisation of the law of secured transactions all over the world, including in European Union countries with highly developed

14 See http://www.ag.gov.au/pps.
15 See http://www.lawcom.gov.uk/docs/lc296.pdf.
16 See http://www.unidroit.org/english/conventions/1988factoring/main.htm.
17 Model Law on Secured Transactions, published by the European Bank for Reconstruction and Development in London in 1994.
18 See http://www.ebrd.com/country/sector/law/st/core/model/core.htm.
19 See http://www.ohada.com/textes.php?categorie=458.
20 See *Law and Policy Reform at the Asian Development Bank 2000*, Volume I (April 2000), *Law and Policy Reform at the Asian Development Bank 2000*, Volume II (December 2000) and *Law and Policy Reform at the Asian Development Bank–A Guide to Movables Registries* (December 2002).
21 United Nations publication, Sales No. E.04.V.14.
22 Cape Town Convention and Aircraft Protocol, Acts and Proceedings of the Cape Town Diplomatic Conference, 2006, International Institute for the Unification of Private Law (UNIDROIT), Rome.
23 See http://www.oas.org/dil/cidip-vi-securedtransactions_eng.htm.
24 See fn. 2 above.
25 *Proceedings of the Nineteenth Session* (2002), Tomo II, Securities, HCCH, 2006.
26 See http://www.unidroit.org/english/workprogramme/study078/main.htm.
27 Philip Wood, *Comparative Law of Security Interests and Title Finance* (London: Sweet and Maxwell; 2007) at chapter 38, pp.38–103.
28 See Gerard McCormack's research hypothesis in http://www.law.leeds.ac.uk/research/projects/internationalisation-secured-credit-law.php. The question should be whether the Guide provides useful guidance to states and not whether it has been influenced by one or the other law, as historically and today with the development of international markets every law is influenced by foreign and international law.

economies like England.[29] Moreover, such assertions about the influence of Article 9 UCC on the Guide fail to take sufficiently into account the flexibility of the commentary of the Guide and the nature of the Guide as 'soft law'. They also fail to take into account that some of the most important chapters of the Guide have very little to do with Article 9 UCC. For example, the chapter dealing with the treatment of security rights in insolvency follows the principles of the UNCITRAL Insolvency Guide, the chapter on acquisition financing contains a non-unitary approach that is closer to civil law, the chapter on conflict of laws has been prepared in close cooperation with the Permanent Bureau of the Hague Conference on Private International Law and the Guide's recommendations relating to security rights in receivables are based on the provisions of the Receivables Convention.

Background of the Guide

As mentioned above, the Guide is based on a number of national and international legislative texts on secured transactions, including UNCITRAL's earlier project on security interests and the Receivables Convention. With respect to UNCITRAL's earlier security interests' project, it should be noted that, after almost a decade of preparatory work, at its thirteenth session, in 1980, the Commission considered a study that set out the issues to be considered in the preparation of a model law on security interests and made a number of recommendations.[30]

At its thirteenth session, the Commission decided to defer its consideration of the topic of security interests. The reasons given were: that the worldwide unification of the law of security interests was 'in all likelihood unattainable' in view of the complexity of the matter; and the higher priority accorded to other topics.[31] With respect to the complexity of the matter, reference was made to the different understanding in the various legal systems as to the concepts of security interests and retention of title. Reference was also made to the difficulty of unification or harmonisation of bankruptcy law, which would be necessary for a secured transactions law to be effective.[32] A suggestion was made at that session that 'the Commission might wish to await the outcome of the work on retention of title by the Council of Europe and on factoring by the International Institute for the Unification of Private Law (UNIDROIT)'.[33]

Several years later, the Council of Europe discontinued its work on reservation of title[34] and UNIDROIT completed its work on factoring with the adoption of the UNIDROIT Convention on International Factoring at a diplomatic conference in Ottawa in 1988.[35]

29 For the recommendations of the English Law Reform Commission, see footnote 15 above. For a critical discussion of English secured transactions law, see Roy Goode, *Commercial Law*, 3rd edn (London: Penguin Books; 2004) at Part Four, pp. 577–690.

30 See note by the Secretariat, A/CN.9/186 (http://www.uncitral.org/uncitral/en/uncitral_texts/security_past.html)

31 See Report of UNCITRAL on the work of its thirteenth session (1980), A/35/17, paras. 26–28 (http://www.uncitral.org/uncitral/en/commission/sessions/13th.html).

32 Ibid., 26.

33 Ibid., para. 27.

34 CDCJ (84) 55, para. 59.

35 See http://www.unidroit.org/english/conventions/1988factoring/main.htm.

The suggestion for work by the Commission on the assignment of receivables was made at a Congress on International Trade Law which was held in New York in conjunction with the Commission's twenty-fifth session, in 1992.[36] After considering three studies between 1992 and 1995, the Commission decided to prepare a text on the assignment of receivables in view of the economic importance of receivables and the lack of modern legislation on assignment of receivables, which creates a number of problems for international receivables financing transactions.[37] The Commission completed its work on this topic in 2001 with the adoption of a draft Convention on the Assignment of Receivables in International Trade. The Convention was adopted and opened for signature by states with General Assembly resolution 56/81 of 12 December 2001.[38] The main objective of the Convention is to facilitate receivables financing with a view to promoting access to credit at more affordable rates.[39]

The first step towards the preparation of a text on security interests in movable assets was made when the Commission, after considering two reports,[40] one at its thirty-third session, in 2000,[41] and another at its thirty-fourth session, in 2001,[42] decided to refer to Working Group VI (Security Interests) the task of developing an efficient legal regime for security interests in goods involved in a commercial activity, including inventory. At its thirty-fifth session, in 2002, the Commission confirmed that the mandate of the Working Group should be interpreted broadly to ensure an appropriately flexible work product, which should take the form of a legislative guide.[43]

Working Group VI considered the first draft of the Guide in May 2002. The work of the Working Group was developed through 12 one-week sessions,[44] the final session taking place in February 2007. In addition to representatives of the 60 states members of the Commission, representatives of many other states and a number of international organisations, both governmental and non-governmental, participated actively in the preparatory work.[45] Working Group VI closely collaborated with

36 See *Uniform Commercial Law in the Twenty-First Century, Proceedings of the Congress of the United Nations Commission on International Trade Law* (New York, 18–22 May 1992), iv and 156, United Nations publication, Sales No. E.94.V.14.

37 See documents A/CN.9/378/Add.3; A/CN.9/397 and A/CN.9/412 (http://www.uncitral.org/uncitral/en/uncitral_texts/payments/2001Convention_receivables_travaux.html), as well as the report of UNCITRAL on the work of its thirty-fifth session, (A/56/17), para. 358 (http://www.uncitral.org/uncitral/en/commission/sessions/35th.html).

38 See http://www.uncitral.org/uncitral/en/uncitral_texts/payments/2001Convention_receivables.html

39 See Preamble of the Convention.

40 A/CN.9/475 and A/CN.9/496.

41 *Official Records of the General Assembly, Fifty-fifth Session, Supplement No. 17* (A/55/17), paras. 459 and 463

42 Ibid., *Fifty-sixth Session, Supplement No. 17* and corrigendum (A/56/17 and Corr.3), paras. 351 and 358.

43 Ibid., *Fifty-seventh Session, Supplement No. 17* (A/57/17), paras. 202–204.

44 The reports of the Working Group on its work during these 12 sessions are contained in documents A/CN.9/512, A/CN.9/531, A/CN.9/532, A/CN.9/543, A/CN.9/549, A/CN.9/570, A/CN.9/574, A/CN.9/588, A/CN.9/593, A/CN.9/603, A/CN.9/617 and A/CN.9/620. During these sessions, the Working Group considered documents A/CN.9/WG.VI/WP.1–31. These reports of the Working Group were considered by the Commission from its thirty-fifth to fortieth sessions.

45 Those organisations included UNIDROIT, the Hague Conference on Private International Law, the World Bank, the International Monetary Fund, the European Commission, the International Chamber of Commerce, the International Bar Association, the International

Working Group V (insolvency) in order to ensure coordination of the treatment of security interests in insolvency with the UNCITRAL Insolvency Guide. [46]

In addition, Working Group VI closely cooperated with the Permanent Bureau of the Hague Conference on Private International Law in the preparation of the chapter on conflict of laws. Moreover, Working Group VI coordinated with the International Institute on Private International Law (UNIDROIT) to avoid overlap with the Convention on International Interests in Mobile Equipment and UNIDROIT's work on security interests in securities.[47]

At its thirty-ninth session, in 2006, the Commission considered and approved in principle the substance of the recommendations of the Guide.[48] The final negotiations were held during the fortieth session of UNCITRAL, held in Vienna from 25 June to 12 July 2007 (first part),[49] and from 10 to 14 December 2007 (second part),[50] and the Guide was adopted by consensus on 14 December 2007. Subsequently, the General Assembly adopted resolution 63/121 of 11 December 2008. In this resolution, the General Assembly expressed its appreciation to UNCITRAL for the completion and adoption of the Guide, requested the Secretary-General to broadly disseminate the Guide, and recommended to states both the Guide and the United Nations Convention on the Assignment of Receivables in International Trade (the 'Receivables Convention'), the principles of which are also reflected in the Guide.[51]

Key objectives of the Guide

To promote low-cost credit by enhancing the availability of secured credit

The overall objective of the Guide is to promote low-cost credit by enhancing the availability of secured credit (see recommendation 1, subparagraph (a)). The Guide starts from the premise that trade is an important part of economic development and that trade needs credit to grow, in particular, secured credit.

Under the Guide, the main importance of secured credit lies in the fact that the security against the risk of debtor default is likely to result in an increase of the amount of credit available and in a decrease of its cost. In an international context,

Federation of Insolvency Practitioners, the International Insolvency Institute, the Commercial Finance Association, the American Bar Association and others.

46 United Nations publication, Sales No. E.05.V.10. The reports of the two joint sessions of Working Group V and Working Group VI are contained in documents A/CN.9/535 and A/CN.9/550. During these sessions, the working groups considered documents A/CN.9/WG.VI/WP.6/Add.5, A/CN.9/WG.V/WP.70 and A/CN.9/WG.V/WP.71.

47 See http://www.unidroit.org/english/workprogramme/study078/main.htm.

48 *Official Records of the General Assembly, Sixty-first Session, Supplement No. 17* (A/61/17), para. 13. The draft guide was contained in documents A/CN.9/WG.VI/WP.21/Add.3, A/CN.9/WG.VI/WP.24 and Add.5, A/CN.9/WG.VI/WP.26/Add.4–8 and A/CN.9/611 and Add.1 and 2.

49 Ibid., *Sixty-second Session, Supplement No. 17*, (A/62/17 (Part I)), para. 154. The draft guide was contained in documents A/CN.9/631 and Add.1–11.

50 Ibid., *Sixty-second Session, Supplement No. 17* (A/62/17, Part II), paras. 99 and 100. The draft guide was contained in documents A/CN.9/631/Add.1–3 and A/CN.9/637 and Add.1–8.

51 See http://www.uncitral.org/uncitral/en/uncitral_texts/payments/Guide_securedtrans.html.

secured credit becomes even more important as new risks are added. Movable assets cross national borders and rights created in the assets in one jurisdiction may not be recognised in another jurisdiction. In addition, the assets may become subject to rights of third parties in the new jurisdiction. Thus, the importance of secured credit is emphasised by its potential impact on the availability and the cost of credit, that is, factors which are bound to affect the competitiveness of goods and services offered, both in national and international markets.[52]

To allow debtors to use the full value inherent in their assets to support credit

In many jurisdictions,[53] security in movable assets is still based on the notions of possessory pledge and transfer or retention-of-title. While still serving useful purposes, pledge or transfer- and retention-of-title devices cannot accommodate specific needs of a modern economy as they do not permit a debtor to retain possession of encumbered assets, or security to be taken in future assets or to secure future obligations of all types of debtor (for the difficulties associated with possessory pledge, see section D, iv. below).

Specifically, transfer- or retention-of-title devices cannot permit a debtor to use the full value of its assets to obtain credit, as title is vested in the secured creditor/transferee even if the outstanding amount is a fraction of the value of the transferred asset (although, in some jurisdictions, theory and practice accepts that a buyer in a retention-of-title sale, has an expectancy right, amounting to the value of the part of the price paid, which the buyer can use as collateral for credit).

To address all these problems, the Guide allows a security right, possessory or non-possessory, to be taken in a broad array of assets (tangible and intangible; present and future) to secure the widest possible array of obligations (present or future or fluctuating) of as many different types of debtors, creditors and credit transactions as possible (see recommendations 1, subparagraph (b), and 2).

To enable parties to obtain security rights in a simple and efficient manner

In many jurisdictions,[54] a security agreement has to be in a formal writing, signed by the parties or even notarised. Often, the agreement has to be registered in a public registry after it is vetted by a public official, a process that requires time and cost and is exposed to the risk of error and liability.

The Guide recommends a minimum of formalities for the creation of a security right (see recommendation 1, subparagraph (c)). An agreement that reflects the intent of the parties identifies the parties and reasonably describes the secured obligation

52 See Heywood Fleisig, Mehnaz Safavian and Nuria de la Peña, *Reforming Collateral Laws to Expand Access to Finance*, August 2006, and other publications of the Center for the Economic Analysis of Law online at http://www.ceal.org/publications.asp.

53 See Eva-Maria Kieninger (ed.), *Security Rights in Movable Property in European Private Law* (Cambridge: Cambridge University Press), 2004.

54 See Harry C. Sigman and Eva-Maria Kieninger (eds.), *Cross-Border Security over Tangibles* (Selier European Law Publishers; 2007).

and the encumbered asset is sufficient. Written form is required only for the creation of non-possessory security rights. A simple writing (including an electronic record) is sufficient as long as, in itself or together with a course of conduct, indicates the intention of the debtor or other person to create a security right in an asset. A security right can be created in assets that do not exist or do not belong to the debtor at the time of the security agreement as long as they are produced or the debtor acquires them thereafter. A security right may secure a future obligation as long as it arises. It extends in whatever is received in respect of the encumbered assets (proceeds), in attachments and in goods commingled in a mass or processed in to a product (see recommendations 13–22).

To provide for equal treatment of diverse sources of credit and of diverse forms of secured transactions

Even in many civil law jurisdictions, non-possessory security devices developed, in view of the inactivity of the legislator, as a response of practice to concrete needs of practice.[55] Courts had to recognise the effectiveness of these non-possessory security devices, even though some of them (e.g. retention of title or transfer of title), while being useful, can also create costs and undue advantages in favour of some types of creditor and preclude competition to the detriment of the economy as a whole. For example, the rights of a retention-of-title seller may be assigned but only with the purchase price they secure. This assignment is a second financing transaction and the cost associated with it will ultimately most likely be borne by the buyer. In addition, if a retention-of-title right is treated as an ownership right, a secured creditor cannot compete with a retention-of-title seller. As a result, every creditor will try to obtain a retention-of-title right and creditors with a security right will not be certain of their rights.

The Guide starts from the premise that open competition among all potential credit providers is an effective way of reducing the cost of credit. For this reason, it is designed to apply equally to various credit providers: banks, financial institutions and other lenders, manufacturers and suppliers, as well as both domestic and non-domestic credit providers (see recommendation 1, subparagraph (d)). This does not mean that a policy of reasonably favouring suppliers of goods on credit cannot be pursued. It is simply done by giving priority to retention-of-title sellers over secured creditors, provided generally that a notice of the retention-of-title right is registered in the general security rights registry within a short period of time after delivery of the goods (see recommendation 192).

In this regard, it should be noted that the Guide contains a chapter on acquisition financing (chapter IX) and discusses two approaches, a unitary and a non-unitary approach to secured transactions. The unitary approach refers to a unitary notion of a security right and deals with the issues of creation, third-party effectiveness, priority and enforcement of an acquisition security right. The non-unitary approach refers to an acquisition security right, a retention-of-title right and a financial lease right and deals with the same issues. Both approaches are designed to implement one of the fundamental policies of the Guide, that is, to ensure that functionally equivalent devices are treated in the same or very similar way (see recommendation 8).

55 Ibid.,Germany, Julia Rakob, p. 63.

To validate non-possessory security rights in all types of asset

In many jurisdictions, the prototype or main security device is the pledge.[56] The pledge has the advantage that it provides security for the secured creditor in possession of the encumbered asset and limits the commitment of the debtor to that specific asset. However, the pledge has also significant disadvantages. First, it deprives the debtor of the possession of encumbered assets, the use or sale of which may be the only source of income of the debtor (e.g. production equipment or inventory). Second, it requires the secured creditor to make arrangements for the safekeeping of the assets and be exposed to liability for damage or loss caused by the asset (lenders may not be prepared to take possession of encumbered assets). Third, it prevents debtors from using future assets as collateral for credit. Practice and courts had to become very imaginative to invent different types of non-possessory pledges or other arrangements to address these problems.

The Guide addresses these issues directly through a unitary, functional notion of a security right, which includes security rights in a wide array of assets without requiring the debtor to give up possession of the encumbered assets to the secured creditor (see recommendation 1, subparagraph (e)). The Guide does not draw a distinction between possessory and non-possessory security rights except where it recommends different rules. For example, the Guide recommends that: (a) a security agreement need not be reflected in a writing if it is accompanied by the secured creditor's possession of the encumbered asset (see recommendation 15); and (b) a security right in a negotiable instrument or a negotiable document that is made effective against third parties by possession of the instrument or document has priority over a security right in that instrument or document that is made effective against third parties by any other method (see recommendations 101 and 108).

To enhance certainty and transparency by providing for registration of a notice in a general security rights registry

In many jurisdictions, there are no public notice systems with respect to security rights in movable assets.[57] This means that a potential secured creditor has to rely on representations of a potential debtor or on its own independent search to find out whether an asset offered by a debtor as collateral for credit is encumbered by another security right. In other jurisdictions, the security agreement has to be vetted by a public official and registered. The absence of any registration system or the existence of a document registration system often results in delays and costs. In addition, in the case of a document registration system, the confidentiality of a transaction may also be violated even if public access to the registry is limited (which of course will also limit the usefulness of the registry).

To address these problems without unduly interfering with the confidentiality of financing transactions, the Guide provides for a registry system in which only a notice with limited information (the name of the secured creditor or its representative

56 Ibid., France, James Leavy, p. 117; England, Michael Bridge, p. 149; and Netherlands, Michael Veder, p. 194.

57 Ibid., Italy, Anna Veneziano, p. 168.

and the debtor, and a reasonable description of the secured obligation and the encumbered assets) about a transaction is registered (see recommendations 1, subparagraph (f), and 57).

The registry accepts notice without checking or verifying its content, except if it is not accompanied with the required fee or fails to mention the minimum information required by the law (see recommendation 54, subparagraph (c)). The registrar does not require verification of the identity of the registrant or the existence of the authorisation for registration of the notice (see recommendation 54, subparagraph (d)). Of course, if the registration is unauthorised, the grantor of the security right has a right to seek cancellation of the notice through a summary judicial or administrative proceeding (see recommendation 72, subparagraph (b)).

Notices should be indexed and retrieved according to the name or other identifier of the grantor of the security right (see recommendation 54, subparagraph (h)). Fees for registration and searching, if any, should be set at a level no higher that necessary to permit cost recovery (see recommendation 54, subparagraph (i)).The registry system should, to the maximum extent possible, allow notices to be registered and searched for by electronic or similar means (see recommendation 54, subparagraph (j)).

All these recommendations are designed to ensure that registration of a notice of a security right is simple, quick and inexpensive. The Guide makes it clear that only this kind of registration can promote secured credit transactions.

To establish clear and predictable priority rules

As already mentioned, in jurisdictions in which transfer- and retention-of-title devices form the main non-possessory security rights, it is not possible for a debtor to give more than one security right to a secured creditor or, in other words, to use the full value of its assets (although, in some jurisdictions, the buyer in a retention-of-title sale may use its expectancy right as collateral for credit). Once more than one security right may be created in an asset so that the debtor may be able to use all the value of its assets to obtain credit, the question of priority arises (that is which secured creditor will be paid first, if the debtor defaults and the asset's value is not enough to satisfy all secured obligations). A security right will have little value if the secured creditor cannot determine its order of priority before extending credit.

To address this need, the Guide provides a comprehensive set of detailed priority rules dealing with priority conflicts including all types of claimant that may compete with a secured creditor, including unsecured creditors, insolvency administrators, privileged creditors and buyers or lessees of encumbered assets. These rules are based on the time when a secured creditor obtains possession of an encumbered asset, registers a notice of its security right in the general registry or obtains control with respect to a specific type of intangible asset (see recommendations 1, subparagraph (g), and 73–106).

For example, the Guide recommends that priority between competing security rights granted by the same grantor in the same encumbered asset is determined as follows:

(a) If they were made effective against third parties by registration of a notice, priority is determined by the order of registration, regardless of the order of creation of the security rights;
(b) If they were made effective against third parties otherwise than by registration, priority is determined by the order of third-party effectiveness; and

(c) If one security right was made effective against third parties by registration and the other was made effective against third parties otherwise than by registration, priority is determined (regardless of when creation occurs) by the order of registration or third-party effectiveness, whichever occurs first (see recommendation 76).

Also, if an asset that is subject to a security right that is effective against third parties is transferred, leased or licensed, the transferee, lessee or licensee takes its rights subject to the security right (see recommendation 79). There are two exceptions to this rule. The transferee, lessee or licensee takes its rights in the encumbered asset free of the security right, if: (a) the secured creditor authorised the transfer, lease or licence of the encumbered asset free of the security right or the transfer, lease or licence is in the ordinary course of business of the transferor, licensor or lessor and the transferee, lessee or licensee takes its rights in the asset knowing that the transfer, lease or licence violates the rights of the secured creditor under the security agreement (see recommendations 80 and 81).[58]

To facilitate efficient enforcement of a creditor's rights

In many jurisdictions, the enforcement of a security right requires a secured creditor seeking to enforce its security right to obtain a court judgement and follow a formal procedure in disposing of an encumbered asset so as to apply the proceeds to satisfy the secured obligation. This process is often time-consuming and costly, and it often fails to produce the best price for the encumbered asset. Delays and costs in the enforcement process are bound to affect the availability and the cost of credit. This means that some transactions will not take place at all and others will become more expensive.

The Guide provides a set of rules that assist in expediting judicial enforcement proceedings. It also permits extra-judicial enforcement proceedings with appropriate safeguards for the debtor (see recommendations 1, subparagraph (h), and 128–173). For example, a secured creditor may obtain possession of an encumbered asset without having to apply to a court or other authority, provided that: (a) the grantor has consented in the security agreement; (b) the secured creditor has given the grantor any person in possession of the encumbered asset notice; and (c) the grantor and any person in possession do not object at the time the secured creditor seeks to obtain possession of the encumbered asset (see recommendation 148). In addition, after default, the secured creditor is entitled to sell or otherwise dispose, lease or licence the encumbered asset to the extent of the grantor's rights in the asset without having to apply to a court or other authority. In such a case, the secured creditor has to act in good faith and in a commercially reasonable manner (see recommendations 131 and 148).

Moreover, in the case of an extrajudicial disposition of an encumbered asset, the enforcing secured creditor must apply the net proceeds of its enforcement (after deducting costs of enforcement) to the secured obligation and pay any surplus remaining to any subordinate competing claimant that, prior to any distribution of the surplus, notified the enforcing secured creditor of the subordinate competing claimant's claim, to the extent of the amount of that claim. The balance remaining,

58 It should be noted that an intellectual property-specific rule that will modify the rule in recommendation 81, subparagraph (c), is likely to be included in the Supplement to the Guide dealing with security interests in intellectual property.

if any, must be remitted to the grantor (see recommendation 152). Finally, a person that acquires an encumbered asset in the context of an extrajudicial sale takes the asset free of the rights of the enforcing secured creditor and of any subordinate competing claimant but subject to the rights of any senior secured creditor or other competing claimant (see recommendation 161).

The Guide deals with the enforcement of a security right in line with insolvency law and in particular the UNCITRAL Insolvency Guide. So, for example, an encumbered asset is subject to a stay but the secured creditor may seek relief and protection of the value of the encumbered asset (see recommendations 35, 50 and 51 of the UNCITRAL Insolvency Guide). In addition, the effectiveness of a security right is preserved in the case of insolvency of the grantor but is subject to avoidance (see recommendation 238 of the Guide and 87 of the UNCITRAL Insolvency Guide). Similarly, the priority of a security right is preserved in the case of the grantor's insolvency but is subject to preferences established by insolvency law (see recommendation 239 of the Guide and 188 of the UNCITRAL Insolvency Guide).

Moreover, secured creditors may participate in reorganisation proceedings and their rights are not affected unless they have an opportunity to vote on a reorganisation plan (see recommendations 126 and 146 of the UNCITRAL Insolvency Guide). A reorganisation plan may be confirmed by the insolvency court, provided that: (a) the approval process was properly conducted and the necessary approvals were obtained; (b) creditors will receive as much as they would have received in liquidation unless they accepted to receive less; (c) the plan is not contrary to law; (d) administrative claims and expenses have been paid in full, unless otherwise agreed by the holders of the claims; and (e) unless otherwise agreed by affected classes, the class is given full recognition of its ranking (see recommendation 152 of the UNCITRAL Insolvency Guide). Where confirmation by a court is not required and a reorganisation plan is binding upon approval by creditors, affected persons, including secured creditors, may challenge it (see recommendation 153 of the UNCITRAL Insolvency Guide)

Finally, a security right granted after commencement of the insolvency proceedings has no priority unless granted by the insolvency court after hearing the existing secured creditors, the debtor proves that it cannot obtain finance in any other way and the interests of existing secured creditors are protected (see recommendation 67 of the UNCITRAL Insolvency Guide).

To allow parties maximum flexibility to negotiate the terms of their security agreement

In many jurisdictions, rules of law relating to security rights are mandatory. The Guide recognises the need for mandatory rules where rights of third parties are involved. At the same time, the Guide provides sufficient flexibility to parties to tailor their security agreements to meet their precise needs (see recommendation 8).

For example, the priority rules of the Guide are mandatory to the extent rights of third parties are involved, but two competing claimants may agree to change their order of priority as long no third party is affected (that is Secured Creditor A may subordinate its security right to that of Secured Creditor C for the exact amount owed to A; for that amount only, C obtains priority over Secured Creditor B as long as A becomes subordinate to B; see recommendation 91).

In addition, the Guide does not override mandatory provisions of other law. For example, while the Guide applies to consumers, it does not override consumer-protection legislation (see recommendation 2, subparagraph (b)). Similarly, the

Guide does not override statutory limitations to the transferability of assets, such as employment benefits (see recommendation 18).

Moreover, the Guide contains in chapter VI on rights and obligations of the parties to the security agreement and chapter VII on the rights and obligations of third-party obligors a number of mandatory and non-mandatory provisions. For example, on the one hand, the party in possession of an encumbered asset must take reasonable steps to preserve it and upon payment of the secured obligation and termination of any commitment, the secured creditor must return the encumbered asset to the grantor (see recommendations 111 and 112). On the other hand, the secured creditor is entitled to be reimbursed for reasonable maintenance expenses with respect to an encumbered asset or make reasonable use of it, unless otherwise agreed (see recommendation 113).

Finally, the Guide contains a set of detailed rules with respect to the rights and obligations of a debtor of a receivable (in line with the Receivables Convention), the obligor under a negotiable instrument, a depositary bank, the guarantor/issuer of a letter of credit and the issuer of a negotiable document. Most of these rules are subject to contrary agreement by the parties, but some are mandatory. For example, the debtor of a receivable may not waive defences arising from fraudulent acts on the part of the assignee/secured creditor or defences based on the incapacity of the debtor of the receivable (see recommendation 121, subparagraph (b)).

To balance the interests of all affected persons

The Guide recognises that security agreements are not just contractual undertakings affecting only the parties thereto, but have property effects that also affect the rights of third parties (such as secured, privileged and unsecured creditors, purchasers and other transferees of encumbered assets). Thus, the Guide takes into account the legitimate interests of all parties and aims at achieving all the substantive objectives mentioned above, in a balanced way. For example, a retention-of-title seller or financial lessor has to register a notice about the retention-of-title or financial lease transaction in the general security rights registry but obtains priority as of the time of the delivery of the goods (and not just as of the time of registration like any other secured creditor). In principle, this special priority is extended to proceeds of equipment but not to proceeds of inventory (to avoid adverse effects on receivables financing; recommendations 176, 181 and 182).

Similarly, as mentioned above, in the case of insolvency of the grantor, the encumbered assets are part of the estate (subject to stays and other limitations). However, the pre-commencement effectiveness of a security right is respected (subject to any avoidance actions) and so is the pre-commencement priority of a security right (subject to any privileged claims and any decisions of the insolvency court in respect to post-commencement finance). In any case, the value of the security right is to be protected.

To harmonise secured transactions laws, including conflict-of-laws rules relating to secured transactions

One of the problems with security rights in movable assets in cross-border transactions is that a security right in an asset effectively created under the law of one state may not be recognised as being effective under the law of another state in which the asset was moved. For example, once goods subject to retention of title cross national borders, the retention of title may not be recognised even as a normal security right;

or, if an assignment is made and perfected under the law governing the assigned receivable, it may not be treated as effective if the assignor becomes insolvent and the law governing the insolvency proceedings displaces the law governing the receivable as contrary to the public policy of the state where the insolvency proceedings take place.

The Guide provides states with guidance as to how to modernise their secured transactions laws. To the extent states follow the recommendations of the Guide, secured transactions laws will be harmonised with the result that a security right created in one state will be recognised in another state, a result that should promote international trade (see recommendation 1, subparagraph (k)). Harmonisation under the Guide takes place at two levels, the substantive law level and the conflict-of-laws level. With harmonisation of substantive law rules, similar rules will apply under the law of any state. Harmonisation at the level of conflict-of-laws will result in the application of similar applicable-law rules (subject to the limitations of the applicable law being contrary to mandatory rules or the public policy of the forum state). Thus, the Guide contains a comprehensive set of both substantive law and conflict-of law rules.

Here are some examples of the conflict-of-laws recommendations of the Guide. The law applicable to the creation, third-party effectiveness and priority of a security right in a tangible asset is the law of the state in which the asset is located (see recommendation 203). The law applicable to these issues with respect to a security right in an intangible asset is the law of the state in which the grantor is located (see recommendation 208). The grantor is located in the state in which it has its place of business; if the grantor has places of business in more than one state, the grantor's place of business is the place in which the grantor exercises its central administration (see recommendation 219). The law applicable to the enforcement of security right in a tangible asset is the law of the states in which enforcement takes place; the law applicable to the enforcement of a security right in an intangible asset is the law applicable to the priority of the security right, that is, the law of the state in which the grantor is located (see recommendation 218). The law applicable to the mutual rights and obligations of the grantor and the secured creditor is the law chosen by them and, in the absence of a choice of law, the law governing the security agreement (see recommendation 216). Special rules apply to security rights of assets, such as a right to payment of funds credited to a bank account or a right to receive the proceeds under a letter of credit (see recommendations 210 and 212).

Fundamental policies of the Guide

The key objectives just reviewed provide a general policy framework within which states can establish a modern secured transactions regime. The recommendations of the Guide provide a set of detailed rules that may constitute a significant departure from the regime existing in many jurisdictions. In order to provide a link between the key policy objectives of the Guide and the detailed recommendations of the Guide and to explain some fundamental policies, which may be new to many jurisdictions, the Guide sets forth a few fundamental legal principles. These policies are reviewed below.

Comprehensive scope

It is part of reality that practice is faster than the legislator or courts. In the absence of quick action by the legislator or courts, law becomes out of date. This is particularly true for secured financing law, as secured financing is a very dynamic and fast-developing practice. To address this problem, the legislator in many jurisdictions, instead of updating the law in a comprehensive and consistent way has followed a piecemeal approach with the result that there is multiplicity of laws with gaps, uncertainties and inconsistencies or has left it to courts (even in civil law jurisdictions) to apply general principles of secured transactions law so as to fill the gaps in the law.

The Guide addresses this problem with a comprehensive scope that, as far as possible, embraces all forms of secured transactions (regardless of their form or the terminology used by the parties), all categories of grantors and secured creditors (legal and natural persons, including consumers), and a broad range of types of movable asset (goods, equipment, inventory, receivables, negotiable instruments, rights to payment of funds credited to a bank account, rights to receive the proceeds under a letter of credit, intellectual property rights and negotiable documents) and secured obligation (see recommendations 2 and 3). Thus, for example, the Guide devotes a chapter to acquisition financing that includes retention-of-title sales and financial leases. Similarly the Guide includes in each chapter asset-specific recommendations modifying the general recommendations.

Integrated and functional approach

The multiplicity of laws dealing with secured transactions and the resulting gaps and inconsistencies are compounded with different treatment of transactions that essentially perform the same function. For example, in a system where retention-of-title sales and financial leases are not subject to the rules applicable to secured transactions, parties may structure their transaction so as to avoid the application of the secured transactions law. As a result, even parties to transactions that are subject to the secured transactions law may not rely on that law to determine their rights.

The Guide takes the position that, to the maximum extent possible, all transactions that create a right in all types of asset meant to secure the performance of an obligation (that is, fulfil security functions) should be considered as security rights and regulated by the same rules. The main principle in this regard is that in the characterisation of a transaction substance should prevail over form (see recommendations 11 and 12). This is a practical approach that can best facilitate modern secured financing transactions in the sense that it can encompass all types of transactions that serve security purposes and provide equal treatment of all credit providers, thus encouraging competition and potentially affecting in a positive way the availability and the cost of credit. The functional approach can also lead to a harmonisation of secured transactions laws of the various jurisdictions of the world as it facilitates the cross-border recognition of the various security devices based on their function rather than on their name.

Security rights in future assets of a grantor

Many states with traditional pledge-based systems only permit grantors to create security rights in existing assets that they own at the time of the creation of a security right. They are not able to grant a security right in assets not yet in existence or that they have not yet acquired at the time of the conclusion of the secured transaction. The concern is to protect debtors from over-commitment of their assets, in particular their future assets, to secured creditors. Nonetheless, because business grantors may not always have present assets available to secure credit, this limitation prevents them from obtaining many types of credit that are predicated upon a stream of future assets, such as inventory and receivables. Thus, the Guide is premised on the view that, except to the extent that consumer-protection or other legislation provides otherwise, a security right may be created in future assets (see recommendations 17 and 18). Similarly, a notice of a security right may refer to future assets (see recommendation 68), and priority extends to assets covered by the notice, including future assets and to all secured obligations, regardless of the time they are incurred (see recommendations 97 and 99).

Extension of security rights into proceeds

It is in the nature of property (*in rem*) rights to follow the asset in the hands of a transferee. When the grantor of a security right sells or otherwise disposes of an encumbered asset, the buyer acquires the asset subject to the security right (*droit de suite*). Some states also give the secured creditor a right in the proceeds (normally receivables) that may be generated by the sale of the encumbered asset. The reason for this approach is that the value may be in the proceeds rather than in the original collateral and, if the secured creditor could not rely on the proceeds, it could take steps to prevent the debtor from selling or further encumbering the encumbered asset.

The Guide recommends that the security right should be extended into whatever proceeds are received upon the disposition of encumbered assets (defined in a very broad way to include not only proceeds upon a disposition of an asset, but also civil and natural fruits). In any case, the secured creditor will always get no more than the secured obligation, plus interest and costs (see recommendations 19, 39 and 40). The Guide also recommends that, if a security right in an asset is effective against third parties, so is the security right in the proceeds, provided that the proceeds are described in a generic way in the registered notice or consist of money, receivables, negotiable instruments or right to payment of funds credited to a bank account (see recommendation 39). Otherwise, the security right in the proceeds remains effective against third parties for a limited period of time after the proceeds arise and thereafter only if that security right in the proceeds is separately made effective against third parties (see recommendation 40). The Guide also recommends that a security right in the proceeds should have the same priority as the security right in the original encumbered asset (see recommendation 100).

Distinguishing effectiveness as between the parties from effectiveness against third parties

In many states, when a security right is created, it is effective not only between the grantor and the secured creditor but also against third parties (*erga omnes*). As a result, to the extent a publicity act is not required for the purpose of creating a security right, third parties have insufficient notice; to the extent a publicity act is required, creation is burdened with unnecessary formalities. In any case, secured creditors and grantors must always await conclusion of their agreement before taking steps to ensure priority as against competing claimants.

For these reasons, the Guide recommends that a distinction should be drawn between effectiveness as between the parties and effectiveness as against third parties. The Guide also recommends that creation of a security right should be as simple as possible, and that only minimal additional steps should be required to make the security right effective against third parties (see recommendations 13-15). At the same time, the commentary of the Guide discusses other possible approaches, such as, for example, providing that upon its creation a security right is effective against all parties with the exception of other secured creditors with respect to which registration of a notice would be required (see chapter III on the effectiveness of a security right against third parties, para. 8).

Establishment of a general security rights registry

In many jurisdictions, non-possessory security rights are available only on the basis of various statutes for specific types of asset or only for certain types of grantors. In some of these jurisdictions, separate registries or mechanisms of publicity are available for different categories of assets and grantors. Such an approach creates gaps and inconsistencies. It also results on different treatment of credit providers, a result that is likely to have a negative impact on the availability and the cost of credit as it distorts competition. Many of these registration systems require registration of transaction documents, which the registrar has to check before issuing a certificate that provides full or presumptive evidence as to the validity of the transaction. Such systems typically create delays and costs that ultimately debtors have to bear.

The Guide is premised on the view that efficiency will be enhanced if there is a single general security rights registry, in which notices relating to existing or potential security rights may be registered. The Guide thus recommends a single registry, which, to the extent possible, should be electronic, and registration in which should be as simple, quick and inexpensive as possible. Registration is not necessary to create a security right (an effective security agreement is necessary for that result). It merely has third-party and priority effects (see recommendations 54–75). The Guide treats document registries in which registration has constitutive effects and registries with high registration fees as detrimental to secured financing. The Guide also recognises specialised registries, such as registries for ships, aircraft or intellectual property rights and gives priority to a security right registered in such a registry (see recommendations 38 and 77).

Availability of and priority among multiple security rights

In many jurisdictions, multiple non-possessory security rights in the same movable assets are not permitted. This is particularly the case in jurisdictions where transfer- or retention-of-title devices are the main devices for obtaining a non-possessory security right in a movable asset. In some of those jurisdictions, under the theory that the buyer in a retention-of-title sale has a title expectancy may grant a security right in the assets bought even before the buyer acquires title (it is also possible for a bank to acquire the benefit of retention of title through an assignment of the claim for payment of the balance of the purchase price). In any case, the difficulty in the recognition of multiple non-possessory security rights in the same assets means that a debtor may not readily use the full value of its assets to obtain credit from more than one creditor.

In order to facilitate this result, the Guide permits a person to grant multiple security rights in its assets. Furthermore, in order to allow parties to obtain the optimal benefit of granting multiple security rights in their assets, the Guide provides a comprehensive set of detailed and clear rules for determining priority between a security right and the rights of a competing creditor. The Guide takes the position that the order of filing a notice in the registry or of achieving third-party effectiveness (as registration may take place in advance of creation, third-party effectiveness means both creation and an act of registration, possession or control) should be the main basis upon which priority is determined (see recommendation 76).

Priority between a secured creditor and third parties other than secured creditors

The fact that non-possessory security rights in movable assets are available in a jurisdiction or that a registration or other act may be required to make them effective against third parties does not necessarily mean that they will always have priority against all claimants. In many jurisdictions, later-in-time unregistered privileges (such as tax claims or employee claims) outrank security rights. The Guide recommends that states should weigh the benefits expected from such privileged claims against their potential negative impact on the availability and the cost of secured credit, limit such claims and, in any case, proclaim them in a clear and transparent way in the law (see recommendation 83).

The Guide also recommends that a security right has priority over the rights of a judgement creditor unless that creditor obtained a judgement and took steps to acquire rights in the encumbered assets before the security right was made effective against third parties (see recommendation 84).

Facilitative rather than formalistic regulation

In many jurisdictions, the law seeks to control the impact of security rights by restrictively enumerating the types of transaction to which parties could agree (*numerus clausus*) and by regulating in detail not only the conditions for creating such agreements, but also the specific terms that could be included in a security agreement.

The Guide recommends that, in general, parties should be permitted to design their own security agreements, and that any mandatory rules should aim only at ensuring fairness and protecting the legitimate interests of third parties without precluding them from obtaining the benefits of useful transactions (see recommendations 8 and 110–113).

Extra-judicial enforcement

In many jurisdictions, to enforce a security right, a secured creditor is required to apply to a court or other authority, seize and sell encumbered assets in a public auction. Extra-judicial enforcement is either not permitted at all or only in limited cases (for example, in the case of pawnbrokers and creditors holding general company security rights). As a result, even in cases where the debtor and the secured creditor agree (even after default) that the secured creditor may repossess and sell the encumbered asset without recourse to a judicial authority, the secured creditor has no means to enforce its security right other than applying for a court order. As a result, secured creditors take into account delays, costs and other possible problems with enforcement in determining whether to offer credit and at what terms.

To address this problem, the Guide recommends that, as long as the enforcement regime is designed to protect the legitimate interests of grantors and third parties, and can produce more value for an encumbered asset in a more time-and cost-efficient manner, there should be no limitation on a secured creditor's right to enforce its security right extra-judicially (see recommendations 142, 147–155). As already mentioned, to protect the interests of the debtor and third parties, the Guide provides specifically that the debtor needs to consent to extra-judicial enforcement in the security agreement, the debtor and third parties should be notified and at the time of enforcement the debtor and any third party in possession of the encumbered asset should not object to extra-judicial enforcement (see recommendation 147).

Equality of treatment of all creditors that provide credit to enable grantors to acquire tangible assets

In many jurisdictions, a sharp distinction is drawn between the rights of sellers and the rights of lenders financing the acquisition of tangible assets. In some jurisdictions, sellers are given special rights usually by retaining title to the tangible asset sold until the purchase price is paid in full. Lenders may get the benefit of retention-of-title only by obtaining an assignment of the claim for the outstanding purchase price. This is bound to raise the cost of credit as the addition of another creditor will most likely add the cost of the assets to the end-buyer.

The Guide recommends that, to encourage competition, the law should treat sellers and lenders that provide credit to enable a buyer to acquire tangible assets in the same way. As a result, retention-of-title sellers will be able to benefit from the complete range of rights given to secured creditors, which in some ways exceed the rights available to retention-of-title sellers under existing law in many states. At the same time, in recognition of the importance of acquisition credit, the Guide provides special priority rules for acquisition financiers, including lenders, retention-of-title sellers and financial lessors (see recommendation 180).

Conclusions

The recommendations of the Guide form in effect the basis of a model secured transactions law for the world. They are accompanied with commentary explaining not just the recommendations but also other possible workable approaches with their relative advantages and disadvantages. The Guide is comprehensive in its scope and detailed in its treatment of the issues covered. Thus, the Guide combines the certainty of the recommendations with the flexibility of the commentary, and provides complete guidance to states. In order to modernise secured credit law, and thus facilitate secured credit, the Guide follows pragmatic and practical approaches, such as the approach for a comprehensive, integrated and functional notion of security right.

However, at the same time, the Guide balances carefully the interests of different stakeholders, such as secured, unsecured and privileged creditors and also establishes a coordinated regime in order to avoid tensions with general contract or property and insolvency law. It is particularly important that the treatment of security rights in insolvency in the Guide is consistent and supplemented by the UNCITRAL Insolvency Guide.

The Guide may serve as a vehicle for modernisation but also harmonisation of secured financing law in states with different legal systems and at different stages of economic development.[59] This process will necessarily be protracted but even if substantive secured financing law is harmonised other issues will remain. Most notable of these, concerns the conflict-of-laws rules which will be necessary to address issues such as the question where to register a notice about a secured transaction.

59 A brief look at the secured financing law in the world is sufficient to show that secured financing law, even in countries with developed and sophisticated markets, is out of date or defective; see further Roy Goode, op. cit., fn. 29.

Appendix 1
Work of the Law Commissions of England and Wales and Scotland 2002–2005

A. The work of the Law Commission of England and Wales:[1]

1. Law Commission Consultation Paper No. 164 'Registration of Security Interests: Company Charges and Property other than Land' (London: TSO, 2002)
2. Law Commission Consultation Paper No. 176 'Company Security Interests: a Consultative Report' (London: TSO, 2004)
3. Law Commission Report No. 296 'Company Security Interests' Cm 6654 (London: TSO, 2005)

B. The work of the Scottish Law Commission:[2]

1. Scottish Law Commission Discussion Paper No. 121 'Registration of Rights in Security by Companies' (Edinburgh: TSO, 2002)
2. Scottish Law Commission Report No. 197 'Registration of Rights in Security by Companies' HC 1003 (Edinburgh: TSO, 2004)

1 All these documents are available at www.lawcom.gov.uk.
2 Both of these documents are available at www.scotlawcom.gov.uk.

Appendix 2
Companies Act 2006
Part 25 Company charges

CHAPTER 1

Companies registered in England and Wales or Northern Ireland

Requirement to register company charges

860 Charges created by a company

(1) A company that creates a charge to which this section applies must deliver the prescribed particulars of the charge, together with the instrument (if any) by which the charge is created or evidenced, to the registrar for registration before the end of the period allowed for registration.
(2) Registration of a charge to which this section applies may instead be effected on the application of a person interested in it.
(3) Where registration is effected on the application of some person other than the company, that person is entitled to recover from the company the amount of any fees properly paid by him to the registrar on registration.
(4) If a company fails to comply with subsection (1), an offence is committed by–

  (a) the company, and
  (b) every officer of it who is in default.

(5) A person guilty of an offence under this section is liable–

  (a) on conviction on indictment, to a fine;
  (b) on summary conviction, to a fine not exceeding the statutory maximum.

(6) Subsection (4) does not apply if registration of the charge has been effected on the application of some other person.
(7) This section applies to the following charges–

  (a) a charge on land or any interest in land, other than a charge for any rent or other periodical sum issuing out of land,
  (b) a charge created or evidenced by an instrument which, if executed by an individual, would require registration as a bill of sale,
  (c) a charge for the purposes of securing any issue of debentures,
  (d) a charge on uncalled share capital of the company,
  (e) a charge on calls made but not paid,

(f) a charge on book debts of the company,
(g) a floating charge on the company's property or undertaking,
(h) a charge on a ship or aircraft, or any share in a ship,
(i) a charge on goodwill or on any intellectual property.

861 Charges which have to be registered: supplementary

(1) The holding of debentures entitling the holder to a charge on land is not, for the purposes of section 860(7)(a), an interest in the land.
(2) It is immaterial for the purposes of this Chapter where land subject to a charge is situated.
(3) The deposit by way of security of a negotiable instrument given to secure the payment of book debts is not, for the purposes of section 860(7)(f), a charge on those book debts.
(4) For the purposes of section 860(7)(i), 'intellectual property' means–

(a) any patent, trade mark, registered design, copyright or design right;
(b) any licence under or in respect of any such right.

(5) In this Chapter–

'charge' includes mortgage, and
'company' means a company registered in England and Wales or in Northern Ireland.

862 Charges existing on property acquired

(1) This section applies where a company acquires property which is subject to a charge of a kind which would, if it had been created by the company after the acquisition of the property, have been required to be registered under this Chapter.
(2) The company must deliver the prescribed particulars of the charge, together with a certified copy of the instrument (if any) by which the charge is created or evidenced, to the registrar for registration.
(3) Subsection (2) must be complied with before the end of the period allowed for registration.
(4) If default is made in complying with this section, an offence is committed by–

(a) the company, and
(b) every officer of it who is in default.

(5) A person guilty of an offence under this section is liable–

(a) on conviction on indictment, to a fine;
(b) on summary conviction, to a fine not exceeding the statutory maximum.

Special rules about debentures

863 Charge in series of debentures

(1) Where a series of debentures containing, or giving by reference to another instrument, any charge to the benefit of which debenture holders of that series are entitled *pari passu* is created by a company, it is for the purposes of section 860(1) sufficient if the required particulars, together with the deed containing the charge

(or, if there is no such deed, one of the debentures of the series), are delivered to the registrar before the end of the period allowed for registration.

(2) The following are the required particulars–

(a) the total amount secured by the whole series, and
(b) the dates of the resolutions authorising the issue of the series and the date of the covering deed (if any) by which the series is created or defined, and
(c) a general description of the property charged, and
(d) the names of the trustees (if any) for the debenture holders.

(3) Particulars of the date and amount of each issue of debentures of a series of the kind mentioned in subsection (1) must be sent to the registrar for entry in the register of charges.
(4) Failure to comply with subsection (3) does not affect the validity of the debentures issued.
(5) Subsections (2) to (6) of section 860 apply for the purposes of this section as they apply for the purposes of that section, but as if references to the registration of a charge were references to the registration of a series of debentures.

864 Additional registration requirement for commission etc. in relation to debentures

(1) Where any commission, allowance or discount has been paid or made either directly or indirectly by a company to a person in consideration of his–

(a) subscribing or agreeing to subscribe, whether absolutely or conditionally, for debentures in a company, or
(b) procuring or agreeing to procure subscriptions, whether absolute or conditional, for such debentures, the particulars required to be sent for registration under section 860 shall include particulars as to the amount or rate per cent of the commission, discount or allowance so paid or made.

(2) The deposit of debentures as security for a debt of the company is not, for the purposes of this section, treated as the issue of debentures at a discount.
(3) Failure to comply with this section does not affect the validity of the debentures issued.

865 Endorsement of certificate on debentures

(1) The company shall cause a copy of every certificate of registration given under section 869 to be endorsed on every debenture or certificate of debenture stock which is issued by the company, and the payment of which is secured by the charge so registered.
(2) But this does not require a company to cause a certificate of registration of any charge so given to be endorsed on any debenture or certificate of debenture stock issued by the company before the charge was created.
(3) If a person knowingly and wilfully authorises or permits the delivery of a debenture or certificate of debenture stock which under this section is required to have endorsed on it a copy of a certificate of registration, without the copy being so endorsed upon it, he commits an offence.
(4) A person guilty of an offence under this section is liable on summary conviction to a fine not exceeding level 3 on the standard scale.

Charges in other jurisdictions

866 Charges created in, or over property in, jurisdictions outside the United Kingdom

(1) Where a charge is created outside the United Kingdom comprising property situated outside the United Kingdom, the delivery to the registrar of a verified copy of the instrument by which the charge is created or evidenced has the same effect for the purposes of this Chapter as the delivery of the instrument itself.
(2) Where a charge is created in the United Kingdom but comprises property outside the United Kingdom, the instrument creating or purporting to create the charge may be sent for registration under section 860 even if further proceedings may be necessary to make the charge valid or effectual according to the law of the country in which the property is situated.

867 Charges created in, or over property in, another United Kingdom jurisdiction

(1) Subsection (2) applies where–

  (a) a charge comprises property situated in a part of the United Kingdom other than the part in which the company is registered, and
  (b) registration in that other part is necessary to make the charge valid or effectual under the law of that part of the United Kingdom.

(2) The delivery to the registrar of a verified copy of the instrument by which the charge is created or evidenced, together with a certificate stating that the charge was presented for registration in that other part of the United Kingdom on the date on which it was so presented has, for the purposes of this Chapter, the same effect as the delivery of the instrument itself.

Orders charging land: Northern Ireland

868 Northern Ireland: registration of certain charges etc. affecting land

(1) Where a charge imposed by an order under Article 46 of the 1981 Order or notice of such a charge is registered in the Land Registry against registered land or any estate in registered land of a company, the Registrar of Titles shall as soon as may be cause two copies of the order made under Article 46 of that Order or of any notice under Article 48 of that Order to be delivered to the registrar.
(2) Where a charge imposed by an order under Article 46 of the 1981 Order is registered in the Registry of Deeds against any unregistered land or estate in land of a company, the Registrar of Deeds shall as soon as may be cause two copies of the order to be delivered to the registrar.
(3) On delivery of copies under this section, the registrar shall–

  (a) register one of them in accordance with section 869, and
  (b) not later than 7 days from that date of delivery, cause the other copy together with a certificate of registration under section 869(5) to be sent to the company against which judgment was given.

(4) Where a charge to which subsection (1) or (2) applies is vacated, the Registrar of Titles or, as the case may be, the Registrar of Deeds shall cause a certified copy

of the certificate of satisfaction lodged under Article 132(1) of the 1981 Order to be delivered to the registrar for entry of a memorandum of satisfaction in accordance with section 872.

(5) In this section–

'the 1981 Order' means the Judgments Enforcement (Northern Ireland) Order 1981 (S.I. 1981/226 (N.I. 6));

'the Registrar of Deeds' means the registrar appointed under the Registration of Deeds Act (Northern Ireland) 1970 (c. 25);

'Registry of Deeds' has the same meaning as in the Registration of Deeds Acts;

'Registration of Deeds Acts' means the Registration of Deeds Act (Northern Ireland) 1970 and every statutory provision for the time being in force amending that Act or otherwise relating to the registry of deeds, or the registration of deeds, orders or other instruments or documents in such registry;

'the Land Registry' and 'the Registrar of Titles' are to be construed in accordance with section 1 of the Land Registration Act (Northern Ireland) 1970 (c. 18);

'registered land' and 'unregistered land' have the same meaning as in Part 3 of the Land Registration Act (Northern Ireland) 1970.

The register of charges

869 Register of charges to be kept by registrar

(1) The registrar shall keep, with respect to each company, a register of all the charges requiring registration under this Chapter.

(2) In the case of a charge to the benefit of which holders of a series of debentures are entitled, the registrar shall enter in the register the required particulars specified in section 863(2).

(3) In the case of a charge imposed by the Enforcement of Judgments Office under Article 46 of the Judgments Enforcement (Northern Ireland) Order 1981, the registrar shall enter in the register the date on which the charge became effective.

(4) In the case of any other charge, the registrar shall enter in the register the following particulars–

(a) if it is a charge created by a company, the date of its creation and, if it is a charge which was existing on property acquired by the company, the date of the acquisition,

(b) the amount secured by the charge,

(c) short particulars of the property charged, and

(d) the persons entitled to the charge.

(5) The registrar shall give a certificate of the registration of any charge registered in pursuance of this Chapter, stating the amount secured by the charge.

(6) The certificate–

(a) shall be signed by the registrar or authenticated by the registrar's official seal, and

(b) is conclusive evidence that the requirements of this Chapter as to registration have been satisfied.

(7) The register kept in pursuance of this section shall be open to inspection by any person.

870 The period allowed for registration

(1) The period allowed for registration of a charge created by a company is–

(a) 21 days beginning with the day after the day on which the charge is created, or
(b) if the charge is created outside the United Kingdom, 21 days beginning with the day after the day on which the instrument by which the charge is created or evidenced (or a copy of it) could, in due course of post (and if despatched with due diligence) have been received in the United Kingdom.

(2) The period allowed for registration of a charge to which property acquired by a company is subject is–

(a) 21 days beginning with the day after the day on which the acquisition is completed, or
(b) if the property is situated and the charge was created outside the United Kingdom, 21 days beginning with the day after the day on which the instrument by which the charge is created or evidenced (or a copy of it) could, in due course of post (and if despatched with due diligence) have been received in the United Kingdom.

(3) The period allowed for registration of particulars of a series of debentures as a result of section 863 is–

(a) if there is a deed containing the charge mentioned in section 863(1), 21 days beginning with the day after the day on which that deed is executed, or
(b) if there is no such deed, 21 days beginning with the day after the day on which the first debenture of the series is executed.

871 Registration of enforcement of security

(1) If a person obtains an order for the appointment of a receiver or manager of a company's property, or appoints such a receiver or manager under powers contained in an instrument, he shall within 7 days of the order or of the appointment under those powers, give notice of the fact to the registrar.
(2) Where a person appointed receiver or manager of a company's property under powers contained in an instrument ceases to act as such receiver or manager, he shall, on so ceasing, give the registrar notice to that effect.
(3) The registrar must enter a fact of which he is given notice under this section in the register of charges.
(4) A person who makes default in complying with the requirements of this section commits an offence.
(5) A person guilty of an offence under this section is liable on summary conviction to a fine not exceeding level 3 on the standard scale and, for continued contravention, a daily default fine not exceeding one-tenth of level 3 on the standard scale.

872 Entries of satisfaction and release

(1) Subsection (2) applies if a statement is delivered to the registrar verifying with respect to a registered charge–

(a) that the debt for which the charge was given has been paid or satisfied in whole or in part, or
(b) that part of the property or undertaking charged has been released from the charge or has ceased to form part of the company's property or undertaking.

(2) The registrar may enter on the register a memorandum of satisfaction in whole or in part, or of the fact part of the property or undertaking has been released from the charge or has ceased to form part of the company's property or undertaking (as the case may be).
(3) Where the registrar enters a memorandum of satisfaction in whole, the registrar shall if required send the company a copy of it.

873 Rectification of register of charges

(1) Subsection (2) applies if the court is satisfied–

(a) that the failure to register a charge before the end of the period allowed for registration, or the omission or mis-statement of any particular with respect to any such charge or in a memorandum of satisfaction–

(i) was accidental or due to inadvertence or to some other sufficient cause, or
(ii) is not of a nature to prejudice the position of creditors or shareholders of the company, or

(b) that on other grounds it is just and equitable to grant relief.

(2) The court may, on the application of the company or a person interested, and on such terms and conditions as seem to the court just and expedient, order that the period allowed for registration shall be extended or, as the case may be, that the omission or mis-statement shall be rectified.

Avoidance of certain charges

874 Consequence of failure to register charges created by a company

(1) If a company creates a charge to which section 860 applies, the charge is void (so far as any security on the company's property or undertaking is conferred by it) against–

(a) a liquidator of the company,
(b) an administrator of the company, and
(c) a creditor of the company, unless that section is complied with.

(2) Subsection (1) is subject to the provisions of this Chapter.
(3) Subsection (1) is without prejudice to any contract or obligation for repayment of the money secured by the charge; and when a charge becomes void under this section, the money secured by it immediately becomes payable.

Companies' records and registers

875 Companies to keep copies of instruments creating charges

(1) A company must keep available for inspection a copy of every instrument creating a charge requiring registration under this Chapter, including any document delivered to the company under section 868(3)(b) (Northern Ireland: orders imposing charges affecting land).
(2) In the case of a series of uniform debentures, a copy of one of the debentures of the series is sufficient.

876 Company's register of charges

(1) Every limited company shall keep available for inspection a register of charges and enter in it–

 (a) all charges specifically affecting property of the company, and
 (b) all floating charges on the whole or part of the company's property or undertaking.

(2) The entry shall in each case give a short description of the property charged, the amount of the charge and, except in the cases of securities to bearer, the names of the persons entitled to it.
(3) If an officer of the company knowingly and wilfully authorises or permits the omission of an entry required to be made in pursuance of this section, he commits an offence.
(4) A person guilty of an offence under this section is liable–

 (a) on conviction on indictment, to a fine;
 (b) on summary conviction, to a fine not exceeding the statutory maximum.

877 Instruments creating charges and register of charges to be available for inspection

(1) This section applies to–

 (a) documents required to be kept available for inspection under section 875 (copies of instruments creating charges), and
 (b) a company's register of charges kept in pursuance of section 876.

(2) The documents and register must be kept available for inspection–

 (a) at the company's registered office, or
 (b) at a place specified in regulations under section 1136.

(3) The company must give notice to the registrar–

 (a) of the place at which the documents and register are kept available for inspection, and
 (b) of any change in that place, unless they have at all times been kept at the company's registered office.

(4) The documents and register shall be open to the inspection–

 (a) of any creditor or member of the company without charge, and
 (b) of any other person on payment of such fee as may be prescribed.

(5) If default is made for 14 days in complying with subsection (3) or an inspection required under subsection (4) is refused, an offence is committed by–

(a) the company, and
(b) every officer of the company who is in default.

(6) A person guilty of an offence under this section is liable on summary conviction to a fine not exceeding level 3 on the standard scale and, for continued contravention, a daily default fine not exceeding one-tenth of level 3 on the standard scale.
(7) If an inspection required under subsection (4) is refused the court may by order compel an immediate inspection.

CHAPTER 2

Companies registered in Scotland

Charges requiring registration

878 Charges created by a company

(1) A company that creates a charge to which this section applies must deliver the prescribed particulars of the charge, together with a copy certified as a correct copy of the instrument (if any) by which the charge is created or evidenced, to the registrar for registration before the end of the period allowed for registration.
(2) Registration of a charge to which this section applies may instead be effected on the application of a person interested in it.
(3) Where registration is effected on the application of some person other than the company, that person is entitled to recover from the company the amount of any fees properly paid by him to the registrar on the registration.
(4) If a company fails to comply with subsection (1), an offence is committed by–

(a) the company, and
(b) every officer of the company who is in default.

(5) A person guilty of an offence under this section is liable–

(a) on conviction on indictment, to a fine;
(b) on summary conviction, to a fine not exceeding the statutory maximum.

(6) Subsection (4) does not apply if registration of the charge has been effected on the application of some other person.
(7) This section applies to the following charges–

(a) a charge on land or any interest in such land, other than a charge for any rent or other periodical sum payable in respect of the land,
(b) a security over incorporeal moveable property of any of the following categories–

(i) goodwill,
(ii) a patent or a licence under a patent,
(iii) a trademark,

- (iv) a copyright or a licence under a copyright,
- (v) a registered design or a licence in respect of such a design,
- (vi) a design right or a licence under a design right,
- (vii) the book debts (whether book debts of the company or assigned to it), and
- (viii) uncalled share capital of the company or calls made but not paid,

- (c) a security over a ship or aircraft or any share in a ship,
- (d) a floating charge.

879 Charges which have to be registered: supplementary

(1) A charge on land, for the purposes of section 878(7)(a), includes a charge created by a heritable security within the meaning of section 9(8) of the Conveyancing and Feudal Reform (Scotland) Act 1970 (c. 35).
(2) The holding of debentures entitling the holder to a charge on land is not, for the purposes of section 878(7)(a), deemed to be an interest in land.
(3) It is immaterial for the purposes of this Chapter where land subject to a charge is situated.
(4) The deposit by way of security of a negotiable instrument given to secure the payment of book debts is not, for the purposes of section 878(7)(b)(vii), to be treated as a charge on those book debts.
(5) References in this Chapter to the date of the creation of a charge are–

- (a) in the case of a floating charge, the date on which the instrument creating the floating charge was executed by the company creating the charge, and
- (b) in any other case, the date on which the right of the person entitled to the benefit of the charge was constituted as a real right.

(6) In this Chapter 'company' means an incorporated company registered in Scotland.

880 Duty to register charges existing on property acquired

(1) Subsection (2) applies where a company acquires any property which is subject to a charge of any kind as would, if it had been created by the company after the acquisition of the property, have been required to be registered under this Chapter.
(2) The company must deliver the prescribed particulars of the charge, together with a copy (certified to be a correct copy) of the instrument (if any) by which the charge was created or is evidenced, to the registrar for registration before the end of the period allowed for registration.
(3) If default is made in complying with this section, an offence is committed by–

- (a) the company, and
- (b) every officer of it who is in default.

(4) A person guilty of an offence under this section is liable–

- (a) on conviction on indictment, to a fine;
- (b) on summary conviction, to a fine not exceeding the statutory maximum.

881 Charge by way of ex facie absolute disposition, etc.

(1) For the avoidance of doubt, it is hereby declared that, in the case of a charge created by way of an *ex facie* absolute disposition or assignation qualified by a back letter or other agreement, or by a standard security qualified by an agreement, compliance with section 878(1) does not of itself render the charge unavailable as security for indebtedness incurred after the date of compliance.
(2) Where the amount secured by a charge so created is purported to be increased by a further back letter or agreement, a further charge is held to have been created by the *ex facie* absolute disposition or assignation or (as the case may be) by the standard security, as qualified by the further back letter or agreement.
(3) In that case, the provisions of this Chapter apply to the further charge as if–

  (a) references in this Chapter (other than in this section) to a charge were references to the further charge, and
  (b) references to the date of the creation of a charge were references to the date on which the further back letter or agreement was executed.

Special rules about debentures

882 Charge in series of debentures

(1) Where a series of debentures containing, or giving by reference to any other instrument, any charge to the benefit of which the debenture-holders of that series are entitled *pari passu*, is created by a company, it is sufficient for purposes of section 878 if the required particulars, together with a copy of the deed containing the charge (or, if there is no such deed, of one of the debentures of the series) are delivered to the registrar before the end of the period allowed for registration.
(2) The following are the required particulars–

  (a) the total amount secured by the whole series,
  (b) the dates of the resolutions authorising the issue of the series and the date of the covering deed (if any) by which the security is created or defined,
  (c) a general description of the property charged,
  (d) the names of the trustees (if any) for the debenture-holders, and
  (e) in the case of a floating charge, a statement of any provisions of the charge and of any instrument relating to it which prohibit or restrict or regulate the power of the company to grant further securities ranking in priority to, or *pari passu* with, the floating charge, or which vary or otherwise regulate the order of ranking of the floating charge in relation to subsisting securities.

(3) Where more than one issue is made of debentures in the series, particulars of the date and amount of each issue of debentures of the series must be sent to the registrar for entry in the register of charges.
(4) Failure to comply with subsection (3) does not affect the validity of any of those debentures.
(5) Subsections (2) to (6) of section 878 apply for the purposes of this section as they apply for the purposes of that section but as if for the reference to the registration of the charge there was substituted a reference to the registration of the series of debentures.

883 Additional registration requirement for commission etc. in relation to debentures

(1) Where any commission, allowance or discount has been paid or made either directly or indirectly by a company to a person in consideration of his–

  (a) subscribing or agreeing to subscribe, whether absolutely or conditionally, for debentures in a company, or
  (b) procuring or agreeing to procure subscriptions, whether absolute or conditional, for such debentures, the particulars required to be sent for registration under section 878 shall include particulars as to the amount or rate per cent of the commission, discount or allowance so paid or made.

(2) The deposit of debentures as security for a debt of the company is not, for the purposes of this section, treated as the issue of debentures at a discount.
(3) Failure to comply with this section does not affect the validity of the debentures issued.

Charges on property outside the United Kingdom

884 Charges on property outside United Kingdom

Where a charge is created in the United Kingdom but comprises property outside the United Kingdom, the copy of the instrument creating or purporting to create the charge may be sent for registration under section 878 even if further proceedings may be necessary to make the charge valid or effectual according to the law of the country in which the property is situated.

The register of charges

885 Register of charges to be kept by registrar

(1) The registrar shall keep, with respect to each company, a register of all the charges requiring registration under this Chapter.
(2) In the case of a charge to the benefit of which holders of a series of debentures are entitled, the registrar shall enter in the register the required particulars specified in section 882(2).
(3) In the case of any other charge, the registrar shall enter in the register the following particulars–

  (a) if it is a charge created by a company, the date of its creation and, if it is a charge which was existing on property acquired by the company, the date of the acquisition,
  (b) the amount secured by the charge,
  (c) short particulars of the property charged,
  (d) the persons entitled to the charge, and
  (e) in the case of a floating charge, a statement of any of the provisions of the charge and of any instrument relating to it which prohibit or restrict or regulate the company's power to grant further securities ranking in priority to, or *pari passu* with, the floating charge, or which vary or otherwise regulate the order of ranking of the floating charge in relation to subsisting securities.

(4) The registrar shall give a certificate of the registration of any charge registered in pursuance of this Chapter, stating–

(a) the name of the company and the person first-named in the charge among those entitled to the benefit of the charge (or, in the case of a series of debentures, the name of the holder of the first such debenture issued), and
(b) the amount secured by the charge.

(5) The certificate–

(a) shall be signed by the registrar or authenticated by the registrar's official seal, and
(b) is conclusive evidence that the requirements of this Chapter as to registration have been satisfied.

(6) The register kept in pursuance of this section shall be open to inspection by any person.

886 The period allowed for registration

(1) The period allowed for registration of a charge created by a company is–

(a) 21 days beginning with the day after the day on which the charge is created, or
(b) if the charge is created outside the United Kingdom, 21 days beginning with the day after the day on which a copy of the instrument by which the charge is created or evidenced could, in due course of post (and if despatched with due diligence) have been received in the United Kingdom.

(2) The period allowed for registration of a charge to which property acquired by a company is subject is–

(a) 21 days beginning with the day after the day on which the transaction is settled, or
(b) if the property is situated and the charge was created outside the United Kingdom, 21 days beginning with the day after the day on which a copy of the instrument by which the charge is created or evidenced could, in due course of post (and if despatched with due diligence) have been received in the United Kingdom.

(3) The period allowed for registration of particulars of a series of debentures as a result of section 882 is–

(a) if there is a deed containing the charge mentioned in section 882(1), 21 days beginning with the day after the day on which that deed is executed, or
(b) if there is no such deed, 21 days beginning with the day after the day on which the first debenture of the series is executed.

887 Entries of satisfaction and relief

(1) Subsection (2) applies if a statement is delivered to the registrar verifying with respect to any registered charge–

(a) that the debt for which the charge was given has been paid or satisfied in whole or in part, or

(b) that part of the property charged has been released from the charge or has ceased to form part of the company's property.

(2) If the charge is a floating charge, the statement must be accompanied by either–

(a) a statement by the creditor entitled to the benefit of the charge, or a person authorised by him for the purpose, verifying that the statement mentioned in subsection (1) is correct, or
(b) a direction obtained from the court, on the ground that the statement by the creditor mentioned in paragraph (a) could not be readily obtained, dispensing with the need for that statement.

(3) The registrar may enter on the register a memorandum of satisfaction (in whole or in part) regarding the fact contained in the statement mentioned in subsection (1).
(4) Where the registrar enters a memorandum of satisfaction in whole, he shall, if required, furnish the company with a copy of the memorandum.
(5) Nothing in this section requires the company to submit particulars with respect to the entry in the register of a memorandum of satisfaction where the company, having created a floating charge over all or any part of its property, disposes of part of the property subject to the floating charge.

888 Rectification of register of charges

(1) Subsection (2) applies if the court is satisfied–

(a) that the failure to register a charge before the end of the period allowed for registration, or the omission or mis-statement of any particular with respect to any such charge or in a memorandum of satisfaction–

(i) was accidental or due to inadvertence or to some other sufficient cause, or
(ii) is not of a nature to prejudice the position of creditors or shareholders of the company, or

(b) that on other grounds it is just and equitable to grant relief.

(2) The court may, on the application of the company or a person interested, and on such terms and conditions as seem to the court just and expedient, order that the period allowed for registration shall be extended or, as the case may be, that the omission or mis-statement shall be rectified.

Avoidance of certain charges

889 Charges void unless registered

(1) If a company creates a charge to which section 878 applies, the charge is void (so far as any security on the company's property or any part of it is conferred by the charge) against–

(a) the liquidator of the company,
(b) an administrator of the company, and
(c) any creditor of the company unless that section is complied with.

(2) Subsection (1) is without prejudice to any contract or obligation for repayment of the money secured by the charge; and when a charge becomes void under this section the money secured by it immediately becomes payable.

Companies' records and registers

890 Copies of instruments creating charges to be kept by company

(1) Every company shall cause a copy of every instrument creating a charge requiring registration under this Chapter to be kept available for inspection.
(2) In the case of a series of uniform debentures, a copy of one debenture of the series is sufficient.

891 Company's register of charges

(1) Every company shall keep available for inspection a register of charges and enter in it all charges specifically affecting property of the company, and all floating charges on any property of the company.
(2) There shall be given in each case a short description of the property charged, the amount of the charge and, except in the case of securities to bearer, the names of the persons entitled to it.
(3) If an officer of the company knowingly and wilfully authorises or permits the omission of an entry required to be made in pursuance of this section, he commits an offence.
(4) A person guilty of an offence under this section is liable–

    (a) on conviction on indictment, to a fine;
    (b) on summary conviction, to a fine not exceeding the statutory maximum.

892 Instruments creating charges and register of charges to be available for inspection

(1) This section applies to–

    (a) documents required to be kept available for inspection under section 890 (copies of instruments creating charges), and
    (b) a company's register of charges kept in pursuance of section 891.

(2) The documents and register must be kept available for inspection–

    (a) at the company's registered office, or
    (b) at a place specified in regulations under section 1136.

(3) The company must give notice to the registrar–

    (a) of the place at which the documents and register are kept available for inspection, and
    (b) of any change in that place, unless they have at all times been kept at the company's registered office.

(4) The documents and register shall be open to the inspection–

    (a) of any creditor or member of the company without charge, and
    (b) of any other person on payment of such fee as may be prescribed.

(5) If default is made for 14 days in complying with subsection (3) or an inspection required under subsection (4) is refused, an offence is committed by–

(a) the company, and
(b) every officer of the company who is in default.

(6) A person guilty of an offence under this section is liable on summary conviction to a fine not exceeding level 3 on the standard scale and, for continued contravention, a daily default fine not exceeding one-tenth of level 3 on the standard scale.
(7) If an inspection required under subsection (4) is refused the court may by order compel an immediate inspection.

CHAPTER 3

Powers of the Secretary of State

893 Power to make provision for effect of registration in special register

(1) In this section a 'special register' means a register, other than the register of charges kept under this Part, in which a charge to which Chapter 1 or Chapter 2 applies is required or authorised to be registered.
(2) The Secretary of State may by order make provision for facilitating the making of information-sharing arrangements between the person responsible for maintaining a special register ('the responsible person') and the registrar that meet the requirement in subsection (4). 'Information-sharing arrangements' are arrangements to share and make use of information held by the registrar or by the responsible person.
(3) If the Secretary of State is satisfied that appropriate information-sharing arrangements have been made, he may by order provide that–

(a) the registrar is authorised not to register a charge of a specified description under Chapter 1 or Chapter 2,
(b) a charge of a specified description that is registered in the special register within a specified period is to be treated as if it had been registered (and certified by the registrar as registered) in accordance with the requirements of Chapter 1 or, as the case may be, Chapter 2, and
(c) the other provisions of Chapter 1 or, as the case may be, Chapter 2 apply to a charge so treated with specified modifications.

(4) The information-sharing arrangements must ensure that persons inspecting the register of charges–

(a) are made aware, in a manner appropriate to the inspection, of the existence of charges in the special register which are treated in accordance with provision so made, and
(b) are able to obtain information from the special register about any such charge.

(5) An order under this section may–

(a) modify any enactment or rule of law which would otherwise restrict or prevent the responsible person from entering into or giving effect to information-sharing arrangements,
(b) authorise the responsible person to require information to be provided to him for the purposes of the arrangements,
(c) make provision about–

(i) the charging by the responsible person of fees in connection with the arrangements and the destination of such fees (including provision modifying any enactment which would otherwise apply in relation to fees payable to the responsible person), and
(ii) the making of payments under the arrangements by the registrar to the responsible person,

(d) require the registrar to make copies of the arrangements available to the public (in hard copy or electronic form).

(6) In this section 'specified' means specified in an order under this section.
(7) A description of charge may be specified, in particular, by reference to one or more of the following–

(a) the type of company by which it is created,
(b) the form of charge which it is,
(c) the description of assets over which it is granted,
(d) the length of the period between the date of its registration in the special register and the date of its creation.

(8) Provision may be made under this section relating to registers maintained under the law of a country or territory outside the United Kingdom.
(9) An order under this section is subject to negative resolution procedure.

894 General power to make amendments to this Part

(1) The Secretary of State may by regulations under this section–

(a) amend this Part by altering, adding or repealing provisions,
(b) make consequential amendments or repeals in this Act or any other enactment (whether passed or made before or after this Act).

(2) Regulations under this section are subject to affirmative resolution procedure.

Appendix 3
Companies Act 1985
Part XII Registration of charges

Annotations:
Amendments (Textual)

F1Ss. 395–424 repealed by Companies Act 2006 (c. 46), ss. 1295, 1300, Sch. 16

Modifications etc. (not altering text)

C1Pt.XII (ss. 395–424) extended (with modifications) by S.I. 1989/638, regs. 18, 21, Sch. 4 para. 4

Chapter I Registration of charges (England and Wales)

395 Certain charges void if not registered

(1) Subject to the provisions of this Chapter, a charge created by a company registered in England and Wales and being a charge to which this section applies is, so far as any security on the company's property or undertaking is conferred by the charge, void against the liquidator [**F1** or administrator] and any creditor of the company, unless the prescribed particulars of the charge together with the instrument (if any) by which the charge is created or evidenced, are delivered to or received by the registrar of companies for registration in the manner required by this Chapter within 21 days after the date of the charge's creation.

(2) Subsection (1) is without prejudice to any contract or obligation for repayment of the money secured by the charge; and when a charge becomes void under this section, the money secured by it immediately becomes payable.

Annotations:
Amendments (Textual)

F1Words inserted by Insolvency Act 1985 (c. 65, SIF 27), s. 109, Sch. 6 para. 10

Modifications etc. (not altering text)

C1S. 395 applied (with modifications) (6.4.2001) by S.I. 2001/1090, reg. 4, Sch. 2 Pt. I

C2S. 395 excluded (26.12.2003) by The Financial Collateral Arrangements (No.2) Regulations 2003 (S.I. 2003/3226), reg. 4(4)

396 Charges which have to be registered

(1) Section 395 applies to the following charges–

(a) a charge for the purpose of securing any issue of debentures,
(b) a charge on uncalled share capital of the company,
(c) a charge created or evidenced by an instrument which, if executed by an individual, would require registration as a bill of sale,
(d) a charge on land (wherever situated) or any interest in it, but not including a charge for any rent or other periodical sum issuing out of the land,
(e) a charge on book debts of the company,
(f) a floating charge on the company's undertaking or property,
(g) a charge on calls made but not paid,
(h) a charge on a ship or aircraft, or any share in a ship,
(j) a charge on goodwill, [**F1**or on any intellectual property].

(2) Where a negotiable instrument has been given to secure the payment of any book debts of a company, the deposit of the instrument for the purpose of securing an advance to the company is not, for purposes of section 395, to be treated as a charge on those book debts.
(3) The holding of debentures entitling the holder to a charge on land is not for purposes of this section deemed to be an interest in land.
[**F2**(3A) The following are 'intellectual property' for the purposes of this section–

(a) any patent, trade mark, **F3**. . . registered design, copyright or design right;
(b) any licence under or in respect of any such right.]

(4) In this Chapter, 'charge' includes mortgage.

Annotations:
Amendments (Textual)

F1Words substituted by Copyright, Designs and Patents Act 1988 (c. 48, SIF 67A), s. 303(1), Sch. 7 para. 31(2)
F2S. 396(3A) inserted by Copyright, Designs and Patents Act 1988 (c. 48, SIF 67A), s. 303(1), Sch. 7 para. 31(2)
F3Words in s. 396(3A)(a) repealed (31.10.1994) by 1994 c. 26, s. 106(2), Sch. 5; S.I. 1994/2550, art. 2

Modifications etc. (not altering text)

C1S. 396 applied (with modifications) (6.4.2001) by S.I. 2001/1090, reg. 4, Sch. 2 Pt. I
C2S. 396(1)(*j*) extended by Patents, Designs and Marks Act 1986 (c. 39, SIF 67A), s. 2, Sch. 2 Pt. I para. 1(*k*)(i)
C3S. 396(3A)(a) amended (31.10.1994) by 1994 c. 26, s. 106(1), Sch. 4 para. 1(2); S.I. 1994/2550, art. 2

397 Formalities of registration (debentures)

(1) Where a series of debentures containing, or giving by reference to another instrument, any charge to the benefit of which the debenture holders of that

series are entitled pari passu is created by a company, it is for purposes of section 395 sufficient if there are delivered to or received by the registrar, within 21 days after the execution of the deed containing the charge (or, if there is no such deed, after the execution of any debentures of the series), the following particulars in the prescribed form–

(a) the total amount secured by the whole series, and
(b) the dates of the resolutions authorising the issue of the series and the date of the covering deed (if any) by which the security is created or defined, and
(c) a general description of the property charged, and
(d) the names of the trustees (if any) for the debenture holders,

together with the deed containing the charge or, if there is no such deed, one of the debentures of the series:
Provided that there shall be sent to the registrar of companies, for entry in the register, particulars in the prescribed form of the date and amount of each issue of debentures of the series, but any omission to do this does not affect the validity of any of those debentures.

(2) Where any commission, allowance or discount has been paid or made either directly or indirectly by a company to a person in consideration of his–

(a) subscribing or agreeing to subscribe, whether absolutely or conditionally, for debentures of the company, or
(b) procuring or agreeing to procure subscriptions, whether absolute or conditional, for such debentures,

the particulars required to be sent for registration under section 395 shall include particulars as to the amount or rate per cent of the commission, discount or allowance so paid or made, but omission to do this does not affect the validity of the debentures issued.

(3) The deposit of debentures as security for a debt of the company is not, for the purposes of subsection (2), treated as the issue of the debentures at a discount.

Annotations:
Modifications etc. (not altering text)

C1S. 397 applied (with modifications) (6.4.2001) by S.I. 2001/1090, reg. 4, Sch. 2 Pt. I

398 Verification of charge on property outside United Kingdom

(1) In the case of a charge created out of the United Kingdom comprising property situated outside the United Kingdom, the delivery to and the receipt by the registrar of companies of a copy (verified in the prescribed manner) of the instrument by which the charge is created or evidenced has the same effect for purposes of sections 395 to 398 as the delivery and receipt of the instrument itself.
(2) In that case, 21 days after the date on which the instrument or copy could, in due course of post (and if despatched with due diligence), have been received in the United Kingdom are substituted for the 21 days mentioned in section 395(1) (or as the case may be, section 397(1)) as the time within which the particulars and instrument or copy are to be delivered to the registrar.
(3) Where a charge is created in the United Kingdom but comprises property outside the United Kingdom, the instrument creating or purporting to create

the charge may be sent for registration under section 395 notwithstanding that further proceedings may be necessary to make the charge valid or effectual according to the law of the country in which the property is situated.

(4) Where a charge comprises property situated in Scotland or Northern Ireland and registration in the country where the property is situated is necessary to make the charge valid or effectual according to the law of that country, the delivery to and the receipt by the registrar of a copy (verified in the prescribed manner) of the instrument by which the charge is created or evidenced, together with a certificate in the prescribed form stating that the charge was presented for registration in Scotland or Northern Ireland (as the case may be) on the date on which it was so presented has, for purposes of sections 395 to 398, the same effect as the delivery and receipt of the instrument itself.

Annotations:
Modifications etc. (not altering text)

C1S. 398 applied (with modifications) (6.4.2001) by S.I. 2001/1090, reg. 4, Sch. 2 Pt. I

399 Company's duty to register charges it creates

(1) It is a company's duty to send to the registrar of companies for registration the particulars of every charge created by the company and of the issues of debentures of a series requiring registration under sections 395 to 398; but registration of any such charge may be effected on the application of any person interested in it.

(2) Where registration is effected on the application of some person other than the company, that person is entitled to recover from the company the amount of any fees properly paid by him to the registrar on the registration.

(3) If a company fails to comply with subsection (1), then, unless the registration has been effected on the application of some other person, the company and every officer of it who is in default is liable to a fine and, for continued contravention, to a daily default fine.

Annotations:
Modifications etc. (not altering text)

C1S. 399 applied (with modifications) (6.4.2001) by S.I. 2001/1090, reg. 4, Sch. 2 Pt. I

400 Charges existing on property acquired

(1) This section applies where a company is registered in England and Wales acquires property which is subject to a charge of any such kind as would, if it had been created by the company after the acquisition of the property, have been required to be registered under this Chapter.

(2) The company shall cause the prescribed particulars of the charge, together with a copy (certified in the prescribed manner to be a correct copy) of the instrument (if any) by which the charge was created or is evidenced, to be delivered to the registrar of companies for registration in manner required by this Chapter within 21 days after the date on which the acquisition is completed.

(3) However, if the property is situated and the charge was created outside Great Britain, 21 days after the date on which the copy of the instrument could in

due course of post, and if despatched with due diligence, have been received in the United Kingdom is substituted for the 21 days above-mentioned as the time within which the particulars and copy of the instrument are to be delivered to the registrar.

(4) If default is made in complying with this section, the company and every officer of it who is in default is liable to a fine and, for continued contravention, to a daily default fine.

Annotations:
Modifications etc. (not altering text)

C1S. 400 applied (with modifications) (6.4.2001) by S.I. 2001/1090, reg. 4, Sch. 2 Pt. I

401 Register of charges to be kept by registrar of companies

(1) The registrar of companies shall keep, with respect to each company, a register in the prescribed form of all the charges requiring registration under this Chapter; and he shall enter in the register with respect to such charges the following particulars–

(a) in the case of a charge to the benefit of which the holders of a series of debentures are entitled, the particulars specified in section 397(1),
(b) in the case of any other charge–

(i) if it is a charge created by the company, the date of its creation, and if it is a charge which was existing on property acquired by the company, the date of the acquisition of the property, and
(ii) the amount secured by the charge, and
(iii) short particulars of the property charged, and
(iv) the persons entitled to the charge.

(2) The registrar shall give a certificate of the registration of any charge registered in pursuance of this Chapter, stating the amount secured by the charge.
The certificate–

(a) shall be either signed by the registrar, or authenticated by his official seal, and
(b) is conclusive evidence that the requirements of this Chapter as to registration have been satisfied.

(3) The register kept in pursuance of this section shall be open to inspection by any person.

Annotations:
Modifications etc. (not altering text)

C1S. 401 applied (with modifications) (6.4.2001) by S.I. 2001/1090, reg. 4, Sch. 2 Pt. I

402 Endorsement of certificate on debentures

(1) The company shall cause a copy of every certificate of registration given under section 401 to be endorsed on every debenture or certificate of debenture stock which is issued by the company, and the payment of which is secured by the charge so registered.

(2) But this does not require a company to cause a certificate of registration of any charge so given to be endorsed on any debenture or certificate of debenture stock issued by the company before the charge was created.

(3) If a person knowingly and wilfully authorises or permits the delivery of a debenture or certificate of debenture stock which under this section is required to have endorsed on it a copy of a certificate of registration, without the copy being so endorsed upon it, he is liable (without prejudice to any other liability) to a fine.

Annotations:

Modifications etc. (not altering text)

C1S. 402 applied (with modifications) (6.4.2001) by S.I. 2001/1090, reg. 4, Sch. 2 Pt. I

C2S. 402 excluded (12.2.1992) by S.I. 1992/225, reg. 91(1).

403 Entries of satisfaction and release

(1) [**F1**Subject to subsection (1A), the registrar] of companies, on receipt of a statutory declaration in the prescribed form verifying, with respect to a registered charge,–

(a) that the debt for which the charge was given has been paid or satisfied in whole or in part, or

(b) that part of the property or undertaking charged has been released from the charge or has ceased to form part of the company's property or undertaking,

may enter on the register a memorandum of satisfaction in whole or in part, or of the fact that part of the property or undertaking has been released from the charge or has ceased to form part of the company's property or undertaking (as the case may be).

[**F2**(1A) The registrar of companies may make any such entry as is mentioned in subsection (1) where, instead of receiving such a statutory declaration as is mentioned in that subsection, he receives a statement by a director, secretary, administrator or administrative receiver of the company which is contained in an electronic communication and that statement–

(a) verifies the matters set out in paragraph (a) or (b) of that subsection,

(b) contains a description of the charge,

(c) states the date of creation of the charge and the date of its registration under this Chapter,

(d) states the name and address of the chargee or, in the case of a debenture, trustee, and

(e) where paragraph (b) of subsection (1) applies, contains short particulars of the property or undertaking which has been released from the charge, or which has ceased to form part of the company's property or undertaking (as the case may be).]

(2) Where the registrar enters a memorandum of satisfaction in whole, he shall if required furnish the company with a copy of it.

[**F3**(2A) Any person who makes a false statement under subsection (1A) which he knows to be false or does not believe to be true is liable to imprisonment or a fine, or both.]

Annotations:
Amendments (Textual)

F1Words in s. 403(1) substituted (22.12.2000) by S.I. 2000/3373, art. 22(1)(2)
F2S. 403(1A) inserted (22.12.2000) by S.I. 2000/3373, art. 22(1)(3)
F3S. 403(2A) inserted (22.12.2000) by S.I. 2000/3373, art. 22(1)(4)

Modifications etc. (not altering text)

C1S. 403 applied (with modifications) (6.4.2001) by S.I. 2001/1090, reg. 4, Sch. 2 Pt. I

404 Rectification of register of charges

(1) The following applies if the court is satisfied that the omission to register a charge within the time required by this Chapter or that the omission or mis-statement of any particular with respect to any such charge or in a memorandum of satisfaction was accidental, or due to inadvertence or to some other sufficient cause, or is not of a nature to prejudice the position of creditors or shareholders of the company, or that on other grounds it is just and equitable to grant relief.
(2) The court may, on the application of the company or a person interested, and on such terms and conditions as seem to the court just and expedient, order that the time for registration shall be extended or, as the case may be, that the omission or mis-statement shall be rectified.

Annotations:
Modifications etc. (not altering text)

C1S. 404 applied (with modifications) (6.4.2001) by S.I. 2001/1090, reg. 4, Sch. 2 Pt. I

405 Registration of enforcement of security

(1) If a person obtains an order for the appointment of a receiver or manager of a company's property, or appoints such a receiver or manager under powers contained in an instrument, he shall within 7 days of the order or of the appointment under those powers, give notice of the fact to the registrar of companies; and the registrar shall enter the fact in the register of charges.
(2) Where a person appointed receiver or manager of a company's property under powers contained in an instrument ceases to act as such receiver or manager, he shall, on so ceasing, give the registrar notice to that effect, and the registrar shall enter the fact in the register of charges.
(3) A notice under this section shall be in the prescribed form.
(4) If a person makes default in complying with the requirements of this section, he is liable to a fine and, for continued contravention, to a daily default fine.

Annotations:
Modifications etc. (not altering text)

C1S. 405 applied (with modifications) (6.4.2001) by S.I. 2001/1090, reg. 4, Sch. 2 Pt. I

406 Companies to keep copies of instruments creating charges

(1) Every company shall cause a copy of every instrument creating a charge requiring registration under this Chapter to be kept at its registered office.
(2) In the case of a series of uniform debentures, a copy of one debenture of the series is sufficient.

Annotations:
Modifications etc. (not altering text)
C1S. 406 applied (with modifications) (6.4.2001) by S.I. 2001/1090, reg. 4, Sch. 2 Pt. I

407 Company's register of charges

(1) Every limited company shall keep at its registered office a register of charges and enter in it all charges specifically affecting property of the company and all floating charges on the company's undertaking or any of its property.
(2) The entry shall in each case give a short description of the property charged, the amount of the charge and, except in the case of securities to bearer, the names of the persons entitled to it.
(3) If an officer of the company knowingly and wilfully authorises or permits the omission of an entry required to be made in pursuance of this section, he is liable to a fine.

Annotations:
Modifications etc. (not altering text)
C1S. 407 applied (with modifications) (6.4.2001) by S.I. 2001/1090, reg. 4, Sch. 2 Pt. I

408 Right to inspect instruments which create charges, etc.

(1) The copies of instruments creating any charge requiring registration under this Chapter with the registrar of companies, and the register of charges kept in pursuance of section 407, shall be open during business hours (but subject to such reasonable restrictions as the company in general meeting may impose, so that not less than 2 hours in each day be allowed for inspection) to the inspection of any creditor or member of the company without fee.
(2) The register of charges shall also be open to the inspection of any other person on payment of such fee, not exceeding 5 pence, for each inspection, as the company may prescribe.
(3) If inspection of the copies referred to, or of the register, is refused, every officer of the company who is in default is liable to a fine and, for continued contravention, to a daily default fine.
(4) If such a refusal occurs in relation to a company registered in England and Wales, the court may by order compel an immediate inspection of the copies or register.

Annotations:
Modifications etc. (not altering text)
C1S. 408 applied (with modifications) (6.4.2001) by S.I. 2001/1090, reg. 4, Sch. 2 Pt. I

409 Charges on property in England and Wales created by oversea company

(1) This Chapter extends to charges on property in England and Wales which are created, and to charges on property in England and Wales which is acquired, by a company (whether a company within the meaning of this Act or not) incorporated outside Great Britain which has an established place of business in England and Wales.
(2) In relation to such a company, sections 406 and 407 apply with the substitution, for the reference to the company's registered office, of a reference to its principal place of business in England and Wales.

Chapter II Registration of Charges (Scotland)

410 Charges void unless registered

(1) The following provisions of this Chapter have effect for the purpose of securing the registration in Scotland of charges created by companies.
(2) Every charge created by a company, being a charge to which this section applies, is, so far as any security on the company's property or any part of it is conferred by the charge, void against the liquidator [**F1** or administrator] and any creditor of the company unless the prescribed particulars of the charge, together with a copy (certified in the prescribed manner to be a correct copy) of the instrument (if any) by which the charge is created or evidenced, are delivered to or received by the registrar of companies for registration in the manner required by this Chapter within 21 days after the date of the creation of the charge.
(3) Subsection (2) is without prejudice to any contract or obligation for repayment of the money secured by the charge; and when a charge becomes void under this section the money secured by it immediately becomes payable.
(4) This section applies to the following charges–

   (a) a charge on land wherever situated, or any interest in such land (not including a charge for any rent [**F2**, ground annual] or other periodical sum payable in respect of the land, but including a charge created by a heritable security within the meaning of section 9(8) of the **M1**Conveyancing and Feudal Reform (Scotland) Act 1970),
   (b) a security over the uncalled share capital of the company,
   (c) a security over incorporeal moveable property of any of the following categories–

      (i) the book debts of the company,
      (ii) calls made but not paid,
      (iii) goodwill,
      (iv) a patent or a licence under a patent,
      (v) a trademark,
      (vi) a copyright or a licence under a copyright,
      [**F3**(vii) a registered design or a licence in respect of such a design,
      (viii) a design right or a licence under a design right,]

   (d) a security over a ship or aircraft or any share in a ship, and
   (e) a floating charge.

(5) In this Chapter 'company' (except in section 424) means an incorporated company registered in Scotland; 'registrar of companies' means the registrar or other officer performing under this Act the duty of registration of companies in Scotland; and references to the date of creation of a charge are–

(a) in the case of a floating charge, the date on which the instrument creating the floating charge was executed by the company creating the charge, and
(b) in any other case, the date on which the right of the person entitled to the benefit of the charge was constituted as a real right.

Annotations:
Amendments (Textual)

F1Words inserted by Insolvency Act 1985 (c. 65, SIF 27), s. 109, Sch. 6 para. 10
F2Words in s. 410(4)(a) repealed (S.) (28.11.2004 with effect as mentioned in Sch. 12 para. 46(3)(4) of the amending Act) by 2000 asp 5, ss. 76(1)(2), 77(4), Sch. 12 Pt. 1 para. 46(2)(b), Sch. 13 Pt. 1 (with ss. 58, 62, 75); S.S.I. 2003/456, art. 2
F3S. 410(4)(*c*)(vii)(viii) inserted by Copyright, Designs and Patents Act 1988 (c. 48, SIF 67A), s. 303(1), Sch. 7 para. 31(3)

Modifications etc. (not altering text)

C1S. 410 applied (with modifications) (6.4.2001) by S.I. 2001/1090, reg. 4, Sch. 2 Pt. I
C2S. 410 excluded (26.12.2003) by The Financial Collateral Arrangements (No.2) Regulations 2003 (S.I. 2003/3226), reg. 5
C3S. 410(4)(*c*) extended by Patents, Designs and Marks Act 1986 (c. 39, SIF 67A), s. 2, Sch. 2 Pt. I para. 1(*k*)(i)
C4S. 410(4)(c)(v) amended (31.10.1994) by 1994 c. 26, s. 106(1), Sch. 4 para. 1(2); S.I. 1994/2550, art. 2

Marginal Citations

M11970 c. 35.

411 Charges on property outside United Kingdom

(1) In the case of a charge created out of the United Kingdom comprising property situated outside the United Kingdom, the period of 21 days after the date on which the copy of the instrument creating it could (in due course of post, and if despatched with due diligence) have been received in the United Kingdom is substituted for the period of 21 days after the date of the creation of the charge as the time within which, under section 410(2), the particulars and copy are to be delivered to the registrar.
(2) Where a charge is created in the United Kingdom but comprises property outside the United Kingdom, the copy of the instrument creating or purporting to create the charge may be sent for registration under section 410 notwithstanding that further proceedings may be necessary to make the charge valid or effectual according to the law of the country in which the property is situated.

Annotations:
Modifications etc. (not altering text)

C1S. 411 applied (with modifications) (6.4.2001) by S.I. 2001/1090, reg. 4, Sch. 2 Pt. I

412 Negotiable instrument to secure book debts

Where a negotiable instrument has been given to secure the payment of any book debts of a company, the deposit of the instrument for the purpose of securing an advance to the company is not, for purposes of section 410, to be treated as a charge on those book debts.

Annotations:
Modifications etc. (not altering text)

C1S. 412 applied (with modifications) (6.4.2001) by S.I. 2001/1090, reg. 4, Sch. 2 Pt. I

413 Charges associated with debentures

(1) The holding of debentures entitling the holder to a charge on land is not, for the purposes of section 410, deemed to be an interest in land.
(2) Where a series of debentures containing, or giving by reference to any other instrument, any charge to the benefit of which the debenture-holders of that series are entitled pari passu, is created by a company, it is sufficient for purposes of section 410 if there are delivered to or received by the registrar of companies within 21 days after the execution of the deed containing the charge or, if there is no such deed, after the execution of any debentures of the series, the following particulars in the prescribed form–

    (a) the total amount secured by the whole series,
    (b) the dates of the resolutions authorising the issue of the series and the date of the covering deed (if any) by which the security is created or defined,
    (c) a general description of the property charged,
    (d) the names of the trustees (if any) for the debenture holders, and
    (e) in the case of a floating charge, a statement of any provisions of the charge and of any instrument relating to it which prohibit or restrict or regulate the power of the company to grant further securities ranking in priority to, or pari passu with, the floating charge, or which vary or otherwise regulate the order of ranking of the floating charge in relation to subsisting securities,

    together with a copy of the deed containing the charge or, if there is no such deed, of one of the debentures of the series:
    Provided that, where more than one issue is made of debentures in the series, there shall be sent to the registrar of companies for entry in the register particulars (in the prescribed form) of the date and amount of each issue of debentures of the series, but any omission to do this does not affect the validity of any of those debentures.
(3) Where any commission, allowance or discount has been paid or made, either directly or indirectly, by a company to any person in consideration of his subscribing or agreeing to subscribe, whether absolutely or conditionally, for any debentures of the company, or procuring or agreeing to procure subscriptions (whether absolute or conditional) for any such debentures, the particulars

required to be sent for registration under section 410 include particulars as to the amount or rate per cent of the commission, discount or allowance so paid or made; but any omission to do this does not affect the validity of the debentures issued.
The deposit of any debentures as security for any debt of the company is not, for purposes of this subsection, treated as the issue of the debentures at a discount.

Annotations:
Modifications etc. (not altering text)

C1S. 413 applied (with modifications) (6.4.2001) by S.I. 2001/1090, reg. 4, Sch. 2 Pt. I

414 Charge by way of ex facie absolute disposition, etc.

(1) For the avoidance of doubt, it is hereby declared that, in the case of a charge created by way of an ex facie absolute disposition or assignation qualified by a back letter or other agreement, or by a standard security qualified by an agreement, compliance with section 410(2) does not of itself render the charge unavailable as security for indebtedness incurred after the date of compliance.
(2) Where the amount secured by a charge so created is purported to be increased by a further back letter or agreement, a further charge is held to have been created by the ex facie absolute disposition or assignation or (as the case may be) by the standard security, as qualified by the further back letter or agreement; and the provisions of this Chapter apply to the further charge as if–

  (a) references in this Chapter (other than in this section) to the charge were references to the further charge, and
  (b) references to the date of the creation of the charge were references to the date on which the further back letter or agreement was executed.

Annotations:
Modifications etc. (not altering text)

C1S. 414 applied (with modifications) (6.4.2001) by S.I. 2001/1090, reg. 4, Sch. 2 Pt. I

415 Company's duty to register charges created by it

(1) It is a company's duty to send to the registrar of companies for registration the particulars of every charge created by the company and of the issues of debentures of a series requiring registration under sections 410 to 414; but registration of any such charge may be effected on the application of any person interested in it.
(2) Where registration is effected on the application of some person other than the company, that person is entitled to recover from the company the amount of any fees properly paid by him to the registrar on the registration.
(3) If a company makes default in sending to the registrar for registration the particulars of any charge created by the company or of the issues of debentures of a series requiring registration as above mentioned, then, unless the registration has been effected on the application of some other person, the company and every officer of it who is in default is liable to a fine and, for continued contravention, to a daily default fine.

Annotations:
Modifications etc. (not altering text)

C1S. 415 applied (with modifications) (6.4.2001) by S.I. 2001/1090, reg. 4, Sch. 2 Pt. I

416 Duty to register charges existing on property acquired

(1) Where a company acquires any property which is subject to a charge of any kind as would, if it had been created by the company after the acquisition of the property, have been required to be registered under this Chapter, the company shall cause the prescribed particulars of the charge, together with a copy (certified in the prescribed manner to be a correct copy) of the instrument (if any) by which the charge was created or is evidenced, to be delivered to the registrar of companies for registration in the manner required by this Chapter within 21 days after the date on which the transaction was settled.
(2) If, however, the property is situated and the charge was created outside Great Britain, 21 days after the date on which the copy of the instrument could (in due course of post, and if despatched with due diligence) have been received in the United Kingdom are substituted for 21 days after the settlement of the transaction as the time within which the particulars and the copy of the instrument are to be delivered to the registrar.
(3) If default is made in complying with this section, the company and every officer of it who is in default is liable to a fine and, for continued contravention, to a daily default fine.

Annotations:
Modifications etc. (not altering text)

C1S. 416 applied (with modifications) (6.4.2001) by S.I. 2001/1090, reg. 4, Sch. 2 Pt. I

417 Register of charges to be kept by registrar of companies

(1) The registrar of companies shall keep, with respect to each company, a register in the prescribed form of all the charges requiring registration under this Chapter, and shall enter in the register with respect to such charges the particulars specified below.
(2) In the case of a charge to the benefit of which the holders of a series of debentures are entitled, there shall be entered in the register the particulars specified in section 413(2).
(3) In the case of any other charge, there shall be entered–

 (a) if it is a charge created by the company, the date of its creation, and if it was a charge existing on property acquired by the company, the date of the acquisition of the property,
 (b) the amount secured by the charge,
 (c) short particulars of the property charged,
 (d) the persons entitled to the charge, and
 (e) in the case of a floating charge, a statement of any of the provisions of the charge and of any instrument relating to it which prohibit or restrict or regulate the company's power to grant further securities ranking in priority to, or pari passu with, the floating charge, or which vary or otherwise

regulate the order of ranking of the floating charge in relation to subsisting securities.

(4) The register kept in pursuance of this section shall be open to inspection by any person.

Annotations:
Modifications etc. (not altering text)

C1S. 417 applied (with modifications) (6.4.2001) by S.I. 2001/1090, reg. 4, Sch. 2 Pt. I

418 Certificate of registration to be issued

(1) The registrar of companies shall give a certificate of the registration of any charge registered in pursuance of this Chapter.
(2) The certificate–

(a) shall be either signed by the registrar, or authenticated by his official seal,
(b) shall state the name of the company and the person first-named in the charge among those entitled to the benefit of the charge (or, in the case of a series of debentures, the name of the holder of the first such debenture to be issued) and the amount secured by the charge, and
(c) is conclusive evidence that the requirements of this Chapter as to registration have been complied with.

Annotations:
Modifications etc. (not altering text)

C1S. 418 applied (with modifications) (6.4.2001) by S.I. 2001/1090, reg. 4, Sch. 2 Pt. I

419 Entries of satisfaction and relief

(1) [**F1**Subject to subsections (1A) and (1B), the registrar] of companies, on application being made to him in the prescribed form, and on receipt of a statutory declaration in the prescribed form verifying, with respect to any registered charge,–

(a) that the debt for which the charge was given has been paid or satisfied in whole or in part, or
(b) that part of the property charged has been released from the charge or has ceased to form part of the company's property,

may enter on the register a memorandum of satisfaction (in whole or in part) regarding that fact.

[**F2**(1A) On an application being made to him in the prescribed form, the registrar of companies may make any such entry as is mentioned in subsection (1) where, instead of receiving such a statutory declaration as is mentioned in that subsection, he receives a statement by a director, secretary, liquidator, receiver or administrator of the company which is contained in an electronic communication and that statement–

(a) verifies the matters set out in paragraph (a) or (b) of that subsection,
(b) contains a description of the charge,
(c) states the date of creation of the charge and the date of its registration under this Chapter,

(d) states the name and address of the chargee or, in the case of a debenture, trustee, and
(e) where paragraph (b) of subsection (1) applies, contains short particulars of the property which has been released from the charge, or which has ceased to form part of the company's property (as the case may be).

F2(1B)Where the statement under subsection (1A) concerns the satisfaction of a floating charge, then there shall be delivered to the registrar a further statement which–

(a) is made by the creditor entitled to the benefit of the floating charge or a person authorised to act on his behalf;
(b) is incorporated into, or logically associated with, the electronic communication containing the statement; and
(c) certifies that the particulars contained in the statement are correct.]

(2) Where the registrar enters a memorandum of satisfaction in whole, he shall, if required, furnish the company with a copy of the memorandum.
(3) Without prejudice to the registrar's duty under this section to require to be satisfied as above mentioned, he shall not be so satisfied unless–

(a) the creditor entitled to the benefit of the floating charge, or a person authorised to do so on his behalf, certifies as correct the particulars submitted to the registrar with respect to the entry on the register of a memorandum under this section, or
(b) the court, on being satisfied that such certification cannot readily be obtained, directs him accordingly.

(4) Nothing in this section requires the company to submit particulars with respect to the entry in the register of a memorandum of satisfaction where the company, having created a floating charge over all or any part of its property, disposes of part of the property subject to the floating charge.
(5) A memorandum or certification required for the purposes of this section shall be in such form as may be prescribed.
[**F3**(5A)Any person who makes a false statement under subsection (1A) or (1B) which he knows to be false or does not believe to be true is liable to imprisonment or a fine, or both.]

Annotations:
Amendments (Textual)

F1Words in s. 419(1) substituted (22.12.2000) by S.I. 2000/3373, art. 23(1)(2)
F2S. 419(1A)(1B) inserted (22.12.2000) by S.I. 2000/3373, art. 23(1)(3)
F3S. 419(5A) inserted (22.12.2000) by S.I. 2000/3373, art. 23(1)(4)

Modifications etc. (not altering text)

C1S. 419 applied (with modifications) (6.4.2001) by S.I. 2001/1090, reg. 4, Sch. 2 Pt. I

420 Rectification of register

The court, on being satisfied that the omission to register a charge within the time required by this Act or that the omission or mis-statement of any particular with respect to any such charge or in a memorandum of satisfaction was accidental, or due to inadvertence or to some other sufficient cause, or is not of a nature to prejudice the position of creditors or shareholders of the company, or that it is on other grounds just and equitable to grant relief, may, on the application of the company or any person interested, and on such terms and conditions as seem to the court just and expedient, order that the time for registration shall be extended or (as the case may be) that the omission or mis-statement shall be rectified.

Annotations:
Modifications etc. (not altering text)

C1S. 420 applied (with modifications) (6.4.2001) by S.I. 2001/1090, reg. 4, Sch. 2 Pt. I

421 Copies of instruments creating charges to be kept by company

(1) Every company shall cause a copy of every instrument creating a charge requiring registration under this Chapter to be kept at the company's registered office.
(2) In the case of a series of uniform debentures, a copy of one debenture of the series is sufficient.

Annotations:
Modifications etc. (not altering text)

C1S. 421 applied (with modifications) (6.4.2001) by S.I. 2001/1090, reg. 4, Sch. 2 Pt. I

422 Company's register of charges

(1) Every company shall keep at its registered office a register of charges and enter in it all charges specifically affecting property of the company, and all floating charges on any property of the company.
(2) There shall be given in each case a short description of the property charged, the amount of the charge and, except in the case of securities to bearer, the names of the persons entitled to it.
(3) If an officer of the company knowingly and wilfully authorises or permits the omission of an entry required to be made in pursuance of this section, he is liable to a fine.

Annotations:
Modifications etc. (not altering text)

C1S. 422 applied (with modifications) (6.4.2001) by S.I. 2001/1090, reg. 4, Sch. 2 Pt. I

423 Right to inspect copies of instruments, and company's register

(1) The copies of instruments creating charges requiring registration under this Chapter with the registrar of companies, and the register of charges kept in pursuance of section 422, shall be open during business hours (but subject to such reasonable restrictions as the company in general meeting may impose, so that not less than 2 hours in each day be allowed for inspection) to the inspection of any creditor or member of the company without fee.
(2) The register of charges shall be open to the inspection of any other person on payment of such fee, not exceeding 5 pence for each inspection, as the company may prescribe.

(3) If inspection of the copies or register is refused, every officer of the company who is in default is liable to a fine and, for continued contravention, to a daily default fine.
(4) If such a refusal occurs in relation to a company, the court may by order compel an immediate inspection of the copies or register.

Annotations:
Modifications etc. (not altering text)

C1S. 423 applied (with modifications) (6.4.2001) by S.I. 2001/1090, reg. 4, Sch. 2 Pt. I

424 Extension of Chapter II

(1) This Chapter extends to charges on property in Scotland which are created, and to charges on property in Scotland which is acquired, by a company incorporated outside Great Britain which has a place of business in Scotland.
(2) In relation to such a company, sections 421 and 422 apply with the substitution, for the reference to the company's registered office, of a reference to its principal place of business in Scotland.

Index

For Product Safety Concerns and Information please contact our EU representative GPSR@taylorandfrancis.com Taylor & Francis Verlag GmbH, Kaufingerstraße 24, 80331 München, Germany